CURRENT PERSPECTIVES
ON SEX
Crimes

CURRENT PERSPECTIVES ON SEX Crimes

Edited by

Ronald M. Holmes
University of Louisville

Stephen T. Holmes
University of Central Florida

Sage Publications
International Educational and Professional Publisher
Thousand Oaks ▪ London ▪ New Delhi

For information:

Sage Publications, Inc.
2455 Teller Road
Thousand Oaks, California 91320
E-mail: order@sagepub.com

Sage Publications Ltd.
6 Bonhill Street
London EC2A 4PU
United Kingdom

Sage Publications India Pvt. Ltd.
M-32 Market
Greater Kailash I
New Delhi 110 048 India

Printed in the United States of America

Library of Congress Cataloging-in-Publication Data

Current perspectives on sex crimes / edited by Ronald M. Holmes and
Stephen T. Holmes.
    p. cm.
  Includes bibliographical references and index.
  ISBN 0-7619-2557-0 (c)
  ISBN 0-7619-2416-7 (p)
  1. Sex crimes. 2. Sex offenders. I. Holmes, Ronald M. II. Holmes,
Stephen T.
HV6556.C87   2002
364.15'3—dc21   2001005398

06   07   7   6   5   4   3   2

Contents

Preface
and Acknowledgments

ABOUT THIS BOOK

This book has a manifest purpose of presenting readings that deal with specific sexual behaviors. The reader will instantly note that most of the readings have been published within the past 2 years. Certainly, there are appropriate articles written before this time, but we have taken special care in examining writings that are not only new but, more importantly, timely. Also, we have included original writings of several authors that have been solicited for this book. Coupling the articles from the past and the ones written especially for this book, we hope that this book will fill a void that exists. There are books and readers that deal with particular subjects such as serial murder (including our own), child abuse, child victims, and so on. But this book is unique in its content and focus. We are hopeful that it will fill the void.

We wish to thank some individuals in our discipline for their interest in and support of our work. When one lists people to thank, there is always the chance that a name or two is omitted. So, we wish to apologize in advance for this. Nevertheless, we thank Sgt. David Rivers, Metro-Dade (Florida) Sheriff's Office; Drs. David Fabianic and Bernie McCarthy, University of Central Florida; Parole Officer James Massie, Louisville, Kentucky; Dr. Eric Hickey, California State University at Fresno; and Dr. Jack Levin, Northeastern University. In addition, we talked with some individuals who gave us some inside information: Lt. George Barret (ret.) of the Louisville Police Department; Sheriff Charles Cox, Miami County, Ohio; Major Henry Ott, Louisville Fire Department; Rick Sanders, Drug Enforcement Administration; and Thomas Harris, author.

Our families deserve special attention. Even as we are writing this section, our wives are shopping at Bed, Bath, and Beyond. They deserve special attention and praise, we think.

—Ronald M. Holmes
University of Louisville
—Stephen T. Holmes
University of Central Florida

UNIT 1

—▬—

A BASIC OVERVIEW

1

Sex in the 21st Century

RONALD M. HOLMES

University of Louisville

STEPHEN T. HOLMES

University of Central Florida

Sex is a hotly debated topic. How do we discuss this vital human topic truly and accurately? In one respect, sex is a behavior that we acknowledge is important and should be discussed in a personal, rational, and scientific manner. But again, how honest are we when we speak of it even to our most intimate partner? One part of us demands a discussion, whereas another part pleads for some protection from the invasion of our most private fantasies. We do not wish to truly risk our own personal vulnerability. If we lower our guard, will people think less of us? Are our own sexual proclivities beyond the realm of sexual normalcy?

We judge our sexual practices to be normal. But many forms of sex behaviors are beyond the realm of what many consider normal, and some are even illegal. In the second edition of our sex crimes book, we examine several forms of sex behaviors and sex crimes. Initially, we examine the incidences of sex behaviors and crimes that many consider normal under various standards: statistical, cultural, religious, and subjective. Using these four standards as a measure of what is "normal," we examined various forms of behaviors and crimes, many of which are known and some of which are relatively unknown. We devoted one chapter to nuisance sex crimes (exhibitionism, voyeurism, frottage, mysophilia, bestiality, zoophilia, and many others). Other chapters covered subjects such as rape, pedophilia, incest, child pornography, adult pornography, dangerous sex crimes, victims of sexual assaults, and the treatment of sex offenders.

Within each of these chapters, various modes of behavior were discussed. Additionally, we included a chapter on the history of sexual expressions and repression, and the importance of the family and other social institutions in shaping personality and the sexual component within the personality. How did we do that? We examined the institution of the family with the interplay of society, culture, and religious institutions as formative elements. Using history as a framework for analysis, we discussed the evolving family types and how they influenced our thoughts regarding sex. This was true especially for the early Christian family. But the other types had an impact on our own ethos of family and the sexual themes and practices extant in families of today.

Thus, the purpose of the second edition of our book, *Sex Crimes,* is to serve as an introduction to the subject of sex behaviors and sex crimes. Its aim is to examine the topics using a broad perspective while attempting to cover as many topics as possible.

When we wrote the second edition of *Sex Crimes,* we realized that other works existed that were written by academics, researchers, and practitioners. We also understood that several articles were important to cite, and that we needed to alert serious readers to their existence. Thus, the reader as a companion to *Sex Crimes* was envisioned. We believe that these articles deserve exposure for the sake of the value they provide as well as an understanding of the material itself. We deliberated which articles to include, and many were deserving. But, of course, due to space constraints, we were limited in the number of articles we could include. The scope and focus of the reader were difficult, because the more we researched, the more apparent it became that narrowing down the articles would be no easy task. What finally became deciding factors for selection were the appropriateness and timeliness of the articles themselves. Some of the articles were solicited especially for this reader. Other articles were selected from previously published sources. Within the sections we created, we believed it was important to closely mirror the contents of *Sex Crimes, Second Edition.* Thus, there are sections devoted to the topics of nuisance sex crimes, homosexuality, transvestism, transsexualism, juvenile sex crimes, dangerous sex crimes, rape, and special issues and concerns of sex behaviors and crimes.

But before we could decide upon the articles, we needed to examine the current state of sexual affairs to determine the content of the articles. This was our next task.

THE STATE OF SEX IN THE 21ST CENTURY

The appropriateness of certain sexual behaviors in America's 21st century is different certainly from other times and other cultures. In the second edition of *Sex Crimes,* various sexual behaviors are included. Some may disagree with our inclusion of some of these behaviors. For example, some people may argue that prostitution is a moral outrage. Others may say that prostitution is an affront to the dignity of women; and others may argue that those involved in prostitution are using the power of their gender to victimize their customers. Two readings in this book address these concerns.

Voyeurism is another topic about which many people disagree regarding its label as a nuisance behavior. We believe that voyeurism is not only inappropriate but also criminal. The voyeur invades the privacy of another person. In fact, some people believe that seeing another person nude or in a state of undress is an invasion of their being as well as their privacy.

What we have done with the nuisance section, as well as other sections we have included in *Sex Crimes, Second Edition,* is to provide readings that address such behaviors and the issues they present. For example, we have included articles that inspect to varying degrees the sexual behaviors of homosexuality, transvestism, and transsexualism. Although we do not consider these human sexual behaviors to be sex crimes, we do recognize that they can lead to victimization not only in same-sex institutions (e.g., jails, prisons, etc.), but also in our communities and towns by a small but sometimes predatory group of individuals. We also decided to include these topics because of many people's confusion about the differences among the three.

The topic of children and sex is also discussed in this book. Issues of the sexual abuse of children, the Internet and child selection and later victimization, and child sex and the law are examined. As addressed in *Sex Crimes, Second Edition,* the victimization of children is an abomination, and thus a grave and vital social concern. True, children have been sexually victimized by adults since recorded history. Once, children were viewed as chattel to be used and discarded, but today, children are viewed in a much different light. The death of JonBenét Ramsey has highlighted such interest. As a currently unsolved homicide, the murder of the young beauty queen occupied media headlines for months; some people think that the parents are prime suspects. Polly Klaas is another such child victim. The investigation into her death eventually led to the arrest and conviction of her killer. Adam Walsh's death touched the hearts of us all. The killing of three children by Westley Dodd enraged people from one part of our country to another. Even Dodd's execution did not appease many who believed that the death sentence was too easy a punishment for this sadistic child offender.

Most people cannot understand how someone can fatally assault a child. Perhaps even more appalling is that national organizations exist that lobby for the legalization of sex with children. Organizations such as the North American Man-Boy Love Association, the Rene Guyon Society, and the Pedophile Liberation Front demand the revision of laws that make it illegal for an adult to have sex with a child. Such groups make one pause to consider the legal, moral, and ethical issues of such an action.

Society has been touched by crimes against children, and some law enforcement endeavors, such as the National Center for Missing and Exploited Children, seek to protect our precious assets. Federally funded and with its own Web site, this organization dedicates its resources to fighting for the rights of children. Truly, we have come a long way since the early part of this century.

Dangerous sex crimes are also discussed in *Sex Crimes.* We have mirrored that treatment in this reader with articles that discuss these serious sex crimes and behaviors. Serial murder, rape, infibulation, and other kinds of sex behaviors present us with challenges and concerns that address our own safety. Today, we are probably little closer to understanding the psyche of the sexual predator, regardless of the manner in which the offender preys upon others, than we were a few decades ago. We are aware of such infamous sex offenders as Ted Bundy, John Wayne Gacy, Douglas David Clark, and Kenneth Bianchi, but to truly understand them is quite another story. We may have theories (and we do), and we may try to come to some understanding of the etiology of the sexual predator, but in reality, we are barely scratching the surface. The etiology of the sex offender is a vital concern that needs to be addressed. Communities are paralyzed with fear when a sexual predator is active in their areas, and this is evident in the media stories that are often pandered to the public.

When a sexual offender is arrested, adjudicated, and incarcerated, we are then faced with another dilemma. What should be done with this person? Are we really at the point where rehabilitation is the primary aim? If so, what do we do with the offender if he or she is mentally ill or suffers from some type of character defect? What is society's role in the incapacitation and possible rehabilitation of such offenders? Some may believe that warehousing is the answer. Others may believe that society has a responsibility to change the offender into a contributing member of society. Still others adopt a more middle-of-the-road approach. Their stand allows for rehabilitation only after some type of guarantee of public safety. Perhaps some part of that plan involves not only predicting who will someday be a danger to others but also developing some type of realistic strategy to notify citizens when a sex offender is released from a correctional setting. This practice occurs now in many jurisdictions. What we are trying to say, in a rather convoluted way, is that we are dealing with sex offenders in a much different way than we ever have before in human history.

What is the current state of affairs in sex behaviors? True, we are concerned with sexually transmitted diseases, especially HIV/AIDS. We are also concerned with those who sexually abuse our children. This concern spills into the areas of rape, lust murder, and even those sexual behaviors we have taken the liberty of calling "nuisances." This is a big battle, especially in terms of 21st-century technology.

What we have tried to do with this book is to deliberately avoid articles that are theoretical in nature, with the one exception of the article on the exploration of the mind of the serial killer, "Fractured Identity Syndrome: A New Theory of Serial Murder." The other articles are not theoretical in content; they are articles for understanding the latest thoughts and research regarding the sex offender.

CURRENT STATISTICS ON SEX CRIMES

The Uniform Crime Report from 1999 to 2000 (press release, December 18, 2000) states that violent crime has declined in the past year. This does not include forcible rape, which has gradually increased. Regional differences exist, however, with western and northeastern rates increasing and southern rates decreasing. The *Sourcebook of Criminal Justice Statistics 1999* (Bureau of Justice Statistics, 2000) reports that 17.6% of women in the United States have experienced a completed (14.8%) or attempted (2.8%) rape. In 1998, there were 21,922 arrests for rape, 68,536 arrests for prostitution, and 65,536 arrests for other types of sex crimes. These are formidable statistics for any country, and the figures represent arrests only. Obviously, the report does not contain data on the rates of occurrence of these crimes, which would obviously be much higher. Much is made of the drop in the violent crime rate in this country. But in examining the numbers involved, we can see that sex crimes still represent a monumental and formidable problem.

With rape, we normally think of the perpetrator as an oversexed male who victimizes helpless women. In many cases, the depiction of a woman as helpless is true, but not always. In Arkansas, Joshua Brown, 23, was convicted in the rape and murder of a 13-year-old boy whom he suffocated. The victim was drugged, bound, raped, and sodomized at Brown's apartment, which he shared with his gay lover (Skoloff, 2001). Too often, this scenario involves a mysoped and a child. The section on juvenile sex crimes addresses some of the concerns about the apparent rise in the number of children who are sexually victimized by adults.

In some cases, rape is one element in domestic or partner abuse. The number of women and men who are victims of sexual abuse in intimate partner relationships is unknown, mainly because of unreported incidents, but certainly, the number is in the thousands. APBnews.com (May 17, 2000) reports that this number is more than 1 million. In a similar vein, the same media (January 10, 2000) reported that, on the average, nearly four American women are killed each day by a husband, ex-husband, or boyfriend.[1] The number of victims reported in the article does not include the partner abuse of men, which may be more of an underreported crime. It also does not include fathers and stepfathers who rape their children. APBnews.com reports that a man in West Virginia repeatedly raped his 13-year-old daughter in order to teach her about sex and birth control. He said that he raped her as a loving parent who was concerned about teaching her the facts of life. The judge disagreed and sentenced him to prison from 10 to 20 years ("Father Says He Raped Girl," 2001).

Many sex crimes are not reported. Some behaviors are not legally proscribed but may lead to other sex behaviors that are crimes. Most cases of mysophilia coupled with bestiality are never reported unless the sanitary conditions of the premises are so poor that neighbors call the health department. Many times, the health department then calls the police because some type of intervention is required. Transvestism is another sexual behavior that is seldom reported unless a law has been broken, such as a law that forbids cross-dressing in public. Formicophilia, zoophilia, triolism, and other such sex behaviors are usually "closeted" behaviors and do not present themselves to the criminal justice system, so the actual figures, which might be quite high, are low in incidences and even lower in arrests.

CONCLUSION

The contents of this book reflect many of the current issues and behaviors of sex in the 21st century. Some behaviors occur more frequently than others, and some are more serious than others. Some behaviors occur between consenting adults, and others are sex crimes perpetrated against unwilling, unprotected, and vulnerable victims.

Sex will remain an integral part of relationships between people. That is a given. How these behaviors will change over time is left to serious researchers. What we have tried to show here is the current state of sex affairs in the United States in the 21st century.

NOTE

1. For further information, visit the APBnews.com archives at http://www.apbnews.com.

UNIT 2

NUISANCE SEX BEHAVIORS
AND CRIME

In this first series of readings, we are concerned with those behaviors that are neither dangerous nor threatening to society. We have deliberately chosen readings that reflect various forms of sexual behaviors.

The first reading, "Swinging: A Functional Alternative to Prostitution," deals with co-marital sexual behavior. Relying upon past research while working on his doctorate degree at Indiana University, coupled with additional current research and interviews, Ronald Holmes offers a glimpse into the world of fun moralists, or swingers. The original research was based on interviews with 268 swingers in the Midwest. Now, 20 years later, other swingers were interviewed, along with five couples from the original group. For several years, swinging was in a moribund state, but Holmes has found that it is once again in a viable state. The fear of sexually transmitted diseases, including AIDS, was at least a partial influence on many who had thought of swinging. This fear has now passed, and swinging is alive and well and continues to be a functional alternative to prostitution and possibly other forms of sexual activities. The traits and characteristics of the various types of swingers and swinging are explored. For example, most swingers appear to be white, middle-class parents of young children. The husband coerces the wife into swinging, but typically, he is the one who wishes to stop first. Other interesting findings are discussed.

The next article, "The Transformative Power of Sex Work," examines a controversial position. For example, some people believe that women are objectified by the sex work industry. They are used as pawns for the sexual gratification of men. However, Alissa Perrucci offers a different point of view. In her article, she offers the possibility that the sex industry actually empowers women, but not at the expense of men. Considering the strip club as a microcosm of society, both men and women experience power and objectification, and the experience reflects the contradictions of life in this society. In this article, women are not seen as pawns in the hands of men; rather, they control their destiny and gain both power and authority from the achieved status as a worker in some form of sex industry. This article will prove worthy of a healthy discussion.

Nova Sweet and Richard Tewksbury explore the world of women strippers. Their article, "Entry, Maintenance and Departure From a Career in the Sex Industry: Strippers' Experience of Occupational Costs and Rewards," explores the avenues of entry, maintenance, and departure of the sex industry for the female stripper. Sweet, a stripper in college, and Tewksbury, her academic mentor, examine the hidden and secretive world of the adult sex industry, especially stripping and, in too many cases, prostitution. Carefully examining the work of the stripper, the authors also speak of the economic and psychological losses and gains of this form of occupation. What makes this article so important is that it is co-authored by a former worker in the industry. Addressed are actions and issues that were confronted on a firsthand basis. As the authors say,

> Strippers have mixed feelings about their occupational choice, and the degree to which an individual stripper focuses on the rewards and costs vary with time. However, as she accumulates experience, she typically sees the costs coming to outweigh the rewards.

There are obvious psychological gains as well as material gains. Maybe, as the authors suggest, the stripper is more concerned about being in an occupation that provides "a sense of comfort, an appreciation from others, and an enjoyable, 'fun' work environment." Of course, some effects are negative, which the authors also examine.

"Prostitution, the Sex Industry, and Sex Tourism," by Jody Miller and Dheeshana Jayasundera, examines prostitution from a different perspective. Unlike Sweet and Tewksbury's article, this commentary deals with the very real danger of personal violence to which prostitutes are exposed almost daily. How the legal system and social experiences shape the self-perception of the prostitute is also examined. This article offers a unique insight into the world of prostitution; the experiences that the women undergo; the manner in which prostitutes must interact with the legal system; and other psychological, economic, and social issues and concerns. Additionally, the authors discuss the role of prostitution and other forms of the sex industry as entry points into a world of violence directed specifically toward women.

Joseph Davis's original article, "Voyeurism: A Criminal Precursor and Diagnostic Indicator to a Much Larger Sexual Predatory Problem in Our Community," deals with the sexual behavior of voyeurism as a forerunner and possible indicator of later sexually deviant behaviors. Although this article has been placed in the "nuisance" category of this reader, it is important to remember that this form of sexual behavior, also known as scoptophilia, may be a definitive sign of more serious sexual crimes in the future, including predatory sexual crimes of rape, fetish burglary, and frottage. Davis offers information on the backgrounds of voyeurs with the rationale that these signs should be considered "red flags" for future acts of sexual predation as well as tracking strategies for the protection of society. Additionally, Davis stresses that the serial "peeper" may pose a great danger to others in the future unless the criminal justice system and those in the helping professions intervene.

In the final reading in this unit, "Lookin' for Love in All the Wrong Places: Men Who Patronize Prostitutes," the authors, Richard Tewksbury and Patricia Gagné, examine the sex industry from a different perspective. The authors acknowledge that most research on this topic focuses upon the harm that prostitution can do to society, the near exclusiveness of women involved in prostitution, and, finally, the research dedicated to prostitutes themselves. This article is different in that its focus is on the men who patronize prostitutes. Noting that one in five men has a relationship with a prostitute at some time during his adult life, this study devotes itself to examining who these men are, what their motivations are, and what they anticipate getting out of the relationship. In other words, what do the men want, why do they want it, and what do they hope to realize from the transactions in prostitution?

These readings examine sexual behaviors not considered to be dangerous. However, we do stress that, left untreated or ignored, these behaviors may lead to other, dangerous forms of sexual predations. Ted Bundy told Dr. Ronald Holmes that he was a voyeur in his early teenage years. Ann Rule, in her book on the alleged serial killer Randy Woodfield, reported in *The I-5 Killer* that when he was a young teenager, Woodfield was brought before the juvenile justice system on two occasions for indecent exposure. Rule also reported in another book, *The Lust Killer,* that as a teenager, Jerry Brudos, a killer of four women in Oregon, made two young women disrobe so that he could take nude photos of them. Although the early experiences of Bundy, Woodfield, and Brudos were not life-threatening at the time, these men later developed murderous personalities. Perhaps if more attention had been paid at the time, their later actions could have been circumvented. So it is with many nuisance sex crimes.

2

Swinging

A Functional Alternative to Prostitution

———————■———————

RONALD M. HOLMES

University of Louisville

Swinging dates back to the 1950s. Initially, personal ads were the only way for swingers to connect with one another. With the formation of the Sexual Freedom League in the 1960s, this organization paved the way for experimentation in alternative lifestyles. Various sexual behaviors and lifestyles became visible to social and behavioral scientists. Group marriage, trial marriages, communal living, experiments in polygamy, and swinging were but a few of the attempts to change conservative sexual practices. Of course, it was not only sex behaviors that were part of the counterculture of the time. The Vietnam War, draft evaders, the Nixon Watergate scandal, and other social actions were reflecting the mood of the nation. Was there something also occurring in the sexual arena? It appears so.

Swinging was launched into the nation's consciousness by the media. *Bob and Carol and Ted and Alice* emerged from the Hollywood studios with a message that swinging can be a desirable and functional alternative to monogamy. Even though the two couples never actually completed their exchange of partners, the message was still clear. Swinging had now become a visible form of sexual behavior in which "respectable" people were engaged. It was no longer restricted to those who were previously viewed and judged to be sexually perverse and morally degenerate. And it may have personal and societal benefits.

WHAT IS SWINGING?

Swinging is co-marital sexual activity, or the consensual exchange of marital partners for sexual purposes. It can also be viewed as a form of recreational sex between consenting adults, commonly consisting of male-female couples meeting with other male-female couples for sex and, to a much lesser degree, social relationships. What is discussed here is married couples who, with the knowledge and consent of the partner, are actively engaged in the exchange of sex with others on a regular basis. This is different from clandestine, adulterous relationships done without the knowledge or the consent of the partner. Swinging may be less dangerous to the marriage than adulterous activity because both are aware of the activity and are, on one level, consenting to a temporary sexual relationship with another, sometimes a stranger, sometimes not. This latter statement was a common theme arising from the various interviews with current married swingers.

WHAT IS SWINGING?

Swinging is a social and sexual intercourse with someone other than your mate, boyfriend, or girlfriend. In this section, swinging will be confined to those sexual activities between married or cohabiting males and females.

Single swingers will not be discussed here. The dynamics of single swingers may be different from those who are in dyadic, committed relationships. Single swingers may also be different from married swingers in their motives and anticipated gains. The ways in which sexual partners are sometimes selected may be similar to those that are used by married or committed partners, but there are other distinguishing traits and characteristics that separate the various types of swingers. If only for that purpose, this chapter will deal only with married couples who are involved in co-marital sexual activity.

THE EXTENT OF SWINGING

What is the extent of swinging in the United States in the new millennium? This is not an easy question to answer. William and Jerry Breedlove (1970) estimated that there were 10,000 swingers (married couples) active in the late 1960s and early 1970s. This number was gleaned from several sources. The authors extrapolated this number from advertisements that appeared in various swinging magazines. One, for example, *Select*, had advertisements that contained, in one issue, 5,000 people interested in meeting other people who were interested in this form of alternative lifestyle. Other magazines were consulted, such as *American Swinger* and *Kindred Spirits*. Each of the publications held advertisements from single people, divorced people, and married (or committed) couples, but the exact number was unknown. Many swingers remained hidden from open society because there were potentially severe problems associated with being a "mate swapper" in that time in American society.

The extent of swingers currently involved is still unknown. Jenks (1995) believes that the number will never be known because of the social and cultural inhibitions against those who live such an alternative lifestyle. However, despite a reduced number involved in this behavior in the 1980s due to the risk of sexually transmitted diseases, including AIDS, it appears now that the number of couples involved is increasing again. One way to measure this increase, if only in interest, is the number of Web sites devoted to swinging.

THE DECISION TO
BECOME INVOLVED IN SWINGING

Why does one become involved in swinging? Obviously, there are no simple reasons. The answers are varied and, in many cases, complex. Some couples may decide to enter the swinging scene because of a reason that never occurred to others. One couple interviewed stated that they decided to swing because their sexual relationship with each other had become uninteresting. During the interview with Jim and Marlene, conducted in their living room, the couple stated that they had been swinging for the past 15 years. They became involved as a result of an affair that Jim was having with a neighbor. Marlene decided that one way to get back at Jim was to have an affair of her own. This led to several adulterous relationships before each decided to confront the other with what he or she had done. Talking about the affairs, according to both, was a painful experience. But what they learned was that they had enjoyed the sexual part of the affairs, and they decided that they could still experience the sexual, recreational aspects while declining the relationship parts of the events. They started their swinging experience by going to a local swinging bar, then joined a national swinging magazine and attended a few swinging conferences in nearby large cities. I asked them about the extent of their swinging partners, and Jim believed that the number of his partners was 2,000. Marlene estimated hers to be as many as 5,000.

Jim and Marlene are not typical swingers. Their children are aware of their sexual lifestyle. Their neighbors are also cognizant of their sexual activities. They are "open swingers," not restricting themselves to few partners. They are also atypical as far as their length of time involved in swinging.

Swingers become involved in co-marital sexual activities for other reasons as well.

• *Bored With Marriage.* Some couples involve themselves in swinging because they believe they are in a marriage that lacks vitality and vigor. In other words, the spark seems to be gone from their marriage, and swinging may be one way to rekindle the old flame that was once part of their union. Several couples in the sample stated that they had become somewhat routinized in their relationships, and that behaviors became predictable both of a personal and sexual nature. By even deciding to explore the possibility of swinging, this initial decision appeared to be enlivening their relationship and became a focal part of their discussion and planning.

• *Bored With Marital Sex.* Almost without exception, the sample of 276 married couples admitted that their sexual lives with one another had become predictable. As several said, they could not only reliably predict when the partner would be sexually approachable, but also what would be the next move in their sexual scripts with one another. In other words, what was at one time spontaneous and unexpected was now planned, often after the evening news. What many were trying to recapture was the sexual scenario that was a part of their younger days with each other when sex was new and, for want of a better word, unanticipated.

• *Consensual Adultery.* Many swingers voice an opinion that swinging is not adultery because it is done with the knowledge and consent of the partner. Most say that they would not consider a clandestine sexual affair because it would be a fraud against their partner.

What they do consider with swinging is a sexual relationship with a person, sometimes with their partner in the same room, so there is no fraud, no hypocrisy, and no need to lie about their sexual activities. In essence, then, what swingers are saying is that, at least on one level, a decision to become involved in co-marital, consensual sex with others is not considered a form of adultery because of the knowledge and permission of one's partner.

• *Recreational and Inexpensive.* The decision to become involved in a swinging relationship with another couple or in the open swinging scene is, for some couples, based on the recreational and expense elements. For example, some couples believe that sex and love can be compartmentalized. Thus, for these couples, sex can be viewed as a form of recreation, no different from playing golf or tennis with another couple or a series of couples. This is very difficult to understand for those who do not share their fun morality sexual philosophy. Additionally, many believe that swinging is a very inexpensive form of entertainment. If one couple joins another couple for a swinging evening, then the expense is minor compared to the traditional evening of dining out, a movie, and other minor expenses. One couple interviewed stated that the whole evening's expense may be one bottle of wine.

• *Outlet for Sexual Deviancy.* For many people, talking openly about their sexual desires to their most intimate partner is difficult. For this reason, becoming involved with relative strangers in a swinging scene affords the individual an opportunity to voice a preference for a certain type of sex that one would not share with a partner. As one swinger related in my conversation with him, his propensity was to pretend to have sex with a corpse. He asks his female partner that evening to be very still, or "asleep," as he penetrates her. He said that he would never ask his wife to do that because he believed she would think him to be weird or perverted. Another preference of this same person is his desire for anal sex, something to which his wife is totally opposed. He has found some of his partners to be very willing, whereas others are not. Nevertheless, he said, he does risk personal rejection when asking his swinging partner, but this rejection is only temporary. If his wife rejects him, their marriage is at stake.

Many males have a fantasy of seeing women involved in lesbian behavior. One husband stated that it is a great visual aphrodisiac for him to watch his wife involved sexually with another woman. The wife related that she was somewhat curious about her own sexuality, and when she was first sexually involved with another woman at a party, she discovered that it was not repugnant. Instead, she enjoyed this experience.

Society judges other forms of behaviors to be deviant, but the swinging scene offers a situation in which many believe they can be free with their desires as long as others are willing partners. The only exception I have found is the reluctance and even refusal of swingers to allow males to engage sexually with other males.

TYPES OF SWINGING

Basically, there are two types of swingers: open and closed. Although swingers have preferences that distinguish them from other people, initially, they are involved in swinging with a variety of people, mostly strangers, but sometimes with couples they have known for some time.

Open swingers are more blatant when seeking sexual partners. For example, open swingers are more likely to advertise in magazines or on the Internet, seek people from local bars, attend conventions/socials, or seek out people they have met through other acquaintances or even neighbors.

Closed swingers are more conservative in their approach when selecting sexual partners. Typically, closed swingers know the couples with whom they will be involved, couples with whom they have been friends for some time. They are more likely to have fewer sexual partners and to have partners with whom they are personally acquainted. Some may have been in school together or have lived close to each other for some time.

Some swingers, still either open or closed, have certain sexual proclivities and seek out those with similar sexual interests. Some are interested in sadism and masochism, and some are devotees of urolagnia, coprolagnia, or other forms of sexual paraphilias. These types of sexual interests will be mentioned later during this chapter.

THE DEVELOPMENT OF A SWINGING LIFESTYLE

Becoming involved in an alternative sexual lifestyle such as swinging is not something that is immediately thought of and then acted upon. There is a process of deciding to do this. In interviewing 276 married couples who are swingers in a large, midwestern city, I found that a swinging personality was something that developed. First of all, it appears that in most cases, the husband convinces the wife to experiment with the swinging experience. But then, in the majority of cases, the wife wishes to continue with the swinging. Once the wife makes the decision to swing, she is more determined that she has made the correct choice and that it is for the good of the marriage (Holmes, 1972).

Once a couple decides to become involved in co-marital sexual activity, whatever the elements are that lead to that judgment, means and methods exist to seek sexual partners. Some of the ways could lead to the swingers' lifestyle being discovered, and the effects can be damaging. Regardless, some are willing to risk discovery, possibly by their children, and loss of job, among other things. The decision is made to proceed to a sexual involvement with friends (closed swinging) or strangers (open swinging).

Methods of Recruitment

Personal Recruitment

Perhaps the most risky manner in which to find other swingers is personal recruitment. This is prevalent especially among the closed swingers, who will solicit potential partners from friends and/or neighbors who appear to be at least interested in discussing the possibility of involvement.

One couple interviewed stated that they talked with a couple who were neighbors. The women went shopping and then to lunch. At the luncheon, the swinger broached the subject and then made a proposition. The neighbor was offended by this proposal, and soon, word got around the subdivision that the couple were swingers. It affected both the couple and their two children, who were in the neighborhood elementary school. The couple felt pressured to move and relocated in another section of the community. Eventually, they moved to another state, where they currently reside.

TABLE 2.1   Annual Swinger National Conventions

Name of Organization	Location	E-mail or Web Address
Visions	Ft. Pierce, Florida	visions@cadv.com
Happenings	Flint, Michigan	tp38@aol.com
Wind & Waves	Lynnwood, Washington	peoples@premier1.net
Lifestyles Convention	Buena Park, California	convention@lifestyles.org
Swing Fling	Madison, Wisconsin	WISwingstock.com@aol.com
Chicago Adventure	Vernon Hills, Illinois	clubadventure@clubadventure.org

Clubs and Socials and Cyberspace Recruitment

There are large and small swinging organizations that sponsor swinging clubs and socials or conventions. In the 1970s, national conventions of swingers were sponsored by *Select*. These conventions were held almost monthly in large cities throughout the United States—Chicago, Baltimore, New York, and so on. The conventions sponsored workshops on topics such as safe sex and sex techniques, as well as dinners, dances, and other opportunities to meet like-minded people.

With the rise in technology, the Internet has become a site for advertisements for national conventions. Table 2.1 contains a sample convention list. The conventions also advertise the activities that are unique to the occasion. For example, one advertised the following:

> Annual international convention since 1973. The largest gathering of PlayCouples in the world. Academic and experiential presentations on lifestyles, relationships. Sexuality, topical subjects, Adult MarketPlace exhibits; Erotic Arts Exhibit; games, theme dances; Ms. Lifestyles Swimsuit Pageant, Evening of Caressive Intimacy and Erotic Masquerade Banquet & Ball. Some events are sponsored by resorts, airlines and other corporations. All couples welcome. Expected attendance 1800+ couples. This year's convention is set for the Famous Las Vegas Tropicana.

The conferences and socials are not only a means to alert swingers to others who share a common lifestyle, but they have also become big business for those who sponsor such conventions.

Magazines

As swinging emerged in the late 1960s and early 1970s, so did an abundance of magazines. These magazines listed ads and photographs of swingers who advertised their availability. The ads were usually accompanied by a description of what the couple desired, their location, and other pertinent information. For example, the following is an ad from *Select*, a national swinger's magazine:

C35-393. Couple new to swinging, wish to meet other like-minded couples. Can travel within 50 mile radius of Nashville. No B&D or S&M. Wife is versatile, husband is safe. Photo & phone. All photos will be returned.

The number in the ad begins with the letter C which stands for "Couple." A letter M denotes a male advertising and F indicates a female ad. B&D stands for bondage and discipline; S&M means sadism and masochism. The wife is bisexual (versatile), and the husband has a vasectomy (safe).

In 1972, the author placed an ad in *Select* as part of a study. From this one ad, without a picture, 276 replies were received from couples in a three-state area around Kentucky. Some replies to the letter, sent first to the *Select* mailing address and then forwarded to the person(s) placing the ad, contained photos, home addresses, telephone numbers, and other personal information. This information was sent even though the sender knew only what had appeared in the advertisement in the magazine.

Other magazines, including *Kindred Spirits, American Swinger,* and *Swinger News,* followed the same format as *Select.*

BENEFITS OF SWINGING

The literature suggests certain benefits for swingers. These benefits are those reported by those currently involved in the alternative lifestyles and must be viewed with some skepticism because of their present involvement.

• *Enhances Marriages.* From the research by those already cited in this chapter, and also from the interviews I conducted, many swingers believe that their marriages have been helped by their involvement in co-marital sexual activity. They state that their lines of verbal communication used to be limited to the everyday, mundane missives about children, home, bills, yard work, and so on. But since swinging, they have many other things to speak about with each other, albeit sexual stories of their own involvement sexually with others. Because the relationships are not clandestine, the couples believe they can speak of their own behaviors openly with each other, and this openness extends now to other areas of their lives together. This point is further covered in a following section.

The couples state that they look at each other differently now. For example, one husband remarked that his wife has gotten more attractive since they started to swing. He said that she is more aware of her own appearance, has lost weight, dresses more fashionably, and has undertaken a health enhancement program. He has lost weight and engages in an exercise program of his own. Both stated that the quality of their sex life together has grown better, and the frequency of their sex encounters together has increased. But how typical are their results?

What needs to occur is a longitudinal study to measure in some respect the validity of their argument. Three couples whom I know have been swinging since the early 1970s. All three are still married at this time. Their children are not aware of their swinging experiences, and the couples all say that swinging has been and continues to be a healthy and remedial experience in their married lives.

• *Enhanced Sexual Techniques.* Some swingers complain of a boring sex life with their partners prior to swinging. In the swinging scene, these same people state that their involvement with swinging has taught them some sexual techniques that they bring to their own marriage bed and that enhance their own sex lives. These techniques involve oral and anal sex, intercourse, foreplay, sex games, and, with some of the women, lesbian sex.

• *Increased Communication With Spouse.* Many swingers complain about the lack of personal communication that exists between the partners. However, after their involvement in swinging, the sense and level of communication is reported to increase. True, the content of the communication may involve their activities in swinging, but nevertheless, the swingers report that they have a great deal more to discuss than before their involvement, including both sex activities and other items of personal concern. The swingers report that they are more likely to return to a communication level that was present earlier in their married life. In other words, they talk about personal and nonpersonal items that had been neglected for some time prior to their involvement in co-marital sexual activity.

• *Manner of Meeting New Acquaintances.*   There is no doubt that swingers open a gateway for meeting new people who share a similar perspective on extramarital sexual relationships. These new acquaintances often have other things in common. Many are professionals (often middle class) of about the same age, parents of young children, and just starting on their careers or married lives. Thus, they have many things to discuss and can share common experiences and concerns. These new acquaintances offer an opportunity for swingers to widen their range of activities with an increasing range of newly acquainted people that, under ordinary circumstances, they would have never met. This is especially true for open swingers. For example, if a newly committed couple attends a social or convention, as mentioned earlier, one can see that the people they meet at that convention would have remained complete strangers in ordinary circumstances.

• *Lowering Sexual Inhibitions.* Many swingers report that their partners, especially the wives, are sexually inexperienced and naive in sexual matters. Many others state that their partners—again, especially the wives—are sexually inhibited, that is, not willing to try new sexual techniques or games. However, once one makes the decision to swing, these inhibitions may be lowered the more one is involved in this act, leading one to become dedicated to the lifestyle of swinging. This point of view is reinforced by the works of Jenks (1995), Dixon (1985a, 1985b), and Fang (1976). It may be true that once one decides to become a swinger and is involved in a swinging episode(s), sexual inhibitions are lowered and one is more willing to do some sexual acts that previously would have been judged too risqué. This is very evident in sex between women. Among the swingers in my study, I found that few of the women had been involved sexually with another woman. However, in swinging, lesbian sex is encouraged by the men, and many women become involved to the extent that it becomes an integral part of the swinging parties.

• *Decrease in Divorce Rates.* Sometimes, swingers make remarks concerning the low divorce rate among those who practice this lifestyle, and this was indeed the case among the local group I studied, where the divorce rate was less than 20%. If sexual monotony is lessened, if clandestine adulterous relationships are rare, if communication is increased, and if other matters are improved in the marriage, then it is easy to see that the divorce rate would decrease. However, this issue does need further study.

LIABILITIES OF SWINGING

As with other forms of human behavior, swinging does have its liabilities. Swingers report the following as some of the difficulties encountered.

• *Others' Indiscretions.* Perhaps the greatest fear of swingers is that others will discover their involvement. "Others" would include their employers, families, friends, acquaintances, and neighbors. This has obvious negative ramifications, because an employer would react to such news with the termination of employment. This scenario was especially true in the case of a local minister and his wife who were involved in an open swinger situation. The discovery was made by a nonswinger who had been talking with a swinger, and the swinger mentioned the minister's name. The nonswinger went to the local association of his Christian faith and demanded that the minister be terminated immediately. The association did so after a meeting with the minister and his wife. The couple moved to another state. The risk of discovery looms heavy in the minds of most swingers, but again with most, it does not deter them.

• *Unwanted Pregnancy.* Although not as much a concern as it once was, the fear of an unwanted pregnancy is still present. With the advances of the medical field in controlling fertilization, this fear has greatly diminished. Regardless, it is still a concern for some swingers. In one unusual situation, four couples in my sample were involved in closed swinging for at least 2 years each. Their minister had told them that they could exchange partners for sex because in their situation, it was not adultery. However, they were not allowed to practice any form of birth control!

• *Contracting Unwanted Disease.* Traditionally, venereal disease has been an issue that swingers have had to address. The diseases were usually syphilis and gonorrhea. However, the past two decades have alerted swingers and others who feel the need to become involved with multiple partners to the possibility of contracting AIDS. At one time, AIDS was responsible for a drastic reduction in the number of swingers, but this reduced membership, especially in the open swinger category, seems to have reached its low point. Swingers appear to be more comfortable now in their acceptance of the risk of contracting this disease. Thus, AIDS does not appear to be the deterrent it once was.

One manner in which the swinging enterprise has tried to cope with the problem of contracting sexually transmitted diseases (STDs) is through education. As mentioned earlier, conventions are one such means to alert swingers not only to the prevalence of STDs but also to the methods of early identification and medical treatment.

• *Forced Membership.* In most cases of couples involved in swinging, the husband attempts to persuade the wife to become involved. This forced membership situation is often mentioned by partners who were initially opposed to the idea. The partner who was coerced admitted that the spouse's mention of the activity was devastating at the time, but as time went on and other discussions followed, including threats of divorce, the partner decided to appease the spouse and try it at least one time.

The forced membership issue is one that many spouses mention as being especially traumatic, but at the same time, had it not been for such an ultimatum, they probably would have never become involved.

• *Children's Discovery.* This appears to be the most important of all the concerns of married swingers. Preventing discovery by their children looms as a priority for most. They may keep the swingers magazines hidden, place parental controls on the Web sites that deal with the swinging scene, and make certain that children do not walk into a swinging party that they host.

In my interviews with the swingers, I found only one couple whose children knew of their parents' involvement. In that family, the daughter was 18 and the son was 17. The parents stated that the children had known for several years about their involvement. The children had not participated in any form of sexual play with others at the many swinger parties hosted by the couple. The swingers stated that the children could involve themselves later in their lives as swingers, but that was a concern for each child and the child's spouse when that time came. They also stated that under no circumstances would they involve themselves in swinging with their children; they considered that incest, and that was a taboo taken seriously by all swingers.

• *Marital Difficulty and Establishment of Relationships.* Swingers sometimes involve themselves in co-marital sexual activity in an attempt to solve an unhappy marriage. This is hardly a positive reason to swing. As mentioned by one swinger, if one is in an unhappy marriage, swinging will only destroy it further. The reason to swing is to enjoy a healthy sexual relationship with others without the hypocrisy and clandestine activities that occur with typical adulterous affairs.

Additionally, swingers mention that one of their concerns with swinging is the possibility of meeting someone else and developing a positive emotional relationship with that person. This relationship could lead to a strain or a break with the spouse, especially if the reason for swinging was to try to remedy a marriage in trouble. This is one reason that many swingers go to some length to avoid knowing the others on an intimate, personal level. For example, many open swingers know the other couples only by first names. Answers to ads are often directed to post office box numbers rather than home addresses. One swinger mentioned that he was becoming concerned about one couple whom he and his wife had met at a party and with whom they had swung on several occasions. He said that they had met the couple on several nonsexual occasions (i.e., dinner, movie, etc.), and that he and his wife were becoming very fond of them. He was concerned that they were falling in love with the other couple. To salvage their marriage, they decided that they should not see the other couple again. To pursue such a relationship runs counter to the swingers' impersonal sex philosophy.

• *Sexual Boredom.* Swingers admit that one of the reasons for their initial involvement in swinging is to resolve sexual boredom. Yet this is also a potential problem for those already involved in swinging. For example, several swingers in this sample admitted that they had learned a great deal concerning sexual techniques. Some tried to bring those lessons to their own marriage bed, with varying degrees of success. One couple mentioned that although they had learned to experiment sexually with other couples, their own sex life had not kept up with the sex they shared with their swinging partners.

Thus, some couples feel pressure to try new techniques that they have learned in swinging sessions, but they have met with resistance from their own marital partners. This has led some swingers to evaluate their sexual life with their partner. Honest communication must be developed to meet this potential obstacle in their marriage.

CONCLUSION

Swinging as a social and sexual lifestyle has been with us in American society for the past several decades, and there is no sign that it is in a moribund state. Rather, with the fun morality philosophy of many couples; the different avenues through which to advertise their availability (magazines, socials and conventions, bars, the Internet); and the advances made in the medical field in the fight against STDs, there may be an increase in the number of couples who involve themselves in this alternative sexual lifestyle. There is no doubt that swinging is not for everyone; certain social, cultural, religious, and subjective proscriptions serve as functional deterrents. But to some, swinging is a rewarding and recreational activity that does not appear to interfere with their marriages in any detrimental way.

3

The Transformative Power
of Sex Work

———■———

ALISSA C. PERRUCCI

Duquesne University

✿

REFLEXIVE STATEMENT

Women's subjectivity—their feelings and expressions of themselves as persons—is complicated by the ways in which women's sexuality is deemed transgressive. Women become sexual beings in a world of conflicted messages and double binds. They are taught that they must contain their sexuality at the same time that they are rewarded for augmenting their sexual desirability. For both workers and customers, the world of sex work is typically seen as a deviant expression of sexual desire. However, the gendered dynamics within this world are often not so different from those in everyday sexual relationships. The context of sex work highlights the dynamics of power (for men) and objectification (of women), but a closer look reveals that sex workers are indeed expressing a sense of empowerment. It is tempting for academic feminism to declare that any feelings of empowerment are evidence of a false consciousness or rationalizations for their choice of work. Our task becomes to not only acknowledge that human experience is conflicted but also search for the catalysts for such conflicts within the social discourse on feminine sexuality. A serious and genuine consideration of the voices of persons that are marginalized within a culture is key to changing that discourse. Subversion of any repressive understanding of sexuality must begin with an understanding of the social construction of sexuality and desire, and that objectification and empowerment coexist for all genders.

INTRODUCTION

Sex work is a context that can transform the power dynamics of gendered interactions. This transformation is accomplished through aspects of the sex worker's subjectivity: her sense of

Author's Note: This article first appeared in *Humanity and Society,* Vol. 24 No. 4, November 2000, pp. 323-337. Reprinted with permission of *Humanity and Society.*

privacy, and her sexuality. The way a woman chooses to embody her sexuality in the context of her work transforms the discourse of masculine and feminine desire, and sexuality. A woman's feelings about doing sex work, and the revelation or concealment of those feelings in the context of that work, are aspects of her agency and ultimately, her subjectivity. This paper is based on interviews with five exotic dancers in the Pittsburgh area. Interviews focused on the dancers' experience of privacy, how they protected their privacy, and the significance of violated privacy. A qualitative analysis of the data revealed that dancers consider body parts and processes, feelings and desires, personal information, and role identities to be private. A sense of privacy is possible when a dancer can control the revelation and concealment of these aspects of body and self. A sense of control is significant because it is tied to one's sense of autonomy and agency; a woman's personhood is acknowledged and legitimates her ability to make choices regarding her sexuality. Specifically, the choice to reveal or conceal aspects of self and body is empowering. In the seductive play of the strip club, both participants—customer and dancer—engage in differing degrees of self-disclosure and self-concealment. If this play is kept within the boundaries of the club's rules, privacy remains intact. Dancer and customer then have the freedom to inhabit a mutually satisfying space of sexual expression. In contrast, the customer's concealment of his motivations and desires is problematic for the dancer's sense of control and, ultimately, her privacy.

For some dancers, it is important to conceal certain body parts and keep aspects of their personal lives separate from their jobs. For others, the context of sex work is a site of liberation, and freedom from repressive notions of feminine sexuality. Sex work becomes the possibility for the public expression of sexuality precisely because it exists within the realm of fantasy. The play of exotic dancing depends in part on the mystery that surrounds both participants and their willingness to engage with one another within the boundaries and rules of the club. The transformative power of sex work originates in the dancer's control over what she reveals and/or conceals during the customer-dancer encounter. The sense of control gives way to a sense of privacy and agency and is ultimately the grounds by which she can feel empowered.

The structure of the strip club is founded upon a set of rules that both limits and facilitates the customer's fantasy. The interactions between dancers and customers are constructed in part by discourses that govern heterosexual interactions. In order to keep the structure of fantasy intact, the dancer must, at times, conceal personal feelings and desires. If she enjoys dancing, she may find that her desire shows itself when she is at work. If she dislikes her job she will most likely conceal her true feelings. The revelation and concealment of these feelings is her choice, just as it was her choice to be a dancer. Women become sex workers for many reasons. Some enjoy the work, some want a flexible schedule and a high hourly wage, while others have few alternatives. Those who state that sex work is not part of feminist discourse believe that women are degraded no matter what they experience. However, whether or not a woman enjoys dancing, she can decide what stance she will take toward the dynamics within that system.

Kappeler (1986) maintains that sex workers do not have power. The structure of representation in society, specifically pornographic representation, is such that it confines women to positions of subordination and elevates men to positions of power. These gender-specific positions are infused in the language and images of both pornography and the everyday world. Of central importance to the anti pornography debate is that pornography, through the objectification of women, radically distorts attitudes about and behaviors toward women. Objectification—the limitation of women's actions, freedoms, and possibilities—perpetuates socially constructed gender inequality by narrowing the conceptualization of the feminine. The images and fantasies of pornography seduce the viewer into subscribing to a new reality of feminine sexuality. More than a mere representation of actual sexual practices, pornography constructs and perpetuates a skewed picture of feminine sexuality and desire. What is represented in pornography comes to reside in the world along with other objects and things; it is not simply fantasy. For Kappeler, there is no freedom for the subject to create her own sexual reality within pornography.

Many feminists who support pornography propose that the variation of its images and scripts provide for the possibility that men can be objects for women, and that men can be dominated and objectified. Kappeler argues that there cannot be "equal exploitation" (1986;50), because the model for objectification is based on women and is ultimately created by, and for, men. A man need not be the actual viewer or maker of pornography, but the man-as-subject stands, for Kappeler, as the third term in every pornographic relation. No matter how creative pornography becomes, nor how many images portray women in positions of supposed dominance and power, it is impossible to place objectification on equal terms between the genders. Men depend upon the representation of women to demonstrate their power, as well as their very existence. The fantasies and images of pornography are reality, and not just in the sexual arena; the residue of representation is everywhere. The viewing and self-expression that is involved in watching pornography is an action that exists in the world and shapes reality.

Feminists have long struggled with the possibility of a positive side to pornography and sex work, and many are caught between the belief that pornography is detrimental while at the same time experiencing pleasure and power through it (Williams, 1989). It offers an arena of sexual freedom where a woman is encouraged to explore her sexuality without shame or stigma (McElroy, 1995). It liberates a space for sexuality and fantasy much in the same manner as did the feminist movement. Paglia scolds the "middle class feminist mentality of arrogance, conceit, and prudery" (1994;57) that portrays the sex worker as a victim. Instead of serving to imprison women in roles of submission and objectification, pornography profoundly demonstrates "men's excruciating obsession with and subordination to women" (1994;58). The prostitute becomes "the ultimate liberated woman, who lives on the edge and whose sexuality belongs to no one" (1994;58). She rejects the interpretation that pornography only serves to denigrate and shame women, and limit their sexual and individual freedom: "Sexual objectification is characteristically human and indistinguishable from the art impulse. There is nothing degrading in the display of any part of the human body" (1990;62). To characterize pornography as deviant or immoral upholds misogynist, repressive views of women's sexuality. The dancer personifies the mystery of feminine sexuality because in the act of stripping the reproductive organs can never be fully seen (Paglia, 1994). While Kappeler sees power as an impossibility for women in pornography, Paglia views women as clearly dominant in this realm of sexual expression.

On stage, dancers command the attention of customers who follow their every move. Men come to the strip bar night after night to drink and watch dancers. They stand at the edge of the stage with dollar bills extended, waiting patiently for the dancers to attend to them. Some men sit at the bar and watch because they are too shy to tip. Others spend their entire paychecks and overdraw their credit cards. However, a customer can violate a dancer's privacy. At times, she may feel "like a piece of meat or a piece of shit" from the way that he looks at her or tries to touch her. Objectification is a possibility for the dancer just as are feelings of power. Most importantly, a shared feeling of respect and mutual understanding that coexists between dancer and customer is essential to a balance of power and the existence of a shared space of sexual expression.

THE MYSTERY OF THE DANCER'S DESIRE

The persona of the exotic dancer involves the creation and projection of a particular embodied sexuality; this is part of her performance. To be successful, a dancer must entice customers to pay for individual attention. Her dance routine, makeup, and costumes are chosen to reflect customers' preferences, as well as her own. A dancer must pay attention to tipping customers, even if she finds them disagreeable. At times, it is the mystery of the dancer's desire that fascinates the customer. He may pursue the truth of her thoughts, feelings, and personal life. He might ask her personal questions or try to touch her. Most customers, however, follow the rules and take responsibility for constructing their fantasies within these perimeters. In the tension between her own and her customers' desires, a dancer must, at times, "swallow [her] pride" and go out on stage. At times, dancers strive to create the appearance of feeling seductive or attracted to a customer, even if their true feelings are contrary.

> A lot of times if you're not in the mood, you've got cramps or whatever or if you're sick, the way I get into my dancing I think of my boyfriend. You know, making love to him or how he turns me on and that actually helps me dance better.

Despite what her customers might be imagining, Erica was, at times, thinking of her boyfriend in order to dance more seductively. Other times, she felt sick or uncomfortable in her body. Nevertheless, she projected an aura of coolness and control. Erica professed a love for dancing. It was better than "killing [her]self working two jobs" for less pay; it enabled the lifestyle that she enjoyed, and helped her plan financially for her future once she stopped dancing. She was angered by customers who conflated her performance on stage with her nondancer identity. She considered herself to be a performer and relished this aspect of her job. She created the illusion of sexual desire for customers, and this gave her a feeling of power. Erica enjoyed the game that occurred within the boundaries of the club's rules and having license to "jack off" customers. This expression is slang for teasing or playing around with another's expectations. Erica enjoyed the flirtations that occurred with her customers, but she also had regular customers with whom she sat and conversed.

> People tell me I enjoy my job too much. I love teasing guys! I mean think about it. I'm getting paid just to jack 'em off, you know! And if I want to, I can drink and party a little bit. As long as you can control yourself, you're fine.

In slight contrast, Shelley preferred to feel comfortable and "relaxed" while on stage dancing; she considered herself to be an entertainer. It was less important to her to try to be "sexy," because that did not feel natural to her. Regardless of her customers' interpretations of her performance, Shelley stated that she did not always intend to appear seductive or overtly sexual.

I feel like I'm here to entertain. I like to have a good time. I like to dance and most of the time I'm more relaxed than I am sexy because I try to be sexy and then I'll just burst out laughing because I can't handle it.

Shelley was not ashamed of her costume because it was similar to a bathing suit and athletic gear. Although she would never show her genitals, she was not as worried about her breasts because they were small, and her nipples were covered by pasties. She felt that her small breasts made her body less sexual. Having less flesh to conceal, she was less of a sexual object, and even less like an exotic dancer. By comparing her costume to a bathing suit, dancing became more like a public behavior and less like a revelation of private body parts.

As long as I have my G-string on I feel cool. I feel like I'm in basically nothing more than a bathing suit. Some of my bathing suits probably show more. And when I'm working out at the gym I'm in about the same attire, you know? And I don't have big breasts so I don't feel like I'm really showing anything there.

Brooke differed from the other participants in that she enjoyed dancing nude, and she did not stress the importance of separating a private self from her exotic dancer persona. Brooke was outspoken, assertive, and took on somewhat of a supervisory role with her co-workers. She had strong ethics of self-control and responsibility. Her certainty that customers took pleasure in her nudity gave her the confidence to present herself in a way that she considered to be authentic. This confidence was not equaled when she danced in pasties and a G-string.

I enjoy being naked. When I dance totally nude I enjoy being naked. It lets me express myself the way I wanted to express myself. Because what you see is what you get! There ain't no hiding nothing.

Brooke was true to herself from her full disclosure of her body and her feelings about being naked. Although there were times when she felt self-conscious about her body, she believed that there were remedies to help conceal flaws and accentuate stronger features. In contrast, Shelley believed that showing her genitals to strangers was too intimate. Erica had "no problem dancing nude." She emphasized that she did not do so by choice. Both Erica and Shelley enjoyed the performance aspect of their jobs. They considered themselves to be skilled entertainers and relished the seductive play of dancing. They also expressed more of a need for privacy in terms of a separation between private self and dancer persona. It was important to Erica that her job remained a secret from her family, and she had a hard time "staying in character" when persons that she knew from her everyday life came into the club. Although Shelley did not describe a conflict between her worlds, she did state that she had begun to drink more heavily at work in order to tolerate customers' insensitive remarks. All three women stressed the importance of a mutual respect between dancer and customer that was necessary for each to be comfortable in her or his role. When this was not possible, each stressed that there were times when true feelings were covered over in order to protect themselves from the customers' violating behaviors.

Just as dancers expected customers to leave their fantasies at the door when the night was over, they assumed that intimate others would not subject them to the demands of work once they arrived at home. It was difficult for Nicole's boyfriend to understand that the character she created at work was not who she wanted to be at home, nor was it representative of her sexuality within their relationship. He expected the same favors and attention that Nicole granted her customers.

> [My boyfriend] expects me to come home and dance for him. I keep telling him, "Look, it's my job. I don't like it and I sure as hell don't want to do it when I'm done with five or six hours of work." [He says,] "If I was a mechanic, you'd want me to fix your car." I said that's different. I said that ain't a mind game. Being a mechanic you get your fingers dirty. I said I can go be a mechanic and I'll work on your car.

The reality, or truth, of Nicole's desire was a mystery to her partner. He was jealous of the type of attention that Nicole granted her customers, believing that she withheld her true sexuality from him. He treated her like a dancer when she was at home, pursuing the truth of her desire. Nicole was unable to fully separate her dancer life from her everyday life. She felt that the two worlds had contaminated one another. Being an exotic dancer was something that she wanted to hide from her kids, and she wanted customers to stay out of her everyday life. Six months prior to our interview a customer had been stalking her, and he was recently allowed back into the club. She felt that her hold on personal safety was tenuous and adamantly declared that she had "no privacy." The mystery of Nicole's desire was sought by both customers and intimate others. She had little recourse to protecting her privacy, but she continued to dance. However, she had positive relationships with many of her regular customers because they respected her boundaries.

THE MYSTERY OF THE CUSTOMER'S DESIRE

A dancer's ability to maintain an aura of ambiguity surrounding her own desires facilitates her sense of privacy. The ambiguity of the customer's desires, on the other hand, is detrimental to a sense of control and privacy, because dancers depend upon the customer's predictability in order to plan their self-presentation. Nicole was often disturbed by the mystery of a customer's thoughts. Usually, she was conscious of the fact that he was staring at her body. The unknown aspects of his thoughts and feelings detracted from her sense of control.

> It's having to deal with the fact that people are standing there looking at you totally naked with whatever's going through their mind and they don't even have the decency to tip you for it.

It was especially unnerving to consider that a customer might be focusing on a flaw, or a particular characteristic of her body. In these moments, she became self-conscious. However, she quickly resigned herself to the task at hand by focusing on making money. She could "block out" an undesirable interaction with a customer if she concentrated on the desirable financial outcome.

Dancers expected customers to follow the club's rules so that the intimate nature of the relationship would remain on the level of fantasy. Any uncertainty regarding the customer's expectations inhibited a dancer's ability to prepare herself for an interaction. New customers presented the possibility of unusual demands or expectations. Regular customers required little assessment on the part of the dancers because their behaviors were predictable.

It was less likely that a regular customer would try to break the rules by touching or asking personal, intrusive questions. Regular customers made the job pleasant because they were friendly, happy to see the dancers, always tipped, and sometimes even brought them gifts. An unfamiliar face meant that a dancer had to assess the new person's motivations and anticipate his reactions. Brooke always remained attentive and alert when she approached a new customer, particularly during a lap dance where she would be more vulnerable to intrusions of privacy.

> You read the guy. If you're doing stage work you really don't worry about it. But in a private dance, you read the guy and you never let your guard down because even the nicest person can turn into a Mr. Hyde. They might be really nice and sweet and give you a five-dollar tip up front and then turn around and expect you to do something to them instead of just for them.

Participants agreed that it was easier to dance for female customers than male customers, because women did not usually have the same impulse to ask personal questions, make rude remarks, or demand favors. According to Nicole, the motivations of heterosexual female customers were usually simple and clear.

> The girls that'll come in as girls and tip you—there's nothing to it. It don't bother me at all. . . . It's actually more comfortable because I know the girls ain't trying to score. They ain't in here to get a piece of ass. They're just in here because they know you're working and they're here to have a beer or they're in here to see their friends. They know you're in here for the money so they'll give you a dollar or two.

Erica, Nicole, and Brooke felt that female customers had a better understanding of a woman's motivations for being an exotic dancer. They believed that female customers were sympathetic to the fact that the dancers' seductive behavior was part of their job and was a performance. Female customers were generally more supportive and did not make their work more difficult by pursuing a fantasy relationship with them. In addition, participants said that it was easy to dance for me because my intentions were clear and they understood my expectations. Of my presence in the club, Erica stated, "Girls like you, you're just— you're cool. You're there to have a good time, to party."

Erica and Brooke felt uncomfortable the first time that they danced for a female customer, especially if it was a private dance, but with time it became less awkward. After Brooke ascertained the customer's preferences, the situation became immediately less ambiguous, and she regained a sense of control.

> There's an awkwardness. . . . You also got to remember it's awkward for her. Especially if she's not . . . both ways, you know, it's awkward for her. She's looking around this way and this way. If you do something she's interested in by not showing all and just being seductive and dancing for both of them they enjoy that a lot better and then you feel more comfortable.

A female customer, who was not bisexual, and was at the club with her boyfriend or friends, was uncomfortable when Brooke approached her aggressively. Such a woman might find it difficult to make eye contact with the dancer. A woman in this situation might be more comfortable if Brooke kept a greater distance from her. When dancers knew what female customers expected from them, they were able to stay comfortably in character because they could prepare how to approach them. Thus, it was important to assess a female customer's motivations. Brooke used this information to adjust her own behavior, make the woman feel more comfortable, and give the woman the type of attention that she preferred.

> When a woman comes in and she's not with a man . . . you need to find out why she's there. You need to talk to her. . . . Now the ones that come in with their boyfriends to get excited, you just dance sexy for them. You don't necessarily do it to them and then they appreciate that a lot better than if you were doing it to them because they don't really want you to do it to them.

Knowing that there were many different reasons why a woman might come to a strip club, Brooke watched her customers carefully to gauge their reactions. A female customer could be there unwillingly and feel awkward or embarrassed if the dancer gave her too much attention, or she might be dissatisfied unless she was "treated like a man," received a lap dance, and was touched by the dancer.

When the gender or sexual orientation of a customer was unclear or unknown, dancers had less information with which to prepare themselves. Nicole was initially uncomfortable when a customer's gender identity was ambiguous. In such instances, she had less information to ascertain the motivations of that particular customer. Sometimes Nicole did not realize that there were lesbians in the club, because they appeared to be very masculine. She did not like being surprised by the gender or sexual orientation of a customer, because "when someone comes in and they're not who they're supposed to be . . . it just catches you off guard." She needed information about gender to gauge the interaction. The ambiguity or mystery of their gender identity made their desire a mystery as well. It became more difficult for her to embody her character in a way that promoted a sense of power and privacy.

> The one thing I didn't like is when I was working at a club and there were girls dressed up as guys. They were straight up wanna-be dudes. And I actually, honest-to-God thought they were guys. And they're sitting at the stage and they're tipping me like crazy. I'm like, cool! And I'm trying to talk to one and it was a female voice. [I became] totally uncomfortable. I didn't expect it. And you're just sitting there like, "Now, how do I actually talk to this person?"

It did not matter to Nicole which preference a customer had, as long as she knew it in advance. She stated that she felt comfortable dancing and changing in front of a transgendered person who used to work at her club, because she knew what gender that person wanted to be. Nicole's comfort with a transgendered coworker was cemented once she understood that person's sexual orientation. Brooke and Erica, while acknowledging the initial awkwardness of dancing for lesbian and bisexual women, adjusted their stance toward these customers in such a way that they met the needs of both parties.

Dancers relied on cultural norms of male heterosexual desire in order to predict how a male customer would behave toward them. Unfamiliar male customers were a source of anxiety, because dancers were familiar with the ways that men tended to violate their privacy. But regular male customers were a pleasure, because their behavior was predictable and respectful of dancers' privacy. Even though women tended to be hassle-free customers, they still warranted close inspection until the dancer was sure of their motivations and expectations. Persons become intelligible subjects through their conformity or nonconformity to gender roles (Butler, 1990). Even in the context of dancing for women, the customer's desires and motivations can be a mystery to the dancer. Although from experience they knew that women were less likely to violate their privacy, every situation merited caution on the part of the dancer. Dancers simply wanted to know what kind of desire their customers were approaching them with, no matter what their gender or sexual orientation. In sex work, as in the everyday world, a person's gender identity is the primary source of information in determining their desire (Schwartz and Rutter, 1998). Dancers know and predict differences in customers' behaviors based on their experiences, as well as cultural understandings and sexual behaviors.

PRIVACY, DESIRE, AND POWER

Deciphering the dynamic of power between men and women in the world of sex work must begin by acknowledging that desire, libido, and sexual drives have historically been characterized as essentially masculine (Chodorow, 1989; Fink, 1995; Freud, 1989; Irigaray, 1985). Feminine sexuality is the "natural" recipient of that desire. If the strip club is envisioned as a system that operates solely on male desire and men's fantasies, then there is no possibility for the freedom of women's desire to exist as authentic or self-creating. Being a sex worker means that at times one must indeed focus on the customer's desire, while at other times one can explore one's own sexual possibilities. The means by which sexual freedoms are limited in sex work occur when both participants—dancer and customer—inhabit roles that define particular styles of sexual interaction. For example, the body types of dancers reflect the dominant trends in what is considered to be sexually appealing for men, and the fetishistic quality of clothes and shoes worn by the dancers may appear, to some, to be limitations of sexual expression. However, if one visits enough clubs one begins to see variation even in these areas.

The club's rules, and the breaking of those rules, are also ways of participating in a game that recreates and perpetuates norms of gendered desire. Women are coy, seductive, and inherently desirable. The customer's desire must be controlled by the imposition of limits on physical contact. The dancer's sexuality is created within this context in the same way that the customers' behaviors are modeled after society's expectations of masculinity. A reality of masculine and feminine desires and behaviors is generated accordingly. This reality may correspond with, or deviate from, the dancer's own felt sense of her sexuality. In this way, the dancer's acquiescence to these dominant trends reinforces stereotypes, especially if her own true feelings are incongruent with the way that she expresses herself. However, it is too simplistic to view sex workers as being the "perpetrators" of this style of (hetero)sexual interaction.

If we listen to the narratives of women who enjoy sex work, we see evidence of transformation through the freedom of self-expression. If we cannot even entertain the possibility of an authentic transformation of power in gendered interaction, we continue to limit women's (as well as men's) possibilities in the expression of desire. Ironically, this view denies the sex worker her subjectivity and her freedom, which is the very act that many accuse the male customer of committing on a nightly basis. To subscribe to a theory that excludes the possibility of power for sex workers divides women into mutually exclusive groups by virtue of their degree of sexual promiscuity. Modesty, virginity, and chastity become the measure of a woman's worth as a person and whether or not she is a feminist (Pendleton, 1997). This logic assumes that the female body has an essential value that is preserved only when its sexual expression is concealed and guarded, and limits the contexts in which said sexual desire is deemed authentic and appropriate. It also characterizes men as sexual pred-ators against whom women must fight to preserve their chastity.

In the everyday world, women suppress their desire in congruence with the dominant sexual morality (Queen, 1997). In the context of sex work, the possibility arises that the expression of desire becomes the locus of power. On the other hand, when the dancer's pri-vacy is violated, her creation of the appearance of intimacy and eroticism is her power. Her power then resides in the mystery of her body, her hidden sexuality, and her skill of seduc-tion. The dancer's ability to manipulate the appearances of intimacy, desire, and eroticism becomes a dynamic of power. This ability to manipulate appearances is akin to Enck and Preston's (1988) description of creating the "illusion of intimacy" (1988;370) as well as Boles and Garbin's term "counterfeit intimacy" (1974;136). However, deeming the cus-tomer-dancer interaction as inauthentic or manipulative on the part of either of its par-ticipants obscures the possibility that much of the time dancer and customer desire and acknowledge this very "illusion" as a form of being in relationship to one another. The very essence of the roles of dancer and customer can be mutually satisfying to both participants, particularly when both preserve the limits of the relationship by following rules and re-specting one another. Of course, there are many customers who are frustrated by the rules of the club (Erickson and Tewksbury, 2000), and dancers for whom sex work exposes the performative nature of heterosexual courting, masculinity, and femininity (Delacoste and Alexander, 1987; Nagle, 1997; Ronai, 1992). Thus, both the withholding, as well as the expression of sexuality, are ways that men and women are together in relationship both in sex work as well as socially legitimated sexual unions. Each style of relating has gains and losses. Because masculinity and femininity do not occur in a vacuum, but instead in the cul-turally infused space of being with others, persons may call upon a sense of privacy in order to preserve integrity of body and self. While negotiating an uncertain space with another person, control over self-exposure balances feelings of objectification and power.

The cultural discourse of feminine sexuality is infused with the rhetoric of shame and repression in an effort to limit women's sexual freedom. Historically, women's worth as persons has been measured in terms of an adherence to sexual practices created for the sole purpose of reducing their value to their (re)productive capabilities (Rubin, 1975). By limit-ing women's sexual freedom, the culture maintains a system of personal liberty and eco-nomic freedom for men. Motivated by punitive shame, the culture continues to margin-alize sex workers. As a result, all women internalize society's shame regarding expressions of feminine sexuality (Queen, 1997). A radical sex work movement might prefer that sex workers disclose their choice of occupation for political reasons. Keeping one's identity hidden is seen as complicit with society's wish to silence sex workers. However, one must consider a woman's reasons for concealing aspects of her identity. Sex workers who do not have the support of partners and family, and suffer a hostile work environment, have fewer motivations to self-disclose, and do not enjoy the privilege of understanding their work as political or transformative. For these women, the realm of privacy becomes the locus of sub-version and part of the process of integrating feminism, feminine sexuality, and sex work. Butler (1990) states that the subversion of a system of power relations is only possible within that system; there is no subject that transcends the situation.

There is no self that is prior to the convergence or who maintains an "integrity" prior to its entrance into this conflictual cultural field. There is only a taking up of the tools where they lie, where the very "taking up" is enabled by the tool lying there. (1990;145)

A "taking up of the tools," I believe, includes both the dancer's tactics to protect her privacy and the customer's attempts to violate it. The dancer's privacy—what she conceals, keeps hidden, or keeps for herself—may include her desire. Her sense of privacy is what makes her a subject; it also makes her a person. The mystery within which a dancer shrouds a private sexuality can be empowering. Or she may choose to reveal herself, as Brooke did, in order to feel truly liberated. Her privacy, as part of her subjectivity, is her way of making something her own within the context of her work. If she employs a sense of privacy to protect aspects of body and self, she can inhabit multiple social roles, and conceal the discrepancies of desires and behaviors between roles. When a woman has a persona, she is part of the public realm; she is a person (Brown, 1966). If a woman is figured to have no persona or no public face, she can be controlled. With no recourse to the persona, and no distinction between public and private, she cannot move freely in either context. When one has privacy, one can occupy several roles as a sexual being and as a whole person. To deny a dancer's experience of privacy is to deny her personhood. It is to objectify her just as she is objectified in her work situation and to negate the value of her existence.

The context of the strip club is the scene of a potential gender-power transformation. On the surface, we find familiar themes of feminist discourse: the naked body, the gaze, active subject and passive object, commodification, subjugation, perversion, and desire. These terms generally allocate power to one gender and powerlessness to the other. This dichotomy limits forms of gendered interaction. Sex work subverts this dichotomy. It grants a space for a different sexuality for women: one that is not exclusively procreative, one where women are in control of how they show themselves to others. It becomes the foundation of subjectivity and freedom.

The strip club is a cultural artifact where gender and sexual relations are created, re-created, and perpetuated. I do not believe that it is so different from other contexts, just that the dynamics are more transparent. The strip club is not simply a place for sexual release, nor is it a subculture that fosters crime and deviancy. On the surface, the world of sex work represents the enactment and perpetuation of stereotypes of gender and sexual behavior, the "eternal mystery" of feminine sexuality that men hope to solve a dollar at a time. But both customers and dancers return to the club, night after night. Each participant experiences power and objectification. The phenomenology of the strip club and the exotic dancers' experience deepens our understanding of the sometimes conflicted and ambiguous way that we live out the construction of gendered behaviors, while at the same time subverting and transcending them. An awareness of the true complexities and inherent contradictions within gendered interaction is a first step for greater tolerance in the movement toward gender and sexual freedom.

4

Entry, Maintenance, and Departure From a Career in the Sex Industry

Strippers' Experiences of Occupational Costs and Rewards

NOVA SWEET
RICHARD TEWKSBURY
University of Louisville

REFLEXIVE STATEMENT

The sex industry today includes, but is not limited to, pornographic pictures and magazines, prostitution, nude Web sites, pornographic movies, and stripping. For those who are employed in these lucrative positions, there is the widely anticipated risk of being socially ostracized. Outsiders' curiosities may ensue when contemplating why certain individuals would choose such an employment path, considering the attached stigmatizations guaranteed to follow. Clearly, there are costs that are experienced by commercial sex workers, as well as important rewards. It is the ways that the encountering of these costs and rewards influence occupational decisions and experiences that is the focus of this research. Through a discussion of employment practices, motivational forms and levels, costs, rewards, and the reliances on rewards, this article seeks to provide readers with a greater understanding of the experiences of women who work in the commercial sex industry as strippers.

In general, people strive for acceptance and approval among their peers. Few, if any, of us make a conscious decision to become an outcast from the social mainstream. However, due to a lack of foresight or inability to anticipate societal rejection, or simply a lack of concern, many individuals do find themselves socially ostracized and stigmatized. One variety of person likely to be set apart as such are those who work, live, or have connections with the commercial sex industry. This paper is concerned with one specific occupation in the commercial sex industry—stripping—and the women who populate the field.

Authors' Note: This article was first published in *Humanity and Society,* Vol. 24 No. 2, May 2000, pp. 136-161. Reprinted with permission of *Humanity and Society.*

Strippers oftentimes do not carefully consider the decision and consequences of whether or not it is socially beneficial to embark on a career in which judgments, shame, and disgrace are common themes. Rather, stripping is often seen as an occupational choice that will provide not only financial rewards, but also a sense of comfort, an appreciation from others, and an enjoyable, "fun" work environment. These are not the only rewards workers in the sex industry can anticipate. There are a range of attractive inducements for both men and women strippers, the most salient of these being economic gain and a desirable lifestyle. However, despite its many attractions, work as a stripper is fraught with myriad challenges, difficulties, disappointments, and hardships. This includes hardships created both directly and indirectly by the illegal nature of prostitution (Sanchez, 1998). It is these aspects that structure the life of a stripper, and which will be the focus of this article.

The first part of the discussion will provide a detailed explanation of practices common among strippers and review the similarities and differences that separate and unite male and female strippers. Next, we illustrate the factors that serve to both draw women into stripping and facilitate a developing reliance on such work. Consideration is given to what female strippers identify as the primary forms of rewards and costs of their work, and explanations for how, when, and why careers are terminated. Finally, we examine strippers' accounts of how they manage the negative labels they believe are imposed on them because of their occupational choice, and what strippers believe are important and necessary attributes for succeeding and successfully negotiating the structure and culture of working in this branch of the commercial sex industry.

OCCUPATIONAL STRATEGIES AND CHARACTERISTICS

Perhaps the most significant area of interest for scholars and laypersons alike is the interactional strategies used by strippers to maximize their monetary gain. What has been clearly shown in previous research is that central to these strategies is the "cynical performance" which creates "counterfeit intimacy" (i.e., the illusion of sexual, physical, and emotional intimacy) (Goffman, 1959; Sijuwade, 1995). Goffman's (1959) dramaturgical metaphor of life as theater is commonly relied on and includes the notion of the "cynical performance" to describe a social actor with little belief in her/his performance, but who nonetheless uses the performances and elicited responses of the audience to achieve other ends. Strippers are widely believed to rely on such a strategy for maximizing their income.

A cynical performance is an occupational strategy of self-presentation and impression management done for the purpose of preserving an actor's real self-identity while simultaneously selling the act as sincere (Sijuwade, 1995). Successful dancers manipulate the sexual fantasies of their customers through the creation of counterfeit intimacy (Boles & Garbin, 1974), and the illusion that sexual intimacy is possible if customers have the necessary charm and money (Sijuwade, 1995). By creating this false sense of intimacy, strippers will not only provide a more pleasing interaction for customers, but will also likely increase their earnings, which are primarily generated through tips from patrons. However, it is important to recognize that these are not necessarily "naturally" occurring forms of interactions. Most (if not all) strippers need to learn these techniques from more experienced peers (Lewis, 1998).

Research suggests that customers knowingly pay for counterfeit intimacy because the "legitimate" institution for intimacy fails to provide the benefits they think appropriate

(Sijuwade, 1995). Rather than the customer surrendering his expectations of intimacy in legitimate institutions (i.e., marriage and courting relationships), he seeks fulfillment, and sometimes knowingly pays for the fulfillment, in some alternative setting (see also Erickson & Tewksbury, 2000). In the strip club, intimacy is gained via a cynical performance created specifically for people who share sexual and intimate frustrations (Sijuwade, 1995). Both female and male strippers work to create an air of counterfeit intimacy when working with patrons, primarily so as to enhance their own financial status (Boles & Garbin, 1974; Lewis, 1998; Sijuwade, 1995; Tewksbury, 1994a, 1994b). There are additional similarities and differences, however, which individualize the male and female stripper's role.

First, male strippers consciously pursue stripping as a supplemental occupation, in addition to a regular job (Tewksbury, 1994a). Men's decisions to begin stripping are often promoted and supported by significant persons—friends and family—who themselves have knowledge or experience in a sex industry, entertainment occupation (Dressel & Petersen, 1982a). For women, however, the situation is slightly different. Although most female strippers usually have a close relationship with the person who introduces them to the industry, the person's encouragement is not the reason they get involved (Sanchez, 1998).

Second, few male strippers engage in sexual encounters with members of the audience, and even rarer is sex exchanged for money (Tewksbury, 1994a). This is in contrast to data on female strippers, which suggests that prostitution is an occasional, and often common, way to supplement their income (Prus & Irini, 1980; Ronai & Ellis, 1989; Salutin, 1971; Sanchez, 1998; Skipper & McCaghy, 1970).

There are also two situational contingencies regarding induction to the field for female strippers that do not apply to men. First, the experience of a major personal crisis (typically financial) is a factor in becoming a stripper for women. None of the male strippers interviewed by Dressel and Petersen (1982a) or Tewksbury (1994a) were compelled to strip through a crisis situation. Second, the female stripper has a greater likelihood of having been involved in previous jobs which required some display of the body (Boles & Garbin, 1974; Dressel & Petersen, 1982a; Prus & Irini, 1980; Ronai & Ellis, 1989; Skipper & McCaghy, 1970; Thompson & Harred, 1992; however, also see Lewis, 1998). However, neither Dressel and Petersen (1982a, 1982b; Petersen & Dressel, 1982) nor Tewksbury (1994a, 1994b) found male strippers who had previous work experience requiring body display. The implication is that for females, stripping is more directly tied to sexuality and sexual activity, while for males it is more socially normative (and more socially acceptable) to work as a stripper (Tewksbury, 1994a).

Within the strip club, behaviors that would be seen as deviant in everyday life are viewed as normative (Thompson & Harred, 1992). So, how do strippers manage the apparent dissonance created by immersion in two very different social worlds? For one thing, dancers consciously and consistently work to maintain their privacy. Dancers use stage names and customers enjoy total anonymity, so that no hint of stigma or deviance can be associated with their actions outside the club (Tewksbury, 1994a, 1994b; Thompson & Harred, 1992). As Thompson and Harred (1992) explain, when individuals are vulnerable to being stigmatized by their work, there are two common approaches to managing such a situation: (1) dividing the social world, and (2) techniques of neutralization (Sykes & Matza, 1957). The specific ways one responds to and handles stigma will be at least somewhat influenced by the socialization provided by more experienced strippers (Lewis, 1998).

Dividing the social world, as described by Goffman (1963), involves information control. This means establishing a small group with which discrediting information is shared, while keeping the same information hidden from the rest of the world. For example, many dancers claim a public identity as a waitress, because it is the most convenient employment excuse (Thompson & Harred, 1992). While strippers admit they do hide their deviant occupation, they are also quick to point out that they do not see anything wrong with what they are doing (Thompson & Harred, 1992). However, they recognize the potential difficulties they could encounter if they were completely open with others.

Some dancers feel they have won the ultimate game in American society, which continues to judge the value of women by their attractiveness and seductiveness (Ronai & Ellis, 1989). Dancers receive money, attention, and validation for their displays of appropriately feminine characteristics and argue they are doing nothing more than most women do (Ronai & Ellis, 1989). In the view of dancers, they are winning the game because they have achieved the supreme gratification, attention, affection, and payment for being beautiful. However, the world of stripping is not a thoroughly positive environment. Moreover, if strippers could make the same money and have the same freedom in a different occupation, most would opt for an alternate career. However, most strippers believe they cannot and, therefore, do not (Prus & Irini, 1980; Robboy, 1985; Ronai & Ellis, 1989).

METHODS

The present research was based on in-depth, qualitative interviews conducted with a sample of women currently employed as strippers. All interviews were conducted between August and December 1998.

Description of Sample

The twenty women in this sample were, for the most part, experienced strippers. Only 15% of the interviewees had been dancing for less than 1 year, 70% had between 1 and 4 years of experience, and 15% had more than 4 years' experience. These women lived and worked in a variety of cities, including Chicago, Boston, Atlanta, Las Vegas, New York, Tampa, Orlando, St. Louis, Phoenix, San Francisco, Charlotte, Houston, and Louisville. The sample ranged in age from 18 to 34 years old. The majority of the sample was Caucasian (60%), while the other 40% of the sample identified as African American, Asian, Hispanic, and mixed race women. Most (60%) of the sample were short in stature, between 5'0"-5'4", while the other 40% were between 5'4"-5'4". Most of the sample reported hazel/green eyes and brown hair.

Of the 20 women interviewed, 50% were mothers; 60% of these women became mothers during their teenage years. Currently, most of the sample were in some kind of relationship; 60% reported having a steady boyfriend, 20% reported being single/never married, 10% had a steady girlfriend, 5% were married, and the other 5% were divorced.

Research Process

All interviews were conducted by the first author, who solicited interviews through the course of her work in strip clubs. No requests for interviews were denied, although several women who initially volunteered were unable to schedule time.

Interviews were conducted in hotel rooms, homes, automobiles, and by telephone; scheduling constraints and privacy considerations guided the choice of locale. Interviews ranged from one to two hours in length. A semi-structured format was used, all interviews were audiotape-recorded, and analysis was based on verbatim transcripts.

All interviewees were guaranteed confidentiality; all interview tapes were identified by first name only and were destroyed at the conclusion of the project. All names used in this article are pseudonyms.

An analytic-inductive process was used in organizing and interpreting the interviews (Miles & Huberman, 1984). Data analysis included three activities: data reduction, which included the process of identifying emergent themes in the data; data display, the process of organizing and clustering the information to be used for deriving conclusions; and con-clusion drawing and verification, the process of deciding what experiences mean, noting patterns and explanations, and verifying the findings (Miles & Huberman, 1984).

LIFESTYLES AND EMOTIONAL EFFECTS OF LABELS

Prior research suggests strippers suffer from identity problems (Ronai & Ellis, 1989) when they internalize mainstream society's negative images regarding their occupation. Identity problems derive from a person's concept of self, which is based on two personal identities—the perceived and ideal self—both of which are dependent upon one's definition of the sit-uation. The perceived self is what individuals see themselves as being, and is affected by outsiders' positive and negative reinforcements. The ideal self, on the other hand, is how in-dividuals think they should be, and how they should act around others so as to be liked and respected. Clearly, however a stripper feels about her occupation and her involvement in the sex industry has a great deal to do with how she sees herself, how she believes she can/should gain the acceptance of others, and how she believes others perceive her.

It is when a stripper leaves work that outsiders' opinions and reinforcements may effect the discrepancy between her perceived and ideal selves. It is at this juncture that she may recognize and perhaps internalize labels of deviance. In the present sample, only one in five strippers indicates an internalized designation as "deviant"; however, this is only an occa-sional self-identification. Sara, a stripper who said there were times her work makes her feel like a social outcast, explains why,

> I think it's bad because we're taking our clothes off for twenty dollars. Sometimes when I look at a guy and he gives me two or three hundred dollars, I'm just like wow, what if he's ad-dicted and wants more after the dance? What if he had kids or is married? I don't want to be a home wrecker, but I'm not making him spend that money either. I'm just entertaining.

On the other hand, strippers were much more likely to report no feelings of inappropri-ateness or shame due to their occupation. Central here is the fact that these strippers claim the views of others and the labels imposed on them have little, if any, effect on their self-perceptions. In large part, the strippers in the present study justified and explained their work and identities by condemning their condemners and pointing to the practicalities of their work.

Primary concerns and motivations for strippers to begin and remain in stripping center on financial needs and "freedom." Stripping is a job, and making money is the primary, if not only, concern for these women. Issues of others' views and attempts to label them are not consciously considered. The majority of the strippers in this sample expressed neither pride nor shame about their work. Rather, their work was simply an occupation, a means to an end rather than an encompassing lifestyle and identity. For example, in Brenda's case, she believed stripping was an honest way to make a living, but she would never brag about it because of what others may think.

> It's an honest way to make a living. I wouldn't say I'm proud of it. I wouldn't brag about it, and I don't want to do it forever. I'm somewhere in the middle, I'm not ashamed, but I'm not proud of it.

In a similar manner, Leslie reported that she did not think of her work in terms of being proud or ashamed, rather as a means to support herself. Nonetheless, she said she felt a sense of disappointment with herself.

> I'm not ashamed, but I'm not particularly proud because I know I'm capable of much more. A lot of times I'm disappointed with myself. Especially when I wake up the next morning at seven o'clock and I feel like shit. I've come to grips with it when I'm able to pay my bills. This is what I have to do at this particular time.

Higher levels of discrepancy between the perceived self and the ideal self result in lower emotional stability. Such a discrepancy may be evidenced in more shame, anxiety, guilt, and depression (Peretti & O'Connor, 1989). Only two of the strippers in this study claimed to feel a sense of shame regarding stripping. Sable was not proud of stripping, but she believed she had to do whatever it took for her and her family to survive, again emphasizing the critical issue of money.

> I'll never be proud of it. I need the money to survive. It would never go any further than that. It's all about the money.

Women with a low discrepancy between their perceived and ideal selves often report a higher degree of job satisfaction, more self-worth, more self-acceptance, and a better overall quality of life. Fully one third of this sample claimed a sense of pride in stripping. Two reasons these strippers had a low degree of discrepancy between selves were centered in their lengthy experience as entertainers and their reported emotionally supportive ties with families, friends, and significant others. Although prior research (Peretti & O'Connor, 1989) suggests that stripping negatively affects the emotional stability of dancers, the experiences of this sample do not support this conclusion.

Despite their proclaimed lack of shame (and for some, pride), very few of these strippers tell others what they do for a living. Here it appears that although few women indicate internalized discrepancies, most, if not all, readily recognize that many in society are likely to perceive their attitudes, work, and entire world as "different" and most likely "wrong," "inferior," or "deviant." Brandy was one of these women; she steadfastly declared she has nothing to hide, but readily recognized that many others were likely to look down on her because of her chosen occupation.

> If somebody asks me what I do, I'll tell them. I don't see anything wrong with what I do, and I have an outlook on life that if somebody has a problem with dancing or with me, then they don't need to be around me.

Typically, one's work as a stripper is carefully hidden from outsiders. Reasons for keeping their occupation "quiet" include a belief that others will be disappointed with them, a fear that they will be looked down on, have their character questioned, or that they will be labeled as "sleazy" or promiscuous. In short, it is the fear of labeling that motivates many strippers to keep their work secret. This fear was clear in the words of Monica, who explained that she was very selective regarding to whom she confessed her occupation.

> Especially when you meet a guy, you tell him you're a dancer, then you can just tell automatically in their heads they think we're easy.

Explicit and implicit reminders that one is perceived to be a "prostitute, slut, druggie, or lazy" cause many strippers to question their self-concepts and, after repeated denigrations, internalize the public's opinion of them. What she believed were prejudiced stereotypes motivated Melanie to hide her occupation.

> I think outsiders' guard goes up a bit. They know that when you're at work you're naked, so instantly they're like "She gets naked for a living." They think about what they think goes on in strip bars, and they think you're doin' those things. They probably picture you as conniving. They probably think you don't give a shit about anybody else. I think they just assume that you're a selfish person. I think it totally intimidates them.

What this reveals is a sense of dissonance on the part of many strippers; although they typically report no personal sense of wrong-doing, they hide their profession from outsiders because of both real and anticipated stereotyping. For the most part, the women in this sample reported significant comfort with themselves and their occupational choices. However, they chose to maintain this significant aspect of their lives as a secret from those they feared could restrict their opportunities.

While the fact that one is a stripper was kept from many acquaintances, it was not hidden from their immediate family members. The majority of dancers in this research told at least some members of their families of their work. For many, it simply became too difficult to keep the secret; in these instances, this information was shared with one or a few trusted family members (usually siblings or mother) who were in turn coerced or convinced to conspire to keep the secret from the rest of the family. Ferrah explains why she did not want to tell her mother at first:

> It took me awhile to tell my mother. I felt like I was letting her down. She's like a Catholic Bible study teacher, she's a very Christian woman. She told me I'm going to burn in hell for what I do for a living. I wasn't even allowed in their house on Thanksgiving for what I do. She still loves me, she'll still come and see me, but I can't go to her house.

In contrast, other strippers believed that their families would be supportive of them, even if their support was not immediately expressed or demonstrated. Such was the case for Barbara, who informed her family from the outset about her job as a stripper.

My family has always known. I have a very close relationship with my family, especially with my parents. They weren't crazy about it when I first started doing it, but they realized after awhile that it's just a job, it doesn't affect me when I'm not there.

Those strippers who had not informed their families about their career choice cited reasons including cultural barriers, shaming, and not knowing how to break such "shocking" news. Victoria felt she would disappoint her family and, therefore, devoted much energy to keeping her secret.

They would be disappointed. My family wouldn't disown me, but they would be extremely disappointed, and I don't want to disappoint them. It would be something they would be scared of, they wouldn't understand.

A stripper's self-concept, although not wholly reshaped, is effected by the discrepancy between her self-identity and her perceptions about society's views. Contingent on the degree of discrepancy is the severity of its effects, which cause a fluctuation in a stripper's self-identity. It would seem that a stripper, in order to construct a more positive experience in her profession, needs to identify ways in which she can bridge correspondence between her goals and ideals with her means of pursuing such. In large part, this means not internalizing negative, externally imposed labels and also focusing on how her own definition of self varies from the stereotypes others may attempt to impose on her. However, where problems arise is that many women do internalize labels and allow their definitions of self to be reshaped, thereby altering their daily routines and emotions. We will now turn to an examination of previously neglected aspects of how strippers' personal and professional lives overlap.

ENTRY AND MAINTENANCE ISSUES

One important, widely shared trait among the strippers interviewed was their reason for entering the sex industry. Previous literature consistently argues that the primary reason women get into exotic dancing is because of a financial crisis in their lives (Peretti & O'Connor, 1989; Prus & Irini, 1980; Ronai & Ellis, 1989; Salutin, 1971; Skipper & McCaghy, 1970; Thompson & Harred, 1992). This study found financial reasons were critical to this decision, but they were not necessarily "crises" that led women to stripping. While many of these women reported their primary reason for entry into stripping was due to a financial crisis, need, or desire, it was most often a desire for greater financial opportunities, rather than a true crisis. Most often the financial situation that drew women to the potentially lucrative occupation of stripping was a set of aspirations: the desire to live a "high-class" lifestyle, have nice things, and do "fun stuff." Brenda explained this attraction and why she set out to strip:

I wasn't really hard up for money necessarily. I wasn't doing anything else in my life. I guess I was stuck in those teenage party years. Making that much money, it's like WOW, I'm the shit. I just dance, take my clothes off and make lots of money. It was cool.

For other women, the attraction was the income potential and the possibility of easing financial pressures. These women "needed" money, but they were not desperate and they rejected the idea of having been in crisis. According to Vicki, who was typical of this sample, she needed the money stripping provided to pay bills and live comfortably:

> I started out dancing occasionally for extra money to pay my bills, pay my car payment, and still try to do other things in my life. The mindset of everybody in that environment sucked me in. I was chasing the money, I guess.

One of the financial needs that drew some women to stripping was a way to pay for college. Others had needs arising from being a single parent and/or becoming pregnant, not wanting to go on welfare, and in the extreme, being homeless. Victoria reflected on her experiences as an unemployed, low-skilled young woman who found stripping both financially attractive and easy to enter.

> I started dancing because I lost my job and I needed money. At the time, almost all my friends danced. It seemed like an easy way to make money, make my own hours, and I still could do other things.

Or in Monica's situation, financial need was also the critical factor, although her "crisis" arose very differently.

> I started dancing about a month after high school graduation. My father had kicked me out; we were not on good terms. I was working at a restaurant waitressing, not making a lot of money, and I had my own car, apartment, and college tuition to pay for.

Whatever the specific dynamics of the crisis or "need" may be, dancers' decisions almost always center on the perceived opportunities to earn large amounts of money in relatively short periods of time. Stripping is also seen as an attractive option because it not only offers a high income potential, but flexible work schedules, a "fun" working environment, and a great deal of independence.

The degree, frequency, and longevity of an individual's involvement in stripping is based on numerous factors including commitment levels, personal desires, achievement levels, and personal goals, as well as the types and degree of support/socialization they received from experienced strippers (Lewis, 1998). According to the data in the current research, although similar factors and circumstances draw women into stripping and they begin their careers with similar aspirations and experiences, with time, dancers typically see their aspirations and approach to their work change. Generally speaking, we have identified three ideal types of approaches to stripping that account for a dancer's attitudes and means of carrying out her work. The three ideal types of strippers are: 1) Career Dancers, 2) Party Dancers, and 3) Power Dancers. These are only ideal types. Few, if any, dancers who stay in the business beyond a couple of months are static in their attitudes and activities, and motivations often fluctuate over a career. First, however, we will discuss the initial aspirations of strippers, the common ground from which strippers embark on their sex industry career.

Initial Aspirations

Almost all of the strippers began their careers with a similar set of aspirations, intentions, and motivations. Initially, the dancers believed stripping will be only a temporary, short-term situation. Entry into stripping was largely driven by a desire or perceived "need" for extra money. Seeing an opportunity to make large amounts of money in a short time period, while exerting less energy in an "exciting" environment, drew the women into stripping. Such work was simply a means to an end during this period. Elaine reminisced on her early days as a stripper.

> I wanted to go to college, and I was broke. My parents were too wealthy for me to get financial aid, and I wasn't getting money from them, so there's not really any other way to make this kind of money. So I started stripping.

When starting out, women often work only part-time; this may mean working for a season (summer, over the holidays, or during special events in their community) or during times when they need extra cash. Whatever her personal situation entails, dancing provides sufficient amounts of cash in almost every circumstance. These women feel they cannot dedicate enough time in their daily lives to a profession and/or they lack the necessary skills to acquire an alternate, financially rewarding career.

If a woman does not take her earnings and move on, she will find herself working more frequently and developing one of three forms of reliance on stripping. For some, the money becomes too strong of an attraction to leave. For others, the lifestyle becomes engrossing. Finally, for others, the psychological/emotional rewards outdistance any previously known and function to hold the woman in the business.

Career Dancer

Women who find the financial aspects of stripping to be above and beyond what they have previously known, or realistically aspired to, will often increase their working frequency and devote increasing energy and time to developing a true career in the field. Dancing becomes a part of these women's lives for extended periods, typically a minimum of four years. Career dancers can pursue one of two general career tracks. A woman can simply work many hours and cultivate a regular clientele in a single club. Or, a decision can be made to pursue a high-profile (and potential six-figure income) status as a "feature dancer."

Working as a feature dancer is the top achievement with the greatest rewards in the stripping industry. Featuring, however, requires both a significant time commitment and a change in lifestyle. Feature dancers do more than simply dance and remove their clothing; they develop marketable personas and gimmicks for their performances. Consequently, many hours of rehearsal are required, and large amounts of money must be put into costumes, props, and special effects. On average, feature dancers typically work fewer days a month than regular dancers, and commonly make in excess of $100,000 a year. Deidra, the only featured entertainer in this sample, explained what it was like trying to leave the business for a "normal" job.

When I got into dancing, I told myself I'd only do it for a short time, to catch up on my bills. I danced for four years, then I quit for a year. I got into real estate, and I was a sales assistant making $7.50 an hour. It was horrible, I hated it. I decided to come back to dancing and featuring, and that's when I realized this is a career. In order to leave the business, I would have to make the money I'm making right now, and to do that, I'd have to own a business and invest my money. I could not only not go back to making less money, I could never work for someone else.

However, non-feature career dancers often find themselves simply evolving into regular performers, not necessarily making a conscious decision to pursue stripping on a full-time, long-term basis. For these women, their careers are more a matter of evolution and circumstances than they are products of a career choice. Regardless of the specifics, career dancers often find themselves "being caught up" in the industry. They come to recognize the limited alternative opportunities available to support them at a similar financial level. As Jessica explained, she did not plan on stripping for such a long time, it just happened to go that way.

It was a week before my 18th birthday when I started dancing. I was homeless; I had a one-year-old son; and I needed to survive. I've been dancing for four years now. I didn't plan on dancing this long, it was just a way to make more money, spend more time with my son, and a way to get on my own quicker. I'm thinking I'll be done dancing in about two more years.

Party Dancer

An alternative form of reliance on stripping centers on the lifestyle, not the financial rewards, that accompanies work as a stripper. These women evolve from their initial aspirations and experiences to look at stripping as an opportunity to socialize, drink, dance, and recreate. For some, being a party dancer is only a temporary stage on the path to financial reliance, while for others, the lifestyle becomes all-encompassing. Among women whose work as a stripper focuses on the party atmosphere and lifestyle, stripping is pursued for the primary purpose of being able to consume alcohol or drugs on a regular or even daily basis. Laura explained why she thought she could afford to party on the job.

I own my house, and my car. I'm financially situated. My daughter is almost sixteen. I don't dance to pay my rent. I dance to buy new clothes, pay a few bills, and to party!

The party-based lifestyle for these women often bleeds over to their lives outside of the strip club. It is not uncommon for such women to spend extravagant amounts of money on street and dance clothes, makeup, nails, tanning, traveling, and flashy jewelry. The lifestyle of the party dancer is the most akin of any strippers to common stereotypes about strippers. These women report that they often sleep all day, rising only to return to the club and "party some more." One downside to this approach to stripping is that these women are widely believed to age more quickly because of the frequent consumption of large quantities of alcohol, smoke, and drugs—which subsequently curtails income, thereby leading women to believe it is necessary to work more. As a result, strippers whose reliance centers on the party lifestyle cultivated inside strip clubs may find themselves caught in a cycle where they spend increasing time, money, and energy in an attempt to maintain their lifestyle and income. In essence, the reliance on the party lifestyle is often analogous to addiction.

Power Dancer

A third form of reliance is that which highlights the psychological and emotional rewards women take from their work. These rewards are largely related to a developing sense of power and a perceived ability to control the actions of others and their own interactions. Interestingly, strippers who find their work attractive primarily because of these forms of rewards are those who are most likely to report abusive (sexual, mental, physical) backgrounds. A perceived sense of power over men, power over sex, and power over money can be compelling forces, strong enough to hold women in the business. For some women, the strip club begins to be perceived as a safe haven, because it is a place where rather than being openly denigrated and abused, they are objects of desire. As such, it is possible for these women to feel in control and able to determine and direct their own interactions. Deidra explained her commitment to stripping, believing that it was strongly related to her childhood.

> I think that subconsciously, there are some reasons that have drawn me into the business and kept me in, like having control over men, and then the ego boost that you get from men telling you how beautiful you are, and the attention you gain from the guys. I think a lot of that comes from childhood problems.

It is important to keep in mind that these forms of reliance are simply ideal types of commitments. Many women will enter stripping for short periods, but only a minority will remain in the business for more than a couple of months. During various stages of one's career, there may be varying forms and degrees of reliance that hold an individual woman in a strip club. Moreover, stripping is an occupation that can last only so long, and exiting the field can be the result of several factors.

EXITING

The number of women who work for only a short time as strippers is quite high; turnover among dancers in a club is considered the norm. In other words, a majority of women who try stripping end up leaving the industry in short order. The general agreement among this sample is that the women who leave stripping right away realize they are not cut out for the competition, judgments, and what some define as perversion within the strip club. Those women consciously decide that the negative components outweigh the primary attraction: the money. For some, it is believed that they leave the occupation due to fears that their families may discover their choice of occupation; and they believe it would be too difficult to confront the presumed shame and disappointment their loved ones may express. Barbara summarized these views in her explanation for why turnover among strippers was so high.

> A lot of girls, if they don't stay long, they have an internal conflict like they're not comfortable with themselves for doing what they're doing, or they're afraid their parent(s) are going to find out, or they're just not cut out for it.

Across all strippers interviewed in the current research, there was consensus that they had every intention of getting out of the business at some point. No interviewee expressed complete satisfaction with her current situation and insisted that stripping was merely a temporary condition. Motivations for leaving the business included physical aging and fatigue, wanting more for one's children, living a life free of stigma, and hoping for a "normal, loving relationship." For some strippers, leaving the business was perceived not necessarily as a choice to be made, but rather as a necessity due to physical aging and a constant influx of younger women. Leslie was one stripper who believed her time as a stripper was limited, largely because of the toll her work had taken on her body during the year and a half she had worked as a stripper.

> I'm twenty-seven years old, I'm not going to be able to do it much longer. I've aged more in the last year and a half than I have in the last five years probably. The hours, I never drink at home, at work I smoke like a freight train and I drink. It's rough on you. My skin, the wrinkles.

For others, it was not the physical changes in their body/appearance that limited their tenure as strippers, but social pressures. In Jessica's case, although she did not enjoy societal stigmas, her chief concern was her son. Her responsibilities for him were pushing her to exit the stripping world. Jessica believed that although she could continue to strip and make a good income, the accompanying costs of her work/lifestyle would be too great. Specifically, she worried that if she continued to dance, there would be negative repercussions for her son.

> Because of my son, for one. I'm tired of it, for two. The way other people look at me, most of the time I don't care unless it's my family. Mainly for my son.

Regardless of what aspects of stripping an individual woman has come to be reliant on (finances, lifestyle, or psychological rewards), she will often begin to suffer from burn-out and come to believe that stripping—although presently rewarding—is not her most beneficial career choice. When a woman develops such a view, she begins to look for opportunities to change occupations. For many strippers, this is a return to their initial set of aspirations, intentions, and motivations, but with a very different perspective than they held during the peak points of their careers. A stripper's career, then, often takes a cyclical pattern: She begins with intentions of working to get through a financially difficult time, develops a reliance on some aspect of the work, and eventually sees the costs outweighing the benefits of the work and seeks to get out "as soon as I can make it work financially."

It was common to hear strippers express with resignation, "I wish I had known better what I was getting myself into." Stripping, while initially perceived as exciting, challenging, and highly rewarding, evolved into a tiring, monotonous, and discouraging job. This is clearly not unique to the field of stripping; such a cycle can easily be seen in many occupations and professions. Therefore, just as with most any career choice, in order for a woman to make the most of a stripping career, it is important that those considering this field of work understand both the array of rewards and costs that stripping can introduce into one's life. Therefore, our final discussion focuses on strippers' recommendations and advice to those looking at stripping as a potential occupational/career option.

REWARDS AND COSTS OF STRIPPING

Rewards

Stripping offers several highly desired benefits—material, physical, and emotional—for women who elect to work as dancers. Although most women who stay in stripping reap various forms of rewards, each individual finds her primary form of reward in either financial, lifestyle, or psychological benefits/attractions. However, by far the most common and most important rewards reported were related to the income one can make stripping. The annual average income in this sample was $36,000. When considered in light of the training required to strip, the time one spends working, and the other opportunities available to these women, the income is highly attractive. However, as some research has suggested, a stripper's income potential can be limited by the emergence of more strip clubs in a community and other dancers' willingness to "do more" for tips (Sanchez, 1998).

A second often-cited reward from stripping directly related to lifestyle issues was the opportunity to meet new and different people. Strippers widely attributed their work with teaching them important lessons about people and social interaction. These women reported they felt more streetwise, smarter, and stronger due to their experiences stripping. Because of their experiences managing interactions with both individual and groups of male patrons, as well as issues with club management and other dancers, strippers commonly reported that they quickly learned to stand up for themselves. If a dancer did not take a strong stance with club management and patrons, she would risk being exploited, conned, and cheated out of income. Therefore, the dancer needs to gain and exert assertiveness and a sense of personal strength, or she will most likely leave the industry out of frustration.

Most strippers also cited the attention one receives, especially the attention from men, as a valued reward of their work. These rewards appeared directly related to psychological forms of reliance that hold many women in the stripping industry. Dancers reveled in the feelings of having captured the attention of a crowd, especially one that showered her with praise and money. For many, such experiences can be extremely empowering. It is easy to understand how a woman may feel empowered when she performs for an audience that she perceives as worshipping and complimenting her, while she also feels an ability to control or direct the actions of audience members. Such experiences forge strong bonds of attachment to the industry. Accompanying the psychological and emotional benefits, the fact that she is paid large amounts of money just because of her body and good looks provides a strong boost to self-esteem and a sense of accomplishment. According to Sophie, applause was the absolute best part of dancing.

> When men applaud, it gives you self-confidence. As a stripper, you never run out of people who want to know about you.

Almost without exception, the women in this sample reported that dancing boosted their self-esteem and self-confidence, and made them feel sexy and pretty. Monica elaborated on how her self-esteem was boosted from stripping.

> I crave to be beautiful, and I want to show off my body. When I dance, I feel beautiful, popular, and everyone wants to talk to you.

The strippers liked feeling and being told they are beautiful, sexy, and desirable. Being the center of attention, at least for a few moments while performing, was previously unknown to many strippers. For some strippers, this meant that stripping provided them with previously unknown feelings of being loved and praised. These feelings, in turn, led to a perception of enhanced opportunities for self-expression and a development of a sense of strong will. The women interviewed for this research reported that stripping brought them a rarely before experienced sense of happiness, open-mindedness, and comfort with themselves. For women from emotionally impoverished and perhaps abusive backgrounds, these can be cherished rewards.

An additional emotional reward common for many strippers is the structured set of opportunities for establishing relationships with other women—colleagues and coworkers comprising a peer group. As others have shown for numerous occupational groups, a sibling-like (i.e., sisterhood) bond forms among strippers because they feel they can relate to one another, have shared experiences, and faced similar daily challenges. Melanie discussed the sisterhood she has in her club:

> You can build bonds with the girls you work with. It's like a sisterhood. You have a bunch of girls doing the same thing you are, probably close to the same kind of lifestyle you have.

Lifestyle rewards dancers attribute to stripping include a fun work environment, entertaining different people, listening to music, and "dancing the night away." Many strippers, especially those with a heavy reliance on the financial, psychological, and lifestyle aspects of stripping, suggested that they cannot envision a better way to earn an income. The strip club affords them a comfortable setting in which to work and have fun where they can realistically expect positive reinforcements, all while earning what is defined as a good income. Having a flexible work schedule, traveling, staying in shape, and learning new "sales techniques" are also aspects of stripping that women cite as attractive and rewarding. Despite the rewards, however, there are also a host of costs that strippers must be prepared to manage. If the costs are not perceived as outweighed by the rewards, stripping will not be a lengthy experience, and individuals can be expected to leave the industry fairly quickly.

Costs

In addition to the financial, lifestyle, and psychological/emotional rewards, there are also several problematic issues, or costs, encountered by women in the stripping industry. By far the most commonly cited "cost" of stripping centers on the actions of the men who patronize strip clubs. Specifically, strippers object to ever-present and unwanted touching, violence, explicitly and implicitly presented attitudes about women, rude and hurtful comments, pick-up lines, and propositions (Sanchez, 1998). Sexual propositions are the most vexing aspect of a stripper's work. Not only are propositions considered bothersome, but so too are the ways men attempt to engage women seen as rude, silly, or simply a "ridiculous routine." Nonetheless, it is not only the fact that male patrons attempt to gain sexual access to a stripper that is defined as an occupational cost. In some instances, it is not only male patrons, but also men in authority, such as management positions, who harass and exploit strippers (Sanchez, 1998). For many men, it would appear that the actual person of the stripper is seen as not present, although her body is present (Erickson & Tewksbury, 2000). When this situation occurs, male patrons essentially ignore the person but consume her body. It is commonly accompanied by a running commentary on what the patrons perceive as both the positive and negative facets of the stripper's body. Many times, these comments and statements are less than flattering. Ferrah explained that hearing customers' commentaries on her body and their associated beliefs about her as a person has been emotionally draining,

> It's brutal on you. There are days I go in there and I try not to take anything these people say to me to heart, but sometimes you hear things. You try not to let it get you down. Sometimes guys put you down. They'll say things about dancers, how we're whores and sluts, it gets to you. It's a beating emotionally.

Interestingly, one of the most frequently cited rewards of stripping was the opportunity presented to meet a variety and range of new persons. Clearly, at least some of these "opportunities" are less than optimal and rewarding, and in fact are occupational costs.

Another area in which occupational rewards and costs overlap is in the area of the overall lifestyle and working atmosphere provided by sex industry jobs, such as work in a strip club. Strippers tend to work late hours and find themselves, peers, customers, and supervisors/management drinking, drugging, and smoking. Combining a work environment that is smoky, attracting inebriated individuals, and busiest (most physically taxing) at late hours with disruptions of normal sleeping patterns yields an individual that quickly becomes physically, psychologically, and emotionally worn out. The physical demands of the job are difficult and often overlooked by both casual and professional observers. Dancers' work entails long periods of repeatedly bending over, kneeling, jumping, kicking, climbing, hanging, and flipping. These activities can take a severe toll on one's body, especially on joints, bones, and muscles. When a stripper's body suffers, so too are her mind and attitude affected, almost always negatively.

An additionally cited cost of stripping is directly related to the above-discussed rewards: money. This is not to suggest that earning a respectable income is seen as a cost; rather, when strippers grow accustomed to making a certain amount of money, they develop an expectation for a similar income on a regular basis. In some ways, this may be interpreted as simple greed; however, a more positive view would simply see this as a naturally developing consistent expectation once a particular level of income is attained. When a dancer does not bring in her self-determined "quota" for the night, she feels not only disappointment and perhaps anger, but also a sense of failure and shame. Nevertheless, as the more reflective strippers in this sample explained, a "failure" to earn a specified amount of money in one night may simply be due to an unexplained bad night, a bad week, or some completely unrelated reason (weather, other events in town, etc.). Vicki, who had been dancing for several years, had to struggle to maintain her perspective on money and the ebbs and flows of her income. As she reflected, it was possible to become "spoiled in the business," and come to expect ever-increasing amounts of money for the same or less effort.

> Once you're in it for awhile, you get kind of spoiled as a woman, having guys just hand you money like that.

As a final primary cost of stripping, and building on the rewarding aspects of stripping, for some strippers, the atmosphere and clientele can be undesirable aspects of the work. Specifically, some strippers complain about the many "bad influences" that can be found in strip clubs at almost any hour of any day, sometimes in sizeable numbers. These undesirable influences include drug dealers, pimps, "perverts," and men who "just won't take no for an answer." Leslie provided a useful reflection on this cost of stripping. In her words, she had been negatively affected by her work in the stripping industry in many ways, but most importantly,

> it's depleted my trust and faith in people. The way you see relationships, unfaithful men, who are turning their pagers and cell phones off.

Not only do strippers come to view their customers in largely negative lights, but so too do some show evidence of becoming desensitized to activities that in other settings and environments would clearly be defined as "deviant." Some strip clubs frequently play host to rowdy, obnoxious, and drunk men, many of whom engage in illegal behaviors and frequently not within parameters strippers would define as "good taste" (Erickson & Tewksbury, 2000). In many instances, strippers are encouraged, expected, or coerced to go beyond legal limits with patrons, in the interest of making more money for herself and especially the club in which she dances (Sanchez, 1998).

Largely because of the environment and population with whom strippers work, maintaining an intimate relationship outside the club is not necessarily an easy task. Because of the nature of the stripper subculture, it is hard for those outside the business to understand or cope with the daily routines and priorities of strippers. Ferrah was just one of many women who thought her relationships with men suffered because of her stripping career,

> I am the wonder of three-month relationships. It is so hard to have a boyfriend that is going to trust you. I go in there every night in front of strange men and talk and be friendly with them. It's tough for guys to understand and deal with that.

Some strippers may develop eating disorders, see their motivational levels drop, become increasingly less responsible, become desensitized sexually, and, as a result of the attention they receive focused on their bodies and appearance, alter their ways of perceiving and interpreting the world around them.

Although the positive rewards from stripping can be strong enough to hold some women in the industry for long periods of time, strippers themselves generally claim that the costs of their work have a more direct and lasting effect on their lives. The degree to which an individual stripper experiences each of these rewards and manages the costs vary depending upon her personality, management of problematic issues from childhood, and current strength and stability of identity. Where the picture becomes most interesting is to look at how women currently working as strippers perceive their work and their worlds and use their experiences to formulate advice for those women considering embarking on a career in the stripping industry. It is to these issues that we turn next.

ADVICE FOR OTHERS

Strippers strongly advise other women considering entering the stripping industry to carefully consider their decision and suggest that this option is not a desirable occupational choice. This caution is not due to a desire to limit competition or extend the time that a woman can continue to make money, but rather it is based on a sincere desire to see other women effectively avoid the costs that most strippers see coming from their occupation. Such cautionary advice, however, is not universal. It is those women who have been in the business the longest who are most adamant that stripping is to be avoided. As length of experience increases, the likelihood of discouraging others from entering the sex industry also increases.

It appears to be only those women who are at the earliest stages of their careers and presumably have had the least experience with the costs of stripping who offer encouragement to others. This perspective seems to center from their perception of stripping as fun, an easy way to make a lot of money, an opportunity to meet new people, and an exciting lifestyle. These women essentially see the rewards of stripping as far outweighing the identified costs. According to the current study, these women who say they would recommend their line of work to others also experienced complete support from their families, continued to actively pursue other long-term goals while dancing, and steadfastly held to their belief that other people's convictions did not matter to them. In other words, the commonly identified costs of the occupation were not yet fully realized by these women.

Those who would definitely not recommend stripping to other women emphasized that with time, the costs of the industry far outweighed the rewards. When probed to elaborate on why they would discourage others from pursuing stripping, these women discussed their own experiences with what they defined as emotional scars, physical hardships, stresses from working long nights, a lack of appreciation for the value of money, and pressures and restrictions created by outsiders' judgments. Although valuing their income, these women make clear that the financial rewards generated by stripping do not, and in fact cannot, moderate the frustrations and harm it provides. Although they readily acknowledged that they made a "decent living," if it were not for the money, they would have left the industry. The money is "not worth what you have to do for it." Illustrating this view was Alisha, who hated "the business," especially how tired it made her feel.

> I hate it, it's long nights, and you're so tired, one day you'll make a lot of money and the next you won't, it's bullshit. It's not all it's cracked up to be.

The costs of working in the sex industry impose hardships and pain in both the long and short term for many dancers. However, it is the reliance on the financial rewards, lifestyle, and psychological/emotional benefits that keeps women in the industry. Most compelling, though, are the financial rewards. As commonly expressed by strippers in this sample, if a woman can avoid the lifestyle that stripping "always" brings, she should. This is why Leslie urged other women to stay away.

> You see women get caught up in the things you got caught up in. A friend of mine, she's a young girl who strips and she's got into drugs and other things, and she no longer has her child because of it. That hurts. People say to me all the time, "You have four kids and they are all still with you?" That's what hurts me the most, I see women come in and get caught up in the drugs and alcohol, and I see them leave with a different guy two or three nights a week.

Some strippers, however, are less convinced that stripping is a bad occupational choice and suggest that their work might, in fact, be manageable for the "right type of woman." It is only those who possess the "right" set of personality attributes and who bring a minimum of troubling background and childhood issues who should consider becoming a stripper. Otherwise, the culture of the industry, and the others with whom a stripper will find herself interacting, can present too strong of a negative force, leading to "inevitable" lifestyle changes. The recurring theme for the type of woman that a stripper might recommend for stripping includes a strong belief in the need for a significant degree of personal strength; the ability and habit of making good, responsible decisions; high self-esteem; a true financial need or crisis; confidence with her sexuality; not easily influenced by others; and clear goals for entering the business.

Clearly, then, women who work as strippers are at best hesitant, and at worst adamantly opposed to, recommending other young women follow in their professional footsteps. Unless specified personality traits (all related to strength of character and convictions) are possessed by the woman considering entry to stripping, this is seen as a potentially dangerous occupational choice. However, most women who become strippers do not seek out the advice of those currently in the field, and therefore, this point becomes somewhat moot.

Strippers do have advice for those about to enter, or who have just recently entered, the stripper's corner of the sex industry. The one universal piece of advice offered by the strippers in this sample was that better preparation for a stripping career will result in fewer and less severe emotional scars, more positive adventures, and increased tangible property at the end of one's career. Knowing what you are getting into, why you are entering this occupation, and what you want to take away from it are critical to surviving and succeeding in the stripping world.

A recurring piece of advice these women had to offer centered on the income potential of stripping. Not only can a woman make a sizable income by stripping, but she may also have the potential to turn her stripping income into long-term income, if she invests her money rather than squanders it. Most strippers do not do this, however. In simple, yet insightful words, "Do not become frivolous with spending, just because payday is every day." Nearly all strippers urge others (despite their own actions) to deposit a portion of their earnings in savings or investments. Strippers are professionals with a significant income potential and should handle their money in much the same way as any other professional: form a financial plan, work toward long-term goals, and be sure to manage expenses efficiently. Brenda focused her advice on saving from the very beginning.

> Watch your money. Don't blow it. Save a little out of every night's earnings, and you'll be set. Save from the very beginning, even though it's going to feel cool having all that money. You have to save some of it and you'll be okay.

Additionally, women currently working in the stripping industry suggested that a woman considering entering the field should identify strategies for keeping her "perspective." Whereas for some dancers, the "lifestyle" of a stripper is a valued reward, most strippers interviewed believed that when one develops a reliance on the lifestyle, such changes are a serious cost of the occupation. Therefore, those just entering the business are advised to maintain a perspective that conceptualizes stripping as an occupation, not a lifestyle. Some entertainers may escape into the subculture of stripping, where working, partying, and socializing are interchangeable. To maintain a mainstream lifestyle—as well as garner the respect of family, friends, and "society"—strippers generally believe it is important to "keep a level head" and not lose sight of long-term goals. Without such an approach, it is believed that a new stripper will be "lost" to the party-centered lifestyle of strip clubs.

One of the best ways to ensure that a new stripper does not fall into the "darker side" of the stripping industry and subculture is to "take it slow" when starting out. For many newcomers, this can be difficult, especially considering the rush of excitement from the usually previously unavailable amounts of money one can earn. The financial rewards can push women to work more often and delay intentions of getting out of the business. When coupled with the "excitement" of the strip club, some women may be at risk of "losing themselves" to the stripper world. Explaining how this can happen, Vicki provided a vivid explanation of this situation in her advice to women new to the stripping industry:

> Be sure about themselves, and make their own decisions. It's their life, it's their body, it's their money to make. You run into a lot of people that don't have the right intentions, and probably want to cause you harm or have you doing things that should be your decision whether you want to do those things or not.

On a more practical level, the strippers also strongly suggested that newcomers pay close attention to their bodies, being certain to stay healthy. As discussed above, stripping can be a physically demanding job; it is important that dancers take special care of themselves. This means avoiding the temptation of drugs and drinking on a daily basis. Temptations to drink and use drugs can be strong; one works long hours, the setting can be physically and emotionally stressful, and at times the work fairly dull. Partying on the job may make time pass more quickly, but in the eyes of experienced strippers, in the long run, adopting such a perspective will induce serious and lasting consequences.

Perhaps the best approach for maintaining a proper perspective is to have a plan for not only how one will structure and strategize her work, but to also enter the industry with the knowledge of what lengths one is willing to go to for money. Strip club patrons can be expected to push a stripper's limits and offer money for a variety of "extra" services and interactions (Erickson & Tewksbury, 2000). A new stripper needs to be aware that the time will come when her limits will be pushed, with substantial amounts of money being offered for fulfilling patrons' requests. It is for this reason that experienced strippers advise newcomers to the industry to be knowledgeable and have established limits in mind from the outset. What many strippers advise, although few have done so themselves, is to maintain a connection to the world outside the stripping industry and to have a backup plan, meaning keeping another job while stripping. Maintaining another job while stripping not only guarantees an income, but it also allows for a connection to the everyday, normal working routine in society. In short, these strippers believe it is critical to avoid becoming reliant on the lifestyle.

CONCLUSION

In the end, the accounts provided by these female strippers provide us with a confirming, albeit slightly different, view of what has been previously reported in the social science literature, as well as some additional insights regarding the ways and means by which women enter, experience, and exit one portion of the commercial sex industry. Strippers become strippers for a variety of reasons, although they are primarily pursuing an occupational choice for financial reasons. When first embarking on a career in stripping, the decision is seen as a short-term solution to a financial need; few, if any, women become strippers because they believe this will be a rewarding long-term career. For many, it is, in fact, a fairly short-lived occupational foray; however, for others, the experience itself—balancing the rewards and the costs of the work—establishes a hold on the individual, and she becomes reliant on at least one of the primary rewards.

Whether it is a financial, lifestyle, or psychological/emotional reliance, the experience provides opportunities to both succeed and suffer. Once a woman comes to recognize her reliance on the rewards of her work, she is likely to become increasingly aware of the costs of her work and seek to either minimize the costs in contrast to the rewards (and seek to become a feature dancer or develop a regular clientele) or work to find and realize alternative options. Most often, it is the latter that is pursued.

Strippers have mixed feelings about their occupational choice, and the degree to which an individual stripper focuses on the rewards and costs varies with time. However, as she accumulates experience, she typically sees the costs coming to outweigh the rewards. Hence, strippers typically do not see stripping as a choice that others should make. In the end, strippers believe that they are simply hard-working, misunderstood service workers. The glamour is faint, the income dwindles and is often used in less than optimal ways, and the reactions both anticipated and realized from others are negative.

Stripping can be financially rewarding, periodically enjoyable, and at times psychologically satisfying. But these rewards are not lasting. Costs of stripping, on the other hand, mount and intensify. Perceptions of exploitation build, frustrations grate, and individuals come to question the worth and consequence of their occupational pursuits. Stripping can provide women with rewards, but in the end, the costs are almost always perceived to significantly overshadow any and all remuneration.

5

Prostitution, the Sex Industry, and Sex Tourism

———◼———

JODY MILLER
DHEESHANA JAYASUNDERA

The adage "prostitution is the world's oldest profession" may read as a tired cliché, but it highlights key issues salient for understanding women's experiences in the commercial sex industry. Explicit in the adage is recognition that prostitution is an enactment of sexual labor, and one that is deeply rooted across societies. The particular nature of the industry takes a variety of forms historically as well as within and across nations. However, a common thread in the organization and control of the sex industry is that it is characterized by gender, race, and class inequalities, as well as power imbalances resulting from colonial and imperialist relations across nations (see Maher, 1997; Truong, 1990). As sociologist Eleanor Miller (1991) notes, prostitution is work that would have no value were it not for the conditions of economic and sexual inequality under which it is performed (p. 8; see also Overall, 1992).[1]

In recent years, there have been a number of significant shifts in the organization of the commercial sex industry, each relevant to women's experience of violence within prostitution. In the United States, the arrival of crack cocaine in urban markets in the mid-1980s considerably altered the conditions under which sex work is performed, with many scholars suggesting that these changes have been to women's detriment (see Maher, 1997; Miller, 1995a; Ratner, 1993). Internationally, the last decades of the 20th century witnessed a tremendous growth in what is known as sex tourism: the development and expansion of industries providing sexual services, catering primarily to Western and Japanese men who travel to Third World countries for business or leisure activities (see Truong, 1990). In conjunction with the development and expansion of sex tourism has been a rise in trafficking of individuals for prostitution and the widespread involvement of children in the sex tourism industry.

Authors' Note: This article first appeared in Renzetti, C., Edleson, J., & Bergen, R. K. (Eds.) (2001). *Sourcebook on Violence Against Women* (pp. 459-480). Thousand Oaks, CA: Sage. Used with permission.

This chapter provides an overview of the commercial sex industry within the United States and internationally, highlighting the impact of legal responses and organizational features in shaping women's experiences within prostitution, particularly their experiences of violence. Linda Fairstein (1993), a Manhattan sex crimes prosecutor, argues that it is unlikely that any occupation or lifestyle exposes a woman to the threat of assault and gratuitous violence as constantly and completely as prostitution (p. 171). Our goal is to illuminate how and why this is the case.

DEFINITIONAL CONCERNS

Definitions of prostitution, along with appropriate interventions, are hotly contested. Social definitions largely concentrate on the exchange of sexual relations for monetary payment or barter, characterized by promiscuity or lack of emotional attachment (Flowers, 1998, p. 6). However, contemporary debate centers on the issue of prostitution as forced or chosen: violence against women versus a form of work. In recent years, women engaged in the sex industry have been at the forefront in arguing that prostitution should be defined as sex work (see Bell, 1987; Jenness, 1993; Kempadoo & Doezema, 1998). For example, the U.S.-based prostitutes' rights movement, COYOTE (Call Off Your Old Tired Ethics), asserts that laws against prostitution are at the heart of sex workers' victimization, and that prostitution is voluntary. COYOTE argues that prostitution should be decriminalized, destigmatized, and recognized as a legitimate form of service work (Jenness, 1993). In sharp contrast, some feminist groups, most notably WHISPER (Women Hurt in Systems of Prostitution) and CATW (Coalition Against Trafficking in Women), characterize prostitution by definition as a form of violence against women. Drawing on the language of the anti-rape movement, they refer to women as survivors of prostitution and reject the claim of prostitution as work (see Barry, 1979, 1995; Giobbe, 1991).

Although many feminists do not take the hard-line stand of groups such as WHISPER, they nonetheless have difficulty accepting wholeheartedly the position of groups such as COYOTE and some international sex workers' rights organizations (see Kempadoo & Doezema, 1998, for a number of examples). Most feminists highlight the larger patriarchal contexts in which prostitution occurs, suggesting that prostitution both results from and contributes to the sexual objectification of women and the sexual double standard. Moreover, given economic and employment inequalities based on gender, race, class, and nation, they argue that it is difficult to know how many women would choose sex work if a wider range of employment options was available. Thus, while maintaining a crucial moral distinction between prostitutes as sex workers and prostitution as a practice and institution (Overall, 1992, p. 708), many feminists defend prostitutes' entitlement to do their work but [do not] defend prostitution itself as a practice under patriarchy (Overall, 1992, p. 723; see also Chancer, 1993; Cooper, 1989).

These debates are played out within the international arena as well. Early international conventions distinguished between prostitution as a personal choice and slavery-like prostitution due to coercion or trafficking in people. These conventions prohibited international trafficking and regarded prostitution as a human rights violation only if it involved overt coercion or exploitation (Lim, 1998). Successive international instruments also followed this approach. However, the Convention for the Suppression of Traffic in Persons and the Exploitation of the Prostitution of Others, adopted by the United Nations in 1949, took an abolitionist approach. This convention viewed the prostitute as a victim and did not distinguish between forced and voluntary prostitution (Lim, 1998).

After the 1949 Convention, both feminist and international concern for prostitution and the traffic in women abated for a time (Doezema, 1998, p. 36). It was not until the 1980s, in conjunction with the rise in sex tourism, that trafficking and prostitution again received international attention. Some more recent international instruments also take the abolitionist approach outlined in the 1949 Convention (Lim, 1998). However, supporters of sex workers' rights argue that many adults make relatively free decisions to enter the trade; thus, voluntary prostitution should be distinguished from prostitution resulting from trafficking, which involves overt pressure or coercion from third parties in the form of deception, violence, or debt bondage (Foundation Against Trafficking in Women, International Human Rights Law Group, and Global Alliance against Traffic in Women, 1999).

In fact, some argue that the tendency to view Third World sex workers primarily as victims, while accepting that Western women can choose sex work, is a continuation of colonial legacies that define Third World women as inferior, needing guidance, assistance, and help (Kempadoo, 1998, p. 11). Instead, these authors argue that despite the marginality and vulnerability of sex workers internationally (Kempadoo, 1998, p. 8), the conceptualization of Third World sex workers exclusively as victims should be rejected. Consequently, even the forced/voluntary dichotomy recently has been challenged. A number of activists argue that this remains a limited framework for dealing with sex work, as it often results in policies aimed only at rescuing trafficked women; women who are voluntarily involved in the sex industry continue to face exploitation and human rights violations that remain unaddressed by current intervention strategies (Doezema, 1998).

Our own position parallels that of Kempadoo and Doezema. Although we use the terms prostitution and sex work interchangeably throughout the chapter, we nonetheless recognize prostitution as a form of sexual labor and sex workers as human agents despite their subjection to stigma, victimization, and exploitation. Without taking an ethical position on the legitimacy of prostitution or its functions in support of patriarchal capitalism,[2] our concern in this chapter is with the legal, social, and economic conditions under which prostitution occurs within racist, patriarchal, capitalist systems. Again, our particular focus is how these conditions promote and contribute to violence against sex workers.

LEGAL RESPONSES TO THE SEX INDUSTRY

Four legal paradigms have been identified to address prostitution: prohibition, abolition, legalization/regulation, and decriminalization (Coomaraswamy, 1997). In fact, these paradigms speak to the definitional concerns highlighted in the previous section. In the prohibitionist model, prostitution is a crime. Technically, all parties involved are criminalized, including the sex worker, client, and others who profit (e.g., pimps, brokers, traffickers, managers). However, with few exceptions, it is primarily sex workers themselves who are arrested and prosecuted under these laws. The United States currently adopts the prohibitionist model, as do China, Iceland, Japan, Malta, Nepal, the Philippines, Romania, Slovenia, Sri Lanka, Tanzania, Uganda, and Vietnam (Wijers & Lap-Chew, 1997).

The prohibition model is widely believed to be the most oppressive for sex workers (see Scibelli, 1987). This approach leaves women with no legal apparatus to defend themselves. Rarely do states enforce laws against traffickers, pimps, or clients, although women are routinely subject to arrest and incarceration. Moreover, because of the illegal nature of their work, many women are hesitant to go to law enforcement when they are crime victims and conduct their work so as to conceal their activities, which increases their risk of victimization (Miller, 1997).

The abolitionist approach calls for the elimination of laws against prostitution itself. It criminalizes third parties, rather than the actual transaction. As noted earlier, this is the approach adopted by the U.N. Convention of 1949. Abolitionism decriminalizes women's involvement in prostitution and does not distinguish between voluntary and forced prostitution. Instead, prostitutes are defined as victims. As such, the abolitionist approach does not recognize women's right to choose prostitution as a legitimate occupation. Most countries in Western Europe adopt a predominantly abolitionist approach, including Belgium, Denmark, Finland, France, Ireland, Italy, Norway, Portugal, Spain, Sweden, and the United Kingdom. In addition, Bangladesh, Bulgaria, Cameroon, Canada, Czechoslovakia, Colombia, the Dominican Republic, Hong Kong, India, Lithuania, Nigeria, Poland, Thailand, and the Ukraine follow a primarily abolitionist model (Hoigard & Finstad, 1992; Petersson, personal communication, 1999; Wijers & Lap-Chew, 1997). In fact, in January 1999, Sweden, which previously only criminalized third parties, passed a new law that criminalizes sex workers' clients. Although other Scandinavian countries are considering the legislation, there was just one successful conviction in the year following passage of the legislation (Petersson, personal communication, September 12, 1999).

It is important to clarify that no country has adopted a purely abolitionist approach; typically, whereas the act of prostitution itself is not criminalized, such acts as street solicitation, loitering, and curb-crawling remain criminal offenses (e.g., see Hatty, 1989, regarding Australia; Lowman, 1990, regarding Canada; Scibelli, 1987, regarding France and Thailand). In fact, Thailand is a case worth discussing. Some authors classify Thailand as adopting a prohibitionist approach (Scibelli, 1987), in part because of the contradictory nature of laws governing the industry there. In her detailed analysis of sex tourism in Thailand, social researcher Thanh-Dam Truong (1990) documents these contradictions:

> Sexual services are produced on the edge of legal ambiguity. Prostitution is criminalized under the Penal Code. At the same time, it is formalized under the law governing industries. Under the Penal Code it is defined as a crime of promiscuity. It is defined as personal services under business law, and as special services by the Police Department. The law recognizes personal services as a business and ensures privileges to investors, and at the same time criminalizes workers in the business. Given the contradiction between the legality of personal service enterprises and the illegality of prostitution, the relations of power and production in prostitution are complex and diverse. (p. 180)

Legalization/regulation is the third legal paradigm dealing with prostitution. This is the predominant approach in a number of Western countries, including Australia, Austria, Germany, Greece, the Netherlands, and Switzerland, as well as Curacao, Ecuador, Peru, and Turkey (Wijers & Lap-Chew, 1997). This is also the approach found in some counties in Nevada (Scibelli, 1987). Under this model, there is state tolerance of prostitution through government regulatory schemes. Regulation includes direct government interventions such as the registration of brothel houses, as well as neo-regulatory systems such as mandatory health exams and taxation. Under this model, sex workers rather than other parties are subject to regulation. Registration is often compulsory, and unregistered women are considered to be committing an illegal act. And whereas sex workers are typically required to undergo medical exams for sexually transmitted diseases (STDs), their customers are not. Failure to attend mandatory medical exams makes women liable to prosecution (Wijers & Lap-Chew, 1997). Moreover, women's mobility is severely restricted, with regulations governing when and with whom they can be in public space (see Scibelli, 1987).

Decriminalization is the paradigm advocated by many sex workers' rights organizations, including COYOTE (Jenness, 1993). In contrast to the abolitionist model, the argument for decriminalization emphasizes the view that prostitution is work and rejects the notion that sex workers are, by definition, victims. Instead, this model aims to criminalize exploitation, coercion, and violence by third parties against sex workers, while defining sex work as a legitimate occupation. To highlight the distinction between decriminalization and the abolitionist approach, consider again Sweden's new law against clients. Under the decriminalization paradigm, such laws are discriminatory, even though sex workers themselves are not targeted. The laws challenge the legitimacy of the work, may deter clients from seeking the services of sex workers, and thus have an adverse effect on their business. Moreover, the abolitionist model has been critiqued for failing to distinguish between pimps and brokers, on the one hand, and women's partners and boyfriends, on the other. Anyone who profits from sex workers' labor legally qualifies as a pimp, even if the relationship is not based on coercion (see Hoigard & Finstad, 1992).

Decriminalization is a fundamentally liberal approach; key issues include challenging the sexual double standard of morality as a means to destigmatize prostitution, as well as combating discriminatory labor practices and exploitative working conditions (see Truong, 1990, pp. 48-50). Some advocates do not critique the sex industry as a feature of patriarchal capitalism (see Jenness, 1993), whereas others view decriminalization as a short-term solution to improve sex workers' lives, with the goal of eliminating prostitution in an ideal nonpatriarchal society (see Chancer, 1993; James, 1978; Overall, 1992; Scibelli, 1987).

Before moving on, two additional legal issues are noteworthy. First is the harmful impact of immigration laws on transnational sex workers; second, we will briefly discuss current legal interventions on the international child sex trade. A number of sex workers' rights organizations have argued that besides laws against prostitution, immigration laws also contribute to the coercive, exploitative features of the transnational sex industry (see Kempadoo & Doezema, 1998). Many Third World and Eastern European women who are trafficked or go abroad to work in the sex industry do so as illegal immigrants. Thus, the threat of deportation remains a serious concern that keeps many sex workers in dependent relationships with third parties. Even though deportation at first glance appears to be a solution, in many cases, women find that traffickers are waiting for them when they arrive home, or they face rejection from their families and communities when the nature of their work is discovered. As Kempadoo and Doezema (1998) summarize,

> It is important to recognize that trafficked women are first and foremost migrant persons seeking economic, social, and political opportunities away from home yet, due to restrictive laws and policies and limited opportunities for women, are relegated to informal sector work. State policies and laws furthermore serve to position migrant women as undesirable aliens and criminals, yet yield benefits for traffickers. (p. 32)

Moreover, these laws allow third parties to dispense with women who are no longer viewed as economically viable (for instance, if they contract STDs such as HIV) by turning them in to authorities for arrest and/or deportation (see Kempadoo & Doezema, 1998; Truong, 1990).

With regard to children's involvement in the sex industry, there is near-uniform agreement that an abolitionist model is best, at least in theory. Children are defined as victims of the sex industry, and third parties as well as clients should be criminalized and prosecuted. Child sex tourism has become a grave international concern, resulting in both national and international efforts to ameliorate it. The United Nations Convention on the Rights of the Child has as one goal the protection of children from sexual exploitation. A number of Western nations have passed new laws to prosecute citizens for sex crimes against children committed abroad; however, evidentiary and cross-jurisdiction problems have thus far made these efforts difficult (Berkman, 1996; Bureau of International Labor Affairs, 1996; Healy, 1995).

In addition, most of the countries where child sex tourism occurs have adopted stringent laws prohibiting the trade. In Sri Lanka, for example, new laws were passed in 1995 to curb child sex tourism by raising the minimum age of consent to 18 for boys and 16 for girls, making sexual activities with youths under those ages a crime, and providing a minimum 5-year jail term for pimps and clients (Gunasekera, 1996; Samarasinghe, 1996, 1997). Several European tourists have been prosecuted under the new laws, although there is no evidence in the short term of a significant deterrent effect of the laws. For the most part, enforcement has been quite lax in most countries.

In addition, it is important to note that some argue that the issue of children's involvement in the sex industry should be defined more broadly to explicitly emphasize poverty and economic inequalities exacerbated by Western imperialism. As noted previously, developmental processes have contributed to a rise in the earning activities of children globally; attempts to ameliorate children's participation in the sex industry without addressing the global exploitation of children's labor more broadly provide a truncated approach, with likely harmful effects for the children involved (see Kempadoo, 1998; Montgomery, 1998).

In the remaining sections of this chapter, we will provide overviews of the sex industry in the United States, as well as sex tourism, child sex tourism, trafficking, and transnational sex work. As we do so, we turn our attention to the exploitation of and violence against sex workers in these contexts. We will pay particular attention to the impact of legal and social responses to sex work as entrenched features of the industry's organization, further highlighting the role these play in contributing to sex workers' exploitation and abuse. Particularly in the West, the extent of violence and of women's ability to protect themselves varies across sectors of the industry, with women working in indoor settings generally afforded greater protection, at least from violence at the hands of clients.[3] Within the sex tourism industry and among transnational sex workers, this distinction is less meaningful. As we will discuss further below, sex workers in these contexts often face a wide range of abuses in the context of brothel and other indoor work, including illegal confinement, forced or coerced labor, and sexual and physical abuse (Kempadoo & Doezema, 1998).

PROSTITUTION AND VIOLENCE AGAINST STREET SEX WORKERS IN THE UNITED STATES[4]

As noted previously, with the exception of several counties in Nevada, prostitution remains criminalized in the United States. Because of the illicit nature of prostitution in the United States, it is not possible to obtain accurate estimates of its prevalence. In 1996, there were

48,591 arrests of women for prostitution or commercialized vice in the United States (Maguire & Pastore, 1997, p. 336). This increase from 33,306 arrests 20 years earlier (see James, 1978) is not necessarily a result of a rise in prostitution; it may rather be an outcome of the dominant law-and-order philosophies characteristic of criminal justice policies in the 1980s and 1990s. In 1996, the bulk of these arrests (61%) were of women between the ages of 25 and 39 (Maguire & Pastore, 1997, p. 335); African Americans accounted for 38% of those arrested for prostitution and commercialized vice in 1996 (Maguire & Pastore, 1997, p. 338).[5]

These figures are of limited utility, however, as they only document arrests (and may include multiple arrests of the same women) and are widely recognized as overrepresenting women working on the streets, who are most vulnerable to law enforcement efforts. Priscilla Alexander (1988), a sex workers' rights advocate and researcher, estimates that only 10% to 20% of sex workers work in this sector of the industry. In addition, sex work occurs in massage clinics, bars, hotels, brothels, and outcall sectors (e.g., escort services, call girls) (see Alexander, 1988). Scholars estimate that from 250,000 to 500,000 women are involved in prostitution in the United States (Scarpitti & Andersen, 1989; Scibelli, 1987).

However, most research on prostitution in the United States has focused on women's experiences in the lower echelons of the sex industry: the streets, and more recently crack houses and other drug environments (see Carmen & Moody, 1985; Inciardi, Lockwood, & Pottieger, 1993; Maher, 1997; Miller, 1986; Ratner, 1993; Zausner, 1986). This is partly a result of greater ease of access to these populations, as other forms of sex work remain hidden. In addition, it is because street prostitution has often been defined as the most problematic form of sex work in the United States and elsewhere because it occurs in public settings and often in areas characterized by high rates of crime. Street prostitution is also widely recognized as the most dangerous setting for sex workers themselves, a topic we will return to shortly. Notably, social definitions of prostitution in the United States so pervasively emphasize the actions of only sex workers that virtually no research has been conducted on clientele (see Chancer, 1993; but see Prasad, 1999).

The sex industry is not only characterized by different sectors but by status and economic hierarchies across them. Generally speaking, women working on the streets are among the lowest paid and socially stigmatized, with the recent exception of women engaged in sex-for-crack exchanges and/or who work in crack houses. Women working through escort services or as call girls are at the high end. Not surprisingly, poor women and women of color are disproportionately represented on the streets and in the lower levels of prostitution, in part because of the low value assigned to their sexuality within racist constructs of desire (Austin, 1992, p. 272; see also Kempadoo, 1998). In fact, in her ethnography of a Brooklyn drug market, sociologist Lisa Maher (1997) reports hierarchy among street-level sex workers, with white women able to attract more and higher-paying clientele than their African American and Latina counterparts.

Most scholars, activists, and sex workers agree that, in the United States and elsewhere, women's primary motivation for involvement in the industry is economic. In markets characterized by intense gender, race, and class hierarchies, prostitution provides a sometimes viable economic alternative among the limited options available. Both in the United States and abroad, despite the risks associated with sex work, no other occupation available to unskilled women provides an income comparable to that provided by prostitution. It is also important to note that in one person's lifetime, sex work is commonly just one of the multiple activities employed for generating income, and very few stay in prostitution for their entire adulthood (Kempadoo, 1998, p. 4; see also Austin, 1992, p. 272; Maher, 1997; Miller,

1986). Nonetheless, prostitute often becomes a master status for women involved in sex work, contributing to problems such as law enforcement discrimination, stigmatization, and violence.

In the United States, street prostitution is widely believed to be the most dangerous setting for sex work. Women engaged in street prostitution face widespread physical and sexual violence. For example, in the early 1980s, researchers Mimi Silbert and Ayala Pines (1982) conducted one of the largest studies of violence against street prostitutes in the United States, interviewing 200 women and girls in the San Francisco Bay area. They reported that 70% of their sample had been raped by clients, 65% were beaten by clients, 66% were physically abused by pimps, and 73% had experienced rapes totally unrelated to their work as prostitutes (p. 128). When women were identified as prostitutes by their rapists, the rapes tended to be more brutal, and the victims sustained more serious injuries.

Likewise, sociologist Jody Miller's (1997) study of street prostitution in Columbus, Ohio, in the early 1990s reported that 94% of the women had been sexually assaulted, including 75% who were raped by clients and 63% who were raped in other contexts on the streets. In addition, 88% reported having been physically assaulted: 61% had been beaten up, nearly a third had been stabbed or slashed, a quarter had been hit with an object such as a baseball bat or brick, and 38% reported having been kidnapped and held captive. In this sample of just 16 women, two reported having been choked, three had suffered serious injuries such as broken bones, one had her head rammed through a glass door, and one had been tortured with electric shock (Miller & Schwartz, 1995, p. 8).

These studies report the prevalence of violence, but this is only the tip of the iceberg, as women working on the streets describe much of this kind of violence as routine (Miller, 1986, 1997; Miller & Schwartz, 1995; Silbert & Pines, 1981; Zausner, 1986). Moreover, street-level sex workers experience violence, not just at the hands of clients, but also from pimps, drug dealers and users, the police, and others within the street environment (see Bracey, 1983; Maher, 1997; Miller, 1995a). Outside the United States, similar findings have also been reported, for instance, in the United Kingdom (Cunnington, 1984), Scotland (McKeganey & Barnard, 1996), Canada (Lowman & Fraser, 1995), and Norway (Hoigard & Finstad, 1992).

As noted previously, a wealth of evidence suggests that shifts resulting from the introduction of crack cocaine into the U.S. urban street scene have had detrimental effects on women engaged in sex work in these settings. For example, in her monograph, *Sexed Work*, Lisa Maher (1997) documents a rigid gender division of labor in the crack economy, shaped along racial lines, in which women find sex work one of the only available options for supporting their drug use. Changes in the economy brought about by crack have disadvantaged street sex workers further, resulting in lower payments, increased competition between women, and an intensification of their degradation and mistreatment. In addition, sexual exchanges in crack houses, particularly sex-for-crack exchanges, are believed to be among the most exploitative for drug-addicted women (see Bourgois & Dunlap, 1993; Goldstein, Ouellet, & Fendrich, 1992; Inciardi et al., 1993).

The intensity of violence against women working on the streets is a result of at least two sets of factors. First is the way in which the organization and criminalization of street prostitution make women particularly vulnerable to violent attack. Often, women who work on the streets have as one primary goal the avoidance of police detection. So, for example, they get into cars with clients hurriedly to minimize the possibility of being seen, they conduct transactions in isolated spots such as dark alleys or side streets, and they have clients drop them off in these areas to decrease visibility. However, these strategies often put women in

greater physical danger. Because they are unable to conduct their work openly, their vulnerability to violence is increased. Although women also have strategies to avoid victimization,
the nature of the work makes vulnerability to violence a structural feature (see Miller,
1997). Consequently, street-level sex workers are primary targets for serial killers as well
(Klinger, personal communication, October 27, 1999). In the 8 months following Miller's
research in Columbus, Ohio, five street sex workers were murdered by a serial killer who
was never caught (see also The Black Coalition Fighting Back Serial Murders, n.d.;
Cunnington, 1984; Lowman & Fraser, 1995).

Additional contributions to violence are ideologies that stigmatize sex workers, and
street sex workers in particular (see Austin, 1992), marking violence against them as in-
significant, deserved, and/or justified (Miller, 1995a, p. 437). Miller and Schwartz (1995)
suggest that a particular set of ideological beliefs or rape myths concerning prostitution allow clients to justify or excuse their sexual violence against sex workers and also limit sex
workers' access to legal assistance. First is the belief that prostitutes cannot be raped: The
fact that prostitutes are available for sexual negotiation [is interpreted to] mean that they
are available for sexual harassment or rape (Hatty, 1989, p. 236; see also Rubin, 1984). Second is the belief that no harm was done: Through a confusion of sex with violence, rape is
defined simply as a bad business transaction. Third is a belief that prostitutes deserve
violence against them because of their violation of normative expectations of appropriate
femininity.

Finally, the notion of collective liability (see Black, 1983; Scully, 1990) is brought to
bear on sex workers. For instance, women in Miller and Schwartz's (1995) study reported
being held responsible for the actions of their counterparts: A client angry at one sex
worker would pick up another woman and take his aggression out on her. Although they
recognized the pervasiveness of these beliefs, the women in Miller and Schwartz's study rejected each of them. As one put it, "Being prostitutes, we still know the difference between
rape and not getting raped." Another said, "Just because I'm working the streets, it's not
casual to me, it's still a traumatic thing."

Besides overt violence, women working on the streets encounter a number of additional problems. Most notable is discriminatory law enforcement, both with regard to the
sometimes indiscriminate arrest of street sex workers and the handling of (and participation in) their victimization by criminal justice officials. We will begin with a focus on the latter. The extent of women's legal protection from sexual violence is shaped by the extent to
which they adhere to the standards of normative femininity. In the United States, this means
being white, middle class, and chaste; as Bumiller (1990) suggests, protection is governed
by women's ability to present themselves as fallen angels (see also Estrich, 1987; Frohmann,
1997). Because sex workers fall at the far end of this continuum, some scholars have suggested that rape of prostitutes goes unpunished (see Frohmann, 1997; Miller & Schwartz,
1995). Fairstein (1993) reports that in many U.S. communities, complaints brought by sex
workers are automatically dismissed. Moreover, many sex workers do not go to the police
when they are victimized for fear of criminal sanctions, because they have outstanding warrants for prostitution-related charges, or simply because they don't believe the criminal
justice system will take their victimization seriously (Miller, 1997).

As noted, attitudes about sex workers play an important role in this process. When
Miller was completing her research in Columbus, one vice officer told her that the attitude
among police when a prostitute is found dead is, who really cares? You're dealing with a girl
who's a zero. The Black Coalition Fighting Back Serial Killers (n.d.) was formed in the mid-

1980s to raise awareness about police inattention and mishandling of the case of the Southside Slayer, a serial killer in South Central Los Angeles who targeted primarily African American women working as street sex workers. The police didn't bring the murders to public attention until 10 women had been killed and, specifically, until white women had been targeted. Moreover, early in the investigation, several officers referred to them as cheap homicides, and one officer was overheard saying, The slayer is doing a better job cleaning up the streets than we are (Prescod, 1990).

In addition, as noted earlier, discriminatory law enforcement also occurs when it comes to the arrest and prosecution of street-level sex workers. There are often reports of police officers demanding free sex in exchange for avoiding arrest. In fact, in Miller's (1997) study, nearly half of the women she spoke with reported having been forced or coerced into having sex with men who identified themselves as police officers (see also Carmen & Moody, 1985). Other problems are noteworthy as well. As stated previously, sex workers bear the brunt of laws against prostitution, even where there is formal equality under the law criminalizing all parties involved (see Lowman, 1990). Even when clients are arrested, the penalties they face are not as harsh, and charges often are dropped if they agree to testify against the sex workers (Scibelli, 1987). In some places, entrapment is legal, so that an undercover officer can approach a woman, quote a sexual act and a price, and if she consents, she is subject to arrest for solicitation.

Even when entrapment is not legal, it is nearly impossible for a known prostitute to credibly challenge the word of a police officer. Consequently, women often plead guilty rather than undergo prosecution. Once a woman has a record for prostitution, she is subject to indiscriminate arrest under loitering laws, which criminalize the movement of known prostitutes in public spaces (Scibelli, 1987). There is evidence of a great deal of abuse in the application of loitering laws, with police using arbitrary arrest tactics to harass women who are known prostitutes. Women have reported being arrested for walking to the store, for dressing a certain way, and for carrying condoms with them (Carmen & Moody, 1985; Miller, 1997). The process becomes cyclical: The more often women are arrested, the longer their record of prostitution becomes, making it more and more difficult to escape criminal labeling (Scibelli, 1987).

This section has documented some of the myriad problems faced by women working at the lower levels of the sex industry, particularly in the United States. In the remainder of the chapter, we turn our attention to the international sex industry, focusing on sex tourism, as well as trafficking and transnational sex work. Although many of the problems documented in the previous section apply to women working in the international sex industry, sex workers in the transnational sexual economy face a number of unique dangers tied to organizational features of the global industry.

VIOLENCE, COERCION, AND EXPLOITATION WITHIN THE INTERNATIONAL SEX INDUSTRY

Sex Tourism and Child Sex Tourism

According to the United Nations World Tourism Organization, tourism is fast becoming the single most important global economic activity (Enloe, 1989, p. 20). Tourism has been promoted extensively as a developmental strategy, resulting particularly from Western developmental policies, the influence of multinational corporations, and the economic impact of the U.S. military presence abroad (Campagna & Poffenberger, 1988; Enloe, 1989; Mies, 1986; Truong, 1990; Wood, 1981). Local governments, too, have actively promoted tourism, as it has become increasingly important in sustaining their economies. Worldwide, tourism is a $3.4 trillion industry (Kattoulas, 1995).

This is the context in which sex tourism has flourished. As we have defined it, sex tourism generally refers to the development and expansion of industries providing sexual services, catering primarily to Western and Japanese men who travel for business or leisure activities. Although prostitution and sex tourism are global phenomena, the growth in sex tourism in recent decades has been particularly pronounced in Asia. Prostitution has a long history in the region, but sex tourism is in part an outgrowth of U.S. military bases and rest and recreation centers established there during the Vietnam War (Enloe, 1989; Mies, 1986; Phongpaichit, 1982). The growth in international tourism, linked to the production of leisure services, occurred simultaneously with the placement of American troops in the region. The infrastructures put in place were well suited to the expansion of the tourist industry when the soldiers withdrew (see Truong, 1990).

Western imperialism, colonial legacies, and racialized notions of sexuality continue to shape the structure and operation of the sex tourism industry (Kempadoo & Doezema, 1998). For instance, the promotion of tourism and sex tourism, including packaged sex tours, advertises the sexual availability of young women and girls to tourists, highlighting the notion that Asian women are submissive, exotic, and thus sexually desirable. Moreover, sex tourism is often framed as beneficial to both Third World economies and individual sex workers and their families, thus assuaging possible guilt on the part of sex tourists (see Kempadoo & Doezema, 1998; Miller, 1995b; Truong, 1990). Sex tourism is well documented in a number of countries, including Thailand, the Philippines, China, Vietnam, Laos, Cambodia, Brazil, and the Dominican Republic (Flowers, 1998).

In Thailand, for instance, an estimated 500,000 to 700,000 women work in the commercial sex industry, the vast majority in Bangkok (Lim, 1998; Scibelli, 1987). A third are believed to be minors (Lim, 1998). If these estimates are accurate, upward of 10% of young women in Thailand between the ages of 15 and 25 are involved in the industry (see Scibelli, 1987). Young women from impoverished rural areas migrate or are trafficked to Bangkok to work in the sex industry as a means of supporting their families. There are direct routes from villages in the North to brothels in red-light zones in the Suthisarn and Saphan Kwai and from all regions to Patpong and Pattaya. Often, these young women are the main or even sole breadwinners in their families. It is important to note that estimates of the size of the commercial sex industry in various places do not distinguish between women working in tourist versus local markets. Although the thrust of public and research attention has been on sex tourism, many sex workers in Third World countries also provide services to local clientele (see Kempadoo & Doezema, 1998; Miller, 1999).

There is evidence that many young women are sold, outright or into debt bondage, in exchange for money provided to their families (Lim, 1998). Growing consumerism in the Third World is also cited as a factor; families in rural areas, able to purchase consumer goods from the profits of their daughters' labor, often obtain status within their communities (see Kempadoo & Doezema, 1998; Truong, 1990). As in other Southeast Asian countries, young women's sense of obligation to their families, and in some cases the economic benefits they receive, often result in their acceptance of the circumstances of their work. Moreover, as will be discussed shortly, they often have little recourse to resist because of the stigma attached to the work, its criminalization, and the coercive features of the industry.

Linked with tourism, prostitution is often recognized as a way to increase foreign revenue to a country, despite the fact that the majority of profits generated from tourism are channeled to Western multinationals (Truong, 1990). For example, a recent study conducted in Thailand suggests that prostitution is the largest underground industry in that country, generating between 10% and 14% of the country's gross national product (see Lim, 1998). The result is a tacit acceptance of the industry, despite the criminalization of sex workers (see Truong, 1990). Consequently, whereas women and other providers of sexual services are stigmatized and face law enforcement sanctions, the infrastructures of the industry and those who profit from it remain untouched. This is not just the case in Thailand; it is a global phenomenon (see Kempadoo & Doezema, 1998).

One outgrowth of sex tourism industries has been a rise in the involvement of children in these markets. Experts suggest that child sex tourism in particular has grown in recent years, as Western tourists who fear AIDS among adult prostitutes increasingly demand younger children (Boyes, 1996; Kattoulas, 1995). In addition, there is some evidence of organized pedophile networks in the West, exacerbated by the Internet, which provide information and organize tours abroad for the purpose of sexually abusing children (Boyes, 1996; EPCAT, 1997; McGirk, 1996). Moreover, developmental processes within the global economy have contributed to a rise in the earning activity of Third World children in a variety of settings. Thus, the rise in children's involvement in sex tourism and prostitution must be addressed in the context of the global exploitation of child labor (Kempadoo, 1998, p. 7).

Again, most available data focus on the Asian context, whereas child prostitution remains a global problem. According to a recent estimate by the U.N. International Labor Organization, upward of 1 million children in Asia are involved in the sex trade (Kaban, 1996; see also Healy, 1995). Thailand, Sri Lanka, the Philippines, Cambodia, and India are believed to be among the main centers of child sex tourism (Boyes, 1996; McGirk, 1996). Evidence suggests that in contrast to the West, where most child prostitution involves runaways (Davis, 1993), in Asia, many youths work in the sex industry to support their families (Montgomery, 1998; Truong, 1990). Sex tourists from Western Europe as well as Australia, Japan, and the United States travel to Asia to partake in the child sex trade. There is evidence that the production of pornographic publications featuring children has increased as well.

As is the case with the sex tourism industry more generally, the root causes of the problem appear to be a host of economic, social, and cultural factors that developing countries face, as well as the demand generated by thousands of men who travel to the region annually to purchase sexual services from children; multinational infrastructures support the trade. Poverty is often cited as a primary cause for the increase in the number of children involved. This is the case both for parents who are induced to sell their children and for youths who see the sex industry as a viable means of earning money when compared to the limited alternatives available (see Montgomery, 1998). Gender discrimination and the lesser value of female children also contribute to a climate in which the sexual exploitation of girls flourishes, although there is evidence of the involvement of boys in the sex industry as well (Montgomery, 1998). As previously discussed, a number of legal remedies have recently been introduced to curtail child sex tourism in particular; however, there is limited evidence of their success.

Trafficking and Transnational Sex Work

In conjunction with globalization and sex tourism, there has been a documented rise in trafficking and the movement of sex workers across international borders. The most recent definition given by the Global Alliance Against Traffic in Women, in cooperation with other agencies, defines trafficking as all acts and attempted acts involved in the recruitment, transportation within or across borders, purchase, sale, transfer, receipt, or harboring of a person (a) involving the use of deception, coercion, or debt bondage; (b) for the purpose of placing or holding such person, whether for pay or not, in involuntary servitude, in forced or bonded labor, or in slavery-like conditions, in a community other than the one in which such person lived at the time of the original deception, coercion, or debt bondage (Foundation Against Trafficking in Women, International Human Rights Law Group, and Global Alliance Against Traffic in Women, 1999).

However, as noted previously, a number of activists argue against the voluntary versus forced dichotomy, noting that it remains a limited framework for dealing with transnational sex work. For example, as a result of both immigration laws and laws against prostitution, women who voluntarily migrate for prostitution often find themselves in situations of coercion, dependence, and debt bondage. Because their decision to engage in sex work was voluntary, they receive less public sympathy and inadequate assistance or support (Kempadoo & Doezema, 1998). Thus, it is important to note that many of the problems associated with trafficking are also faced by women who migrate voluntarily for prostitution.

Evidence suggests that every year, hundreds of thousands of women are trafficked and exploited within the transnational prostitution industry. Although accurate data are difficult to come by, the International Organization for Migration estimates that traffickers move as many as 4 million illegal migrants each year. Trafficking may take place within national boundaries as well as across international borders. International trafficking involves both legal and illegal migration. Although much attention is currently paid to international trafficking, particularly across Asian countries, rural-urban migration patterns are long established within national boundaries, as noted above with regard to Thailand. Calcutta is a well-known receiving zone in India, with land routes through West Bengal, Bombay, and Punjab.

Although the trafficking of women for prostitution is a global activity, trafficking is believed to be highest within and from Asia. Nonetheless, trafficking can be found in Latin America and the Caribbean, in Africa, and to and from North America, the Middle East, Europe, and Australia. The collapse of the Soviet Union, with the resultant opening of borders and economic decline, has resulted in highly organized Russian crime groups that also send women abroad to work in the commercial sex industry. Russian sex workers are found throughout the world, most notably in Japan, China, the Middle East, and Western Europe (Brussa, 1998; Flowers, 1998). Although there are common patterns in sex workers' experiences in various locations, cultural patterns and differences in laws pertaining to migration and prostitution also create unique problems that are site-specific for sex workers (see Kempadoo & Doezema, 1998). We will touch on some of these issues below.

Where trafficking across borders is concerned, it is notable that the same country can serve as a sending, destination, or transit country. For example, in Thailand, there is evidence that women are trafficked from China to Hong Kong, from Burma to Thailand, and from Thailand to Japan (Wijers & Lap-Chew, 1997). Thus, there does not appear to be one set pattern to trafficking. Instead, trafficking routes change in response to economic and political changes. Typically, women and girls are trafficked to a destination via overland routes; where more sophisticated crime groups are involved, they are also transferred by air to overseas markets.

In most instances, developed or developing countries with well-established sex industries are receiving countries. These include Japan, Germany, the United States, and the Netherlands, along with Thailand, Taiwan, Korea, and India. For instance, evidence suggests that the majority of sex workers in Western Europe today are migrants from Third World and Eastern European countries (Brussa, 1998). Poorer countries, with the lowest levels of development, are more likely to send women and children abroad; the historical pattern continues to be outmigration from poorer to wealthier countries. Wealth disparities between First and Third World countries, as well as the marginalization of women in the latter, are factors. As mentioned with regard to sex tourism more broadly, developmental strategies have contributed immensely to the growth in international trafficking. In addition, Western notions of the exotic sexuality of Asian, African, and Latin American women contribute to demand (Kempadoo & Doezema, 1998; Miller, 1995b).

The extent and nature of trafficking is best documented in Asia. It encompasses a large spectrum of countries, with diverse cultures and economies. Within the region, Japan is a major receiving country. It is estimated that 150,000 non-Japanese women, mainly from Thailand and the Philippines, are working as prostitutes in Japan. Japanese men constitute the largest number of sex tourists in Asia (Lim, 1998). Thailand is also a major receiving country in Asia, in part because of its well-developed tourism industry. It receives women mainly from the Philippines, China, Hong Kong, and Burma. In South Asia, Bangladeshi women are usually trafficked via India to Pakistan, and massive trafficking of women and girls takes place across Nepal into India. It is estimated that over 100,000 Nepalese women and girls work in brothels in India. About a quarter of sex workers in India are believed to be underage (Lim, 1998).

Asia includes a large number of poor countries as well as economically well-developed countries. This, along with the growth in tourism, helps explain the high rate of trafficking within the region. High rates of illiteracy, lack of employment opportunities, and cultural religious ideologies and patriarchal family structures that place unmarried, separated, divorced, or widowed women outside the protective confines of the social system make them most liable for trafficking. Trafficking usually takes place from rural to urban settings and from cities to other countries. Unfamiliarity with their surroundings makes it difficult for women to return home.

It is important to note that women who are trafficked and/or who migrate for sex work are not only found in tourist markets. Instead, their sexual services are made available to indigenous men, too (Kempadoo & Doezema, 1998). In Sri Lanka, for instance, where a great deal of internal trafficking occurs (e.g., women migrate and are tricked or coerced from rural to urban areas within the country), the vast majority of women describe their clientele as almost exclusively local men, despite Sri Lanka's reputation for sex tourism. Moreover, women who migrate into the country from Russia, Thailand, and elsewhere routinely provide sexual services to Sri Lankan businessmen (Miller, 1999).

It is estimated that traffickers generate gross earnings of U.S. $5 billion to $7 billion per year (Office for Drug Control and Crime Prevention, United Nations Interregional Crime and Justice Research Institute, and Centre for International Crime Prevention, 1998). Trafficking today is well structured and is often controlled by organized crime groups. Recruiting agents may be job agencies, acquaintances, family friends, or relatives. Recruitment methods usually involve deceit or debt bondage, but they can also involve violence. Most often, women are deceived about the conditions of work rather than its nature, although it is not uncommon for women to be deceived about the nature of the work as well. Some are brought over with promises of jobs as waitresses, domestic helpers, or similar service workers; sometimes, false marriages are promised or arranged.

Even when women know they are migrating for sex work, they are often unprepared for the working conditions they discover. For example, trafficking often generates a system of debt bondage. This occurs when women borrow money for the cost of travel, visas, false documents, and employment location; they are, then, charged exorbitant interest and required to work off the debt before accumulating their own earnings. It is not uncommon for women's debt to be sold by one employer to another, or for women's visas and passports to be confiscated as security on the loan. In some instances, particularly cases involving the traffic in young women or children, an advance payment is given to the family, which the individual is required to pay off with interest. Even when migration is voluntary, women's status as illegal immigrants makes them vulnerable to exploitation and coercion in these markets (Kempadoo & Doezema, 1998).

Violence and Exploitation Within Sex Tourism and Transnational Sex Work

Evidence regarding sex tourism and transnational sex work tends to be more anecdotal than the research discussed above from the United States. Nonetheless, it consistently points to similar patterns of violence and discriminatory law enforcement, in addition to coercion, exploitation, and violence in the context of inside work (e.g., brothels, lodges, outcall services), as a result of the structural features of the international sex industry. Trafficking, as we have previously discussed, is a process through which migrant women are brought into prostitution through the use of violence, coercion, deceit, [or] abuse, and are denied human rights and freedoms (Kempadoo & Doezema, 1998, p. 21). As noted, trafficking can occur within or across national borders. In addition, women who voluntarily migrate for sex work also sometimes find themselves working in slavery-like conditions in which their mobility is restricted and they are not given the right to control the conditions of their work, including the choice of which or how many customers they see. Moreover, many women work under conditions of debt bondage, as previously described.

Documenting how slavery finds its way into the sex industry, sex workers' advocate Jo Bindman (1998) notes,

> Most people who work in [sex] establishments lack formal contracts with the owners or managers but are subject to their control. Those who work in the sex industry are commonly excluded from mainstream society. They are thereby denied whatever international, national, or customary protection from abuse is available to others as citizens, women, or workers. The lack of international and local protection renders sex workers vulnerable to exploitation in the workplace and to violence at the hands of management, customers, law enforcement officials, and the public. (p. 67)

As a consequence of conditions of illegal confinement and forced labor, women are subject to a range of abuses, including physical and sexual assault, as well as exposure to HIV and other STDs. Health care is minimal, and women who contract diseases are often simply discarded. For instance, Truong (1990) reports that in Thailand, brothel owners often arrange police raids and the arrest of unwanted women. Sex workers are often blamed for the spread of AIDS and other STDs. Just as historian Judith Walkowitz (1980) documented regarding the spread and control of syphilis in the 19th century, sex workers today are placed under scrutiny, subject to intense campaigning and . . . define[d] as the vectors and transmitters of disease (Kempadoo, 1998, p. 18). In some countries, such as Sri Lanka, women found to have STDs are remanded to detention facilities (Miller, 1999). Most often, migrant women are deported on discovery that they are HIV-positive, and they face intense stigma on return to their homelands. In fact, there is a fairly well-substantiated rumor that HIV-positive Burmese women returned to Burma [e.g., deported] have been executed by the ruling SLORC authorities (Murray, 1998, p. 56).

Again, many argue that strict migration laws in conjunction with legal statutes governing the sex industry allow this system to flourish and increase sex workers' dependence on outside agents (Kempadoo & Doezema, 1998). Brokers, managers, traffickers, recruiters, and middle men, as well as legitimate businesses such as hotels and travel agencies, continue to profit from the industry, whereas sex workers face distinct disadvantages that undermine their ability to control their labor and make them dependent on individuals and organizations who exploit them (see Kempadoo & Doezema, 1998; Truong, 1990). In addition, police corruption, bribery schemes, and government collusion are well documented (Miller, 1999; Truong, 1990). Several particularly gruesome cases highlight the seriousness of violence against women in the international sex industry. One is a well-publicized brothel fire in Thailand, where the charred remains of women were found chained to beds. Legal analyst Margaret Healy (1995) opens her analysis of laws against child sex tourism with the horrifying case of a 12-year-old Filipino girl who was brutalized by an Australian doctor, who forcibly inserted an electric vibrator into [her] vagina (p. 1985), where it broke and became lodged. The girl did not receive medical treatment and died 7 months later. Although the doctor originally received a life sentence for the crime, the Supreme Court in the Philippines eventually reversed the decision and acquitted the doctor, who remains a free man. It is difficult to know how typical cases such as these are, but clearly, around the world, sex workers are imprisoned and detained, subjected to cruel and degrading mistreatment, [and] suffer violence at the hands of the state or by private individuals with the state's support (Doezema, 1998, p. 46). Because many of the women subject to this exploitation made the initial decision to engage in sex work, they do not receive public support. As yet, no international conventions or anti-trafficking organizations exist that explicitly support sex workers' human rights (Kempadoo & Doezema, 1998, p. 30), particularly if they are voluntarily involved in the industry.

CONCLUSION

This chapter has provided an overview of the commercial sex industry in the United States and internationally, focusing on how the organization and control of the industry facilitates the abuse and mistreatment of sex workers. The sex industry is built on gender, race, and class inequalities, as well as power imbalances between Western and Third World nations. Profits generated from the sex industry, as well as a sexual double standard that defines sex workers as deviant and therefore outside the realm of legitimate society and its protections, allows the industry to thrive on the backs of sex workers themselves. As we have detailed, the law plays a critical role in determining the physical vulnerability of prostitute women (Hatty, 1989, p. 235). Legal responses, whether they emphasize prohibition, abolition, or regulation, jeopardize the rights and safety of women involved in the industry in various but systematic ways.

As noted, most activists and researchers agree that the key to improving the situation of women in the sex trade is to recognize the legitimacy of their work and to sanction those who exploit them. Sometimes, this approach is viewed merely as a short-term solution by people who remain critical of the industry itself (see Overall, 1992), and in other cases, it is a long-term goal that seeks recognition of prostitution as a legitimate service industry (see Jenness, 1993). Given the economic benefits derived from sex workers' exploitation by individuals, multinational corporations, and governments, as well as the gendered hierarchies on which the industry is built, the likelihood of this occurring in the short term is minimal. Nonetheless, the recent development of sex workers' rights organizations throughout the world is reason to maintain hope.

NOTES

1. Here, we should clarify precisely what our chapter will and will not cover. Although we recognize that a minority of sex workers are men, our focus is on women in the sex industry. In addition, although we will provide a brief overview of children's involvement in sex tourism markets, it is beyond the scope of this chapter to deal systematically with the array of distinct and additional problems associated with this facet of the industry. Thus, our primary emphasis is on adults. Finally, although a number of activities fall under the umbrella term sex work, including pornography, erotic dance, stripping, and phone sex work, we limit our analysis to prostitution.

2. This is necessary, as the coauthors do not share an identical position regarding these questions. One is more sympathetic to feminist critiques of prostitution as an institution that contributes to women's oppression; the other's position falls closer to that of prostitutes rights' groups, which posit that prostitution is legitimate service work. Moreover, to focus on this debate at length distracts from the primary goal of this chapter, which is to highlight the contemporary nature of violence against sex workers. The authors agree, however, that the terms of the previous debate are inadequate to address the child sex trade.

3. An ironic exception is the recent case of Queensland, Australia, where laws were changed in a seeming move to afford greater control to sex workers. As a result, women were legally permitted to work as call girls, but third-party involvement was strictly prohibited. A number of call girls were subsequently murdered by clients in their apartments, acting on the knowledge that the women were working alone (Arnot-Bradshaw, personal communication, April 14, 1999).

4. We do not have data to address estimated prevalence rates of prostitution in other Western industrialized countries. Where data are available, various facets of the commercial sex industry in these countries will be discussed.

5. The *Sourcebook of Criminal Justice Statistics 1997* did not provide a breakdown of arrests by race and gender; thus, this figure includes both male and female arrestees.

6

Voyeurism

A Criminal Precursor and Diagnostic Indicator to a Much Larger Sexual Predatory Problem in Our Community

———————

JOSEPH DAVIS

California State University, San Diego

Sexual assault is one of the most serious and fastest growing violent crimes in the United States. The National Victim Center, located in Bethesda, Maryland, reported that more than 700,000 women are raped or sexually assaulted annually (American Medical Association, 1995). Furthermore, there is the growing concern regarding serial rape and sexually related homicide (Prentky et al., 1989). All sexual acts, paraphilias, and sexually related crimes, organized or disorganized, begin with fantasy, and when an individual suffers from sexual aberrations or perversions, the fantasy and corresponding behaviors often take on a deviant sexual nature (Freud, 1938; Hazelwood & Warren, 1995a). Considerable care should be taken in identifying and isolating the antecedent behavioral predictors of sexual offenders (McCall, 1993). Paraphilias, particularly voyeurism, are common to sexual offenders. By recognizing these public order sexual offenses that contribute to and reinforce violent sexual fantasies, the early identification of, intervention with, and potential prosecution of these offenders can occur prior to any future sexual offenses being committed (Davis, 1996; Hazelwood & Warren, 1995a).

THE HUMAN SEXUAL MOTIVE AND DRIVE

Criminological Causality and Psychosocial Stressors

Less has been written about voyeurism than about any other sexual deviation noted in the medical and psychiatric literature. Drs. Otto Fenichel (1945) and von Krafft-Ebing

Author's Note: I would like to acknowledge the research support of a former graduate student, Brian R. Lewin, MFS, and assistance with this chapter. Mr. Lewin is now a Special Agent assigned to the U.S. Secret Service Field Office located in San Diego, CA.

(1965) suggested that voyeurism as a disorder is a symptom of psychosexual infantilism. That is, achieving sexual gratification principally from the act of peeping at a woman undressing often results in masturbating, found represented in a very rudimentary level of sexuality. Furthermore, voyeurism is seen as an overcompensation for sexual immaturity, suggesting an arrested psychosexual development (Fenichel, 1945; von Krafft-Ebing, 1965).

People who make obscene phone calls (also a paraphilia), called telephone scatologia or scatophilia, and those who write obscene letters, called written or graphical docuphilia, share the same problems as the voyeurist. Davis (1992) proposed that these deviations are also compensatory sexual activities often representing the efforts of voyeuristic men (because most voyeurs studied have been male) who possess sexual desires but have no confidence in their interpersonal psychosexual development and communication skills to relate or express them in an appropriate social manner.

There are three principle components of the human sexual drive: biological, physiological, and psychosocial. The biological element in humans is analogous to the instinct to take in nourishment when hungry. This element is shared with other forms of mammalian life. The physiological component occurs when the human body responds to stimuli in a sexual manner. These two components have limited relevance to sexual crime investigations. The psychosexual element, however, is an integration of various factors involving the cognitive, affective, and behavioral elements of an individual. Deriving from both internal fantasy and external behavior, the interrelated elements of sexuality shape an individual's unique sexual character (Hazelwood & Warren, 1995a). Freud (1938) termed the psychological representation of the inner somatic source of sexualized stimulation and the individual's sexual aim or desire as the human "sexual instinct and libidinal urge." He distinguished sexual instinct from a sexual stimulus, which comes from combined external excitations. Sexual instinct has a definite sexual object—the person from whom the sexual attraction emanates— and sexual aim—the aim toward which the instinct strives. The deviations, in reference to both the sexual object and the sexual aim, can provide the criminal investigator with crucial information about a sexual offender (Freud, 1938; Hazelwood & Warren, 1995a).

SEXUAL DEVIANCE AND HUMAN ABERRATION

Certain intermediary relations to the sexual object exist that are connected with copulation and are intended to enhance sexual arousal. Touching or rubbing (if the intent of the behavior is deviant, it is called "toucherism" or "frotteurism") and looking (voyeurism) are both recognized as normal preliminaries to the sexual aim. However, when an individual lingers in intermediary relations to a sexual object and becomes fixated on the sexual (precursory) aberrations (described as perversions by Freud), the resulting behavior is often deviant sexual behaviors and fantasies (Freud, 1938).

Looking, or sight, has been identified as the primary component of the human male's sexual response to excite the sexual drive (libido). Touching, which Freud stated as being analogous to looking, is an important sensory input mechanism related to sexual arousal and sexual gratification (Freud, 1938). Furthermore, many voyeurs engage in autoerotic, masturbatory activities, where the impulse is directed not to other people but to their own gratification (Hazelwood & Warren, 1995a). According to Freud, the desire to look becomes a perversion when (a) it is limited exclusively to the genitals; (b) it becomes connected with the overwhelming response of loathing (voyeurism); and (c) the individual suppresses it instead of preparing for the normal sexual aim (Fenichel, 1945; Freud, 1938). Such sexually deviant, fantasy-derived or -driven behaviors are common to serial rapists and sexual murderers (Hazelwood, Dietz, & Warren, 1995; Hazelwood & Warren, 1995b).

GENDER IDENTITY DISORDER AND THE PARAPHILIAS

Diagnostically, a paraphilia is a compulsive condition responsive to, and predicated and dependent upon, an unusual and personally or socially unacceptable stimulus that is perceived in the visual imagery of fantasy for optimal initiation and maintenance of erotosexual arousal and the facilitation or attainment of orgasm (University of Washington, 1996). Furthermore, a paraphilia ("para," meaning the intended object or type of deviant behavior attracted to, and "philia," meaning next to, beyond, or close to love) is a perversion of behavior (usually a sexual deviancy). In the clinical nomenclature, a paraphilia (e.g., voyeurism) is typically considered to be associated with unusual or bizarre sexual practices and attachments. The essential diagnostic features of a paraphilia (considered a sexual and gender identity disorder) as determined by the *Diagnostic and Statistical Manual of Mental Disorders, Fourth Edition* (*DSM-IV*) (American Psychiatric Association, 1994), are (a) recurrent, intensely sexually arousing fantasies, sexual urges, or behaviors; (b) the possible involvement of nonhuman objects; (c) the involvement of real or imagined suffering or humiliation of one's self or one's partner; and (d) the possible involvement of children, adolescents, or other nonconsenting partners.

The paraphilias listed in the *DSM-IV* include exhibitionism; fetishism; frotteurism; pedophilia; sexual masochism; sexual sadism; transvestic fetishism; telephone scatology or scatologia; voyeurism (Peeping-Tomism, inspectionalism, scoptophilia); and atypical paraphilias not otherwise specified (*DSM-IV* NOS), such as necrophilia, autoerotica (also referred to as asphyxophilia, hypoxyphilia, psychosexual asphyxia, sexual asphyxia, autoerotic asphyxia fatality, Kotzwarraism, and Susanna Hill Syndrome), and even cannibalism. The most predominant paraphilias treated in psychiatric forensic inpatient clinics or hospitals are voyeurism, exhibitionism, and pedophilia (American Psychiatric Association, 1994). Abel et al. (1988) (as cited in Hazelwood et al., 1995) documented that people tend to suffer from multiple paraphilias, and that individuals identified as having one paraphilia generally suffered from two or three additional forms of sexual deviation (Hazelwood & Warren, 1995a). These fantasy-derived, paraphilic-related behaviors, often referred to in the law enforcement community as public order offenses, are commonly acted out and exhibited during sexual crimes (Hazelwood & Warren, 1995b).

VOYEURISM AS A PARAPHILIA

Yalom (1960, as cited in Lester, 1975) defined the term *voyeurism* as an "exaggerated desire to see by stealth, a member of the opposite sex (generally) in some stage of undress, redress, in a sexual act or the act of excretion" (p. 22) and "a wanton desire which is so intense that it surpasses in importance the sexual act" (p. 23) often driven by obsession and compulsion. Davis (1992) viewed voyeurism as an "ego-syntonic" compulsion (meaning in the desired direction of thinking that is acceptable to one's ego) that an individual does not object to, but only yields to, in terms of a compulsive or ritualistic abreaction or action (a psychological excitement and subconscious intrapersonal thrill of "acting out a peeping fantasy on a unsuspecting victim" without getting caught). Furthermore, according to Davis (1992), voyeurs rarely, if ever, seek out psychiatric or mental health services on their own. Many voyeurs who receive treatment typically do so as a direct result of a public safety issue and police involvement as it relates often to court-mandated or enforced treatment in an outpatient or inpatient forensic mental health setting (Davis, 1992, 1996; Yalom, 1960).

The paraphilic focus of voyeurism involves the achievement of sexual stimulation and pleasure through seclusion while in the unsuspected act of looking. In the clinical vernacular and nomenclature, voyeurs and voyeurism are often referred to as Peeping Toms, Peeping-Tomism, or inspectionism (Bartol, 1995). Due to the attainment of intrapersonal pleasure through a clandestine act of peeping (i.e., typically young male heterosexuals looking in women's windows), peepers experience sexual gratification through covertly (by stealth) observing unsuspecting individuals. Usually targeting female strangers, voyeurs enjoy viewing women who are in the process of disrobing, those who are partially nude or nude, and those who are about to engage in consensual sexual activity. Generally, the voyeur obtains most of his sexual gratification through the act of looking and does not seek out real sexual activity with the observed person (American Psychiatric Association, 1994; Forrest, 1994). However, the voyeur will fantasize and imagine having compulsory sexual relations (often leading to imagined or real masturbation and a climax with the unsuspecting victim) as represented in the postcognitive fantasy process of the perpetrator on or after leaving the victim's personal property (Forrest, 1994).

The essential diagnostic features to determine voyeurism, as outlined by the *DSM-IV*, are (a) a pattern of exhibited behavior no less than 6 months in duration; (b) recurring and intensely sexually arousing fantasies, sexual urges, or behaviors involving the act of observing an unsuspecting person who is naked, in the process of disrobing, or engaging in sexual activity; and (c) fantasies, sexual urges, or behaviors that cause clinically significant distress or impairment in social, occupational, or other important areas of functioning (American Psychiatric Association, 1994). However, Hazelwood and colleagues (Hazelwood et al., 1995; Hazelwood & Warren, 1995a, 1995b) noted that even though the first two clinical features outlined here are represented, serial voyeurists often feel very little distress or impairment other than an "excitatory autonomic physiological response" from viewing. Furthermore, voyeurists show habitual patterns of ritualistic behavior much like those of drug addicts in performing ritualistic or routine peepings while trolling through targeted neighborhoods for unsuspecting victims (Davis, 1992, 1996). Some had referred to voyeurism as an addiction of activity or an activity addiction involving a ritual of routine behavior that has some gratification attached to it (Davis, 1992, 1996; Hazelwood et al., 1995).

Voyeurism is a form of compulsion—a behavioral pattern that stems from the thoughts of extremely sexually perverse acts, termed obsessions. Many crimes that appear to be sexually motivated or related have their origins in such obsessive-compulsive, ritualistic behaviors. Obsessions are often irrational or unwanted cognitive thoughts that relentlessly persist and are forced into the individual's stream of consciousness and psyche. Furthermore, the voyeurist may develop a maladjusted lifestyle as a direct result of the relentless obsessions (Reese, 1979). Voyeurs feel compelled to peep by engaging in this sexually deviant behavior repeatedly (much like a ritualistic process).

Voyeuristic behavior is often accompanied by autoerotic, masturbatory activities during the voyeuristic process or in a latent response to the cognitive trace memory of the visualized and directed sexual arousal and subsequent excitement witnessed (see Appendix A) (Forrest, 1994).

Voyeurism and other sexual deviations have been established and traced through impressions received during psychosexual development in childhood. Conditioning, reinforcement, and overlearning as factors contribute to the early development of voyeurism (Forrest, 1994). Sigmund Freud (1938) concluded that there is something inherent or congenital (possibly biological) about voyeurism. He also believed that many sexual deviations in certain individuals are a direct result from being predisposed to perversions as they are brought into prominence by powerful maternal and paternal influences during abnormal psychosexual development. Moreover, he stated that many people have these perversions, and that the internal substrate of all perversions or sexual deviations is demonstrable in childhood. (Although all impulses manifest themselves in moderate intensity, many never reach a level that involve breaking the law.) Later in life, sexual deviates fail to repress (a protective ego defense mechanism) their primary process-centered or -oriented thinking and their impulses, and they are believed to either conserve the infantile state of their sexuality or regress to it sexually (Fenichel, 1945; Freud, 1938). Forrest (1994) also indicated that voyeurism is an infantile or childhood sexual fixation. Based on this theory of psychosexual regression, the experiences during the infantile state and childhood pertaining to the process of sexual development should be examined (Freud, 1938).

DEMOGRAPHIC PROFILES OF THE VOYEURIST PARAPHILE

Davis and Bernstein (1996) completed a review of the psychiatric and medical literature on sexual deviancy. Davis (1992), Gebhard, Gagnon, Pomeroy, and Christensen (1965), and Yalom (1960) established demographic backgrounds and profiles of the voyeurist. Characteristics of the voyeurist background are found in the accompanying appendix (see Appendix B).

In 1984, the Office of Juvenile Justice and Delinquency Prevention funded a study focusing on serial rape. The research and study were a collaborative effort by the Federal Bureau of Investigation's National Center for the Analysis of Violent Crime (NCAVC) and Ann Wolbert Burgess, a professor of mental health and nursing science at the University of Pennsylvania. Forty-one incarcerated serial rapists who were responsible for 837 rapes and more than 400 attempted rapes were clinically interviewed. The psychosexual development of the subjects (one of the primary interests and foci of the study) determined that voyeurism was the predominant past or present sexual behavior in these predators (68%), which began during their childhood or adolescence (Hazelwood & Warren, 1995b).

CASE #1

Troy, one of the subjects, began window peeping at the age of 14. At 17, he spied on a 24-year-old woman and found her especially appealing sexually. He began to focus his voyeuristic activities on her and eventually observed her making love to her boyfriend. This so enraged him that he decided to rape her. After she had gone to sleep one evening, he entered through an unlocked window and jumped on her. She awoke and began screaming. In a panic, he grabbed a handful of tissues from the bedside table, pushed them in her mouth, and accidentally suffocated her. Five days later, he was arrested for voyeurism in the same neighborhood. He was not questioned about the death because he was "just a peeper." Seven years later, he confessed to the unsolved crime, but he was not believed until he gave information about the death scene that only the killer would have known. (Hazelwood & Warren, 1995b)

Voyeurs are frequently detected by law enforcement or the person or people being watched (Forrest, 1994). Because of repetitive masturbation, voyeurs are often arrested for indecent exposure or public indecency (a lewd exposure of the body done with the intent to arouse or to satisfy the sexual desire of the voyeur) (Reese, 1979). Moreover, voyeurism is also considered an invasion of privacy, which tends to cause emotional distress to many victims, as compared to exhibitionism (Posner, 1992). Sexual offenses such as voyeurism, exhibitionism, fetishism, and obscene phone calls are referred to in the law enforcement community as nuisance or public order offenses. However, because of the nature of voyeur-istic activities, serial or repetitive voyeurism is correlated with violent behavior. Despite the correlation with violent behavior, voyeurs are rarely psychopaths or sexual predatory criminals. However, voyeurism does include an element of sexually related sadism (Forrest, 1994).

Similar to voyeurism, the conception of sadistic sexual behavior occurs during child-hood. Freud (1938) stated that when children witness sexual acts between adults and can-not understand the acts, they conceive of the sexual act as maltreating or overpowering. This childhood impression contributes to the sadistic disposition toward the sexual in-stinct. The sexuality of most men shows aggression—the desire to subdue their sexual object by any means other than normal courting—and suggests that sadism would then cor-respond to the aggressive component of the sexual instinct (Freud, 1938).

In a study assessing aggression in violent offenders, Dr. Dewey Cornell and colleagues at the University of Virginia determined that aggression was correlated with criminal psychopathology and a history of violent offenses (Cornell, Hawk, & Warren, 1996). Fur-thermore, Serin and colleagues (Serin, Malcolm, Khanna, & Barbaree, 1994) found in their study of 81 incarcerated sexual offenders that a significant relationship existed between psychopathy, as defined by the Hare Psychopathy Checklist-Revised (Hare, 1980), and deviant sexual arousal. Additionally, Hazelwood and Warren (1995a) stated that aggres-sion, sex, and power are the underlying motivations for sexual assault and are expressed in complex sexual fantasies.

CASE #2

As a teenager, one sexual sadist peeped throughout his neighborhood, masturbating as he watched women undressing or having sex. At home, he masturbated repeatedly to fantasies in which he incorporated what he had seen while peeping. As a young adult, he made ob-scene phone calls, which led to his first arrest when he agreed to meet a victim (who had informed the police prior to the meeting). He later exposed himself to a series of victims, which he eventually explained was for the purpose of eliciting their reaction of "shock and fear." He followed women home from shopping malls, determined how much cover was available for peeping and entering the home, and eventually raped a series of women. In his early rapes, he depended on weapons of opportunity, but later carried with him a rape kit, which consisted of adhesive duct tape, handcuffs, precut lengths of rope, and a .45-caliber semiautomatic handgun. He became progressively more violent in his sexual assaults, torturing his victims by beating, burning, and pulling their breasts. His violence escalated to the point that he pummeled one victim so severely that she lost both breasts. He forcibly raped more than 50 women and was actually contemplating murder when he was finally apprehended. (Hazelwood et al., 1995)

Courtship disorders directly refer to the underlying disturbances involving voyeurism, frotteurism (rubbing or touching), preferential rape, and exhibitionism. A study by Freund (1990) determined that men with courtship disorders did not differ from rapists in their responses during phallometric testing. Additionally, these authors found that 57% of their subjects ($n = 195$), rapists, admitted to engaging in a paraphilic act of voyeurism, frotteurism, sadism, or exhibitionism. Furthermore, Abel and colleagues (see Hazelwood et al., 1995) reported that 53% of their sample population also showed paraphilic behavior (Seto & Kuban, 1996). Investigators should not be misled by the fact that the sexual sadist usually has a history of nuisance offenses (Hazelwood & Warren, 1995b).

Voyeurs usually operate in a circular pattern, close to or near the neighborhood in which they reside. They tend to develop a pattern or route in which they patrol the neighborhood. Often, voyeurs operate or troll at the same time each evening (Reese, 1979). In a recent study conducted at the University of Virginia's Institute of Law, Psychiatry and Public Policy in Charlottesville, Virginia, in collaboration with the Federal Bureau of Investigation's Behavioral Science Services Unit and NCAVC, on the temporal sequencing and cognitive mapping of serial rapists, the researchers and agencies reported that the majority of their subjects ($n = 108$) attacked victims within a half-mile of the subjects' homes. Furthermore, the rapists who lived in one city and committed the crime of rape or attempted rape generally lived within 3.14 miles of their offenses and did not travel further than 4.93 miles (Warren, Reboussin, & Hazelwood, 1996).

When analyzing serial sexual crimes, investigators can determine certain components of an offender's fantasy from his actual criminal behavior displayed at the crime scene. Indoor rape, specifically, is a highly planned, ritualized, premeditated offense that is often preceded by voyeuristic activities (see Appendix C) (Reese, 1979).

FANTASY AND BEHAVIOR

Sexual acts, whether considered normal or perverse, originate in fantasy (Hazelwood & Warren, 1995a). Although deviant sexual fantasies are common to even normal individuals, these individuals usually repress (as a defense mechanism) their instinctual impulses and, instead, abide by contrived culturally and socially acceptable behaviors (Forrest, 1994; Freud, 1938; von Krafft-Ebing, 1965). Furthermore, the sexual offender disregards society's rules and acts freely upon his sexual impulses and desires (Freud, 1938).

Similar to an artist whose visualizations, as expressed through a certain artistic medium, are transformed from an abstract mental image to a tangible and real creation, voyeuristic behavior originates in visualizations and fantasies. This suggests an element of creativity (in an aesthetic sense) in the cognitive processes of the voyeuristic offender (Gendel & Bonner, 1984). Just as a killer leaves his signature at a crime scene, I believe that the sexual offender's fantasy is "painted with his own brush," meaning that the design and construction of his fantasy is as unique to him as were the often distorted and abstract creations of artists like Pablo Picasso or Salvador Dalí (Lewin, 1996). No matter which medium the offender chooses to transfer his unique and personal sexual interests, the crime is usually the product of the voyeuristic offender's fantasy (just as the painting is the product of an artist's visualization).

The cognitive-behavioral relationship between fantasy and the resulting behavior—whether voyeurism, serial rape, or sexual homicide—is bidirectional. The internal fantasy sets the parameters for such behaviors. Also, the procedural steps to follow along with the prescribed acts to be done (symbolically done in fantasy), as well as the actual behaviors when carried out, help to redefine, refine, improve, and vividly vitalize the fantasy, eventually leading to an acting-out (abreaction) on that fantasy as a crime. Much time is spent on developing and ruminating in fantasy, often leading the offender to harbor such deviant sexual desires and instincts since his childhood (Freud, 1938; von Krafft-Ebing, 1965). Most often, in the initial phase of fantasy development, the future offender will spend time thinking about and rehearsing the sexual act itself. The victims of the acts are often just imaginary and faceless. As the compulsion amplifies, the faceless victims often no longer suffice. The offender begins to eroticize his fantasy by acting out his craving through compulsory behavior to see real, unsuspecting people in their homes. Usually, the first real people he places in his fantasy are those around him, in his neighborhood, workplace, or school. For the first time, the offender begins to look at people as objects and not as human beings (Holmes & Holmes, 1996). This is similar to Freud's concept of the "libidinal sexual object," with the exception that there is no intention at all of any normalcy in the relationship created within the fantasy (Freud, 1938; von Krafft-Ebing, 1965). The offender is almighty and omnipotent with each successful peep. He is the one in control as the object (unsuspecting victim) is provided for his pleasure, to do with as he desires (Holmes & Holmes, 1996). As an example, early in his criminal career, a young Ted Bundy prowled local neighborhoods, looking at unsuspecting women in the midst of their sexual acts or while undressing. Subsequently, these early images and developmental stages helped fuel Bundy's need to further his violent fantasies, which would later be used as an internalized cognitive script for his own sexually driven sadistic crimes (Davis, 1996).

Paraphilias are fantasy-driven behaviors (Hazelwood & Warren, 1995a). As the voyeur observes his victims, he actively fantasizes about joining in sexual activities with them. A voyeur will often fantasize over having one or more sexual experiences with the observed person, but in reality, his observations are a replacement for his own unmet sexual needs and acts (Davis, 1992; Forrest, 1994; von Krafft-Ebing, 1965). Prentky et al. (1989) defined fantasy as an elaborate set of cognition or thoughts, characterized by mental preoccupation, rehearsal, and an anchored emotion originating in semilucid daydreaming. As previously mentioned, voyeurism, as reported by Freud (1938) and von Krafft-Ebing (1965), is the fixation of a prescribed, precursory sexual aim; an aim toward fulfilling the ungratified sexual instinct and drive. Deviation to the sexual aim in voyeurs can be seen as an artistic sublimation (a defense mechanism to protect the violated, fragile ego state). In the same way an artist is influenced by his or her surroundings to create the image that he or she sees, so too is the voyeur. The deviant sexual excitations, developed by the process of sublimation, are manifested, used, and acted out in other areas of the voyeur's life (Freud, 1938; von Krafft-Ebing, 1965).

It is well reported in the literature that violent sex offenders fantasize about their crimes well in advance of acting out on them (Hazelwood et al., 1995; Hazelwood & Warren, 1995a, 1995b; Holmes & Holmes, 1996; Prentky et al., 1989; Ressler et al., 1988; Serin et al., 1994). In a study involving sexually sadistic serial murderers, Dr. Janet Warren, a professor at the University of Virginia, and her colleagues (Warren et al., 1996) reported that 85% of the subjects ($n = 20$) revealed consistent violent fantasies—featuring a ritualized, repetitive core fantasy—in addition to multiple paraphilic behaviors. The fantasy provided an internal script that they followed during the offenses (see Appendix D) (Hazelwood & Warren, 1995a).

CASE #3

Sam, a 24-year-old male, preselected his victims through peeping activities. He then watched his victim's home to establish a pattern of behavior. After deciding to commit rape, he waited until the victim had gone to sleep, entered the home, and placed his hand over her mouth. He advised the victim(s) that he did not intend to harm them if they cooperated. He raped more than 20 women before he was apprehended. (Hazelwood & Warren, 1995a)

Voyeurism places real people into the offender's mind, and from that point, they are his; he owns them. If he wants to rape, he will, and if he wants to murder, then he will (Holmes & Holmes, 1996). Although a correlation does not mean a certain causation, research on serial rapists and sexual murderers has shown that a majority of the perpetrators studied have histories of voyeuristic-type behavior. Through the investigation of serial sexual offenders and sexually related murderers, research has shown a high correlation between fantasy and serial rape or sexually related homicide (Hazelwood et al., 1995; Hazelwood & Warren, 1995b). The fantasy acts as a script, which these types of offenders follow to the last detail. Moreover, the criminal behavior displayed in these offenses provides investigators with an astute insight into the violent fantasies harbored within the offender's psyche (Holmes & Holmes, 1996).

CONCLUSION

Overall, voyeurism does not always generalize to serial rape or sexual homicide, but such fantasy-driven behaviors are common to a majority of serial rapists and sexual murderers (Hazelwood et al., 1995; Hazelwood & Warren, 1995b). Although correlation does not mean a certainty of causation, such characteristic behaviors, like voyeurism, should be considered, both clinically and legally, red flags for other sexually deviant offenses. Considering that voyeurism is classified as a *DSM,* Axis-I Gender Identity Disorder in the *DSM-IV* (American Psychiatric Association, 1994), the offender should be evaluated psychologically by also identifying, in addition to voyeurism, other potential mental disorders as outlined in the *DSM-IV,* such as Axis-II, Personality Disorders. Instead of treating the voyeur as a nuisance, public order, or misdemeanant sex offender, the voyeur should be assessed for probable dangerousness and future predatory threat, as well as the potential to commit a physical act of violence upon another person. Although individuals who are diagnosed with a mental disease, defect, or illness are not statistically noted to be violent per se (about 1% of the mental health population is recognized to be potentially violent), such a condition could exacerbate violent behavior for individuals with a propensity toward violence (Bartol, 1995; Davis, 1992, 1996; Lewin, 1996).

By recognizing the antecedent events that contribute to the development and reinforcement of deviant sexual fantasies, early identification and intervention with potential and actual offenders (i.e., treatment, incarceration, or both) is imperative in order to limit or decrease "first-strike" offenses or additional strike offenses from being carried out (Davis, 1996; Hazelwood & Warren, 1995a). Finally, as the projected frequency of public order offenses increases, more aggressive legal sanctions and penalties in terms of punishment must be legislatively orchestrated, designed, and implemented into our current system of justice. Also, an early identification system identifying potential offenders—both first-time and repeat offenders—is pertinent and instrumental to the prevention of future sexually related offenses.

APPENDIX A   Offender Sex Experiences in Childhood

Category	% Rank
Pornography	81
Autoerotic practices	79
Sexually stressful events	73
Voyeurism	71
Admission of rape fantasy	61
Childhood sexual abuse	43
Fetishism	72
Consenting sex	56
First rape fantasies prior to 12 to 14 years of age	50
Sexual incompetence	44
Witnessing disturbing sex acts	42
No peer consenting sex	44

SOURCES: FBI research study, 1978-1982; Ressler et al. (1988).

APPENDIX B Demographic and Clinical Profile of the Voyeurist

Category	Reported Data
Offender Gender	Typically almost all male
Targeted Object	Typical intended target is females
Female Voyeurs	Rare (often underreported)
Homosexual Voyeurs	Rare (often underreported)
Previous Record of Offenses	Yes, public order offenses
Common Age Range of First Offenders	r (range) = 15 to 33 years of age
Developmental History	Starting with peeping at mother or caregiver
Ego-Syntonic Impressions	Thoughts of superiority over victim
Clinical Diagnosis	Alcoholism, personality disorder of gender identity
Sexual Development	Inadequate sexual experiences
Viewpoint Toward Victim	Victim seen as "prey"
Masturbation While Peeping	Yes, about 60% reported
Marital Status	Overall, very few voyeurs marry
When Married	30% remain married, 70% divorce or separate
Intelligence Factor (IQ)	Full-scale range from 105 to 125 (WAIS-R)
Birth Order	90% have no older sibling (male)
Familial Relations	Only or youngest child, no sisters
Parental Relations	Had functional relations with parent(s)
Female Friends in Development	Rarely had female friends when growing up
Sadism	Correlated with the act of being viewed
Masochism	Rarely seen as a common practice
Subsequent Crimes From Voyeuristic Act	Rape, assault, fetish-type burglary and arson
Other Related Public Order Crimes	Paraphilia such as exhibitionism (flashing)

SOURCES: Davis and Bernstein (1996); Gebhard et al. (1965); Yalom (1960).

APPENDIX C   Serial Rapists, Sexual History, and Current Sexual Behavior

Category	n	%	N
Childhood or adolescent sexual trauma			
Witnessing sexual violence of others	8	25	32
Witnessing disturbing sexual activity on part of parents	17	44	39
Witnessing disturbing sexual activity on part of other family members or friends	9	25	36
Physical injury to sexual organs; venereal disease	5	14	36
Multiple sexual assault	11	31	35
Sex stress situations (e.g., punitive parental reaction to masturbation)	17	46	37
Adult sexual behavior			
Marked inhibition/aversion to sexual activity	4	10	40
Compulsive masturbation	21	54	39
Exhibitionism (paraphilia)	12	29	41

SOURCE: Hazelwood and Warren (1995a).

APPENDIX D   Descriptive Characteristics of Serial Versus Single Sexual Murderers (Prentky et al., 1989)

Characteristics	Serial Subjects (n = 25)			Single Subjects (n = 17)			
	n	%	n		%	$c2$ (df = 1)	p
Fantasies of rape, murder, or both	19	86	3		23	14.02	.001
Paraphilias (typical or atypical)							
Compulsive masturbation	14	70	6		50	1.28	.26
Indecent exposure	5	25	1		7	1.81	.19
Voyeurism	15	75	6		43	3.60	.06
Fetishism	15	71	4		33	4.54	.03
Cross-dressing	5	25	0		0	4.38	.05
Organized crime scene							
Organized	17	68	4		24	8.00	.005
Planned	10	42	7		41	—	—

NOTE: N = 42.

7

Lookin' for Love
in All the Wrong Places

Men Who Patronize Prostitutes

———————

RICHARD TEWKSBURY
PATRICIA GAGNÉ
University of Louisville

One of the most pronounced aspects of life in the United States today is the pervasive presence of sex. Whether on television, in movies, in advertising, or in our day-to-day interactions, sex and images of sexuality are everywhere. In fact, the advertising industry in the United States is predicated on the idea that sex sells. Yet when individuals turn that simple concept around and "sell sex," they are labeled as deviant and marginalized in U.S. society. Prostitution, "the world's oldest profession," has been around for centuries. Still, the depth of understanding that social scientists, law enforcement officials, and the public at large have tends to be only superficial and is based frequently on myths and misunderstandings. In this chapter, we examine one of the least understood aspects of the prostitution industry: the clients.

Most research on prostitution focuses on one of three issues. First, is the harm and cost to society. Many researchers, policymakers, and citizens consider prostitution to be a social problem, something that is harmful to individuals, society, and major social institutions, especially the family. From this perspective, prostitution is a common crime and is thought to constitute a quality-of-life problem in many urban areas. Each year, thousands of hours of law enforcement effort and millions of dollars are devoted to enforcing prostitution laws in American cities. As reported in 1987 (Pearl, 1987), the 16 largest American cities spent an average of $7.5 million on prostitution enforcement. Although prostitution is often officially considered a serious urban problem, critics question expending resources to police it and seriously question the harm it allegedly causes.

A second focus of research on prostitution is the near-exclusive concentration on female prostitutes. This focus is based, in part, on assumptions that women have lower sex drives than men, and that men are more predatory than women when it comes to sex. In addition, social homophobia has led some researchers to overlook male prostitutes who serve a male clientele. Thus, prostitution is often thought to consist primarily of men paying women for sex. For many, the thought of women paying men for sex is absurd, and men's paying other men for sex is unthinkable. Nevertheless, research has shown that both types of prostitution do exist, although studies of them tend to be fewer than those of female prostitutes (Calhoun, 1992; Morse, Simon, Bause, Balson, & Osofsky, 1992; Nelson & Robinson, 1996; Van der Poel, 1992; West, 1998).

Finally, the third focus is on prostitutes themselves, with a tendency to overlook those who patronize them. This focus is undoubtedly affected by social attitudes that have traditionally considered (female) prostitutes as deviant, while viewing those (men) who patronize them as pursuing natural, biologically driven goals, although perhaps in a slightly deviant way.[1] Based on these assumptions, there is little to be learned by including the customers of prostitutes in research because they are not typically seen as the "problem."

The work we discuss here breaks from these directions in prostitution research. Rather than conceiving of commercialized sex as problematic, we view prostitution as a commercial activity that has been socially constructed as deviant. Despite the deviant label, however, patronizing prostitutes is not a statistically rare event; rather, nearly one of every five adult men (18%) report having paid for sex (Sullivan & Simon, 1998).

The prostitution on which our research is based involves both male and female sex workers, as well as police decoys of both sexes, but the focus of our analysis is on the men who patronize them. Clearly, this is a neglected area of scholarly inquiry, although sound scholarly and practical reasons exist for understanding the clients of prostitutes. As summarized by Atchison, Fraser, and Lowman (1998):

> From a theoretical point of view, the client is central to the study of prostitution. Without him, there is no sex trade. Politically, the client is central because prostitution is held out to be the quintessential instance of the male sexualization, commodification, and exploitation of women. From the point of view of policymakers, the client is central because he represents an obvious site of social intervention, be it in the name of protecting neighborhoods and preventing nuisance and/or preventing sexual exploitation of children and violence against women who prostitute. Yet we know very little about the client. (p. 172)

An even greater unknown is the client of the male prostitute, yet "there continues to be a dearth of social science literature on male prostitutes" (Snell, 1995, p. 12). The literature that is available is skewed heavily toward the study of juvenile male prostitutes (Calhoun, 1992; Snell, 1995; Weisburg, 1985; West, 1998). However, this is not surprising because social scientists, working from a social problems perspective, are most likely to focus on the "problematic categories of male prostitution" and individuals on the margins of the vocation (Van der Poel, 1992). This typically includes juveniles and prostitutes working in the most visible and dangerous segments of the commercial sex industry. In almost all instances, researchers have disregarded successful male prostitutes (however, see Adams, 1998, and Van der Poel, 1992) and failed to consider the clients of male prostitutes as anything beyond "vectors of transmission" for sexually transmitted diseases (most notably HIV) (McKeganey, 1994; Morse, Simon, Osofsky, Balson, & Gaumer, 1991; Plumridge, Chetwynd, Reed, & Gifford, 1996; Sawyer, Rosser, & Schroeder, 1998).

THE HIERARCHY OF PROSTITUTES

Prostitution, as with any occupational category, is characterized by a stratified system of workers and work environments. The four general varieties of male prostitution (in order of ascending status and income opportunities) are street hustling, bar hustling, escort services, and call boys (Adams, 1998; Luckenbill, 1986; Van der Poel, 1992). For the vast majority of male prostitutes in the United States, street hustling is the point of entry to the occupation because it is the bottom rung of male prostitution (Luckenbill, 1986; West, 1998). Males who work selling sex on the streets—like their counterparts in the drug industry (Adler, 1985; Jacobs, 1999)—possess the lowest level of skill and professionalism, have the lowest income potential (Adams, 1998; Van der Poel, 1992; West, 1998), face the greatest dangers of arrest and physical victimization (Miller, 1993; Miller & Schwartz, 1995), are most likely to have arrest records (Weisburd, 1985), and generally are those who bear the brunt of society's stigmas regarding "whores." Perhaps as a consequence of these negative attributes and experiences, most male prostitutes who work via street hustling are polysubstance users (Morse, Simon, Baus, et al., 1992). Male prostitutes who self-identify as heterosexual and possess negative attitudes toward gay men are those who are most likely to use alcohol and drugs while working (Morse, Simon, Baus, et al., 1992), which in turn places these men at increased risk of both physical victimization and viral infection. Also, not unexpectedly, those who use drugs or alcohol more frequently and intensely, in turn, have a greater dependency on prostitution (Morse, Simon, Baus, et al., 1992).

Among female prostitutes, a hierarchy of workers exists that is similar to that seen among male sex workers. These include, in ascending order, streetwalkers and bar prostitutes, brothel prostitutes, massage parlor sex workers, women who work for escort services, and call girls (Edgley, 1989; Greenwald, 1970; Prus & Irini, 1980; Rasmussen & Kuhn, 1976). The majority of female prostitutes are streetwalkers. Among female prostitutes, this group runs the greatest risk of arrest, as well as violence at the hands of customers, pimps, and others on the street (Carmen & Moody, 1985; Diana, 1985).

CUSTOMERS OF PROSTITUTES

Researchers have not completely ignored the customers of prostitutes, although what is known is almost exclusively in regard to men who patronize female prostitutes (see Sullivan & Simon, 1998). The primary focus in this literature in recent years has been on issues of public health and ways to intervene with regard to sexually transmitted diseases and HIV. What we do know about prostitutes' customers is that, demographically, they are diverse in age, are typically employed and are high school graduates, and more often than not are involved in a long-term relationship (Atchison et al., 1998; Campbell, 1998b; Diana, 1985; McKeganey & Barnard, 1996; Sawyer et al., 1998; Sullivan & Simon, 1998). Anecdotal mentions of male prostitutes' customers suggest that these characteristics hold, regardless of the sex of the prostitute. Contrary to common assumptions, men who pay other men for sex most often self-identify as heterosexual (or bisexual) rather than gay. Furthermore, preliminary findings reported by Atchison et al. (1998) indicate that men who purchase sex are more likely to have initiated sexual activities at earlier ages than are men who do not. Adding complexity to the issue, some researchers have suggested that male prostitutes typically self-identify as heterosexual and are frequently married (Morse et al., 1991). This suggests that in many instances where a man propositions another man on the street for a sex-for-money exchange, both parties self-identify as heterosexual. As might be expected, then, many men who patronize prostitutes report feelings of internal conflict regarding basic values, morals, and their sexuality (Sawyer et al., 1998). Therefore, the exchange of money for sex between men is a much more complex interaction than might be expected.

One final aspect of exchanges between prostitutes and their customers adds an additional, perhaps ironic, twist to the picture. Men who visit prostitutes often do so for reasons that have little, if anything, to do with sex (McKeganey & Barnard, 1996; Winick, 1962). Rather, they seek out prostitutes in pursuit of social and interpersonal contact and bonding (McKeganey, 1994; Sawyer et al., 1998; Snell, 1995). More than one quarter of the male prostitutes in Snell's (1995) study reported having "fun times" with customers in completely nonsexual ways. This finding is not unique to interactions with prostitutes, whether male or female. Research has shown that men patronize a wide range of sexual settings, such as show bars and adult bookstores, for purposes other than sexual release (Erickson & Tewksbury, 2000; Styles, 1979; Tattleman, 1999; Tewksbury, 1990, 1995). Nevertheless, when sex is the primary reason for seeking a prostitute, customers are often motivated by a desire for sexual activities not available to them in their relationships, or they want to add different partners or forms of sexual enjoyment to the sexual experience.

In perhaps the best review of the literature to date on customers of prostitutes, Atchison et al. (1998) conclude that there are six primary reasons why men seek out prostitutes: (a) their own physical unattractiveness, (b) their social unattractiveness, (c) their psychopathology and retarded sexual development, (d) their desire to fulfill cultural expectations of sexual promiscuity, (e) their inability to obtain sex without gender role responsibilities, and (f) their expression of power over others (usually women). In addition, prostitutes' clients report that the impersonal nature of the exchange allows them to engage in sexual acts that they would be uncomfortable asking a regular partner to perform, and such men are also motivated by a desire to have sex with a number of different partners or partners with a particular image (McKeganey & Barnard, 1996).

DANGERS INVOLVED IN PROSTITUTION

Dangers plague the sex-for-money exchange both legally and extralegally. As an illegal commercial exchange, the threat of arrest, for both prostitutes and those who patronize them, is an ever-present possibility. But the dangers that may pose more serious and lasting consequences are those beyond the possibility of arrest.

The Danger to Prostitutes

Research shows that female prostitutes often suffer victimization from male clients, including physical assault, rape, robbery, and verbal denigration (Barnard, 1993; Miller, 1993; Miller & Schwartz, 1995; Sanchez, 1998; Silbert & Pines, 1981, 1982). The fact that clients victimize prostitutes should not be surprising. Clients report that they see the prostitute not as a person, but rather simply as a sexual outlet, one over which the monetary exchange entitles the client to power over the person and the encounter (McKeganey & Barnard, 1996). When victimized, prostitutes almost never report the incident to law enforcement authorities (McKeganey & Barnard, 1996; Miller, 1993; Miller & Schwartz, 1995; Silbert & Pines, 1982). Still, they engage in a number of strategies to minimize danger and reduce its severity or to retaliate for violence once it occurs (Miller, 1993; Sanchez, 1998).

Arrest is a risk that prostitutes face. According to the U.S. Department of Justice (1999a), in 1998, there were 68,536 arrests for prostitution. Of those arrested, 42% were men and 58% were women. (These statistics also suggest that male prostitution is more prevalent than previous research would suggest.) Broken down by age, 1.5% of arrests for prostitution were of individuals under the age of 18, 18% were of individuals between 18 and 24, 59% were of individuals between 25 and 39, and the remaining 21% were of individuals age 40 and older. Despite the risk of being arrested, most prostitutes say that they are not afraid of arrest (McKeganey & Barnard, 1996; Snell, 1995).

Social stigma is another risk prostitutes face, but fear of the damage to one's reputation appears to be greater among male prostitutes than females. Perhaps because street hustlers are marginal to the life of prostitution, many have a significant level of concern about maintaining the secrecy of their hustling activities. Thus, they must devote a great deal of effort to trying to distinguish between real customers and the police, as well as those who are safe.

An additional risk faced by prostitutes is exposure to sexually transmitted diseases. Although research has repeatedly shown that prostitutes do have high rates of sexually transmitted disease (including HIV) infection (Castro et al., 1988; McCoy & Inciardi, 1995), their continued participation in the trade suggests that this is a risk they are willing to take. Nevertheless, research suggests that some prostitutes do take measures to reduce their risk of exposure, including the use of condoms and their refusal to engage in certain high-risk sexual activities (Miller, 1993).

Danger to Customers

Customers of prostitutes also face dangers, including the possibility of arrest, a significant other learning about the solicitation, robbery, and exposure to sexually transmitted diseases. The primary concern about which clients talk most often is the possibility of contracting a sexually transmitted disease, including HIV. A second important concern is that a significant other will learn of the solicitation. Still, the limited research on clients suggests that, although customers might acknowledge these risks, their concerns do not deter them from seeking prostitutes. This is despite the fact that men who patronize male prostitutes engage in a great deal of high-risk sexual activity and drug use with prostitutes (Morse, Simon, Balson, & Osofsky, 1992).

McKeganey (1994) reports that even though men who patronize female prostitutes know that HIV is widespread among that population, they do not believe they are personally at risk. Clients of female prostitutes in one study (McKeganey & Barnard, 1996) estimated that between 33% and 80% of prostitutes were infected with HIV; however, "hardly any" felt that they were personally at risk of infection. Similarly, Levine (1988) shows that in the state of Florida (a state with one of the highest rates of HIV infection), health concerns did not discourage men from patronizing prostitutes in the mid- to late 1980s. Perhaps the greatest risks come in instances of sex-for-drugs exchanges, especially when the drug involved is crack cocaine. As Inciardi (1989; Inciardi, Lockwood, & Pottieger, 1993) has shown, sex-for-drug exchanges are almost always unprotected sex, and those who trade sex for drugs tend to do so with a higher number of clients than do prostitutes who exchange sex for money. Moreover, as Estep and Waldorf (1989) have shown, male streetwalkers are the male prostitutes least likely to practice safe sex and those who engage most frequently in high-risk sexual practices. Although knowledge about HIV/AIDS and safe sex is related to the practice of safe sex, it is also dependent on the social class of the prostitute: Those from lower socioeconomic backgrounds are less likely to practice safe sex, and to have a greater number of customers. Therefore, street-working male prostitutes appear to present the greatest danger of HIV (and other sexually transmitted disease) infection. Yet customers seem to psychologically deny or minimize the risks, even when they are fully aware of them, believing they can avoid danger by using certain strategies.

The ways that clients attempt to avoid exposure to sexually transmitted diseases and HIV are poorly thought out and, in all probability, not very effective. Generally, clients attempt to identify prostitutes possessing attributes they believe would put the prostitute at greatest risk of being infected, and then avoid these prostitutes. Translated into action, men who patronize prostitutes and massage parlors report restricting themselves to those who seem "clean" (McKeganey & Barnard, 1996; Plumridge et al., 1996). The assessment of cleanliness includes her or his general appearance, prices charged, whether he or she washes between clients, and how he or she contacts clients (McKeganey & Barnard, 1996).

DYNAMICS OF THE
SEX-FOR-MONEY EXCHANGE

Because of the potential risks and dangers involved in the sex-for-money exchange, prostitutes and customers attempt to read each other in an effort to determine if the transaction should be conducted and whether the other is safe (Calhoun, 1992). In addition to clients attempting to determine whether the prostitute has a sexually transmitted disease, customers try to determine whether the prostitute is a police decoy, at the same time that prostitutes read the potential "date" for signs that he may become violent (Miller, 1993).

In a study based on observations of and interviews with male street hustlers, Calhoun (1992) outlines the following sequence of events that a typical interaction between a prostitute and customer follows, although he notes that some stages may be skipped. These are initial contact, confirmation, negotiation of the sexual act and fees, and negotiation of location.

During the initial contact stage, the prostitute must read a potential customer and make it known to the client that he is available without explicitly stating that he is a prostitute until the customer has expressed his interest in a sex-for-money exchange. Generally, the customer will cruise by a prostitute several times, during which he attempts to determine whether the person he is watching is, indeed, a prostitute. With each pass, he expresses an interest in the individual by staring. Once the prostitute has noticed the attention, he nods his head or waves, indicating a willingness to talk with the potential customer. At this point, neither is sure that the other is interested in a sex-for-money exchange, so each is vague, asking for a cigarette, a light, or the time of day. Once the prostitute is satisfied that the individual is a potential customer, he is likely to ask whether the individual is a police officer and what he is looking for. Still, the messages remain vague so that they may be interpreted more than one way. Once the prostitute finds the potential customer acceptable, they negotiate the fee and the sexual act to be performed and decide on a location.

Similarly, Luckenbill (1984) outlines seven stages of the prostitute-customer interaction: making the initial contact, assessing each other's suitability, agreeing to a sale, coming to terms on the conditions of the sale, moving to a protected setting, making the exchange of money and sex, and terminating interaction and leaving each other's presence. To manage the risks each party sees as possible in the sale, each must rely on her or his own knowledge and instincts to protect her- or himself (Calhoun, 1992; Luckenbill, 1984).

To publicize their availability and recruit business, prostitutes engage in a simultaneous process of reading potential customers and managing their presentation of self so that potential customers are more likely to read them as available, safe, and catering to the potential customer's desires (Kamel, 1983). Undercover law enforcement officers employ these same methods when they successfully work undercover sting operations. The undercover officer needs to engage in "imaging practices" (Kamel, 1983) that communicate to potential solicitors that they are available, safe, and real.

THE PRESENT STUDY

This study focuses on men's motivations for seeking street prostitutes, as well as interactions between customers and actual and decoy male and female street prostitutes. As the earlier review of literature shows, a fair amount is known about prostitutes; the costs and dangers of prostitution for prostitutes, customers, and communities; and the negotiation processes of prostitutes and their clients. Nevertheless, relatively little is known about the motives, perceptions, and experiences of prostitutes' customers (see McCleod, 1982). This is especially true for men who patronize male prostitutes.

Our first goal in this research is to identify the ways that men who patronize male street hustlers learn where to find prostitutes and how to initiate the purchase of sexual services. Second, we will explain how patrons determine the amount of money to offer a prostitute. Third, we will discuss whether specific concerns about disease influence patrons' choices of prostitutes, and fourth, we will examine men's strategies for approaching and soliciting prostitutes. Based on the information we learned by interviewing men caught in the act of trying to solicit a prostitute, we hope to add to understandings about the dynamics of the full range of the sex-for-money exchange. It is our goal to educate consumers of commercial sex about effective (and safe) approaches to soliciting sex, as well as to inform law enforcement officials about how to plan and implement effective undercover operations.

METHODS

This research involves observation of 14 men in the process of soliciting presumed or actual prostitutes, as well as interviews with 12 of those men. We carried out these observations from July 1999 to December 1999 in naturalistic settings in a mid-sized, midwestern city. We carried out the research in conjunction with an urban law enforcement agency conducting a special detail designed to identify and apprehend clients of prostitutes. Specifically, we observed from undercover vehicles and listened in on conversations between police decoys, who were wearing hidden microphones and transmitters, and potential customers. Through the use of decoy officers, as well as undercover surveillance of known prostitutes, the law enforcement agency identified men who were soliciting actual or presumed prostitutes. Once the law enforcement officers identified themselves as such and the customer was apprehended, the first author approached the man and invited him to participate in a brief, on-the-spot interview. For individuals who consented, we explained the purpose of the project to him and invited him to participate in our research. If the customer accepted, we conducted a brief audiotape-recorded interview.

Interviews ranged from 5 to 15 minutes in length. We conducted all of the interviews on site at the location where the arrest or citation was made, away from the police officers, permitting confidentiality for the research subjects. We did not provide any audiotapes or interview content to anyone associated with law enforcement. Once the interviews were transcribed in full, we analyzed them for content themes using principles of analytic induction (Charmaz, 1983; Miles & Huberman, 1994).

Sampling among men who patronize prostitutes is extremely difficult. Indeed, as Campbell (1998b) asserts, "The taboo related to buying and selling sex still persists" (p. 156). This taboo is an important reason why finding and gaining access to the population of men who patronize street prostitutes (and, indeed, any sex workers) is so difficult (McKeganey, 1994). Carrying out on-the-spot interviews with men who were caught in the act of trying to pay for sex was one way to overcome some of the barriers to conducting research on this population. Although some difficulties exist in doing research this way (e.g., the men were understandably quite nervous during the interview), this method did help us overcome some of the problems other researchers have experienced.

Some researchers have been successful in gaining access to customers of prostitutes through personal introductions by prostitutes and subsequent snowball sampling methods (McCleod, 1982; Thomas, Plant, & Plant, 1990). In one study (McKeganey & Barnard, 1996), the researchers were able to talk with clients of female prostitutes by approaching men in a red-light district and requesting interviews. However, the authors reported this to be an extremely time-consuming and difficult approach, yielding only nine interviews that had an "edgy quality" to them. Consequently, they found it necessary to recruit men through health clinics and newspaper advertisements. Other researchers (Gemme, Murphy, Bourque, Nemeh, & Payment, 1984) have advertised for research participants; however, such an approach raises serious questions about validity and generalizability of data. That is, there is likely something different about men who would reply to an advertisement when compared to the larger population of men who have hired prostitutes. Furthermore, asking men to talk about their experiences long after they have occurred has the potential to make them less accurate. The fact that our research was conducted in a naturalistic setting, during and immediately after the solicitation, makes it more valid and generalizable than research conducted after the fact, based upon recall or upon a sample of volunteers responding to advertisements.

Still, there are limitations to our method. Most of the men we interviewed were extremely anxious about being arrested or about significant others learning of their attempts to hire a prostitute. Although we made it clear to each subject that we were not affiliated with the police and would not share our data with them, most appeared to be apprehensive, with one refusing to be interviewed and another calling off the interview shortly after it began. Thus, like the data gathered by McKeganey and Barnard (1996), our interview data have an "edgy quality" and are more cursory in nature than what might be obtained once the customer knew that he would not be arrested and that his reputation was no longer in jeopardy.

FINDINGS

In undercover police operations, only the first three stages of solicitation as identified by Luckenbill (1984) need to be completed. That is, the prostitute (or decoy) must make an initial contact, the pair must assess each other's suitability, and agree to a sale. Typically, for pragmatic reasons, a police decoy will progress through Stage 4—coming to terms on the conditions of the sale—and then progress to Stage 5—moving to a protected setting—by sending a customer to a secluded location (e.g., an alleyway), where police will then apprehend him. This is done to allow the decoy to keep working without others determining that he or she is an undercover police officer. For the operation to be effective, it is important for the decoy to get the customer to work through any apprehensions about possible dangers the customer may see in the decoy (as outlined by Luckenbill, 1984). However, as discussed later, customers who get arrested or cited have not worked effectively through this process: Rather than successfully perceiving and avoiding the danger of detention, the men we observed and interviewed were deceived by the decoy and apprehended.

The Client

The customers in our sample were largely a cross section of the larger community, although they were limited in racial and ethnic background to whites and African Americans, despite the relatively large population of Asians and Hispanics residing in the area. The men we interviewed ranged in age from 28 to 82 years and held a full range of occupations and careers, from low-level, blue-collar workers to professional and managerial workers. Most, although not all, were married or involved in long-term relationships. Only one identified as gay, although nearly half had solicited sex with a male decoy.

Learning Where the Action Is

Most of the men in our study said they had learned where to find prostitutes from someone else or had learned about the reputation of a certain area from other people or the media. For example, when asked how they knew where to look for prostitutes, one man said, "Somebody just told me about it out here. You know how guys will get together and talk." Another explained, "I heard you know, news, 7 or 8 months ago, you know, how guys pick you up." In talking further with them about what brought them out that evening in search of prostitutes, we learned that the men who knew where to find prostitutes were more likely than those who did not know to say that their search was planned. A second way that men learned where to find prostitutes was to simply "stumble upon" an area frequented by streetwalkers. Such men were likely to attempt to seek sex for money on impulse. One such impulse buyer explained, "It was just one of those impulses. I was laying down. I just got up and came on." These men typically approached men or women who were on the street who appeared to have no other reason to be loitering in the area. Of course, it is incumbent upon the prostitute or decoy to make it obvious to potential customers that she or he is there for only one reason.

Takin' It to the Street:
How Prostitutes Present Themselves

To be successful in luring potential customers, prostitutes must do a number of things that can enhance their trade. First, they must make themselves visible in a location where there is no other obvious reason for them to be there. The importance of this was confirmed for us when the police placed a male decoy in a bus shelter one night. Not one person attempted to solicit him, despite the fact that he was there for several hours and had let a number of buses pass. Successful decoys and prostitutes positioned themselves on sidewalks, as close to the street as possible, and in a location where they could be seen by motorists for long distances. Second, prostitutes and decoys enhanced their trade when they made eye contact with drivers or pedestrians or waved to motorists who slowed down or repeatedly cruised by them. For a prostitute or decoy to succeed, they must be good at making themselves seen and spotting potential customers. In short, a prostitute's business is dependent upon seeing and being seen. Third, the prostitute or decoy must look like he or she needs money and is interested in sex. One of the most successful female decoys we observed accomplished this by refraining from bathing for 3 days before the detail and by wearing old, dirty clothing, which included a sweatshirt cut off to reveal her bare midriff. The successful male decoys we observed communicated a need for money and an interest in sex by presenting an image that they hoped would be interpreted by potential customers as gay. That is, they wore tight-fitting jeans, boots, and pastel-colored shirts, and, perhaps more important, engaged in masculine "camp." This presentation involved making direct eye contact with men who approached or passed by them, with no break in eye contact or other signals of backing down. Once eye contact was made, male decoys, unlike female officers, initiated contact with men, thus coming on to them in ways in which men do not normally engage. In taking their business to the streets, prostitutes and decoys must be accomplished at understanding and being able to communicate to potential customers by using the signals of the trade and relying upon common stereotypes of what a prostitute looks and acts like. Of course, making contact is only the first step in the negotiation process.

Checkin' It Out

Once a prostitute or police decoy has attracted the attention of a potential customer, a negotiation process begins (Calhoun, 1992; Luckenbill, 1984). Among the interactions we observed, these negotiations typically begin with a "feeling-out" process in which the customer and decoy assessed or sized up each other. Conversations between female decoys and customers were always initiated by the potential client. A typical conversation began with the customer asking the decoy a vague question, such as, "Hey, what's goin' on?" To that, the decoy replied in such a way that had the potential to be interpreted two ways, such as "Oh, you know, I'm lookin' to party," or "Hey, you know, just workin'." The customer typically then tried to keep the conversation going by throwing the ball back into the prostitute's court. For example, one replied to the decoy's assertion that she was "just workin' " by saying, "Yea, I just got off work myself." At that point, it becomes incumbent upon the decoy to get more direct by asking the potential client questions that can create a conversational opening for him to proposition her. For example, one female officer asked a potential customer what he was looking for, to which he responded that he was looking for a date. She replied that she was hoping for a date as well, but, "you know, I'm workin'."

Once this process of mutual evaluation is accomplished, the customer might offer alcohol or drugs. A real prostitute is likely to get in the car and, while drinking or using drugs, then proposition the customer. For safety reasons, however, a decoy will never get in a car with a potential customer because it would be too easy for her or him to lose connections with backup officers. Instead, the decoys we observed responded to offers of drugs or alcohol by saying, "Yea, that sounds fun, but I'm workin'," thus leading the customer to make a direct offer. If the client is really looking only for someone with whom to socialize, he is likely to look elsewhere. But when he was seeking a prostitute, an assertion that one is interested in partying but also has to work was interpreted as a clear signal that the customer has found someone to solicit. It is at this point that customers made direct offers. Such offers often are simple, straightforward propositions, such as "How much for a blow job?"

As previous research has shown, prostitutes attempt to evaluate customers to assess their potential for danger (Calhoun, 1992; Miller 1993). Although our research was not focused on interviewing actual street prostitutes, our fieldwork presented us with the opportunity to talk with one African American woman who was cited for soliciting. She affirmed many of Miller's findings, saying that she preferred older men; she would not "date" Black men; and she was always on the lookout for signs that potential customers were too drunk or too high. She also looked for signs that they would become aggressive or violent, or that they would rob her after the sexual encounter. These apprehensions are logical and fit well with informed assumptions such as this woman's preference for a customer who appeared to be nervous or afraid of getting caught, because she felt she had more control over the interaction and thus was in less danger.

The negotiation process between a customer and a real prostitute or police decoy involves a "circling" process wherein each person is checking out the other. The customer is seeking to avoid the embarrassment of soliciting a woman who is not a prostitute, as well as the inconvenience, humiliation, and potential negative consequences of being arrested or cited. Real prostitutes want to avoid the danger of violence and robbery, whereas decoys are more concerned about being detected as police officers. One way that the decoys we observed avoided being detected was by communicating concern that the potential customer was a police officer. In most instances, if a customer asked, "You're not a cop, are you?" the decoy's response was, "No, are you?" Interestingly, all the would-be customers we interviewed (erroneously) assumed the officer was under a legal obligation to tell the truth (see *Lewis v. United States,* 1966, and *United States v. Russell,* 1973).

Efforts to negotiate a sex-for-money exchange are based on a desire by customers to purchase something they want and, presumably, by prostitutes to maximize their profits while minimizing their expenditures of time and effort. In the next section, we examine what the men in our study wanted from prostitutes, before turning our attention to pricing issues.

What Men Want

Most of the men we interviewed did not indicate that they were looking specifically for a male or a female prostitute or one with any other characteristics. Whether the venture was planned or spur-of-the-moment, most indicated that their decision to solicit a particular prostitute was based first on the fact that he or she was available, and second on their perceptions of risk. For example, when asked what attracted him to the male police decoy he had solicited, one man, who ended the interview before we could learn his sexual orientation, replied, "He was there." When we asked another man what attracted him to a female decoy, he said, "I don't even know, man. Stupid stuff. I was coming through and saw her on the corner and just stopped. I just wanted someone." Another self-identified heterosexual man who had solicited a male decoy explained that he preferred to solicit male prostitutes because "[there's] too much stuff goin' around, man." Fearing sexually transmitted diseases, he felt that it was safer to have sex with male rather than female prostitutes. He added that he was very cautious and thought he could tell if a prostitute had a disease, saying, "I try to be extremely careful. I follow my instinct. I'm not saying I'm any better than anybody else, but if the person is all ragged, eyes all bulged and all that [then I just leave them alone]." We asked another man, who was apprehended soliciting a female prostitute, what he usually looked for. He replied, "Somebody who looks decent. Somebody that's not, like I said, skanky-looking."

With some men, the fact that the prostitute had particular physical features was an added attraction, not a determining factor, in their decision to solicit. One man said that he was attracted to a particular male prostitute "because he was Black," whereas another said that he tried to pick up a female prostitute "because she was blonde and built like I like them." Although finding a prostitute who fit one's personal tastes was a bonus, most attempts at solicitation were based upon perceived opportunity and safety. Even among self-identified married men with children or grandchildren, the deciding factor in attempting to pick up a male or a female prostitute was who was on the street that evening and whether or not they looked safe.

Just as men went out without a clear-cut idea of who they were looking for, most did not articulate a clear idea of the type of sexual activity they were seeking or what they would have to pay for it. Instead, the men we interviewed said they thought the sexual activities to be performed, as well as the price, would be negotiated between themselves and the prostitute. Only one man had a specific idea of what sexual activity he was seeking. He said, "I'm not saying I would have sex with her. But you know, I just like to get off [masturbate] in front of a girl." When we asked him what he would expect to pay for the service, he said, "She said she would take 20." Similarly, another man, who had offered $25 to a prostitute, said that it was his sense that $20 to $25 was the prevailing rate. When asked why he offered that much, rather than, say, $10, he replied, "It doesn't make any sense. All the girls I know say, like, 20, 25, that I've known." When we asked another man how he knew how much to offer a male prostitute, he replied, "I didn't know. I had 10 bucks. I actually had about 17 bucks. I spent for a Coke and a sandwich. I just had eight dollars, you know." So, eight dollars is what he offered.

The only difference between men trying to pick up male prostitutes and those soliciting females was that men cruising male prostitutes first tried to establish a liaison without paying for sex. When they failed to pick up a man without offering to pay for sex, some gave up and left. Others, realizing they could not have services without paying for them, then offered to pay. A few men do offer to pay for a prostitute's time or services in drugs, but this is not the norm. Whether seeking a male or a female prostitute, none of the men we interviewed articulated a clearly defined idea of the type of sexual activity they desired. Rather, in their negotiations, they tried to determine what their choices were before offering a certain amount of money for a particular act.

Why Men Want It

The men we interviewed gave a variety of reasons for seeking prostitutes. Perhaps one of the more surprising findings from our research was that emotional motives appeared to play a larger role than sexual desires in men's decisions to look for prostitutes. Anger and emotional frustration motivated some men, who had gotten into arguments with wives or girlfriends. Some went out looking for prostitutes in an effort to retaliate against their partners. When asked why he had come out looking for someone that particular night, one man said, "Ain't done nothin' all week, fighting with the old lady." Another man, who refused to talk with us, told the police that he had just had a big fight with his wife. This motive appears to coincide with research that has found that some men seek out prostitutes as an act of power. However, it appears that the power being displayed here is as much toward one's significant other as over the prostitute, even though all of the men we interviewed were extremely concerned that their partners would find out about their efforts to solicit.

Loneliness is another motive that led some men to seek the companionship of prostitutes. For example, one man said,

> I'm sick and my wife works, and I took a ride over to [city]. It was somewhere to go. I just drove up, and I rode around here. . . . I know I'm a damn fool. I'm 82 years old. What the hell. . . . You get my age, you just don't fool around too much.

Similarly, when we asked why he was looking for a prostitute, another younger man said, "I don't know. I don't have anybody to hang out with." And another man, who was a divorced plumber who lived out of his pickup truck, told of trying to date a prostitute he had picked up but with whom he had not had sex. He said that he had said to her,

> Why don't we, you know, why don't we go out on a date? And she told me, she was like, "No. I'm a crackhead. You wouldn't go out with me." And I was like, "I don't care if you're into drugs, you know, you seem like a nice person. I would just like to go out with you." Which, really that's not right. But man! The work that I have. I don't meet that many people.

Although some of the men we interviewed were motivated by a desire to purchase quick, anonymous sex, many looked upon the potential encounter as an opportunity for companionship, with sex a potential added attraction. For them, prostitutes offered an important social service, as much as serving as a sexual outlet.

CONCLUSION

Men who patronize prostitutes represent a cross section of American society. Despite myths, media images, and stereotypes about such men, this research has shown that customers of prostitutes are, in fact, very "normal." Men who solicit prostitutes—both female and male prostitutes—identify primarily as heterosexual. This contradicts a significant popular assumption that men who pay other men for sex are gay. In fact, this research shows just the opposite.

Soliciting a prostitute is a process. The process involves a series of tasks or stages that focuses on first identifying someone who appears to be a prostitute; interacting with that person to determine if, in fact, he or she is a prostitute; and making an actual proposition of money (or drugs) for a sexual act. This process, and the ways that customers negotiate their way through it, is an important aspect for all involved to understand. Customers obviously need to understand how to safely identify, approach, and engage a prostitute. Prostitutes need to know what to expect from potential customers. And law enforcement officials need to know how the process works if they hope to police such encounters effectively and efficiently.

The process is a learned one. Typically, it is learned through observation and trial-and-error. For some people, learning the process is very important. If a customer cannot, or does not, learn how to approach a prostitute properly, he is unlikely to secure someone's services. If a prostitute is not attuned to how men initiate contacts, he or she is unlikely to be very busy. And if law enforcement officials—especially officers working undercover—do not learn the process correctly and quickly, they are likely to be suspected as police and, consequently, be ineffective in their mission.

Prostitution is a social, legal, and public health issue that receives a significant degree of attention in our society. However, the attention that is devoted to prostitution is often of a reactionary or exploitative nature. Sound social scientific understandings of the individuals involved (especially customers) and the dynamics of interactions between prostitutes and customers are not all that common. This research, focusing on advancing our understandings of men who patronize prostitutes, as well as the dynamic process of identifying and engaging prostitutes, offers an important step in filling this gap in our knowledge.

NOTE

1. Early research (Glover, 1943) conceptualized customers of prostitutes as suffering a psychopathological condition and being regressed to the infant stage of sexual development with a sexual desire for one's opposite-sex parent. Similarly, in the late 1960s and 1970s, Masters and Johnson (1970) reaffirmed the popular belief that clients of prostitutes were psychologically defective and disturbed.

UNIT 3

———

HOMOSEXUALITY, TRANSVESTISM, AND TRANSSEXUALISM

A great amount of confusion exists concerning the terms and definitions of homosexuality, transvestism, and transsexualism. Although we do not believe that any of the three should be considered a sex crime simply because one may be a homosexual, a transvestite, or a pre- or postop transsexual, some people may place themselves or find themselves in situations where they may be victimized. Thus, we have selected three articles that illustrate the problem or scenario that may contain an agenda for a serious sexual predation of those who are varied in their sexual orientation or activity.

The first article, "Developmental Implications of Victimization of Lesbian, Gay, and Bisexual Youths," is by Anthony D'Augelli. In this article, the author examines the sexual orientation victimization of lesbian, gay, and bisexual youths. First, the author reports that youth are more likely to be victimized, and the victimizations are more severe than those of their adult counterparts. Whatever the reason for the victimization, even the increasing visibility of the cohort's existence, youths in general are more apt to be victimized than adults. Often, lesbians, gays, and bisexuals place themselves in situations where violence is more likely to occur. Additionally, these groups are more aware of their orientations and more apt to "come out of the closet" than in previous times. Because of all of these reasons, perhaps, the victimizations increase in number and quality of violence. American society must be ready to meet the problems of youth. HIV/AIDS, physical violence, and sexual violence must be recognized as consequences of victimization, and social and mental health support systems must be developed to aid the victimized as they move into the adult world.

The second article, by Robert Dumond, is "Inmate Sexual Assault: The Plague That Persists." Noting that the population of incarcerated inmates has risen and continues to do so, Dumond says that the problem of sexual assaults in correctional facilities will likely also increase. Noting that everyone in a correctional facility is at risk of a sexual assault, these assaults present problems to correctional staff as far as medical, physical, psychological, and social consequences are concerned. Taking the victimization to an additional level, the author suggests that the correctional staff may also contribute to the victimization. Calling upon the staff to recognize the problem of inmate sexual assaults as well as staff assaults—

whether sexual, physical, or psychological—the author says that staff must be especially aware of the problem and develop training efforts, policies and procedures, and intervention techniques to combat it.

The third article, by Alarid, examines sexual assaults and coercion in a female correctional facility. In this article, "Sexual Assault and Coercion Among Incarcerated Women Prisoners: Excerpts From Prison Letters," the author examines the extent of, motivations for, and anticipated gains from these assaults by women upon other women. One woman offered a subjective report by a former inmate of a female correctional facility through letters written in a prison. As reported, "The present research attempts . . . a qualitative case study approach to examine situations and behaviors underlying sexual coercion and sexual assault among incarcerated women." The survey queried women about sexual assaults and the reasons for the reported and mostly unreported assaults. The principal reporter is a 41-year-old mother of three children who was serving a 25-year sentence for her third felony conviction. The report suggests that many women are approached when they are first institutionalized, and many experience a lessening pressure when they refuse the advances. However, the report continues, some women continue to be victimized, for a variety of reasons, throughout their incarceration. Obviously, the report has important policy implications for correctional facilities of all types.

Victimizations of lesbians, gays, and bisexuals will continue. Youths, too, will continue to be victims of those who are intolerant of different sexual orientations, as well as variant types of sexual paraphilias, including tranvestism and transsexualism. These articles examine different levels of these forms of behaviors. While not casting any aspersion on the practices discussed in this section, we believe they do deserve special attention and consideration. One transsexual we know spent years as a male consumed with anger and aggression. Jack said that he knew there was something wrong with him as early as 5 years of age. Married twice, divorced twice, he finally went into counseling and decided that he was not homosexual but transsexual. He underwent a sex change operation, and for the past several years has been on hormone therapy that she will continue for the rest of her life. More calm, and more happy, this person had, throughout her life, thought that she was a homosexual, practiced transvestism, and finally matched her gender with her body. Confused early in life, she will now live her remaining years with a sense of inner peace, despite the harsh comments she still overhears in public places concerning her appearance.

8

Developmental Implications of Victimization of Lesbian, Gay, and Bisexual Youth

ANTHONY R. D'AUGELLI

Pennsylvania State University

Studies of bias-related violence that document victimization based on sexual orientation generally provide information about different types of incidents that have occurred to the lesbian, gay, and bisexual people sampled within time frames that vary in their specificity and duration. An analysis of the cumulative experience of being targeted over the course of one's life for unpleasant events ranging from hostile verbal comments to murderous assaults must minimally account for the frequency of events and for the particular kinds of sexual orientation victimization (SOV) experienced: Fifty homophobic comments are surely worse than one; and one vicious assault is more likely to be traumatizing than fifty common epithets.

But many other factors must be ascertained as well to arrive at an understanding of the psychological impact of SOV. Theories of the impact of violence on victims suggest that the characteristics of the person victimized as well as the characteristics of the victimizer (or victimizers), the actions that occurred, and the meanings and consequences of the event for the victim will determine whether someone else's action is experienced as trivial, traumatic, or transformative (Frieze, Hymer, & Greenberg, 1987; Janoff-Bulman & Frieze, 1983; McCann, Sakhcirn, & Abrahamson, 1988). The age of the victim at the time of the attack is one important factor in the impact of the victimization.

In this chapter, I review current research about SOV directed toward lesbian, gay, and bisexual youths. In contrast to lesbian, gay, and bisexual adults, youths are more likely to be victimized, and the psychological consequences of their victimization may be more severe. There are several reasons youths are more often victimized. First, adolescents in general are at greater risk of experiencing violence than are adults (Hammond & Yung, 1993; U.S. House of Representatives, 1989; Whitaker & Bastian, 1991). Second, lesbian, gay, and

Author's Note: This article first appeared in Herek, G. (Ed.). (1998). *Stigma and Sexual Orientation: Understanding Prejudice Against Lesbians, Gay Men, and Bisexuals* (pp. 187-210). Thousand Oaks, CA: Sage. Used with permission.

bisexual youths are more subject to violence because of their presence in settings in which SOV is most prevalent, such as lesbian/gay-identified neighborhoods in urban areas. Within these neighborhoods, they are more likely to attend social activities than are older lesbian, gay, and bisexual people. Third, lesbian, gay, and bisexual youths are victimized because of their association with the HIV epidemic (Herek & Glunt, 1988). Finally, lesbian, gay, and bisexual youths are victimized as a result of backlash resulting from the greater visibility of lesbian, gay, and bisexual people in society (Berrill, 1990; Hunter, 1990).

With increasing social acceptance of same-sex sexual orientation, more lesbian, gay, and bisexual youths are aware of their sexual orientation at earlier ages, have language to articulate their identities, disclose their identities ("come out") to others earlier, and find greater support from similar youths and from their families (Herdt, 1989; Savin-Williams, 1990, 1995). These factors create a strong personal identity from which to make their lives known to others. In contrast to earlier cohorts, in which shame about sexual orientation interfered with public acknowledgment, contemporary lesbian, gay, and bisexual youths develop in a context of lesbian, gay, and bisexual pride. Thus, lesbian, gay, and bisexual youths are more assertive about their identities and more confrontational than are members of prior generations (Leck, 1994; Schulman, 1994; Signorile, 1993). Their increased assertiveness, however, often puts them in direct conflict with others, including family and peers, as well as with traditional social institutions such as "the family," organized religion, and, most important, schools (Rofes, 1989, 1994). Contemporary youths' affirmative stance provides the personal resilience and the social support required to buffer the many forms of victimization that can follow open assertion of lesbian, gay, or bisexual identity. Nonetheless, the combination of earlier acknowledgment of sexual identity and earlier exposure to different kinds of victimization makes this generation of lesbian, gay, and bisexual youths vulnerable to psychological risks unknown to earlier cohorts. These risks are exacerbated by the HIV epidemic, which has had a profound impact on how lesbian, gay, and bisexual youths develop (Rotheram-Borus, Hunter, & Rosanio, 1995).

DEVELOPMENTAL CHALLENGES FOR LESBIAN, GAY, AND BISEXUAL YOUTHS

The amplified social vulnerability to victimization of lesbian, gay, and bisexual youths results from the distinctive character of their adolescent years (Savin-Williams, 1994, 1995). The physiological, psychological, and social changes related to pubertal development are difficult for many adolescents, but lesbian, gay, and bisexual youths face even more difficult challenges in developing a positive sexual identity in proximal (parents, family, peers, teachers) and distal (neighborhood, community) environments that are generally conditioned by heterosexist assumptions.

Although no research based on representative samples has explicitly focused on sexual orientation prior to puberty, the conclusion of recent studies is that personal awareness of same-sex erotic feelings often occurs in early adolescence and becomes increasingly crystallized at puberty spurred in part by advances in cognitive development (D'Augelli & Hershberger, 1993; Herdt & Boxer, 1993; Savin-Williams, 1990). It is entirely possible that same-sex orientation evolves following the same developmental pattern as gender development, but its expression in early childhood is so severely sanctioned that its further elaboration is inhibited, suppressed until feelings reemerge at puberty or later.

The later same-sex feelings emerge, the more extensive has been the person's exposure to (and psychological commitment to) heterosexual socialization expectations. Research suggests, for example, that unconventional gender-related behavior (usually called gender nonconformity) in young boys is met with greater sanctions than is nonconventionality in young girls (Archer, 1984; Katz & Ksansnak, 1994), perhaps because girls' exceptional behavior mimics conventional "masculine" characteristics. Indeed, early childhood discouragement of emotional attachments to the same sex may be the first SOV experienced by all youths, regardless of their later sexual identity. The "appropriate" heteroerotic scripts for the development of sexual attachments are established implicitly, but the inappropriateness of homoerotic attachments is communicated explicitly when they occur in early childhood. Not only do parents discourage boys from fantasies and play in which they "marry" other boys, but teachers do as well. Homosociability is the only acceptable way to express same-sex interests, but there are clear social scripts for its expression. For boys, sports participation is the socially sanctioned script for ritualized (and thus controlled) same-sex affection. For girls, traditional female sex role development contains same-sex affection in a way that diffuses its erotic elements.

By the end of elementary school, children in American society have learned that heterosexuality is natural and that homoeroticism is shameful. Indeed, the same behaviors that researchers on adult SOV call "verbal attacks" (e.g., "You're a fag" or "You're so gay!") are normative childhood banter, seldom subject to adult sanction. Unfortunately, these adult-validated comments are sometimes directed to children with emerging homoerotic attachments. Such comments are also often provoked by unconventional gender-related behavior. Retrospective accounts of lesbians and gay men often include vivid memories of others' punitive responses to early signs of an emerging same-sex orientation, generally cued by their acting like the opposite sex (see, for example, Brimnier, 1995; Due, 1995). Many of these early incidents are traced to family sanctioning at particular ages—ordinarily when children enter preschool or elementary school. As children's behavior patterns become less fluid with age, parents presume the future stability of the patterns. A socially stigmatized pattern of gender atypicality raises parental concern—not only for a child who might be taunted by peers, but also for the family, whose "product" reflects upon them. Thus, a confluence of concern and anticipatory shame leads parents to monitor and forcefully extinguish "nonconforming" behavior, especially in boys. In most children, the behavioral patterns that are associated with negative reactions will be suppressed and alternatives attempted; feelings will be relabeled, repressed, or denied. Children who manifest extremely atypical gender-related behavior take on psychosocial careers as "sissy boys" or "tomboys."

The biological processes of puberty accelerate the intensity of same-sex orientation, while the increasingly demanding heterosexual social pressures of adolescence preclude its expression. The tension between physiological drives (which propel the eroticizing of others and of social bonds) and the channeling of eroticism into heterosexual social scripts (which mark objects for eroticizing) makes early adolescence, the teen-age years, and young adulthood turbulent developmental periods, for if eroticism becomes decreasingly pansexual in the first decade of life, the heterosexual master script becomes increasingly powerful in the second decade. During the second decade of life, the expression of repressed and underdeveloped homoerotic feelings is inevitable and conflictual for all. How the homoerotic/heteroerotic tension is resolved during this part of life strongly predicts adult sexual orientation self-identification.

Positive resolution of the developmental dilemma of puberty by an age-appropriate expression and exploration of homoerotic social and sexual bonds does not typically occur for lesbian, gay, and bisexual youths because of stigmatization. For most lesbian, gay, and bisexual youths, the risks associated with expressing their feelings are learned vicariously as they observe penalties that open lesbian, gay, and bisexual youths and adults experience. Young adults who are lesbian or gay commonly remember that they maintained secrecy during their high school years because they knew what would happen at home or in school. But their reflections may be colored by the experiences of adulthood. It is unlikely that the processes of social perusal, reflection, decision making, and action occurred at the time in the same way they are remembered in adulthood. This silent victimization is nearly universal for those youths who are aware that they are interested in their own sex. Even applying the labels to oneself has costs—particularly given the prevalence of myths about lesbian, gay, and bisexual life that youths with such feelings may have internalized. Thus, if developmental opportunity loss is the first type of victimization lesbian, gay, and bisexual youths experience, self-doubt induced by cultural heterosexism is the second. We know from retrospective reports the negative consequences for youths of years of denial—constriction of affect, escalating social vigilance, turning away of social opportunities, and inauthentic heterosexual role playing (Hetnick & Martin, 1988; Martin, 1982; Remafedi, 1987c). Unfortunately, we have no reliable empirical information on the adult consequences of living the years of one's adolescence and early adulthood in uncertainty, fear, and alienation from self.

Self-acknowledgment of homoerotic feelings, itself the endpoint of a complex developmental process, instigates other processes of identity consolidation that are fundamentally social. Coming out to oneself usually leads to disclosure to someone else. Ordinarily, telling another person for the first time is experienced as extremely difficult, and this disclosure may follow self-awareness and self-labeling by many years. This first disclosure then creates momentum for more disclosures. There are multiple, overlapping processes involved in removing others' presumptions of heterosexuality, such as telling family (parents, siblings, extended family); friends (ranging from casual acquaintances to close friends); and important others in one's social network (such as coworkers, religious leaders, teachers, and coaches). These disclosure processes facilitate an exiting from heterosexual identity and its lifelong social expectations.

Exits from cultural heterosexuality are stressful both for the person who has been socialized within a heterosexual model and for her or his social network, whose previously unchallenged expectations are violated. Coming out to others initiates a lifetime of complex challenges—opportunities as well as problems—associated with the public knowledge of homoerotic interests. Indeed, if the silent victimization prior to disclosure to someone else exacts its costs, public openness about homoerotic orientation sets up the possibility of a lifetime of untoward events, ranging from religious condemnation to employment discrimination (Badgett, 1995). Indeed, public acknowledgment—even to friends and family—is an admission of criminal status in the states that retain anti-sodomy statutes. And, under current Department of Defense regulations, the verbal admission of same-sex orientation requires evidence that homosexual behavior has not occurred and will not occur to avoid separation from military service. This institutional victimization is the third form of victimization that lesbian, gay, and bisexual people must cope with.

Past writing about coming out has not focused on chronological age at disclosure as a crucial individual difference variable. Yet coming to terms with one's sexual orientation and the many complex dilemmas involved is considerably different for a 14-year-old than it is for a 24-year-old or a 34-year-old, for example. We have only begun the systematic process of understanding identity development for lesbian, gay, and bisexual youths, and we are surely conditioned by an "adultocentric" model wherein ways in which adult lesbian, gay, and bisexual people of earlier cohorts have developed are presumed to be relevant for teenagers, who occupy a very different and rapidly changing cultural space. Extrapolation of thinking about lesbian, gay, and bisexual adults to youths is similarly difficult. Not only do we have less information about such victimization compared with the victimization of lesbian, gay, and bisexual adults, but we know little about how youths successfully cope.

NORMATIVE VICTIMIZATION
OF LESBIAN, GAY, AND BISEXUAL YOUTHS

Many stressors in the lives of lesbian, gay, and bisexual youths occur only because of their sexual orientation. This kind of victimization—which makes heterosexuality normal and homoeroticism deviant—shapes how lesbian, gay, and bisexual youths develop. In this section, I will review three common cultural experiences that have developmental consequences for lesbian, gay, and bisexual youths: marginalization, coping with familial responses to disclosure of sexual orientation, and the impact of HIV/AIDS.

Marginalization

In contrast to heterosexual youths, lesbian, gay, and bisexual youths have few opportunities to explore their developing identities without risk. The earliest phenomenological experience of a young lesbian, gay male, or bisexual person is a sense of difference. This sense of "otherness" results from isolation from those with similar feelings and from messages that homoerotic feelings are shameworthy. Feeling different (and often not being able to understand the feeling), these youths withdraw from others or try to act "straight," with varying degrees of success. This process widens the gap between private identity and public identity and intensifies social vigilance, lest others figure out one's "true" identity. That homoerotic identity is socially stigmatized is shown by the results of a recent study of sexual harassment in high school, which found that being called "gay" by others was deemed the most upsetting form of sexual harassment (American Association of University Women, 1993).

During the initial period of recognition and labeling of homoerotic feelings, most lesbian, gay, and bisexual youths have little support from peers. In fact, the development of a supportive peer network occurs very slowly for most lesbian, gay, and bisexual youths. An intense fear of rejection by heterosexual peers is commonplace. A recent national survey of males 15 to 19 years of age found that few (12%) felt they could have a gay friend and that most (89%) considered sex between males to be "disgusting" (Marsiglio, 1993). Many lesbian, gay, and bisexual youths become dependent on small networks of friends who know of their sexual orientation. Having a small network of knowing friends while hiding one's sexuality from everyone else (including parents, siblings, and teachers) reinforces marginality and can increase stress. Without the opportunity to discuss their feelings, lesbian, gay, and bisexual youths may further internalize the negative views of society.

The internalization of a devalued marginality can erode coping efforts. Thus, it comes as no surprise that all available research points to a higher than expected frequency of problem behavior among many lesbian, gay, and bisexual youths. Savin-Williams's (1994) review found these major problem areas: (a) Lesbian, gay, and bisexual youths have school problems because of harassment from other students, leading to excessive absences, poor academic performance, and dropping out; (b) lesbian, gay, and bisexual youths run away from home, and some end up homeless; (c) many gay and bisexual male youths engage in conduct problems that bring them into contact with authorities; and (d) lesbian, gay, and bisexual youths abuse alcohol, drugs, and other substances to cope with daily stressors and with facing the future as a member of a stigmatized group.

Coping With Familial Responses to Disclosure of Sexual Orientation

Many problems of lesbian, gay, and bisexual youths are exacerbated by the lack of parental, sibling, and extended family support. The presumption of heterosexuality leaves families unprepared for homoeroticism, and youths' understanding that disclosure will not be greeted enthusiastically maximizes secrecy. Whereas most youths from historically disenfranchised groups rely on family support in the face of victimization, because of their stigmatized identity, lesbian, gay, and bisexual youths often cannot. Indeed, if they are victimized, lesbian, gay, and bisexual youths often hesitate to tell their families because of fear of disclosure of their sexual orientation. Youths who reside at home or who are dependent upon their families for food, shelter, and financial support are even less likely to risk rejection if they are attacked than are other youths.

Fears of lesbian, gay, and bisexual youths about family reactions to disclosure of their sexual orientation seem justified. Research on parental reactions to disclosure of sexual orientation reveals considerable upset among parents, many of whom respond negatively at first (Strommen, 1989). Remafedi (1987b) found that 43% of a sample of gay male adolescents reported strong negative reactions from parents about their sexual orientation. Rotheram-Borus, Hunter, and Rosario (1994) found that youths experienced coming out to parents and siblings, being discovered as gay by parents or siblings, telling friends or being discovered by friends, and being ridiculed for being gay as the most common gay-related stressors. Using an adult gay male sample, Cramer and Roach (1988) found that 55% of the men's mothers and 42% of their fathers had initially negative responses. Robinson, Walters, and Skeen (1989) sampled parents of lesbian and gay adults through a national support group for parents and found that many reported initial sadness, regret, and depression, as well as fear for their children's well-being. Boxer, Cook, and Herdt (1991) studied parents of lesbian, gay, and bisexual youths aged 21 and younger, and found that more youths had disclosed to their mothers than to their fathers. Of the lesbian youths, 63% had disclosed to mothers and 37% to fathers; of the males, 54% had disclosed to mothers and 28% to fathers. Parents reported considerable family disruption after the initial disclosure. Herdt and Boxer (1993) found that most youths first disclose their orientation to friends, with more males finding this difficult than females. D'Augelli, Hershberger, and Pilkington (in press) found that three quarters of the youths in their study who lived at home had told their parents about their sexual orientation. Those who had disclosed received mixed acceptance; half of youths' mothers were accepting, but only one quarter of their fathers were. Other research has found that those youths who have secure relationships with their families may experience increased closeness over time following disclosure (Holtzen, Kenny, & Mahalik, 1995).

The Impact of HIV/AIDS

Feelings of marginality and conflicts with family appear to be nearly universal experiences of growing up as a lesbian, gay, or bisexual person. The historical anomaly of the HIV/AIDS epidemic augments these common stressors with challenges unknown prior to the early 1980s (Cranston, 1991; Rotheram-Borus et al., 1995). Issues related to HIV/AIDS are now major normative stressors in the lives of lesbian, gay, and bisexual youths. The most troublesome conflict occurs at the intersection of HIV risk and the expression of homoeroticism through sexual behavior. Male youths who have unsafe sex with other males (receptive anal intercourse without a condom and, at a considerably lower level of risk, receptive oral sex with ingestion) risk HIV infection regardless of their self-identification. Sexual identity depends upon sexual behavior; the psychological experience of sexual behavior helps to confirm self-identification or helps to resolve ambiguity. For young males who wish to engage in sexual activity with other males, fear of HIV infection may be an overpowering obstacle. How a young gay or bisexual male calculates his risk (or avoids the calculation) depends on many factors, another example of a highly critical life challenge for youths already burdened with intense dilemmas.

Recent studies have documented seroprevalence rates for HIV among urban young gay men varying from 7% to 12%, and unprotected intercourse rates of 10% to 40% (Davies et al., 1992; Dean & Meyer, 1995; Lemp et al., 1994; Meyer & Dean, 1995; Remafedi, 1994; Rotheram-Borus, Rosario, et al., 1994; Silvestre et al., 1993; Stall et al., 1992). Hoover et al. (1991) have estimated that sero negative 20-year-old urban gay males have a 20% chance of sero conversion before age 25. It is a developmental requirement that a young gay or bisexual male know how to negotiate a sexual experience with a new partner, yet such a process requires considerable social skill, especially assertiveness. For many gay and bisexual male youths, however, such negotiations are difficult (Grossman, 1994).

A related concern is HIV risk among young lesbians and bisexual females. A recent study by Cochran and Mays (1996) found a low HIV prevalence rate (0.5%) in two samples of 18- to 24-year-old bisexual and lesbian women. More than one fourth of the sample reported heterosexual intercourse in the previous year. Of bisexually identified women, 10% had had sex with a gay male partner within the year. Of the entire sample, 2.8% reported having had sex with a gay male partner within the past 3 months. The women who had had sex with gay men were those in the younger part of the sample, and many were teenagers. As Cochran and Mays also found that heterosexual sexual behavior was associated with having a sexually transmitted disease, further exploration of the relationship between young lesbians' and bisexual women's sexual behavior and HIV risk is clearly important.

It is beyond the scope of this chapter to review the history of HIV/AIDS and its impact on lesbian, gay, and bisexual youths. However, several comments are warranted. Historically, many gay and bisexual men became infected with HIV at least 10 years before they displayed symptoms. The infections occurred for some when they were teenagers or in their early 20s. In contrast to the generation who became adults (21+) in 1980, the generation now approaching 20 years of age was less than 10 years old when the first cases of AIDS were reported in 1981. They became teenagers and young adults during the HIV/AIDS epidemic. For many, coming to an awareness of their own identity occurred amidst enormous cultural controversy about the relationship of homoeroticism to AIDS. Their adolescence was also lived at a time when lesbian and gay people were more visible than ever before. Many were instructed about the existence of gay men within the context of AIDS education in schools. Whereas some of this socialization may have been helpful, the implicit message conflated sexual orientation and sexual behavior: Being gay involves risk for AIDS. The burden of feeling that one's sexual orientation puts one at risk for a potentially lethal infection (even though it is one's sexual and drug-using behaviors and the serostatuses of one's sexual partners that create the literal risk) is a special stress that HIV/AIDS has superimposed on lesbian, gay, and bisexual youth development.

BIAS- AND HATE-MOTIVATED ATTACKS
ON LESBIAN, GAY, AND BISEXUAL YOUTHS

The fourth type of victimization experienced by lesbian, gay, and bisexual people takes the form of direct attacks in which the attackers know, suspect, or presume that their targets are lesbian, gay, or bisexual.

Research suggests that young lesbian, gay, and bisexual people are often the victims of assaults (D'Augelli & Dark, 1995; Dean, Wu, & Martin, 1992). Dean et al. (1992) have shown that young gay men (aged 18 to 24) in New York are attacked more frequently than are older men. Victimization was found to be highest among women ages 18 to 24 in the National Lesbian and Gay Health Foundation study; 29% reported physical abuse, 50% reported rape and sexual assault, and 18% reported incest (Bradford, Ryan, & Rothblum, 1994). Violence directed at open lesbian, gay, and bisexual college and university students has also been documented (D'Augelli, 1992; Evans & D'Augelli, 1995). In Comstock's (1991) analysis of victimization patterns among college students, 22% reported having been chased or followed; 15% had had objects thrown at them; 4% had been punched, hit, kicked, or beaten; 11% had been the targets of vandalism or arson; 3% had been spat upon; and 1% had been assaulted with a weapon. Comstock concluded that lesbian, gay, and bisexual students are victimized at a rate four times higher than the rate reported by the general college student population. In a study of New York City lesbian, gay, and bisexual youths from a social services agency, 41% had suffered from physical attacks, nearly half of which were provoked by the youths' sexual orientation (Hunter, 1990).

Lesbian, gay, and bisexual youths appear to be the victims of childhood physical or sexual abuse more frequently than do heterosexual youths, although direct comparisons between studies of lesbian, gay, and bisexual youths and youths in general (see Finkelhor & Dziuba-Leatherman, 1994) are difficult. Boney-McCoy and Finkelhor (1995) reported that 2.6% of females and 1.9% of males in a national telephone sample of 10- to 16-year-olds said they were physically attacked by their parents. In addition, 15.3% of female youths and 5.9% of male youths reported past sexual assault. In contrast, Bradford et al. (1994) reported that 24% of their sample of 1,925 lesbians had been harshly beaten or physically abused while growing up, 21% reported rape or sexual molestation in childhood, and 19% reported childhood incest. Of 1,001 adult gay and bisexual males attending sexually transmitted disease clinics, Doll and her colleagues (1992) found that 37% said they had been encouraged or forced to have sexual contact (mostly with older men) before age 19. Using the same sample, Barthalow et al. (1994) reported a significant association between past sexual abuse and current depression, suicidality, risky sexual behavior, and HIV-positive serostatus.

Attacks Within the Family

The home is often not a safe haven for lesbian, gay, and bisexual youths, especially if they tell their families about themselves. Many parents believe that they are responsible for their offspring's sexual orientation, a belief that puts the family and the youths in conflict that may lead to abuse and violence (Hunter & Schaecher, 1987). For many youths, their families' religious commitments set the stage for rejections of different kinds, ranging from begrudging acknowledgment to forceful ejection from the household. In community surveys of antilesbian/antigay abuse by relatives, 19% to 41% of respondents had experienced verbal insults or threats, and 4% to 7% had encountered physical violence (Berrill, 1990). In a study of lesbian and gay youths at a New York City social service agency dedicated to their needs, Hunter (1990) found that 61% of the violence youths reported as occurring because of their sexual orientation had happened at home. One fourth said that fear of future victimization at home affected their openness about their sexual orientation. Pilkington and D'Augelli (1995) found that more than one third of their lesbian, gay, and bisexual youth sample had been verbally abused by a family member, and 10% were physically assaulted by a family member because of their sexual orientation. Of those youths in this study who were still living at home, one quarter of the males and one third of the females who had disclosed their sexual orientation said that their mothers were verbally abusive; fathers were reported to be verbally abusive by 20% of the disclosed youths (D'Augelli et al., in press). Disclosed lesbian youths living at home were physically attacked by their parents (10% by mothers, 5% by fathers) more often than were disclosed male youths (3% by mothers, 2% by fathers). Many reported fear of verbal or physical abuse at home. Harry (1989a) found that gay males were more likely to be physically abused during adolescence than were heterosexual males, especially if they had histories of childhood femininity and poor relationships with their fathers. The National Lesbian and Gay Health Foundation survey found that 70% of all women beaten or abused as children were attacked by unspecified male relatives, and 45% were attacked by female relatives (Bradford et al., 1994). Of those women raped or sexually attacked as children, 31% were attacked by male relatives and 45% by other males they knew. Of those who ever experienced incest (19% of the total sample), 34% of the perpetrators were brothers, 28% were fathers, 27% were uncles, and 18% were cousins.

Attacks in Community Settings

In addition to familial conflicts and violence, lesbian, gay, and bisexual youths who are open about their sexual orientation (or who are assumed to be lesbian or gay) face verbal harassment and physical attacks in community settings. More than half of the gay male youths in Remafedi's (1987a) study reported peer verbal abuse, and nearly one third reported physical assaults. Nearly 40% of the male youths in Remafedi, Farrow, and Deisher's (1991) study said that they had experienced physical violence. In the Bradford et al. (1994) study, 52% of the young lesbians said that they had been verbally attacked, and 6% said that they had been physically attacked. Pilkington and D'Augelli (1995) found that 80% of the lesbian, gay, and bisexual youths in their study reported verbal abuse based on their sexual orientation; 48% reported that such abuse had occurred more than twice. Gay male youths reported significantly more verbal abuse. Of the total group, 44% had been threatened with physical violence; 23% had had personal property damaged; 33% had had objects thrown at them; 30% had been chased, 16% more than once; and 13% had been spat upon. As for more serious attacks, 17% had been assaulted (punched, kicked, or beaten); 10% had been assaulted with a weapon; and 22% reported sexual assault. More than half of the male youths in Remafedi's (1987c) study reported peer verbal abuse, and nearly one third (30%) reported physical assault. Nearly 40% of the male youths in the Remafedi et al. (1991) study said that they had experienced physical violence. Physical attacks by family members, peers, or strangers were reported by 41% of the lesbian and gay youths surveyed by Hunter (1990), with nearly half of the attacks attributable to sexual orientation. In a study of gay male youths drawn from the same social service agency used by Hunter (1990), Rotheram-Borus, Rosario, and Koopman (1991) found that 27% reported physical assault, 14% reported rape or sexual assault, and 55% said that they had been ridiculed by someone because of their sexual orientation. In the National Lesbian and Gay Health Foundation study, 52% of the total sample of women said that they had been verbally attacked, and 6% said that they had been physically attacked (Bradford et al., 1994). Nearly half (44%) of another sample of lesbian and gay youths said that they were either physically or emotionally abused, with sexual orientation the primary reason for the abuse (Hammelman, 1993).

Attacks in Schools

In addition to familial conflicts and victimization in the community, open lesbian, gay, and bisexual youths face verbal harassment and physical attacks in schools. Because young people spend so much time in schools, and because of the relationship between academic achievement and later accomplishments, these settings are of crucial importance to our understanding of lesbian, gay, and bisexual youths' transitions into early adulthood. Many school problems of lesbian, gay, and bisexual students, such as poor academic performance, truancy, and dropping out of school, are direct or indirect results of verbal and physical abuse perpetrated by peers or others in schools (Uribe & Harbeck, 1991). Up to half of lesbian and gay male adults report having experienced some form of victimization in school (Berrill, 1990). Gross, Aurand, and Adessa (1988) found that 50% of a sample of gay men reported victimization in junior high school and 59% in high school; of lesbians sampled, 12% were victimized in junior high school and 21% in high school. These findings were corroborated in a later survey (Gross & Aurand, 1992). In 1991, 37% of lesbians and gay men surveyed by the National Gay and Lesbian Task Force Policy Institute (1994) reported experiencing harassment, threats, or actual violence in junior and senior high school. A survey of New York State junior and senior high school students showed that nearly one third witnessed acts of violence directed at students or teachers thought to be lesbian or gay (White, 1988). In the Pilkington and D'Augelli (1995) study, 31% of the youths feared verbal abuse at school, and 26% feared physical abuse at school.

THE IMPACT OF
VICTIMIZATION ON MENTAL HEALTH

The four forms of SOV that I have described—developmental opportunity loss, self-doubt, institutional victimization, and direct attacks—increase adjustment difficulties that can lead to mental health problems for some youths. General population surveys have shown that youths victimized by assaults show more symptoms, posttraumatic stress reactions, and sadness than do youths who are not attacked, and that symptomatology is worse among survivors of sexual assault (Boney-McCoy & Finkelhor, 1995). There is every reason to assume that these relationships are further intensified for lesbian, gay, and bisexual youths. The evidence of significant stressors in this population is compelling. In the Bradford et al. (1994) study, mental health problems were common among 17- to 24-year-old lesbians. Nearly two thirds (62%) had received counseling. The concerns most frequently taken to counselors were family problems, depression, problems in relationships, and anxiety. Remafedi (1987a) found that nearly three quarters of a sample of adolescent gay males had received mental health services. A study of young gay university males revealed many personal and emotional concerns, the most frequently reported of which were dealing with parents about sexual orientation (93% reported it to be a concern), relationship problems, worry about AIDS, anxiety, and depression (D'Augelli, 1991).

The available evidence also suggests a disproportionately high incidence of suicide attempts among lesbian, gay, and bisexual youths compared with findings for youths in general. Lewinsohn, Rohde, and Seeley (1996) have noted that lifetime suicide attempt rates in studies of high school students range from 6% to 10%. All of the available research on suicide attempts among lesbian, gay, and bisexual youths shows higher rates. An early study of gay male youths found that 31% had made a suicide attempt (Roesler & Deisher, 1972). The first Kinsey report devoted exclusively to homosexuality found that 20% of the gay men studied reported a suicide attempt prior to age 20 (Bell & Weinberg, 1978). A decade later, Hetrick and Martin (1988) found that 21% of their clients at a social service agency for troubled youth had made a suicide attempt. Harry (1989b) concluded that lesbians and gay men are more likely to make suicide attempts at times of conflicts about sexual orientation, especially in adolescence.

Recent empirical studies have come to similar conclusions about elevated risk for suicide among lesbian, gay, and bisexual youths. Remafedi (1987a) found that 34% of his gay male adolescent sample had attempted suicide. In a later study with a larger sample, Remafedi et al. (1991) found that 30% had made a suicide attempt. Those who had attempted suicide were younger, had more feminine gender role concepts, and were more likely to report drug and alcohol abuse. Remafedi et al. found that nearly half of the gay male youths studied reported that their suicide attempts were precipitated by "family problems." Another study of gay male youths found that 23% had attempted suicide at least once, and that 59% evidenced serious suicidal thinking (Schneider, Farberow, & Kruks, 1989). Schneider et al. (1989) found that suicide attempters had not yet established a stable sexual identity, and that attempts occurred most often before youths acknowledged their sexual identity to others. They also found that early awareness of sexual orientation was associated with suicide attempts. Of the young women in the National Lesbian and Gay Health Foundation survey, only 41% said that they had never contemplated suicide, and about one quarter had made an attempt (Bradford et al., 1994). Herdt and Boxer (1993) found that 29% of lesbian, gay, and bisexual youths in a Chicago youth support group program had made a suicide attempt. More than half (53%) of the lesbian youths reported suicide attempts, compared with 20% of the gay male youths. In the D'Augelli and Hershberger (1993) study, 42% of the 194 youths reported a past suicide attempt. Attempters were aware of their sexual attractions at an earlier age, were more open about themselves, had lower self-esteem, and showed more current symptoms. Attempters were also more often victimized than were nonattempters. The strongest correlations with past suicide attempts were the loss of friends due to sexual orientation and low self-esteem (Hershberger, Pilkington, & D'Augelli, 1997).

Many lesbian, gay, and bisexual youths—whether in school or not—cope with the challenges of victimization on their own, or with the help of a small network of others whose confidence is predictable. Some, especially those who are seriously hurt as a result of an assault, may have no choice but to turn to others, such as parents, teachers, or religious leaders, who may be unaccepting of their sexual orientation. For some youths, attacks lead to the precipitous disclosure of their sexual orientation. For others, a fragile equilibrium in which neither they nor their families have confronted the issue of sexual orientation may be shattered by victimization (Boxer et al., 1991). Thus, youths may experience additional difficulties in the process of seeking help after being attacked, whether the victimization is routine mistreatment or a direct physical attack. Some lesbian, gay, and bisexual adults experience increased vulnerability, intensified internalized homophobia, depression, guilt, and self-blame as a consequence of victimization (Garnets, Herek, & Levy, 1990). Herek, Gillis, Cogan, and Glunt (1997) found that lesbian, gay, and bisexual adult victims of antilesbian/antigay bias crimes were more psychologically distressed than were victims of other kinds of crimes. An extension of this research to lesbian, gay, and bisexual youths is very much needed. It may be hypothesized that negative reactions to victimization based on sexual orientation would be more common among lesbian, gay, and bisexual youths than among adults, especially for those youths who have low self-esteem, who have little family support, and who have not found support in lesbian, gay, and bisexual community settings.

RESEARCH QUESTIONS

The first generation of research about victimization directed to lesbian, gay, and bisexual youths has been concerned with simple documentation. In a general sense, we know that lesbian, gay, and bisexual young people are verbally insulted and physically hurt; that they appear to be harmed more often than older lesbian, gay, and bisexual people and more often than heterosexual youths; and that they are not free from fear of victimization in their homes, communities, or schools. In families, in communities, and in schools, youths engage in varying degrees of contortion of self to avoid becoming the target of others' hostility. Greater openness—whether by being "identifiable," by telling others about oneself, by being "outed" by others, or by appearing to be lesbian or gay—may lead to more victimization. Honesty may not be the best policy, especially for a young lesbian, gay, or bisexual person living at home with family members who have strong homophobic views. Although there is much left to be learned about victimization of lesbian, gay, and bisexual youths, we know enough about some of the developmental implications of victimization to suggest interventions (D'Augelli, 1993, 1996).

The next generation of research on this topic must address the details. The set of questions ahead differs if one emphasizes patterns of victimization or mechanisms that explain how different kinds of SOV promote or interfere with developmental advancement to adulthood. Studying younger populations compresses the time frame for recall of past experiences, allowing greater accuracy and reflection about victimization. For instance, one could study youths who have recently come out and learn of their experiences prior to their disclosure. From this group, details of early development could be learned, so that we might begin to articulate a developmental model of sexual orientation as well as understand victimization that occurs in childhood. Research on youths who begin to tell others is crucial for identifying the stimuli that provoke victimization based on sexual orientation. Is physical appearance relevant? Can telling one untrustworthy high school peer set into motion a chain of events that leads to attacks? Do certain personality characteristics (sociability, assertiveness, and so on) lead to attacks? Do certain characteristics diminish the chance of attacks? Or is the nature of youths' proximal social environments—the heterosexism of families, schools, neighborhoods—at the core of victimization patterns? This contextualization of victimization may also help disentangle victimization based on other characteristics, such as gender, racial/ethnic background, and socioeconomic status, from attacks related to youths' sexual orientation.

Research on victimized youths must extend its purview over time to encompass developmental sequelae. There are no longitudinal data on lesbian, gay, and bisexual youths that detail patterns of SOV. Which SOVs are perceived as distressing is an important question, as is how lesbian, gay, and bisexual youth networks may help to "neutralize" SOV by warning about typical attacks and suggesting how to cope with them.

Linking patterns of SOV to later adjustment indicators will help us to know how well youths respond to SOV. The coping mechanisms that lesbian, gay, and bisexual youths use to deal with different kinds of victimization must be detailed. Most lesbian, gay, and bisexual youths cope effectively with victimization and become well-adjusted adults. However, when SOV is associated with distress, it is crucial to know the mediating emotional conditions involved. Little is known about how variability in crucial factors such as prior mental health status, personal characteristics (especially self-esteem and coping skills), support from family and friends, and involvement with helping resources of different kinds (especially those affirming youths' sexual orientation) might buffer the impacts of verbal and physical abuse.

CONCLUSIONS

Based on a reading of the available research literature, some general predictions are possible about the future needs of lesbian, gay, and bisexual youths. More youths will be disclosing their sexual orientation to others, and at earlier ages. The junior and senior high school years will become times during which more youths will self-label in a positive way than in past generations. As youths self-label earlier, they will experience greater vulnerability too. The increased cultural visibility of lesbian, gay, and bisexual people will stimulate more negative reactions from heterosexuals. As youths experience more conflict, more of them will seek social support. Some will seek help as a result of the psychological consequences of persistent verbal harassment, and some will need help recovering from physical assaults. More youths will also self-identify as lesbian, gay, and bisexual during their college years, as this is often the first time that parental scrutiny is significantly diminished.

Contemporary lesbian, gay, and bisexual youths, if given access to helping resources such as lesbian, gay, and bisexual peer support and other affirming helping resources, will do well in meeting the challenges of developing into well-functioning lesbian, gay, and bisexual adults. The ideology of "queer" affirmation provides youths with an invigorating model for enhancing personal resilience and developing group solidarity. It is crucial to avoid stereotyping lesbian, gay, and bisexual youths as passive and helpless victims. In fact, youths have provided a visible challenge to older lesbian, gay, and bisexual people to demand fair treatment in society. Yet young lesbian, gay, and bisexual people should not be romanticized. Many lesbian, gay, and bisexual youths have problems, and these problems should not be minimized. The challenges unique to lesbian, gay, and bisexual youths are mostly caused by cultural and institutional victimization as well as direct attacks. Both systemic victimization and direct attacks must be eliminated. Personal and social identities can develop only in safe and supportive social circumstances. Developmental delays and dysfunctions in the processes of identity development are more likely to occur in hostile and heterosexist environments. In hostile contexts, internalized homophobia and social inhibition prevent the development of self-esteem and social integration. And for some lesbian, gay, and bisexual youths, diminished self-esteem and loneliness may lead to despair. Until we know which youths move toward adulthood with resilience and which slide toward self-erasure, which conditions encourage resourcefulness and which deplete it, it is crucial that we consider lesbian, gay, and bisexual young people to be potential targets of victimization who are in need of protection and support.

9

Inmate Sexual Assault

The Plague That Persists

———————

ROBERT W. DUMOND

Franklin Pierce College

THE AMERICAN CORRECTIONAL SYSTEM
STRETCHED BEYOND ITS CAPACITY

As an increasing number of Americans are being incarcerated in the nation's prisons, jails, and correctional facilities—1.86 million (Beck, 2000)—the horror of sexual victimization while incarcerated continues to affect countless individuals. Mental health professionals who serve inmates (both juvenile and adult) within correctional facilities and upon release to the community are in a unique position to address this problem in a number of ways.

Although the problem of inmate sexual assault has been known and examined for the past 30 years, the body of evidence has failed to be translated into effective intervention strategies for treating inmate victims and for ensuring improved correctional practices and management. The situation is further complicated by problems faced by most correctional institutions. Although the rate of incarceration in the United States has doubled within the last decade alone (Bureau of Justice Statistics, 1995), most penal settings are operating well beyond their rated capacity, with problems of overcrowding, understaffing, and inadequate resources being common (Beck & Mumola, 1999; Clark, 1994; U.S. Department of Justice, 1999c). As a result, inmate sexual assault, called by some the "extra punishment anyone sentenced to prison can expect" (Weiss & Friar, 1974), continues to terrorize certain inmates.

Author's Note: This article first appeared in *The Prison Journal,* Vol. 80 No. 4, December 2000, pp. 407-414. Copyright © 2000 Sage Publications, Inc. Used with permission.

THE INCIDENCE OF
INMATE SEXUAL ASSAULT REMAINS UNKNOWN

The actual extent of prison sexual assault is still unknown. The incidence of inmate sexual victimization is quite variable and difficult to predict with accuracy (Dumond, 1992). The research remains sharply divided in epidemiological analysis (Donaldson, 1995). A recent analysis of the Nebraska prison system by Struckman-Johnson, Struckman-Johnson, Rucker, Bumby, and Donaldson (1995, 1996) revealed fairly high rates of forced or coerced sexual activity in confinement (medium or maximum security = 22% of male prisoners; minimum security = 16%). The same study noted that the problem appeared to be aggravated in larger prison systems with more crowded inmate populations with greater ethnic diversity. Cotton and Groth's (1982) observation appears to still retain its validity: "Available statistics must be regarded as very conservative at best, since discovery and documentation of this behavior are compromised by the nature of prison conditions, inmate codes and subculture and staff attitudes" (p. 48).

The problem is further complicated by the complex social-psychological milieu of the incarcerated setting. Coerced sexual assault may take many forms, on a continuum ranging from trading sex for protection ("hooking up") to brutal gang rape (Donaldson, 1993, 1995; Stop Prisoner Rape, 1993). There is a general joining of social status and sexual behavior while incarcerated, which leads many inmates to be cast in a role that can be extremely humiliating.

SOME INMATES MAY BE AT
INCREASED RISK OF SEXUAL VICTIMIZATION

Contrary to popular perception, it must be understood that no inmate is immune from sexual victimization. This being said, certain groups of inmates appear to be more vulnerable. They include (a) young, inexperienced; (b) physically small or weak; (c) inmates suffering from mental illness and/or developmental disabilities; (d) middle-class, not "tough" or "streetwise"; (e) not gang affiliated; (f) known to be homosexual or overtly effeminate (if male); (g) convicted of sexual crimes; (h) violated the "code of silence" or "rats"; (i) disliked by staff/other inmates; (j) previously sexually assaulted (Cotton & Groth, 1982, 1984; Donaldson, 1993, 1995; Dumond, 1992, 1995; Lockwood, 1978, 1980; Scacco, 1975, 1982). The issue of race has also been identified (Lockwood, 1980, 1994; Knowles, 1996; Wooden & Parker, 1982), especially in those settings with disproportionate racial populations and high racial tension.

RESPONDING TO VICTIMS OF
INMATE SEXUAL ASSAULT IS COMPLEX AND DIFFICULT

The effects of sexual victimization are pervasive and devastating, with profound physical, social, and psychological components (Cotton & Groth, 1982, 1984; Fagan, Wennerstrom, & Miller, 1996; Kupers, 1997). These effects are magnified in captivity. The perpetrator's actions and beliefs profoundly influence the psychology of the victim (Herman, 1992), and some inmates experience a systematic, repetitive infliction of psychological trauma, physical/sexual assault, continuation of terror, helplessness, and fear (Toch, 1992). Whatever inmate victims choose to do regarding the sexual assault (reporting the crime, seeking protective custody, protective pairing), it has a profound impact on their future life while incarcerated (Donaldson, 1993; Kupers, 1997). In addition to the physical harm, there are risks of HIV+/sexually transmitted diseases (STDs), medical injuries, post-traumatic stress disorder (PTSD), depression, suicidal ideation, loss of social status in the incarcerated community, labeling, and stigmatization. In addition, they may be vulnerable to further victimization.

Clinicians who respond to inmate victims should be acutely aware of the sequelae of sexual victimization, both physically and psychologically (see Cotton & Groth, 1982, 1984; Fagan et al., 1996; Lockwood, 1978, 1980; Scacco, 1975, 1982). It is interesting that many mental health clinicians may be more familiar with treating sexual predators than understanding and treating victims of sexual assault.

An interdisciplinary approach to care, with special attention to confronting the risk of suicide and to ensuring the ongoing safety and well-being of the inmate following the intervention, must be achieved. Clinicians must be prepared to intercede with security, classification, and administrative staff to effectively manage victim care. Standard P-57 Sexual Assault of the National Commission on Correctional Health Care (1997) should be universally adopted in all correctional settings. Another exemplary, comprehensive model to emulate is PS 5324.04 Sexual Abuse/Assault Prevention and Intervention Programs (updated December 31, 1997) of the Federal Bureau of Prisons (1997) that can be accessed at http://www.bop.gov/progstat/53240104.html.

The issue of HIV and STDs bears additional comment. As noted by Hammett, Harmon, and Maruschak (1999), inmates have disproportionately high rates of infectious disease, substance abuse, high-risk sexual activity, and other health care problems. Although the rate of transmission of HIV/AIDS by coerced sexual assault against inmates is unknown, all victims of sexual assault by inmates while incarcerated face the possibility of an "unadjudicated death sentence" ("Breaking the Silence," 1995), a significant subversion of the intent of the criminal justice system.

INMATE SEXUAL VICTIMIZATION BY STAFF— A CANCER OFTEN OVERLOOKED

The issue of sexual misconduct/abuse/assault by staff on male and female inmates is also an important issue to address. To be sure, most correctional staff members are not involved with such abusive behavior, yet a small minority of staff have inflicted serious harm on inmates. The boundaries between staff and inmates can sometimes get confused in the alienating and negative environment of the prison milieu. Therefore, some staff who are vulnerable may become manipulated and, as a result, may have inappropriate sexual contact with inmates. Even if the exchange between staff and inmate is "consensual," it represents a barrier that cannot be breached. When allegations of sexual misconduct by staff are made, careful investigation must be performed to rule out false complaints or inmate manipulation, which can destroy a correctional staff member's career.

It has also become increasingly apparent that women in confinement face substantial risk of sexual assault by a small number of ruthless male correctional staff members, who use terror, retaliation, and repeated victimization to coerce and intimidate confined women (Amnesty International, 1999; Baro, 1997; Coomaraswamy, 1999; Human Rights Watch, 1996, 1998; Smith, 1998; U.S. Government Accounting Office, 1999). Concerns about this issue led the National Institute of Corrections (U.S. Department of Justice, 1999b) to solicit submissions for the development of "a training curriculum for investigating allegations of staff sexual misconduct with inmates." Such abuses are intolerable. They are fundamental violations of incarceration and defile the guiding principles of correctional environments ("the care, custody, and control of inmates"). Mental health clinicians must be willing to entertain such complaints and act aggressively to pursue justice to protect and treat inmates so victimized. In addition, all correctional institutions incarcerating women should adopt the standards and practice of the Georgia Department of Correction (National Broadcasting Company, 1999).

CONTINUITY OF
INMATE VICTIM CARE IS DIFFICULT

The nature of the incarcerated setting itself complicates continuity and thoroughness of care for the victim. Many inmates face transfer to different institutions, often unexpectedly. It is vital that treating clinicians ensure ongoing care of inmate victims if and when they are transferred from one institution to another. There should also be clear differentiation between the needs of the inmate victim who will be released within a short period of time and those who will be incarcerated for an extended period of time. Clinicians need to plan their treatment strategies accordingly (Dumond, 1992, 1995; Fagan et al., 1996). Finally, inmate victims, upon release, whether to parole or to the community, should be provided competent community intervention and/or treatment.

CORRECTIONAL STAFF TRAINING IS VITAL

Mental health professionals also have an opportunity to have an impact on correctional staff and their attitudes, which, unfortunately, may exacerbate the victimization experience for inmates. Gardner (1986) identified that education and age were factors in correctional officers' attitudes about inmate victims. Eigenberg's (1989) disturbing analysis of officers employed in the Texas Department of Correction found that half of the officers surveyed engaged in victim blaming, and that many were apt to define rape victims as prostitutes and believed that homosexuals "cry rape" if they are caught during the act of intercourse.

In a later amplified analysis, Eigenberg (1994) focused on staff training as a key ingredient to proactively and responsibly dealing with counterproductive staff attitudes. Staff training programs such as those operating in the Massachusetts Department of Correction (Dumond, 1994) and the Federal Bureau of Prisons are important contributions to increasing the professional response toward this issue. (See also an insightful analysis by Dallou [1996] in *Corrections Today* and Donaldson [1993] in *Prisoner Rape Education Program: Overview for Administrators and Staff.*) Staff development officers and trainers may also wish to use an excellent resource video titled *The Correctional Officer: Recognizing and Preventing Closed-Custody Male Sexual Assaults* (AIMS Media, 1995).

MENTAL HEALTH STAFF
MUST HELP FORGE THE REMEDIES

There are no panaceas for such a complex and difficult phenomenon as inmate sexual assault while incarcerated. Mental health practitioners will be increasingly involved in dealing with this issue, in forging more responsive treatment strategies for individual victims themselves, and in helping institutions respond more affirmatively. We are in a pivotal role to shape the training efforts of correctional staff and to improve and enhance the classification system for identifying at-risk inmates. Administrators, government officials, and security staff will look for and expect clinicians to give them insight into this often misunderstood and ill-managed problem. Our inaction in this vital arena portends dire consequences for corrections and American society itself.

10

Sexual Assault and Coercion Among Incarcerated Women Prisoners

Excerpts From Prison Letters

———■———

LEANNE FIFTAL ALARID

University of Missouri–Kansas City

Countless acts of sexual assault, including acts of coerced sex that may appear consensual, have occurred in U.S. prisons. Sexual assault and coercion jeopardize both individual safety and institutional security. Although not all sex in prison is coerced, it is estimated that in 1995, there were approximately 359,000 male victims and 5,000 female victims who were sexually assaulted while doing time in U.S. prisons (Donaldson, 1995). Incidents of coerced sex in prison and jail are related to individual and group violence, offender adjustment problems, and health complications (Struckman-Johnson & Struckman-Johnson, 1999, 2000; Tewksbury, 1989a; Wooden & Parker, 1982). There is a clear need for more research in this area so that administrators can better understand the nature and effects of prison sex. Increased understanding may lead to enhanced staff awareness, improved institutional control, and a decrease in uses of force.

Previous lines of inquiry have focused either on sexual assault in the community (e.g., Bevacqua, 2000; Odem & Clay-Warner, 1998; Russell, 1984; Schwartz & DeKeseredy, 1997; Scully, 1990; Searles & Berger, 1995; Stanko, 1985) or male sexual assault inside male correctional institutions (e.g., Chonco, 1989; Cotton & Groth, 1982; Dumond, 1992; Eigenberg, 1989; Groth & Burgess, 1980; Jones & Schmid, 1989; Lockwood, 1985; Nacci & Kane, 1983, 1984; Saum, Surratt, Inciardi, & Bennett, 1995; Smith & Batiuk, 1989; Tewksbury, 1989a, 1989b; Wooden & Parker, 1982). Both bodies of literature have ignored the prevalence and nature of sexual assault of incarcerated women.

Author's Note: The author wishes to thank Velmarine Oliphant Szabo for sharing her personal experiences and observations from prison during the past 5 years and for bringing to the criminal justice community an awareness and better understanding of female sexual coercion.

Academic experts in the area of female prisoner subcultures have only recently acknowledged the possibility of female prisoner sexual assault (Bowker, 1981, 1982; Pollock-Byrne, 1990). Since the 1960s, previous studies have found that many women prisoners participate consensually in play families, intimate (nonsexual) dyads, and/or same-sex couple relationships (for a review of these studies, see Alarid, 1996). Most recently, Owen (1998) described involvement in play families and nonsexual friendships as a way to avoid "the mix." The mix is defined as "any behavior that can bring trouble and conflict with staff and other prisoners," which includes reduction of good time, restriction of privileges, or solitary confinement (Owen, 1998, p. 179). The three overlapping behaviors of the mix that most often led to trouble were involvement in homosexuality ("playing around"), drugs, and fighting. Most women interviewed by Owen did not admit to currently being in the mix, only that they used to be involved or that they strongly advised staying out of the mix. Exploitative relationships of an economical and/or emotional nature were found to exist among women prisoners involved in the mix. However, there was little mention of sexual coercion and sexual assault associated with the "homosexual mix" (Owen, 1998).

Outside of academic circles, increased attention has been paid to female offenders who were sexually coerced or sexually assaulted by correctional staff (Amnesty International, 1999; APBnews.com, October 10, 1999; Human Rights Watch, 1996; Smith, 1998; U.S. General Accounting Office, 1999). Women prisoners are more likely to be sexually abused by correctional staff than are men prisoners (Donaldson, Dumond, Knopp, Struckman-Johnson, & Thompson, 1995).[1]

REVIEW OF THE LITERATURE

There are few existing studies, however, that address the prevalence and nature of sexual coercion and sexual assault of women offenders by other incarcerated women. Two known studies were conducted by Cindy and Dave Struckman-Johnson in 1994 and 1998. The first study was conducted statewide in three men's prisons and one female prison in Nebraska. The study found, via anonymous mail surveys, that 22.0% of men and 7.7% of women reported that they experienced being "pressured or forced into sexual contact in a state prison facility" (Struckman-Johnson, Struckman-Johnson, Rucker, Bumby, & Donaldson, 1996, p. 74).[2] Of this number, only 29% of prisoners actually reported the incident to prison staff.

A follow-up study was conducted in 1998 with 2,051 inmates and 518 staff members at seven men's prisons and three female prison units in other midwestern states. The researchers found that the sexual coercion rates reported by female inmates (those who reported at least one incident of sexual coercion) varied among the three facilities: at 6%, 8%, and 19% (Struckman-Johnson & Struckman-Johnson, 1999, 2000). A second major finding was that between 55% and 80% of all sexual coercion in the three women's units was committed by other women offenders, which is notably more than that committed by correctional staff. Incidents described by the women offenders were defined and classified by the researchers. The sexual coercion ranged from "pressure tactics" and genital touching to "force tactics" such as gang rape. Rape rates for women varied from 0% to 5% of the female offender population. Thus, most of the sexual coercion incidents were committed by other women offenders who fondled, seduced, or somehow pressured women inmates into oral and/or vaginal sex. These studies suggest that sexual coercion rates of women prisoners varied by institution. Institutional factors included institutional size, housing type, and type of offender. Female institutions that were larger, had barracks or dorm-style housing, and housed offenders who were convicted of crimes against persons were more likely to have higher rates of sexual coercion (Struckman-Johnson & Struckman-Johnson, 1999, 2000).

METHOD

Sexual misconduct among women inmates is particularly sensitive and difficult to study by outside researchers. Barriers to studying prison sexual coercion and assault include inmates' fears of the subculture, which prohibits offenders from disclosing misconduct by other inmates; the stigma of admitting involvement in the mix; lack of sensitivity from correctional officers; a researcher's limited institutional access; and resistance from prison administrators (Alarid, 1999; Eigenberg, 1989; Struckman-Johnson et al., 1996).

The present research attempts to overcome some of these barriers by using a qualitative case study approach to examine situations and behaviors underlying sexual coercion and sexual assault among incarcerated women. Surveys were initially disseminated to women in a large urban county jail in the South. The surveys asked women about a variety of attitudes and behaviors relative to the institutional subculture, the inmate code, play families, and sexual and economic behaviors (see Alarid, 1996, for detailed methodology). The survey data unexpectedly uncovered information that suggested that sexual harassment and sexual coercion were present among women offenders in the jail. To further investigate this question, a random group of 25 women offenders who had previously participated in the survey were asked to mail back additional information on sexual coercion. Contact with most of the women was eventually lost as they were transferred or released from jail. One woman, Velmarine,[3] maintained weekly contact through the mail for 5 years, as she transferred between four or five different female units. Velmarine conducted observations of all aspects of the prison subculture and recorded them in written letters she mailed on a weekly basis. Velmarine is a 41-year-old African American mother of three children who is serving a 25-year prison term for her third felony conviction. Although Velmarine has been attending college and trying to keep to herself, she has admitted involvement in the mix. Velmarine detailed her own experiences of sexual coercion and rape, as well as observations of others inside various prison units as they occurred. These experiences and observations were later indexed by the author according to certain themes that emerged and compared to the existing literature.

In this study, sexual assault is distinct from the definition of sexual coercion. Sexual assault is forced sex, and it ranges from unwanted genital touching to oral, vaginal, and/or anal sex. Sexual coercion is pressuring another to have sex, ranging from verbal harassment to extortion to obtain sex (Struckman-Johnson & Struckman-Johnson, 1999, 2000).

FINDINGS

The data indicate an association between involvement in the mix and sexual coercion, in that the chances of sexual coercion and sexual assault seem to increase during the time women are involved in the mix. Although many women are approached for sex or sexually harassed when they first come to prison, the pressure eventually subsides for unaffiliated women or "prison Christians" who "don't play." However, the vast majority (75% to 80%) of women in jails and prisons have been or are currently "in the homosexual mix," in that they experiment with, or are involved in, coupling or relationships that include sexual favors. Many of these women are involved in both play families and sexual liaisons. Women of all races and ethnic backgrounds who are involved in sexual liaisons most often prefer the "femme"[4] role, whereas the outnumbered "stud"[5] role is occupied primarily by African American women. Identified lesbians are obligated to play the stud role because most prisons have a low supply of studs compared with the high number of femmes.

Four themes emerged from the data of observations and experiences relative to sexual coercion and sexual assault among women offenders. The themes were (a) apathy toward sexual coercion and sexual assault, (b) the "jailhouse turnout femme" as the sexual aggressor, (c) insight to one rape situation, and (d) institutional factors contributing to sexual coercion.

Apathy Toward Sexual Coercion and Sexual Assault

The data excerpted from the letters indicate first that the official (reported) sexual assault rate among women prisoners is fairly low in women's prisons. In other words, sexual assault occurs between prisoners, but it is not reported. The reasons for the low reported rate may be that women inmates may be desensitized to definitions of coerced sex. Due to women offenders' past history of molestation, sexual assault, or various other sexually demeaning relationships that many have had as a child or as an adult with previous partners, these women may be overlooking the fact that they have been coerced into committing various sexual acts or have been victims of sexual assault.

> Most [women here] have no concept of a healthy relationship to begin with, and thus do not recognize coerced responses. This I've ascertained via conversations with other women. The saddest component . . . is the female prisoner basically accepts these relationship behavioral problems in prison, as well as out in society, as "okay." (August 21, 1997)

A second reason why forced sex may be lower among women prisoners is illustrated by another one of Velmarine's observations: "If it were not for the fact that most female inmates capitulate with coercion, there would be more forced sex acts or threats of violence, thereby causing recognizable rape to be a more common occurrence among women prisoners" (8/21/97). In other words, the letters suggest that some of the more passive women inmates reluctantly submit to subtle or blatant verbal coercion by getting involved in relationships of a sexual nature. The passive women may not wish to be involved in the relationship but do so for two reasons. Many incarcerated women hold a strong desire to belong to some sort of group. This need for belonging is not for protection, like in men's prisons, but for companionship and to combat loneliness, which makes doing time seemingly less painful. The problem with women in this situation is that they tend to give in to peer pressure more easily, which can cause more difficulties for them later on.

A second explanation for why women become involved in sexual relationships is that they may be intimidated by threats of violence, property destruction, or "setups." An example of a common setup is while the victim's dorm cubicle is unoccupied, the perpetrator hides contraband (a shank, bleach, etc.) and then reports the contraband to a staff member. The more passive woman, then, is trying to avoid a physical confrontation and possible fight with the perpetrator, having her own property stolen or destroyed, or losing privileges and good time for receiving a disciplinary report. In their reluctance to become involved, the issue of consent may become blurred for these women.

Throughout the past 5 years, Velmarine documented many cases of sexual coercion in which she was victimized and that she witnessed happening to other inmates. For some women, being a target of sexual coercion by a few female perpetrators was a daily experience. Common incidents of sexual coercion included loud verbal sexual harassment, genital exhibition, and masturbation. It appeared that some forms of sexual coercion, if ignored by the target, escalated to other forms of violence: "My first alert to rape danger was when one of my bunkmates began sexually propositioning me, via genital exhibition, then making threats of bodily harm . . . calling me a 'punk' while threatening to 'kick my ass' " (9/9/96).

Sometimes, the escalation of sexual coercion did not always involve bodily harm. The letters were full of incidents where one woman destroyed another inmate's property.

Velmarine discusses a second incident that illustrates the importance of learning how to deal with sexual coercion:

Women were waking me up out of good, deep, sleeps to see if I was "ready" or interested [in having sex]. Of course this angered me, but I've learned over the years that there's a thin line to tread to avoid fights or getting "ganged" when rejecting the sexual overtures of incarcerated women. I used to tactlessly speak my mind, not caring how my words made them feel as long as they left me alone. The results were usually derision in return and physical group attacks in retaliation. (January 14, 1998)

The "Jailhouse Turnout Femme" as the Sexual Aggressor

In this study, the heterosexual "jailhouse turnout femmes"[6] were more often sexually aggressive than studs. One cause of jailhouse turnout aggression was the perception that studs should always be involved with someone. Thus, studs should not ignore sexual advances from femmes. An example of the effects of unreciprocated love follows:

I felt pressured to select a black sexual "playmate" to avoid pressure from such women as "Carolyn," an unattractive, odious, obese and tall, black woman. . . . In all of her vulgarity, Carolyn would openly begin masturbating whenever she thought that I may have been looking in her general direction. . . . Carolyn stood a good 5'10" and weighed over 300 pounds. . . . She threw a cup of hot coffee at me, and luckily missed. I believed that there's some things that we just don't back down from in life especially in jail. My acceptance of this treatment from Carolyn in front of the entire dorm would have labeled me as a coward to have anything done with, and to, that anyone might have wished. My commissary, "head" (oral sex), and nothing else would have remained mine to control. . . . As Carolyn raised her left arm and made a fist, she lumbered towards me. I picked up a sharpened pencil from my mattress. As Carolyn swung down, I side-stepped her and jumped up onto her massive body. . . . I drove the pencil deeply into the flesh of her left upper arm before I felt the pencil snap. . . . Due to the fact that the Warden had actually seen what occurred . . . I was allowed to explain why and how Carolyn had come to a peak of bullying based upon sexual coercion because they hadn't fully understood the reasons for what they'd seen via the two-way mirror. (January 20, 1998)

Sometimes, verbal threats and sexual harassment by femmes can lead to physical alter-cations (e.g., property destruction, scalding with hot liquid, assault) of a stud. One of the re-sults of this situation is that studs, perceiving the need to uphold their reputations, may spend more time in a restriction dorm or solitary confinement for fighting. These situations occur, in part, because effeminate-looking heterosexual women may be favored by correc-tional staff over other women perceived to be gay or masculine looking (Eigenberg, 1989). In any case, it appears that femmes currently have many advantages over studs, as indicated by Velmarine:

> Forceful persuasion is used by the femmes against the "studs" for participation or sexual fa-vors if the stud is unwilling. Currently, femmes tend to attack their studs for suspected infi-delity or what they term as disrespect, e.g., flirting with other femmes. I've often observed the "stud" (often but not in all cases) back away from the femme that turns her attentions to another "stud." (February 8, 1997)

Studs who ignore femmes who express sexual interest in them means rejection in the form of personal disrespect. As a result of the perceived disrespect, some femmes unite as a group and in retaliation, they become involved in sexual extortion—fabricating stories to correctional officers that a stud is causing them problems. The stud broad might receive a disciplinary report. The extortion would continue until the stud broad "agreed" to be sexu-ally involved in a relationship. Velmarine writes,

> There's a prevalent perverse idea [by the officers and inmates] that if a lesbian gets involved with an obsessive woman who wishes to continue to harass after the involvement has ended, then that obsessive behavior [by the perpetrator] is alright. In other words, if a feminine-looking woman is physically attacking a tomboyish or masculine-looking woman, that is seen as alright because she [the femme] only wants the sex that the other should never have offered. (August 2, 1996)

In sum, sexual pressuring, unreciprocated love, and jealousy are the basis of most female prison violence. These were the same reasons for many incidents of male prison violence (Nacci & Kane, 1983).

Like most male offenders, some women attempt to ward off sexual victimization by emphasizing toughness and de-emphasizing characteristics that are considered weak or feminine. A display of kindness or caring through giving away commissary is considered weak and tends to open up the woman to being seen as a target (Smith & Batiuk, 1989). Velmarine remembers one example:

> When "Roberta" [a femme] first entered the dorm [transferred from another unit], she made a pass at me and every stud (which I don't consider myself) in the dorm. I was given the privilege of rejecting her first. After she made her rounds, she came back with a sympathy "poor me" ploy. . . . After I rejected her offer of cunnilingus, Roberta developed a nasty atti-tude with me . . . so I called her to the square (challenged her to a physical fight). She backed down and left me alone. (August 21, 1997)

Homosexual alliances were often formed by studs as a form of protection from sexual advances and assaults. Most of these relationships were destructive and short-lived:

Some stud broads reacted to the harassment by disrespecting their femme during the short-term relationship. After using them for sex, some stud broads would go to great lengths to rid themselves of the femme in hopes that they seem less appealing to other potential harassers. Verbal abuse in public was the most common form of disrespect between feuding partners. (September 12, 1998)

For the most part, female studs seem to deal with femme harassment in isolation. Studs do not form play families as protective liaisons against femme harassment.

The reluctant sexual submission of women offenders to other, more aggressive women inmates while in prison mirrors past experiences of coerced relationships with men outside of prison. Furthermore, the lesbian target and the female heterosexual aggressor observed in this study were similar to the roles found in Wooden and Parker's (1982) study of domineering male heterosexual "jockers" who targeted gay men for sex.

Insight Into One Rape Situation

Based on the data obtained during the 5-year period, rape occurred at a much lower rate than other forms of sexual behavior. However, when rapes did occur among women offenders, there were multiple perpetrators rather than a single female offender. Davis (1968) found that many male sexual liaisons developed after inmates were threatened with gang rape or following a gang rape incident. This does not appear to be the case for women. In this situation, it is likely that gang rape was used as the instrument to express feelings of resentment and anger that other inmates had toward their target. The following situation depicts the events that preceded Velmarine's rape, the trauma of the rape itself, and the aftermath:

Back in July of 1991, the . . . jail was extremely overcrowded. There were three women crammed into cells designed to house one or two women. I was sharing a cell with two Hispanic women, "Valerie" and "Anna." Valerie was more feminine and Anna, her lover, was more masculine. Nonetheless, Anna had made it clear on several occasions that she was attracted to me. I decided to give a little attention to "Sherylynn," a woman in the cell next to ours who had been subtly flirting for quite a while. . . . In spite of Anna's quiet protest, I moved into Sherylynn's cell that same night just before our doors were racked.

After one fantastic night with Sherylynn, I made out my commissary list using most of my allocated order spaces on her. What I had not counted on was Sherylynn being one of the women that has been in such abusive relationships with men that they can't accept someone loving and being kind to them. . . . Sherylynn had to have mates fighting over her to make herself feel worth something. Once Sherylynn had the commissary I'd purchased for her, she . . . pitted Anna against me and threw me out [of her cell]. Sherylynn wasn't getting [the reaction] that she wanted from Anna, so she began playing back up to me. Anna caught on to what Sherylynn was doing and quickly made amends with me. . . . [Anna] let me move back into the cell with her and Valerie. The next week, when I couldn't make store, Anna would spend on me like I was accustomed to doing for others.

One night after Anna latched on to my hand in her sleep, I found myself allowing Sherylynn to join me in the shower. Anna was so infuriated that she called 15-20 women in the tank to observe Sherylynn and I, while Anna threw my belongings out of my cell. . . . I moved into a cell with an older harmless Caucasian woman.

Three days later . . . while I was standing at the bars of the dayroom [and Valerie and two other inmates left to go to the law library], a stocky black woman named "Joniqua" (a friend of Sherylynn's) grabbed me from behind. When I began to struggle, Sherylynn and one other woman grabbed my arms. Anna was directing them to "Bring her into my cell, c'mon hurry, bring her in here!" I felt the weight of three more women pushing me into the cell. Joniqua got my panties off and threw them into the dayroom. I realized then that this was no practical joke or game. I was stripped of my bra and county dress (all women wore one piece dresses in the County Jail at that time). While four women were holding me down, Anna ordered one grotesque female to sit on my face and to force me to perform an act of cunnilingus. When I refused to cooperate, and threatened to bite her if she tried, they moved me to a smaller cell. As I struggled on the floor of Cell #7, I felt fists pummeling my legs and thighs. When I relaxed under the blows, Anna straddled my face while begging me to "just stick your tongue out a little bit." If I would have complied with Anna's pleas, (I found out later) that Sherylynn and Joniqua would have forced as many women to try to have me in the same manner. To add to my humiliation, Anna had secreted vaginal fluids all over my nose and mouth, which seemed to appeal to the animalistic frenzy these women had worked themselves into.

The girl who was in Cell #7 was ordered out, and it was given to me. When my grievance about the rape incident was completely ignored [by staff], I began to be asked to be racked in my cell all day except for meals and showers to keep Anna, Sherylynn, and Joniqua from fondling me whenever they felt the safe urge. Everytime I'd come out for a shower, I'd get fondled or dragged out naked to the dayroom. After about two weeks of this living hell, a nurse came to my rescue. I was in the shower, and Sherylynn and Joniqua were fondling my nipples, when the nurse wheeled in the medicine cart. I suddenly got brave and shouted: "Get your hands off my tits!" Sherylynn and Joniqua didn't see the nurse, and began to assault me. The nurse wheeled her cart out of the vestibule as if escaping a fire. The nurse ran straight to a Deputy and said "There's an inmate about to be raped in there!" I was moved out of the tank [the same day].

When I got transferred to prison [from the County Jail], Sherylynn was there and laughingly told me how she and Joniqua charmed the Deputies at the disciplinary hearing and only received 10 days loss of privileges (no commissary or visits), with no segregation or loss of good time. Anna's excuse later given to me [for the rape] was: "None of this would have ever happened if you hadn't been bragging about how good you were." (August 2, 1996)

This incident demonstrates that continued sexual harassment and fondling occurred weeks after the rape, until Velmarine saw an opportunity to obtain a transfer to a different part of the jail. These incidents seem to follow offenders to prison, where victimization is likely to continue.

Institutional Factors Contributing to Sexual Coercion

As previously mentioned, Velmarine did time in at least five different prison units in a period of 5 years, and she was therefore able to compare various institutional environments. The data in the letters indicated that there were two main institutional factors that contributed to increasing incidences of sexual coercion and sexual assault among women prisoners: (a) open dormitory-style housing and (b) correctional staff ignoring or encouraging offender sexual behavior.

Institutions with a greater proportion of open dormitory-style housing seemed to have more incidences of sexual coercion and sexual assault than areas with one- or two-person cells. In addition to having open dormitory housing, there were some prison units that had entire areas with dorms or cubicles for women on "restriction." The restriction dorm is the place where women are housed for temporary loss of privileges for prison rule violations. Velmarine pointed out that more inmate rapes occur in the restriction dorm, where the deprivation factor is temporarily intensified for all inmates, due to no television, no outside recreation time, no scrabble/cards/dominoes, or other activities. Below is an example of one such witnessed incident:

> On the date of 9/1/96, I observed two Black "stud broads," one White "stud," and four black femmes grab a Hispanic femme and half carry, half drag, her off into a corner of Restriction Dorm where there was no camera coverage, nor were the Officers able to view the scenario from the outside of the dorm.
>
> After they stripped her out of her clothes, one of the Black stud broads vaginally penetrated the Victim with her fingers, the other Black stud administered passion marks to the victim's neck while the White "stud" continued to help hold the victim down. Several femmes looked on and gave loud blow-by-blow descriptions of what was transpiring. After about five minutes of this commotion, the victim was called out by Officers amid yells from the dorm inmates to "cover up her neck." The victim . . . screamed and hollered "no" every step of the way. This leads me to believe that an involuntary sexual act had taken place with force, which equals rape irregardless of how the victim later explained it to inquiring staff. The inmate chose not to tell (for good reason), came back into the dorm trying to smile or "grin it off," although she still appeared a bit shaken. So ends another episode of sexual exploitation among women. It saddens me to realize that these victims are not always able to recognize the fact that they've been victimized. The same Black "stud" that gave the "hicky" to that inmate was the same one that grabbed my buttocks a few mornings later while I was returning from breakfast.
>
> Had I tried to go to any Officer about some of the stressful things I was experiencing in Restriction Dorm (a.k.a. the Butt Naked Club—called that by Officers and Inmates alike), I would have been laughed away from their presence. (September 6, 1996)

The actions (or inactions) of some correctional officers have been shown to contribute to the problem of offender sexual coercion in men's prisons (Eigenberg, 1989). This problem seems to be present in women's institutions as well. The correctional officers who are part of the problem tend to be undereducated about sexual coercion and sexual assault, less rigid and less consistent about rule enforcement, and may even encourage unruly behavior to "have fun" or to "play" with inmates. For example, sexually victimized inmates who attempt to prevent an incident are sometimes stigmatized through laughter and name-calling by correctional officers, even in the presence of inmates. A more serious form of officer misconduct is encouragement from correctional officers and other inmates to engage in sexual behavior. Velmarine writes about an incident in which another inmate ["Yvonne"] is attempting to coerce her into sexual activity:

With the CO's [correctional officers] joking around with Yvonne, and telling her she is doing the right thing, [and with] inmates telling Yvonne that I'll come around, I don't have a chance in hell of deterring Yvonne's attempted affections or threats.

Correctional officers who are advocates of prisoners' welfare are held in disdain by other correctional officers (Lockwood, 1980). The same situation seems to hold true in women's prisons. Velmarine offers a suggestion that would likely decrease sexual coercion and assault:

CO's who perform their jobs well are often resented by inmates, but they're respected. The officer's rigid adherence to the rules eradicates most otherwise intended criminal behavior during their assigned work area and shift with simply their visibility, as these officers are known for their zero tolerance for rule infractions. I presume that a good officer's presence would counter . . . coerced and consensual sexual acts among women. (August 21, 1997)

SUMMARY AND IMPLICATIONS

This qualitative study examined themes of sexual coercion and sexual assault among women offenders that surfaced in prison letters sent by an incarcerated woman during a 5-year period. One caveat is that this study was not meant to represent all situations of sexual misconduct behind bars—only the situations that were directly experienced or observed by one offender. Experiences of women targets in prison varied among small samples of women in other studies (Struckman-Johnson et al., 1996).

This study found that sexual pressuring and sexual harassment were much more prevalent than sexual assault in women's prisons. Although many women prisoners experienced sexual coercion at some point while in prison, women who participated in homosexual liaisons, particularly in the masculine role of the stud, were more likely to experience repeated incidences of sexual coercion.

A related finding was that sexual pressure tactics may be a related factor in later incidences of physical violence and sexual assault among women offenders. These findings suggest that to prevent incidences of sexual assault among offenders, correctional staff may wish to focus on identifying and curbing sexual coercion. Ignoring or encouraging sexual coercion may contribute to volatile and potentially violent situations.

A third finding was the dynamics between sexually aggressive heterosexual femmes and their targeted studs. Femmes seem to have become more sexually aggressive because there are few current restraints on their behavior. Heterosexual women possessing feminine qualities do not seem to be perceived by officers as an institutional threat. This situation might be prevented by correctional-staff education and consistent reprimand of all parties involved.

Because sexual coercion in women's prisons is an underresearched topic, the implications of the data were meant to suggest new ways for researchers to further examine the nature and prevalence of sexual coercion and sexual assault in women's jails and prisons. Social learning theory has been suggested as an explanation of women's sexual aggression. Using social learning theory, Anderson (1998) found that college women who had been sexually abused in the past and/or who viewed sexual relationships as adversarial were more likely to be sexually aggressive than nonabused, nonadversarial women. Allgeier and Lamping (1998) suggest methods of measuring sexual coercion that might be applied to women in prison.

The role that correctional institutions and prison administrators have played regarding prevention, intervention, and prosecution of sexual assaults has been slowly improving. Identifying and segregating targets from perpetrators has been suggested as a prevention tactic. Segregation has resulted in increased institutional safety for some targets, such as gay and bisexual men, but incidents of sexual coercion still occur in protective custody (Alarid, 2000). Others have suggested that to prevent sexual coercion, facilities may wish to increase surveillance in vulnerable areas where assaults have been known to occur. These areas include "transportation vans, holding tanks, shower rooms, stairways and storage areas" (Cotton & Groth, 1982, p. 54). This study suggests that in vulnerable areas, such as restriction dorms, prison administrators should install and make regular use of more cameras.

Finally, prosecuting perpetrators of pressured or forced sex has drawn increased attention. It has been suggested that facilities should inform new inmates of the probability they may be sexually assaulted while incarcerated. Information should be given to new inmates about how to avoid becoming a target and what medical, legal, and/or psychological help is available if someone is targeted (Cotton & Groth, 1982; Dallao, 1996; Lockwood, 1985).

NOTES

1. On March 4, 1999, Amnesty International launched a campaign to pass laws to criminalize the sexual misconduct of prison staff in 13 states. As a result of their efforts, six states enacted laws. As of June 2000, seven states still did not have any laws against sexual misconduct in prison: Alabama, Kentucky, Minnesota, Oregon, Utah, Vermont, and Wisconsin (Amnesty International, 1999).

2. In 1999, there were approximately 138,000 women behind bars (Bureau of Justice Statistics, 1999). If we assume that 7.7% of women in prison are sexually assaulted, there would be more than 10,600 women victims.

3. All participant names and places have been changed to fictitious names to protect the confidentiality of individuals. Written permission was granted to use Velmarine Oliphant Szabo's real name.

4. A "femme" is a slang term used by prisoners for a female inmate who plays the feminine role in the sexual/courting relationship (Alarid, 1996).

5. "Stud," "butch," "little boy," or "mac daddy" are slang terms used for female inmates who speak, dress, and play a masculine role in a sexual/courting relationship. A stud may initially coax a femme with commissary to become interested in a sexual liaison. Once the two become a couple, the stud then demands goods (commissary) and services (clean the cell, wash clothes) from the femme. The stud may threaten to deny sex or physically abuse the femme in some way if the stud does not get what "he" wants (Alarid, 1996).

6. A "jailhouse turnout" or "douche bag" is a woman who experiments with homosexual sex for the first time while in jail or prison. A jailhouse turnout chooses either a femme or a butch role, and may move between both roles.

UNIT 4

——■——

JUVENILE SEX CRIMES AND BEHAVIORS
OFFENDERS AND VICTIMS

This series of readings concerns the sexual offending behavior of youth or those who prey on society's youth. While we present on article on the self-reporting behavior of juvenile sexual offenders, our primary focus is on those individuals that sexually abuse children.

The first reading, "The Creation of and Considerations Surrounding Megan's Law," deals with the societal and political reactions to adult offenders who prey on children. In this article, Tad Hughes details the history behind the passage of the first sex offender registry law in Massachusetts. This piece of legislation, better known as "Megan's Law," was passed following the brutal and bizarre murder of Megan Kankas in 1994. After Megan's death, petitions were passed throughout the community, town, and state, and a law was signed requiring all convicted and adjudicated sex offenders to register with the police.

As this article points out, the enactment of this law and others like it placates public opinion and serves political needs, but there is little evidence to date that such laws are an effective deterrent to the future victimization of children. Although communal notification does make people feel better and safer in their communities, the courts are continuing their investigation of whether communal notification after the courts have handed down their penalty results in the imposition of additional penalties long after the sentence.

The second reading examines the number of cognitive distortions (life adjustment problems) among women who report being a childhood victim of sexual abuse. The basic premise of the article by Owens and Chard, "Cognitive Distortions Among Women Reporting Childhood Sexual Abuse," is that individuals who are victims of childhood sexual abuse are more likely to have problems trusting others, less likely to feel safe in their environment, and likely to feel powerless about the world around them. They also typically suffer from low self-esteem and have problems in intimate relationships as they mature.

The authors take this hypothesis a step further by asking the respondents a battery of questions designed to measure the presence of indicators of posttraumatic stress disorder (PTSD). They posit that those who score high on the PTSD scales will experience greater problems in life related to the aforementioned indicators and will also blame the outside world and environment for the problems that they experience in life.

One of the most important findings of this article is that victims of child sexual abuse do not develop the distrust of the world and their environment to the same level that many rape victims do. This may be due to the fact that in most cases, the perpetrator was often a member of the victim's immediate family. Despite these findings, the implications are clear. The authors claim that treatment for child sexual abuse survivors should focus more on ways in which treatment officials can help the survivors understand that the resulting victimization was not their fault, and hence, they are not to blame for the incident, instead of focusing efforts on retraining these victims to understand that the world they live in is not as dark and evil a place as we assume they would believe.

The third article in this section, "The Self-Reported Behaviors of Juvenile Sexual Offenders," deals with the scope, type, and variety of sexual offenses that juvenile offenders undertake. This article is important for many reasons, but paramount among them is the baseline figures it provides for those interested in the etiology of the offenses.

The findings of this study provide further proof that sexually abusive behavior toward children is not just an offense undertaken by adult men, but rather an offense that is common across both the young and the old. In this article, Zolondek, Abel, Northey, and Jordan report that in their national sample of 485 juvenile sex offenders, more than 60% reported involvement in sexual molestation on children.

Regarding the etiology of the assaults against other children, these authors found that more than 73% of the time, the youth used some type of physical or psychological coercion to initiate the sexual abuse on the other child. Furthermore, just under 75% of the time, when the victim was a child, the offender was a sibling or other family member.

A second part of the study examined the frequency of paraphiliac involvement between the authors' sample of juvenile sexual offenders and a similar sample of more than 5,000 adult males. They found that their sample of juveniles reported a higher frequency of fetishism, obscene phone calls, child molestation, and phone sex. Furthermore, although there were no differences between child and adult self-reported participation in exhibitionism, voyeurism, masochism, sadism, pornography, transsexualism, and transvestism, these are all sexual paraphilias that we do not commonly associate with juvenile behavior, much less early sexual behavior.

The final article, "Misuse of the Internet by Pedophiles: Implications for Law Enforcement and Probation Practice," deals with use of the Internet by pedophiles to troll for and locate child victims or to ascertain or distribute child pornography. There is perhaps no greater concern for any parent today than the concern over with whom their child interacts on the Internet. Today, more than 50% of all homes are equipped with a computer and subscribe to some form of Internet service. This article delves specifically into just how pedophiles and others with a sexual interest in children are now using the Internet and e-mail to locate potential victims, distribute child pornography, and join virtual communities where these offenders can share their fantasies and collaborate in any one of many forbidden activities. Although this article is somewhat dated (it was first published in 1997), the issues are as true today as they were just 5 short years ago.

Since this article's publication, law enforcement agencies have made great strides in their efforts to police and patrol chat rooms, but much remains to be done. The problems with victims and offenders in multiple jurisdictions still hound many efforts by law enforcement officials to bring these offenders to justice. Although not mentioned specifically in the article or even thought of at the time, one contemporary perspective regarding pedophiles cruising on the Internet is that their active engagement in these forums may serve as a safety valve, where those with a proclivity toward children may be able to live out their fantasies and not actually physically violate our nation's youth. However, this does not mean that the police should relax their enforcement efforts; it just means that more research needs to be done that looks at and compares the trends of child sexual victimization by adults and the proliferation of the Internet.

This collection of readings represents a cross section of the research that has been done looking at juvenile sex crimes. Although there may be no offense as serious or as egregious as the sexual victimization of a child, more research needs to be conducted in this area in order to help criminal justice officials and treatment practitioners better understand this class of offenders and stop the potential escalation of violence and offending behavior before these offenders reach adulthood.

11

The Creation of and Considerations Surrounding Megan's Law

The D.A. Can't Get No Relief

———

TOM "TAD" HUGHES

University of Louisville

The creation and proliferation of sex offender registration and community notification laws are a recent occurrence in the area of American criminal justice. Such laws, often known as a "Megan's Law," appear to be the result of the confluence of several powerful and disturbing factors.[1] This chapter seeks to explore this phenomenon in more detail. First, some of the unique challenges posed by sex crimes will be discussed. Second, the emotional and political salience surrounding the death of a child will be explored. Third, a review of the sad events that led to the creation of Megan's Law will be examined. Next, the requirements of Megan's Law will be defined. Fifth, the strengths and weaknesses associated with the law will be discussed. Six, the legal consternation surrounding Megan's Law will be enumerated. Finally, the general nature of registration and notification laws across the United States will be examined.

SEX OFFENSES AND OFFENDERS

Sex offenders and the consequences of their crimes represent a unique class of concerns and problems for the criminal justice system. Sadly, sexual victimization is not a rarity in our society. Such victimization results in extreme physical and emotional damage to the victim of the crime. The private nature and stigma associated with sexual victimization make reporting of victimizations as well as recovering from crimes difficult. Moreover, a substantial number of those who are sexually victimized are children (Greissman, 1996). In the cases where children are harmed, difficulties regarding reporting and recovery would seem to be particularly acute.

Sex offenders also represent difficult challenges for the criminal justice system. First, sex offenders do display some common characteristics, but they may vary greatly in their individual characteristics. For example, sex offenders can vary on economic, racial, and marital status variables. Thus, it appears that a strong and distinctive general profile for sex offenders is not possible. A second factor that makes sex offenders a difficult clientele for the criminal justice system concerns reoffending. Although the literature on recidivism of sex offenders is complex, sex offenders seem to reoffend at higher rates than do other criminal actors. Indeed, it appears that sex offenders do not "age out" of crime over time, as many other types of offenders do (D. Feldman, 1997; Greissman, 1996). The personal and social costs associated with sex crimes, as well as the unique challenges posed by sex offenders, combine to draw both attention and emotion to the area of sex offender legislation.

DEATH AND POLITICAL SALIENCE

The death of a child is a tragic event. Such a death certainly takes a devastating toll on the child's parents and family. Moreover, most people within the local community also feel such a death vicariously. In the aftermath of such a painful loss, parents, family, friends, and other citizens seek to understand how and why a young and fragile life was ended. Understanding the cause of the loss, however, is often not the end of the grieving process. Occasionally, parents and other concerned citizens seek to address some factual situation that caused the death of the child. These parties seek to create new rules that will never allow such a tragic event to happen again. These efforts often take the form of proposed laws that will alter some factual aspect involved in the child's death. It seems that the need to do something intersects with the American ideal that the law can be used to prevent similar occurrences in the future.

Few incidents have greater ability to generate political salience than the death of a child. This power is not lost on local, state, and national politicians. When these officials receive proposals for new legal rules from aggrieved parents and other concerned citizens, the moral suasion of these proposals is evident. Elected officials know that opposition to such emotionally charged appeals would inflict substantial damage on their political careers. Who wants to be remembered as the elected official who said "no" to a grieving mother and father when the next election cycles around? Thus, it seems that proposed legislation that flows from the tragic deaths of children moves through the legislative process with a speed and strength unlike other propositions.[2] Such harried movement through the legislature facilitates passage of new laws without careful consideration. Such expedience can result in legislators failing to consider the new law's likely actual impact; its ability to be enforced by the authorities; and any negative, unintended consequence that may result. Furthermore, the salience of the issue may result in the laws being adopted in a number of jurisdictions across the country. In short, the amazing political power of legislation generated by and associated with the death of a child seems to result in the quick creation and spread of laws.

THE CREATION OF MEGAN'S LAW

The sad events that lead to the creation of Megan's Law came to pass in Hamilton Township, New Jersey. On July 29, 1994, at approximately 6:30 p.m., 7-year-old Megan Kanka went out of her home to see a friend who lived down the street. Her sister went to find Megan several minutes later but learned she did not arrive at her destination. Frantically, the Kanka family, police, and neighbors searched for Megan. Twenty-three hours later, the police informed the Kankas that Megan had been found dead in a park several miles away from their home. The Kankas then had to undergo the grim task of identifying their daughter's body. Megan had been sodomized and raped. The attacker also strangled her with a belt and placed her head in a plastic bag to kill her (Cannon, 1996).

The attacker, Jesse Timmendequas, lived across the street at 27 Barbara Lee Drive. The 33-year-old man shared the residence with two other convicted sex offenders. Timmendequas had a prior record for the attempted sexual assault of both a 7-year-old and a 5-year-old girl. None of the residents in the area knew of Timmendequas's criminal record or his criminal sexual tendencies (O'Shaughnessy, 1995).[3]

Motivated by Megan's death, the Kankas and others sought to change the legal landscape in such a way that would allow members of a community to know when a convicted sex offender was moving into the area. The goal of this law was to arm local residents with the knowledge that a sex offender was in the area and thereby prompt them to take precautions that would reduce the chances of future victimization. The goal of the campaign was encapsulated in the simple phrase, "the right to know." The groundswell of support for this initiative was massive. In 1 week, 100,000 signatures were gathered on petitions in support of the law (Schneider, 1997). In just 2 months, 400,000 signatures were collected. The measure became law in New Jersey 89 days after Megan's murder (Cannon, 1996).

THE REQUIREMENTS OF MEGAN'S LAW

As originally enacted, Megan's Law was a 10-bill bundle of legislation. In essence, the legislation concerns registration of freed sex offenders and community notification regarding offenders who pose a substantial risk of reoffending.

The registration requirement of the law required that people who were convicted, found delinquent, or found not guilty due to insanity of sex offenses register with the police. This registration requirement also applied to sex offenders who were no longer incarcerated at the time of the statute's enactment but who had committed sex offenses prior to its effective date. These various groups of convicted people had 120 days from the date of the statute's enactment to register with the local police department. Furthermore, those placed on probation for sex offenses, as well as individuals who were convicted of sex offenses in other jurisdictions and wished to come into the State of New Jersey, also had to register within 120 days of entering the jurisdiction. Once registered, should a person wish to move, he or she was required to register anew with the local police department in his or her new community 10 days prior to taking up residence. Individuals who were required to register were able to apply to the superior court to end their obligation. A termination of the registration requirement required that the offender demonstrate that he or she had not committed an offense for at least 15 years following his or her conviction or release from a correctional facility and that he or she was not likely to reoffend (Martin, 1996).

The responsibility of community notification was given to local police chiefs. Notification consisted of providing the offender's name, physical description, photograph, address, place of employment or schooling, and vehicle description (Martin, 1996). The extent of notification required was shaped by the potential danger that the offender posed to the community. Offender risk levels were classified into three tiers. Those with low risks were labeled Tier 1. A police chief was required to notify local law enforcement of the presence of Tier 1 offenders. Those with moderate risks were classified as Tier 2. A police chief was required to notify local law enforcement and local community groups (e.g., schools) regarding the presence of a Tier 2 offender. Tier 3 was reserved for those who had a high risk of reoffending. In a Tier 3 situation, the police chief had to notify local law enforcement, community groups, and the public.

The responsibility of designing a community notification plan as well as classification of offenders into the tier system was given to county prosecutors. The statute provided a list of factors to be considered by the classifying prosecutor. These factors were divided into facts that were thought to either lower or raise a risk of recidivism. For example, an offender who was under some form of supervision or treatment or who had a serious physical illness was be thought to be of a lower risk. Factors that would tend to elevate a risk assessment included the use of a weapon by the offender during the sex offense, the number of prior victimizations, and psychiatric evaluations that warned of reoffending (Martin, 1996).

STRENGTHS AND WEAKNESSES OF MEGAN'S LAW

Megan's Law has engendered both supporters and detractors. Those in favor of the law claim several benefits from its existence. First, supporters maintain that the law increases public safety. It is hoped that armed with the knowledge regarding the presence of sex offenders in the neighborhood, police, government officials, and citizens will alter their behavior and reduce the chances of sexual victimization. Second, it is thought that registration and notification regarding the presence of sex offenders may aid the police in criminal investigations. Each state in the union has passed legislation that requires some form of registration of sex offenders. Such a registration scheme provides an organized accounting of sex offenders and their location. The existence of an organized database of sex offenders provides the police with a preexisting list of suspects to investigate when sex crimes occur. Thus, registration and the information it creates saves the police from having to cull names, locations, and other relevant information from court documents when investigating a reported sex offense (D. Feldman, 1997).[4] Third, it is hoped that the registration process will act as a deterrent. Here, the notion is that registered sex offenders will be less likely to reoffend because they are aware that the police have their information on file (Arnone, 2000). Finally, many believe that the law reduces the opportunities for sex offenders to recidivate. The argument here focuses upon the quick apprehension of a sex offender who starts to recidivate. Individuals armed with the knowledge of local sex offenders may well be able to identify them quickly, which would allow the quick apprehension of a sex offender who has either begun inappropriate contact that is the precursor to a new sex offense or who has actually begun to recidivate. A quicker mobilization of the police and resulting response would deny sex offenders the time necessary to victimize anew (D. Feldman, 1997).

Those who oppose Megan's Law have averred that the law will have several negative effects. First, opponents of the law fear that it deters sex offenders from rehabilitative programs (Martin, 1996; Schopf, 1995). That is, offenders will not seek out help to overcome their problems and thus will be a continued threat to the community. The difficulty in rehabilitating sex offenders must be remembered. However, if Megan's Law does result in offenders shying away from treatment, any possible gains that flow from rehabilitation would be lost.

The second concern of opponents to Megan's Law focuses upon displacement of sex offenders. Critics contend that the implementation of Megan's Law may drive predatory behavior to an area where the offender has not been identified (Schopf, 1995). An offender bent on recidivism may reside in one area where he or she has been identified and engage in criminality in another where he or she is unknown.

A third concern focuses upon the ability of Megan's Law to foster vigilantism (Martin, 1996). Examples of community residents taking the law into their own hands have occurred. In one community, the proposed home of a sex offender was the target of arson. In another community, two men attacked a man they mistook for a sex offender staying at the same residence (Schopf, 1995). Community protests have also resulted in sex offenders deciding to move away from a proposed residence to another community (C. Feldman, 1997). These actions may indeed drive sex offenders away from a notified community, but remember that extreme actions by community members could be illegal. Furthermore, such community action would seem to result in the displacement of the offenders to communities that cannot mobilize to deter the offender's presence. Thus, an effect of community protest and action may be a concentration of offenders in communities that lack a strong social structure and that already experience a host of social ills.

A final concern surrounding the law focuses on the creation of an unfounded sense of security in the community (Martin, 1996). Members of the community may believe that the notification process will inform them of all criminal sexual threats in their neighborhood. However, the reality is that many threats would remain even with community notification. Authorities or the public will not know sexual predators who have not been caught by the police or who have not been convicted by the courts. Moreover, the public generally will be made aware of only those sex offenders who have been classified as high risks to reoffend. The process of predicting future human behavior is very difficult and complex. Such predictions are often well beyond the most learned psychological minds. Under Megan's Law, the classification process is performed by public officials who likely have little education regarding the prediction of future criminality (Greissman, 1996). Under such circumstances, mistaken classification may occur. Perhaps most important, community notification provides information about new people coming into the neighborhood. Such knowledge can protect a child against potential danger associated with a stranger new to the area. However, research indicates that approximately 80% of sex offenders are known to their victims. Under these circumstances, community notification may foster a belief among parents and children that they are aware of significant risks of victimization when, in reality, they are not. In short, the promise of community notification may make the public believe that it is aware of all substantial threats regarding sexual victimization (Hudson, 1998). However, due to the imperfect nature of the classification process and the reality that Megan's Law does not account for all sex offenders, the public will likely remain exposed to threats of sexual victimization to which it is unaware.

LEGAL CHALLENGES TO MEGAN'S LAW

Almost from its inception, Megan's Law has been subject to a host of constitutional concerns and challenges (Martin, 1996). These legal challenges have focused on the registration and notification requirements of Megan's Law and have been of limited effectiveness in striking down the law (Greissman, 1996). Challenges that focus on the aspect of sex offender registration have generally been unsuccessful (D. Feldman, 1997).

Challenges to registration and notification have been based on several constitutional principles. Specifically, Megan's Law has been challenged based upon the Eighth Amendment prohibition against cruel and unusual punishment, noncompliance with the requirements of procedural due process, a violation of equal protection of the laws, the rule against double jeopardy, and a violation of the right to privacy (Chen, 1996; D. Feldman, 1997; Schopf, 1995).

Perhaps the most common and difficult legal concern regarding laws like Megan's Law flows from the rule against ex post facto laws (C. Feldman, 1997). The U.S. Constitution prohibits both states and the federal government from enacting an ex post facto law (Article I, §10, cl. 1 and Article I, §9, cl. 3, respectively). The case of *Calder v. Bull* (1789) described four laws that would violate this constitutional principle: a law that makes conduct that was legal when done illegal and punishes the conduct; a law that increases the seriousness of a crime to a higher level than when the act was committed; a law that increases punishment to a higher level than when the crime was committed; and a law that alters the legal rules of evidence used to convict the perpetrator between the time he or she committed the act and his or her adjudication. The ex post facto prohibition allows defendants protection from the government changing the legal rules surrounding conduct for which they are being tried. In effect, a defendant locks in the legality of the act, rules of evidence, level of offense, and punishment receivable at the time the act is committed (Loewy, 1987).[5] Based upon the ex post facto clause, those convicted of sex offenses could argue that at the time they committed their crime, the law did not provide for the additional punishments of registration and community notification (Schopf, 1995). The linchpin of this argument is that registration and/or community notification be considered punishment. If these requirements are not construed by the law to be punishment, then the ex post facto clause would not apply and the provisions would comply with the Constitution. As with other legal challenges to Megan's Law, results based on this argument have been mixed.

THE PROLIFERATION AND EXTENT OF MEGAN'S LAW

Laws requiring the registration of sex offenders and the potential for community notification regarding their presence have spread across the United States in the past 10 years. Between 1990 and 1995, 29 states added legislation concerning registration and notification (Schopf, 1995). On May 8, 1996, then-President Clinton signed into effect federal legislation encouraging states to create laws regarding community notification about local sex offenders (Cannon, 1996). The ideas behind Megan's Law moved from a state statute to a federal standard in less than 2 years. The federal legislation encourages such state legislation by punishing those states that do not comply with reduced federal funding opportunities. By November 1996, 40 states were in compliance with the requirement (D. Feldman, 1997).

An examination of the states' requirements concerning registration and public notification finds substantial variation. In determining whether or not a registration requirement applies to a specific offender, state statutes generally consider the type of sex crime, age of offender, and age of victims. Other factors that may require a person to register in a jurisdiction include a conviction of some specific non-sex crimes, being found not guilty of a sex crime due to insanity, and being convicted of a sex crime and working in a jurisdiction though not residing there.

The extent and methods of community notification vary more than registration requirements. Levels of community notification range from notification of the local police to information conveyed directly to the general public. When notification of the public is mandated, it is often tied to a risk assessment. Typically, when a risk assessment results in the conclusion that an offender poses a high risk to community members, some form of direct communication to the community is required. However, some states place the onus of community notification on citizens. For example, some states provide open records that are available for public inspection at the local police or sheriff's office. Similarly, other states allow for the release of information upon written request or phone call of a citizen. Restrictive jurisdictions leave the question of community notification to the discretion of the local police, prosecutor, or school. Finally, some states make sex offender registration material available only to local police.

The approved methods of community notification are also divergent. Specific methods of community notification include the use of mail, telephone, descriptive flyers, CD-ROMs, newspapers, community meetings, postings at the offender's residence, door-to-door notification by the police, and the World Wide Web.[6] The use of Web-based notification appears to be a coming trend. As of May 2000, 21 states had placed their sex offender registrations on the Internet, with several others planning to implement Web sites in the near future (Zielbauer, 2000). It should be remembered that the legal requirements concerning registration and community notification for sex offenders are dynamic. The impact of court challenges, referenda, and statutory amendments makes this a protean area of criminal justice.

CONCLUSION

In the past decade, states and the federal government have passed legislation concerning both the registration of convicted sex offenders and public notification regarding sex offenders located in the community. In many instances, these laws were sparked by the tragic death of Megan Kanka and frequently bear her name. These laws have engendered supporters and detractors and have been subjected to frequent, divergent legal challenges. Although the federal government has mandated registration and community notification, an examination of state laws in this area shows great variation in which sex offenders are required to register and how the community is notified of their presence.

NOTES

1. Although sex offender registration and notification are commonly considered a Megan's Law, the registration of sex offenders is not a new concept. Indeed, the first sex offender registry was started in California in 1947 (Zielbauer, 2000). As indicated infra, the true distinction of Megan's Law concerns community notification regarding the presence of a sex offender in the area.

2. Fritz (1999) notes several laws and legal movements that are the result of the death of children: The death of Polly Klass was used to support the need for "three strikes" legislation; Aimee's Law concerns compensation from repeat offenders; Jenna's Law focuses on truth in sentencing; Bryan's Law requires a university to notify a student's parents if a student is missing; and Lizzie's Law deals with child visitation with a parent who murders the child's other parent.

3. Timmendequas was subsequently convicted of murder and is awaiting execution on New Jersey's death row (Kanka, 2000).

4. Feldman notes that the existence of a sex offender registration list does create the danger of creating a list of "usual suspects." The idea of police relying on usual suspects is potentially damaging in two ways. First, such lists may perpetuate the suspicion associated with a reformed offender. Second, such lists may focus police on preexisting offenders to the exclusion of new offenders.

5. These restrictions do not apply to changes that aid or help the defendant (Loewy, 1987).

6. This information regarding the variation of registration and notification requirements was drawn from an examination of the KlassKids Foundation home page, located at www.klasskids.org. This page contains brief descriptions of Megan's Law in all 50 states.

12

Cognitive Distortions Among Women Reporting Childhood Sexual Abuse

———■———

GINA P. OWENS
KATHLEEN M. CHARD
University of Kentucky

Recent literature has suggested that many of the psychological effects of childhood sexual abuse, such as self-destructive behaviors, posttraumatic stress disorder (PTSD), anxiety, interpersonal difficulties, and sexual dysfunction, may begin with cognitive distortions about the self and the world that become part of a child's cognitive schema (Smucker, Dancu, Foa, & Niederee, 1995). Further research proposes that these schema distortions may contribute to the emotional distress experienced by many adult survivors of sexual abuse (Briere & Elliott, 1994).

Specific areas of cognitive distortions resulting from the trauma of sexual abuse typically occur around five principal areas: safety, trust, power, esteem, and intimacy (McCann, Sakheim, & Abrahamson, 1988). These five areas of distortions are associated with certain psychological responses, including anxiety, social withdrawal, avoidant behavior, fear of betrayal, isolation, passivity, anger, and feelings of powerlessness and weakness. In addition, Briere and Runtz (1993) proposed that the cognitive distortions of childhood sexual abuse (CSA) survivors often include an exaggeration of the possibility of danger or difficulty in the world and a decreased view of the person's self-efficacy and self-worth.

Despite these recent schema conceptualization developments, the information available on the distortions of CSA survivors is in need of further examination. Research on the

Authors' Note: Data from this article are part of a larger treatment study on cognitive processing therapy for childhood sexual abuse conducted at the Center for Traumatic Stress Research at the University of Kentucky. The present research was funded by National Institute of Mental Health Grant 1R21MH56633-01. We thank Dawn Johnson for assistance with statistical analysis. Correspondence concerning this article should be addressed to Kathleen M. Chard, Department of Educational and Counseling Psychology, University of Kentucky, 235 Dickey Hall, Lexington, KY 40506-0017; e-mail: kchard@pop.uky.edu.

relationship of PTSD severity to cognitive distortions of sexual abuse survivors is sparse. Moreover, little research with this population has used two recently developed cognitive measures, the Personal Beliefs and Reactions Scale (PBRS) (Resick, Schnicke, & Markway, 1991) and the World Assumptions Scale (WAS) (Janoff-Bulman, 1989). Wenninger and Ehlers (1998) examined the cognitive distortions of German and American samples of sexual abuse survivors using the PBRS. Results of this study indicated that a greater number of cognitive distortions was associated with higher symptom scores. Mechanic and Resick (1993) investigated cognitive distortions of rape victims using the PBRS and WAS. Their results suggested that rape victims having more positive beliefs about the benevolence of the world and self-worth on the WAS were more likely to have healthier beliefs as indicated by the PBRS. Although the PBRS and WAS have been used together in studies with rape victims, the two instruments have not been used simultaneously to examine the cognitive distortions of CSA survivors. The aforementioned findings emphasize the need to further investigate the cognitive distortions of adult survivors of sexual abuse in the hope of finding useful means of identifying and addressing these particular distortions during any cognitive-based treatment.

The present study was part of a larger treatment study involving cognitive processing therapy for sexual abuse survivors, or CPT-SA (Chard, Weaver, & Resick, 1997). Cognitive processing therapy focuses on alleviating symptoms arising from past sexual abuse, including PTSD, one of the more prevalent psychological reactions to CSA (Briere, 1992; Briggs & Joyce, 1997). The purpose of this study was to determine whether survivors with a greater number of cognitive distortions at the time of treatment request also have a greater severity of PTSD symptoms as indicated by the PBRS, the WAS, and Clinician Administered PTSD Scale (CAPS-SX). A further purpose was to identify how the PBRS and WAS correlate within a sample of adult survivors of CSA.

METHOD

Participants

Seventy-nine female adults reporting a history of CSA were recruited through fliers posted throughout the community and mailings to service providers in a moderately sized midwestern city. The mean age of the sample was 32.32 years, with a range of 18 to 55 and standard deviation of 8.70. Eighty-two percent of the sample was Caucasian, 11% African American, 5% Hispanic, and 2% other ethnic groups. The mean for years of education was 14.04 ($SD = 2.25$).

Specific characteristics of the sexual abuse experience were also obtained. The mean age of onset of abuse was 6.3 years ($SD = 2.76$), with a range from 1 year to 12 years. Ninety-six percent of participants reported kissing or fondling during the abuse, 58% reported that penetration occurred, and 66% of participants reported oral sexual contact. Thirty-seven percent of participants were abused by both a nonrelative and a relative, 48% were abused by a relative, and 15% were abused by a nonrelative. Twenty percent of participants had 5 or fewer incidents of abuse, 13% had between 6 and 10 abuse incidents, 9% had between 15 and 30 incidents, and 58% of the sample experienced 100 or more incidents of abuse.

Assessment Instruments

CAPS. The CAPS-2 is a structured clinical interview for assessment of PTSD (Blake et al., 1990). The more current unpublished version, the CAPS-SX (One Week Symptom Status Version) (Blake et al., 1996), was used in the present study. Questions pertain to the 17 symptoms of PTSD contained in the *Diagnostic and Statistical Manual of Mental Disorders (DSM-III-R)* (American Psychiatric Association, 1987) as well as eight additional items associated with PTSD, including global ratings of validity, severity, and symptom improvement; survivor guilt; guilt concerning acts of commission or omission; reduced awareness of surroundings; derealization; and depersonalization. Blake (1994) reported that the CAPS is consistent with the *DSM-IV* (American Psychiatric Association, 1994). Each of the 17 symptoms is rated according to both frequency and intensity on a scale from 0 to 4. A score of at least 1 for frequency and 2 for intensity must be obtained for a symptom to be considered significant. The total score on the CAPS (frequency + intensity) indicates the severity of PTSD symptoms.

Although the CAPS has had limited use in CSA studies, it has been used extensively in PTSD research with rape survivors (Resick, Nishith, & Astin, 1996) and combat veterans (Weathers & Litz, 1994). The CAPS-1 was originally administered to 25 combat veterans (Blake et al., 1990). Results indicated that the CAPS was a reliable instrument, with reliability coefficients for frequency and intensity scores of the PTSD symptom clusters ranging from .92 to .99. Results also suggested the CAPS was valid because correlation coefficients between the CAPS and both the Mississippi Scale for Combat-Related PTSD (Keane, Caddell, & Taylor, 1988) and the PTSD subscale of the Minnesota Multiphasic Personality Inventory (Keane, Malloy, & Fairbank, 1984) were fairly high, ranging from .70 to .84, respectively.

PBRS. The PBRS was originally developed to detect disruptions in the cognitive schemas of rape victims. The PBRS consists of 55 statements that the respondent rates from 0 (*not at all true for you*) to 6 (*completely true for you*). Higher scores on the PBRS indicate less distorted cognitive schemas. Minor changes were made in the wording of 14 of the original PBRS items, such as replacing the words *rape* or *raped* with either *sexual abuse* or *sexually abused*. Eight subscales are represented, including safety, trust, power, esteem, intimacy, negative (rape/sexual abuse) beliefs, self-blame, and undoing.

To investigate the reliability and validity of the PBRS, Mechanic and Resick (1993) administered several self-report measures to three samples of rape victims (*N* = 114), including the Rape Aftermath Symptom Test (RAST) (Kilpatrick, 1988), Impact of Events Scale (IES) (Horowitz, Wilner, & Alvarez, 1979), Coping Strategies Inventory (CSI) (Tobin, Holroyd, Reynolds, & Wigal, 1989), and WAS. Test-retest reliability for the PBRS was .81. Nonsignificant correlations between the RAST and the PBRS indicated the PBRS detects more than global distress levels. Significant correlations between PBRS subscales and the IES Intrusion and Avoidance scales supported the ability of the PBRS to detect cognitive distortions. Correlations between the PBRS and the CSI indicated that the PBRS is able to ascertain the content of cognitive schemas, inasmuch as engagement strategies such as cognitive restructuring were related to healthier cognitive schemas and disengagement strategies were associated with more distorted beliefs. Correlations between the PBRS and the WAS suggested that the PBRS is a valid instrument for detecting distortions in the cognitive schemas of rape victims. The Mechanic and Resick (1993) study also indicated that the

PBRS can differentiate between rape victims with and without PTSD, lending further support to the measure's validity.

Wenninger and Ehlers (1998) conducted studies using the PBRS with both an American sample ($N = 72$) and a German sample ($N = 35$) to investigate the relationship between dysfunctional cognitions and adult psychological functioning among survivors of CSA. Results from both the American and German samples indicated that five of the eight PBRS subscales (safety, esteem, intimacy, self, and others; $p < .006$ for American sample, $p < .007$ for German sample) were significantly correlated with two symptom measures, the PTSD Symptom Scale, self-report version (PSS-SR) (Foa, Riggs, Dancu, & Rothbaum, 1993) and the Trauma Symptom Checklist (TSC-33) (Briere & Runtz, 1989). The trust subscale was also significantly correlated with symptom scales with the American sample, but only marginally so in the German sample. Results suggested that greater symptom scores were associated with more dysfunctional beliefs.

WAS. The WAS was developed for use with victims of past traumatic events such as death of a relative, incest, or rape. The respondent rates the 32 items on the scale from 1 (*strongly disagree*) to 6 (*strongly agree*). Higher scores on the WAS indicate a stronger belief. The WAS consists of eight subscales including benevolence of the world, benevolence of people, luck, justice, randomness, control, self-worth, and self-control. Three basic assumptions are proposed to be represented by the scale: benevolence of the world, meaningfulness of the world, and worthiness of self. For the three higher order scales, reliability coefficients ranged from .76 to .87. Reliability coefficients of the eight subscales ranged from .66 to .76. Results indicated that victims and nonvictims differed significantly in their assumptions concerning self-worth and benevolence of the world.

Ullman (1997a) conducted a study with a convenience sample of adult female sexual assault survivors ($N = 155$) who were sexually victimized in childhood, adulthood, or both. Questionnaires included items concerning attributions of blame, the search for meaning, and the WAS in its entirety. Alpha coefficients for the three scales of the WAS were .86 (benevolence of the world), .74 (meaningfulness of the world), and .87 (worthiness of self). Results suggested that external attributions of blame were associated with a decreased belief in self-worth, $r = -.18$, $p < .05$, and perceptions of the world as less benevolent, $r = -.20$, $p < .01$. In contrast, self-blame was associated with greater meaningfulness of the world, $r = .15$, $p < .05$. On the WAS, greater self-worth was associated with perceptions of the world as more benevolent, $r = .33$, $p < .001$ (one-tailed), and meaningful, $r = .18$, $p < .05$.

In Mechanic and Resick's (1993) study with rape victims, correlations were calculated between the PBRS and WAS. Results indicated that more positive assumptions about the benevolence of the world and self-worth on the WAS were associated with healthier beliefs on the PBRS. The highest correlation coefficients were found between the WAS scale, worthiness of self, and the PBRS esteem, $r = .70$, $p < .01$, and intimacy, $r = .66$, $p < .01$, subscales. Correlations were also high for the WAS scale, benevolence of the world, and the PBRS intimacy, $r = .56$, $p < .01$, and trust, $r = .52$, $p < .01$, subscales. PBRS subscales were not significantly associated with assumptions about the meaningfulness of the world on the WAS.

Procedures

A battery of assessment measures was administered by trained doctoral- and master's-level students as part of a larger CPT-SA treatment study (Chard, 2000). CPT-SA is an adaptation of Resick's cognitive processing therapy for rape victims (Resick & Schnicke, 1993) and consists of a combination of individual and group therapy occurring over the course of 17 weeks. Treatment focuses on alleviating symptoms commonly found among CSA survivors, including PTSD, depression, and disruptive cognitions.

After contacting the primary researcher, participants were informed that the study's purpose was to assess the effectiveness of a new treatment for PTSD and other symptoms for individuals having a CSA history. Requirements for participation included having at least one concrete memory of abuse, no new assault/abuse/trauma in the past 3 months, no current substance dependence, and current PTSD as determined by the CAPS-SX during the initial assessment. Individuals were asked to complete an initial assessment session designed to assist in identifying their current symptoms. Assessment sessions were conducted at the Center for Traumatic Stress Research on the campus of the University of Kentucky using a standardized administration format. Sessions lasted approximately 3 to 4 hours, and individuals were paid $50 for their participation. Several self-report measures were given to participants, including specific measures pertaining to cognitive distortions: the PBRS and the WAS.

Participants who met criteria for PTSD according to the CAPS-SX ($N = 72$) were randomly assigned to one of two conditions, treatment or minimal attention. Minimal attention subjects were offered treatment after a 17-week waiting period. Assessment sessions occurred prior to the beginning of therapy (or minimal attention condition). Seven participants did not meet criteria for PTSD during the initial assessment and were referred for treatment to other agencies after the assessment session was completed. All participants assessed were used for data analyses in this article to reflect a treatment-seeking sample.

RESULTS

Reliability of Cognitive Measures

Internal consistency coefficients were calculated for both the PBRS and the WAS subscales. Reliability coefficients for PBRS subscales ranged from .42 (beliefs) to .75 (self-blame). Reliability coefficients for the three higher order scales of the WAS were .62 (meaningfulness of the world), .76 (benevolence of the world), and .68 (worthiness of self). Subscales of the WAS ranged from .40 (justice) to .82 (self-worth). Reliability coefficients for both the PBRS and WAS are presented in Table 12.1.

Relationship Between PTSD Severity and Cognitive Distortions

Pearson correlation coefficients were calculated between the CAPS-SX severity scores and the PBRS and WAS subscales. A Bonferroni correction, $p = .003$, was applied for the most conservative criteria for significance. The strongest relationships were found between PTSD severity and the PBRS subscales of safety, trust, power, esteem, intimacy, and beliefs, $p = .003$. The undoing and self-blame subscales of the PBRS were also significantly related to PTSD severity, $p = .01$. As PTSD severity increased, scores on the PBRS subscales decreased, indicating more disrupted cognitive schemas. A significant negative correlation was found between the Worthiness of Self Scale of the WAS and PTSD severity, $r = -.422$, $p = .003$. The three subscales that constitute the Worthiness of Self Scale, self-worth, luck,

TABLE 12.1   Internal Consistency of Personal Beliefs and Reactions Scale (PBRS) and
World Assumptions Scale (WAS) Subscales

PBRS Subscale (N = 79)	Alpha Coefficient	WAS Subscale (N = 79)	Alpha Coefficient
Safety	.66	Higher-order scales	
Trust	.68	Benevolence of the world	.76
Power	.51	Meaningfulness of the world	.62
Esteem	.71	Worthiness of self	.68
Intimacy	.60	Subscales	
Beliefs	.42	Justice	.40
Undoing	.58	Self-control	.71
Self-blame	.75	Control	.66
		Luck	.78
		Randomness	.54
		Benevolence of the world	.71
		Benevolence of people	.60
		Self-worth	.82

and self-control, were also significant (self-worth and luck, $p = .003$; self-control, $p < .05$, two-tailed). None of the other higher order scales or subscales were significantly related to PTSD severity. Pearson correlation coefficients are shown in Table 12.2.

Prediction of PTSD Severity Based on Cognitive Measures

A linear regression was performed to test whether pretreatment cognitive distortions, represented by the eight subscales of the PBRS and the three higher order scales of the WAS, could predict pretreatment PTSD severity. Subscales of the PBRS and WAS that were significantly correlated to PTSD severity were entered into a regression analysis. No significant relationship was found between WAS subscales and PTSD severity. However, the subscales of beliefs, $p = .011$, safety, $p = .005$, and power, $p = .000$, on the PBRS predicted PTSD severity. A stepwise regression was performed to obtain the final model, including the three PBRS subscales, beliefs, safety, and power, $F(3, 74) = 21.44$, $p = .000$, adjusted $R^2 = .44$. Beta values for each factor are included in Table 12.3.

Prediction of Cognitive Distortions From Event Characteristics

Regression analyses were used to test whether event characteristics (e.g., whether penetration occurred or identity of the perpetrator) could predict pre-treatment cognitive distortions. Subscales of the PBRS and WAS that were significantly correlated to event characteristics were entered into regression analyses. Only one event characteristic (penetration) was significantly correlated with any PBRS (trust and power) or WAS (worthiness of self) subscale. Penetration was used to predict each of these distortion subscales individually. Penetration predicted 19% of the variance in the Worthiness of Self subscale of the WAS, $F(1, 78) = 18.68$, $p = .000$, adjusted $R^2 = .19$. Twelve percent of the variance on the trust

TABLE 12.2   Pearson Correlation Coefficients Between Personal Beliefs and Reactions Scale (PBRS), World Assumptions Scale (WAS), and Clinician Administered Post-Traumatic Stress Disorder Scale (CAPS-SX) Total Scores

PBRS Subscale (N = 79)	CAPS-SX	WAS Subscale (N = 79)	CAPS-SX
Safety	−.550***	Higher-order scales	
Trust	−.536***	Benevolence of the world	−.071
Power	−.586***	Meaningfulness of the world	−.009
Esteem	−.486***	Worthiness of self	−.429***
Intimacy	−.462***	Subscales	
Beliefs	−.364***	Justice	−.034
Undoing	−.322**	Self-control	−.283*
Self-blame	−.309**	Control	−.018
		Luck	−.347***
		Randomness	−.030
		Benevolence of people	.033
		Benevolence of the world	−.138
		Self-worth	−.346***

*$p \leq .05$; **$p \leq .01$; ***$p \leq .003$.

TABLE 12.3   Prediction of Post-Traumatic Stress Disorder From Cognitive Distortions (N = 79)

	Beta	p
Personal Beliefs and Reactions Scale subscale		
Beliefs	−.227	.011
Safety	−.289	.005
Power	−.402	.000
Adjusted R^2	.44	

subscale of the PBRS was explained by the penetration predictor, $F(1, 78) = 11.74$, $p = .001$, adjusted $R^2 = .12$. Penetration predicted 20% of the variance on the power subscale of the PBRS, $F(1, 78) = 20.72$, $p = .000$, adjusted $R^2 = .20$.

Relationship Between Cognitive Measures

Pearson correlation coefficients were calculated to determine the relationship between the PBRS subscales and the three higher order WAS scales. A Bonferroni correction, $p = .005$, was used for the most conservative significance criteria. Beliefs about worthiness

TABLE 12.4   Pearson Correlation Coefficients Between Personal Beliefs and Reactions
Scale (PBRS) and the World Assumptions Scale (WAS)

| PBRS Subscale (N = 79) | WAS Scale (N = 79) | | |
	Benevolence of the World	Meaningfulness of the World	Self-Worth
Safety	.131	.021	.390***
Trust	.325**	.045	.653***
Power	.182	.029	.499***
Esteem	.208	.002	.582***
Intimacy	.196	.007	.394***
Beliefs	.003	−.045	.162
Undoing	−.020	−.094	.164
Self-blame	−.034	−.002	.226*

$*p \le .05$; $**p \le .01$; $***p \le .005$.

of self (WAS) were significantly associated with the PBRS subscales of safety, trust, power, esteem, and intimacy, $p = .005$. As beliefs in these five areas of the PBRS became less distorted, positive assumptions about self-worth on the WAS increased. A significant correlation was found between the WAS benevolence of the world scale and the PBRS trust subscale, $p = .01$, two-tailed. Correlations between the PBRS subscales and the WAS scales are presented in Table 12.4.

DISCUSSION

The results indicated that PTSD symptoms increased with a higher number of cognitive distortions. The CSA survivors with more severe PTSD levels had more distortions in all areas included on the PBRS and also had more distorted beliefs about self-worth on the WAS. Stronger associations were indicated by regression analyses, which suggested that certain PBRS subscales and higher order WAS scales can predict PTSD severity. Specifically, the beliefs, safety, and trust subscales of the PBRS predicted PTSD severity in this treatment-seeking sample. These results also support data on the PBRS by Mechanic and Resick (1993) and Wenninger and Ehlers (1998), both indicating that the level of cognitive disruptions affects the severity of PTSD symptoms among rape and sexual abuse survivors. Thus, survivors' current interpretations of the abuse seem to play a major role in the severity of PTSD symptoms experienced. Although the current study focused only on cognitions in relation to PTSD, other factors also have been found to have an effect on PTSD severity, such as dissociation at the time of the abuse (Johnson, Pike, & Chard, in press) and coping strategies used by survivors (Blount, Sheahan, Johnson, & Chard, in press). In addition, only one characteristic of the abuse, whether penetration occurred, appears to have some effect on the development of cognitive distortions. In this sample, the survivor's beliefs about power, trust, and self-worth were more disruptive if penetration occurred. The current findings regarding participants' beliefs about the abuse and the impact of abuse characteristics on disruptive cognitions, combined with results from factors such as dissociation and coping strategies, are critical to note in applications of cognitive therapy to the alleviation of PTSD.

The PBRS and WAS contributed new information about the beliefs held by CSA survivors, information that is particularly useful to any treatment using cognitive therapy. Important to the psychological health of the abuse survivor is the finding that healthier beliefs concerning five of the cognitive areas on the PBRS (safety, trust, power, esteem, and intimacy) appeared to be moderately associated with more positive beliefs about worthiness of the self on the WAS. Because these five areas were identical to those proposed by McCann et al. (1988) for trauma victims, the importance of having treatment address these cognitive domains is reinforced by the present data. The results are similar to data from Mechanic and Resick (1993) with rape victims, wherein seven PBRS subscales were significantly correlated with worthiness of self on the WAS. Although the magnitude of the correlations between self-worth and PBRS subscales was smaller than that indicated by Mechanic and Resick, significance levels were as high as those found with rape survivors.

However, unlike Mechanic and Resick's (1993) findings that seven PBRS subscales were associated with the benevolence of the world assumption on the WAS, only one PBRS subscale, trust, was associated with this assumption in the present sample. Combined with the data concerning self-worth, this result is interesting in that it suggests some differences between the beliefs of rape victims versus sexual abuse survivors. Survivors of CSA appear to focus more on self-attributions in the processing of the abuse, as indicated by the correlations between McCann et al.'s (1988) five areas of cognitive distortions represented on the PBRS and self-worth on the WAS. With rape survivors, on the other hand, distortions seem to be distributed between assumptions formed about the world and the self. Thus, with sexual abuse survivors, it would seem of greater benefit to focus more of therapy on the survivor's disruptive cognitions related to the self and self-blame and less on disruptive schemas about the world and others.

The reliability coefficients obtained for some of the PBRS and WAS subscales were relatively low in this study. Particularly low reliability coefficients were found for the justice and randomness subscales on the WAS as well as the beliefs and power subscales of the PBRS. Reliability may have been lowered because some subscales contained a small number of items (eight or fewer). The sample size may also have affected the reliability of the measures. However, based on recent research (Wenninger & Ehlers, 1998) and results from the present study, the PBRS does seem capable of detecting cognitive distortions of sexual abuse survivors.

The results of this study suggest several directions for future research. Because PTSD symptoms were shown to increase with an increasing amount of cognitive distortions, decreasing the number of cognitive distortions may help to decrease PTSD symptoms and possibly alleviate some of the distress experienced. This possibility highlights the need to continue to focus on treatment of both PTSD symptoms and the cognitive processing of the abuse. Future research should also work to further establish the PBRS and WAS with sexual abuse survivors inasmuch as reliability coefficients with this sample were moderate overall. Continued research on the correlations between the PBRS and WAS with CSA survivors using a larger sample is recommended to determine whether the results obtained were simply an artifact of the population used in the present study or whether a distinct cognitive difference exists between rape victims and survivors of sexual abuse. Also, in light of the regression findings, research using a larger sample to examine other predictors of PTSD severity along with the cognitive predictors should be conducted.

In summary, results from the present study indicate that the severity of PTSD symptoms correlates with the amount of cognitive distortions found among adult survivors of CSA. More specifically, as the number of cognitive distortions on the PBRS and WAS increases, severity of PTSD symptoms increases as well. Overall, moderate levels of internal consistency were found for both PBRS and WAS subscales with this population.

13

The Self-Reported Behaviors
of Juvenile Sexual Offenders

STACEY C. ZOLONDEK

Behavioral Medicine Institute of Atlanta and Emory University

GENE G. ABEL

*Behavioral Medicine Institute of Atlanta, Emory University,
and Morehouse School of Medicine*

WILLIAM F. NORTHEY, JR.

American Association for Marriage and Family Therapy

ALAN D. JORDAN

Behavioral Medicine Institute of Atlanta

Sexually abusive behavior has traditionally been viewed as perpetrated exclusively by adult men. However, more recent crime statistics and research on sexual offenses have consistently shown that this is not the case, and in the past 15 years, sexual abuse perpetrated by juvenile sexual offenders (JSOs) has received increased attention. Conservative estimates indicate that between 15% and 20% of all sexual offenses are committed by youth younger than 18, and as many as 50% of all molestations may be committed by youth younger than 18 (Davis & Leitenberg, 1987; Furby, Weinrott, & Blackshaw, 1989). Furthermore, many adult sex offenders began their offending as juveniles (Abel, Mittelman, & Becker, 1985).

The only fairly definitive conclusion that can be drawn to date is that JSOs are a very heterogeneous group. As Weinrott (1996) noted, "There is great variation in victim characteristics, degree of force, chronicity, variety of sexual outlets (i.e., other paraphilias), arousal profiles, and motivation and intent" (p. 20). Numerous studies and literature reviews have summarized the data about JSOs (Davis & Leitenberg, 1987; Ryan, Miyoshi, Metzner, Krugman, & Fryer, 1996; Vizard, Monck, & Misch, 1995; Weinrott, 1996), and

This article first appeared in *Journal of Interpersonal Violence*, Vol. 16 No. 1, January 2001, pp. 73-85. Copyright © 2001 Sage Publications, Inc. Used with permission.

findings have indicated that often, multiple paraphilias are demonstrated by the same individual, providing evidence that sexually exploitative behaviors may be contained within a single continuum (Abel & Osborn, 1992; Ryan, 1997). Unfortunately, this continuum, although potentially useful, is generally reduced to categorization of offenses into hands-off, hands-on, and pedophilic offenses (Becker, Harris, & Sales, 1993). A thorough description of juveniles' sexual offenses is necessary to paint a more complete picture of who these juveniles are and what they are doing.

Molestation of children is the highest frequency offense reported in samples of JSOs, and JSOs who molest children report the highest number of victims (Davis & Leitenberg, 1987; Ryan et al., 1996; Weinrott, 1996). Few studies report data on other sexual offenses perpetrated by JSOs. This may be due to the fact that other sexual offenses rarely result in arrests compared to hands-on offenses (Abel et al., 1987). Ryan et al. (1996) did find that between 35% and 50% of hands-off JSOs had also sexually abused a child.

The modal age of offenders reported in studies tends to be 14 to 15 years, with a first offense most likely to occur at age 13 or 14. However, there is some evidence indicating that about 25% of JSO samples had engaged in sexually abusive behaviors before age 12 (Metzner & Ryan, 1995; Ryan et al., 1996; Weinrott, 1996). In his review of the JSO literature, Weinrott (1996) concluded that it is rare for juvenile child molesters to have both male and female victims. Victims are most likely to be female acquaintances or siblings; rarely are they strangers. In general, the victims of JSOs are at least acquainted with the perpetrator. Reports consistently indicate that more than 50% of perpetrators know their victim, and in cases of child molestation, 75% of victims were either related to or acquaintances of the perpetrator (Davis & Leitenberg, 1987). Ryan et al. (1996) reported that almost 40% of the JSOs in their national sample were blood relatives of the victims, and that sexual victimization of strangers only accounted for 6% of the cases.

Most offenses committed by JSOs are verbally coercive rather than overtly aggressive or violent (Ryan et al., 1996; Weinrott, 1996), and the intensity of the coercion may increase with the age of the victim (Becker, Cunningham-Rathner, & Kaplan, 1986). Finkelhor and Dziuba-Leatherman (1994) found that only a small fraction of JSOs commit crimes that result in physical injury, and generally no more force is used than is necessary to complete the act. Although about one third of offenders blame the victim for their offense, most offenders report using some coercion, ranging from bribes and promises to some level of force to gain compliance (Metzner & Ryan, 1995). Prevalence of conduct disorder is reportedly high among juvenile child molesters. Whereas serious delinquency, substance abuse problems, and interpersonal aggression are relatively uncommon, some researchers have reported that general delinquent behavior is often quite common pre- and post-adjudication for a sexual offense. For example, nonsexual criminal activity has been reported by 29% to nearly two thirds (Ryan et al., 1996) of JSOs. Furthermore, there is a significantly greater chance that JSOs will engage in a nonsexual offense after treatment than a sexual offense (Bourduin, Henggeler, Blaske, & Stein, 1990; Brannon & Troyer, 1991; Davis & Leitenberg, 1987; Furby et al., 1989; Kahn & Lafond, 1988). Many JSOs have been exposed to neglect, abuse, family violence, and early sexualization. Ryan et al. (1996) indicated that 42% of their sample reported physical abuse, 39% sexual abuse, 26% neglect, and 63% had been witness to some form of family violence. Similar findings have been found by other researchers (Awad & Saunders, 1991; Hunter & Santos, 1990; Kahn & Lafond, 1988).

In a recent review of the literature on JSOs, Vizard et al. (1995) concluded that "there is a long way to go before we fully understand or effectively meet the needs of these young people" (p. 749). Unfortunately, much of what is known about JSOs comes from clinical writings and from studies using small samples of offenders, which calls into question their representativeness. Furthermore, some studies use retrospective information reported by adult sexual offenders. It is unknown whether the information reported by youth differs from that given by adult offenders reporting about their youth. Few studies replicate measures used by others and instead rely predominantly on self-report or subjective clinical impressions, rarely using standardized instrumentation. The largest study to date described a sample of 1,600 JSOs. Ryan et al. (1996) described the findings of the National Adolescent Perpetrator Network (NAPN), which had requested that its members complete a standard data collection instrument in regard to characteristics of their JSOs. Because decisions about who to include were left to program administrators, it is difficult to assess the representativeness of this sample. The NAPN questionnaire was completed by clinicians rather than by the JSOs themselves, and criteria for eliciting reports of JSOs' behavior were not standardized. Finally, literature rarely differentiates juveniles' sexual behaviors into the specific categories of sexual offenses found in adult samples.

The purpose of the present study is to describe a national sample of 485 male JSOs using a standardized protocol. To date, there are no studies of JSOs that use self-report data from a sample this large. This study differs from Ryan et al. (1996) in that it uses a self-report, paper-and-pencil instrument rather than clinician report. The literature suggests that adolescents report more deviant behaviors when paper-and-pencil assessments are used than during face-to-face interviews (Erdman, Klein, & Greist, 1985; Ochs, Meana, Pare, Mah, & Binik, 1994; Weinrott & Saylor, 1991). The data from JSOs are also compared to adult sexual offender data. Although there is some evidence that once caught, juveniles are more likely to admit to their offenses than are adults, this assumption may be premature. Little is known about the truthfulness of information collected from JSOs and the effect that social desirability has on responding. This study also examines the utility of incorporating a social desirability scale into measures of juvenile sexual behavior by exploring possible differences in reporting between boys high and low in social desirability.

We predict that JSOs undergoing this assessment will report a variety of sexual offenses and that their offenses will be similar to those of adult sexual offenders. Furthermore, we expect that the frequency of committing the reported sexual behaviors will be high and that JSOs will report engaging in their reported behavior several times. It is expected that juveniles who score higher on a social desirability measure will report less engagement in sexual offenses and that these JSOs will have friends who engage in similar levels of nonsexual antisocial behaviors.

METHOD

Participants

Participants in this study were 485 boys between the ages of 11 and 17 who were seeking either evaluation or treatment for possible sexually deviant behaviors and interests at several locations in 29 of the United States and in Canada. Of the 485 participants, 42.7%

were assessed in sites in the Southeast, 19.4% were assessed in sites in the Southwest, 9.3% were assessed in sites in the Midwest, 9.1% were assessed in sites in the Northwest, 8.5% were assessed at sites in the Northeast, 4.8% were assessed in sites in Hawaii, 1.8% were assessed in sites in Canada, and 5.4% were assessed elsewhere. Forty-eight percent reported that they were assessed in treatment centers, 35.7% reported that they completed the assessment in their clinician's office, 3.7% reported that they completed the questionnaire in a detention center or jail, 3% indicated that they were being assessed because they had been the victims of sexual abuse, and 8.8% reported that they were filling out the questionnaire for other reasons. These categories were not mutually exclusive.

In this sample, 56.3% of the boys were Caucasian, 21.5% were African American, 9.8% were Hispanic, 3.8% were American Indian, 0.8% were Asian, and 7.6% were of another racial group. Participants reported that 2.5% had completed high school, 27.4% had completed some high school, 17.3% had completed junior high school through the ninth grade, 38.6% had completed the seventh or eighth grade, and 12.8% had only completed grade school. Most of the JSOs (60.2%) reported that their parents owned their homes. The JSOs in this sample mostly lived in small homes; 60.3% had between 1 and 5 rooms in their home, 28.2% had 6 to 10 rooms in their home, and only 6.6% had more than 10 rooms in their homes. According to their reports, 28% of the adults that the JSOs lived with engaged in some type of skilled labor (carpenter, painter, fireman, clerk, and skilled worker) for a living, 24.5% made a living through unskilled labor (factory, gas station, waitress, and house cleaning), 17.3% of the adults they lived with made a living as professionals (doctor, lawyer, accountant, teacher, and nurse), 10.3% owned their own businesses, 12% were unemployed and/or on welfare, and 2.1% had military occupations.

Procedure

As part of the clinical assessment, the boys completed a standard self-report questionnaire (Abel, 1995). This questionnaire comprises four sections. The first section consists of 58 questions assessing demographics, nondeviant sexual experiences, delinquent behaviors, and drug use. Part 2 contains questions on 13 sexual behaviors, including exhibitionism, fetishism, voyeurism, bestiality, obscene phone calls, masochism, child molestation, unwanted touching, transvestitism, sadism, telephone sex, use of pornography, and transsexualism. Unwanted touching included both frottage and rape as testing has indicated that many JSOs do not view their hands-on behaviors as rape. Part 3 contains questions on sexual victimization of the participant, and Part 4 includes various vignettes describing sexual activities that a juvenile may endorse as sexually arousing to him and a set of questions dealing with issues of social desirability. The 20 social desirability questions measure the juvenile's willingness to admit to violations of common social mores and includes questions such as: I would never to lie to others just to get what I want, I have not lied about my feelings for someone in order to have sex with them, Sometimes I have sex with a partner just for my own pleasure, I seldom insist on getting my own way, and I always admit when I am wrong. The score can range from 0 to 100, with 100 indicating that all questions were answered in a socially desirable way. This scale displays internal consistency; Cronbach's alpha = .81, and item-to-total correlations range from .24 to .57.

The JSOs spent, on average, 60.9 (SD = 26.5) minutes completing the questionnaire.

TABLE 13.1 Percentage of Juvenile Sexual Offenders Engaging in Behaviors

Behavior	Percentage Reporting	Age of Onset	Number of Victims	Number of Acts
Exhibitionism	11.5	11.4	6.0	11.1
Fetishism	26.4	10.8	NA	46.0
Voyeurism	17.0	11.0	8.8	16.9
Zoophilia	5.0	10.8	Unknown	11.6
Obscene phone calls	16.4	12.3	10.0	Unknown
Masochism	1.9	9.7	NA	40.9
Child molestation	60.8	11.9	4.2	11.1
Unwanted rubbing/touching	17.0	11.7	9.1	15.4
Sadism	2.1	11.0	2.4	11.2
Transvestism	4.6	11.5	NA	9.4[a]
Phone sex	15.4	12.4	Unknown	11.7
Pornography	31.6	11.4	NA	22.9
Transsexualism	3.3	10.1	NA	NA

a. Mean number of times per month.

RESULTS

Table 13.1 shows the percentage of JSOs who reported engaging in various paraphilic behaviors, age of onset of these behaviors, mean number of victims, and the mean number of times that they engaged in the behaviors. The percentage of JSOs engaging in sexual behaviors differed from those self-reported by 5,063 adult men on a similar questionnaire (Abel & Osborn, in press). Juveniles reported higher frequencies than adults for fetishism (26.4% vs. 11.8%, $\chi^2 = 84.5, p < .001$), obscene phone calls (16.4% vs. 6.3%, $\chi^2 = 71.2, p < .001$), child molestation (60.8% vs. 34.4%, $\chi^2 = 130.7, p < .001$), and phone sex (15.4% vs. 5.1%, $\chi^2 = 77.3, p < .001$). Fewer juveniles than adults reported engaging in zoophilia (5.0% vs. 8.4%, $\chi^2 = 5.8, p = .016$), and frequencies of exhibitionism, voyeurism, masochism, sadism, use of pornography, transsexualism, and transvestitism did not differ for juveniles and adults.

The mean sum of social desirability items was 48.0 ($SD = 21.4$). Juveniles were divided based on whether they scored low (below 35), medium (between 35 and 54), or high (above 54) on social desirability. Percentage of JSOs engaging in paraphilic behaviors was calculated for JSOs falling into each of the three levels of social desirability. Participants who were low in social desirability reported a greater frequency of participation in all paraphilic behaviors. As indicated in Table 13.2, there were statistically significant differences in paraphilic behaviors between groups. Participants with low social desirability scores reported engaging in more paraphilic behaviors, across all categories of behavior, than those with medium social desirability scores, and those with medium social desirability scores reported higher frequencies of paraphilic behaviors than those who were high in social desirability.

Table 13.3 shows the frequency that JSOs report engaging in a variety of anti-social behaviors and the frequencies at which they report their friends engaging in antisocial behaviors. JSOs indicated that they engage in delinquent behaviors at higher frequencies than

TABLE 13.2   Self-Reported Sexual Behaviors Based on Social Desirability

Behavior	Level of Social Desirability			
	Percentage Low	Percentage Medium	Percentage High	Chi-Square
Exhibitionism	30.2	8.5	8.3	10.9*
Fetishism	33.9	30.0	16.0	13.6**
Voyeurism	25.7	20.0	8.9	14.6**
Zoophilia	12.8	4.6	0.6	17.9**
Obscene phone calls	30.3	16.9	7.1	25.9**
Masochism	5.5	0.8	0.6	9.7*
Child molestation	72.5	62.3	52.7	10.9*
Unwanted rubbing/touching	28.4	16.9	9.5	22.5**
Sadism	6.4	0.8	0.6	183.1**
Transvestism	7.3	3.1	3.0	3.7
Phone sex	31.2	15.4	8.9	23.8**
Pornography	52.3	27.7	21.9	29.7**
Transsexualism	6.4	3.1	2.4	106.4**

$*p \le .01; **p \le .001.$

their peers do. Furthermore, Table 13.4 shows that JSOs do not report engaging in high rates of substance use. With the exception of alcohol and marijuana, fewer than 10% of the JSOs reported that they had tried drugs or that they used drugs more than 10 times. Slightly more than half of the JSOs had never tried marijuana, and 34% reported never trying alcohol.

Juveniles were asked to self-report on who they were accused of victimizing; 8% had been blamed for touching an adult woman, 2% an adult man, 13% a girl the same age or older, 7% a boy the same age or older, 14% a girl 1 or 2 years younger, 8% a boy 1 or 2 years younger, 15% a girl 3 or 4 years younger, 10% a boy 3 or 4 years younger, 28% a much younger girl (5 or more years younger), 24% a much younger boy (5 or more years younger), and 19% had not been blamed for touching another person. These percentages may add up to more than 100, as many JSOs were accused of more than one offense; therefore, these categories were not mutually exclusive.

Participants who reported molesting a child ($n = 292$) were also asked to report the degree of coercion and force used to gain compliance in sexual activities with a much younger child (5 or more years younger than the perpetrator) and to indicate all responses that applied; 14% claimed that the activity was initiated by the child; 34.9% reported that activity was mutual; 24.3% promised the child candy, money, a toy, and so on; 29.8% tricked the child; 10.3% threatened the child; 5.1% roughed up the child a bit; 4.1% roughed up the child a lot; and 0.2% reported that the child died.

Of those who had molested a child, 43.2% of the JSOs indicated offending against a younger sibling, 30.1% against another family member, 33.6% against a non-family member whom they knew, and 7.5% against a foster sibling. Only 8.2% of the sample reported offending against a stranger.

TABLE 13.3 Percentage of Juvenile Sex Offenders (JSOs) and Their Friends Who Engage in Antisocial Behaviors

Behavior	Percentage Reporting Behaviors		Chi-Square
	JSOs	Friends	
Fighting	69.9	43.7	68.14**
Get arrested	54.4	26.8	77.08**
Kicked out of school	37.5	29.9	6.34*
Stealing	53.6	30.5	53.23**
Robbing people	17.7	12.0	6.20*
Beat up people	33.3	24.3	9.32**
Carry knives and guns	27.0	21.4	4.03*
Belong to gangs	17.1	20.0	2.66
Quit school	10.5	18.1	11.50**
Do unwanted sexual touching	42.7	8.2	146.54**
None of the above	15.1	33.6	45.49**

$*p \leq .01; *p \leq .001.$

TABLE 13.4 Reported Substance Abuse of Juvenile Sexual Offenders

Substance	Frequency of Substance Use		
	Percentage Not at All	Percentage Some Use	Percentage More Than 10 Times
Alcohol	34.3	36.0	29.7
Marijuana	51.8	21.0	25.4
Barbituates	91.9	5.8	2.3
Cocaine	90.9	6.5	2.6
Narcotics	94.6	3.6	1.7
Hallucinogens	87.4	7.7	4.7
Amphetamines	90.0	6.6	3.4

Juveniles were asked to indicate whether they had been blamed for molesting a child and how well the characteristics of the actual offense matched what they had been blamed for. Overall, 27.4% of the JSOs who had been blamed for molesting a child reported that the characteristics of the offense were exactly as the child had reported. However, 13.2% reported that they were blamed but had not committed the offense or been near the child; 16.7% reported they were blamed, had been near the child, but did not commit the offense; 11.1% reported they were blamed but the child had wanted the sexual activity to occur; 17.5% reported they been blamed but had actually done less than the child reported; and 5.6% reported that they had been blamed but had touched the child more than the child reported.

Of the 27.6% (*n* = 134) of JSOs who had never been blamed for molesting a much younger child, 41.5% reported that they had in fact molested a much younger child. The social desirability scores of the unblamed JSOs who reported molesting a child did not differ from those who did not report molesting a child.

During Parts 1 and 4 of the questionnaire, participants were asked to indicate how honest they had been in answering the questions. When asked in Part 1, 89.2% reported that they had been absolutely honest, 9.1% reported fairly honest, and 1.5% reported that they had not been very honest. When completing Part 4, 83.8% reported that they had been absolutely honest, 14.2% reported fairly honest, and 1.6% reported they had not been very honest. These reports differed slightly based on social desirability; participants with high social desirability scores reported more honesty in responding when questioned at the end of the questionnaire. When first questioned, 85.5% of boys with low social desirability, 90% of boys with medium social desirability scores, and 91.1% of boys with high social desirability scores reported total honesty in responding. When questioned at the end of the questionnaire, 78% low social desirability, 76.9% medium social desirability, and 85.8% high social desirability reported total honesty in responding.

DISCUSSION

In this study, the self-reported characteristics of a large sample of adolescent sex offenders from throughout the United States were obtained using a standardized evaluation. In this sample, JSOs reported that with the exception of quitting school and belonging to gangs, they were engaging in various delinquent behaviors more frequently than were their friends. However, many of the JSOs did report having peers who engaged in a variety of delinquent behaviors. Substance use and abuse was not high. Less than a third of the sample used marijuana or alcohol, and very few had experimented with other substances. Juvenile sexual offending could be related to an overall antisocial lifestyle; however, substance abuse does not appear to play a major role.

Molestation of children was the most commonly reported offense, endorsed by more than 60% of the sample. More than 30% of the sample reported using pornography, more than a quarter of the sample reported fetishism, and between 10% and 20% reported engaging in voyeurism, obscene phone calls, unwanted rubbing or touching, and phone sex. Zoophilia, masochism, sadism, transvestitism, and transsexualism were less common; each was reported by fewer than 5% of the sample. The proportion of juveniles engaging in fetishism, obscene phone calls, child molestation, and phone sex was higher than that of adults. Hands-off offenses including fetishism, voyeurism, and pornography use had a higher mean number of acts than hands-on offenses such as child molestation and unwanted rubbing and touching. In this sample, child-molesting juveniles had fewer victims than JSOs engaging in voyeurism, exhibitionism, and unwanted rubbing or touching.

Although participants overwhelmingly reported that they had been honest in their responding to the items on the questionnaire, participants who demonstrated greater concern with reporting socially desirable responses also reported engaging in fewer paraphilic behaviors. In addition, more participants with high social desirability scores reported total honesty. This may be an example of giving a socially desirable response. In studying sexual offenders, this highlights the importance of assessing and controlling for social desirability. Self-reports of honesty in responding may be confounded by a desire to provide socially desirable responses and may not provide an accurate measure of how honest JSOs actually are. Because of socially desirable responding, self-report data obtained from juveniles are probably minimal values. JSOs who respond in ways that they perceive as socially desirable on the social desirability scale may also be responding to other questions in this manner, and our data indicate that they are less likely to admit to engaging in paraphilic behaviors. When assessing JSOs, it is crucial to perform an assessment that takes into account socially desirable responding and denying or minimalizing behaviors. Results of studies with juvenile offenders must be anchored to a measure of social desirability, or researchers must approach JSOs in such a way that they are able to obtain more accuracy in collection of data, such as using a certificate of confidentiality, which has been shown to increase reporting of paraphilic behaviors in adult samples (Abel et al., 1987).

Molestation of children tends to involve younger siblings or known nonfamily members, and JSOs tend to coerce or trick rather than threaten or rough up the child. This indicates that JSOs select victims who are easily accessible and with whom they have a relationship. Whereas most of the JSOs in this sample had molested children, more than a quarter of the JSOs had not been blamed for molesting a child, and 20% percent of the boys in the sample had never been blamed for a hands-on offense. However, of the quarter that had not been blamed for molesting a child, 42% indicated that they had in fact molested a child. Many JSOs engage in behaviors that go undetected. Therefore, to understand the full nature of the JSOs' presenting problem, it is important to assess JSOs for paraphilic behaviors other than their index offenses.

The average age of onset of the various behaviors ranged from 9.7 to 12.4 years, which is considerably younger than what is reported (Abel et al., 1985; Weinrott, 1996). However, previous studies have relied heavily on retrospective reports of adult offenders. Therefore, it is possible that either the adolescents are beginning their sexual offending careers earlier, adult offenders may not accurately recall the age at which they began their sexually abusive behavior, or some combination of both. In either instance, the current study highlights the importance of gathering information from juveniles as soon as they are identified. On identification, JSOs are likely to have committed several offenses with several victims. When investigating age of onset of sexual behaviors, clinicians and researchers must be careful to go back to preadolescent years. Deviant sexual patterns exhibited in preadolescent boys must be taken seriously to prevent later sexual offending and to understand the etiology of paraphilic behavior.

14

Misuse of the Internet by Pedophiles

Implications for Law Enforcement and Probation Practice

KEITH F. DURKIN

McNeese State University

INTRODUCTION

Child sexual abuse is widely recognized as an especially serious problem in the United States. A voluminous body of scientific literature indicates that children who are sexually molested suffer a variety of physical, psychological, and social damage because of their victimization (see Browne & Finkelhor, 1986; Burgess & Lottes, 1988; Conte & Berliner, 1988; Lurigio, Jones, & Smith, 1995). Adults who sexually abuse children are considered to be among the most serious deviants in our society. Consequently, they often come to the attention of criminal justice agencies. Because of prison overcrowding, probation is a common punishment for child sex abusers. However, the supervision of individuals who have been convicted of sexually abusing children poses serious challenges to probation departments since these individuals are difficult to manage and frequently recidivate (Lurigio et al., 1995). Recent developments involving the misuse of the Internet by pedophiles—adult males whose sexual preference is for children[1]—further complicate this already problematic situation.

Advances in telecommunication technology have made possible the existence of vast computer networks collectively referred to as the Internet or the "information superhighway." An estimated 30 to 40 million people in more than 160 nations have access to the Internet (Elmer-Dewitt, 1995). This global network consists of tens of thousands of interconnected computer networks, including those at academic, government, and business facilities, as well as commercial on-line services (e.g., America On-Line, Prodigy, and Compuserve) and private bulletin board systems. There appear to be four ways in which pedophiles are misusing the Internet: to traffic child pornography, to locate children to molest, to engage in inappropriate sexual communication with children, and to communicate with other pedophiles.

Author's Note: This article first appeared in *Federal Probation*, Vol. 61 (Sept. 1997), pp. 14-18.

The abuse of the Internet by pedophiles has received a modest amount of attention lately. Recent criminal investigations have led to the arrest of numerous pedophiles for trafficking child pornography and soliciting sex from children on-line. For example, in September 1995, as part of a law enforcement operation dubbed "Innocent Images," FBI agents arrested more than a dozen people for transmitting child pornography and soliciting children for sexual purposes via America On-Line, the nation's largest commercial service provider. The impetus for this investigation was the case of a missing 10-year-old Maryland boy who was lured from his home by on-line pedophiles (Marshall, 1995). In a statement about this investigation, Attorney General Janet Reno said, "We are not going to let exciting new technology be misused to exploit and injure children" (Swisher, 1995, p. A1).

The purpose of this article is to document the ways in which the Internet is being misused by pedophiles. Special consideration is afforded to the implications that these deviant activities have for law enforcement and probation practice. In a recent article, Davis, McShane, and Williams (1995) called attention to the need to control the computer access of child sexual abusers who are on probation. Although these authors briefly mentioned a few of the ways in which pedophiles are misusing computer technology, their primary focus was on the development of valid conditions of probation to limit or prohibit computer access for these offenders. The information presented here reinforces the need to restrict the computer access of convicted child sexual abusers who are on probation. An adequate understanding of the ways in which pedophiles can misuse the Internet certainly will be useful to probation officers in supervising pedophiles and to law enforcement personnel in developing investigative strategies to combat the problem.

PEDOPHILES ON THE INTERNET

One of the primary ways in which pedophiles are misusing the Internet is to exchange child pornography. Traditionally, pedophiles would traffic this material via clandestine newsletters or other tightly controlled exchange networks (Carter, 1995). Now pornographic pictures can be transmitted through computer networks. For instance, in a 1993 law enforcement effort called "Operation Long Arm," federal agents served over 30 warrants against individuals who were using computer networks to import illegal child pornography from Denmark (Durkin & Bryant, 1995). Pedophiles also can obtain text stories with pedophiliac themes from the Internet. Although such textual descriptions of children participating in various types of sexual activities are not illegal, pedophiles collect these narratives for prurient purposes (Lanning, 1992). These stories are fairly common on the Internet. One study estimated that they comprised approximately 10 percent of the content of one of the major Internet newsgroups dedicated to "erotica" (Williams & McShane, 1995).

A trend of particular concern is pedophiles' use of the Internet to locate children to molest. One prosecuting attorney remarked that "instead of hanging around the playground looking for the loneliest kid, potential child molesters simply have to log on" (Kantrowitz, King, & Rosenberg, 1994, p. 40). Through the "chat rooms" available on many commercial Internet services, some pedophiles seek to contact youngsters to arrange meetings for sexual purposes.[2] Consequently, the number of reports of children being molested by pedophiles they met via the Internet is growing. Recently, "a number of people have been arrested for traveling across state lines to meet undercover agents posing as minors they had met on-line" (Swisher, 1995, p. A13).

Another way in which pedophiles are misusing the Internet is to engage in inappropriate sexual communication with children. The anonymity of the Internet affords a pedophile the ability to misrepresent his identity. He can assume the identity of a young person and attempt to engage in sexually explicit on-line discussions with youngsters that he meets in computer chat rooms. Moreover, there also have been reports of children who use the Internet receiving unsolicited computer files containing pornographic pictures that were sent to them by adult users (Rubenstein, 1996).

Pedophiles also can use the Internet to correspond with each other. Regarding this communicative potential of computer networks, Lanning (1992) wrote, "There is a modern invention that is of invaluable assistance to the pedophile: the computer. . . . Now instead of putting a stamp on a letter or package, they can use their computers to exchange information" (p. 30).

This communication can transpire via chat rooms or Internet newsgroups dedicated to discussions for pedophiles, as well as directly through e-mail. One particularly noteworthy example of this phenomenon is the Usenet newsgroup alt.support.boy-lovers.[3] According to this newsgroup's frequently asked questions list (FAQ), which is regularly posted to acquaint new users with the purpose of this particular computer forum,

> alt.support.boy-lovers is a forum for males to discuss their feelings towards boys. It is intended to provide a sense of peer support for those having difficulties with their feelings, for boy-lovers who feel isolated with their orientation, and for those who have no other avenue of discussion than via a group such as this. This Internet newsgroup receives between 150 and 200 message postings each month.

Durkin (1996) examined a sample of this newsgroup's postings. He determined that this computer forum serves two major functions for pedophiles. First, it appears to serve a validation function for its users. Pedophiles have a need for such validation (Lanning, 1992). Individuals who posted to this newsgroup frequently provided advice and encouragement to other users. Some pedophiles posted messages in which they sought personal support from other users. For instance, one indicated that he felt so isolated that he was experiencing suicidal ideations. Another wrote of how his car was burned by neighbors who had discovered his deviant sexual orientation. Other pedophiles offered support and encouragement to these individuals in subsequent postings. Other users may conceivably receive vicarious validation from reading these postings. These pedophiles probably are not the only users who have experienced suicidal ideations or had their property vandalized because of their pedophiliac orientation. The support that these two particular pedophiles received may have provided affirmation to other pedophiles.

The overall tone and demeanor of this newsgroup also may serve a validation function. In the context of this computer forum, pedophiles are referred to as "boy-lovers." In fact, this newsgroup is called alt.support.boy-lovers. However, in the context of the larger society, pedophiles typically are referred to with such pejorative appellations as "perverts" and "child molesters." The use of the term "boy-lover" may help pedophiles maintain a positive self-concept despite such strong societal condemnation.

Durkin (1996) also found that this newsgroup appears to serve an information function for its users. A wide assortment of information of interest to pedophiles was regularly posted to this forum. There were frequent postings that provided users with instructions on how to obtain novels, poetry, and comic books for pedophiles via mail order or computer.

Postings that contained information about the North American Man/Boy Love Association (NAMBLA) also were quite common. NAMBLA is a pedophile organization that advocates the abolition of laws regarding the age of consent, as well as the release of all men incarcerated for "non-coercive" sexual contacts with minors (de Young, 1984). This group, with an estimated membership of 1,000, has its organizational headquarters in New York City and local chapters in Boston, Los Angeles, San Francisco, and Toronto (Vito & Holmes, 1994). These postings contained excerpts from NAMBLA publications, as well as information on how to become a member of this organization.

SIGNIFICANCE OF
INTERNET MISUSE BY PEDOPHILES

The misuse of the Internet by pedophiles constitutes a significant development in the area of sexual deviance which has several problematic aspects. First, pedophiles are using the Internet as an outlet for deviant sexual gratification. Because of the existence of the Internet, a motivated pedophile now can obtain child pornography through his computer rather than via mail order. Most pedophiles derive sexual gratification from this material (Vito & Holmes, 1994). Additionally, pictorial child pornography, such as that available on the Internet, can be used as a tool in child molestation by desensitizing the victim to nudity and sexual activity (Lanning, 1992). One especially troubling way in which pedophiles are using the Internet as an outlet for deviant sexual gratification is to locate children to molest. The Internet affords a pedophile the opportunity to contact children from the privacy of his home and arrange meetings with them for sexual purposes. The apparent purpose of using the Internet to engage in inappropriate sexual discussions with minors is also of a sexual nature.

An additional aspect of this phenomenon that is significant is the fact that the Internet is serving as a social consolidation mechanism for these sexual deviants. Durkin and Bryant (1995) observed that the Internet can provide an enormous, and extremely rapid, contact network for people of related interests, including those related to sexual deviancy. Individuals can seek, identify, and communicate with fellow deviants of a similar carnal persuasion across the country, and even around the world. Information from deviant subcultures can be broadly disseminated, and interested new persons can be recruited (p. 187).

It normally has been assumed that most pedophiles are isolated individuals with little or no social contact with agemates (Prendergast, 1991). Computer forums such as alt. support.boy-lovers constitute a supportive social context in which pedophiles can provide validation to each other. This appears to be an unprecedented development in the area of pedophiliac behavior. Moreover, members of pedophile organizations such as NAMBLA can use the Internet to proselytize and thus expose hundreds of other pedophiles to their group's deviant ideology.

Another significant aspect of this phenomenon is the distinct possibility that the supportive social context afforded by the Internet may encourage some pedophiles to molest children. The Internet provides an unprecedented source of support and information for these individuals. There is the distinct possibility that some pedophiles may refine or act upon their deviant proclivities because of their exposure to the Internet. Pedophiles who participate in these computer groups also may conspire with each other to victimize children. For example, two Virginia men used a computer bulletin board in an attempt to locate a young boy to use in a "snuff film" (Durkin & Bryant, 1995). Fortunately, a law enforcement agent was monitoring this computer service and discovered their despicable plot. When these men were arrested, police found that one of the two pedophiles had a supply of muriatic acid to apply to the youngster's corpse.

DISCUSSION

There are tremendous difficulties associated with investigating criminal activities regarding misuse of the Internet by pedophiles. As with most forms of criminal and deviant behavior that are related to computer technology, the actions of pedophiles have far outpaced the ability of the law enforcement community to respond effectively (Carter, 1995). Most agencies are simply ill equipped to deal with high-tech crimes (Coutorie, 1995). Since the misuse of the Internet by pedophiles is a relatively new phenomenon, most law enforcement agencies, particularly at the state and local levels, lack the experience and expertise to confront this problem. Although it is relatively easy for pedophiles to traffic child pornography on the Internet, it is difficult for law enforcement personnel to track this material (Reske, 1994). Moreover, whenever a pedophile uses a computer in an effort to find children to molest, he is typically doing so anonymously from the privacy of his residence. Additionally, because the Internet transcends geographical boundaries, criminal cases related to pedophiles' misuse of the Internet typically involve the jurisdiction of more than one law enforcement agency.

Davis et al. (1995) suggested that a key element in locating pedophiles "who misuse computers is adequate training and awareness by criminal justice agencies" (p. 47). A strong commitment to cooperation among members of the law enforcement community is imperative. Those officers and agencies with expertise in this area must be willing to share their knowledge with others. Such cooperation not only will be useful in disseminating information between various agencies, but will help prevent any conflicts between agencies from different jurisdictions that may occur during the course of an investigation.

Although misuse of the Internet by pedophiles poses serious challenges to law enforcement agencies, it presents important opportunities as well. Investigators should be aware that any pedophile with computer access may engage in the type of activities described in this article. As Kosid-Uthe (1992) recommended, the search warrant for the residence of a pedophile who is suspected of involvement in illegal activities should specify computer equipment and files. This should be done whether or not the impetus for the investigation was illegal activities associated with the suspect's Internet use. This type of search can yield evidence of criminal activity such as computer files that contain child pornography. Computer files also may contain copies of correspondence in which the pedophile was trying to arrange meetings with children for sexual purposes. In a study of messages posted to an Internet newsgroup frequented by pedophiles, Durkin (1996) found that some of these postings appeared to be tantamount to admissions of child molestation. If a pedophile posted such a message, a copy of it may be in his computer files.

An important way in which the law enforcement community can combat the problem of Internet misuse by pedophiles is through educating parents about practical steps they can take to prevent their children from being victimized by on-line pedophiles. Parents should be encouraged to monitor closely the computer activities of their children.

Also, they should forbid their children from giving out any personal information, such as the child's last name, address, and phone number, to anyone on-line. Moreover, parents should instruct their children never to agree to an in-person meeting with someone from the Internet. Parents also should be urged to report any suspicious activity (e.g., adults attempting to solicit sex from or sending obscene materials to their children) to police immediately.

Misuse of the Internet by pedophiles also presents problems for probation agencies. Probation is a particularly common punishment for individuals who sexually abuse children. However, these individuals are difficult to manage and frequently recidivate (Lurigio et al., 1995). Recent trends in Internet misuse present additional problems for the management of pedophiles who are on probation. The Internet may serve as a conduit for illegal or otherwise deviant activities that constitute a violation of the general terms of a pedophile's probation. He can obtain illegal child pornography or arrange meetings with children for sexual purposes through the Internet. A pedophile also can obtain text stories which describe children engaging in sexual activity via the Internet. Although this child "erotica" is not technically illegal, the possession of such material may constitute a probation violation. Additionally, a pedophile typically is forbidden from associating with minors as a term of his probation. However, a pedophile can readily interact with youngsters on the Internet. As previously mentioned, this computer interaction may include inappropriate sexual communications. For instance, a pedophile can assume the on-line identity of a 13-year-old boy and enter the computer chat rooms frequented by youngsters and attempt to engage in sexual discussions with them. However, these probation violations involving Internet misuse are difficult to detect due to the privacy and anonymity associated with computer technology.

A common disposition for convicted sex offenders is probation with mandated treatment (Furby, Weinrott, & Blackshaw, 1989). However, compared to other sex offenders, pedophiles are the most difficult to treat (Prendergast, 1991; Vito & Holmes, 1994). There is the distinct possibility that use of the Internet by pedophiles may undermine the treatment efforts that are a condition of probation. For instance, cognitive therapy is currently a very popular type of treatment for pedophiles. The target of this therapy is cognitions "that promote their deviant activities and allow them to deny, minimize, and rationalize their behavior" (Lurigio et al., 1995, p. 73). Cognitive therapies operate on the assumption that cognitions cause behavior (Jenkins-Hall, 1989). However, an offender on probation can participate in the Internet discussion groups that provide a supportive social environment for pedophiles. In a study of one of these groups, Durkin (1996) found that many of these postings contained statements that attempted to rationalize child molestation and pedophilia. Exposure to these forums would certainly be detrimental to cognitive treatment efforts.

It is imperative that probation officers are familiar with the various ways in which pedophiles are misusing the Internet. A pedophile can participate in illegal or otherwise deviant activities via the Internet that constitute a violation of the general terms of his probation. Moreover, there is a strong likelihood that the use of the Internet by a convicted pedophile may subvert treatment efforts. Consequently, it is important that the Internet access of a pedophile who is on probation be restricted. In order to construct specific terms of probation concerning computer use, the reader is directed to the insightful discussion of Davis et al. (1995) on this crucial matter.

CONCLUSION

Recent developments in computer technology have made possible the existence of the Internet or "information superhighway." While millions of people use the Internet, the misuse of this medium by pedophiles is clearly reason for concern. Pedophiles are misusing the Internet in several ways: to traffic child pornography, to locate children to molest, to engage in inappropriate sexual communication with children, and to communicate with other pedophiles. The use of the Internet by pedophiles constitutes a significant development in pedophiliac behavior. Pedophiles are using the Internet as an outlet for deviant sexual gratification and as a social consolidation mechanism. Moreover, the supportive social context afforded by the Internet may encourage some pedophiles to victimize children.

These developments present serious challenges to law enforcement. Most agencies are not prepared to deal with this problem. Furthermore, the activities of pedophiles on the Internet are difficult to detect. Adequate training programs and cooperation between agencies are needed to deal with the problem. Investigators need to be aware that any pedophile with Internet access may be involved in the activities described in this article. A careful search of a pedophile's computer equipment and files may yield important evidence of criminal activity. Also, law enforcement agencies need to undertake a campaign to educate parents about steps they can take to prevent their children from being victimized by pedophiles who use the Internet.

The misuse of the Internet by pedophiles also presents difficulties for probation agencies. A pedophile can use the Internet to engage in activities that constitute a violation of the general terms of his probation. The use of the Internet by a pedophile also may undermine the treatment efforts that are a mandated condition of his probation. It is important that probation officers are aware of the possible problems associated with the Internet use of pedophiles under their supervision. It is strongly recommended that the Internet access of any pedophile who is on probation be restricted or prohibited.

NOTES

1. The terms pedophile and child molester are frequently confused. The term "pedophilia" typically refers to a sexual orientation or preference (Faller, 1990), whereas the term "child molestation" normally refers to actual behavior. A pedophile is an adult "whose sexual fantasies and erotic imagery focuses on children as sexual partners" (Lanning, 1992, p. 2). On the other hand, a child molester is an adult "who engages in any type of sexual activity with individuals legally defined as children" (Burgess & Lottes, 1988, p. 6). Not all pedophiles commit acts of child molestation. However, even if a pedophile does not molest children, he may participate in related activities that are unlawful, such as the possession of child pornography (Prendergast, 1991; Lanning, 1992). Although there have been a few cases of women committing acts of child molestation, virtually all pedophiles are male. For instance, Faller (1990) noted that she had never encountered a female offender who fit the definition of pedophilia. Therefore, masculine pronouns will be used to refer to pedophiles in this article.

2. Computer "chat rooms" are interactive discussion groups. These groups are "actually a window in which comments from many users scroll by" (Markoff, 1992, p. A5). Many of the commercial services, such as America On-Line and CompuServe, have these chat rooms. These chat rooms

cater to individuals with similar characteristics or interests such as teenagers, senior citizens, or various hobbyists.

3. Usenet is a collection of thousands of discussion groups, known as newsgroups, distributed over the Internet. They are devoted to nearly every possible topic ranging from astronomy to yoga. Some of these groups are dedicated to discussions of sexual deviance. There are groups dedicated to nearly every conceivable sexual proclivity including bestiality, transvestism, sadomasochism, and pedophilia. The user of one of these groups can read and post messages. These postings are organized in an archival format and can be read in a fashion similar to the daily newspaper.

UNIT 5

DANGEROUS SEX CRIMES

In this section, we will examine dangerous sex crimes practices through articles dealing with serial murder, pyromania, arson, lust-motivated murder, psychopathology of incarcerated sex offenders, and marital homicide and marital rape. This sections deals with perhaps the most serious of sex crimes and behaviors.

Dangerous sex crimes have become a fascination. Films such as *Hannibal, Copy Cat, Kiss the Girls,* and others attempt to capture the essence of the sexual predator in film for an analysis of the sequential violent offender. Books written about true and fictional offenders are almost guaranteed to be best-sellers if for no other reason than the topic itself. A cottage industry has been established by those who have recently retired from the FBI because they show us the inner workings of the Bureau as well as what it takes to be a successful crime fighter and psychological profiler. Why is there such a demand? Maybe it is fascination with the dark side of evil, and we can read it or view it from a safe perspective in the family room of our home or the safe setting of the theater.

Regardless, dangerous sex is a threat to many and a particular concern for those who study, research, and write about it. In our careers, we have met many authors who write both fiction and true crime. We have also had the privilege of interacting with others of the academic community. True, their perspectives are different, and with the license the former group possesses, their publications are perhaps more interesting but not as realistic in their approach to the understanding of the human condition. Yes, there is no true Hannibal Lecter despite the human and monstrous qualities attributed by the author, Thomas Harris, in *Silence of the Lambs, Red Dragon,* and *Hannibal*. Dr. Kay Scarpetta is a figment of Patricia Cornwell's imagination in *Black Notice, Post Mortem, Body Farm,* and others. In *Kiss the Girls* and other books by James Patterson, Dr. Alex Cross solves murders with an insight into the psyche of the offender. Caleb Carr moves the reader swiftly into a resolution of murder cases in *The Alienist* and *The Angel of Darkness*. But in reality, there is no shortcut to the successful resolution as depicted. It is usually a long process, and one that demands an understanding of the human condition.

What we are attempting to do in this section is to examine the dangerous sex crimes of serial killers, pyromaniacs, and other such people and acts. For example, in the first article, "Fractured Identity Syndrome: A New Theory of Serial Murder," Holmes, Tewksbury, and

Holmes admit that relatively little is known about the mentality of the serial killer. Additionally, little is known about the intrinsic motivation and etiology of the serial killer. This article examines current theories and how these theories offer little more than a listing of traits and characteristics of serial murderers. In this article, the authors propose a new theory of serial murder merging elements of Cooley's looking-glass self and Goffman's virtual and actual social identity, calling it "fractured identity syndrome."

Davis and Lauber examine the deadly acts of arson, pyromania, and serial fire-setting in their article, "Criminal Behavioral Assessment of Arsonists, Pyromaniacs, and Multiple Firesetters." Recognizing the dangerous elements in such acts, the exercise of power in each form of fire-setter, the authors take great care in trying to explain the basic motivations behind the act of setting fire for different motivations and anticipated gains. This obsession with fire needs a great deal more empirical research, and this article will provide a suitable plan for intervention and possible treatment.

The next article, "Profiles of Psychopathy in Incarcerated Sexual Offenders," deals with the psychopathology of sex offenders in correctional facilities. The offenders included rapists and child molesters. The researchers reported that antisocial personality types were more prevalent in the samples of rapists/molesters and rapists than the "simple" child molesters. These findings have important implications for policy administration in a correctional facility as well as the treatment of the individuals researched in this study.

In "Prevalence and Consequences of Male-to-Female and Female-to-Male Intimate Partner Violence as Measured by the National Violence Against Women Survey," Tjaden and Thoennes discuss the prevalence of sexual violence within a committed marital relationship and living arrangement. The study was based on telephone interviews with both males and females, and the general findings indicate what we would anticipate. For example, the findings indicate that married/cohabiting women were more likely to experience marital violence (including rape) than married/cohabiting men. The authors further report that women reported more frequent and longer lasting victimization; fear of bodily injury; time lost from work; injuries; and use of medical, mental health, and justice system services.

What we have chosen in this section deals with very violent behaviors among intimates as well as strangers. Serial killers, partner violence among intimates, and the psychology of sex offenders themselves are covered in this section. Another form of sexual violence, rape, follows in the next section.

15

Fractured Identity Syndrome

A New Theory of Serial Murder

———■———

STEPHEN T. HOLMES

University of Central Florida

RICHARD TEWKSBURY

RONALD M. HOLMES

University of Louisville

"A part of me was hidden all the time."
Ted Bundy, January 24, 1989

INTRODUCTION

Serial murder as a fatal behavior has fascinated and galvanized the interest of the American citizenry since the early 1970s. The names of the serial killers are well-known: Brudos, Bundy, Gacy, Bianchi, Lucas, Berkowitz, Eyler, Kemper, and many others. Newer names join this list: Andrew Cunanan, Glenn Rogers, Larry Evans, Westley Dodd, Kenneth McDuff, and others. The victims are unknown, but the killers have become a part of America's pop culture. What else explains the interest in our "entertainment" industry? The monetary success of movies and books that deal with serial murder almost are imperious to failure. Books of fiction that feature a serial murder theme, such as Thomas Harris's *The Red Dragon* (1984) and *The Silence of the Lambs* (1988), Patricia Cornwell's *The Body Farm* (1994) and *Cause of Death* (1996), John Sandforth's *Sudden Prey* (1996), James Patterson's *Kiss the Girls* (1995), Caleb Carr's *The Alienist* (1994) and *The Angel of Darkness* (1997), and other books have become a part of our written culture. Nonfiction books also contribute to our fascination of serial murder (see Table 15.1). Such books have highlighted careers of serial killers. These books include: Michaud and Aynesworth's *The Only Living Witness* (1983);

———

Authors' Note: This article originally appeared in the *Journal of Criminal Justice*, Vol. 15 No. 3, August 1999, pp. 262-272. Copyright © 1999 Sage Publications, Inc. Used with permission.

TABLE 15.1   Selected Nonfiction Serial Murder Books

Author	Name of Book	Serial Killer
Chris Anderson & Sharon McGehee	*Bodies of Evidence*	Judias Buenoano
Ed Bauman	*Step Into My Parlor*	Jeffrey Dahmer
Daniel Blackburn	*Human Harvest*	Dorothea Puente
Anthony Bruno	*The Ice Man*	Richard Kuklinski
Graham Chester	*Berserk*	Various killers
Peter Conradi	*The Red Ripper*	Andrei Chikatilo
Joyce Egginton	*From Cradle to Grave*	Marybeth Tinning
Bruce Gibney	*The Beauty Queen Killer*	Chris Wilder
Robert Gollmar	*Edward Gein*	Edward Gein
Delores Kennedy	*On a Killing Day*	Aileen Wuornos
Clifford Linedecker	*Nurses Who Kill*	Various killers
William A. Burt & Richard Lourie	*Hunting the Devil*	Andrei Chikatilo
Jack Olsen	*The Misbegotten Son*	Arthur Shawcross
Bruce Paley	*Jack the Ripper: The Simple Truth*	Jack the Ripper
John Philpin & John Donnelly	*Beyond Murder*	Danny Rollin
Donald Rumbelow	*The Complete Jack the Ripper*	Jack the Ripper
Ann Rule	*The Stranger Beside Me*	Ted Bundy
Eric van Hoffmann	*A Venom in the Blood*	Gerald Gallego & Charlene Gallego

Jackman and Cole's *Rites of Burial* (1992), and Bruno's *The Iceman* (1993). Movies such as *Seven, Copycat, The Manhunter, The Silence of the Lambs,* and others offer a temporary satisfaction to the insatiable appetite the public has for serial murder and the serial killer.

The academic community has nurtured an abiding interest in serial murder. Several academics have come to the forefront as the leading experts: Hickey (1997), Egger (1990b), Jenkins (1994), and a very few others. They are considered to be the ones who have an insight into the serial murder problem and have written articles and books on the topic. Hickey's *The Serial Killer and His Victims* (1997), now in its second edition, is often heralded as the classic publication in serial homicide. Egger's *Serial Murder: The Elusive Phenomenon* (1990b) and *The Killers Among Us* (1997) have added important knowledge to the field of serial murder. Phillip Jenkins's *Using Homicide: The Social Construction of Homicide* (1994) has received critical acclaim as a leading academic publication into the social problem of serial murder. An early publication by Holmes and DeBurger, *Serial Murder* (1988), was one of the first books that alerted the academic community as to the real and potential dangers of the serial killer.

Despite the best of intentions of these authors, and several others (Canter, 1994; James, 1991; Leibman, 1989; Rappaport, 1988; Sears, 1991), none of the publications has satisfactorily explained the etiology of the serial killer. This is the purpose of this paper. We will examine several "theories of serial murder" and shall see that the theories are little more than a description of the traits or characteristics of the serial murderer. What is needed and what we do in this paper is provide the academic community with a theory of serial murder. We call this theory "fractured identity syndrome."

LITERATURE REVIEW

The interest of the academic community quickly followed the "discovery" of a "serial murder problem." The early serial murder cases of Jerry Brudos, Ted Bundy, The Hillside Stranglers (Ken Bianchi and Angelo Buono), and others in the 1970s and early 1980s caused a fury to explain this phenomenon. Holmes and DeBurger (1985, 1988) published an article and a book that developed a typology of serial killers: Visionary, Mission, Hedonistic, and Power/Control. This typology has since been cited across the world as a starting point in the understanding of the serial killer mentality.

In an attempt to differentiate the various types of killers, Holmes and DeBurger (1985, 1988) stated that there were serial murderers who killed for different motivations and for various anticipated gains. Killers were not all the same despite some similarities. There were internal and external motivating factors to become a sequential killer; there were also different anticipated gains, either psychological or material. In Holmes and Holmes's (1994) work, professional hit men would be serial killers because they realized a material or monetary gain from the fatal dispatchment of a number of people. This is well-illustrated by the case of Richard Kuklinski, who was a suspect in scores of murders. His killings were committed for material gain, either for himself or for families of organized crime. He admitted that he probably should feel some remorse for what he had done but felt none (Bruno, 1993).

Attempts to move understandings beyond simple definitions have proven to be slow and to provide only small increments in understanding. Here we see that the majority of academic work available has focused upon describing patterns of activities and attempting to identify similarities across serial killings and killers. Illustrating the general failure of academics to explain serial murder, Levin and Fox's *Mass Murder* (1985) offers what is presented as the basic understanding of the major and discriminatory factors in serial murder. However, these differentiations in actuality fail to distinguish between forms of multiple homicides; neither do they adequately show how psychological conditions are transformed to actual killings. The etiology of the "mass murderer," they contend, must rest within the world of the "insane mind." Levin and Fox base their argument upon the work of Dr. Donald Lunde (1976), who insisted that serial killers suffer from paranoid schizophrenia and sexual sadism. In both sources (Levin and Fox, and Lunde), however, no distinction is made between the mass and serial killers. This failure to distinguish between serial and mass murder is significant, however, as they are clearly very different phenomena (Egger, 1990b; Hickey, 1997; Holmes & Holmes, 1994; Jenkins, 1994).

In another attempt to explain serial killing, Sears (1994) reports the serial killer murders for reasons we do not understand. Consequently, no theory is offered in his book *To Kill Again*. He does list traits of a serial killer that include: raised in an unstable home, lack of self-worth, self-centered, abuses alcohol and drugs, started his killings in his early 20s and early 30s, and several other traits. This same criticism could be said of the work of James (1991).

Rappaport (1988) reports that the serial killer kills to control the inner conflict that controls him. Moreover, he kills to demonstrate a sense of power and control. He further adds the traits of the serial killer. But there is no adequate explanation of the etiology of the inner conflict and the need to express power and control. Liebman (1989) also lists traits of the serial killer and adds the premise that the serial killer kills from an "ego-dystonic" state.

The motives, thoughts, and the murder itself are unacceptable to the killer. Because of this, the killer feels extreme guilt over his actions but still feels drawn to commit the act of sequential homicide, and often has no memory of the acts themselves. Canter (1994) adds that the serial killer displays personality traits consistent with an antisocial personality with traits of narcissism. But again, the basic development of a theory strictly for the serial killer personality is missing.

Hickey (1997), based on interviews with several serial killers, believes that the etiology of the serial killer rests within an unstable home environment where abuse and other forms of dysfunction were apparent. These experiences and scenarios are termed "traumatizations." He then lists three main facilitators: alcohol, drugs, and pornography; addiction to pornography; and a sexual fantasy. But again, there is no theory development despite the admirable work of Hickey. In his work, he is more comfortable in explaining the possible making of the serial killer mentality using a sociological approach: social process or social structure. Neither is an appropriate explanation for the serial killer.

There have been also applications of biological concepts and process in attempts to explain serial killings. One such effort has been the work of Norris (1988). Developing a so-called "profile of a serial killer" (with no supporting documentation), Norris proclaimed that each serial killer in his sample had received a blow to the head as an adolescent and this became an integral part of the process of becoming a serial murderer. This theory quickly became popular but fell to the sideline as other constitutional theories have fallen, including the work of Lombroso, Sheldon, and phrenologists who attempted to explain criminality from a physical perspective. In short, both documentation and the establishment of a causative link have failed to be uncovered.

There is no theory, sociological, psychological, or constitutional, that adequately addresses the question of the etiology of the serial killer. What actually are currently passing as theories are little more than a listing of alleged serial killer traits or characteristics. What is needed is a theory that helps explain this unique form of sequential predation and its developmental process of a serial killer. What we have chosen here is the application of the works of Cooley and Goffman's "Actual Social Identity" and "Virtual Social Identity" perspectives as they may be applicable to the development of the serial killer mentality.

THE FRACTURED SOCIAL IDENTITY

Our work is an application and extension of the work of Cooley (1902/1964) and Goffman (1959, 1963), especially Goffman's concepts of the actual and virtual social identity, for explaining why serial killers develop homicidal propensities, and why these inclinations are brought to bear upon a particular class of victims.

Cooley offered a personality theory founded on the individual's subjective self-evaluation, as well as the individual's reaction to others' perceived evaluations. The "looking glass self" concept was an early attempt to explain personality development by a movement from a subjective to an objective evaluation. The introduction of this concept was a substantial departure from other propositions offered by the unconscious school of thought. Cooley's theory allowed the individual a result role in one's own personality development. The person examines his/her own personality and makes a subjective judgment of value. He seeks out information from those in his meaningful world and makes a determination whether these persons are worthy of judgment. Then a decision to make changes in the personality, predicated upon the "worth" of those significant persons, is made. If the person hears a judgment about his own personality, but cares little about the person making the judgment, there will be little or no changes made. However, if the person making the judgment is valued (i.e., in a primary group relationship with the individual), certain changes in attitude and behavior may be more apt to occur.

Goffman (1959, 1963) builds upon Cooley's ideas to offer a more refined, and more active, perspective. Goffman theorized that an individual may change behavior when something (or someone) of significance enters the life of the person at particularly vulnerable times. This may result in radical departures of behavior. Goffman further offers two views of social identity: the virtual social identity and the actual social identity (1963, p. 3). The virtual social identity is the aspect of self that is managed and presented for public view. The actual social identity is who the person "truly" is, and whom the individual knows himself to be; the actual social identity is not managed and is generally known only to the individual and to the truest of confidants. It is the virtual social identity, or at least one form of it, with which observers are familiar.

Social scientists have long theorized that the deviants in society have been traumatized (see Hickey, 1997). This process of traumatization affects people in a variety of ways. For some, these acts of trauma are of small consequence. For others, a life of crime becomes the aftermath of such an experience. Fortunately for a very few, fragmentation sets the stage for a developing serial murder personality. In this instance, the serial murderer will learn he has an "inborn stigma," and become socialized into an "actual social identity" even while the killer learns what is normal (Goffman, pp. 32-33). No one is raised in a societal vacuum. Society plays a great role in a developing personality. The serial killer will become aware of internal feelings that include reasons, motivations, and rationalizations for sequential homicide (Holmes and Holmes, 1998b).

Serial killers are much like everyone else during the primary years of personality development. This position is reinforced by many who have been friends and relatives of serial killers early in the lives of the serial offenders, as well as professional research (Egger, 1990b; Hickey, 1997; Holmes and DeBurger, 1985, 1988; Holmes and Holmes, 1998a). The killers lead "normal" lives, and there was nothing in their early years that would have prepared them for the events of sequential predation that will occur later in their lives. What does happen, and it appears often in the adolescent years, is a social event, or a series of events, that results in a "fracturing" of the personality of the serial killer.

First, let us examine the term "fracture." This term means there is a small breakage of the personality. It is not a total destruction; the old personality is not ravished. A small but potent and destructive segment takes its place alongside the total personality. More often, the "fracture" is not visible to the outside world. It is only felt by the serialist. To the outside world he appears "normal." There are many examples of this phenomenon. For example, Bundy was a young Republican and active on a committee to reelect the governor in the state of Washington. Andrew Cunanan surprised his friends by being identified as a serial killer. John Gacy was a minor politician in Chicago and an owner of his own construction company. Donald Harvey was thought to be a dedicated health care provider. Mary Beth Tinning was considered to be a caring mother who had the misfortune to have her children die in infancy. These serial killers exposed only their public faces. The "fractured" part of the personality is hidden from public view. He can feel the "pain," the "fracture" so to speak. Not only can he feel the pain caused by the event, he can recall the social event that caused the small lesion in his personality. This was witnessed by a serial killer who remarked to one author (RMH) about the "Great Banana Incident." His father wrongly accused him of eating a banana that his father was "saving" for breakfast. The killer, age 9, was punished for a "crime" he did not commit. Moreover, as he recalled the incident thirty years later, he learned the value of lying and deceit at that time. He was angry with his father for the punishment, but he was more angry with his mother, who refused to intercede. He decided to admit to the eating of the banana (which was a lie) only after spending eight hours in a corner. He learned that by lying he was able to influence his own behavior, getting out of the corner, and said had it not been for this incident, he might have not killed "scores and scores of women" (Author's files). There is a great deal of doubt that this one incident "caused" him to be a serial killer. What is more possible is that one incident caused a small fissure in his personality, and the other incidents that followed in his life caused the fissure to explode into a "fractured identity" personality. Certainly most other persons can account for a severe treatment incident done by their parents that caused them discomfort but never to the point of being the sole precipitating cause of sequential fatal violence.

We must add here that the FIS is not simply another name for dissociation. With the work of Carlisle (1993) discussing the existence of the "dark side" of the serial killer and the dissociation on the part of the personality, this dissociation becomes a defense for the killer to psychologically insulate the personality and to offer some protection for the killer. In the FIS, however, we are saying that there is in existence within the personality a damage element that will arise because of "damages" that existed for some time, usually in the childhood of the adult killer.

Other serial killers talk about their hidden or fractured selves. In interviewing one killer currently incarcerated for life in a southwest prison, he related to one author:

> I knew there was something wrong with me when I was as young as 6. I quickly became aware of my dark side, my part of my overall personality that was bent on destruction of human life. I learned very quickly to kill. I only was impelled to kill when my compulsion demanded me to kill. As I grew into my twenties I gave it a name. My me, my "beast," announced the time and the circumstances for my killing. It also announced the type of victim for me to stalk and murder. It had to be a certain type with certain physical attributes. Blonde-haired, blue eyes, unmistakably young, very definitely female, cheerleader type. No others would do. My beast would not accept any substitute unless I had not fed it the meal for a long period of time.

A serial killer from another western state remarked, "I woke up that morning knowing I was going to kill. It was that awful, raging, eating feeling that was eating me up alive. It, my shadow demanded an offering."

Ted Bundy told one author, "There was something deep inside of me, something I could not control." (Bundy called it the entity.) Bundy told his mother the day before he was executed, "A part of me was hidden all the time."

Let us examine a few other serial killers to see how this might have occurred in their early lives. Ted Bundy, for example, in his early years lived a lifestyle that was no different from other young boys in his age group. He, however, discovered at about the age of 13 that he was illegitimate (Michaud and Aynesworth, 1983; personal interview [RMH]). Shortly after that discovery, Bundy turned to pornography, age 13½, and then 2 years later killed his first victim. Was it the discovery of his illegitimacy that was the instrument of his fracturing? Certainly other young men and women discovered their own illegitimacies and never reacted to fatal sequential victimizations. Ken Bianchi (one of the Hillside Stranglers) discovered he was adopted (O'Brien, 1988). Did this contribute to his personality as a serial killer? Jerry Brudos was aware of his secondary status in his mother's eyes, who much preferred his older brother. Other serial killers could also be cited, but these three celebrated and infamous serialists certainly illustrate the point.

The argument is well taken that others undergo similar social events in their young lives that do not lead them to serial murder. They do not undergo lives of serialists unless they determine a dreadful wrong has occurred in their personality development and sequential homicide is the acceptable manner to remedy their "unnatural passion" or "abomination of the body" (Goffman, p. 4). This "wrong" may be real or imagined. Just as important may be the sequence in which the events take place and the special timing of the "fracturing" event in the life. So, it is not only the common experiences that all undergo, it is the unique experiences and the timing of the "fracturing" event that is crucial.

Serial murderers, just as others affected by fractured identities, learn to live with their pain and knowledge of their stigmata, and they learn how best to conceal it. As Goffman states, the deviant (in this instance, the serial killer) is ". . . afraid to engage in long conversations" (1963, p. 15), because to do so might threaten the potency of the killer's virtual social identity. Serial killers have exerted great energies to keep their fractured identities secret. A managed identity is constructed and consistency presented in social encounters; this virtual social identity presents the individual as a "regular" or "normal" member of society. The fractured identity is hidden from public view. Additionally, long-lasting relationships are avoided if for no other reason than to lessen the risk of someone discovering the part that is hidden, the fractured identity.

The only person(s) to witness the fractured identity component of the actual social identity is the victim(s) of the serial killer. The energies that are expended in this most important of identity management routines are quite great, and at times the individual feels a need to be true and to relax the management. It is during these episodes that the victim is the chosen subject who is "privileged" to witness the actual social identity and to identify the fractured elements of the identity structure. In essence, at the time of the murder, the killer exposes his actual social identity, laying bare his fractured identity. The hidden, destructive part becomes visible only for a short period of time, the time necessary to commit the act of murder. The revealing of the fracture is comforting for the killer, and yet also an experience of such vulnerability that any and all who might have knowledge of the vulnerability (and how to exploit it) must be controlled. This is the reason for the witness-to-the-fracture to be killed. With the killing, the fractured identity temporarily returns to comfort with the actual social identity where it once again lays in wait for the opportunity to manifest itself at the time of the next killing.

CONCLUSION

The research concerning the basic etiology and behavior of the serial murderer is in its infancy. It has been only in the last 25 years that we as a society have been made aware of the dangers of the serial murderer. Over these decades a significant amount of research and writing has been produced regarding case histories of known serial killers, demographic and behavioral profiles of offenders and attempts to locate patterns within the characteristics and traits of victims.

However, what has remained essentially absent from this body of work has been a serious attempt at developing a theoretical understanding of how and why such offenses occur. The "theories" of serial murder that have been previously offered have been primarily cataloguing of traits or characteristics of the murderers. For instance, we know that most serial killers are white males, usually in their 20s or 30s, come from unstable homes, and often have histories of using/abusing alcohol and drugs. The only other "explanations" for serial killing have suggested that offenders suffer from sociopathic or psychotic personality disorders, and/or sexual sadists. Only a decade ago, the first move toward serious theoretical development appeared with Holmes and DeBurger's (1985, 1988) examination of motives, anticipated gains, and victim selection patterns. However, as has become clear since the appearance of those works, an integral component was missing: the manner in which the basic identity structure of the serial killer develops/emerges.

The development of the personality of the serial killer has been the focus of this paper. A basic theoretical construct has been suggested as at the core of the phenomenon, relying on a micro-level, social conception. Specifically, we suggest that those persons in significant relationships with individuals who are capable of influencing personality and identity constructions have significant influence on the developmental health of the future sequential predator. If one could identify those social events that influence and contribute to the fracturing of the serial killer's identity structure, the first step could be taken in the early identification (and perhaps intervention) of the serial killer identity.

16

Criminal Behavioral Assessment of Arsonists, Pyromaniacs, and Multiple Firesetters

The Burning Question

—■—

JOSEPH A. DAVIS

Center for Applied Forensic-Behavioral Sciences, San Diego, California

KELLI M. LAUBER

San Diego, California

In order to fully understand and appreciate the context presented here, it is first necessary to operationalize the concept that is the basis for this article. *Arson* may be described as "the willful or malicious burning or attempt to burn, with or without intent to defraud, a dwelling house, public building, motor vehicle or aircraft, personal property of another, etc." (Department of Justice, 1980). *Firesetting* is a broader, more general term because the act does not require intent on the part of the individual. Thus, a person can engage in firesetting behavior by accident (i.e., careless smoking). In contrast, the phrase *deliberate firesetting* is often used synonymously with arson and is predicated on the relevance of intent. *Pyromania* is another term used in conjunction with arson. Pyromaniacs, however, "have a persistent compulsion to set fires. They receive no material benefit from the act and lack conscious motivation for it" (Bennett & Hess, 1984). Pyromania eventually received official recognition when it was incorporated into the *DSM-III* (American Psychological Association, 1980) as a disorder of impulse control.

The estimates on the percentage of deliberate firesetters who are pyromaniacs are extremely varied and controversial. Some estimates are as high as 40% (Mavromatis & Lion, 1977), whereas others claim that pyromania is very rare, especially cases involving those individuals who obtain sexual gratification from the act (Geller, Erlen, & Pinkus, 1986; MacDonald, 1977; Rice & Harris, 1991). *Fire-bug* is a term coined by Lewis and Yarnell (1951), who in 1951 conducted the most extensive study ever undertaken on criminals and

Authors' Note: This article first appeared in *Journal of Contemporary Criminal Justice,* Vol. 15 No. 3, August 1999, pp. 273-290. Copyright © 1999 Sage Publications, Inc. Used with permission.

their association with fire. Fire-bugs are "those offenders who said they set their fires for no practical reasons and received no material help for the act" (Lewis & Yarnell, 1951). An additional category is reserved for the hired torch. The hired torch is a "professional who sets fires for financial profit" (Bennett & Hess, 1984). Other subcategories continue to be teased out of the literature as the database on arson continues to develop. These distinct categories include psychotic firesetters, female firesetters, juvenile and adolescent firesetters, nonpsychologically motivated firesetters, personality-disordered firesetters, group firesetters, and so forth. In reviewing the literature on arson and firesetting, it was readily apparent that there was a lack of consistency and cohesiveness in the attempts to provide an adequate classification schemata.

The historical significance of arson and its penalties is lengthy and diverse. Prior to the French Revolution, arson in France was punishable by death, and in a few documented cases, the arsonist was burned alive (Steinbach, 1986). During the turn of the 19th century, attempts were made in Germany and France, and eventually Britain and America, to understand pathologic arson. In 1833, Marc introduced the concept of *monomanie incendiare,* or pyromania, as a condition suffered by pathologic arsonists (Pilgrim, 1885).

Germany and France were the first countries to designate pyromania as a form of insanity, which led to the enactment of legal clauses whereby those individuals diagnosed with pyromania could avoid the death penalty. Isaac Ray was the first American to use the term pyromania when, in 1844, he used the term in the second edition of *A Treatise on the Medical Jurisprudence of Insanity.* Ray described pyromania as a "distinct form of insanity, annulling the responsibility for the acts to which it leads." In the early 20th century, arson was adopted into a psychoanalytical framework by Freud (1932), as well as by Stekel, who, in *Peculiarities of Behavior* (1924), wrote about the "sexual root of pyromania." Freud, in particular, postulated the idea of disordered psychosexual development, with a specific mention of fixation (or regression) to the phallic-urethral stage of psychosexual development. Freud's interpretations were laden with references to homosexuality, the similarities of the flames in action to the phallus in motion, and the overwhelming desire to extinguish the flames with a stream of urine (Freud, 1932; Zeegers, 1984).

STATISTICS ON THE
CRIME OF ARSON IN AMERICA

On a per capita basis, the United States has one of the most extensive arson problems in the world. Between the years of 1983 and 1989, more than 2 million fires, 5,800 civilian deaths and 28,500 civilian injuries occurred, and 8 billion dollars in property loss occurred annually between these years (Federal Emergency Management Agency, 1988). In 1989, 97,000 fires were attributed to suspicious origins, which led to an estimated 1.5 billion dollars in property damage (Karter, 1990). Arson was also the third leading cause of residential fires, the second leading cause of residential fire fatalities, and the leading cause of nonresidential fires. However, during that same year, only 15% of arson-related offenses were solved by arrest, and of these, 50% were never prosecuted, and roughly one third of those prosecuted were found not guilty. Therefore, only approximately 3% of arson offenses led to convictions (Blumberg, 1981; Hall, 1990).

In the past 10 years, arson has ranked within the three leading causes of fires in five countries. In 1990, it was the leading cause of major fires in the United Kingdom and the major cause of insurance loss in Germany. In Japan, 21% of all structural fire deaths between the years of 1983 and 1987 were direct results of incendiary suicide (Hall, 1990). During the year of 1989, in the United States, a fire department responded to a fire every 15 seconds. In addition, many of these fires were of a suspicious nature; these accounted for roughly 30% of all fires (Karter, 1990). Statistics such as these are endless, and they help to promote the need for an understanding of arson and arson-related behavior so that effective treatment programs can be implemented.

CHARACTERISTICS OF ARSONISTS

Regardless of how much information has been gathered about arsonists, the behavioral science profession still does not have a complete understanding of this aberrant behavior. It is important to note that there is not a typical arsonist per se; there are only certain characteristics that may be common among those who engage in deliberate firesetting activities. Arson is an extremely complex and multifaceted phenomenon; therefore, the psychological clues gathered from an individual who participates in such an activity may be present in one circumstance and only partly present, or completely absent, in another. Therefore, they represent generalizations that may or may not apply to all cases. There are also problems with obtaining information on arsonists. Anthony Rider (1980) divided this problem into the following five areas: (a) the problem of apprehending arsonists; (b) the legal disposition of arson crimes with the few who are incarcerated; (c) the source of arson statistics was not centralized until 1978; (d) the legal constraints on information exchange; and (e) the focus and conclusion of past research. Even with this in mind, behavioral science has been able to draw on certain clues and inherent traits that have led to the advent of arsonist profiles much like those of sexual homicide perpetrators, pedophiles, or rapists. A summary of the variables (see Table 16.1) will be introduced here, with a more extensive list in the form of profiles of two categories of arsonists, a pyromaniac and a hired torch (outlined in Appendix A and Appendix B).

A final variable worth revisiting is that of gender. Much of the data on arsonists has traditionally focused on males due to their involvement in the majority of arson-related crimes. Some studies have concentrated their research more specifically on female arsonists and have yielded some interesting results. A study by Bourget and Bradford (1989) claimed that female arsonists' motives, although similar to those of male arsonists, are often more dangerous and dramatic. For example, there are cases of revenge firesetting and cases of destruction of property that holds some symbolic tie with the woman. Female adolescents often display more concrete motives, such as a rebellion against parental authority or a show of attention-seeking behavior (Bourget & Bradford, 1989). Another variable that was researched in this study was the relationship between the time when the crime was committed and the phases of the menstrual cycle (no correlation was found). A separate research project focusing solely on women concluded that none of the female arsonists studied displayed any evidence of sexual arousal as a result of arson; this is a trait that has been discussed in the male arsonist literature (Stewart, 1993).

CRIMINAL MOTIVES AND METHODS

The motives for arson are subjective and diverse. Much of the literature on arson motives contains innumerable classifications and categories, and many of the typologies are flawed,

TABLE 16.1   Arsonist Characteristics

Age	The data varies over an extremely wide range on this component; however, according to one study, the mean age for men was 25 years, and the mean age for women was 31 years (Rix, 1994). One summary of firesetting behavior listed an age range of 4 to 73 (Barker, 1994).
Race	Most studies listed subjects as predominately Caucasian.
Gender	The vast majority of arsonists are male.
Environment	Arsonists frequently come from "disruptive, frustrating, harsh, broken, or unstable homes. Families are often large and in the lower socioeconomic levels. One or both parents are frequently absent from the home. Many come from homes in which the father was absent and the mother was domineering, overly protective, rejecting, or abusive" (Bennett & Hess, 1984). If the father was present, he was typically indifferent, unresponsive, or rejecting (Vreeland & Levin, 1980). A recent study listed a background of parental abuse in 63% of arsonists (Harris & Rice, 1996).
Prior criminal history	Most studies of incarcerated arsonists listed extensive criminal histories; however, not all previous arson offenses resulted in criminal convictions.
Intelligence	Many studies listed intelligence levels that are below average or showed arsonists to be mentally deficient. Of course, it is speculated that this category of arsonist is the one that is most often detected by law enforcement, whereas the intelligent arsonists often get away with their crimes for a longer period of time.
Academic performance	As it relates to the intelligence factor, arsonists often have low academic performances and a high rate of grade failure due to poor study habits.
Social relationships	"Many arsonists are socially maladjusted and loners, lacking the social skills needed for good interpersonal relationships. For most arsonists, relationships with all people are difficult, especially relationships with women" (Bennett & Hess, 1984; Leong, 1992).
Martial ties	Due to the consequences outlined in social relationships, it is expected that numerous arsonists lack marital ties. Many express or hide a fear or hatred of women. Those who are married typically lack the necessary skills for a healthy interpersonal relationship with their partners.

(Continued)

due in large part to the enormous complexity of the task. However, from the data, several motives do overlap, and they will be discussed here. The predominate motives behind arson include variables ranging from revenge, excitement (including sexual), vandalism, vagrancy, cry for help, attempted suicide, rehousing, psychosis, carelessness, insurance fraud, cover-up, heroism, arson by proxy, vanity, political arson, pathological jealousy, antidepressant,

TABLE 16.1   (Continued)

Employment history	Arsonists are typically unemployed or work in unskilled positions, and they often display poor work habits. Difficulties with coworkers and people in authoritative positions are apparent. Often, they will drift from job to job.
Physical deformities and defects	"Arsonists have exhibited a high incidence of physical abnormalities and deformities, sufficiently so that it may be a factor in producing a stressful environment that sets the occasion for activities such as arson" (Bennett & Hess, 1984).
Alcoholism	Several arsonists reported intoxication at the time that they set the fire. According to one study, approximately 43% of institutionalized arsonists reported an alcohol problem in the last year (Rice & Harris, 1991). Another study reported that 56 out of 58 violent offenders and impulsive firesetters fulfilled the *DSM-III* (American Psychological Association, 1980) criteria for alcohol abuse, and 44 out of 54 subjects had first- or second-degree blood relatives with alcoholism (Linnoila, DeJong, & Virkkunen, 1989). Another study stated that as many as 84% of the arsonists studied have an alcohol problem (Rasanen, Hakko, & Vaisanen, 1995).
Sexual disturbance	It has been the subject of controversial speculation that sexual perversions are associated with arsonists. However, the exact nature of this is unknown. Arson may act as a sexual substitute, and many pyromaniacs have reported a correlation between sexual excitement and arson. As a side note, in one study a positive history of sexual abuse was found in 18% of the men and 44% of the women (Puri, Baxter, & Cordess, 1995).
Emotional disturbances	"Firesetters are frequently described as psychiatrically disturbed, emotionally distressed, maladjusted, and lacking self-control and self-confidence. They often exhibit significant distress and tension, and they may manifest psychopathic, neurotic, or psychotic disorders" (Bennett & Hess, 1984).

fire buff, hero syndrome, other manipulations, and unknown or no obvious motive arson. One classification of motives for arson has been proposed by Prins, Tennent, and Trick (1985). This classification system tends to encompass the majority of motives that are found throughout the literature. This classification system is as follows:

A) Arson committed for financial reward
B) Arson committed to cover up another crime
C) Arson committed for political purposes (e.g., for specific terrorist or similar activities)
D) Self-immolation as a political gesture
E) Arson committed for mixed motives (e.g., in a state of minor depression [reactive], as a cry for help, or under the influence of alcohol)

F) Arson due to the presence of an actual mental or associated disorder
    (1) Severe major or recurring depression
    (2) Paranoid schizophrenia
    (3) Organic disorders (e.g., brain tumor, head injury, temporal lobe epilepsy, demented processes, disturbed metabolic processes)
    (4) Mental subnormality (retardation)
G) Arson due to motives of revenge
    (1) Against an individual or a group of individuals—specific
    (2) Against society or others—general
H) Arson committed as an attention-seeking act (but excluding motives set out under E)
I) Arson committed as a means of deriving sexual satisfaction or excitement
J) Arson committed by young adults (17 years and older)
K) Arson committed by children (Prins, Tennent, & Trick, 1985, pp. 275-278)

Revenge or anger is an extremely common motive for arson, accounting for as much as 40% in some cases (Rice & Harris, 1991). It is a particularly common motive in Western countries, where it can take the form of revenge directed at one individual (the boss who fired the arsonist, the lover who rejected the arsonist) or, in a larger perspective, directed toward society in general (Davis & Milton, 1997; Inciardi, 1970; O'Connor, 1987; Prins, 1986). Jealousy often plays an integral role in conjunction with revenge.

Communicative arson is a popular buzzword that inevitably makes its way into the arson literature. Communicative arson is not a diagnosis; rather, it is a descriptive term used to describe firesetting behavior that expresses a desire, wish, or need. According to Jeffrey Geller (1992b), a psychiatrist who has extensively studied the nature of firesetting behaviors, "fire is a good medium of expression for such persons (those lacking in social skills), because firesetting is non-confrontational and requires no verbal exchange or direct communication of any kind."

Although, in a historical sense, fire has had a long, enduring relationship with sexual components, the literature backing this affiliation is rare, and there exist some researchers who discredit the correlation altogether. "All of the evidence for the sexual motivation of firesetting consists of case studies, anecdotes, literary analyses, and uncontrolled group studies" (Quinsey, Chaplain, & Upfold, 1989). It is argued that sexually motivated pyromaniacs, although true to life, make up only a small percentage of the arsonist population (Bradford, 1985; Hill et al., 1982; Scott, 1974a). Indeed, much of the data involving sex and fire is derived from case studies that typically involve fire fetishism. A fetish, by definition, is an object that evokes devotion and respect, and is worshipped as magical by primitive peoples. However, it also means an object abnormally stimulating to sexual desires. The vast majority of case studies involving fire fetishes focused on the perpetrator watching the results of his arsonist act while engaging in masturbation. It is not uncommon, in many cases, for the arsonist to report seeing images of certain individuals dancing in the flames (Bourget & Bradford, 1987). One study involved orgasmic reconditioning coupled with covert sensitization in the treatment of a fire fetish. The subject, a 20-year-old male, reported a history of masturbation associated with firesetting. He claimed that this was his only sexual outlet. Measures involving physiological and subjective tests indicated a greater sexual arousal to photographic slides of fires than to slides of nude females. Via reconditioning therapy, the subject reoriented his sexual arousal from stimuli involving fire to stimuli involving women (Lande, 1980).

PSYCHOLOGICAL ASSESSMENT
AND DIAGNOSTIC CONSIDERATIONS

In order to rationalize the behavior of an arsonist, it is often presumed by law enforcement, firefighters, and the lay public that the individual must be psycho or crazy in some aspect. However, arsonists, on the whole, are not mentally ill. Roughly 2% of arsonists receive a court hospital order each year, and of those arrested for arson, only approximately 10% are considered to be mentally ill (Barker, 1994). Even with these relatively low percentages, arson does have an association with mental disorders, as well as medical and neurologic disorders that are included in the following summary (Geller, 1992a). Many tests have been used in the assessment of arsonists, these tests include the WAIS-R, WISC-R, Rorschach, MMPI, and MMPI-2. However, to date, no standardized psychometric approach to the study of arson has provided adequate cross-comparison results. Other problems, such as inadequate study designs, discrepancies in subject population, and methodological approaches, have also impeded the quest for new data (Davis & Milton, 1997).

A) Disorders of thought or perception
   1) Delusions as a component of schizophrenia, bipolar affective disorder, and other psychotic disorders (Geller, 1984; Koson & Dvoskin, 1982; Prins, 1986)
   2) Hallucinations as a component of schizophrenia or alcoholic hallucinosis (Geller, 1984; Scott, 1974b)
B) Disorders of mood
   1) Depression (arson reported secondary to major depressive disorder, dysthymia, and the depression of bipolar affective disorder) (Berelowitz, 1986; Moore, Thompson-Pope, & Whited, 1996; O'Sullivan & Kelleher, 1987; Wiklund, 1987)
   2) Mania (arson reported secondary to hypomania or mania in bipolar affective disorder) (Geller, 1987; Prins, 1986)
C) Disorders of judgment
   1) Developmental disorders (mental retardation) (Bradford, 1982; Day, 1990; Harris & Rice, 1984)
   2) Dementia
   3) Psychoactive substance induced
D) Disorders of impulse control
   1) Intermittent explosive disorder
   2) Pyromania
E) Chromosomal disorders (arson reported in association with Klinefelter's syndrome and with XYY syndrome) (Eberle, 1989; Miller & Sulkes, 1988; Nielsen, 1970)
F) Central nervous system disorders in association with epilepsy, head trauma, and brain tumors (Byrne & Walsh, 1989; Tonkonogy & Geller, 1992)
G) Infectious diseases (reported with HIV-associated dementia) (Cohen, Aladjem, & Bremin, 1990)
H) Endocrine and metabolic disorders (in association with diabetes) (Linnoila, DeJong, & Virkkunen, 1989)

The current data fluctuate greatly as to what percentage of the arsonist population is driven by psychotic motivation. One study concluded that only 6% of the arsonist subjects could be diagnosed with psychosis, whereas 54% displayed a personality disorder, 12% a mental handicap, 3% a depressive disorder, and the remaining 25% fell into various other categories (Rix, 1994). Another study claimed that 25% of arsonists could be described as psychotic (Koson & Dvoskin, 1982).

Some other interesting studies involving psychobiological variables have been conducted as well. Most notably, five separate studies conducted on pathological firesetters have suggested metabolic or neurotransmitted abnormalities. In particular, these five studies implied that the arsonists all showed significantly lower concentrations of cerebrospinal fluid monamine metabolite levels, specifically 3-methoxy-4-hydroxyphenylglycol (MHPG) and 5-hydroxyindoleacetic acid (5-HIAA) (Barnett & Spitzer, 1994; Virkkunen, DeJong, Bartko, Goodwin, & Linnoila, 1989; Virkkunen, DeJong, Bartko, & Linnoila, 1989; Virkkunen, Nuutila, Goodwin, & Linnoila, 1987). It has been hypothesized that a low 5-HIAA concentration in the cerebrospinal fluid correlates with disorders of impulse control. Pyromania, as mentioned earlier, is classified under this category. Behavioral criteria for pyromania include (a) a recurrent failure to resist impulses to set fires; (b) an increasing sense of tension before setting the fire; (c) an experience of either intense pleasure, gratification, or release at the time of committing the act; (d) a lack of motivation, such as monetary gain or sociopolitical ideology for setting fires; and (e) not due to another disorder (American Psychiatric Association, 1980). This undoubtedly raises some interesting questions in regards to the legal context.

MENTAL DISORDER, MITIGATING CIRCUMSTANCES, AND CRIMINAL CULPABILITY

Labeling someone diagnostically as a pyromaniac has historically been one method of absolving the individual from the crime. However, firesetting is rarely found under the McNaughten, or the irresistible impulse, test, and because few firesetters are insane by the legal standard, the main point worth debating is whether they are a future risk to society and whether they are treatable (Davis & Milton, 1997).

CONCLUSION

In conclusion, arson is a complex and difficult phenomenon to understand, and it is responsible for the loss of lives and the loss of billions of dollars of property annually. Various complications concerning designs, subjects, and legal access to data have impeded the quest to better comprehend the arsonist and his or her behavior. Despite the problems, a significant amount of valid information has been collected, thus allowing attempts to be made with regards to classification, antecedent environmental conditions, arsonist behavioral traits, recidivism, organismic variables, and the possible implementation of intervention and treatment programs. Using a behavioral assessment model, numerous traits of the arsonist have been outlined, including common motives for engaging in deliberate firesetting activities. Biological models as well as theories based on inadequate social learning skills were also reviewed. Psychologically, arson is a difficult offense to evaluate. Historically, the legal system has viewed the act of arson as a willful and malicious act; however, with the recent data being obtained specifically in regards to psychobiological variables, we could see the further development of legal loopholes through which arsonists may be exonerated from their crimes. It is important for the applied criminologist, psychiatrist, or psychologist to not become overly preoccupied with specific diagnoses or labels, such as pyromania; instead, they should look at the sum total of variables involved in the behavior, and progress from there to obtain the most thorough and complete assessment possible.

Arson, unlike other crimes, is unique in the sense that the magnitude of its power is often unknown, even to the arsonist. A gunman can choose the number of rounds to expend, and a knife-wielding perpetrator can make a conscious choice as to the number of wounds to inflict, but an arsonist surrenders the power of choice once the fire takes on a mind of its own. Fire chooses its own course of destiny based on several environmental factors; it is no longer dictated by the malevolent wishes of the individual who gave it life. This makes it one of the most deadly and potent forms of criminal behavior. It is therefore worthy of any and all attempts aimed at successful arson prevention.

APPENDIX A   Profile of the Pyromaniac

Age	The heaviest concentration was between ages 16 to 28, with the highest frequency at age 17.
Gender	Male
Race	Predominately White
Intelligence	The pyromaniac can range from being mentally defective to being a genius (approximately 22% of those with no explanation for their firesetting were low-grade defectives).
Physical defects	These were found to be frequently present.
Enuresis	This was present in some.
Mental disorders	Psychopathy, as well as psychotic disorders, were identified within this category; the compulsive urge also appears to reflect a neurotic obsessive-compulsive pattern of behavior.
Academic adjustment	They have poor educational adjustment, although some pyromaniacs were intellectually bright. Their academic performance was marginal or scholastically retarded; they were underachievers.
Rearing environment	A pathological, broken, and harsh rearing environment with inconsistent discipline and parental neglect was typical. Pyromaniacs noted an unhappy home life.
Social class structure	Some pyromaniacs emerged from middle or even upper socioeconomic levels, whereas others were products of lower-class environments.
Social adjustment	They are socially maladjusted. They have severe problems in developing and maintaining interpersonal relationships.
Marital adjustment	Although some pyromaniacs are married, their marital relationships were poorly adjusted.
Sexual adjustment	Sexually maladjusted and inadequate, they have limited contact with women.
Occupation or employment history	Most frequently, they are unskilled laborers, if they were employed at all. Many accepted subservient positions and became resentful when they realized that their work was degrading.

Personality	The pyromaniac has been described as a hopeless misfit; a feeble person; and a physical coward with feelings of inadequacy, inferiority, insufficiency, and self-consciousness. They are introverted, reclusive, aloof, frustrated, and lonely people. They have unconscious fears of being unwanted and unloved, and they suffer from a wounded self-esteem and a lack of pride and prestige. They often project an image of calmness and indifference (although anxiety and tension are still present). However, they have vague feelings that their defenses will fail them and that these repressed impulses will emerge. They tend to be defensive and obstinate in attitude, and they feel ambivalent toward authority. Although they have an inner dependence on authority, they also have contempt for authority. In fact, they have repressed their rage and hatred toward society and authority figures. They lack ambition and aggressiveness. Some have stated that they did not want to really hurt anyone. They are apologetic, yet ashamed for being apologetic. They seek expression through excitement. Some pyromaniacs have been found to be quite intelligent, neat, and methodical in their behavior. They have a craving for power and prestige. Some have failed to express remorse or to accept responsibility for their firesetting behavior.
Criminal history	Many had histories of delinquency and criminal behavior that includes running away, burglary, theft, and other property offenses.
Use of alcohol	Alcohol was frequently used as a method of escape and as a way to remove social inhibitions, but they did not set fires because they drank. Of the 447 who offered no explanation for their firesetting, except for an "irresistible impulse,," 70 were alcoholic (approximately 16%).
Suicide motives	Some attempted suicide after their arrest and incarceration. The exact motivation in each case was unknown; however, the following motives were identified: 1. They have a desire to be a hero and the center of attention (craving for excitement and prestige), to play detective at the fire, to render first aid, to help rescue victims, and to assist firefighters. 2. They have a desire to show themselves to be sufficiently clever to cause the experts, the firefighters and detectives, problems and to render them helpless. They have grandiose ambitions to be the executive who directs the fire fighting activity and puts the firefighters into action. 3. They enjoy the destruction of property (vagrants exhibiting pyromania receive pleasure in watching the destruction of buildings). 4. They have an irresistible impulse (they could not offer an explanation except that they were driven by an unexplainable force or impulse to set fires). 5. Revenge, although not consciously present, was also considered to be a possible factor. 6. Sexual satisfaction (this was noted in only 40 cases).
Irresistible impulse	No single precipitating factor produced this impulse. It was believed to be the result of an accumulation of problems that caused stress, frustration, and tension. Examples include thwarted sexual desires, loss of employment, death of a parent or loved one, threats to personal security and masculinity, explosive protest over the imagined immorality or promiscuousness of a mother or spouse, fear of impotency, and other.

Firesetting experience

Type of fires	Their fires were generally made in haste and in a disorganized fashion, often set in rubbish; basements; and in and around inhabited dwellings such as office buildings, schools, hotels, and other structures in thickly populated sections of cities. Frequently, they were made in rapid succession. Matches, newspapers, and other available materials were used in starting the fires.
Number of fires	Frequently, they started numerous fires, sometimes hundreds of fires, before they were caught.
False alarms	They were also known to set false alarms.
Time of day	Their fires were often nocturnal.
Regard for life	They have no regard for life (fires were frequently set in and around occupied buildings).
Type of firesetter	They were usually solitary (an insignificant number set fires in groups or with a partner).
Emotional state and behavior after the firesetting	Pyromaniacs frequently expressed the following symptoms preceding their firesetting: mounting tension and anxiety; restlessness and an urge for motion; conversion symptoms, such as headaches, pressure in the head, dizziness, ringing in the ears, and palpitations; a sense that the personality was merging into a state of unreality; and an uncontrollable urge or irresistible impulse to set fires.
Emotional state and behavior during the firesetting	While setting the fire, pyromaniacs felt that the act was so little their own that they described an emergence of a dissociative state (a transient sensation of being controlled by an external force—a feeling of being automated). They recognized that the firesetting was senseless, but they did not have the control to prevent it. To a casual observer, they would appear normal and in control.
Emotional state and behavior after the firesetting	Pyromaniacs expressed a sense of relief and even exaltation. After setting a fire, their tension subsided. Few expressed sexual satisfaction in setting fires. They often stayed at or near the fire to watch, or to assist the responding firefighters by rendering first aid, or to rescue victims from the fire. Some enjoyed playing detective at the fire scene. Some pyromaniacs, after setting the fire and ensuring that the firefighters would respond, went home to a restful sleep.
Arrest	Some pyromaniacs ensured that they would be identified and arrested; some even turned themselves in to the police. Many continued to set fires until they were apprehended. The arrest seemed to release the magical hold that the irresistible impulse had on them. It was a relief for them to be stopped from setting fires.
Confession	Pyromaniacs often readily confessed or admitted guilt, although they expressed no remorse or regret for their behavior; they did not generally accept responsibility for their firesetting activity. They were most often quiet and cooperative under arrest.
Selection of target	Firesetting targets are often randomly selected for no apparent reason.
Recidivism	There was a 28% recidivistic rate in the study.

NOTE. Compiled by the FBI, based on studies conducted by Lewis and Yarnell (1951).

APPENDIX B   Profile of the Hired Torch

Age	The age may vary from late 20s to late 60s. However, the age will generally be concentrated between early 30s and mid 50s. The psychopath may begin to burn out between 45 and 50 years of age.
Gender	Male
Race	Typically, the professional hired torch is Caucasian. This will vary, of course, with the area of the country and the location of the arson activity.
Intelligence	They tend to have average to above-average intelligence (often very cunning and streetwise).
Personality style	They have a psychopathic (antisocial) style of personality, with such common characteristics as egocentricity; manipulative and exploitative behavior; deceitfulness; pathological sense of confidence; impulsiveness; lack of anxiety, remorse, and guilt; propensity for high-risk living. The hired torch is a schemer and a con man.
Marital status	It is not common to be single, separated, or divorced.
Marital stability	The marriage is often unstable due to the hired torch's personality and impulsive lifestyle.
Lifestyle	Their lifestyle is somewhat impulsive and erratic. It can often be characterized by high-risk living and excitement-seeking. They are possibly nomadic, and they are prone to be nocturnal.
Socioeconomic level	They often belong to the middle class, but they are prone to be in heavy debt or financially overextended.
Use of alcohol	Alcohol use is common (excessive drinking is common, but not during the torching activity; the hired torch is frequently a heavy social drinker).
Occupation or employment	The hired torch may be employed in a variety of capacities, from being a professional businessperson to being an unskilled laborer. The hired torch is frequently employed by others. If the hired torch owns or operates a business, it will frequently be financially marginal.
Work habits	They tend to have irregular and marginal work habits.
Prior criminal history	Although there may not have been an arrest history, the hired torch may have been a suspect in a variety of crimes that range from fraud to homicide. The hired torch may have an arrest history for such offenses, but without any accompanying criminal convictions. The hired torch may have only one or two criminal convictions, but is a suspect in numerous other criminal activities. The hired torch may also have an extensive criminal record, with convictions for fraud, assault, and even murder.
Firesetting	They are rationally motivated by economic incentives.
Arson planning	The arson is premeditated and is often carefully planned to avoid detection.
Solitary or group firesetting	If the hired torch is an affiliate or a member of a loosely knitted or structured criminal enterprise, he or she may work with one or more other arsonists. If the hired torch is an independent, he or she will most often function as a solitary arsonist.
Behavior before the firesetting	They often prepare the facility for burning a day or so before the firesetting in order to ensure that it burns as intended.
Behavior at the firesetting	As little time as possible is spent in the structure at the time of the firesetting. The fire is usually timed in order to provide for a departure prior to the incendiarism.
Behavior after the firesetting	They commonly depart the fire scene immediately, before the arrival of the fire service. They often return home, to a bar, or to another planned activity to establish an alibi (Rider, 1980).

17

Profiles of Psychopathy in Incarcerated Sexual Offenders

STEPHEN PORTER

Dalhousie University

DAVID FAIRWEATHER
JEFF DRUGGE

Correctional Service of Canada

HUGUES HERVÉ
ANGELA BIRT

University of British Columbia

DOUGLAS P. BOER

Correctional Service of Canada

With the tremendous increase in reports of sexual crimes in recent years, the problem of sexual violence has never been so clear. Surveys indicate that about one in eight males and one in four females have been sexually assaulted in childhood (e.g., Finkelhor, Hotaling, Lewis, & Smith, 1990), whereas 10% to 25% of women report an adulthood rape experience (e.g., Koss, 1993a). Reflecting the increasing numbers of disclosures, the rate of incarceration for sexual offenses has been steadily rising. For example, by 1996, 21% of federal offenders in the Canadian correctional system had been convicted of a sexual offense (Motiuk & Belcourt, 1997). This pattern has highlighted the need to better understand sexual violence and develop improved risk management strategies. Because most sex offenders are conditionally released before the end of their sentences, the accurate assessment of their dangerousness has become an important agenda of corrections. Furthermore, sexual offenders must be screened for their treatment prognosis. Only a small proportion of sex offenders are expected to benefit significantly from treatment (e.g., Furby, Weinrott, &

This article first appeared in *Criminal Justice and Behavior,* Vol. 27 No. 2, April 2000, pp. 216-233. Copyright © 2000 Sage Publications, Inc. Used with permission.

Blackshaw, 1989; Hall, 1995) and, in general, the recidivism rate of sex offenders appears to be high (e.g., Doren, 1998). In this article, we explore how psychopathy might contribute to the understanding of sexual violence.

THE HETEROGENEITY OF SEXUAL VIOLENCE

There is a growing recognition that sexual offenders are heterogeneous in their risk, criminal diversity, treatment needs, and personality profiles (e.g., Boer, Wilson, Gauthier, & Hart, 1997). Research has focused on differences between sexually aggressive and nonsexually aggressive men (e.g., Lalumière & Quinsey, 1996), sexual and nonsexual offenders (e.g., Hanson & Scott, 1994), and types of sexual offenders (e.g., Prentky & Knight, 1986, 1991). Within the sex offender population, the most parsimonious classification system uses victim age, giving a dichotomy of child molesters and rapists. Using this typology, several differences within sex offenders have been found. For example, molesters appear to be motivated more by sexual aspects of the offense (e.g., Malcolm, Andrews, & Quinsey, 1993), whereas rapists appear to be motivated more by violence and anger (e.g., Barbaree, Seto, Serin, Amos, & Preston, 1994; Serin, Malcolm, Khanna, & Barbaree, 1994). Molesters have been found to be more socially inept and more unassertive than rapists (e.g., Prentky & Knight, 1991); rapists show more serious antisocial histories and higher rates of general and violent recidivism (Hanson & Scott, 1994; Prentky, Lee, Knight, & Cerce, 1997; Quinsey, Rice, & Harris, 1995). Prentky et al. (1997) found that most crimes by rapists were nonsexual, whereas those of child molesters usually were limited to sexual violence, indicating very different criminal motivations. There are also variations within molester and rapist subgroups. For example, incest offenders show a lower recidivism rate than either extrafamilial offenders or rapists (e.g., Forth & Kroner, 1995). Sex offenders with strong affective (e.g., empathy) deficits appear to use more aggression than those without such deficits (e.g., Lisak & Ivan, 1995; Paris, Yuille, Walker, & Porter, 1999).

Much of this diversity (e.g., criminal diversity, impulsivity, degree of empathy) appears to relate to clinical features of psychopathy leading to the possibility that the disorder may play a role in sexual violence.

THE IMPORTANCE OF PSYCHOPATHY IN UNDERSTANDING CRIMINAL BEHAVIOR

A large body of research has demonstrated that psychopathy is an important contributor to criminal behavior (e.g., Hare, 1996). Although showing a prevalence of about 1% in the general population, psychopaths comprise about 15% to 25% of offenders in federal correctional settings (e.g., Hare, 1998). A key feature of the disorder is a profound affective deficit and an accompanying lack of respect for social mores and the rights of others (e.g., Hart & Hare, 1997; Porter, 1996). Accordingly, psychopaths are dangerous individuals who repeatedly victimize others in diverse ways (e.g., Hart & Hare, 1997). Relative to other offenders, they begin committing crimes at a younger age and go on to commit a wider variety of crimes, including violent crimes (e.g., Forth, Hart, & Hare, 1990; Haapasalo, 1994). Psychopaths also reoffend faster, violate parole sooner, perpetrate a higher degree of violence, and commit more institutional violence (e.g., Cornell et al., 1996; Hare & McPherson,

1984; Hart, Kropp, & Hare, 1988; Serin, 1991). Not surprisingly, psychopathy is one of the best predictors of criminal behavior (e.g., Harris, Rice, & Cormier, 1991; Hemphill, Hare, & Wong, 1998). Furthermore, psychopaths show lower motivation in treatment programs (e.g., Ogloff, Wong, & Greenwood, 1990), and the recidivism rate of treated psychopaths tends not to be reduced following treatment (e.g., Hemphill, 1992; Rice, Harris, & Cormier, 1992). Treatment participation by many psychopaths may be superficial, intended mainly for impression management.

EVIDENCE FOR A RELATIONSHIP
BETWEEN PSYCHOPATHY AND SEXUAL VIOLENCE

A recent review identified psychopathy as a theoretically important factor in understanding and predicting sexual violence (Boer et al., 1997). One line of research has found an association between sadistic sexual arousal and psychopathy (Rice, Harris, & Quinsey, 1990; Serin et al., 1994). Quinsey et al. (1995) followed 178 rapists and molesters (a psychiatric sample) and found that psychopathy functioned as a predictor of sexual and violent recidivism. In both adolescents and adults, higher scores on the Psychopathy Checklist-Revised (PCL-R) (Hare, 1991) are associated with higher levels of violence in the commission of sex offenses (Gretton, McBride, Lewis, O'Shaughnessy, & Hare, 1994; Miller, Geddings, Levenston, & Patrick, 1994). Psychopathy-related traits have been found to predict both sexual and nonsexual aggression in noncriminal samples (e.g., Kosson, Kelly, & White, 1997). Further evidence for a relationship between psychopathy and sexual violence comes from studies of specific risk assessment tools that incorporate psychopathy (see Boer et al., 1997; Hemphill et al., 1998). The Violence Risk Assessment Guide (VRAG), one of the most widely used risk assessment tools, includes psychopathy as its most heavily weighted predictor (Webster, Harris, Rice, Cormier, & Quinsey, 1994). The VRAG has been shown to have utility in predicting sexual recidivism (Rice & Harris, 1997).

Other evidence indicates a complex relationship between psychopathy and sexual offending. Brown and Forth (1997) found that PCL-R scores in 60 rapists correlated with the number of previous nonsexual offenses ($r = .51$) but not with sexual offenses. Rapists appear to have a higher prevalence of psychopathy than molesters (Forth & Kroner, 1995; Serin et al., 1994). Forth and Kroner (1995) examined 456 adult sex offenders and found that rapists had the highest base rate of psychopathy (26.1%). Psychopathic rapists had a more extensive criminal history and were more opportunistic than their nonpsychopathic counterparts. However, psychopathy was not closely related to sexual offense history and was negatively related to the total number of sexual victims. Rice and Harris (1997) found that sex offenders who offended against multiple types of victims were the most dangerous, as indexed by their faster rate of violent recidivism. Overall, despite the fairly direct relationship between PCL-R scores and general and violent recidivism (see Hemphill et al., 1998), the relation between psychopathy and sexual violence is complex and requires further attention.

The objective of the present study was to investigate profiles of psychopathy and its two core elements among a large, diverse sample of sex offenders. We were allowed the opportunity to study psychopathy in a diverse sample representing 10% of all Canadian federal incarcerated sex offenders and some nonsexual offenders in a common institution. This would permit an examination of profiles of psychopathy in various offender groups.

Because psychopaths engage in a wide range of risk taking and antisocial activities (e.g., Ellis, 1987), it was predicted that they would be overrepresented in offenders who offend against diverse victim types. From clinical experience, it was hypothesized that some offenders are dominant, manipulative individuals characterized by an impulsive, risk-taking, and antisocial lifestyle, who obtain their greatest thrill from diverse sexual gratification and target diverse victims over time. Nonpsychopathic molesters (many with a paraphilia) were expected to be more likely to restrict their offending to one victim type.

METHOD

Participants and Data Collection

Since 1996, all psychologists working in the Pacific region of the Canadian federal correctional system must be thoroughly trained in the application of the PCL-R (Hare, 1991). Before conducting assessments for decision-making purposes, all psychologists are required to attend an in-depth PCL-R workshop given by an expert (usually the originator) with periodic follow-up advanced workshops. Within the Correctional Service of Canada, the training is expected to continue by having interrater reliability measured for the first several assessments conducted by the psychologist.

Files on federal offenders are generally extensive, detailed, and multifaceted. A file search was conducted to obtain the results of all available PCL-R assessments from 1995 to 1997 for offenders incarcerated in a common medium-security Canadian prison in western Canada (Mountain Institution). This institution houses approximately 10% of the entire federally incarcerated adult sex offender population in Canada. It also holds a number of nonsexual offenders at risk in other institutions, usually relating to drug involvement or an informant history. A PCL-R assessment was available for 80% of offenders ($N = 329$). (The Canadian correctional system requires that a risk assessment, including a PCL-R, be conducted for all offenders who have committed serious offenses. Most offenders in medium-security institutions will fall into this category.) The PCL-R assessments were usually based on file information plus an interview (there were no differences on PCL-R full or factor scores for file only vs. file plus interview; Fs ranged from .77 to .94, $p > .05$). The validity of file-only PCL-R assessments has been previously demonstrated (e.g., Wong, 1988), yielding very similar scores to assessments that include an interview.

The institutional files of all offenders in the sample were examined for PCL-R total, Factor 1, and Factor 2 scores as recorded in their risk assessment reports. The offense history was examined from the case management files, in particular the Criminal Profile Reports (CPRs), which document each violent or sexual crime in the offender's adult criminal history. The files were accessed through the computerized Offender Management System. Offenders were classified according to offenses listed on their official criminal record on the Fingerprint Sheet and double checked against their CPR crime descriptions. An examination of the CPR ensured that a sexual aspect of an offense would not be missed. For example, in some homicide cases, the court will hand down a conviction only on the most serious offense (e.g., first-degree murder) due to plea bargaining or the fact that the maximum sentence available in Canada is 25 years to life. This may not reveal that a sexual assault preceded the homicide. However, a detailed description of all serious offenses in the offender's adult history is available in the CPR file, which also records the age of the victim.

The age of 14 was selected as the cut-off for defining a child victim in consideration of previous sexual preference testing research (see Marshall, 1997). Of the 329 offenders, 228 (69.4%) had served time for at least one sexual offense as adults. Based on offense history, an offender was coded as one of the following:

Extrafamilial (EF) Molester: one or more victims of sexual assault 14 years of age or less, and all outside of the offender's family.

Intrafamilial (IF) Molester: one or more victims of sexual assault 14 years of age or less and all within the offender's family. This includes the offender's children or stepchildren, the offender's grandchildren, the offender's younger sibling, the offender's siblings' children or their children's children (i.e., child, stepchild, grandchild, niece, nephew, sibling).

Mixed Intra/Extrafamilial (E/I) Molester: at least one child victim within and one child victim outside of the offender's family.

Rapist: one or more victims of sexual assault older than the age of 14 years with no victims of or younger than the age of 14 years.

Mixed Rapist/Molester: at least one victim older than the age of 14 years and one victim of 14 years of age or less.

Nonsexual Offender: no sexual offenses in adult history.

Materials

The PCL-R has been widely adopted in the study of psychopathy in prison and forensic psychiatric populations (Hart & Hare, 1997). It contains items that fall into two correlated but distinct factors. Factor 1 consists of items that measure the affective and interpersonal features of the disorder. Complementing this personality style, Factor 2 consists of items describing a chronically impulsive, antisocial, and unstable lifestyle. Although correlated, the factors have distinct associations with clinical, personality, behavioral, and physiological measures, supporting the two-factor conceptualization. Factor 1 items include glibness/superficial charm, grandiosity, pathological lying, lack of remorse, shallow affect, lack of empathy, and failure to accept responsibility. Factor 2 items tap a need for stimulation or a proneness to boredom, poor behavioral controls, promiscuity, early behavioral problems, lack of realistic goals, impulsivity, irresponsibility, juvenile delinquency, and revocation of conditional release. The PCL-R is completed on the basis of a semi-structured interview and file information or on the basis of file information alone, provided that the file material is extensive and detailed. The total score, ranging from 0 to 40, is consistent over time, and the psychometric and predictive qualities of the instrument are excellent (e.g., Fulero, 1995; Stone, 1995). The PCL-R measures the extent to which an individual matches a prototypical psychopath. Although the PCL-R gives a dimensional score, a cut-off score of 30 is recommended for a diagnosis (Hare, 1991, 1998).

RESULTS

In terms of ethnicity, the sample was composed of 70.9% Caucasian, 22.7% North American Native, 2.2% Black, 0.6% Asian, and 3.4% "other" or offenders with unknown ethnicity. The 329 offenders had a mean age of 43.6 years ($SD = 11.62$), with no age differences

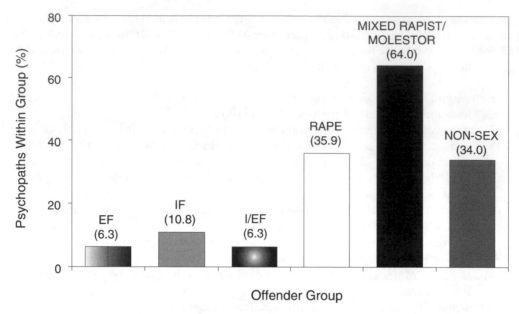

Figure 17.1. Proportion of Psychopaths Within the Offender Groups
NOTE: EF = extrafamilial; IF = intrafamilial; I/EF = mixed intra/extrafamilial.

between the offender groups ($p > .05$). All offenders were male. The breakdown of the offenders by offense type was as follows: 48 EF molesters (14.6%), 37 IF molesters (11.2%), 16 mixed E/I molesters (4.9%), 103 rapists (31.3%), 25 mixed rapist/molesters (7.6%), and 100 nonsexual offenders (30.4%).

Prevalence of Psychopathy as a Function of Offender Type

The groups were first dichotomized as psychopaths and nonpsychopaths according to the recommended diagnostic cut-off score of 30 (e.g., Hare, 1991). With the exception of the mixed rapist/molester group, all groups had more nonpsychopaths than psychopaths. As Figure 17.1 indicates, the child molester groups had low rates of psychopathy. Rapists and nonsexual offenders had moderately high rates, whereas the highest rate by far was evidenced in the mixed rapist/molester group (64.0%).

Victims of Psychopaths and Nonpsychopaths

The types of victims targeted by psychopaths and nonpsychopaths were examined. Of the 95 psychopathic offenders, 38.9% had raped only adult victims, 16.8% had offended against both children and adults, 4.2% had committed only incest, 3.2% had molested children outside the family, and 1.1% had molested children both in and out of the family. Overall, 35.8% of the psychopaths had committed nonsexual offenses only. In contrast, of the 234 nonpsychopaths, 28.2% had raped only adult victims, 28.2% had committed nonsexual crimes only, 19.2% had molested only children outside the family, 14.1% had committed only incest, 6.4% had molested children both in and out of the family, and 3.8% had offended against both children and adults.

A Comparison of Full PCL-R and Factor Profiles in the Offender Groups

To examine possible group differences in overall PCL-R scores and factor scores among the groups, a MANOVA (with offense type as the independent variable and PCL-R scores as the dependent variables) was conducted.[1] The MANOVA was significant, $F(15, 932) = 7.86, p < .01$. Follow-up ANOVAs indicated that there were significant differences in overall PCL-R scores, $F(5, 314) = 9.79, p < .01$, and Factor 2 scores, $F(5, 314) = 17.98, p < .01$. Factor 1 scores did not differ, $F(5, 314) = 1.83, p = .107$.

Full PCL-R Score Differences. The mean PCL-R score for the sample was 24.61 ($SD = 6.80$). The breakdown of the mean PCL-R scores is given in Table 17.1. To examine where full PCL-R score differences were emerging, Tukey comparisons ($p < .05$) were conducted. Rapists scored significantly higher than both the IF and EF molester groups. The mixed rapist/molesters scored the highest and significantly higher than the IF, EF, and mixed E/I molester groups. Finally, nonsexual offenders scored significantly higher than both the IF and EF child molesters. Broken down by ethnic group, the mean PCL-R scores were the following: Caucasian, $M = 24.72$ ($SD = 6.94$); North American Native, $M = 24.83$ ($SD = 6.10$); Black, $M = 23.11$ ($SD = 10.35$); Asian, $M = 18.50$ ($SD = 9.19$); and other/unknown, $M = 23.35$ ($SD = 7.28$). Although the size of the latter three groups precluded mean difference testing, there was no difference in the mean scores of Caucasians and North American Natives, $t(298) = 0.90, p > .05$.

Factor 1 Score Differences. The mean Factor 1 score for the entire sample was 10.04 ($SD = 3.53$). The breakdown of mean scores by offense type is given in Table 17.1. Because of the result of the univariate multiple comparisons were not conducted. However, overall, the mixed rapist/molester group scored the highest and the EF molesters the lowest on this measure of callous personality.

Factor 2 Score Differences. The mean Factor 2 score for the sample was 10.99 ($SD = 4.14$) and the breakdown of mean scores is provided in Table 17.1. To examine where Factor 2 score differences were emerging, Tukey comparisons ($p < .05$) were conducted. The rapist group scored significantly higher than the IF, EF, and mixed E/I molester groups. The mixed rapist/molesters and nonsex offender groups showed similar patterns (each scored higher than the molester groups) but did not significantly differ from each other (or from the rapists). Thus, rapists, mixed offenders, and nonsexual offenders scored significantly higher than molesters on Factor 2.

Relation Between Factor 1 and Factor 2 Scores

The above pattern of results suggested a possible interaction effect of factor scores by offender type. The interaction between offender type (sexual vs. nonsexual offender) by factor score (Factor 1 vs. Factor 2) was tested with a 2 × 2 factorial ANOVA. The ANOVA yielded a significant interaction, $F(1, 317) = 18.56, p < .01$. That is, sex offenders tended

TABLE 17.1   Different Mean Psychopathy Checklist—Revised Scores and Standard Deviations in the Offender Groups

Offense Group	Full Score		Factor 1		Factor 2	
	M	(SD)	M	(SD)	M	(SD)
a. EF molester	20.93	(6.05)	9.27	(3.61)	8.31	(3.96)
b. IF molester	21.17	(6.38)	10.17	(3.19)	7.59	(4.49)
c. Mixed E/I molester	21.24	(6.23)	10.14	(2.77)	8.16	(4.04)
d. Rapist	25.92	(5.87)$_{ab}$	10.06	(3.36)	12.04	(3.27)$_{abc}$
e. Mixed rapist/molester	29.0	(6.48)$_{abc}$	11.84	(4.21)	12.26	(2.96)$_{abc}$
f. Nonsexual offender	25.75	(6.99)$_{ab}$	9.86	(3.61)	12.46	(3.69)$_{abc}$

NOTE: A letter subscript indicates that the given mean was signifcantly ($p \leq .05$) higher than the mean of the group associated with the particular letter.

EF = extramarital; IF = intrafamilial; E/I = intra/extrafamilial.

to have higher Factor 1 than Factor 2 scores, whereas nonsexual offenders showed the opposite pattern.

Correlations between Factor 1 and Factor 2 have been estimated at .50. Over the entire sample, Factor 1 and Factor 2 scores were significantly correlated, $r(322) = .25, p < .01$. For the EF molesters, $r(46) = .03, p > .05$; IF molesters, $r(37) = .06, p > .05$; and mixed E/I molester group, $r(14) = .51, p > .05$, the factors were not significantly correlated. For the mixed rapist/molester group, the correlation was higher but not significant, $r(25) = .30$, $p > .05$. However, for the rapist group, the factors significantly correlated, $r(100) = .31$, $p < .01$. Overall, for the molester groups, the correlation was significant but low, $r(223) = .22, p < .01$, and for the nonsex offender group, there was a significant and higher correlation, $r(99) = .38, p < .01$, closer to correlations found in previous research (e.g., Hare, 1998).

DISCUSSION

Given its relation to crime and violence, psychopathy is arguably one of the most important psychological constructs in the criminal justice system. However, the nature of its relationship with sexual violence had not been sufficiently addressed. The results here, building on previous findings (e.g., Brown & Forth, 1997), clearly demonstrate that patterns of psychopathy differ in various sex offender groups. The rapists and mixed rapist/molesters all scored higher on the PCL-R than offenders who had victimized children exclusively. Furthermore, offenders who had sexually victimized both children and adults were between 2 and 10 times as likely as other offenders to be psychopaths.

Our results indicate that there is no clear relationship between molesting and psychopathy except that many molesters score high on Factor 1. In light of the high reoffense rates of molesters in general (e.g., Prentky et al., 1997), psychopathy may add little to the prediction of their sexual reoffending except to reinforce an assessment of elevated dangerousness. In fact, psychopathy is considerably less common in molesters than in the general prison population. As in previous research (e.g., Quinsey et al., 1995), rapists showed a considerably higher prevalence of psychopathy than molesters. They nearly always scored at least in the medium range on the PCL-R, suggesting a "criminal" lifestyle relative to the more specialized molesters.

An examination of factor scores revealed different patterns of interpersonal and behavioral deviance among the sex offenders. All Factor 1 means found in this sample were higher than the 50th percentile rank from the published norms on offenders in general (Hare, 1991). The mixed rapist/molesters' average score was at approximately the 75th percentile, according to the published norms. Substantial differences emerged on Factor 2, reflecting variations in the degree of aggressive and antisocial behavior. The mixed rapist/molesters, rapists, and nonsexual offenders all scored significantly higher than the molester groups. This indicates that the former groups had more chronic and diverse antisocial lifestyles than molesters. There was also a significant interaction between factor scores and type of offending (sexual vs. nonsexual). That is, Factor 2 scores tended to be higher in nonsexual offenders, whereas the opposite trend was evidenced with sex offenders.

An interesting finding came from the examination of factor correlations. For the nonsexual offenders, there was a significant positive correlation between the two factors (similar to previous research). Other than rapists, the sex offender groups (individually) did not show significant factor correlations. This pattern suggests that callousness in many molesters is manifested mainly in sexual offending, dissimilar to the more generalized pattern of rapists and nonsexual offenders. This is in accord with clinical observations that many molesters maintain an otherwise "normal" existence while preying on children.

Most offenders who crossed the line from child to adult victims (or vice versa) were psychopaths. These offenders also had the highest Factor 1 scores, indicating a ruthless and callous personality. This profile is indicative of a very dangerous group of offenders with a potentially high rate of violent reoffending. We speculate that the mixed rapist/molesters are generally psychopathic offenders whose thrill-seeking and impulsive propensities include a sexual component (without ruling out a sexual deviancy), offenders who can appropriately be called sexual psychopaths. In the absence of empathy or remorse, these offenders can victimize different types of victims when the opportunity arises or when they grow bored.

Exemplifying the sexual psychopath concept, Mr. C. (included in this study) was a middle-aged offender who had been designated a Dangerous Offender. (In Canada, following a conviction for a "serious personal injury offense," either a sexual assault, violent, or otherwise psychologically damaging offense, the Crown prosecution may apply for a hearing to determine whether the offender's level of dangerousness warrants an indefinite period of incarceration) (*Pocket Criminal Code 1999*, 1998). Mr. C.'s most recent offenses included repeatedly sexually assaulting three young teenage girls over a 1-year period, in the context of a "master-slave" relationship. His previous sexual offenses included the serial rapes of adult females, assaults on children, and even bestiality. His pattern was to focus on one victim type for a lengthy period and than move on to another victim type, admittedly "when (I) got bored." He also had been convicted of numerous other serious and sometimes violent offenses. In prison, he was suspected of perpetrating sexual assaults on inmates and was frequently inappropriate with female staff. It was reported in multiple psychological assessments that he was a "textbook psychopath." From our perspective, Mr. C. may have been a sexual psychopath whose excitement or "turn-on" came from victimizing others in a sexual manner.

There are a number of limitations in this study. First, the data were derived from psychological assessments from institutional files. Because the PCL-R assessments were conducted by several psychologists in the 2-year period, it is not known if they were equally proficient in administering the instrument. However, their competence was likely acceptable, given that they had all been similarly trained in PCL-R administration, after which their reliability was tested. Furthermore, because the assessments held considerable consequences (e.g., parole decisions), it can be assumed that the psychologists would be circumspect and motivated to be accurate. However, if for some reason the psychologists as a group scored liberally on Factor 1, it could explain the elevated scores across the sample. Second, the offenders were categorized according to their convictions. It is recognized that many sexual offenses go unreported or unsolved, raising the possibility that some offenders were misclassified. Finally, there are also some features of this sample that may limit generalizations to other sex offenders. These offenders were incarcerated in a medium-security institution where a majority of inmates were sexual offenders. The nonsexual offenders may differ from their counterparts incarcerated in other institutions because many of them were "protective custody" inmates whose lives were in danger at other facilities (some of them were informants, drug dealers, etc.). Given this background, they may have different characteristics from other nonsexual offenders. Indeed, the prevalence of psychopathy was somewhat higher in this sample than in previous samples.

Despite these possible limitations, this research has implications for heightening our understanding of sexual violence. A group of offenders that shows a high prevalence of psychopathy and that can be expected to offend persistently and perhaps violently across the life span was identified. Further research on this potentially dangerous group of mixed offenders is needed. It is expected that the offenders in this study will be tracked for the next several years to monitor their institutional adjustment, performance on conditional release, and long-term recidivism rates to examine the predictive utility of psychopathy (and other factors).

The dual focus of most existing sex offender programs is on sexual deviancy and cognitive distortions. Perhaps a better approach would be to develop programs to address the heterogeneity of offenders more effectively, especially in consideration of the features of rapists and mixed offenders. There have been few programs put into place aimed specifically at altering the psychopathic personality (although there are descriptions of proposed programs, e.g., Hare, 1992). To successfully address the problems of both recurrent sexual violence and nonsexual violent crime, increased attention to treatment issues relating to psychopathy is greatly needed.

NOTE

1. One reviewer pointed out that due to the different numbers of offenders within the comparison groups and distribution trends, ANOVA may be problematic (even though ANOVA is robust to departures from normality). In the analyses, all variances of the groups' scores were homogeneous. To further examine the possibility that the ANOVA approach biased the results, nonparametric tests (Mann-Whitney) were also conducted by looking at the data in stages (rapists vs. mixed offenders, etc.). Results were very similar to the ANOVA results, with a few additional significant multiple comparison differences (this is a liberal analysis relative to ANOVA). Thus, it appeared that the ANOVA was an appropriate, albeit conservative, approach.

18

Prevalence and Consequences of Male-to-Female and Female-to-Male Intimate Partner Violence as Measured by the National Violence Against Women Survey

———■———

PATRICIA TJADEN
NANCY THOENNES
Center for Policy Research

More than 20 years ago, Straus (1977-1978) reported his controversial finding that women are as violent as men toward their partners. Since then, experts in the field of intimate partner violence have debated whether women's use of violence against their partners is the same as men's. On one side of the debate are those who contend that men and women are similarly victimized by their partners, and that the problem of "battered women" should therefore be reframed to one of "spouse abuse" or "family violence" (McNeely & Mann, 1990; McNeely & Robinson-Simpson, 1987; Shupe, Stacy, & Hazelwood, 1987; Steinmetz, 1977-1978; Straus, 1993; Straus, Gelles, & Steinmetz, 1980). Evidence in support of this position comes primarily from surveys of married, cohabiting, and dating couples that ask respondents to self-report violent acts perpetrated by and against intimate partners (Brush, 1990; Lane & Gwartney-Gibbs, 1985; Laner & Thompson, 1982; Makepeace, 1981, 1983; Meredith, Abbott, & Adams, 1986; Morse, 1995; Nisonoff & Bitman, 1979; Straus, 1977-1978; Straus & Gelles, 1986).

On the other side of the debate are those who contend that men's and women's use of violence against intimate partners differs greatly both qualitatively and quantitatively.

Authors' Note: Research reported in this article was sponsored jointly by the Centers for Disease Control and Prevention and the National Institute of Justice under NIJ Grant Number 93-CX-0012. The opinions and conclusions expressed in this document are solely those of the authors and do not necessarily reflect the views of the funding agencies.

Citing evidence from national crime surveys; police, hospital, and court records; and clinical and shelter sample surveys that show women are overwhelmingly the victims of partner violence and significantly more likely than men to be injured during attacks by intimates, these experts argue that reframing the problem of "wife abuse" to one of "spouse assault" or "family violence" trivializes the plight of battered women and diverts attention from the root causes of wife abuse, namely gender inequality and male dominance (Berk, Berk, Loseke, & Rauma, 1983; Bograd, 1984; Dobash & Dobash, 1977-1978, 1979; Dobash, Dobash, Wilson, & Daly, 1992; Kurz, 1989, 1993; Pleck, Pleck, Grossman, & Bart, 1977-1978; Wardell, Gillespie, & Leffler, 1983). In addition, a growing body of literature shows that a substantial amount of female-perpetrated intimate partner violence is committed in the context of self-defense or fighting back (Follingstad, Wright, Lloyd, & Sebastian, 1991; Makepeace, 1986; Saunders, 1986; Schwartz & DeKeseredy, 1997).

This study compares the prevalence and consequences of violence perpetrated against men and women by marital and opposite-sex cohabiting partners. Information for the study comes from a telephone survey that queried a national representative sample of U.S. men and women about their experiences with rape, physical assault, and stalking by all types of perpetrators, including marital and opposite-sex cohabiting partners. Respondents disclosing victimization were asked detailed questions about the frequency and duration of their victimization; their fear of bodily injury or death; injuries sustained; time lost from work; and use of medical, mental health, and justice system services. Using data generated from the survey, the study addresses the following questions: (a) Do men and women experience similar rates of victimization at the hands of marital/opposite-sex cohabiting partners? (b) Is the frequency and duration of violence suffered at the hands of marital/opposite-sex cohabiting partners similar for men and women? (c) Do men and women who are victimized by marital/opposite-sex cohabiting partners experience similar amounts of threats and fear of bodily injury or death? and (d) Do men and women who are victimized by marital/opposite-sex cohabiting partners suffer similar consequences with respect to injuries sustained; time lost from work; and use of medical, mental health, and criminal justice services?

PREVIOUS RESEARCH

Prevalence of Marital/Cohabiting Partner Violence

Relatively few studies using representative samples have examined either the lifetime prevalence or the annual prevalence of marital/cohabiting partner violence in the United States. Prevalence estimates generated by these studies vary widely. Among the handful of probability studies assessing women's lifetime experiences with marital/cohabiting partner violence, prevalence estimates range from 9% to 30% (Nisonoff & Bitman, 1979; Peterson, 1980; Russell, 1982b; Schulman, 1979; Teske & Parker, 1983). The one study that examined men's lifetime experiences with such violence found that 13% to 16% of men were assaulted by a marital/cohabiting partner at some time in their lifetime (Nisonoff & Bitman, 1979). Two studies did not examine lifetime prevalence against individuals, but reported that 28% to 30% of U.S. couples have experienced some domestic violence during the course of their marriage (Straus, 1977-1978; Straus & Gelles, 1986). The only study that compared men's and women's lifetime experiences with marital/cohabiting partner violence found nearly equal rates of victimization among men and women (Nisonoff & Bitman, 1979).

Estimates from studies examining the annual prevalence of marital/cohabiting partner violence vary even more widely. At the high end of the continuum are estimates generated from the National Youth Survey (NYS) (Morse, 1995), which range from 20% to 37% for male-to-female violence and from 28% to 48% for female-to-male violence (Morse, 1995). These estimates are thought to be high because they are based on representative samples of young adults rather than all adults. Studies assessing the annual prevalence of marital/cohabiting partner violence among adult women of all ages have produced estimates ranging from 8% to 12% (Louis Harris and Associates, 1993; Plichta & Weisman, 1995; Schulman, 1979; Straus, 1977-1978; Straus & Gelles, 1985; Teske & Parker, 1983). Two previous studies that examined marital/cohabiting partner violence among adult men of all ages found that 12% of U.S. men experience intimate partner violence annually (Straus, 1977-1978; Straus & Gelles, 1985). In addition, a study using data from the National Survey of Families and Households (NSFH) found that 3% of U.S. couples experience some domestic violence annually (Brush, 1990). Three studies that compared men's and women's annual experiences with marital/cohabiting partner violence found that men and women had nearly equal rates of victimization (Morse, 1995; Straus, 1977-1978; Straus & Gelles, 1985).

Information comparing men's and women's annual experiences with intimate-perpetrated violence also comes from the Bureau of Justice Statistics' National Crime Victimization Survey (NCVS), which collects information on crimes committed against Americans 12 years and older and tabulates average annual rates of victimization by different types of perpetrators, including intimates. NCVS estimates of the average annual rate of victimization by intimate partners range from 2.7 to 9.3 per 1,000 women aged 12 years and older and from 0.2 to 1.4 per 1,000 men aged 12 years and older (Bachman, 1994; Bachman & Saltzman, 1995, Gaquin, 1977-1978; Klaus & Rand, 1984). Estimates generated from the NCVS consistently show that women are at significantly greater risk of partner violence than are men.

Frequency and Duration of Intimate Partner Violence

Though few studies have compared the frequency and duration of male-to-female and female-to-male intimate partner violence, the available research indicates that men are more likely than women to engage in repeated and long-lasting violence against their partners. Using data from the 1985 National Family Violence Survey (NFVS), Straus (1990a) found that men's average frequency of overall assaults against partners was 21% greater than the frequency of such assaults by women, and 42% greater for severe assaults. Using data from the NYS, Morse (1995) found that women averaged more assaults against partners when all types of assaults were considered; however, the mean frequency for "beating up" a partner was significantly greater for men than women.

Consequences of Partner Violence

Previous research shows that female victims of partner violence suffer more severe consequences than their male counterparts. Several survey studies (Brush, 1990; Langen & Innes, 1986; Morse, 1995; Schwartz, 1987; Straus, 1993), as well as studies using police and hospital records (Berk et al., 1983; Kurz, 1990; McLeer & Anwar, 1989; Stark, Flitcraft, & Frazier, 1979), report that women are overwhelmingly the injured parties in domestic conflicts. Previous research also shows that women constitute the vast majority of crime victims using medical or justice system services. For example, a recent government report found that 84% of the estimated 243,400 persons who were treated by U.S. hospital emergency department personnel in 1995 for injuries from confirmed or suspected intimate partner violence were women (Rand, 1997). In addition, analyses of police and court records in North America and Europe have persistently shown that women constitute more than 90% of partner violence victims reported to the police (Berk et al., 1983; Dobash & Dobash, 1977-1978; McLeod, 1984).

STUDY METHOD

Sample

Data for the present study come from the National Violence Against Women (NVAW) Survey, a telephone survey of men's and women's experiences with violent victimization. The survey was conducted from November 1995 to May 1996 by interviewers at Schulman, Ronca, Bucuvalas, Inc. (SRBI) under the direction of Dr. John Boyle. The authors of this article designed the survey questionnaire and conducted the analysis.

The national sample was drawn by random-digit dialing from households with a telephone in all 50 states and the District of Columbia. The sample was administered by U.S. census region. Within each region, a simple random sample of working residential "hundreds banks" of phone numbers was drawn. (A hundreds bank is the first eight digits of any 10-digit telephone number, e.g., 301-608-38xx.) A randomly generated two-digit number was appended to each randomly sampled hundreds bank to produce the full 10-digit, random-digit number. Separate banks of numbers were generated for male and female respondents. These random-digit numbers were called by SRBI interviewers from their central telephone facility in New York City, where nonworking and nonresidential numbers were screened out. Once a residential household was reached, eligible adults (i.e., women and men 18 years of age and older) in each household were identified. In households with more than one eligible adult, the adult with the most recent birthday was selected as the designated respondent.

A total of 8,000 men and 8,000 women completed the interview. Only female interviewers surveyed female respondents. For male respondents, approximately half of the interviews were conducted by female interviewers and half were conducted by male interviewers. A Spanish-language translation was administered by bilingual interviewers for Spanish-speaking respondents. The survey was introduced to respondents as a survey on "personal safety."

Measures

Victimization

The survey screened respondents for rape, physical assault, and stalking victimization. Rape was defined as an event that occurred without the victim's consent, that involved the use or threat of force to penetrate the victim's vagina or anus by penis, tongue, fingers, or object, or the victim's mouth by penis. The definition included both completed and attempted rape. The following questions, which were adapted from the National Women's

Study (National Victim Center and the Crime Victims Research and Treatment Center, 1992), were used to screen respondents for rape victimization:

- Has a man or boy ever made you have sex by using force or threatening to harm you or someone close to you? Just so there is no mistake, by sex we mean putting a penis in your vagina (female respondents only).
- Has anyone, male or female, ever made you have oral sex by using force or threat of force? Just so there is no mistake, by oral sex we mean that a man or boy put his penis in your mouth (or someone, male or female, penetrated your vagina or anus with their mouth or tongue).
- Has anyone ever made you have anal sex by using force or threat of harm? Just so there is no mistake, by anal sex we mean that a man or boy put his penis in your anus.
- Has anyone, male or female, ever put fingers or objects in your vagina or anus against your will or by using force or threats?
- Has anyone, male or female, ever attempted to make you have vaginal, oral, or anal sex against your will, but intercourse or penetration did not occur?

Physical assault was defined as behaviors that threaten, attempt, or actually inflict physical harm. A modified version of the Conflict Tactics Scale (Straus, 1990b) was used to screen respondents for physical assault they experienced as an adult at the hands of another adult.

- After you became an adult, did any person, male or female, ever:
  - Throw something at you that could hurt?
  - Push, grab, or shove you?
  - Pull your hair?
  - Slap or hit you?
  - Kick or bite you?
  - Choke or attempt to drown you?
  - Hit you with some object?
  - Beat you up?
  - Threaten you with a gun?
  - Threaten you with a knife or other weapon?
  - Use a gun on you?
  - Use a knife or other weapon on you?

Stalking was defined as a course of conduct directed at a specific person that involves repeated visual or physical proximity; nonconsensual communication; verbal, written, or implied threats; or a combination thereof that would cause fear in a reasonable person (with repeated meaning on two or more occasions). The authors developed the following questions to screen respondents for stalking victimization:

- Not including bill collectors, telephone solicitors, or other sales people, has anyone, male or female, ever:
  - Followed or spied on you?
  - Sent you unsolicited letters or written correspondence?
  - Made unsolicited phone calls to you?
  - Showed up at places you were even though he or she had no business being there?

      – Left unwanted items for you to find?
      – Tried to communicate in other ways against your will?
      – Vandalized your property or destroyed something you loved?

Because stalking involves repeated behavior and a high level of fear, only respondents who were followed or harassed on more than one occasion and who experienced a high level of fear were counted as stalking victims.

Victim-Perpetrator Relationship. Respondents who reported being victimized were asked whether their perpetrator was a spouse, ex-spouse, current or former opposite-sex cohabiting partner, current or former same-sex cohabiting partner, current or former date or boyfriend/girlfriend, relative, acquaintance, or stranger. Only respondents who reported being victimized by a current or former spouse or opposite-sex cohabiting partner were included in this study.

Frequency and Duration of Victimization. To generate information on the frequency of victimization, respondents disclosing victimization were asked how many times they were victimized by each perpetrator they identified. To generate information on the duration of victimization, respondents were asked when the first and most recent victimization by each perpetrator they identified had occurred.

Consequences of Victimization. To generate information on the consequences of victimization, respondents disclosing victimization were asked detailed questions about the most recent incident of violence they had experienced at the hands of each perpetrator they identified. Included were questions about whether their perpetrator threatened to kill them, whether they thought they or someone close to them would be seriously harmed or killed, whether they were injured, whether they received medical treatment for their injuries, whether they received mental health counseling, whether they reported their victimization to the police, whether they obtained a restraining order against their perpetrator, and whether they lost time from work.

Analytic Techniques

Data were analyzed using SPSS Base 7.0 for Windows software. Measures of association (e.g., lambda) were calculated between nominal-level independent and dependent variables, and the chi-square statistic was used to test for statistically significant differences between men and women (p value < .05). Any estimates that were based on five or fewer responses were deemed unreliable and therefore were neither tested for statistically significant differences between groups nor presented in the tables.

RESULTS

Prevalence of Marital/Opposite-Sex Cohabiting Partner Violence

The first research question, whether men and women experienced similar rates of victimization at the hands of marital/opposite-sex cohabiting partners, was answered

TABLE 18.1   Percentage of Men and Women Victimized by a Current or Former Marital/Opposite-Sex Cohabitating Partner in Lifetime by Type of Violence

Type of Violence	Men (n = 6,934)	Women (n = 7,278)	Chi-Square	p Value (df = 1)
Forcible rape	0.2	4.5	163.446	.000
Physical assault total	7.0	20.4	961.158	.000
threw something	4.4	7.8	428.862	.000
pushed, grabbed, shoved	5.1	16.9	771.854	.000
pulled hair	2.3	8.5	380.072	.000
slapped, hit	5.3	14.9	709.403	.000
kicked, bit	2.6	5.3	275.174	.000
choked, tried to drown	0.5	6.0	227.360	.000
hit with object	3.2	4.9	282.981	.000
beat up	0.5	8.4	315.670	.000
threatened with gun or knife	1.8	5.2	245.412	.000
used gun or knife	0.9	1.4	78.064	.000
Stalking	0.5	4.1	164.421	.000
Any of the above	7.3	21.7	1,018.242	.000

negatively. The study found that women were significantly more likely than men to report being victimized by a current or former marital/opposite-sex cohabiting partner, whether the time period considered was the individual's lifetime or the 12 months preceding the survey, and whether the type of violence considered was rape, physical assault, or stalking. Among surveyed respondents, 6,934 of the men (87%) and 7,278 of the women (91%) reported that they had ever been married or ever lived as a couple with a person of the opposite sex. As Table 18.1 shows, 0.2% of the men and 4.5% of the women reported being raped by a current or former marital/opposite-sex cohabiting partner at some time in their lifetime; 7% of the men and 20.4% of the women reported being physically assaulted by a current or former marital/opposite-sex cohabiting partner at some time in their lifetime, and 0.5% of the men and 4.1% of the women reported being stalked by a current or former marital/opposite-sex cohabiting partner at some time in their lifetime (see Table 18.1). Thus, women were 22.5 times more likely to report being raped, 2.9 times more likely to report being physically assaulted, and 8.2 times more likely to report being stalked by a current or former marital/opposite-sex cohabiting partner at some time in their lives.

A total of 5,982 of the surveyed men (75%) and 5,655 of the surveyed women (71%) were married or cohabiting with an opposite-sex partner at the time of the interview. As Table 18.2 shows, 0.8% of the men and 1.4% of the women reported being raped, physically assaulted, and/or stalked by a current or former marital/opposite-sex cohabiting partner in the 12 months preceding the survey. Although these annual prevalence estimates for men and women may appear quite similar, the difference between them is statistically significant (χ^2 1, 11,637 = 8.8, $p < .01$).

TABLE 18.2 Percentage of Currently Married/Cohabitating Men and Women Victimized by a Current or Former Marital/Opposite-Sex Cohabitating Partner in Previous 12 Months by Type of Violence

Type of Violence	Men (n = 5,982)	Women (n = 5,655)	Chi-Square	p Value (df = 1)
Forcible rape[a]		0.2		
Physical assault	0.6	1.1	4.250	.039
Stalking	0.1	0.3	3.144	.076
Any of the above	0.8	1.4	8.817	.003

a. The number of male rape victims is insufficient to reliably calculate prevalance estimates and the chi-square statistic.

TABLE 18.3 Duration and Frequency of Physical Assault Perpetrated by Marital/Opposite-Sex Cohabitating Partners by Gender of Victims Sustained by Male and Female Victims of Partner Violence

	Gender of Victim		F Ratio	p Value (df = 1)
	Male	Female		
Duration				
Average number of years assaults lasted	3.3	3.8	3.870	.049
Frequency				
Average number of assaults sustained	4.7	7.1	32.583	.000

Frequency and Duration of Marital/Opposite-Sex Cohabiting Partner Violence

The second research question, whether the frequency and duration of violence suffered at the hands of marital/opposite-sex cohabiting partners is similar for men and women, was also answered negatively. As Table 18.3 shows, among respondents who were physically assaulted by their partners, the average frequency of victimization was significantly greater for women than men (7.1 incidents vs. 4.7 incidents, respectively). The duration of violence, as measured by the average number of years the physical assault occurred, was also significantly greater for women than men (3.8 years vs. 3.3 years, respectively), although the difference between women and men on this variable is much smaller (see Table 18.3). It should be noted that the large number of cases in the female sample compared with the male sample may contribute to the significance found between men's and women's average frequency of physical assault.

TABLE 18.4 Percentage of Male and Female Victims Who Were Threatened or Feared Bodily Injury During Their Most Recent Physical Assault by a Marital/Opposite-Sex Cohabitating Partner

| | Physical Assault Victims | | | |
	Male	Female	Chi-Square	p Value (df = 1)
Perpetrator threatened to harm or kill the victim				
Yes	26.4	32.6	132.024	.016
No	73.6	67.4		
(n)	(425)	(1,294)		
Victim feared bodily injury or death				
Yes	19.6	44.7	166.615	.000
No	80.4	55.3		
(n)	(433)	(1,303)		

Threats and Fear of Harm Among Male and Female Victims

The third research question, whether men and women who are victimized by marital/opposite-sex cohabiting partners experience similar amounts of threats and fear of bodily injury or death, was also answered negatively. As Table 18.4 shows, the study found that female victims of marital/opposite-sex cohabiting partner violence experienced significantly more life threats and fear of bodily injury than did their male counterparts. Specifically, 33% of the women, but only 26% of the men who were physically assaulted by a current or former marital/opposite-sex cohabiting partner said their perpetrator threatened to harm or kill them during their most recent physical assault. And whereas 45% of the women who were physically assaulted by a current or former marital/opposite-sex cohabiting partner said they feared they or someone close to them would be seriously harmed or killed during their most recent physical assault, only 20% of the men did so (see Table 18.4).

Consequences of Marital/ Opposite-Sex Cohabiting Partner Violence

The fourth research question, whether men and women who are victimized by marital/opposite-sex cohabiting partners suffer similar consequences with respect to injuries sustained; time lost from work; and use of medical, mental health, and criminal justice services, was also answered negatively. As Table 18.5 shows, women who were physically assaulted by a current or former marital/opposite-sex cohabiting partner were significantly more likely than their male counterparts to report that they sustained an injury, received medical treatment, were hospitalized, received mental health counseling, lost time from

TABLE 18.5   Percentage Distribution of Male and Female Physical Assault Victims by Consequences of Most Recent Physical Assault

Consequence	Victims of Partner Violence		Chi-Square	p Value (df = 1)
	Male	Female		
Victim sustained injury				
Yes	18.8	41.6	158.500	.000
No	81.2	68.4		
(n)	(441)	(1,323)		
Victim received medical care				
Yes	3.8	11.3	42.061	.000
No	96.2	88.7		
(n)	(446)	(1,346)		
Victim was hospitalized				
Yes	2.9	8.8	32.780	.000
No	97.1	91.2		
(n)	(446)	(1,350)		
Victim recieved counseling				
Yes	21.7	27.4	113.786	.018
No	78.3	72.6		
(n)	(438)	(1,325)		
Victim lost time from work				
Yes	11.4	17.8	71.250	.002
No	88.6	82.2		
(n)	(441)	(1,328)		
Victim reported incident to police				
Yes	13.4	27.8	106.447	.000
No	86.6	72.2		
(n)	(439)	(1,322)		
Victim obtained restraining order				
Yes	3.6	17.9	63.072	.000
No	96.4	82.1		
(n)	(441)	(1,311)		
Perpetrator was prosecuted				
Yes	1.4	7.6	26.682	.000
No	98.6	92.4		
(n)	(441)	(1,311)		

work, reported their victimization to the police, obtained a temporary restraining order against their partner, and thought their partner was criminally prosecuted as a result of their most recent victimization.

DISCUSSION

The NVAW Survey is one of very few surveys providing both lifetime and annual-prevalence estimates of marital/cohabiting partner violence among men and women in the United States. Based on men's and women's responses to the same behaviorally specific screening questions, the survey found that women experience higher rates of violence by marital/ opposite-sex cohabiting partners than do men. Surveyed women were significantly more likely than their male counterparts to report violence by a current or former marital/ opposite-sex cohabiting partner, whether the time period considered was the individual's lifetime or the 12 months preceding the survey, and whether the type of violence considered was rape, physical assault, or stalking. Among respondents reporting physical assault by a current or former marital/opposite-sex cohabiting partner, women reported more frequent and longer lasting violence and more threats and fear of bodily harm. Women who were physically assaulted by a current or former marital/opposite-sex cohabiting partner were also significantly more likely than their male counterparts to report that they had been injured, received medical treatment, received mental health counseling, lost time from work, and sought justice system interventions as a result of their most recent victimization. Thus, information from the NVAW Survey provides compelling evidence that men's and women's experiences with violence at the hands of marital and cohabiting partners differ greatly both qualitatively and quantitatively. Although results from this study contradict findings from some previous studies that show symmetry in men's and women's risk of marital/cohabiting partner violence (Morse, 1995; Nisonoff & Bitman, 1979; Straus, 1977-1978; Straus & Gelles, 1986), they support findings from the Bureau of Justice Statistics' National Crime Victimization Survey that show that women are at greater risk of intimate-perpetrated violence than men (Bachman, 1994; Bachman & Saltzman, 1995; Gaquin, 1977-1978; Klaus & Rand, 1984). Information from the present study also supports findings from previous studies that show violence perpetrated against women by male intimates is more repetitious and physically injurious than violence perpetrated against men by female intimates (Berk et al., 1983; Brush, 1990; Kurz, 1990; Langen & Innes, 1986; McLeer & Anwar, 1989; Morse, 1995; Schwartz, 1987; Stark et al., 1979; Straus, 1993). Finally, findings from this study provide compelling evidence that violence perpetrated against women by male intimates results in greater costs to society in the form of lost productivity and the use of mental health, medical, and justice system services than violence perpetrated against men by female partners.

Although it is beyond the scope of this article to explain why some studies show symmetry in men's and women's risk of partner violence and others show asymmetry, it is important to note that previous studies showing symmetry queried respondents about their experiences with both intimate partner victimization and perpetration (Morse, 1995; Nisonoff & Bitman, 1979; Straus, 1977-1978; Straus & Gelles, 1986), whereas those studies showing asymmetry queried respondents only about intimate partner victimization (Bachman, 1994; Bachman & Saltzman, 1995; Gaquin, 1977-1978; Klaus & Rand, 1984). Thus, differences in survey findings with respect to men's and women's relative risk of intimate-perpetrated violence may be caused, at least in part, by methodological differences, with surveys focusing on victimization and perpetration producing evidence of symmetry between males and females and surveys focusing only on victimization producing evidence of asymmetry.

It is also noteworthy that the 1.4% annual intimate partner violence prevalence estimate for women generated by this study (see Table 18.2) is substantially lower than the 11%
to 12% annual intimate partner violence prevalence estimates for women generated by
Straus and Gelles using data from the 1975 and 1985 NFVS (Straus, 1977-1978; Straus &
Gelles, 1986). However, the 1.4% estimate is only somewhat lower than the 3% partner
violence prevalence estimate for couples generated by the NSFH (Brush, 1990) or the 3%
annual partner violence prevalence estimate for women generated by the recent Canadian
Violence Against Women Survey (Johnson, 1996). And although not directly comparable,
the 1.4% annual partner violence prevalence estimate for women generated by this study is
similar to the annual average partner violence victimization estimate of 9.3 per 1,000
women aged 12 years and older generated from the NCVS (see Bachman & Saltzman,
1995).

It is unclear why annual partner violence victimization estimates generated by different
surveys vary so dramatically. For years, researchers have attributed the relatively low rates
of assaults by both husbands and wives found by the NCVS to the fact the NCVS is administered in the context of a crime survey. Because they reflect only violence perpetrated by intimates that victims are willing to label as criminal and report to interviewers, estimates of
partner violence generated from a crime survey are thought to underestimate the true
amount of intimate-perpetrated violence (Klaus & Rand, 1984; Langen & Innes, 1986;
Straus, 1993). Recent changes in the design of the NCVS have attempted to alleviate these
problems by stating that respondents should report all victimizations, regardless of the
identity of the perpetrator, and by using behaviorally specific screening questions. There is
some evidence that these changes have increased reports of intimate partner violence
among both men and women (Kindermann, Lynch, & Cantor, 1997).

Information from the NVAW Survey suggests that administering questions on intimate-
perpetrated violence in the context of a crime survey may have less of an impact on disclosure rates than previously thought. The NVAW Survey, which was administered in the
context of a survey on personal safety, avoided legalistic phrases such as "crime," "rape,"
"assault," "spousal abuse," and "violence," and used behaviorally specific screening questions adapted from the Conflict Tactics Scale-generated annual partner violence victimization estimates that are only somewhat higher than annual partner violence victimization
estimates generated by the NCVS.

Although it is difficult to speculate why the NVAW Survey (and the NCVS and NSFH)
generated annual partner violence victimization estimates that are much lower than estimates generated by the 1975 and 1985 NFVS, one contributing factor may be the different
ways that screening questions on partner violence were introduced and framed by these respective surveys. In the 1975 and 1985 NFVS, respondents were read the following statement before being asked about specific acts of partner violence they may have perpetrated
or suffered:

> No matter how well a couple gets along, there are times when they disagree on major deci-
> sions, get annoyed about something the other person does, or just have spats or fights be-
> cause they're in a bad mood or tired or for some other reason.

Next, NFVS respondents were told that they would be read a list of things that they or their
partner might do when they have an argument. Finally, NFVS respondents were asked how

many times in the past 12 months they had perpetrated or sustained violent acts contained in the Conflict Tactics Scale, beginning with the least severe behaviors. Whereas acknowledging the pervasiveness of disputes among intimate partners and asking how many times a behavior occurred rather than whether a behavior occurred may be considered appropriate because it gives respondents permission to disclose their own experiences with partner violence, it may also be considered leading.

By contrast, respondents to the NVAW Survey were not read a statement about the pervasiveness of conflict and violence among couples before being asked about specific acts of violence they may have experienced. Nor were they asked how many times they had perpetrated or sustained violence in the past 12 months. Instead, respondents to the NVAW Survey were first asked whether they had ever sustained violent acts contained in the Conflict Tactics Scale. Only those respondents who answered affirmatively were subsequently asked questions about the timing of their victimization. Although this approach may be considered less accepting of partner violence and therefore less likely to result in disclosure of intimate-perpetrated violence, it may also be considered less leading.

Clearly, further research is needed to fully understand what impact introductory statements and question-framing practices have on prevalence estimates generated by surveys using similar behaviorally specific screening questions. In the meantime, it can be assumed that administering a survey in the general context of a crime survey will have less of an impact on intimate partner violence disclosure rates than previously thought.

UNIT 6

—■—

RAPE

This section of readings contains a host of articles relating to the crime of rape—the involvement of alcohol in rape events, how friends can help rape victims cope with their victimization, and the services currently available for rape survivors. The readings in this section present a view of rape with which most students in criminal justice and other related fields are not familiar, and that is how rape is viewed and how those close to survivors can help these victims overcome this traumatic experience.

The first reading, "The Role of Offender Alcohol Use in Rape Attacks; An Analysis of National Crime Victimization Survey Data," deals with a critical issue that many believe precipitates the criminal act of rape—the consumption of alcohol by either the victim or the perpetrator. The authors suggest that because alcohol may lower individuals' inhibitions, it likely plays a major role in a person's susceptibility to becoming a victim, or it may serve as a precipitator of violence. To test this assumption, the authors used data collected as part of the National Crime Victimization Survey from 1992-1996 and found that alcohol itself did not appear to play as significant a role as they suspected. Their results concluded that offenders' preassault alcohol use generally tended to predict fewer completed rapes and was unrelated to physical injury or future medical attention. However, when the offender used alcohol, the attack was most likely to occur at night and outdoors, the offender was a stranger to the victim, and the victim was more likely to resist physically.

The authors conclude with a call for researchers to begin to look past the use of alcohol as a precipitator of rape, and start examining the preassault use of alcohol as a contributing factor that adds to the seriousness of the offense and may contribute indirectly to more victim injury.

The next reading, "Assisting Rape Victims as They Recover From Rape: The Impact on Friends," examines the role of friends and family members as helpers of victims who have been raped or who were victimized by another sexual assault. This is one of the most neglected issues surrounding the crimes of rape and sexual assault. Many articles have been written about these crimes, the perpetrators, and what the victims go through following such an assault, but very little mention has been made of how friends and others can help victims cope with their victimization.

In order to study this phenomenon, the authors collected data on 60 students who reported that they had talked to a friend following the friend's sexual victimization and tried to help and counsel the friend in time of need. One of the most interesting findings of this study was the willingness of these friends to openly state that they were not particularly confused about how to help their friends through these rough times. Most felt that the best thing they could do to help the victim was to listen and offer her support. Thus, these helpers believed their friendship did not suffer as a result of the disclosure, and they assumed that they were of some help to their friend. This finding is important for several reasons, but paramount among them is the idea that unlike family members, the disclosure of information regarding the attack to friends does not significantly change or alter the course of the relationship, as often occurs when family members get involved. When informed of a sexual assault, parents may try to shelter the child, overly comfort her, or simply not allow her enough time and space to heal her physical and emotional wounds. However, when victims relate information to friends, these friends are better able to assist the victims without becoming too emotionally involved with the act or the perpetrator. Thus, close friends or acquaintances may be the best sources of emotional support for victims when trying to overcome a horrible victimization.

The final reading in this section deals with the foundation and evolution of rape crisis centers in this country. This article, "Services for Sexual Assault Survivors: The Role of Rape Crisis Centers," is quite different from the other readings in this section. It does not deal directly with the victimization experience itself, but deals with the foundation and administration of the social service agencies designed and established to help survivors of sexual assault and rape cope with their victimization.

The authors begin with a discussion of the evolution of rape crisis centers and how many of the early rape crisis centers were established by feminists as helping organizations designed to provide support for women who were confused and did not know what to do following their victimization. Many of these early organizations were freestanding, independent agencies where women contributed both their time and money to help others in need. However, when these centers began to seek federal and state assistance to cover their expenses, they began to partner with and associate themselves with larger organizations, such as the YWCA, hospitals, and mental health facilities.

The authors found that despite these changes in the organizational structure, many of the services provided by the centers did not change. They still continued to offer 24-hour telephone hot lines, counseling, and legal and medical advocacy. Previous research by these authors found that the services provided to the victims were very important for the victims. For instance, when victims worked with a rape crisis center advocate, they experienced reduced stress and received more accurate medical and legal advice. In sum, the authors found that these centers and the volunteers employed have been effective not only in healing survivors, but also in changing some of the practices of the criminal justice and medical treatment institutions. which traditionally have not been sensitive to the plight of these victims.

This section provides the reader with a cross section of readings dealing not only with how rape and sexual assault are perceived in the community but how various groups are helping those in need of assistance to get through the formal crime-reporting process and begin the healing more quickly. Once the reader has read the articles in this section, it should be clear that the crimes of rape and sexual assault cannot be forgotten quickly. Victims continue to suffer emotional and physical pain for months, if not years, after the incident. This is an important point that needs to be made clear if students and the general public wish to truly understand the total individual and societal consequences of this type of violent offense.

19

The Role of Offender Alcohol Use in Rape Attacks

An Analysis of National Crime Victimization Survey Data

LEANNE R. BRECKLIN
SARAH E. ULLMAN
University of Illinois at Chicago

Alcohol is present in approximately one third to two thirds of rape incidents (Abbey, 1991; Pernanen, 1991). Although many studies have reported on the prevalence of alcohol use in rape incidents, there has been limited research on the role preassault alcohol use plays in these rapes. Because it is still unclear how offender preassault alcohol use affects the outcomes of sexual assaults (e.g., severity of sexual abuse and physical injury), more research is needed that examines the interactions of assault characteristics and offender alcohol use in the prediction of assault outcomes.

There are several ways in which alcohol may affect the outcomes of rapes. Because alcohol use has been shown to be associated with violence (Collins & Schlenger, 1988), the risk of experiencing severe sexual victimization and physical injuries may be increased when alcohol is involved in the incident. Reviews of experimental studies have shown that alcohol consumption is related to aggressive behavior in laboratory situations (Bushman & Cooper, 1990; Hull & Bond, 1986). It is possible that alcohol may facilitate increased aggression toward the victim by reducing the offender's inhibitions to commit sexual aggression. Whether such inhibition is behavioral and/or physiological (Crowe & George, 1989), if it is released by alcohol use, it may result in a more aggressive attack with a more severe assault

Authors' Note: This research was supported by a grant from the Alcoholic Beverage Medical Research Foundation to Sarah E. Ullman. Please address correspondence to: Leanne R. Brecklin or Sarah E. Ullman, Department of Criminal Justice (M/C 141), University of Illinois at Chicago, 1007 West Harrison Street, Chicago, IL 60607-7140.

outcome to the victim. Offender alcohol use has also been linked with sexual abuse and injuries to victims in field research (Coker, Walls, & Johnson, 1998; Johnson, Gibson, & Linden, 1978; Martin & Bachman, 1998; Ullman & Brecklin, in press; Ullman & Knight, 1993). Alcohol use also appears to be associated with riskier situational contexts (e.g., bars and parties) that are associated with higher risk of completed rape (Testa & Parks, 1996; Ullman, Karabatsos, & Koss, 1999a, 1999b; Ullman & Knight, 1993).

There have been four studies of national samples examining the role of alcohol in sexual assault outcomes. Ullman et al. (1999b) used path analysis in a national sample of college women to analyze the role of victim and offender drinking in predicting severity of sexual victimization as measured by the Sexual Experiences Survey. Offender preassault alcohol use was weakly related to severity of sexual victimization, but it was strongly related to offender aggression, the strongest predictor of sexual victimization severity. This suggests that alcohol may play an indirect role in the outcome of rape. Offender drinking was also related to less intimate victim-offender relationships, spontaneous social situations, and victim drinking. A parallel path analysis conducted with a national sample of college men (Ullman et al., 1999a) showed that offender alcohol use was not directly related to aggression or sexual victimization severity, but it was indirectly related to sexual victimization severity through victim alcohol use. As in the study of college women (Ullman et al., 1999b), college men reported that unplanned social situations and less intimate victim-offender relationships were more likely to involve offender drinking.

Using data from a national sample of American women (Wilsnack, Vogeltanz, Klassen, & Harris, 1997), Ullman and Brecklin (in press) examined the role of both victim and offender drinking on physical injury outcomes of sexual assaults. Offender drinking was related to victim drinking, more stranger assaults, more victim injury, and marginally greater offender aggression. Offender drinking and offender aggression were each associated with increased odds of victim injury, but these two variables did not interact to predict injury. This result appears to be consistent with Cleveland, Koss, and Lyons's (1999) recent study of women's narrative accounts of completed rapes in which alcohol use and aggression were two separate strategies used by offenders to accomplish rape. That study did not, however, examine the effects of these strategies on assault outcomes.

Martin and Bachman (1998) analyzed the effects of offender alcohol use on rape and injury outcomes using 279 sexual assault incidents from the 1992-1994 National Crime Victimization Survey (NCVS). Victims were more likely to be injured and marginally less likely to be raped by offenders who were drinking, but these relationships were not significant in multivariate analyses controlling for demographic and situational characteristics.

Present Study

To further examine the role of alcohol in sexual assaults, the present study analyzed attempted and completed rape incidents from the 1992-1996 NCVS. This study differs from Martin and Bachman's (1998) study by including more years of NCVS data and including a broader range of situational and behavioral factors known to predict assault outcomes. Because the NCVS only collects information on the victim's perception of offender alcohol use, it was not possible to examine the roles of both victim and offender drinking in this sample of rape incidents. However, victim and offender drinking often overlap in rape incidents (Johnson et al., 1978; Ullman & Brecklin, in press; Ullman et al., 1999a, 1999b;

Ullman & Knight, 1993), making it worthwhile to explore the role of offender alcohol use here.

Past research shows that stranger rapes are more likely to involve alcohol use than known-offender rapes (Ullman & Brecklin, in press; Ullman et al., 1999a, 1999b). There-fore, it was expected that offender alcohol use would also be related to offender aggression, more verbal threats by the offender, night assaults, outdoor locations, and more weapon use, all characteristics of stranger attacks. In addition, it was expected that victims of drink-ing offenders would resist more (Atkeson, Calhoun, & Morris, 1989; Ullman et al., 1999b), based on past research showing that victims resist more often when offenders are more vio-lent (Ullman, 1997b) and the hypothesis that drinking offenders would be more violent. To assess the cumulative impact of alcohol, situational factors, and offender and victim behav-iors on assault outcomes (rape outcome, physical injury, and medical attention), multi-variate logistic regression models were calculated to determine whether offender alcohol use predicted assault outcomes controlling for other factors. Offender drinking was ex-pected to be associated with more completed rapes (Ullman & Knight, 1993) and more physical injury (Coker et al., 1998; Johnson et al., 1978; Martin & Bachman, 1998; Ullman & Brecklin, in press).

METHOD

Sample

Data for the present study were drawn from the National Crime Victimization Survey National Sample 1992-1996 Incident-Level Rape Subset (Department of Justice, 1999). The NCVS, an ongoing survey of U.S. households about criminal victimization sponsored by the Bureau of Justice Statistics, includes both crimes reported to the police as well as un-reported crimes.

The current sample of the NCVS is approximately 50,000 housing units, which are selected using a stratified, multistage cluster design (Department of Justice, 1999). All in-dividuals age 12 and older that live in housing units or group quarters in selected U.S. cities are eligible to be interviewed, except for armed forces personnel living in military barracks, institutionalized persons, crew members of vessels, U.S. citizens residing abroad, and for-eign visitors to the United States. Using a rotating panel design, respondents are interviewed every 6 months over a period of 3 years. The first and the fifth interviews are face-to-face and take place in the home of the respondent by employees of the U.S. Census Bureau. The remainder of the interviews are held by telephone. After the seventh interview, the house-hold leaves the panel, and a new household is brought in. The NCVS has an average re-sponse rate of more than 95% (Department of Justice, 1999).

By 1992, the redesigned NCVS was in use in which direct questions about sexual as-sault were added.[1] Another purpose of the redesign was to better estimate offenses perpe-trated by known offenders (Bachman & Taylor, 1994). For the redesign, a question was added to the NCVS screener instrument that asks specifically about victimization incidents committed by friends or family members, and the redesign encouraged reporting an inci-dent even if respondents do not perceive it to be a criminal act.

There are two parts of the questionnaire: the screening section and the incident report. If a screening question elicits a positive response for an attempted or completed victimization in the previous 6 months, an incident report is then filled out to collect details about the characteristics and the circumstances of the incident. Rape was assessed in the NCVS initial screen questionnaire with the question, "Has anyone attacked or threatened you in any of these ways?" which included the response of "any rape, attempted rape, or other type of sexual attack." In addition, respondents were asked the following screening question:

> Incidents involving forced or unwanted sexual acts are often difficult to talk about. (Other than any incidents already mentioned), have you been forced or coerced to engage in un- wanted sexual activity by (a) someone you didn't know before, (b) a casual acquaintance, or (c) someone you know well?

Respondents were also later asked, "Do you mean forced or coerced sexual intercourse including attempts?" to clearly distinguish between the responses of rape and less severe sexual attacks. This study included only completed and attempted rapes and not less severe forms of sexual assaults or sexual coercion because there may be different correlates of less severe sexual assaults as compared to attempted or completed rapes. In addition, for comparison purposes, we wanted to remain consistent with past literature, especially past research using the NCVS (Martin & Bachman, 1998), in our criteria for sample selection.

The data included in this study are the single-offender rape incidents perpetrated by a male aged 15 or older against a female victim aged 15 or older (e.g., adult rape).[2] The multiple-offender incidents (gang rapes) were excluded because past research has shown that gang rapes and single-offender rapes differ significantly on many characteristics and outcomes (Gidycz & Koss, 1990; Ullman, 1999). In addition, it would be difficult to discern which offenders were drinking in a gang rape. The total number of sexual assaults against women reported by NCVS during this period was 436, but the selection criteria noted earlier reduced the sample to 362 offenses.

All tests of statistical significance were conducted using unweighted NCVS data because the use of weighted data generally overestimates the significance level. According to the NCVS codebook, "Weighted data are more typically used to compute representative population estimates of victimization dynamics and to compare victimization patterns over time" (Department of Justice, 1999, p. 44). The present study was not focused on examining the prevalence of sexual assaults in the United States or establishing patterns over time, therefore unweighted data have been used.

Measures

Demographics. Demographic data on the respondents' race was coded 0 for minority (e.g., African American; American Indian, Aleut, or Eskimo; and Asian or Pacific Islander) and 1 for Caucasian. Victim age was assessed in years at the time of the survey. The educational level of the victims was coded in years indicating the highest level of educational attainment. Other sociodemographic characteristics used in this study included victims' employment (0 = unemployed, 1 = employed) and marital status (0 = not married, 1 = married). Victims also reported the offender's race (0 = minority, 1 = Caucasian), and offender age was estimated by respondents using the following categories: 15 to 17, 18 to 20, 21 to 29, and 30 and older.

Offender Preassault Alcohol Use. To assess offender preassault alcohol and/or drug use, respondents were asked, "Was the offender drinking or on drugs, or don't you know?" Respondents who perceived the offenders had used substances were also asked whether the offender was "drinking," "on drugs," "both (drinking and on drugs)," or "drinking or on drugs—could not tell which." Offender preassault alcohol use was coded 1 (yes) if respondents indicated that the offenders were only under the influence of alcohol; otherwise, they were coded 0 (no). Offenders who were perceived to be under the influence of drugs ($N = 13$), both drugs and alcohol ($N = 30$), or undetermined substances ($N = 4$) were designated as missing in order to understand the role of alcohol exclusively in sexual assaults. This was done because it is more consistent with past research to exclude offender drug use from the category of alcohol use (Ullman et al., 1999a, 1999b; Ullman & Knight, 1993). For purposes of comparison, a variable assessing offender preassault substance use was also created with offenders who were drinking and/or on drugs coded as 1 and others not under the influence of any substances coded as 0. The analyses of offender alcohol use were replicated with the offender substance use variable to determine whether there were any differences in results.

Situational Characteristics. In addition, several situational characteristics were coded for this study. Respondents were asked, "Was the offender someone you knew or a stranger you had never seen before?" Victim-offender relationship was coded by dichotomizing responses to this question into known (coded as 0) and stranger categories (coded as 1). Respondents were asked, "Where did this incident happen?" from which assault location was coded 0 for indoors and 1 for outdoors. Victims were also asked, "About what time did the incident happen?" Assaults occurring in the daytime (between 6 a.m. and 6 p.m.) were coded 0, and those occurring at night (between 6 p.m. and 6 a.m.) were coded 1.

To assess offender aggression, respondents were asked, "Did the offender hit you, knock you down or actually attack you in any way?" Responses to this question were limited to no (coded as 0) or yes (coded as 1). Respondents were also asked, "Did the offender have a weapon such as a gun or knife, or something to use as a weapon, such as a bottle or wrench?" from which weapon presence (0 = no, 1 = yes) was coded as an additional measure of aggression. Verbal threat was ascertained by the question, "Did the offender threaten to hurt you before you were actually attacked?" (0 = no, 1 = yes).

Victim Resistance Strategies. To determine if victims used resistance during the sexual assault, respondents were asked, "Was there anything you did or tried to do about the incident while it was going on?" Respondents who said yes to at least one type of resistance were coded as using any resistance (0 = no, 1 = yes). Those victims who attacked or threatened the offender with a gun or other weapon, attacked the offender without a weapon, chased the offender, and/or tried to catch or hold off the offender were coded as using forceful physical resistance. Victims who struggled, ducked, blocked blows, ran or drove away, hid, and/or locked doors were coded as using nonforceful physical resistance. Forceful verbal resistance included those victims who threatened to injure the offender without a weapon, yelled at the offender, turned on lights, called the police or a guard or threatened to, tried to attract attention or help, and/or screamed from pain or fear, whereas nonforceful verbal resistance included victims who cooperated or pretended to, argued, reasoned, pleaded, and/or bargained. Each of these four types of resistance was coded 1 if the victims used that particular type of resistance and 0 if they did not use the strategy.

Injury Outcomes.   Three measures of harm to the victim were analyzed: rape outcome, physical injury, and postassault medical attention. A rape outcome variable was created so that attempted rapes were coded 0 and completed rapes were coded 1. Respondents were asked, "What were the injuries you suffered, if any?" to assess the extent of physical injury sustained due to the victimization. The injury measure was coded as a dichotomous variable with 0 for those not injured (including those respondents reporting only rape-related injuries) and 1 for injured. The injuries assessed included knife or gunshot wounds, broken bones, teeth knocked out, internal injuries, being knocked unconscious, bruises, cuts, black eyes, scratches, swelling, and chipped teeth. Respondents who were injured were then asked, "Were you injured to the extent that you received any medical care, including self treatment?" This served as an additional indicator of the severity of injury with cases coded 1 if victims received medical attention and 0 if they did not receive medical attention.

RESULTS

Sample Characteristics

Most victims were Caucasian (80.9%), whereas 14.9% were African American; 1.9% American Indian, Aleut, or Eskimo; and 2.2% Asian or Pacific Islander. The average age of the female victims in the sample of 362 sexual assaults was 27.92 (*SD* = 10.37), and the average number of years of education completed by the victims was 12.71 (*SD* = 2.33). More than half of the victims were employed (55.1%), and 9.4% of respondents were married at the time of the survey. More than two thirds of offenders were Caucasian (68.9%), whereas 31.1% were other races. Approximately half of the victims estimated the age of their offenders to be 30 years or older (47.3%), whereas the rest were judged to be younger than 30.

Alcohol and/or drugs were used by 60.9% of the offenders according to their victims' reports, of which 75.9% were judged to have used alcohol only. Only 13% of assaults were perpetrated by strangers to the victims, and 86.9% were committed by known offenders. More than three quarters of the sexual assaults occurred indoors (83.5%), and most occurred at night (78.1%). Ninety-seven percent of offenders used physical aggression against their victims, and 14.9% had a weapon during the attack. In one fourth of the assaults (25.5%), the offenders threatened to hurt the victim before the attack. Seventy-three percent of women reported using at least one resistance strategy. Few used forceful physical resistance (16.3%), whereas almost half used nonforceful physical resistance (45.0%). Twenty-four percent of victims used forceful verbal resistance, and one third used nonforceful verbal resistance (30.7%). Most rapes were completed (61.3%), and more than one third of victims sustained some kind of physical injury (37.9%). Almost one third (27.8%) of those injured sought medical attention immediately after the assault.

Comparisons of Assaults With
and Without Offender Alcohol Use

Bivariate analyses were done to determine whether there were differences in demographic and assault situation variables according to whether the offender was drinking. Bivariate chi-square tests were conducted to compare sexual assaults with and without

TABLE 19.1 Demographics and Characteristics of Assault With and Without Offender Preassault Alcohol Use

| | Offender Preassault Alcohol Use | | | | | |
	Percentage Offender Alcohol Use	*Percentage No Offender Alcohol Use*	X^2	*df*	*N*	*p*
Victim demographics						
Caucasian	86.0	78.0	2.81	1	254	.093
Employed	55.4	57.0	0.07	1	244	.798
Married	7.4	9.4	.035	1	253	.557
Offender demographics						
Caucasian	77.0	69.5	1.84	1	253	.175
Situational demographics						
Stranger	16.2	5.9	6.91	1	254	.009
Outdoor	20.7	10.9	4.16	1	231	.041
Night	91.9	66.4	26.55	1	252	.000
Offender aggression	98.5	98.3	0.02	1	254	.886
Offender weapon	11.4	10.3	0.08	1	249	.779
Verbal threat	23.3	25.5	0.14	1	222	.709
Victim resistance strategies						
Any resistance	80.9	69.5	4.44	1	254	.035
Forceful physical	19.1	16.9	0.20	1	254	.654
Nonforceful physical	49.3	39.8	2.28	1	254	.131
Forceful verbal	25.0	20.3	0.78	1	254	.376
Nonforceful verbal	35.3	30.5	0.66	1	254	.418
Injury outcomes						
Completed rape	52.9	71.2	8.98	1	254	.003
Victim injured	40.3	31.0	2.33	1	250	.127
Medical attention	25.7	18.9	1.32	1	200	.251

NOTE: Victim race (0 = minority, 1 = Caucasian); employment (0 = unemployed, 1 = employed); marital status (0 = not married, 1 = married); offender race (0 = minority, 1 = Caucasian); victim-offender relationship (0 = known offender, 1 = stranger); assault location (0 = indoors, 1 = outdoors); time (0 = day, 1 = night); offender aggression (0 = no, 1 = yes); offender weapon (0 = no, 1 = yes); verbal threat (0 = no, 1 = yes); any resistance (0 = no, 1 = yes); forceful physical resistance (0 = no, 1 = yes); nonforceful physical resistance (0 = no, 1 = yes); forceful verbal resistance (0 = no, 1 = yes); nonforceful verbal resistance (0 = no, 1 = yes); rape outcome (0 = attempted rape, 1 = completed rape); physical injury (0 = no, 1 = yes); medical attention (0 = no, 1 = yes).

offender drinking. In addition, two one-way analyses of variances were conducted to examine whether victim age and victim educational level varied according to offender alcohol use. Results of the chi-square tests, including likelihood ratio test statistics and percentages, are presented in Table 19.1.

There were no significant differences in the demographic characteristics of victims or offenders according to whether offenders used alcohol prior to the assault; however, the chi-square test for victim race approached significance ($p < .10$), with more Caucasian victims reporting incidents involving alcohol. Offender drinking was associated with more stranger assaults than cases without offender drinking. Assaults in which offenders were perceived to be drinking were more likely to occur outdoors and at night than assaults by nondrinking offenders. Victims used resistance more often in response to drinking offenders, although there were no differences in victims' use of the specific types of resistance strategies according to offender alcohol use. Fewer completed rapes were associated with offender preassault alcohol use. Offender use of physical aggression, weapons, and verbal threats did not differ according to offender preassault drinking. In addition, no differences were found in victim injury or medical attention according to offender drinking status.

Bivariate analyses were also conducted comparing sexual assaults with and without offender substance use (alcohol and/or drugs). There were few differences in the results of these two sets of analyses. Offenders who were perceived to be under the influence of substances were more likely to have a weapon than those who were not. Offender preassault substance use was associated with more victim injury and more medical attention than cases not involving offender substance use. There was a trend toward significance ($p = .06$) for use of nonforceful physical resistance and forceful verbal resistance, with victims more likely to use these strategies when the offender was using substances.[3]

Logistic Regression Analyses

To assess whether offender preassault alcohol use in combination with other situational characteristics affected the outcomes of assaults, a series of logistic regression models was performed. First, an initial set of three models included demographic variables (e.g., age and race of victim and offender and victim educational, marital, and employment status) and assault characteristics (offender alcohol use, victim-offender relationship, assault location, time of day, offender weapon use, offender verbal threats, victim forceful physical resistance, victim nonforceful physical resistance, victim forceful verbal resistance, and victim nonforceful verbal resistance) as predictors. Offender aggression was a constant in these models (e.g., present in all nonmissing cases) because all attacks had offender violence. Therefore, the role of offender aggression could not be examined in these analyses. Dependent variables were dichotomous assault outcomes of rape, injury, and medical attention. Second, the three models were rerun omitting demographic variables that were not significant in the initial models.[4] Finally, three reduced models were calculated retaining only the significant variables from the previous set of models. Beta weights, odds ratios, and p values for the second full and final reduced models are presented in Tables 19.2 to 19.4.

Odds of completed rape were greater for attacks involving unemployed victims, offenders who were not drinking, known offenders, and victims not using nonforceful physical resistance. The odds of completed rape were reduced by approximately one half if the offender was drinking. Attacks involving employed victims, strangers, and victims using nonforceful physical resistance were approximately one third as likely to be completed. Absence of forceful verbal resistance by victims was marginally related to completed rape ($p = .065$). In the reduced model, the same predictors were significant (see right side of Table 19.2), as in the full model.

In a second regression model predicting victim injury, demographic variables were not significant, but victim use of nonforceful physical resistance and nonforceful verbal resistance were each associated with marginally increased odds of physical injury ($p < .10$). The odds of injury were more than 1.5 times (odds ratios = 1.8 for both variables) greater for

TABLE 19.2   Logistic Regression Analyses Predicting Odds of Completed Rape

Variable	Fall Model (N = 191)			Reduced Model (N = 244)		
	Beta Weight	Odds Ratio	p	Beta Weight	Odds Ratio	p
Demographics						
Employment	−0.97	0.38	.014	−0.75	.47	.013
Assault characteristics						
Offender alcohol use	−0.77	0.47	.042	−0.66	.52	.026
Victim-offender relationship	−1.44	0.24	.016	−1.40	.25	.003
Assault location	−0.33	0.72	.498			
Time	−0.52	0.59	.328			
Offender weapon	0.85	2.34	.255			
Verbal threat	0.65	1.92	.179			
Forceful physical	−0.40	0.67	.365			
Nonforceful physical	−1.12	0.33	.003	−1.06	.35	.000
Forceful verbal	−0.75	0.47	.065	−0.58	.56	.091
Nonforceful verbal	0.46	1.59	.228			
-2 x log likelihood			195.41		280.64	
X^2			50.85		43.69	
df			11		5	
p			.000		.000	

NOTE: Employment (0 = unemployed, 1 = employed); offender alcohol use (0 = no, 1 = yes); victim-offender relationship (0 = known offender, 1 = stranger); assault location (0 = indoors, 1 = outdoors); time (0 = day, 1 = night); offender weapon (0 = no, 1 = yes); verbal threat (0 = no, 1 = yes); forceful physical resistance (0 = no, 1 = yes); nonforceful physical threat (0 = no, 1 = yes); forceful verbal resistance (0 = no, 1 = yes); nonforceful verbal resistance (0 = no, 1 = yes); rape outcome (0 = attempted rape, 1 = completed rape).

attacks involving each of these characteristics, and in the reduced model, both variables became significant (*p* < .05).

In a third model, victims using forceful physical resistance had increased odds of immediate postassault medical attention, whereas nonforceful physical resistance was marginally associated with increased medical attention (*p* = .075). The odds ratios for both variables were more than 2.00, indicating that these relationships were fairly strong. Victim forceful physical resistance remained significant in the reduced model, and nonforceful physical resistance became statistically significant (*p* < .05).

Logistic regression models were also conducted replacing offender alcohol use with offender substance abuse to compare the results. The relationships between offender substance abuse and the three outcome measures (rape completion, victim injury, and medical attention) were similar to those revealed in the models including offender alcohol use. In the model predicting rape completion, substance abuse was related to less rape completion (*p* < .05). Offender substance abuse was unrelated to both victim injury and medical attention.

TABLE 19.3   Logistic Regression Analyses Predicting Odds of Physical Injury

Variable	Full Model (N = 196)			Reduced Model (N = 351)		
	Beta Weight	Odds Ratio	p	Beta Weight	Odds Ratio	p
Assault characteristics						
Offender alcohol use	.28	1.32	.396			
Victim-offender relationship	−.37	0.69	.467			
Assault location	.41	1.50	.364			
Time	.26	1.29	.530			
Offender weapon	.30	1.34	.585			
Verbal threat	.62	1.86	.107			
Forceful physical	.57	1.77	.142			
Nonforceful physical	.60	1.83	.062	.86	2.35	.000
Forceful verbal	.08	1.08	.829			
Nonforceful verbal	.60	1.82	.069	.53	1.71	.026
$-2 \times$ log likelihood		246.85			445.80	
χ^2		17.45			19.99	
df		10			2	
p value		.065			.000	

NOTE: Offender alcohol use (0 = no, 1 = yes); victim-offender relationship (0 = known offender, 1 = stranger); assault location (0 = indoors, 1 = outdoors); time (0 = day, 1 = night); offender weapon (0 = no, 1 = yes); verbal threat (0 = no, 1 = yes); forceful physical resistance (0 = no, 1 = yes); nonforceful physical resistance (0 = no, 1 = yes); forceful verbal resistance (0 = no, 1 = yes); nonforceful verbal resistance (0 = no, 1 = yes); physical injury (0 = no, 1 = yes).

DISCUSSION

The role of offender alcohol use in the outcomes of rape incidents was examined using National Crime Victimization Survey data. This study does not directly support the findings of past research that attacks characterized by offender preassault alcohol use are directly associated with more serious assault outcomes. Rather, in this sample, offender alcohol use predicted less completed rape and was unrelated to victim physical injury and medical attention. Using fewer years of NCVS data, Martin and Bachman (1998) also found a trend in their data showing less rape completion in attacks with offender alcohol use. This relationship may reflect a true effect, or it may be an artifact of the particular sample of rape cases analyzed here, which included only the more severe cases of completed and attempted rapes. However, the present study controlled for many important correlates of attack outcomes in the logistic regression models, thus providing a more conservative test of alcohol's effects, which may account for this finding. Perhaps the relationship between alcohol use and fewer completed rapes is also a function of the associations between offender alcohol use and victim resistance, stranger assaults, and outdoor assaults, each of which is related to fewer completed rapes (Martin & Bachman, 1998; Ullman, 1997b; Ullman & Knight, 1991).

TABLE 19.4 Logistic Regression Analyses Predicting Odds of Seeking Medical Attention

	Full Model (N = 163)			Reduced Model (N = 291)		
Variable	Beta Weight	Odds Ratio	p	Beta Weight	Odds Ratio	p
Assault characteristics						
Offender alcohol use	0.09	1.09	.848			
Victim-offender relationship	0.43	1.54	.519			
Assault location	0.15	1.16	.805			
Time	−.027	0.76	.609			
Offender weapon	0.59	1.81	.338			
Verbal threat	0.75	2.12	.123			
Forceful physical	1.13	3.08	0.15	.71	20.4	.040
Nonforceful physical	0.79	2.21	.075	.85	2.34	.002
Forceful verbal	0.41	1.50	.380			
Nonforceful verbal	0.24	1.27	.589			
−2 × log likelihood		149.61			328.48	
χ^2		22.52			15.71	
df		10			2	
p value		0.13			.000	

NOTE: Offender alcohol use (0 = no, 1 = yes); victim-offender relationship (0 = known offender, 1 = stranger); assault location (0 = indoors, 1 = outdoors); time (0 = day, 1 = night); offender weapon (0 = no, 1 = yes); verbal threat (0 = no, 1 = yes); forceful physical resistance (0 = no, 1 = yes); nonforceful physical resistance (0 = no, 1 = yes); forceful verbal resistance (0 = no, 1 = yes); nonforceful verbal resistance (0 = no, 1 = yes); physical injury (0 = no, 1 = yes).

Results revealed that offender preassault alcohol use was associated with stranger assaults, night assaults, outdoor assaults, and more victim resistance, as hypothesized based on past research (Atkeson et al., 1989; Ullman & Brecklin, in press; Ullman et al., 1999a, 1999b). Offender alcohol use was not related to offender aggression; however, this was most likely due to the high percentage of cases in this sample involving aggression (97.0%). In addition, offender alcohol use was not associated with offender use of weapons or verbal threats. Contrary to some prior research (Ullman & Knight, 1993), offender preassault alcohol use was related to less rape completion both in bivariate and multivariate analyses. Consistent with past research, assaults involving offender alcohol use did involve more victim injury and medical attention (Coker et al., 1998; Johnson et al., 1978; Martin & Bachman, 1998; Ullman & Brecklin, in press), but these relationships failed to reach significance.

Offender aggression has typically been found to be a predictor of severity of sexual victimization (Ullman et al., 1999a, 1999b) and physical injury (Siegel, Sorensen, Golding, Burnam, & Stein, 1989; Ullman & Brecklin, in press; Ullman & Knight, 1991). In the present study, the relationships of offender aggression with rape, injury, and medical attention could not be studied because all of the cases in the multivariate models involved offender aggression. This is most likely an artifact of the more severe sample of rape incidents used in this study and the fact that the NCVS only assesses presence or absence but not severity of aggression. Because this sample only included completed and attempted rapes, the study likely overrepresented completed rapes. This restricted range of the rape outcome variable due to the absence of less severe sexual attacks in this sample may have reduced the power of statistical tests to distinguish these types of assaults.

Some past research also shows that offender aggression is more strongly related to sexual victimization severity and injury in cases without offender alcohol use (Ullman & Brecklin, in press; Ullman et al., 1999b) and that alcohol use and physical aggression may be independent tactics used by offenders (Cleveland et al., 1999). This suggests that the relationships between offender alcohol use and assault outcomes may be stronger in attacks without offender aggression, which may be why alcohol was related to less rape completion in this sample.

This study suggests that offender preassault alcohol use may play an indirect role in contributing to injury outcomes of rape attacks through its association with more dangerous situations (night, outdoors, and stranger). According to Collins and Schlenger (1988), offender use of alcohol is rarely the sole direct cause of violence. In some assault situations, the presence of an offender who has used alcohol prior to the assault may be associated with more severe assault outcomes to victims. For example, the relationship of offender alcohol use and assault outcomes may differ according to specific types of victim-offender relationships (e.g., acquaintances and intimates). The present results are important in suggesting that the role of preassault alcohol use in rape outcomes may be more complicated than has been commonly assumed.

There are several limitations of this study that may have affected the results. Although the National Crime Victimization Survey is a representative sample of adults, the final sample of sexual assault incidents analyzed in this study likely is not. Because biased samples of rape incidents are typically obtained despite representative sampling efforts in rape research, consistency of findings is an important criterion for evaluating the accuracy of results (Ullman, 1997b). Replication across different data sets is therefore of critical importance in rape prevention research.

In this study, victims reported on the presence of offender alcohol use according to their own recollections of their assaults. Victims may have been inaccurate in their assessments of offender preassault drinking. Although these analyses excluded cases in which victims did not provide an answer or said they did not know about their offender's preassault substance use, there was no way to evaluate the accuracy of information about this variable. In addition, information about the amount or type of alcohol consumed by the offender is needed because the extent of drinking may also affect the assault outcome. For example, Muehlenhard and Linton (1987) compared dates that led to sexual assault and those that did not and found that heavy alcohol use was a risk factor for sexual assault. Offender alcohol abuse propensity in general (not available in the NCVS) also may be related to more severe sexual victimization, as shown by Ullman et al. (1999a). In addition, this sample included only single-offender assaults, but alcohol may well play a different role in gang rapes, which should be studied in future research. Researchers may also want to examine the role of alcohol use in less severe sexual assaults (e.g., sexual coercion).

The National Crime Victimization Survey is also limited by a lack of data on the victim's own preassault alcohol use, which made it impossible to assess the impact of victims' alcohol use on assault outcomes. In self-report victimization surveys, it is much more likely that victims can accurately report on their own use of substances than on their assailants' substance use. However, victims are much less likely than offenders to drink during sexual assaults generally, and when victims are drinking, typically offenders also are drinking (Johnson et al., 1978; Ullman & Brecklin, in press; Ullman et al., 1999a, 1999b). Because the effects of victim and offender drinking during sexual assaults may differ, future research should address the role of victim drinking.

Despite these limitations, the present study showed that preassault alcohol use by offenders is associated with riskier rape situations and that it may be associated with more severe injury outcomes indirectly through its relationships with these situational factors. Offender alcohol use was also found to be related to less completed rape. In addition, we examined alcohol's role in both rape and physical injury outcomes, an issue that has only been addressed in one previous study using a national sample (Martin & Bachman, 1998). Other national samples have only examined alcohol's effects on one of these dependent variables: injury (Ullman & Brecklin, in press) or sexual victimization severity (Ullman et al., 1999a, 1999b).

This study also expanded on Martin and Bachman's (1998) study by including more years of the redesigned NCVS, which resulted in a larger sample size. The present study included additional victim and offender demographic characteristics (victim employment, victim marital status, victim level of education, offender age, and offender race) in the logistic regression models. Verbal threat, time of assault, and offender aggression were also added to the present study. The effects of specific resistance strategies were also examined in greater detail in this study, including forceful physical resistance, nonforceful physical resistance, forceful verbal resistance, and nonforceful verbal resistance, whereas Martin and Bachman (1998) used only the categories of physical resistance and verbal resistance. The current study examined the role of offender drinking only, whereas Martin and Bachman's (1998) coding of offender alcohol use included offenders who were "both drinking and on drugs." Cases involving offenders who were both drinking and on drugs were excluded from this study's analyses because we were interested solely in the role of alcohol in sexual assaults. However, when we replicated our analyses using offender preassault substance use, the results did not differ substantially from the analyses conducted using only offender alcohol use. Future research is needed on the different combinations of preassault offender drug and alcohol use to discover how their use affects assault outcomes. However, some past research has shown that the prevalence of drug use is quite low in sexual assaults when respondents are asked to specify whether the incident involved alcohol, drugs, or both (Ullman et al., 1999a, 1999b).

In future research, larger samples of assaults are needed that vary in assault characteristics (e.g., assaults with and without weapons and with and without aggression) to assess the effects of offender and victim behaviors on assault outcomes in different situational contexts. Improved reporting and accuracy of information about both victim and offender preassault alcohol use are needed in representative samples of rape incidents to permit a complete evaluation of the role of alcohol use in both the rape and injury outcomes. Development of effective rape prevention programs depends on knowledge about the dynamics of rape attacks and how preassault behaviors such as alcohol use may affect the outcomes of attacks. Given the fact that the present study provides additional evidence of a high prevalence of alcohol use in rapes, rape prevention programs need to incorporate information about the associations of alcohol use, situational factors, and rape outcomes.

NOTES

1. The redesign of the National Crime Victimization Survey (NCVS) was implemented for 50% of the sample in January 1992 and for the entire sample in July 1993 (Bachman & Taylor, 1994).

2. In the NCVS questionnaire, offender age is only reported by the victims in categories (younger than 12, 12 to 14, 15 to 17, 18 to 20, 21 to 29, and 30 and older), which we restricted for our sample to offenders aged 15 and older. Therefore, we also only included victims aged 15 and older.

3. Results of analyses of offender substance use are available from the authors on request.

4. Due to the dichotomous codings of many NCVS measures, path analysis used in past research (Ullman, Karabatsos, & Koss, 1999a, 1999b) could not be conducted in the present study. Several interactions were tested in the regression models between offender alcohol use and the offense characteristics. However, in many cases, the cell sizes were too small to draw reliable conclusions.

20

Assisting Rape Victims
as They Recover From Rape

The Impact on Friends

COURTNEY E. AHRENS
REBECCA CAMPBELL
University of Illinois at Chicago

After surviving sexual assault, victims often find themselves in need of support (Davis, Brickman, & Baker, 1991; George, Winfield, & Blazer, 1992; Golding, Siegel, Sorenson, Burnam, & Stein, 1989; Kimmerling & Calhoun, 1994; S. E. Ullman, 1996a, 1996b). Yet it is unlikely that friends of rape survivors are any more prepared for this event than survivors. Friends may experience emotional reactions that affect their functioning and ability to support survivors. In this article, we examine how friends react to rape disclosure. First, a review of the literature explores the role of friends and family in providing support. An empirical study is then presented to examine the impact of disclosure on friends of rape survivors. These findings are then integrated with canonical correlation analyses, revealing that some friends are able to be supportive, but others have a more difficult time. Qualitative data are used to illustrate these patterns.

Disclosing Sexual Assault and Social Support

Most rape survivors do not disclose the assault to formal agencies (2% to 20% to police, hospital, or rape crisis centers) (Binder, 1981; Brickman & Briere, 1984; George et al.,

Authors' Note: The authors would like to thank James Kelly, Stephanie Riger, and Sarah Ullman for their feedback on this article, and Deanie Blue, Bradley Egal, Tricia Grining, Rania Omar, Christa Russo, and April Skrine for their assistance with data collection and coding. Correspondence concerning this article should be addressed to Courtney Ahrens, Department of Psychology, University of Illinois at Chicago, 1007 West Harrison, Chicago, IL 60607-7137; e-mail: cahrens@uic.edu

1992; Golding et al., 1989; Koss, Dinero, Seibel, & Cox, 1988; Russell, 1982a; S. E. Ullman, 1996a). Rather, most survivors turn to friends and family (59% to 91%) (George et al., 1992; Golding et al., 1989; S. E. Ullman, 1996a), and support from friends and family is considered more helpful than support from formal agencies (60% to 87% thought family/friends were helpful; 5% to 63% thought police/clergy/doctors were helpful) (Golding et al., 1989; Popiel & Suskind, 1985; Ruch & Chandler, 1983; S. E. Ullman, 1996a). Yet although social support is related to better postrape functioning for some victims (Kimmerling & Calhoun, 1994; Ruch & Leon, 1983; S. E. Ullman, 1996a), other studies find no such relationship (Popiel & Suskind, 1985; Ruch & Leon, 1983; Sales, Baum, & Shore, 1984). Negative social reactions, on the other hand, are consistently related to poorer functioning (Baker, Skolnik, Davis, & Brickman, 1988; Davis et al., 1991; S. E. Ullman, 1996b). These findings suggest that social support may benefit survivors if negative reactions can be avoided.

Such negative reactions include feeling sorry for victims (Popiel & Suskind, 1985), blaming victims, and minimizing/denying the impact of the assault (S. E. Ullman, 1996a). Negative reactions considered harmful by non-sexual assault victims include insensitivity, negative emotional reactions, critical judgments, blaming victims, rejecting/avoiding victims, and discrimination (Dakof & Taylor, 1990; Dunkel-Schetter, 1984; Herbert & Dunkel-Schetter, 1992). Thus, helpers' ability to avoid such negative reactions when assisting victims is crucial.

Helpers' Responses

The ability to be supportive and avoid negative responses may be hampered if helpers are burdened by their own emotions. Table 20.1 summarizes affective and interpersonal reactions reported in the literature. These findings suggest that partners and families of rape victims experience emotions ranging from anger to helplessness. Interpersonal reactions such as distancing and controlling behaviors are also noted. Similar findings from reactions to other victims are reported in Table 20.2, suggesting common experiences when assisting victims.

Victimization Perspective Theory

To disentangle the relationship between how friends feel and how they respond to victims, researchers have proposed a model known as victimization perspective theory (Coates, Wortman, & Abbey, 1979; Dunkel-Schetter & Wortman, 1981; Herbert & Dunkel-Schetter, 1992; Silver, Wortman, & Crofton, 1990). According to this theory, helpers who are confronted with people undergoing stressful life experiences believe they should help but feel helpless and frustrated when their efforts appear ineffective. Their interactions then become strained as helpers become increasingly uncertain about how to act (Silver et al., 1990).

Yet there are several limitations to this literature. First, emotional reactions to rape victims have mainly been assessed through case studies, counselors' reflections, or small studies of partners and family members. This literature has neglected the impact of rape disclosure on friends. Second, research on victimization perspective theory has generally been conducted in laboratory settings rather than real-life situations. This study therefore

TABLE 20.1   Affective and Interpersonal Responses of Partners and Family Members to Rape Disclosure

	Findings	
Study	Affective	Interpersonal
Burge (1983)	Anger	Blame the victim
	Guilt (not protecting)	Communication problems
	Helplessness	Distract victim
	Revenge	Keep it a secret
		Overprotect/patronize victim
		Sexual problems
Emm & McKenry (1988)	Anger	Disturbed communication
	Depression	Overprotective of victim
	Fearfulness	
	Frustration	
	Helplessness	
	Revenge	
Feinauer (1982)	Denial	Avoid discussion
	Guilt (not protecting)	Distract victim
	Inadequate	Overprotective
		Sexual problems
Feinauer & Hippolite (1987)	Denial	Avoid discussion
	Depression	Communication problems
	Guilt (not protecting)	Distract victim
	Helpless	Encourage secrecy
	Humiliation	Overprotective
	Inadequate	Trust destroyed
	Resentment	Withdraw from victim
	Shame	
Figley (1983)	Appreciated	Elevations in tension
	Emotionally drained	Increased arguements
	Needed	
	Upset	
Holmstrom & Burgess (1979)	Hurt	Avoided discussing incident
	If-only reactions	Sexual problems
	Revenge	Took control of reporting
Miller, Williams, & Bernstein (1982)	Angry	Communication problems
		Problems in commitment
		Problems in support
		Sexual problems
Mitchell (1991)	Failure to protect	Protect family
	Loss of security	Treat victim of fragile
Remer & Elliott (1988)	Anger	Feel neglected by her
	Denial	Overprotect/control victim
	Depression	Relationship problems
	Guilty	Sexual problems
	Helpless	

(continued)

TABLE 20.1   (Continued)

Study	Findings	
	Affective	*Interpersonal*
	Loss/grief reactions	
	Loss of view of world as fair	
	Revenge	
	Shock	
	Trapped	
Riggs & Kilpatrick (1997)	Anger	Communication problems
	Anxiety	Commitment problems
	Concern	Doubt victim
	Depression	Problems expressing affection
	Guilt (not protecting)	Sexual difficulties
	Hostility	Withdrawl from victim
	Intrusive thoughts	
	Low self-esteem/self-worth	
	Powerlessness	
	Posttraumatic stress disorder	
	Shame	
	Vulnerability	
Rodkin, Hunt, & Cowan (1982)	Denial	Communication breakdown
	Guilt/self-blame	Impatient with slow recovery
	Fear	Overprotect victim
	Powerlessness	Resentment of dependency
	Self-image threatened	Sexual problems
	Somatic disturbances	
Silverman (1978)	Anger	Blame and doubt the victim
	Helplessness	Distract her
	Rage	Keep it a secret
	Resentment	Overprotect victim
	Physical revulsion	Patronize victim
	Shame	Rally support without permission
	Shock	
	Want violent retribution	
Stone (1980)	Anger	Communication problems
	Depression	Confusion about how to help
	Helplessness	Sexual problems
	Revenge	Withdrawl
	Shame	
White & Rollins (1981)	Anger	Avoid discussing
	Anxiety	Distract victim
	Depression	Minimize her reactions
	Fear/vulnerability	Overprotect victim
	Helplessness	Patronize victim
	Self-blame for not protecting	

TABLE 20.2 Affective and Interpersonal Responses of Significant Others to Other Victims

	Findings	
Study	*Topic*	*Affective*
Burgess (1975)	Homicide	Anger
		Fear
		Grief
		Guilt for not protecting
		Helplessness
		Horror
		If-only thoughts
		Outrage
		Preoccupation
		Revenge
		Somatic symptoms
Friedman, Bischoff, Davis, & Person (1982)	Crime victims	Anxiety
		Burdened
		Fear
		Suspicion of others
		Valued as helper
Greif & Porembski (1988)	AIDS victims	Anger
		Denial
		Depression
		Guilt
		Sadness
		Secrecy
		Shame
Irving, Bot, & Catalan (1985)	AIDS victims	Anxiety
		Depression
		Panic disorder
		Sexual problems

seeks to close these gaps by exploring the effects of disclosure on friends of rape survivors (rather than partners or family members) in actual helping experiences.

THE CURRENT STUDY

This exploratory study recruited friends of rape survivors to clarify the impact of rape disclosure. Friends first characterized their friendships and described the assault. Participants then described their ability to help the survivor, the emotional impact of this experience, and changes that occurred in the friendship. Because previous research suggests that men and women may have different experiences when helping survivors (Davis & Brickman, 1996), gender differences were also examined. Similarly, personal history of assault and length of friendship were examined to determine if friends' experiences varied along these lines.

Although these descriptive findings paint a vivid picture of the impact of rape disclosure on friends, it is likely that friends had diverse experiences. Thus, canonical correlation analysis was conducted to integrate the descriptive findings and reveal how friends' positive beliefs, emotions, and relationship outcomes relate to friends' negative beliefs, emotions, and relationship outcomes. The patterns identified are then illustrated with qualitative data.

METHOD

Sampling Design

A cross-sectional survey design with non-probability sampling was used to locate friends who have helped nonfamilial rape survivors who were at least 14 years old at the time of the assault. Undergraduate students were recruited through fliers, the university newspaper and Internet homepage, classroom and student organization presentations, and the Subject Pool.

Participant Characteristics

Eighty-six students completed a questionnaire, and 60 were retained for final analyses.[1] On average, participants were 21 years old ($SD = 4.46$), female (61%), and of diverse racial backgrounds (43% Caucasian, 21% Asian American, 17% African American, 16% Latino/Hispanic, and 3% multiethnic). Twenty-seven percent disclosed a personal history of sexual assault.

Procedure

Participants who responded to fliers were sent questionnaires in the mail. Others received the measure during presentations or completed a questionnaire in person. Students exchanged completed questionnaires for $5 and information/referral packets.

Measures

Although there is a great deal of theory and anecdotal data on the impact of rape disclosure, established measures are lacking. The following measures were therefore developed for this project, based on literature on victimization perspective theory (e.g., Herbert & Dunkel-Schetter, 1992), significant others' reactions (see Table 20.1), and recovery (e.g., Koss et al., 1994).

Description of the Friendship

Description of the friendships included type of relationship (e.g., best friend, acquaintance, etc.), length of friendship, and frequency of contact. Ratings of closeness and importance were obtained using a 5-point Likert-type scale.

Description of the Assault

A description of the assault included delay in disclosure; type of assault; and the presence of a weapon, alcohol, or injuries.

Perceptions About the Assault

Victim Responsibility.   Four items on a 5-point Likert-type scale (1 = *strongly disagree*, 5 = *strongly agree*) formed the Victim Responsibility Scale (e.g., "I thought she could have done more to protect herself"). Alpha was .82, and corrected item-total correlations ranged from .55 to .77.

Empathy.   Participants rated their agreement on a 5-point Likert-type scale with three statements included in the Empathy Scale (e.g., "I was able to understand what she was going through"). Alpha was .82, and corrected item-total correlations ranged from .66 to .72.

Opinions About Victim Coping.   Using a 5-point Likert-type scale, participants rated four statements on survivors' coping (e.g., "I didn't think she was handling it the right way"); higher scores represent negative opinions. Alpha for the Victim Coping Scale was .64, and corrected item-total correlations ranged from .37 to .48.

General Beliefs About the Impact of Sexual Assault

Participants rated beliefs about the impact of sexual assault (i.e., what participants believed should happen during recovery) by responding to four items on a 5-point Likert-type scale (e.g., "How much do you think rape victims will need to talk about what happened?"). Alpha for the Beliefs About the Immediate Impact Scale was .51, and corrected item-total correlations ranged from .17 to .38.

Perceptions of Their Assistance

Confusion.   Six items formed the Confusion Scale (e.g., "I didn't know what to do to help"). Alpha was .84, and corrected item-total correlations ranged from .51 to .68.

Ineffectiveness.   Six statements on a 5-point Likert-type scale measured participants' perceptions of ineffectiveness (e.g., "I felt that my efforts to help didn't help"). Alpha for the Ineffectiveness Scale was .79, and corrected item-total correlations ranged from .49 to .62.

Impact on Participants of Assisting in the Recovery Process

Emotional Distress.   The Emotional Distress Scale included 24 items reflecting distress (e.g., anger, fear, shock) rated on a 5-point Likert-type scale. Alpha was .88, and corrected item-total correlations ranged from .33 to .66.

Validating Emotions. Participants rated seven statements reflecting validating emotions (e.g., "I did a good job helping") on a 5-point Likert-type scale. The Validating Emotions Scale had an alpha of .80, and corrected item-total correlations ranged from .38 to .66.

Impact on Their Relationship

Positive Cognitive Impact. Participants rated seven statements on the Positive Cognitive Impact Scale on a 5-point Likert-type scale (e.g., "I still consider the victim to be a friend"). Alpha was .83, and corrected item-total correlations ranged from .42 to .73.

Negative Cognitive Impact. Participants rated 12 statements on the Negative Cognitive Impact Scale on a 5-point Likert-type scale (e.g., "I am afraid of upsetting the victim"). Alpha for this scale was .75, and corrected item-total correlations ranged from .30 to .55.

Positive Behavioral Impact. There were five items on the Positive Behavioral Impact Scale (e.g., "We still do the same things together"). Alpha was .82, and corrected item-total correlations ranged from .51 to .75.

Negative Behavioral Impact Scale. Using a 5-point Likert-type scale, participants rated 13 statements on the Negative Behavioral Impact Scale (e.g., "I started to avoid the victim"). Alpha for this scale was .83, and corrected item-total correlations ranged from .34 to .58.

RESULTS

Description of the Friendship

The friendships averaged 8 years in length ($SD = 5.97$), and more than three quarters described the survivor as a good friend. The friendships were described as somewhat close ($M = 3.97$, $SD = 1.18$) and important ($M = 4.29$, $SD = .97$), and 81% saw the survivor once a week.

Description of the Victims

Survivors were young females (98%) from diverse racial backgrounds (48% Caucasian, 18% African American, 13% Asian American, 12% Latino, 5% multiethnic, 2% Native American). On average, survivors were 21 years old ($SD = 2.52$), but only 17 ($SD = 2.04$) when assaulted.

Description of the Assault

An average of 7 months ($SD = 15$) elapsed between assault and disclosure. Most were acquaintance rapes (83%) and did not involve injuries (19%), weapons (7%), or alcohol (29%).

General Beliefs About the Recovery Process

Ratings on the Beliefs About the Immediate Impact Scale indicated that participants expected rape to have a strong impact on survivors' lives immediately after the assault ($M = 3.92$, $SD = .88$).

Perceptions About the Assault

Average ratings on the Victim Responsibility Scale ($M = 2.08$, $SD = .88$) indicated that participants did not blame survivors for the assault. Rather, responses to the Empathy Scale ($M = 3.78$, $SD = .92$) indicated that participants felt empathic toward survivors, and average ratings on the Victim Coping Scale ($M = 2.37$, $SD = .72$) indicated that participants did not perceive the survivors' coping strategies to be particularly ineffective.

Friends' Perceptions of Their Assistance

Average ratings on the Confusion Scale indicated that participants were not particularly confused about how to help ($M = 2.58$, $SD = 1.09$) although they did express uncertainty about what survivors needed (68%) and how to help (40%). Similarly, mean scores on the Ineffective Scale indicated that participants believed their efforts to help were effective ($M = 1.70$, $SD = .64$).

Impact on Friends of Assisting in the Recovery Process

Average ratings on the Emotional Distress Scale ($M = 2.84$, $SD = .72$) indicated that participants did not feel particularly distressed. However, a number of distressing emotions were prevalent among most participants. Table 20.3 shows that most participants were angry at the assailant and wanted revenge. Yet experiencing these negative emotions did not affect participants' feelings of validation. Average ratings on the Validating Emotions Scale ($M = 3.36$, $SD = .77$) indicated that participants felt somewhat positive about the experience; the majority of participants felt they were needed and that the survivor was thankful.

Impact on the Relationship

Cognitive Impact. Average ratings on the Positive Cognitive Impact Scale ($M = 4.23$, $SD = .77$) indicated that participants believed the friendship remained intact or grew closer. Table 20.3 shows that most friends continued to consider the survivor a friend and felt they knew and understood her. Conversely, average ratings on the Negative Cognitive Impact Scale ($M = 1.71$, $SD = .58$) indicated that participants did not begin to think negatively about the friendship. Participants did not agree with any items reflecting negative thinking about the relationship.

Behavioral Impact. Overall, participants agreed with statements included in the Positive Behavioral Impact Scale ($M = 4.07$, $SD = .88$). Most participants believed they still treated the survivor the same and could talk about their own feelings (see Table 20.3). Conversely, average ratings on the Negative Behavioral Impact Scale ($M = 1.87$, $SD = .67$)

TABLE 20.3   Friends' Experiences Helping Rape Victims: High- and Low-Ranked Items

Scale[a]	Percentage Who Agreed	Item Mean	Item SD
Distressing emotions			
Highest			
Angry at the assailant	96.6	4.78	.76
Shocked by what happened	71.7	3.92	1.39
Wanted to get even	68.3	3.73	1.55
Lowest			
Nightmares about the assault	10.0	1.67	1.13
Afraid of what others would think	8.3	1.52	1.07
Felt alone dealing with it	6.7	1.60	.99
Validating emotions			
Highest			
She was thankful	73.3	4.18	.97
Felt needed	70.0	3.97	1.12
Doing a good job	65.0	3.87	1.03
Lowest			
Felt at ease	15.0	2.52	1.26
Felt relaxed	13.3	2.20	1.29
Cognitive changes			
Positive			
Still consider as friend	95.0	4.63	.82
Still know and understand her	85.0	4.40	.87
Relationship grew closer	71.6	4.07	1.22
Negative			
Care less for her	5.0	1.35	.82
She was self-centered	5.0	1.35	.82
She ignored me	3.4	1.22	.72
Behavioral changes			
Positive			
Still treat her the same	81.6	4.23	1.17
She still comes for support	75.0	4.20	1.05
Felt able to talk about own feelings	71.6	3.98	1.17
Negative			
Not myself around her	5.0	1.47	.98
Started to avoid her	5.0	1.30	.83
Ended the relationship	5.0	1.28	.88

a. Sample items reflect the three highest and lowest ranked items from each scale.

indicated there were few negative changes in their interactions following the sexual assault. Virtually none of the relationships ended, and few participants started to avoid the survivor.

Gender, Personal History of Assault, and Length of Friendship

A substantial minority of participants had personal histories of sexual assault (27%). Because survivors of sexual assault might react more positively to victims, comparisons

TABLE 20.4   Significant Differences by Gender, Assault History, and Length of Friendship

Variable	Males (M)	(SD)	Females (M)	(SD)	t Value	df
Victim responsiblity	2.40	.92	1.84	.75	−2.56	57*
Empathy scale	3.34	.91	4.07	.83	3.20	57*
Confusion scale	2.94	.28	2.32	1.00	2.18	57*
Ineffectiveness scale	1.94	.65	1.52	.58	−2.58	57*
Positive cognitive changes	3.98	.85	4.39	.68	−2.05	57*
Negative cognitive changes	1.93	.55	1.55	.57	2.51	57*
Negative behavioral changes	2.14	.76	1.70	.55	2.58	57*

Variable	History of Sexual Assault (M)	(SD)	Non-Assaulted (M)	(SD)	t Value	df/ Chi-Square Value
Immediate impact of sexual assault	4.32	.25	3.80	.19	−2.12	57*
Victim responsibility	1.43	.52	2.29	.85	3.83	57***
Positive cognitive changes	4.55	.52	4.11	.81	−2.00	57*
Negative cognitive changes	1.42	.55	1.80	.57	2.31	57*
Negative behavioral changes	1.58	.52	1.90	.69	2.14	57*

Variable	Friends More Than 5 Years (M)	(SD)	Friends Less Than 5 Years (M)	(SD)	t Value	df
Positive cognitive changes	4.48	.48	3.91	.94	−3.10	58**
Positive behavioral changes	4.36	.62	3.68	1.03	−3.15	58**

*$p < .05$; **$p < .01$; ***$p < .001$.

between participants who had been sexually assaulted and those who had not were conducted. Similarly, the results suggested that many of the friendships were of a relatively long duration ($M = 7.73$). To determine if length of friendship differentially affected participants' reactions to victims, comparisons between participants who had been friends with participants for more than 5 years (55%) and those who had been friends for 5 years or less (45%) were conducted. Similarly, previous literature has suggested that men may react more negatively to rape victims than women (e.g., Davis & Brickman, 1996). Thus, comparisons between male ($n = 23$) and female participants ($n = 36$) were also deemed necessary. Finally, although comparisons between reactions to stranger versus acquaintance rape victims are theoretically warranted, the small number of stranger rape victims in this sample ($n = 10$) renders such comparisons unreliable. Thus, independent sample t tests and chi-square tests were conducted to determine if gender, history of assault, and length of the friendship significantly affected any of the findings.

All significant results are reported in Table 20.4. Compared with women, men blamed the survivor more, were less empathic, more confused, felt more ineffective, experienced fewer positive and more negative changes in the way they thought about the relationship, and demonstrated more negative behavioral changes in the friendship. Friends' own sexual assault histories were related to five measures. Compared with friends who had not been sexually assaulted in the past, friends who had been sexually assaulted expected sexual assault to have a more profound impact on survivors' lives immediately afterward, blamed the victim less, experienced more positive and fewer negative changes in the way they thought about the relationship, and had fewer negative behavioral changes in the relationship. Participants who had been friends with the victim for more than 5 years experienced more positive changes in the way they thought about the relationship and the way they interacted with the survivor.

Integration of Descriptive Findings

To integrate these descriptive findings, canonical correlations were performed to discover how positive beliefs, emotions, and relationship outcomes were related to negative beliefs, emotions, and relationship outcomes.[2] Rather than identifying subgroups of participants (as in cluster analysis), canonical correlation highlights the relationship among variables. Due to the small sample size, comparative analyses based on gender, assault history, and length of friendship were not possible here.

The first set of scales in this analysis reflected the positive aspects of helping survivors recover from sexual assault. This set included the Empathy Scale, the Beliefs About the Immediate Impact Scale, the Validating Emotions Scale, the Positive Cognitive Impact Scale, and the Positive Behavioral Impact Scale. Higher scores on these scales indicated positive beliefs, emotions, or relationship outcomes.

The second set of scales reflected the negative aspects of helping survivors recover from sexual assault. This set included the Victim Coping Scale, the Victim Responsibility Scale, the Confusion Scale, the Ineffective Scale, the Distressing Emotions Scale, the Negative Cognitive Changes Scale, and the Negative Behavioral Impact Scale. Increasingly higher scores on these scales indicated more negative beliefs, emotions, or relationship outcomes.

Zero-order correlations were first conducted on the two sets of variables. As can be seen in Table 20.5, the strongest relationships were between the positive and negative relationship changes scales. The Validating Emotions Scale was also negatively related to a number of scales, including the Confusion Scale, the Ineffective Scale, the Negative Cognitive Changes Scale, and the Negative Behavioral Changes Scale. Furthermore, higher levels of ineffectiveness were negatively related to both positive cognitive and behavioral changes in the relationship, whereas both empathy and believing in the devastating impact of sexual assault were only negatively related to negative cognitive changes in the relationship.

Chi-square tests indicated that there were three significant canonical correlations, or patterns, among the variables. The chi-square test only became nonsignificant when the third canonical correlation was removed: Wilks's lambda = .72, χ^2 (15, $N = 60$) = 17.18, n.s. This indicated that the remaining canonical correlations did not significantly contribute to the overall model. Thus, only the first three canonical correlations significantly accounted for the association between the positive and negative aspects of helping (Tabachnik & Fidell, 1996).

The first canonical correlation was .74 (51% of the variance of Set 1, 28% of the variance of Set 2), the second was .62 (9% of the variance of Set 1, 19% of the variance of Set 2), and the third was .45 (8% of the variance of Set 1, 9% of the variance of Set 2). Table 20.6 presents the canonical loadings for each item, percentage of variance each canonical variate accounted for in its own set, and percentage of variance each canonical variate accounted

TABLE 20.5   Correlations Between Positive and Negative Belief, Emotion, and Relationship Scales

	Negative Scales						
	Negative Opinions About Victim Coping	Confusion Scale	Ineffective Scale	Victim Responsibility Scale	Emotional Distress Scale	Negative Cognitive Changes Scale	Negative Behavioral Changes Scale
Positive scales							
Empathy Scale	.08	−.19	−.18	−.18	−.01	−.41*	−.23
Immediate Impact Scale	−.07	−.23	−.24	−.25	.14	−.37*	−.25
Validating Emotions Scale	−.22	−.49*	−.56*	−.21	−.21	−.38*	−.33*
Positive Cognitive Changes Scale	.01	−.24	−.30*	−.17	.09	−.60*	−.58*
Positive Behavioral Changes Scale	−.11	−.37*	−.30*	−.19	.08	−.60*	−.51*

*$p < .05$.

for in its opposite set (redundancy). Only those variables that correlated at .3 or higher with each canonical variate (canonical loadings) were used for interpretation (Tabachnik & Fidell, 1996).

The canonical correlations revealed three main patterns of relationships among positive and negative beliefs, emotions, and relationship outcomes. Each pattern is described below and illustrated with qualitative narratives from participants that exemplify these patterns.

Positive Experience. More empathy, greater understanding of the devastating impact of sexual assault, more feelings of validation, and more positive cognitive and behavioral changes in the relationship were related to less confusion, fewer feelings of ineffectiveness, less victim blaming, and fewer negative cognitive and behavioral changes in the relationship. In other words, this first pattern of associations drew a picture of participants who believed in the devastating impact of sexual assault, could imagine themselves in the survivor's shoes, and did not blame the survivor for what happened. These participants felt good about their efforts to help, felt they knew what to do, and felt they had been effective. These beliefs and emotions were related to positive, not negative, changes in the relationship.

Open-ended responses from participants whose quantitative data matched this pattern illustrated these findings. One participant described her understanding, empathy, and desire to maintain the relationship:

> I knew exactly what she was going through and I knew what an emotional rollercoaster it was to follow. However, the first thing I did was make sure she was okay talking about it and let her know that no matter what happened, our friendship wouldn't change.

TABLE 20.6   Canonical Correlations Between Positive Beliefs, Emotions, and
Relationship Outcomes and Negative Beliefs, Emotions, and
Relationship Outcomes

| | Canonical Loadings | | | |
	First Canonical	Second Canonical	Third Canonical	Total
Set				
Set 1: Positive beliefs, emotions, and relationship outcomes				
Empathy Scale	.57	.03	.13	
Beliefs About Immediate Impact Scale	.58	.01	.16	
Validating Emotions Scale	.56	.61	−.51	
Positive Cognitive Impact Scale	.90	−.30	−.27	
Positive Behavioral Changes Scale	.88	.02	.15	
Percentage of variance	51%	9%	8%	68%
Redundancy	28%	4%	2%	34%
Set 2: Negative beliefs, emotions, and relationship outcomes				
Victim Coping Scale	−.09	−.51	.03	
Confusion Scale	−.53	−.70	.04	
Ineffective Scale	−.52	−.57	.51	
Victim Responsibility Scale	−.35	−.17	−.11	
Distressing Emotions Scale	.09	−.44	.43	
Negative Cognitive Impact Scale	−.92	−.02	−.01	
Negative Behavioral Changes Scale	−.75	.13	.38	
Percentage of Variance	30%	19%	9%	58%
Redundancy	16%	7%	2%	25%
Canonical correlation		.74	.62	.45

NOTE: Italicized numbers highlight canonical loadings.

Some of the participants indicated that they did not blame the survivor:

I wanted to let her know that it was not her fault.

It was really difficult trying to convince her that it wasn't her fault, that no matter what, she was the victim in the situation.

Some participants also described feelings of validation:

I think talking about it made her feel good, which made me feel good.

Other participants believed their efforts to help had been effective:

The way that I was able to help was by listening, supporting, and loving her.

I feel I was helpful, bringing her to the hospital and answering questions about what I knew.

Many participants felt their friendships with the survivors had remained strong:

It [the friendship] hasn't really changed. We share now and have always shared our deepest, intimate thoughts, secrets, and actions.

Even more participants felt that the friendships had actually grown closer:

We became a lot closer and felt bonded in more ways than we thought possible when we first met.

It made us even closer and helped us to depend on each other and trust one another.

Neutral Experience. The second pattern suggested relatively neutral experiences that nonetheless made friends feel good about helping rape survivors. This pattern revealed low levels of confusion, ineffectiveness, and distress, accompanied by moderate levels of validating emotions. Yet there were no positive or negative changes in the friendships. This suggests that the helping experience for some participants is not negative, only somewhat positive, and may not have a long-term impact on the friendship.

Participants whose scores matched this pattern did not describe feeling distressed, confused, or ineffective. These participants also expressed moderate feelings of validation:

It evoked my protective instincts. I felt that she trusted me. It really did make me feel good.

Yes, [I was able to help] because I am sympathetic and I have compassion and concern for other people's feelings. I also have consoled her while she was in other sticky or bad situations. And I have given her advice plenty of times.

Unlike the positive experiences pattern, this neutral pattern did not include any positive changes in the friendship. On the other hand, negative changes in the friendship did not exist.

Thus, this pattern indicates an absence of negative experiences (i.e., they did not feel confused, ineffective, or upset) and only a moderate level of validation (opposed to the high levels indicated in the positive experiences pattern). Thus, this pattern appears to describe a relatively neutral experience: Both positive and negative experiences appeared to be relatively absent.

Negative Experience. The third pattern indicated that feeling less validated was related to stronger feelings of ineffectiveness, more emotional distress, and more negative behavioral changes in the relationship. These participants experienced high levels of distress, felt ineffective, and did not feel good about helping. These emotions were also related to more negative behavioral changes in the relationship.

Some participants' open-ended responses clearly illustrated such feelings of distress:

Thank God my car was parked because I wouldn't know what would have happened if it was moving. My eyes popped and my jaw fell. Besides being shocked, I was very angry.

It left me with a very sick feeling, like I had to vomit. It was very upsetting.

Participants also described strong feelings of anger and rage toward the perpetrator:

My first reaction was to beat the crap out of him for this.

I wanted to find the guy and rip off his penis and shove it down his throat.

Participants whose scores matched this pattern also discussed their feelings of ineffectiveness:

I felt that I was unable to help her because I couldn't find the right words or thoughts to make everything seem all right because I knew that they weren't all right.

I just stood there listening to her story sort of in a bewildered state. I really did not know what to say or do.

These participants also described negative changes in their friendships:

It made me on call 24-7. She'd call me at the most awkward times. Since graduation, we really haven't seen each other.

I feel like I let her down and I think she feels that she can't count on me no more.

DISCUSSION

Major Findings

To understand the impact of rape disclosure, 60 friends of rape survivors described their experiences helping rape survivors. These friendships were close, important, long-term friendships averaging 7 years in length. The average survivor was female, 21 years old, as likely to be from a minority background as Caucasian, and approximately 17 years old when assaulted.

Survivors waited an average of 7 months before disclosing the assaults to their friends. Although this appears somewhat high, previous research suggests that 13% to 29% of women wait years before disclosing the assault to anyone at all (Cohen & Roth, 1987; Ogletree, 1993; S. E. Ullman, 1996c), and a substantial number of women do not disclose prior to participation in a research project (31% to 72%) (George et al., 1992; Golding et al., 1989; Koss, 1985; Ogletree, 1993; S. E. Ullman, 1996c). Indeed, delayed disclosure appears to be related to stereotypical assault characteristics: Survivors who were subjected to more stereotypical assaults are more likely to disclose immediately after the assault (Frank et al., 1988; Stewart et al., 1987; S. E. Ullman, 1996c). Thus, the high proportion of acquaintance rape victims in this sample may have resulted in longer delays in disclosure. Future research may wish to continue to examine factors related to delayed disclosure to clarify this issue.

Consistent with past research, most of the assaults were acquaintance or date rapes (e.g., Koss et al., 1988), and very few of the cases involved injuries, a weapon, or alcohol use. Most participants did not believe survivors were responsible for the assault, were somewhat able to empathize with survivors, and were optimistic about the way survivors were coping with the assault. These perceptions are consistent with friends' general expectations for sexual assault to have a somewhat significant impact on survivors' lives immediately after the assault.

Friends were not particularly confused about how to assist the survivors and did not believe their efforts to help were ineffective. In addition, participants reported they did not feel distressed; rather, they tended to feel good about helping. However, even though overall levels of distress were low, a number of distressing emotions were prevalent among participants. The vast majority of friends were angry at the assailant and wanted revenge. Most participants were shocked by what had happened and were afraid for the continued safety of the survivor. Finally, participants did not feel the relationship had changed in a negative way and were quite positive about both the cognitive and behavioral aspects of the relationship.

Although there were several significant differences in helpers' experiences based on gender, personal history of assault, and length of the friendship, average scores for these subgroups still suggested fairly positive experiences. For example, even though men and friends without a personal history of sexual assault blamed survivors more than women and friends who had been assaulted in the past, none of these subgroups strongly blamed the survivor for the assault. Similarly, even though longer term friendships evidenced more positive cognitive and behavioral changes in the friendships, friendships of shorter duration still demonstrated fairly high levels of positive relationship changes. This pattern held true for each of the significant differences noted in Table 20.4. Thus, although the magnitude of friends' beliefs and experiences did differ according to gender, history of assault, and length of friendship, this appears to be an issue of degree rather than kind. This finding is consistent with Davis and Brickman's (1996) findings on gender differences in unsupportive behavior: Whereas men are significantly more unsupportive than women, average ratings indicate that such unsupportive behavior is relatively rare. Although the current study was not able to compare experiences based on type of assault (acquaintance vs. stranger rape), such analyses are clearly warranted in future research. Previous research has noted substantial differences in social reactions to victims whose assaults are more stereotypical in nature (Orbuch, Harvey, Davis, & Merbach, 1994; Popiel & Suskind, 1985; S. Ullman & Siegel, 1995; S. E. Ullman, 1996a; Wyatt, Notgrass, & Newcomb, 1990), suggesting that friends' experiences may likewise differ according to type of assault. Overall, these findings suggest that differences in friends' experiences do exist according to gender, personal assault history, and length of friendship. Thus, even though most friends were supportive, education targeted toward men and nonvictims may help to eliminate the differences that do exist in reactions toward rape victims.

Overall, these results paint a fairly positive picture: Friends of rape survivors were not distressed, felt their helping efforts were effective, and believed that these close, long-term friendships were maintained. Yet although this summary characterizes the "average experience," further analyses revealed that this positive picture did not hold true for all participants. Canonical correlation analysis revealed three distinct patterns of experiences helping rape survivors. The first pattern was consistent with this general positive summary: Friends understood the devastating impact of sexual assault, were not distressed, and thought the relationships improved. This is good news for rape survivors who may fear that disclosing the assault to their friends could lead to negative responses or could be harmful to the friendship.

The second pattern that emerged from the canonical correlations may also be good news for survivors. This pattern suggests a fairly neutral experience that nonetheless resulted in validating emotions: Friends did not think the survivor was coping poorly, felt relatively unfazed, and felt able to help rape survivors recover. Yet these participants perceived neither positive nor negative changes in the friendship. This pattern suggests that although this helping experience does not have any negative effect on the friendships, it does not necessarily bring the victim and friend closer together. Thus, some friends seem to experience neither negative emotions nor any powerful long-term consequences from this helping experience. Yet future research is needed to further examine this type of neutral experience to determine if it is indeed neutral or if it suggests emotional disengagement on the part of the friend. If this pattern actually reflects emotional detachment, the long-term implications for both friends and victims may not be so benign. Both longitudinal and in-depth qualitative research on this topic may help further explain the implications of this pattern.

Finally, the last pattern identified by the canonical correlations revealed a pattern of perceived distress, ineffectiveness, and negative changes in the friendship. For some participants, feelings of ineffectiveness and emotional distress seem to relate to negative changes in the relationship, such as avoiding the survivor or ending the relationship. This pattern is clearly the worst case scenario, suggesting negative experiences for both friends and victims. Future research may wish to further examine correlates of these negative experiences in an effort to design effective interventions to prevent such reactions. For example, are there certain assault or personal characteristics that are more frequently associated with such negative experiences? What exactly can be done to help minimize the frequency or impact of these negative experiences? Qualitative research that focuses specifically on friends who have negative experiences and evaluates efforts to alleviate their distress is clearly needed.

There are several limitations to this current research that temper the conclusions that can be drawn. First, the focus of this study was limited to the friends' experience. Although surveying friends of rape survivors is the most informative way to learn about the opinions, emotions, and sense of efficacy held by the friend, it may not provide a complete picture of what happened to the friendship as a result of the disclosure. Similarly, friends may not have been willing to reveal negative responses they had toward the survivor and may have instead responded in a socially desirable manner. Alternatively, it is possible that the friends thought they were helpful; the survivors may agree or disagree. Thus, their answers may be accurate and unbiased, from their perspective. Indeed, Davis and Brickman (1996) noted significant differences between survivors' and helpers' perceptions of support: Helpers reported more supportive behavior than survivors, and victim and supporter reports of unsupportive behavior were only moderately correlated. Future studies interested in the impact of rape disclosure on friendships would therefore be bolstered if they could obtain information from both the friend and the survivor.

These findings may be further limited by the design of the current study. The cross-sectional nature of the design may not fully assess the changes that occurred in the relationships over time. Furthermore, the non-probability sampling technique may temper the confidence we can have in these findings. It is conceivable that only friends who responded positively to survivors volunteered to participate. This would suggest that the positive results in this study may be an artifact of sampling bias rather than a true picture of the impact of rape disclosure. Future studies may therefore wish to use a longitudinal design with probability sampling in an effort to expand on and verify these findings.

Finally, the lack of standardized measures on this topic is problematic. This study attempted to address the lack of available standardized measures by developing scales based on literature on victimization perspective theory (e.g., Herbert & Dunkel-Schetter, 1992), significant others' reactions (see Table 20.1), and recovery from sexual assault (e.g., Koss et al., 1994). Nevertheless, future research may wish to continue the efforts initiated in this study and others (Davis & Brickman, 1996; S. E. Ullman, 1996a, 1996b, 1996c) to fully develop measures to assess the impact that helping survivors has on informal support providers.

Implications and Applications

Contrary to the findings in the counseling literature on significant others' reactions to rape disclosure (see Table 20.1), the majority of friends in this study experienced validating rather than distressing emotions. Nonetheless, participants in this study did express feelings of anger and a desire for revenge, which is similar to reported findings on the emotional reactions of rape survivors' family members (Burge, 1983; Emm & McKenry, 1988; Holmstrom & Burgess, 1979; Miller et al., 1982; Remer & Elliott, 1988; Riggs & Kilpatrick, 1997; Silverman, 1978; Stone, 1980, White & Rollins, 1981) and people attempting to support survivors of other stressful life experiences (Burgess, 1975; Greif & Porembski, 1988). The results of this study suggest that friends of rape survivors may be less distressed than family members but may still experience strong feelings of anger and revenge. Thus, anger may be a common response to learning about the assault of a close friend or loved one. Other distressing emotions such as depression or shame, however, may be specific to more intimate relationships, such as families or partners.

Similarly, the majority of participants in this study did not feel confused or believe that their efforts to help survivors were ineffective. For those friends who did experience these feelings of helplessness and frustration, however, the predictions specified by victimization perspective theory (e.g., Herbert & Dunkel-Schetter, 1992) were partially supported by the third canonical correlation. Consistent with this theory, feelings of helplessness were related to feelings of distress and negative changes in the friendship. These findings suggest that victimization perspective theory is indeed useful for understanding the dynamic of helping rape survivors for some friends, but it does not characterize the experiences of many friends in this study. This discrepancy may be due to the close and long-term nature of the friendships in this sample. In a laboratory setting, participants may react negatively to confederates or believe that they would feel confused if faced with helping a rape survivor. When the rape survivor turns out to be someone they care about, however, they may be able to empathize and improvise more readily. They also may feel less distressed than they would have assumed because they receive positive feedback from the survivor about their helping efforts. Thus, the interactive nature of the helping relationship may cause friends to respond differently in a real-life scenario than students imagine they would respond in a laboratory setting.

The findings of this study have several practical implications. Although the majority of participants reported relatively positive experiences helping rape survivors, canonical correlations uncovered patterns that were not so positive. These results suggest that friends believe they can positively support rape survivors during their recoveries, but that some friends may need support and guidance during this process. Future research may wish to further examine factors that may predict such negative experiences (such as gender, type of assault, previous exposure to information about sexual assault, and previous experience helping rape victims) to develop programs targeting such individuals. For example, feelings of confusion and ineffectiveness can certainly be alleviated through community education and resources for helpers. Rape crisis centers, universities, schools, and community centers could provide ongoing education about how to support survivors of sexual assault. Role plays or other interactive simulations could help to familiarize potential supporters with the listening skills necessary to support rape survivors while educating them on the aftermath of sexual assault. Community agencies could also provide information, advice, and support to friends who are currently trying to help a survivor.

Conclusions

This study has addressed some of the gaps in the literature by describing the impact of rape disclosure on friends. It has also dispelled some commonly held beliefs about rape disclosure by revealing a fairly positive picture of what happens when rape survivors turn to their friends for support. Most of the friends in this sample were very supportive, felt validated by helping, and felt that the friendships grew closer as a result of the experience. Because friends are one of the most immediate forms of support that rape survivors can access, knowing that they are likely to receive a positive response can facilitate survivors' decisions to disclose. Many survivors who might not even consider reporting the assault to a community agency might be willing to talk to their friends if they believe they would get a positive response. Thus, rape survivors' support seeking and recovery can be improved if these positive reactions can be enhanced with community interventions aimed at training significant others to be skillful support providers. With education, training, and support, both rape survivors and their friends can be helped through this difficult time.

NOTES

1. Of the 26 people who did not meet the screening criteria, 13 were friends with someone assaulted by a family member, and 2 were friends with someone assaulted when younger than 14. These victims of childhood sexual assault and incest were excluded because their experiences were expected to substantially differ from the experiences of young adult victims of sexual assault (e.g., timing of disclosure, social reactions to victims, availability of resources/options, etc.). Much of the literature on sexual assault distinguishes between these two groups and limits work to victims of nonfamilial sexual assault that occurred at age 14 or beyond (see Koss et al., 1988), thereby establishing a precedent for this screening criteria. Furthermore, an additional 5 participants who had been dating the victim were excluded from final analyses. This study attempted to fill a gap in the literature by focusing exclusively on friends; the experiences of romantic partners were expected to differ enough from friends' experiences to warrant excluding these cases. Finally, 4 respondents did not know the victim personally and 2 left significant portions of the questionnaire blank; these surveys were likewise excluded from final analyses.

2. Canonical correlation was chosen as an analysis strategy that can describe patterns among the variables in the dataset. This analysis is statistically similar to factor analysis in that it identifies

mathematical relationships among groups of variables. Unlike factor analysis, however, canonical correlation identifies unique patterns based on variations in each variable such that a low score on a variable may be associated with one pattern, and a high score on that same variable may be related to an entirely different pattern. Thus, this analysis strategy allows research to move beyond simple linear relationships to identify several unique patterns among groups of variables.

21

Services for Sexual Assault Survivors

The Role of Rape Crisis Centers

———

REBECCA CAMPBELL

University of Illinois at Chicago

PATRICIA YANCEY MARTIN

INTRODUCTION

Rape crisis centers (RCCs) are remarkable organizations. Characterized by Ferree and Martin (1995) as the harvest of second-wave feminism, RCCs are a consequential feature of contemporary U.S. society, we suggest. Many of these organizations, which were formed through grassroots organizing and volunteer labor, have survived for 20 or more years, and they continue do[ing] the work of the movement (Ferree & Martin, 1995, p. 3). This chapter reviews the circumstances that led to the creation and persistence of RCCs, the services provided for victims by these organizations, and the impact of RCCs on victims and society. With over 1,200 RCCs currently in operation in the United States, an average of 24 per state, services to survivors and to the legal, medical, and mental health systems that work with victims are unlikely to disappear any time soon (see Martin, 1997; Martin & Powell, 1994). Indeed, our review suggests that the effects of RCCs on mainstream society are important not only to anti-rape activists but also to students of social movements and societal change. RCCs provide exemplars of how radical feminist ideology indoctrinates and survives within mainstream human service delivery models.

To explore these issues, this chapter is organized into four sections. First, to set the stage for our discussions on the current work of RCCs, we briefly review the history of the anti-rape movement in the United States, with specific attention to the emergence of RCCs. Second, we turn our attention to contemporary issues in the anti-rape movement, focusing on the existing structures and functions of RCCs. The staff and volunteers of RCCs work

Authors' Note: This article first appeared in Renzetti, C., Edleson, J., and Bergen, R. K. (Eds.). (2001). *Sourcebook on Violence Against Women* (pp. 227-242). Thousand Oaks, CA: Sage. Used with permission.

with the legal, medical, and mental health systems to provide comprehensive services to victims of sexual assault and their families. In addition, these centers provide community education, sponsor rape prevention programs, and engage in institutional advocacy to create systems-level changes. Third, we examine the effectiveness of these activities in facilitating victim recovery and raising community awareness about violence against women. Fourth, in light of the fact that RCCs have been effective in fostering beneficial individual- and societal-level outcomes, we delve into how these organizations are able to assist survivors and their communities. We review the specific mobilizing strategies and tactics that RCCs employ as women's movement, anti-rape organizations concerned with helping victims and with ending rape. We close with a discussion of prospects for the RCCs to continue to have a positive impact on victims and social institutions.

THE HISTORY OF THE ANTI-RAPE MOVEMENT

The Emergence of the First Rape Crisis Centers

The first U.S. RCCs emerged in the 1970s as part of the radical feminist women's movement. Although the academic study of RCCs tends to use phrases such as anti-rape movement, isomorphic dynamics, and affiliational structures, fundamentally, these centers emerged from the emotions and passions of feminist activists (Collins & Whalen, 1989; Schechter, 1982). Anger at widespread violence against women. Fear for the safety of all women and children. Hope for healing and social change. RCCs were formed to provide services to victims in crisis, to educate communities on violence against women, and to mobilize efforts for social change. Truly a grassroots effort, many of the first RCCs were run out of women's own homes with donated materials (e.g., telephones, furniture, printing for flyers) (O'Sullivan, 1978; Pride, 1981). The staff of these early centers were often community volunteers who did not have counseling or professional service backgrounds. Women joined these groups because they were committed to helping victims and to politicizing them to change society (Gornick, Burt, & Pittman, 1985; Matthews, 1994).

In sharp contrast to traditional social service agencies, many of these fledgling centers were run as feminist collectives, where power and decision making were shared among all members of the organization (see Koss & Harvey, 1991). Early RCCs rejected hierarchical organizational practices, such as appointing an executive director or forming a board of directors (Koss & Harvey, 1991). Similarly, these organizations were free-standing agencies, completely autonomous and not affiliated with or dependent on a parent organization (e.g., a YWCA, hospital, mental health agency). In fact, many centers were suspicious of the underlying motives and support offered by mainstream organizations (Byington, Martin, DiNitto, & Maxwell, 1991; Martin, DiNitto, Byington, & Maxwell, 1992; Matthews, 1994; Schechter, 1982). Even without the support of established social service agencies and government funding, RCCs continued to grow in numbers throughout the United States.

Although each center has its unique organizational history, there was remarkable similarity across RCCs with respect to the services they offered rape victims (Gornick et al., 1985; Koss & Harvey, 1991; O'Sullivan, 1978). Most had 24-hour crisis hot lines to provide information, referrals, and crisis counseling. In addition, RCCs trained volunteers as legal and medical advocates to accompany victims to police departments and hospitals. These volunteers provided information to victims about their legal rights and advocated on their behalf. Influenced by the radical feminist women's movement, early RCCs actively supported a social action agenda by sponsoring public demonstrations, protests, and marches, as well as lobbying the state for stronger laws on violence against women (Koss & Harvey, 1991; Martin et al., 1992; O'Sullivan, 1978).

The Evolution of the Anti-Rape Movement

As time passed, many of the original leaders of the anti-rape movement grew tired from years of struggle and overcommitment to the cause (Gornick et al., 1985; Matthews, 1994). As they left, new women came on board who valued a more conventional and apolitical approach. With this new diversity, varied visions emerged for the structure and function of RCCs (Gornick et al., 1985; Koss & Harvey, 1991; O'Sullivan, 1978). This shift from radical social change agencies to social service organizations happened in varying degrees over many years. By the mid-1970s, many centers began applying for and receiving funds from the Law Enforcement Assistance Administration (LEAA) and United Way (Gornick et al., 1985; Matthews, 1994; O'Sullivan, 1978; Pride, 1981). The arrival of government funding in RCCs brought about three interrelated changes. First, many centers moved from collectives to hierarchical organizational structures, designating executive directors; program coordinators; and boards of directors with formal decision-making power over members, programs, and policies (Collins & Whalen, 1989; O'Sullivan, 1978; Pride, 1981). Second, with the move from collectives to traditional structures came a shift in staffing. Government funding sources began stressing the importance of professionally certified personnel. It was no longer enough for staff to be former rape victims committed to empowering women; they now had to be trained and certified as professionals or paraprofessionals (Collins & Whalen, 1989). Third, with the competition for public funding resources came the need for affiliation (Byington et al., 1991). To remain in operation, many formerly freestanding centers affiliated with or were absorbed by agencies such as YWCAs, community mental health centers, hospitals, and district attorney's offices (Gornick et al., 1985; Matthews, 1994; Pride, 1981; Schechter, 1982).

Whereas the anti-rape movement experienced a general shift toward professionalization, individual centers varied in how much they changed their structures and functions. For instance, not all centers changed to hierarchical structures with hired professionals, and many centers were successful in warding off co-optation within a mainstream organization. In one of the first studies on this professionalization shift, O'Sullivan (1978) surveyed 90 completely autonomous RCCs that had been founded prior to 1976. Even though these centers had started receiving substantial government fiscal support, only 43% had boards of directors. Most centers favored steering committees over boards of directors, as they saw this format as less hierarchical and more consistent with feminist collective ideology.

In the 1980s, Gornick et al. (1985) surveyed a sample of 50 nationally representative RCCs (see also Harvey, 1985). In the time since O'Sullivan's research, more variation had emerged with respect to organizational structures, staff composition, and funding sources. Gornick et al. (1985) identified four typologies of rape crisis centers: (a) programs resembling the original feminist collectives of the 1970s, (b) programs more mainstream and traditional in structure, (c) programs embedded in a social service or mental health agency, and (d) programs based in hospital emergency rooms. Furthermore, Gornick et al.'s results revealed that independent centers were more politically active than affiliated centers, and collectively run centers were more service-oriented than bureaucratic centers (see also Bordt,

1997). Matthews (1994) replicated many of these findings in her study of six RCCs in Los Angeles during 1988 and 1989. Matthews (1994) argued that rape crisis work had been influenced by a more conservative service delivery approach because of the ongoing struggle between the anti-rape movement and the state. Centers that started out with different styles and perspectives soon became more similar, as RCCs developed consistent procedures and bureaucratic structures in response to government funding requirements (see DiMaggio & Powell, 1991).

In the 1990s, national work by Campbell, Baker, and Mazurek (1998) continued to find evidence of this shift toward homogenized professionalization. In a study of 168 RCCs throughout the country, Campbell et al. (1998) found a cohort effect that differentiated centers formed at the peak of the anti-rape movement, in 1978 or earlier, from those founded in a more conservative era in U.S. politics, 1979 or later. The older centers had larger budgets and more staff but were more likely to be free-standing collectives. Their internal communication style was more likely to stress participatory decision making, with all members of the organization, from the board of directors to the volunteers and clients, involved. Older centers were also more likely than younger centers to participate in social change activities, such as public demonstrations against violence against women and rape prevention programming. The younger centers had comparatively smaller budgets and staffing levels and were more likely to be hierarchical organizations affiliated with larger social service agencies. Internal decisions in these agencies were made without the participation of the less powerful members of the organization (e.g., volunteers and clients). These younger centers were less likely to be engaged in public demonstrations or prevention work, but they were more likely than the older centers to be involved in lobbying elected politicians. The top-down approach of political lobbying may be more consistent with these younger organizations' philosophies than the grassroots tactics favored by older centers. These results suggest that RCCs have altered their structure and function since the beginnings of the anti-rape movement, but these changes may have been necessary to survive the different political climate of the 1980s and 1990s. The staff at many of these centers may have felt that deradicalizing was key to long-term organizational sustainability in an era of increasingly conservative state politics (see Spalter-Roth & Schreiber, 1995).

THE CURRENT ACTIVITIES OF RAPE CRISIS CENTERS

Services Provided by Rape Crisis Centers

Whereas the political activism of RCCs has tempered over time, the direct services these agencies provide to survivors have remained essentially the same throughout the history of the anti-rape movement. In fact, current funding sources (e.g., state Victims of Crime Act funds) often require agencies to offer three basic services: (a) 24-hour hot line; (b) counseling (individual, group, support groups); and (c) legal and medical advocacy. Crisis hot lines are typically staffed by volunteers who have completed an intensive training program in crisis intervention (Campbell et al., 1998). Counseling services are most commonly provided by licensed professionals (e.g., practitioners at the level of the master's in social work), although some centers still employ paraprofessionals for short-term counseling and support group facilitation (Campbell et al., 1998).

Yet of these three basic services, legal and medical advocacy remain the most challenging tasks for center staff (Campbell, 1996; Martin, 1997). Rape victim advocates have the simultaneous job of assisting rape survivors in crisis and educating staff from other service systems (e.g., police officers, detectives, prosecutors, doctors, nurses). Throughout all aspects of their work, rape victim advocates are trying to prevent the second rape: insensitive, victim-blaming treatment from community system personnel. In what is also termed secondary victimization, rape victims often experience negative treatment from society that mirrors and exacerbates the trauma of the rape (Campbell, 1998a; Campbell & Bybee, 1997; Campbell et al., 1999; Frohmann, 1991; Madigan & Gamble, 1991; Martin & Powell, 1994; Matoesian, 1993; Williams, 1984). The job of rape victim advocates, therefore, is not only to provide direct services to survivors but also to prevent secondary victimization.

Medical/legal advocates are typically volunteers who have completed a comprehensive training program to assist victims in accessing emergency medical services and reporting the assault to the police. The process of reporting and prosecuting a rape can be a long and complicated affair, and in fact, most rape victims never report the assault to the criminal justice system (Campbell et al., 1999; Golding, Siegel, Sorenson, Burnam, & Stein, 1989; Ullman, 1996). For those who do report, their first contact is with police officers and detectives, who record victims' accounts of the assault and conduct a preliminary investigation. At this stage, some jurisdictions automatically forward the report or investigation to the local prosecutor, whereas others allow the police to decide whether to forward the report. The prosecutor then chooses whether to authorize an arrest and press charges. Not all cases are charged as rapes or sexual assaults, as some are charged at lesser offenses (e.g., simple assault, reckless endangerment). If the charges are not dropped, the accused rapist has the choice of pleading guilty to the original offense or, if a bargain has been struck, to a lesser offense, or of going to trial. If he is convicted at the trial, the judge or jury must decide whether probation or jail time will suffice as punishment.

With a system this complex, it is quite likely that some cases will slip through the cracks, and in fact, most rape survivors never get their day in court. Only 25% of reported rapes are accepted for prosecution, 12% of defendants are actually found guilty, and 7% of all cases result in a prison term (Frazier & Haney, 1996). In addition, Campbell (1998a) found that even in cases where survivors had the assistance of a rape victim advocate, 67% of cases were dismissed, and over 80% of the time, this decision was made by legal personnel and contradicted the victims' wishes to prosecute. Thus, the effectiveness of RCC advocates can be limited because widespread, effective prosecution of rape remains elusive.

Besides providing legal advocacy, RCC staff also assist victims with their medical needs (see Martin & DiNitto, 1987; Martin, DiNitto, Harrison, & Maxwell, 1985). After a sexual assault, rape victims may need emergency medical care for several reasons. Victims are sometimes physically injured in the assault (e.g., cuts, bruises, vaginal or anal lacerations), so a medical exam is helpful to detect and treat these problems. In addition, forensic evidence such as semen; blood; and/or samples of hair, fiber, or skin can be collected from victims' bodies during this exam (often called the rape kit) (see Martin et al., 1985). For many women, concern about exposure to sexually transmitted diseases (STDs) and the risk of pregnancy is paramount, and hospital staff can provide information and preventive treatments for these issues (e.g., the morning-after pill to prevent pregnancy). In practice, seeking medical care can be a harrowing experience for rape survivors: disrobing in front of the hospital staff; turning over their clothes to police as evidence; enduring a lengthy pelvic exam (to check for injuries and obtain semen samples); and submitting to other evidence collection (combing pubic hair, scraping under fingernails). In the midst of these procedures, nurses come and go taking blood (for pregnancy tests, STD screening) and bringing medications (morning-after pill, antibiotics). This medical care is typically provided in a hospital emergency room, a trauma-focused setting where the ambience can be quite frenetic (see Ahrens et al., 2001). The job of the medical advocate is to explain these medical procedures and help victims by restoring their sense of control.

Despite these diverse medical needs, current research suggests that many survivors are not receiving adequate care. The National Victim Center's (1992) national survey of female survivors of sexual assault found that 60% of victims were not advised about how to obtain pregnancy testing or how to prevent pregnancy. Although 43% of the women who had been raped within the previous 5 years were very concerned about contracting HIV from the assault, 73% were not given information about testing for exposure to HIV. Another 40% were not given information about the risk of contracting other STDs. Yet working with an RCC medical advocate appears to increase the likelihood of receiving needed medical services. Campbell and Bybee (1997) found that in a sample of rape survivors who had the assistance of an advocate, 67% of the victims who wanted information about STDs actually received such information from hospital staff. Similarly, 70% of the victims who wanted information about pregnancy obtained it, but only 38% of the victims who wanted the morning-after pill to prevent pregnancy actually received this medication, despite intensive efforts of the advocates. These results suggest that RCC medical advocates can be a useful presence in the hospital emergency room, as they may be able to obtain needed resources for rape victims.

The Work of Assisting Rape Survivors in Crisis

Working in an RCC can be quite stressful for staff and volunteers. In their jobs, hot line staff, counselors, and advocates bear witness to the pain and devastation of rape over and over again. In addition, experiences with other community agencies, such as the legal and medical systems, can be frustrating as advocates try to prevent the secondary victimization of rape survivors. As a result of this close contact, the trauma of rape reaches far beyond the lives of its primary victims to also harm those close to survivors. Research in psychology, nursing, and social work has demonstrated that husbands/significant others, family, and friends of rape survivors are also detrimentally affected by sexual assault (see Ahrens & Campbell, 2001; Davis, Taylor, & Bench, 1995). Similarly, when rape survivors turn to community systems for assistance, service providers are also emotionally touched by this crime. The staff and volunteers of RCCs can experience a variety of distressing emotions (e.g., anger, fear, sadness) as a result of their work with rape survivors.

The traumatic effect of working with survivors of violence is most commonly referred to as secondary traumatic stress (Dutton & Rubinstein, 1995), vicarious traumatization (McCann & Pearlman, 1990), or compassion fatigue (Figley, 1995; Joinson, 1992). Figley (1995) noted that people can be traumatized without actually being physically harmed or threatened with harm. That is, they can be traumatized simply by learning about the traumatic event (p. 4). The key cause of compassion fatigue is rooted in the meaning of compassion: a feeling of deep sympathy and sorrow for another who is stricken by suffering or misfortune, accompanied by a strong desire to alleviate the pain or remove its cause. Empathy is a major resource for trauma workers, who must use it to assess victims' problems and develop intervention approaches. Repeated exposure to this pain and the need to empathize continually with survivors' suffering produces psychological distress reactions in trauma service providers. The compassion fatigue model maintains that such distress is not only a normal part of this work, it is essential. By its very nature, the role of trauma service provider requires empathic exploration of painful material.

Consistent with the compassion fatigue model, several researchers have documented that therapists, counselors, and rape victim advocates who work with rape survivors experience many of the same reactions as do victims: anxiety; fear; exaggerated startle response; difficulty sleeping; nightmares; and physical health problems (e.g., gastrointestinal distress, repeated headaches). For example, Schauben and Frazier (1995) studied 220 female counselors and learned that as the percentage of therapists' caseloads devoted to treating sexual assault victims increased, counselors reported more posttraumatic stress symptoms. Similarly, Tyra (1979) and Eberth (1989) found that volunteer rape crisis counselors also reported behavioral, somatic, and psychological reactions to their work. Yet there is a functional role of these negative emotions. For instance, Wasco and Campbell (2000) noted that although rape victim advocates experience a variety of distressing emotions in their work (e.g., sadness, fear, anger), they also engage in a variety of adaptive coping strategies to respond to those stresses. Advocates used cathartic strategies to vent or release these feelings. In addition, advocates focused on the positive aspects of their work and the difference they were able to make in the lives of rape survivors. Similarly, Campbell (1996) found that rape victim advocates are able to withstand the stresses of this kind of work because of the personal satisfaction of assisting rape survivors. Wasco and Campbell (2000) argued that the emotions rape advocates feel as a result of their work are resources for strength and social change. Although these feelings can be distressing, most advocates find useful ways to cope with these emotions and use them as catalysts for their work.

RAPE CRISIS CENTERS' EFFECTIVENESS

Effects on Rape Survivors

Although RCCs have existed since the 1970s, few studies have explicitly examined if and how their services benefit survivors. In many respects, both researchers and anti-rape activists have assumed that RCCs help survivors precisely because the job of rape victim advocate is to intervene and prevent victim-blaming harm to survivors. RCC advocates appear to be successful in helping victims obtain needed resources from community systems (see Campbell, 1998a; Campbell & Bybee, 1997). Yet this evidence provides only indirect support for rape crisis effectiveness, because neither study compared outcomes of victims who did and did not receive help from victim advocates. Thus, one approach to studying the effectiveness of RCC services would be to assess how victims benefit (or do not benefit) as a function of receiving advocacy services. Would the survivors who received RCC advocacy services be better off than those who did not?

As a first step in addressing this question, Campbell et al. (1999) interviewed 102 rape survivors in an urban metropolitan area about their postrape experiences with various community agencies. This sample was carefully recruited through a variety of neighborhood contexts (e.g., public transportation, bookstores, coffee shops, beauty/nail salons, currency exchanges) to maximize racial/ethnic diversity as well as to ensure hearing from women who did and did not report the assault to community agencies, including RCCs. Consistent with prior studies, most victims in this study had not reported the assault to the criminal justice system, sought medical care, or obtained mental health services (only 39% had contact with the legal system, 43% with medical, and 39% with mental health). Only one in five victims had worked with an RCC advocate. These varied reporting/contacting rates allow for direct comparisons between victims who did and did not receive RCC services. Campbell et al. (1999) replicated the results of other researchers (e.g., Madigan & Gamble, 1991; Ullman, 1996; Williams, 1984) who found that, overall, rape victims receive little help from the criminal justice system, and this victim-blaming contact tends to be quite distressing for survivors. This effect was far more pronounced for victims of non-stranger rape (i.e., acquaintance rape, date rape, marital rape), who were at particular risk for secondary victimization. Yet working with an RCC advocate was associated with reduced victim distress (Wasco, Campbell, Barnes, & Ahrens, 1999). This same pattern of findings emerged for victims' experiences with the medical system. In other words, non-stranger rape victims were at considerable risk for poor treatment by legal and medical system personnel, but acquaintance, date, and marital rape victims who worked with RCC advocates experienced significantly less distress than those who did not have the assistance of an advocate. Taken together with the findings from Campbell (1998a) and Campbell and Bybee (1997), this work suggests that RCC advocates are quite successful in helping victims obtain needed services and buffering victims from victim-blaming system personnel.

Effects on Society at Large

Throughout the 1980s and 1990s, RCCs have been challenged by federal, state, and local funders; some academic researchers; and other community service providers to prove that they are effective. On one hand, such challenges appear somewhat absurd: RCCs are helping rape victims; educating police, prosecutor, and hospital staff; making public service announcements about rape; encouraging victims to report rape; and lobbying legislatures to change rape laws. How can these efforts be viewed as less than effective? On the other hand, it is not uncommon for small, local social movement organizations, such as RCCs, to have trouble proving that they are effective (Ferree & Martin, 1995; Katzenstein, 1987; Martin, 1990). Often small in size, dependent on volunteers for their labor power, and vulnerable in terms of human and material resources, RCCs have had little organizational time to devote to formal program evaluation (Byington et al., 1991; Campbell et al., 1998). Furthermore, their primary work is often behind the scenes and, given their political goals, RCCs are frequently unable to take credit for their achievements (Schmitt & Martin, 1999).

Evaluating how RCCs affect society at large is a far more complicated task than determining how the provision of services benefits individual survivors' recovery outcomes. Staggenborg (1995) provided a conceptual framework for understanding the society-level impact of social movement organizations, such as RCCs. Social movement effectiveness must take into account a movement's fluidity (that is, its changeability) and the fact that many movement organizations fail. However, the failure of a particular organization does not equate to a movement's failure. Movement organizations that fail can change their environments by leaving behind legacies, which make future mobilizing work possible. Thus, a particular RCC can fail and still, in the end, change its host community. Effectiveness must be evaluated over a substantial period of time, and researchers and policymakers must resist the impulse to declare a closed RCC a failure. Staggenborg (1995) argued that a movement's effectiveness should be gauged by its impact on its host society:

> Feminist organizations can be effective at the same time that they self-destruct as organizations and fail to achieve changes in public policy. Groups that are unsuccessful in terms of organizational maintenance and policy outcomes may be effective as the centers of movement communities and as the originators of cultural changes. Although the successes of many feminist organizations tend to be hidden, they are likely to have an impact on subsequent rounds of collective action. The women's movement is perpetuated not only by its movement organizations but also by its cultural achievements. (p. 353)

Most debates about the effectiveness of social movements and movement organizations focus on whether a movement changed society in the ways it preferred. Gamson (1990, 1992) defined social movement success somewhat modestly as acceptance of a challenging group as a legitimate representative of a constituency by the target of collective action and new advantages won by a challenger (cited by Staggenborg, 1995, p. 140). Mueller (1987) gauges a movement's effectiveness in terms of its influence on culture in the form of collective consciousness—the awareness and understanding of themes the movement promotes. She argued that the radical feminist women's movement successfully introduced new ideas, values, and practices into mainstream U.S. culture in ways that have made society's collective consciousness sympathetic to many feminist ideals.

Building on these and related discussions of social movement effectiveness, Staggenborg (1995) recommended viewing social movements as having multiple outcomes: (a) political and policy outcomes, (b) mobilization outcomes, and (c) cultural outcomes. First, political and policy outcomes refer to a movement's ability to bring about substantive changes through the political system (p. 341). That is, successful movements are able to influence political decision makers and implementers to adopt policies, laws, and/or regulations that the movement promotes. From this perspective, the U.S. anti-rape movement has been quite successful. Since the mid-1970s, all 50 states have dramatically reformed their rape statutes, removing many of the barriers victims used to face when attempting prosecution (e.g., defense attorneys are no longer allowed to extensively question victims about their prior sexual experiences) (Berger, Searles, & Neuman, 1988; Fischer, 1989). In addition, most jurisdictions now allow expert testimony in rape cases on Rape Trauma Syndrome (RTS) to explain to judges and juries how victims are harmed by sexual assault (Fischer, 1989). Much of the credit for these legal reforms goes to the grassroots organizing efforts of RCCs. For example, Schmitt and Martin's (1999) study of a southern California RCC documents how the center successfully influenced state legislators to pass laws that eliminated a requirement for victims to prove that they physically resisted their attacker. Similarly, Martin et al. (1992) studied how one Florida RCC built relationships with 14 other organizations throughout the state to institute a variety of legal reforms that benefit victimized people.

Second, Staggenborg (1995) defined mobilization outcomes as an ability to carry out collective action (e.g., mobilize people and other resources to support movement aims). Again, there is ample evidence indicating that RCCs have been successful in fund-raising, letter-writing campaigning, and organization of community functions (the specific tactics for such mobilization are covered in a later section of this chapter). A key index of the anti-rape movement's mobilization efforts was the passage of the 1994 federal Violence Against

Women Act (VAWA). Together with advocates for battered women and abused children, anti-rape activists secured millions of dollars in federal funding for services and prevention programs. Similarly, the number of RCCs in the United States and the budgets supporting those centers appear to be steadily increasing (see Martin, 1999), not decreasing as some have suggested (Harvey, 1985; Jensen & Karpos, 1993). On a more local level, RCCs continue to be effective organizers for violence-against-women demonstrations, such as the Take Back the Night March and the Clothesline Project (see Campbell & Ahrens, 1998). Schmitt and Martin (1999) described how one RCC in California obtained vast material resources—money, talent, film-making equipment, and skills from the Hollywood entertainment industry—to launch a national campaign against acquaintance rapes on college and university campuses.

Finally, cultural outcomes refer to a social movement's capacity to change a host society's values. As Mueller (1987) described, these values include social norms, behaviors, and ways of thinking among a public that extends beyond movement constituents or beneficiaries [and the] creation of a collective consciousness among groups such as women (p. 341). The anti-rape movement has raised public awareness about all forms of violence against women, but it has had particular success in gaining recognition for forms of non-stranger rape (acquaintance, date, and marital rape) as being serious crimes (see Koss, 1990, 1992, 1993b). Perhaps one of the most ironic sources of support for the cultural impact of RCCs comes from national data on the number of reported rapes in the United States. Jensen and Karpos (1993) paid a backhanded compliment when they claimed that RCCs have influenced women to increase (they say inflate) reports of acquaintance rape. Their evidence of inflated reports is quite weak, but nevertheless, there does appear to be a substantial increase in the number of reported non-stranger rapes throughout the past two decades. Orcutt and Faison (1988) argued that sex role attitude changes and community education efforts of RCCs explain increased reporting to officials. Increased reporting reflects broader social awareness about sexual assault. Making rapes known to legal-justice officials takes rape out of the closet, acknowledges it as a crime, and directs attention to the prosecution of assailants. The cultural effectiveness of RCCs is reflected by more women and girls reporting more instances of rapes more often than they previously did.

MOBILIZING STRATEGIES AND TACTICS

The individual- and societal-level effectiveness of RCCs is achieved through extensive community organizing and mobilization strategies. Social movement mobilizing is the marshaling of human, material, and symbolic resources on behalf of a movement's aims (see Schmitt & Martin, 1999). Strategies are general approaches, such as favoring public protests or educating the public, whereas tactics refers to specific activities such as teaching high school health classes about rape or drafting rape legislation. In this section, we identify strategies and tactics used by RCCs to mobilize their home communities.

Assisting Mainstream Organizations

In contrast to a stand outside and allocate blame strategy used by many early (and most radical) RCCs (e.g., publicly condemning practices by mainstream organizations), today's RCCs use a strategy of occupy and indoctrinate (Martin, 1999; Schmitt & Martin, 1999).

This strategy entails gaining entry to the legal-justice and medical-therapeutic networks of a community and making themselves useful by helping mainstream organizations with their work. RCCs provide assistance by training police recruits about rape, teaching health education courses in public schools, teaching prosecutors about how to question victims and assailants, and writing legislation for legislative staff (see also Campbell & Ahrens, 1998). As Schmitt and Martin (1999) concluded, training staff of mainstream organizations is an effective way to occupy and indoctrinate.

Conducting Educational Campaigns

To inform the public and specific target groups about rape, many RCCs develop and distribute, often free of charge, materials about rape to the media. The southern California RCC studied by Schmitt and Martin (1999) developed a film, posters, and public service announcements (PSAs), which it made available to the public in its city, state, and the nation. They sold 6,000 copies of the film at cost (for $50) and gave away the posters and PSAs. Similarly, RCCs have developed rape awareness and prevention programs for public schools (see Lonsway, 1996). RCCs' educational efforts are also evident by the expert advice and testimony that center staff provide to various community groups such as the media, government, and private sector, who turn to them for information on violence against women (Fischer, 1989).

Developing Community Connections

In the past 5 years, several new service programs have emerged in a handful of RCCs throughout the country because of extensive, long-term community connections between RCCs and other community agencies (see Campbell & Ahrens, 1998). For example, in some areas, rape crisis counseling is readily available at churches and substance abuse treatment centers (Campbell & Ahrens, 1998). In addition, more communities are offering victims an alternative to traditional emergency room-based medical care: Sexual Assault Nurse Examiner (SANE) programs provide postrape health care by a specially trained nurse in a safe, comfortable environment (e.g., a community clinic or a separate area of the hospital/emergency room) (Ahrens et al., 2001; Ledray, 1999). Similarly, Martin's (1999) research on five Florida communities suggests that RCCs are often a hub in their communities, bringing together other community groups to develop new programs or improve existing services. RCCs have created a niche for themselves, and they exercise considerable influence on mainstream organizations and systems in their communities.

CONCLUSIONS

RCCs appear to be a permanent, or at least long-term manifestation of the radical feminist women's movement. The structure and function of RCCs have changed over time, and many no longer resemble the feminist collectives of the early anti-rape movement. Yet the passions of center staff and volunteers to empower survivors and educate society to end violence against women remain steadfast. Our analysis of RCCs suggests that they have been remarkably flexible and innovative: They have withstood changing political climates and continue to improve services for victims. As a case in point, RCCs were a major force in the early

1980s for establishing standardized postrape emergency room medical care for victims (i.e., the rape kit) (see Martin & DiNitto, 1987; Martin et al., 1985). In the late 1990s, RCCs continued to lead the way in developing more personalized care for survivors, as they have organized alternative programs to emergency room-based care (i.e., SANE programs) (see Ledray, 1999). The ability of RCCs to establish programs and continue to revise and improve on them even if such improvements require radical alterations of their previous work reflects ongoing commitment to help victims and change society's tolerance of rape. RCCs have been effective not only in healing survivors but also in challenging dominant social institutions—the legal, medical, and mental health systems—to address sexist practices. The enduring contribution of the anti-rape movement has been raising the collective consciousness of society to understand violence against women as a political issue in need of political action.

UNIT 7

———■———

SPECIAL ISSUES AND CONCERNS OF
SEX BEHAVIORS AND CRIMES

This final section deals with special issues in sex crimes and behaviors. This section is designed as an inimitable chapter for articles that are unique from the other topical articles in this book. This unit contains readings on a variety of topics ranging from the sexual abuse of women on college campuses, community notification laws, and the link between criminality and mental impairedness, to looking at sexual homicides of elderly female victims, intervention philosophies, and the debate over psychological profiling, science or art.

The first article, "The Sexual Victimization of College Women," examines the serious and often hidden problem of sexual victimization of women on college campuses across the United States. In this study, Fisher, Cullen, and Turner claim that women in colleges and 4-year universities are at a greater risk of victimization than women in the general population in comparable age groups. This finding was further supported and bolstered by Congress, which, in 1992, required all colleges and universities to publish their policies regarding rape awareness and rape prevention policies and procedures. Additionally, they were instructed to keep daily crime logs that can be requested and viewed.

This article was taken from a larger study funded by the National Institute of Justice and the Bureau of Justice Statistics to examine this phenomenon and correct the biases found in previous research. The correction of these biases includes the use of a national representative sample of college women, assessing the full range of sexual victimization, and using a two-stage screen questionnaire that detailed questions about the women's victimizations using plain and explicit language.

The authors found that over the course of a female's typical college career, she runs about a 20% to 25% chance of being a victim of a completed or attempted rape. These percentages are somewhat higher than most would suspect and not the type of data that many colleges and universities would want published. Not only do these statistics seem to be larger than previous official statistics indicate, but when these authors compared their study's findings with similar questions taken from the National Crime Victimization Survey, the results were consistently higher than many other previous estimates.

Furthermore, using multivariate logistic regression models, the authors found that females who frequently drank to get drunk, were unmarried, and had been a victim of a prior sexual assault were the group most likely to be victimized. The authors also found that most sexual victimizations of college-aged women occur at night, with a man they know, and in the privacy of a residence.

The next reading in this section, "Where Should We Intervene? Dynamic Predicators of Sexual Offense Recidivism," examines the predictors of sexual recidivism among convicted sex offenders released into the community for supervision. More specifically, this study examines three sets of predictive elements and their relative strength in predicting whether these sex offenders recidivate or not. The three sets of variables are static (non-changing), acute dynamic (situational factors that change), and stable dynamic (situational factors that are relatively constant) predictive elements.

In order to compare these two groups (recidivists and nonrecidivists), the authors matched the sample on static factors and found that there were substantial differences between the two groups. The recidivists were more likely to have weaker social support networks and attitudes that were tolerant of sexual assault, and they were more likely to live antisocial lifestyles. Furthermore, the authors found that the recidivists were more likely to engage in more diverse deviant sexual behavior, suffer from low intelligence, and have more prior treatment failures, and they were more likely to have been reared in a family environment where there was either sexual or emotional abuse.

The authors conclude by stating that of the three different types of risk factors, the stable dynamic factors were the strongest of the three in predicting future recidivism. What this means is that the authors found that criminal lifestyle variables were stronger predictors than were demographic elements, even sexual deviance. Armed with this knowledge, it is then possible to say that the elements that predict future violence (Quinsey, Harris, Rice, & Cormier, 1998) appear to be the same that predict future sexual offending.

The third article deals with sex offender notification laws as a form of community justice. This article, written by Presser and Gunnison, details how sex offender notification laws and the restorative justice movement are two completely different movements that have little in common. The authors take great pains to differentiate the two based on their principle foundations. They state that sex offender notification laws do little to help the community prevent or solve problems but rather encourage future violence and potential vigilantism.

Among the seven key and critical differences between these two movements is the power and authority of the state. Under the community or restorative justice movement, the state acts as the conduit whereby community wounds can be healed and problems can be solved. However, these authors claim that by and through the use of sex offender notification laws, the state fulfills its responsibility once notification has been conducted. Thus, by notifying citizens, and then not being there to make sure actual community healing and prevention activities occur, the state is shirking its true responsibility vested unto it by the community justice movement. Furthermore, the authors claim that sexual notification laws are flawed in that the community perceives that many of these sex offenders cannot be rehabilitated. Although research has found this not to be true, it is difficult to change people's perceptions, especially when it comes to the perceived threat against children by adult sexual predators. The authors state that in this situation, offenders come to acquire the master status of "sex offender," and that despite the penalties they have paid for the crimes of the past, as well as the treatment that they have undergone, there is little likelihood that the community, much less the offenders' neighbors, will allow them to even attempt to reintegrate back into the community. Hence, from these authors' perspective, sexual offender notification laws become nothing more than an additional punishment by the state to remand these individuals to a second-class status, where the chances are small that they can actually reintegrate and become functioning members of society.

In the article "Criminal Profiling: Real Science or Just Wishful Thinking?" the author offers the reader an inside look at the debate of whether psychological profiling is an art or a science. Quoting several "authorities" in the field, including academics and former agents of the Federal Bureau of Investigation, Muller continues to address the distinctions in an effort to make a case. Citing studies, books, and media depictions, the author concludes that psychological profiling is not a science in the purest definition of the term. For example, developing a useful profile relies heavily on the experience and the intuition of the profiler than on pure scientific method. Thus, Muller adds, there is no verifiable evidence to substantiate a case for science. Noting that not all crimes are suitable for profiling, and also adding that a psychological profile has never, by itself, solved a crime, he believes that it is just one more tool in the investigative process. But, he adds, profiling could potentially reach that stage of a "scientific method." But a better question may be, Do profilers really wish the psychological profiling process to be scientific in the first place? As profilers, we agonize over this question. When we deal with human behavior, can we truly reduce it to a scientific level? Would all humanness then be lost? Muller's article in an excellent one that adds pertinent thoughts to this debate.

22

The Sexual Victimization
of College Women

———■———

BONNIE S. FISHER
FRANCIS T. CULLEN
University of Cincinnati

MICHAEL G. TURNER
Northeastern University

INTRODUCTION

During the past decade, concern over the sexual victimization of female college students has escalated. In part, the interest in this problem has been spurred by increasing attention to the victimization of women in general; until the relatively recent past, female victims received very little attention. However, this is no longer true. Terms such as "date rape" and "domestic violence" have entered the public lexicon and signify the unprecedented, if still insufficient, notice given to women who have been victimized.

Attention to the sexual victimization of college women, however, also has been prompted by the rising fear that college campuses are not ivory towers but, instead, have become hot spots for criminal activity. Researchers have shown that college campuses and their students are not free from the risk of criminal victimization.[1] It is noteworthy that large concentrations of young women come into contact with young men in a variety of public and private settings at various times on college campuses.

Previous research suggests that these women are at greater risk for rape and other forms of sexual assault than women in the general population or in a comparable age group.[2] College women might, therefore, be a group whose victimization warrants special attention.

Recognizing these risks, the U.S. Congress passed the Student Right-to-Know and Campus Security Act of 1990 (hereafter referred to as the act). This legislation mandates

---

Authors' Note: This article previously appeared as Fisher, B., Cullen, F., & Turner, M. (2000). *The sexual victimization of college women* (Research report). Washington, DC: National Institute of Justice and Bureau of Justice Statistics.

that colleges and universities participating in federal student aid programs "prepare, publish, and distribute, through appropriate publications or mailings, to all current students and employees, and to any applicant for enrollment or employment upon request, an annual security report" containing campus security policies and campus crime statistics for that institution (see 20 U.S.C. 1092(f)(1)).[3]

Congress has maintained an interest in campus crime issues, passing legislation that requires higher educational institutions to address the rights of victims of sexual victimization and to collect and publish additional crime statistics (e.g., murder and non-negligent manslaughter, arson). For example, Congress amended the act in 1992 to include the Campus Sexual Assault Victims' Bill of Rights, which requires colleges and universities (1) to develop and publish as part of their annual security report their policies regarding the awareness and prevention of sexual assaults and (2) to afford basic rights to sexual assault victims.[4] The act was amended again in 1998 to include additional reporting obligations, extensive campus security-related provisions, and the requirement to keep a daily public crime log; some states already required a public log (Public Law 105-244).[5] The 1998 amendments also officially changed the name of the act to the Jeanne Clery Disclosure of Campus Security Policy and Campus Crime Statistics Act. In 1999, the U.S. Department of Justice awarded $8.1 million to 21 colleges and universities to combat sexual assault, domestic violence, and stalking.[6] In 2000, 20 additional schools were awarded $6.8 million. Two national-level studies are currently in the field. The first study examines how institutions of higher education respond to the report of a sexual assault. The second one is a multisite evaluation of the programs and policies implemented in the above-mentioned 41 schools.

WHAT WE KNOW ABOUT
SEXUAL VICTIMIZATION OF COLLEGE WOMEN

Like government officials, researchers also have given attention to the sexual victimization of college women and have conducted a number of studies.[7] Although illuminating, much of the research is generally characterized by one or more of the following limitations:

- The failure to use a randomly selected, national sample of college women (Many studies have sampled students at only one college or at a limited number of institutions.)
- The failure to assess the various ways in which women can be victimized (Most studies have focused on a limited number of types of sexual victimization.)
- The failure to use question wording or sufficiently detailed measures that prevent biases that might cause researchers to underestimate or overestimate the extent of sexual victimization
- The failure to collect detailed information on what occurred during the victimization incident
- The failure to explore systematically the factors that place female students at risk for sexual victimization
- The failure to study whether women have been stalked—a victimization that, until recently, had not received systematic research

The National College Women Sexual Victimization (NCWSV) study, described in this report and funded by the National Institute of Justice (NIJ), attempted to build on, and surmount the limitations of, existing research on the sexual victimization of college students by

- Employing a nationally representative sample of college women.
- Assessing a range of sexual victimizations, including stalking.
- Measuring sexual victimization using a two-stage process starting with "behaviorally specific" screen questions that attempted to cue respondents to recall and report to the interviewer different types of sexual victimization experiences they may have had. Those who reported a victimization were then asked a series of questions, called an incident report, to verify what type of sexual victimization, if any, had occurred.
- Acquiring detailed information on each victimization incident, including the type of penetration(s) or unwanted sexual contact experienced and the means of coercion, if any, used by the offender.
- Examining how the risk of being sexually victimized was affected by a variety of variables, including demographic characteristics, lifestyles, prior victimization, and the characteristics of the college or university attended.

In addition, the research project contained a comparison component designed to assess how rape estimates that use the two-stage process (behaviorally specific questions and incident reports) compared with rape estimates drawn from a sample of college women who completed a survey based on the National Crime Victimization Survey (NCVS). The comparison component was funded by the Bureau of Justice Statistics (BJS).[8]

The resulting data furnish perhaps the most systematic analysis of the extent and nature of the sexual victimization of college women in the past decade.

WHO WAS SURVEYED?

NCWSV study results are based on a telephone survey of a randomly selected, national sample of 4,446 women who were attending a 2- or 4-year college or university during fall 1996. The questions were asked between February and May 1997. The sample was limited to schools with at least 1,000 students and was stratified by the size of the total student enrollment (1,000-2,499; 2,500-4,999; 5,000-19,999; 20,000 or more) and the school's location (urban, suburban, or rural). Schools were randomly chosen using a probability proportional with the size of the total female enrollment. Students were then randomly selected using a sampling frame provided by the American Student List Company. This company provided the school address and telephone number for each student in the sample.

Each sample member was sent a letter describing the study and research protocol approximately 2 weeks prior to when a trained female interviewer called using a computer-aided telephone interviewing system.[9] The response rate was 85.6 percent.[10]

The comparison component used the same two-stage methodology as the main study except victimization was measured by using the screen questions and the incident report employed by NCVS. One purpose of the comparison component was to conduct a methodological experiment that would provide insight into the extent to which rape estimates are influenced by survey methods.

HOW WAS SEXUAL VICTIMIZATION MEASURED?

Measurement of sexual victimization was based on responses to "screen questions" and on a reference period for the victimization. In addition to the victimization measures, survey questions and secondary data sources were used to investigate the factors that potentially placed women at risk of being sexually victimized.

Two-Stage Measurement Design: The Screen Question-Incident Report Methodology

With important exceptions noted later, sexual victimization was measured largely by following the two-stage measurement format of NCVS. NCVS first asks a series of screen questions that seek to determine if a respondent has experienced an act that may possibly be a victimization. If the respondent answers "yes," then for each of the times that the act was experienced, the respondent is asked by the interviewer to complete an "incident report." This report contains detailed questions about the nature of the events that occurred in the incident. The report is used to classify the type of victimization that took place; that is, responses to questions in the incident report—not the screen questions—are used to categorize whether a victimization occurred and, if so, what type.

Some researchers have contended that the screen questions as worded in NCVS are not detailed enough to identify all women who have experienced a rape or another type of sexual assault. A respondent may not answer "yes" to a screen question unless it is worded in a way that reflects the experience the respondent has had. To rectify this limitation, researchers have argued that sexual victimization should be measured with screen questions that are both numerous and detailed enough that respondents will not misunderstand what is being asked.[11]

NCWSV, therefore, used a series of behaviorally specific screen questions that sought to assess whether respondents had experienced a range of sexual victimizations. A behaviorally specific question, for example, is one that does not ask simply if a respondent "had been raped"; rather, it describes an incident in graphic language that covers the elements of a criminal offense (e.g., someone "made you have sexual intercourse by using force or threatening to harm you . . . by intercourse I mean putting a penis in your vagina"). The same logic can be used to ask about other forms of sexual victimization, such as sexual coercion or unwanted sexual contact.

Examples of the screen questions used in the NCWSV study are listed in Exhibit 22.1. Each completed rape screen question asks the respondent about a different form of penetration in which force or the threat of harm was used. A statement then follows each question that defines the type of penetration. For example, anal sex is defined as "putting a penis in your anus or rectum." The other screen questions provide examples of the behaviors that respondents were asked about.

The NCWSV rape screen questions are similar, if not identical, to those used by Kilpatrick and his associates[12] and by Tjaden and Thoennes.[13] The use of behaviorally specific screen questions is an important difference between the current survey and NCVS. The NCVS screen questions begin with a reference to a type of criminal victimization that may have been experienced (e.g., "were you attacked or threatened"), which is then followed by a list of short cue responses about the potential victimization. This list includes cues regarding specific places or situations in which the victimization could have occurred (e.g., "at work or at school"); objects that could have been used (e.g., "with any weapon, for instance, a gun or knife"); actions that could have been associated with the victimization (e.g., "face-to-face threats"); actions that constitute a criminal victimization (e.g., "rape, attempted rape, or other types of sexual attack"); and people who might have perpetrated

Exhibit 22.1   Survey Screen Questions

Women may experience a wide range of unwanted sexual experiences in college. Women do not always report unwanted sexual experiences to the police or discuss them with family and firends. The person making the advances is not always a stranger, but can be a friend, boyfriend, fellow student, professor, teaching assistant, supervisor, coworker, someone met off campus, or even a family member. The experience could occur anywhere, on or off campus, in your residence, in your place of employment, or in a public place. You could be awake, or you could be asleep, unconscious, drunk, or otherwise incapacitated. Please keep this in mind as you answer the questions.

Now, I'm going to ask you about different types of unwanted sexual experiences you may have experienced since school began. Because of the nature of unwanted sexual experiences, the language may seem graphic to you. However, this is the only way to assess accurately whether or not the women in this study have had such experiences. You only have to answer "yes" or "no."

- Since school began, has anyone made you have sexual intercourse by using force or threatening to harm you or someone close to you? Just so there is no mistake, by intercourse I mean putting a penis in your vagina.
- Since school began, has anyone made you have oral sex by force or threat of harm? By oral sex, I mean someone's mouth or tongue making contact with your vagina or anus or your mouth or tongue making contact with someone else's genitals or anus.
- Since school began, has anyone made you have anal sex by force or threat of harm? By anal sex, I mean putting a penis in your anus or rectum.
- Since school began, has anyone ever used force or threat of harm to sexually penetrate you with a foreign object? By this, I mean for example, placing a bottle or finger in your vagina or anus.
- Since school began, has anyone attempted but not succeeded in making you take part in any of the unwanted sexual experiences that I have just asked you about? For example, did anyone threaten or try but not succeed to have vaginal, oral, or anal sex with you or try unsucessfully to penetrate your vagina or anus with a foreign object or finger?
- Not counting the types of sexual contact already mentioned, have you experienced any unwanted or uninvited touching of a sexual nature since school began? This includes forced kissing, touching of private parts, grabbing, fondling, and rubbing up against you in a sexual way, even if it is over your clothes.
- Since school began, has anyone attempted but not succeeded in unwanted or uninvited touching of a sexual nature?
- Since school began, has anyone made or tried to make you have sexual intercourse or sexual contact when you did not want to by making threats of nonphysical punishment, such as lowering a grade, being demoted or fired from a job, damaging your reputation, or being excluded from a group for failure to comply with requests for any type of sexual activity?
- Since school began, has anyone made or tried to make you have sexual intercourse or sexual contact with you when you did not want to by making promises of rewards, such as raising a grade, being hired or promoted, being given a ride or class notes, or getting help with coursework from a fellow student if you complied sexually?
- Since school began, has anyone made or tried to make you have sexual intercourse or sexual contact when you did not want to by simply being overwhelmed by someone's continual pestering and verbal pressure?

the criminal act (e.g., "a relative or family member"). There is also a screen question that asks about "incidents involving forced or unwanted sexual acts."[14]

Drawing on the NCVS screen question and incident report methodology, the NCWSV screen questions were followed by a detailed incident report that (1) clarified what type of victimization, if any, had occurred and (2) collected information about various aspects of the incident (e.g., victim-offender relationship, whether the victimization took place on or off the college campus, whether the incident was reported to the police). Responses to the screen questions were not used to classify the type of victimization reported by the respondent. Instead, classification was based on the responses in the incident report to questions about (1) the type of penetration experienced (e.g., penile-vaginal, anal, oral); (2) the type of unwanted sexual contact experienced (e.g., touching, grabbing, or fondling); and (3) the means of coercion used by the perpetrators (e.g., force, threat of force). As in Koss et al. and NCVS, the incidents were classified using a hierarchical algorithm; that is, incidents were classified by the most severe type of sexual victimization that occurred within an incident.[15] For example, if, within an incident report, the victim answered questions indicating she had experienced a completed rape and attempted sexual coercion, the incident was classified as a completed rape.

Reference Period

To limit potential response bias due to recall or memory decay, the NCWSV survey questions used a reference period that had a clear starting date for students. Thus, respondents were asked if they had experienced a sexual victimization "since school began in fall 1996." The survey was conducted in 1997 between late February and early May. On average, the reference period for the victimization covered almost 7 months (6.91 months).[16] To participate in the study, respondents had to be enrolled in a college or university at the start of the 1996 fall semester.

Risk Factors

In addition to the victimization measures, the NCWSV survey contained questions about respondents' demographic characteristics, lifestyles or routine activities, living arrangements, prior sexual victimizations, and so forth. Secondary data sources were used to measure the characteristics of the schools the respondents attended (e.g., size of enrollment, location, crime rate). These individual- and institution-level variables were used in multivariate analyses that investigated which factors potentially placed women at risk of being sexually victimized.

WHAT TYPES OF SEXUAL VICTIMIZATION WERE MEASURED IN THE NCWSV STUDY?

Measures of 12 types of sexual victimization were constructed; they are defined in Exhibit 22.2. Most important, the NCWSV study included measures of both completed and attempted rape as well as threats of rape. The study also measured completed, attempted, and threatened sexual coercion (penetration with the use of nonphysical forms of coercion) and

Exhibit 22.2   Descriptions of Types of Victimizations

Types of Victimization	Definition
Completed rape	Unwanted completed penetration by force or the threat of force. Penetration includes: penile-vaginal, mouth on your genitals, mouth on someone else's genitals, penile-anal, digital-vaginal, digital-anal, object-vaginal, and object-anal.
Attempted rape	Unwanted attempted penetration by force or threat of force. Penetration includes: penile-vaginal, mouth on your genitals, mouth on someone else's genitals, penile-anal, digital-vaginal, digital-anal, object-vaginal, and object-anal.
Completed sexual coercion	Unwanted completed penetration with the threat of nonphysical punishment, promise of reward, or pestering/verbal pressure. Penetration includes: penile-vaginal, mouth on your genitals, mouth on someone else's genitals, penile-anal, digital-vaginal, digital-anal, object-vaginal, and object-anal.
Attempted sexual coercion	Unwanted attempted penetration with the threat of nonphysical punishment, promise of reward, or pestering/verbal pressure. Penetration includes: penile-vaginal, mouth on your genitals, mouth on someone else's genitals, penile-anal, digital-vaginal, digital-anal, object-vaginal, and object-anal.
Completed sexual contact with force or threat of force	Unwanted completed sexual contact (not penetration) with force or threat of force. Sexual contact includes: touching; grabbing or fondling of breasts, buttocks, or genitals, either under or over your clothes; kissing; licking or sucking; or some other form of unwanted sexual contact.
Completed sexual contact without force	Any tupe of unwanted completed sexual contact (not penetration) with the threat of nonphysical punishment, promise of reward, or pestering/verbal pressure. Sexual contact includes: touching; grabbing or fondling of breasts, buttocks, or genitals, either under or over your clothes; kissing; licking or sucking; or some other form of unwanted sexual contact.
Attempted sexual contact with force or threat of force	Unwanted attempted sexual contact (not penetration) with force or the threat of force. Sexual contact includes: touching; grabbing or fondling of breasts, buttocks, or genitals, either under or over your clothes; kissing; licking or sucking; or some other form of unwanted sexual contact.
Attempted sexual contact without force	Unwanted attempted sexual contact (not penetration) with the threat of nonphysical punishment, promise of reward, or pestering/verbal pressure. Sexual contact includes: touching; grabbing or fondling of breasts, buttocks, or genitals, either under or over your clothes; kissing; licking or sucking; or some other form of unwanted sexual contact.

(continued)

Exhibit 22.2 (Continued)	
Threat of rape	Threat of unwanted penetration with force and threat of force. Penetration includes: penil-vaginal, mouth on your genitals, mouth on someone else's genitals, penile-anal, digital-vaginal, digital-anal, object-vaginal, and object-anal.
Threat of contact with force or threat of force	Threat of unwanted sexual contact with force and threat of force. Sexual contact includes: touching; grabbing or fondling of breasts, buttocks, or genitals, either under or over your clothes; kissing; licking or sucking; or some other form of unwanted sexual contact.
Threat of penetration without force	Threat of unwanted penetration with the threat of nonphysical punishment, promise of reward, or pestering/verbal pressure. Penetration includes: penile-vaginal, mouth on your genitals, mouth on someone else's genitals, penile-anal, digital-vaginal, digital-anal, object-vaginal, and object-anal.
Threat of contact without force	Threat of unwanted sexual contact with the threat of nonphysical punishment, promise of reward, or pestering/verbal pressure. Sexual contact includes: touching; grabbing or fondling of breasts, buttocks, or genitals, either under or over your clothes; kissing; licking or sucking; or some other form of unwanted sexual contact.

unwanted sexual contact (sexual contact, but not penetration, with force or threat of force). In addition, the study measured stalking and visual and verbal forms of sexual victimization.

HOW EXTENSIVE IS
RAPE AMONG COLLEGE WOMEN?

Exhibit 22.3 reports the extent of rape found in the NCWSV study. As shown, 2.8 percent of the sample had experienced either a completed rape (1.7 percent) or an attempted rape incident (1.1 percent). The victimization rate was 27.7 rapes per 1,000 female students.

We recognize that a hierarchical scoring procedure is not the only way to count victims and incidents, especially because we have multiple victims. Another estimation procedure is to count the total number of completed rape victims and the total number of attempted rape victims separately. For example, suppose there were two incident records for Respondent 00: One incident was classified as a completed rape, and the other was classified as an attempted rape (recall that using a hierarchical scoring procedure, Respondent 00 would be counted as a completed rape victim). Respondent 00 would now count as a completed rape victim and as an attempted rape victim. Using this "separate" counting procedure, there were 57 attempted rape victims, or 1.3 percent of the sample.

Because some women were victimized more than once, the rate of incidents was higher than the rate of victims (35.3 per 1,000 students). Of the 123 victims, 22.8 percent ($n = 28$) were multiple-rape victims.

Exhibit 22.3   Extent of Rape, by Number of Victims and Number of Incidents, by Type of Victimization Incident

	Victims			Incidents	
Type of Victimization	Number of Victims in Sample	Percentage of Sample	Rate per 1,000 Female Students	Number of Incidents	Rate per 1,000 Female Students
Completed rape	74	1.7	16.6	86	19.3
Attempted rape	49	1.1	11.0	71	16.0
Total	123	2.8	27.7[a]	157	35.3

a. Total has been rounded (from 27.665 to 27.7).

A separate analysis, again using the same hierarchical scoring procedure, found that when rates were computed for only undergraduate students, the percentage of students victimized was 1.8 percent for rape and 1.3 percent for attempted rape. The comparable figures for nonundergraduate students were, respectively, 0.8 percent and 0 percent.[17]

At first glance, one might conclude that the risk of rape victimization for college women is not high; "only" about 1 in 36 college women (2.8 percent) experience a completed rape or attempted rape in an academic year. Such a conclusion, however, misses critical, and potentially disquieting, implications. The figures measure victimization for slightly more than half a year (6.91 months). Projecting results beyond this reference period is problematic for a number of reasons, such as assuming that the risk of victimization is the same during summer months and remains stable over a person's time in college. However, if the 2.8 percent victimization figure is calculated for a 1-year period, the data suggest that nearly 5 percent (4.9 percent) of college women are victimized in any given calendar year. Over the course of a college career—which now lasts an average of 5 years—the percentage of completed or attempted rape victimization among women in higher educational institutions might climb to between one fifth and one quarter.[18]

Furthermore, from a policy perspective, college administrators might be disturbed to learn that for every 1,000 women attending their institutions, there may well be 35 incidents of rape in a given academic year (based on a victimization rate of 35.3 per 1,000 college women). For a campus with 10,000 women, this would mean the number of rapes could exceed 350.

Even more broadly, when projected over the nation's female student population of several million, these figures suggest that rape victimization is a potential problem of large proportion and of public policy interest.

HOW DO THE NCWSV RAPE ESTIMATES COMPARE WITH THE RAPE ESTIMATES BASED ON THE NATIONAL CRIME VICTIMIZATION SURVEY?

The sexual victimization literature contains a great deal of discussion about how rape estimates from the nation's federally sponsored victimization survey, NCVS, compare with estimates from other national surveys. This issue was examined through a comparison component.[19] Like the main NCWSV study, the comparison study was conducted in the 1996-1997 academic year, from late March to mid-May. The sample size was 4,432 college women; the response rate was 91.6 percent.[20]

Every effort was made to ensure that, aside from using different screen and incident report questions, the methodology used in both the main and comparison components was the same. Thus, both components (1) contacted sample members with a letter that explained the purpose of the survey, (2) employed the same sampling design and sampling frame, (3) used the same reference period for victimization ("Since school began in fall 1996 . . ."), and (4) measured victimization using the screen question-incident report methodology. Both components also were conducted by the same survey research firm (see Note 10) and were administered by trained female interviewers using a computer-aided telephone interviewing system.

However, in assessing the influence of different methodologies for measuring sexual victimization, the two studies differed on one methodological issue: the wording of the screen questions and the wording of the incident-level questions used to determine the type of incident. As previously described, the main study substantially modified the NCVS format to include a range of behaviorally specific screen questions. In contrast, the comparison component used a format that was closely aligned with the survey format of NCVS. All of the screen questions used in the comparison component came directly from NCVS, as did the incident-level questions used to determine what type of violent victimization the respondent had experienced.[21] Both components used a hierarchical algorithm to classify the type(s) of victimization that the respondent described in the incident report.

We should note, however, that the methodology used in the comparison component differs from that used in NCVS in one respect. In addition to structured responses to the survey questions, NCVS interviewers record a brief "verbatim description" of the victimization incident from those respondents who report experiencing rape or sexual assault. These verbatim responses are used to clarify what occurred in an incident and to code whether an incident should count as a sexual victimization. Thus, according to BJS staff:

> In the NCVS, all questionnaires for which any rape or sexual assault code is entered in any of the pertinent items are reviewed to determine whether the codes reflect the written entries in the summaries. Where there are clear indications that the coded entries are not correct, they are edited, using guidelines developed by BJS and Bureau of Census staffs. This procedure has proven beneficial towards improving the NCVS estimates of rape and sexual assault by removing, to the extent possible, the discrepancies existing between the coded and written entries.[22]

In our comparison component study, the estimates were not adjusted using verbatim responses.[23] We do not know how much this consideration affects the findings reported for the comparison component that is, again, based on NCVS methodology. None of the Criminal Victimization in the United States annual publications report how much the NCVS estimates are adjusted using verbatim responses, or whether such adjustments cause estimates to increase or decrease compared with estimates coded solely on respondents' answers to the structured screen and incident-report questions.

NCVS defines rape as:

Exhibit 22.4. Comparison of Rape Estimates Between the NCWSV Main Study and Comparison Component Study

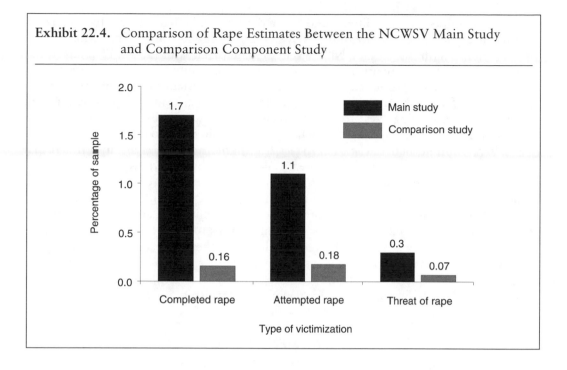

Forced sexual intercourse including both psychological coercion as well as physical force. Forced sexual intercourse means vaginal, anal, or oral penetration by the offender(s). This category also includes incidents where the penetration is from a foreign object such as a bottle. Includes attempted rapes, male as well as female victims, and both heterosexual and homosexual rape. Attempted rape includes verbal threats of rape.

This definition guided the classification of incidents in the comparison study as a completed rape, an attempted rape, or a threat of rape. In the Criminal Victimization in the United States series published by BJS, estimates for attempted rape and threats of rape are reported separately. The same is true in this report so as to compare rape estimates from the two components of the study.

How do the rape estimates from these two studies compare? It should be noted that studies that use behaviorally specific screen questions generally find higher levels of sexual victimization than those reported by NCVS.[24] Most important, this finding has occurred in recent research using a national-level sample and behaviorally specific questions.[25]

Looking at Exhibit 22.4, it is clear that estimates from the comparison study for completed rape, attempted rape, and threats of rape are considerably lower than the respective estimates from the main study. The percentage of the sample that reported experiencing a completed rape in the comparison study was 11 times smaller than the percentage of victims in the main component (0.16 percent compared with 1.7 percent). The attempted rape estimate from the comparison component was six times smaller than the attempted rape estimate (0.18 percent compared with 1.1 percent) from NCWSV. A similar pattern was evident for threats of rape; the estimate based on the comparison component was four times smaller than the NCWSV estimate (0.07 percent compared with 0.3 percent).

What accounts for these differences? Given the similarities between the two studies, it would appear that the differences most likely stem from the wide range of behaviorally specific screen questions used in the NCWSV study. Compared with the NCVS screen questions employed in the comparison component, the use of graphically worded screen questions in NCWSV likely prompted more women who had experienced a sexual victimization to report this fact to the interviewer. Their responses in the incident report determined whether those answering "yes" to a rape screen question were subsequently classified as rape victims.[26] Even so, it appears that behaviorally specific screen questions are more successful in prompting women who have, in fact, been sexually victimized to answer in such a way that they are then "skipped into" the incident report by interviewers.

What is unknown, however, is whether behaviorally specific screen questions produce higher estimates of victimization in general or only higher estimates of sexual victimization. It is possible that, due to the sensitive nature of sexual victimization, graphically descriptive screen questions are needed to prompt reluctant victims to report their victimization to interviewers. The other possibility, however, is that a large set of behaviorally specific questions would result in more victim reports for any type of victimization, including property crimes and other forms of violent crime (e.g., aggravated assault, robbery). Future research on NCVS methodology might profit from exploring this issue.

DO WOMEN DEFINE THEIR VICTIMIZATION AS A RAPE?

In each incident report, respondents were asked, "Do you consider this incident to be a rape?" For the 86 incidents categorized as a completed rape, 46.5 percent ($n = 40$) of the women answered "yes," 48.8 percent ($n = 42$) answered "no," and 4.7 percent ($n = 4$) answered "don't know." Among women who experienced other forms of sexual victimization ($n = 1,318$), it is noteworthy that 3.4 percent ($n = 42$) defined their sexual victimization as a rape and 1.1 percent ($n = 14$) answered "don't know."

Some scholars believe that the failure of women to define a victimization as a rape calls into question whether researchers have truly measured the crime of rape.[27] Others suggest, however, that the true prevalence of rape is best measured by carefully worded questions on victimization surveys, such as NCWSV.[28] Women may not define a victimization as a rape for many reasons (such as embarrassment, not clearly understanding the legal definition of the term, or not wanting to define someone they know who victimized them as a rapist) or because others blame them for their sexual assault.[29] Which of these reasons is more or less correct cannot be definitively substantiated here because little systematic research has examined why women do or do not define as a rape an incident that has met the researcher's criteria for a rape.

HOW EXTENSIVE ARE OTHER FORMS OF SEXUAL VICTIMIZATION?

Exhibit 22.5 presents the extent of victimization across 10 forms of sexual victimization other than rape. Threats of sexual victimization happened less often than other forms of sexual victimization. Across the 10 types of victimization in Exhibit 22.5, the incident rate per 1,000 female students ranged from a low of 9.5 to a high of 66.4.

Exhibit 22.5   Extent of Sexual Victimization

	Victims			Incidents	
Type of Victimization	Number of Victims in Sample	Percentage of Sample	Rate per 1,000 Female Students	Number of Incidents	Rate per 1,000 Female Students
Completed or attempted					
Completed sexual coercion	74	1.7	16.6	107	24.1
Attempted sexual coercion	60	1.3	13.4	114	25.6
Completed sexual contact with force or threat of force	85	1.9	19.1	130	29.2
Completed sexual contact without force	80	1.8	18.0	132	29.7
Attempted sexual contact without force	89	2.0	20.0	166	37.6
Attempted sexual contact without force	133	3.0	29.9	295	66.4
Threats					
Threat of rape	14	.031	3.2	42	9.5
Threat of contact with force or threat of force	8	0.18	1.8	50	11.3
Threat of penetration without force	10	0.22	2.3	50	11.3
Threat of contact without force	15	0.34	3.4	75	16.9
Total	568			1,161	

Exhibit 22.6 presents the data in a slightly different form and contains rape incidents. This exhibit illustrates the percentages of women in the sample who had experienced at least one victimization in three separate categories: (1) physical force, (2) nonphysical force, and (3) either physical or nonphysical force or both. Because the third category includes respondents who have experienced both types of victimization, its percentage is not computed by summing the percentages in the physical and nonphysical categories. As is shown, 15.5 percent of the college women were sexually victimized during the current academic year. In the sample, 7.7 percent experienced an incident involving the use or threat of physical force, and 11.0 percent experienced a victimization that did not involve force.

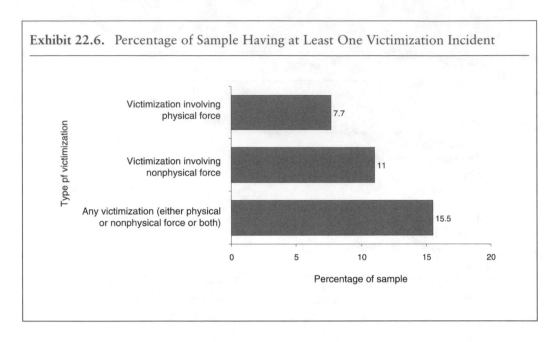

Exhibit 22.6. Percentage of Sample Having at Least One Victimization Incident

HOW EXTENSIVE IS
PRIOR SEXUAL VICTIMIZATION?

Respondents were also asked if they had experienced sexual victimization incidents before starting school in fall 1996. These incidents were measured only with single questions, not incident reports (that is, the two-stage process of screen questions followed by an incident report was not used). To limit bias, we attempted to use the detailed questions shown in Exhibit 22.7. Still, the findings must be assessed in light of this methodological limitation.

As Exhibit 22.7 shows, about 1 in 10 college women said they had experienced a rape, while the same proportion stated that they were victims of an attempted rape. Almost the same proportion also had sexual intercourse or contact in which they were subject to threats of nonphysical punishment or promises of reward. Unwanted or uninvited sexual contacts were widespread, with more than one-third of the sample reporting these incidents.

DO VICTIMS KNOW THEIR OFFENDERS?

Most victims knew the person who sexually victimized them. For both completed and attempted rapes, about 9 in 10 offenders were known to the victim. Most often, a boyfriend, ex-boyfriend, classmate, friend, acquaintance, or coworker sexually victimized the women. College professors were not identified as committing any rapes or sexual coercions, but they were cited as the offender in a low percentage of cases involving unwanted sexual contact. The victim-offender relationship for rape incidents is displayed in Exhibit 22.8.

Exhibit 22.7. **Percent of Sample Who Were Sexually Victimized Before the Start of the 1996 School Year**

Type of Victimization	Yes (percentage)	No (percentage)
Rape[a]	10.1	89.9
Attempted rape[b]	10.9	89.1
Threatened, attempted, or completed unwanted/uninvited sexual contact[c]	35.5	64.5
Sexual intercourse or contact with nonphysical threats/rewards[d]	8.6	91.4
Any other unwanted or uninvited sexual intercourse/contact[e]	5.9	94.1

a. Prior to school starting in fall 1996, did anyone ever make you have vaginal, oral, or anal intercourse—including penetrating you with a penis, a finger, or a foreign object—by using force or threatening to harm you?

b. Prior to school starting in fall 1996. did anyone ever attempt but not succeed in making you have vaginal, oral, or anal intercourse—including penetrating you with a penis, a finger, or a foreign object—by using force or threatening to harm you?

c. Prior to school starting in fall 1996, have you ever experienced any unwanted or uninvited touching of a sexual nature, or threats or attempts of such touching, including forced kissing, touching of private parts, grabbing, fondling, and rubbing up against you in a sexual way?

d. Prior to school starting in fall 1996, has anyone ever tried to make you have sexual intercourse or sexual contact when you did not want to by making either threats of nonphysical punishment or promises of reward if you complied sexually?

e. Prior to school starting in fall 1996, is there any type of unwanted or uninvited sexual intercourse or physical sexual contact that you ever experienced that was not covered in the questions thus far?

Variation in the type of sexual victimization that occurred on a date was evident. With regard to date rape, 12.8 percent of completed rapes, 35.0 percent of attempted rapes, and 22.9 percent of threatened rapes took place on a date.

WHEN DOES SEXUAL VICTIMIZATION OCCUR?

The vast majority of sexual victimizations occurred in the evening (after 6 p.m.). For example, 51.8 percent of completed rapes took place after midnight, 36.5 percent occurred between 6 p.m. and midnight, and only 11.8 percent took place between 6 a.m. and 6 p.m.

WHERE DOES SEXUAL VICTIMIZATION OCCUR?

The majority of sexual victimizations, especially rapes and physically coerced sexual contact, occurred in living quarters. Almost 60 percent of the completed rapes that occurred on campus took place in the victim's residence, 31 percent occurred in other living quarters on campus, and 10.3 percent took place in a fraternity. Off-campus sexual victimizations, especially rapes, also occurred in residences. However, particularly for sexual contacts

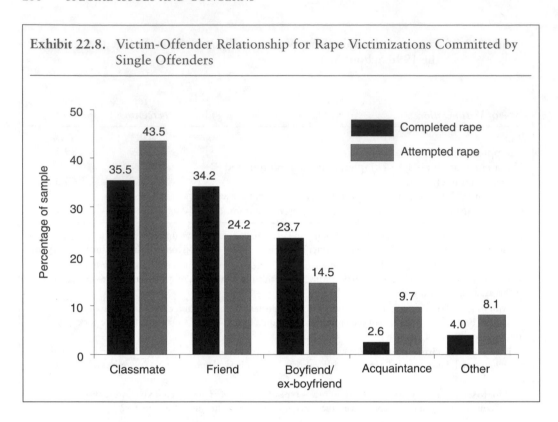

Exhibit 22.8. Victim-Offender Relationship for Rape Victimizations Committed by Single Offenders

and threatened victimizations, incidents also took place in settings such as bars, dance clubs or nightclubs, and work settings.

ARE WOMEN VICTIMIZED ON OR OFF CAMPUS?

College women are victimized both on campus and off campus. For nearly all types of sexual victimization, however, off-campus victimization is more common (Exhibit 22.9). This conclusion must be qualified because off-campus sexual victimizations may take place in bars and nightclubs or in student residences close to campus. Thus, even if a student is victimized off campus, she may be engaged in an activity that is connected to her life as a student at the college she attends.

DO SEXUAL VICTIMS TAKE
PROTECTIVE ACTIONS DURING THE INCIDENT?

As Exhibit 22.10 shows, for nearly all forms of sexual victimization, the majority of female students reported attempting to take protective actions during the incident. For both completed rape and sexual coercion, victims of completed acts were less likely to take protective action than those who experienced attempted victimization. This finding suggests that the intended victim's willingness or ability to use protection might be one reason attempts to rape or coerce sex failed.

Exhibit 22.9. The Location of Victimization by On-Campus and Off-Campus Location, by Type of Victimization

	Location of Victimization[a]	
	On-Campus Percentage (*n*)	Off-Campus Percentage (*n*)
Type of Victimization		
Completed or attempted		
Completed rape	33.7 (29)	66.3 (5.7)
Attempted rape	45.1 (32)	54.9 (39)
Completed sexual coercion	29.0 (31)	71.0 (76)
Attempted sexual coercion	46.5 (53)	53.5 (61)
Completed sexual contact with force or threat of force	34.6 (51)	65.4 (81)
Attempted sexual contact with force or threat of force	33.9 (56)	66.1 (109)
Attempted sexual contact without force	35.9 (106)	64.1 (189)
Threats		
Threats of rape	45.2 (19)	54.8 (23)
Threat of contact with force of threat of force	44.0 (22)	56.0 (28)
Threat of penetration without force	48.0 (24)	52.0 (26)
Threat of contact without force	54.1 (40)	45.9 (34)

a. Don't know (*n* = 2) not included.

Exhibit 22.11 reports the most common forms of protective action taken by victims during rape incidents. Note that the most common protective action was using physical force against the assailant. Nearly 70 percent of victims of attempted rape used this response—again, a plausible reason many of these acts were not completed. Other common physical responses included removing the offender's hand, running away, and trying to avoid the offender. Verbal responses also were common, including pleading with the offender to stop, screaming, and trying to negotiate with the offender.

ARE VICTIMS HURT IN THE VICTIMIZATION INCIDENTS?

Victims in the sample generally did not state that their victimization resulted in physical or emotional injuries. In about one in five rape and attempted rape incidents, victims reported

Exhibit 22.10 Percentage of Victims Taking Protective Action, by Type of Victimization

Type of Victimization	Victim Attempted to Protect Herself (n)
Completed or attempted	
Completed rape	65.1
	(56)
Attempted rape	91.5
	(65)
Completed sexual coercion	46.7
	(50)
Attempted sexual coercion	74.3
	(84)
Completed sexual contact with force or threat of force	87.6
	(113)
Completed sexual contact without force	81.8
	(108)
Attempted sexual contact with force or threat of force	89.8
	(149)
Attempted sexual contact without force	76.6
	(226)
Threats	
Threat of rape	81.0
	(34)
Threat of contact with force of threat of force	86.0
	(43)
Threat of penetration without force	60.0
	(30)
Threat of contact without force	66.7
	(50)

being injured, most often citing the response "bruises, black-eye, cuts, scratches, swelling, or chipped teeth." The percentage injured by other types of victimization was lower, ranging from 0 percent (completed sexual contact without force) to 16.7 percent (threatened rape).

ARE SOME WOMEN MORE AT RISK OF BEING SEXUALLY VICTIMIZED?

Multivariate logit models for each type of sexual victimization measured were estimated to predict the likelihood of having been victimized. Consistent across the models, it was found that four main factors consistently increased the risk of sexual victimization: (1) frequently drinking enough to get drunk, (2) being unmarried, (3) having been a victim of a sexual

Exhibit 22.11. Most Common Forms of Protective Actions Used in Rape Incidents

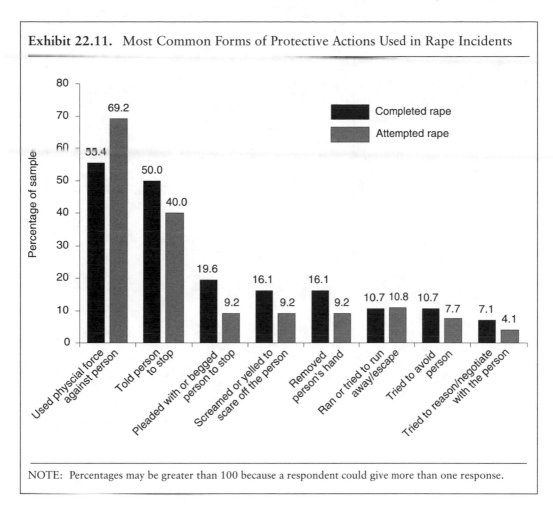

NOTE: Percentages may be greater than 100 because a respondent could give more than one response.

assault before the start of the current school year, and (4) living on campus (for on-campus victimization only).

DO WOMEN REPORT
VICTIMIZATION INCIDENTS TO THE POLICE?

Few incidents of sexual victimization were reported to law enforcement officials. Thus, fewer than 5 percent of completed and attempted rapes were reported to law enforcement officials. In about two-thirds of the rape incidents, however, the victim did tell another person about the incidents. Most often this person was a friend, not a family member or college official.

Victims gave a number of reasons for not reporting their victimizations to law enforcement officials (Exhibit 22.12). Some reasons indicated that they did not see the incidents as harmful or important enough to bring in the authorities. Thus, the common answers

Exhibit 22.12 Reasons for Not Reporting Incident to the Police, by Type of Victimization

Type of incident	Incident was not reported % (n)	Did not want family to know % (n)	Did not want other people to know % (n)	Lack of proof that incident happened % (n)	Fear of being treated with hostility by police % (n)	Fear of being treated with hostility by other parts of justice system % (n)	Not clear it was a crime or that harm was intended % (n)	Did not know how to report % (n)	Police wouldn't think it was serious enough % (n)	Police wouldn't want to be bothered % (n)	Afraid of reprisal by assailant or others % (n)	Did not think it was serious enough to report % (n)	Other % (n)
Completed or attempted													
Completed rape	95.2 (82)	44.4 (36)	46.9 (38)	42.0 (34)	24.7 (20)	6.2 (5)	44.4 (36)	13.6 (11)	27.2 (22)	25.9 (21)	39.5 (32)	65.4 (53)	7.4 (6)
Attempted rape	95.8 (68)	32.4 (22)	32.4 (22)	30.9 (21)	8.8 (6)	1.5 (1)	39.7 (27)	7.4 (5)	33.8 (23)	13.2 (21)	25.0 (32)	76.5 (53)	1.5 (6)
Completed sexual coercion	100.0 (107)	41.9 (44)	43.8 (46)	33.3 (35)	8.6 (9)	1.9 (2)	58.1 (61)	14.3 (15)	24.8 (26)	21.9 (23)	31.4 (33)	71.4 (75)	1.9 (2)
Attempted sexual coercion	100.0 (114)	21.2 (24)	19.5 (22)	15.9 (18)	2.7 (3)	2.7 (3)	46.9 (53)	6.2 (7)	28.3 (32)	18.6 (21)	11.5 (13)	86.7 (98)	0 (0)
Completed sexual contact with force or threat of force	99.2 (128)	19.5 (25)	16.4 (21)	21.9 (28)	9.4 (12)	0 (0)	37.5 (48)	7.0 (9)	37.5 (48)	30.5 (39)	22.7 (29)	81.3 (104)	3.1 (4)
Completed sexual contact without force	98.5 (129)	4.7 (6)	11.7 (15)	18.0 (23)	4.7 (6)	1.6 (2)	43.0 (55)	5.5 (7)	29.7 (38)	18.8 (24)	12.5 (16)	91.4 (117)	0.8 (1)
Attempted sexual contact with force or threat of force	97.0 (160)	13.8 (22)	21.9 (35)	23.1 (37)	8.8 (14)	6.3 (10)	37.5 (60)	10.0 (16)	31.3 (50)	22.5 (36)	23.8 (38)	80.0 (128)	2.5 (4)
Attempted sexual contact without force	99.3 (293)	7.2 (21)	10.2 (30)	18.1 (53)	4.4 (13)	1.4 (4)	39.6 (116)	6.1 (18)	22.9 (67)	18.4 (54)	10.9 (32)	88.4 (259)	2.7 (8)
Threats													
Threat of rape	90.5 (38)	26.3 (10)	34.2 (13)	31.6 (12)	13.2 (5)	7.9 (3)	39.5 (15)	13.2 (5)	34.2 (13)	31.6 (12)	26.3 (10)	65.8 (25)	2.6 (1)
Threat of contact with force or threat of force	90.0 (45)	22.2 (10)	20.0 (9)	20.0 (9)	8.9 (4)	4.4 (2)	51.1 (23)	13.3 (6)	37.8 (17)	26.7 (12)	17.8 (8)	68.9 (31)	4.4 (2)
Threat of penetration without force	100.0 (50)	20.0 (10)	22.0 (11)	24.0 (12)	4.0 (2)	4.0 (2)	46.0 (23)	6.0 (3)	30.0 (15)	30.0 (15)	12.0 (6)	88.0 (44)	2.0 (1)
Threat of contact without force	98.7 (74)	6.8 (5)	8.1 (6)	21.6 (16)	8.1 (6)	6.8 (5)	31.1 (23)	2.7 (2)	21.6 (16)	9.5 (7)	13.5 (10)	83.8 (62)	0 (0)

Reason for Not Reporting Incident[a]

a. Percentages may be greater than 100 because a respondent could give more than one response.

included that the incident was not serious enough to report and that it was not clear that a crime was committed. Other reasons, however, suggested that there were barriers to reporting. Such answers included not wanting family or other people to know about the incident, lack of proof the incident happened, fear of reprisal by the assailant, fear of being treated with hostility by the police, and anticipation that the police would not believe the incident was serious enough and/or would not want to be bothered with the incident.

HOW EXTENSIVE IS STALKING?

In addition to the 12 types of sexual victimization (Exhibit 22.2), this research assessed a form of victimization that has been infrequently studied: stalking. In general, for behavior to qualify as stalking, the attention given to someone must be repeated, and it must create fear in a reasonable person. Accordingly, stalking was measured with this screen question:

> "Since school began in fall 1996, has anyone—from a stranger to an ex-boyfriend— repeatedly followed you, watched you, phoned, written, e-mailed, or communicated with you in other ways that seemed obsessive and made you afraid or concerned for your safety?" If a respondent answered "yes," she was then given an incident report that asked detailed questions about the stalking that occurred.

The survey indicated an incidence rate of 156.5 per 1,000 female students. Indeed, fully 13.1 percent of the female students in the sample ($n = 581$) had been stalked since the school year began. This figure approximates what was found in a pretest of the survey conducted on students attending one university. It also is similar to the 6-month prevalence figure reported by Mustaine and Tewksbury,[30] which, in a survey of 861 women attending nine postsecondary institutions, found that 10.5 percent of the female students reported that they had been stalked.[31]

In contrast, Tjaden and Thoennes's national study of women reports much lower annual rates of stalking: 1 percent to 6 percent, depending on the definition of stalking used.[32] Compared with the current study, the lower extent of stalking in Tjaden and Thoennes's research may be because (1) their study used a more restrictive definition of stalking; (2) their study focused on females across the life course (age 18 to 80 years or older), rather than on younger women among whom stalking is more prevalent; and (3) their study did not focus specifically on college students. It may be that the social domain of college places women in situations and in contact with a range of men that increases the chances of being stalked.

It should be noted, however, that like the study by Tjaden and Thoennes, the estimates in this study of the extent of stalking vary depending on the criteria used to define what counts as stalking victimization.[33] Again, more than 13 percent of the women in the sample were stalked if this victimization is defined as a woman experiencing repeated, obsessive, and frightening behavior that made the victim afraid or concerned for her safety. Even so, if we were to decide that such behavior counts as a stalking victimization only if the person were actually threatened with harm—a requirement for criminal stalking in many states— the extent of stalking victims in the sample falls to 1.96 percent. These results suggest that, in the future, researchers should examine how estimates of the extent of stalking may vary widely depending on the criteria used to define what "counts" as a stalking victimization.

WHAT IS THE NATURE OF STALKING INCIDENTS?

As with other sexual victimizations, four in five victims knew their stalkers. Of the stalkers who were known, they were most often a boyfriend or ex-boyfriend (42.5 percent), classmate (24.5 percent), acquaintance (10.3 percent), friend (5.6 percent), or coworker (5.6 percent). Female students were infrequently stalked by college professors or graduate assistants.

Stalking incidents lasted an average of 60 days. About 30 percent of the female students were stalked only off campus; the remaining victims were stalked either only on campus or both on and off campus. The most common forms of stalking behaviors reported by victims were being telephoned (77.7 percent), having an offender waiting outside or inside places (47.9 percent), being watched from afar (44.0 percent), being followed (42.0 percent), being sent letters (30.7 percent), and being e-mailed (24.7 percent).[34] Almost two thirds of the sample indicated that they were stalked at least two to six times a week.

Although some victims reported being physically injured, the most common consequence was psychological: Almost 3 in 10 women said they were "injured emotionally or psychologically" from being stalked. In 15.3 percent of incidents, victims reported that the stalker either threatened or attempted to harm them. In 10.3 percent of incidents, the victim reported that the stalker "forced or attempted sexual contact."

In nearly three fourths of incidents, victims reported that they had taken "actions as a result of their stalking." Exhibit 22.13 shows actions victims took following stalking incidents. Two of the most common responses were "to avoid the stalker" (43.2 percent) or, conversely, "to confront the stalker" (16.3 percent). Beyond the data in Exhibit 22.13, in about 17 percent of incidents, victims reported the stalker to the police. In contrast, in more than 9 in 10 incidents, victims confided in someone—such as a friend, family member, or roommate—that they were being stalked.

ARE SOME WOMEN MORE AT RISK OF BEING STALKED?

A multivariate logit model was estimated to predict the likelihood of being stalked. The risk of being a stalking victim was increased by a number of factors: the propensity to be in places with alcohol; living alone; being in a dating relationship, especially early in the relationship, as opposed to being married or living with an intimate partner; being an undergraduate; being from an affluent family; and having experienced sexual victimization before the beginning of the current academic year. Also, among racial/ethnic groups, Asian/Pacific Islander women were significantly less likely to be stalked, while American Indian/Alaska Native women were significantly more likely to be stalked compared with women in other racial/ethnic groups. Notably, American Indian/Alaska Native women had the highest likelihood of any racial/ethnic group to experience a stalking. This is consistent with Tjaden and Thoennes's research, which reported that American Indians/Alaska Natives are at greatest risk of being stalked.[35]

WHAT IS THE EXTENT OF VISUAL
AND VERBAL SEXUAL VICTIMIZATION?

Finally, this research measured the extent to which women were involuntarily exposed to visual images and verbal comments that would generally be considered sexually victimizing. Since these relatively "minor" types of victimization were plentiful, it was not possible to ob-

Exhibit 22.13 Actions Taken by Victim as a Result of Stalking Incidents

Actions	Percentage[a]	n
Avoidance		
Avoided or tried to avoid the stalker	43.2	210
Did not acknowledge messages or e-mails	8.8	43
Moved residence	3.3	16
Dropped a class the stalker was in or taught	1.4	7
Quit job	0.8	4
Changed colleges or university	0.4	2
Changed majors	0.2	1
Legal/Judicial		
Sought a restraining order	3.9	19
Filed a grievance or initiated disciplinary action with university officials	3.3	
Went forward with criminal charges	1.9	9
Filed civil charges	1.2	6
Self-Protection		
Got caller ID	4.9	24
Improved security system of residence	4.1	20
Began traveling with companion	3.9	19
Bought a weapon	1.9	9
Took a self-defense class	0.4	2
Psychological		
Became less trustful or more cynical of others	5.6	27
Sought psychological counseling	2.9	14
Confrontation		
Confronted the stalker	16.3	79
Other Actions Taken But Not Specified	21.8	106

a. Percentages may be greater than 100 because a respondent could give more than one response.

tain a detailed report on each incident. Instead, results showed only whether a type of victimization was experienced and, if so, how many times it happened both on and off campus.

As Exhibit 22.14 reveals, most respondents did not experience visual victimization. Still, about 6 percent of female students had been shown pornographic pictures, almost 5 percent had someone expose his sexual organs to them, and 2.4 percent were observed naked without their consent. Verbal victimizations, moreover, were commonplace. About half the respondents were subjected to sexist remarks and to catcalls and whistles with sexual overtones. One in five female students received an obscene telephone call and was asked intrusive questions about her sex or romantic life. One in ten students had false rumors spread about her sex life.

CONCLUSIONS

The sexual victimization of college students has emerged as a controversial issue, pitting feminist scholars who claim that the sexual victimization of women is a serious problem against conservative commentators who claim that such victimization is rare and mostly a

Exhibit 22.14 The Extent of Verbal and Visual Victimization

	Percentage and Number of Victims for Sample	Total Number of Victimizations[a]	Rate per 1,000 Female Students
Type of verbal victimization			
General sexist remarks in front of you	54.3 (2,398)	31,434	7,070.2
Cat calls, whistles about your looks, or noises with sexual overtones	48.2 (2,129)	29,609	6,660.0
Obscene telephone calls or messages	21.9 (97.3)	4,885	1,099.0
Asked questions about sex or romantic life when clearly none of their business	19.0 (844)	4,694	1,055.8
False rumors about sex life with them or other people	9.7 (431)	1,166	262.3
Type of visual victimization			
Someone exposed you to pornographic pictures or materials when you did not agree to see them	6.1 (272)	865	194.6
Someone exposed their sexual organs to you when you did not agree to see them	4.8 (214)	568	127.8
Anyone, without your consent, observed or tried to observe you while you were undressing, nude, or in a sexual act	2.4 (105)	302	67.9
Anyone, without your consent, showed other people or played for other people, photographs, videotapes, or audiotapes of you having sex or in a nude or seminude state	0.3 (15)	18	4.0
Anyone, without your consent, photographed, videotaped, or audiotaped you having sex or in a nude or seminude state	0.2 (8)	9	2.0

(continued)

fictitious creation of ideologically tainted research.[36] The research reported here undoubtedly will not settle this debate; battle lines are solidly entrenched, and how the data are interpreted will, to a degree, lie in the "eye of the beholder." However, the current study attempts to add a judicious voice to this conversation by attempting to furnish a methodologically sound assessment of the extent and nature of the sexual victimization of female students.

To summarize, the national-level survey of 4,446 college women suggests that many students will encounter sexist and harassing comments, will likely receive an obscene phone

Exhibit 22.14 (Continued)

	Number of Victimizations per Victim	Percentage and Number of Victimizations On Campus	Percentage and Number of Victimizations Off Campus
Type of verbal victimization			
General sexist remarks in front of you	13.0	50.6 (15,894)	49.4 (15,540)
Cat calls, whistles about your looks, or noises with sexual overtones	13.9	38.6 (11,423)	61.4 (18,186)
Obscene telephone calls or messages	13.9	59.8 (2,922)	40.2 (1,963)
Asked questions about sex or romantic life when clearly none of their business	5.6	41.2 (1,933)	58.8 (2,761)
False rumors about sex life with them or other people	2.7	59.7 (696)	40.3 (470)
Type of visual victimization			
Someone exposed you to pornographic pictures or materials when you did not agree to see them	3.2	59.9 (518)	40.1 (347)
Someone exposed their sexual organs to you when you did not agree to see them	2.7	34.0 (193)	66.0 (375)
Anyone, without your consent, observed or tried to observe you while you were undressing, nude, or in a sexual act	2.9	44.0 (133)	56.0 (169)
Anyone, without your consent, showed other people or played for other people, photographs, videotapes, or audiotapes of you having sex or in a nude or seminude state	1.2	44.4 (8)	55.6 (10)
Anyone, without your consent, photographed, videotaped, or audiotaped you having sex or in a nude or seminude state	1.1	77.8 (7)	22.2 (2)

a. The distributions for the number of victimization variables are right-censored because they include the value "97 or more."

call, and will have a good chance of being stalked or of enduring some form of coerced sexual contact. During any given academic year, 2.8 percent of women will experience a completed and/or attempted rape. This figure is not based only on broadly worded, behaviorally specific screen questions because all victimization incidents reported in the screen questions were verified through subsequent questions in the incident report. Furthermore, the level of rape and other types of victimization found in the survey becomes an increasing concern when the victimization figures are projected over a full year, a full college career, and the full population of women at one college or at colleges across the nation.

The results also hold important methodological implications. The comparison component study sponsored by the Bureau of Justice Statistics allowed the rare opportunity to conduct a quasi-experiment in how the methods used to measure sexual victimization might potentially affect estimates of victimization. Thus, two randomly selected samples of college women were surveyed using very similar methodology, with one noteworthy exception: A different way of measuring sexual victimization was used with each sample. Results showed that a methodology that uses behaviorally specific screen questions in combination with an incident report yields considerably higher estimates of completed, attempted, and threatened rape than are found using NCVS methodology.

Future research should explore the implications of this finding for NCVS. As noted, it was not determined whether using a number of behaviorally specific screen questions tends to increase estimates of only rape or whether the technique would also increase estimates of other types of victimization (i.e., the more widely in scope and the more closely in detail that possible victimizations are probed, the more victims are prompted to report their victimization to interviewers). However, assuming that the methodology used in this study is defensible, it seems likely that NCVS underestimates the true incidence of rape victimization in the United States.

We should note, however, one other possible factor that might have contributed to the differences in victimization between the main and comparison components: the "context" of the surveys. In the main component of NCWSV, the respondents were instructed in an initial contact letter and in instructions during the interview that the survey was focusing on "unwanted sexual experiences." In contrast, the comparison component was patterned after NCVS, which is a crime survey. In this part of the study, respondents were sent an initial letter that mentioned the "increasing concern about criminal victimizations that women may experience during college," and the interview itself contained questions measuring victimization by other types of criminal offenses. It is conceivable, therefore, that respondents on the main component study were sensitized to report a broad range of sexual victimization incidents they experienced, while those on the NCVS-based comparison component limited their reports to the incidents they defined as criminal. If so, this contextual difference would mean that the comparison component was measuring a much narrower domain of sexual victimization. One caution in this line of reasoning is that, as discussed previously, nearly half of the completed rape victims defined their victimization as a "rape," a clear criminal offense. Even when the count of rape victims is limited to this group, the prevalence of rape victims is several times greater in the main component than in the comparison components. Still, the impact of survey context on respondents' responses to sexual victimization questions remains an area that warrants further research.

Of course, many other methodological issues in addition to the use of behaviorally specific screen questions and survey context will have to be addressed in the quest to design surveys capable of achieving more accurate estimates of rape and other forms of sexual victimization. These would include, but not be limited to, issues such as the differential meaning that words used in questions might have to respondents, the impact of the sequencing of questions on answers, the use of more verbatim descriptions of victimization incidents in coding "what happened" in a sexual assault, and perhaps the use of computer-aided personal interviewing as a means of encouraging respondents to disclose traumatic events. In short, systematic, rigorous experimental research into the factors that affect victim responses and, in turn, victimization estimates—especially in the sensitive area of rape and sexual assault—remains in its beginning stages.

Although exceptions exist, most sexual victimizations occur when college women are alone with a man they know, at night, and in the privacy of a residence. Most women attempt to take protective actions against their assailants but are then reluctant to report their victimization to the police. Although based on fewer cases, these same patterns were found as well in the comparison component survey, which used NCVS methodology,[37] The analysis also revealed that some college women were more at risk of being victimized than others. Several factors appeared to increase various types of victimization: living on campus, being unmarried, getting drunk frequently, and experiencing prior sexual victimization.

Finally, in the aftermath of this study, an important challenge remains: taking the information found and developing programs and policies that may reduce female students' risk of victimization. Minor forms of sexual victimization—sexist statements, harassing catcalls, sexually tainted whistles—appear to be commonplace. How can a more civil environment be achieved without compromising free speech? Much is known about the circumstances under which sexual victimization, including rape, most often occurs. How can this information be used in crime prevention programs, including rape awareness seminars designed for women or rape prevention seminars designed for men? Furthermore, the relatively high prevalence of stalking—a form of victimization often ignored by college officials—is cause for concern. What strategies can women use to prevent or end stalking? What programs might colleges implement to control or counsel men who stalk? More generally, how can the lives of college women—whether on, close to, or off campus—be made safer and thus free from the costs imposed by the experience of sexual victimization?

NOTES

1. Bonnie S. Fisher et al., "Crime in the Ivory Tower: The Level and Sources of Student Victimization," *Criminology* 36 (1998): 671-710.

2. Walter DeKeseredy and Katharine Kelly, "The Incidence and Prevalence of Women Abuse in Canadian University and College Dating Relationships," *Canadian Journal of Sociology* 18 (1993): 137-59; Fisher et al., "Crime in the Ivory Tower"; Mary P. Koss, Christine A. Gidycz, and Nadine Wisniewski, "The Scope of Rape: Incidence and Prevalence of Sexual Aggression and Victimization in a National Sample of Higher Education Students," *Journal of Counseling and Clinical Psychology* 55 (1987): 162-70.

3. John J. Sloan, Bonnie S. Fisher, and Francis T. Cullen, "Assessing the Student Right-to-Know and Campus Security Act of 1990: An Analysis of the Victim Reporting Practices of College and University Students," *Crime and Delinquency* 43 (1997): 248-68.

4. "The Jeanne Clery Act Information Page," at www.campussafety.org (Security On Campus: College and University Campus Safety Information On-Line, maintained by Security on Campus, Inc., King of Prussia, Pennsylvania, 2000).

5. Bonnie S. Fisher, "Campus Crime and Fear of Victimization: Judicial, Legislative, and Administrative Responses," *The Annals of the American Academy of Political and Social Science* 539 (1995): 85-101; Michael C. Griffaton, "State-Level Initiatives and Campus Crime," in *Campus Crime: Legal, Social, and Policy Perspectives,* edited by Bonnie S. Fisher and John J. Sloan III (Springfield, Illinois: Charles C Thomas Publisher, 1995).

6. "Justice Department Awards $8.1 Million to Colleges and Universities to Combat Violence Against Women," edited by Daniel S. Carter, at www.campussafety.org (Security On Campus: College and University Campus Safety Information On-Line, maintained by Security on Campus, Inc., King of Prussia, Pennsylvania, 2000).

7. DeKeseredy and Kelly, "The Incidence and Prevalence of Women Abuse"; Fisher et al., "Crime in the Ivory Tower"; Koss et al., "The Scope of Rape."

8. In the comparison component, the screen questions and incident questions were virtually identical to those used in NCVS. In designing the comparison component, two minor changes were made to NCVS. First, slight word changes or additional responses to the response sets of questions in the incident report were made to capture plausible responses from a college student sample. For example, to determine to which authority the victim reported the victimization, "campus police" was included in the response set. Second, a few questions were added to the NCVS incident report. For example, questions about offender characteristics included a question about fraternity membership.

9. Most of the sample ($n = 4,446$) were full-time students (90.1 percent) and undergraduates (86.1 percent). Freshmen at 4-year schools/first-year students at 2-year schools made up 24.2 percent of the sample; sophomores at 4-year schools/second-year students at 2-year schools, 22.0 percent; juniors, 17.5 percent; seniors, 22.4 percent; graduate students, 12.1 percent; and others (post-doctorate, continuing education, certification programs), 1.7 percent. As expected, the sample was youthful: Slightly more than 76 percent of the sample was between the ages of 17 and 22 years (mean = 21.54, standard deviation = 4.25). Most of the sample was white, non-Hispanic (80.6 percent), followed by African-American, non-Hispanic (7.0 percent), Hispanic (6.2 percent), Asian/Pacific Islander, non-Hispanic (3.4 percent), American Indian/Alaska Native, non-Hispanic (0.8 percent), and mixed or other (1.5 percent). Less than 1 percent (0.5) of respondents refused or did not know their race or ethnicity.

10. The interview was conducted by the firm of Shulman, Ronca, and Bucuvalas, Inc., and lasted an average of 25.9 minutes. This is the same firm that Tjaden and Thoennes (1998) employed for the National Violence Against Women Study.

11. Bonnie S. Fisher and Francis T. Cullen, *The Extent and Nature of Sexual Victimization Among College Women: Results from a National-Level Study* (Unpublished report, Washington, DC: U.S. Department of Justice, National Institute of Justice, 1999); Bonnie S. Fisher and Francis T. Cullen, "Measuring the Sexual Victimization of Women: Evolution, Current Controversies and Future Research," in *Criminal Justice 2000, Volume 4: Measurement and Analysis of Crime,* edited by David Duffee (Washington, DC: U.S. Department of Justice, National Institute of Justice, 2000).

12. Dean G. Kilpatrick, Christine N. Edmunds, and Anne Seymour, *Rape in America: A Report to the Nation* (Arlington, Virginia: National Victim Center, 1992).

13. Patricia Tjaden and Nancy Thoennes, *Stalking in America: Findings From the National Violence Against Women Survey, Research in Brief* (Washington, DC: U.S. Department of Justice, National Institute of Justice, 1998, NCJ 169592).

14. Questionnaires are available in portable document format (pdf) files from the BJS Web site, at www.ojp.usdoj.gov/bjs/quest.htm (July 24, 2000).

15. Koss et al., "The Scope of Rape."

16. The minimum reference period was 6 months, and the maximum was 8 months (standard deviation = 20.3 days).

17. Nonundergraduates made up 13.8 percent of the sample. They included graduate students, postdoctorate fellows, continuing education students, certification students, and others.

18. These projections are suggestive. To assess accurately the victimization risk for women throughout a college career, longitudinal research following a cohort of female students across time is needed.

19. Bonnie S. Fisher and Frances T. Cullen, *Violent Victimization Against College Women: Results From a National-Level Study* (Unpublished report, Washington, DC: U.S. Department of Justice, Bureau of Justice Statistics, 1999).

20. The interviews lasted, on average, 12.7 minutes. Most of the sample ($N = 4,432$) were full-time students (89.3 percent) and undergraduates (82.1 percent). Freshmen at 4-year schools/first-year students at 2-year schools made up 19.9 percent of the sample; sophomores at 4-year schools/second-year students at 2-year schools, 19.5 percent; juniors, 17.3 percent; seniors, 25.4 percent; graduate students, 16.6 percent; and others (postdoctorate, continuing education, certification programs), 1.6 percent. As expected, the sample was youthful; 61 percent of the sample was between the ages of 17 and 22 years (mean = 23.18, standard deviation = 4.79). Most of the sample was white, non-Hispanic (81.6 percent), followed by African-American, non-Hispanic (6.9 percent); Hispanic (5.1 percent); Asian/Pacific Islander, non-Hispanic (3.5 percent); American Indian/Alaska Native, non-Hispanic (0.7 percent); and mixed or other (1.8 percent). Less than 1 percent (0.5) of respondents refused or did not know their race or ethnicity.

21. Some of the incident-level questions had to be modified to reflect the characteristics of a college sample. For example, locations where an incident occurred included on-campus locations, such as a residence hall room or the library.

22. Personal communication with Jan Chaiken and Michael Rand, April 14, 2000.

23. In the comparison component study, we collected verbatim responses for all incidents. We subsequently explored how the use of verbatim responses can potentially affect estimates of completed rape, attempted rape, and threat of rape. See Fisher and Cullen, *Criminal Justice 2000*.

24. DeKeseredy and Kelly, "The Incidence and Prevalence of Women Violence"; Koss et al., "The Scope of Rape"; Nancy A. Crowell and Ann W. Burgess, editors, *Understanding Violence Against Women,* by the Panel on Violence Against Women, National Research Council (Washington, DC: National Academy Press, 1996).

25. Tjaden and Thoennes, *Stalking in America.*

26. Rape victims also have screened into an incident report based on a "yes" to other sexual victimization screen questions (Fisher and Cullen, *Criminal Justice 2000*).

27. Neil Gilbert, "Advocacy Research and Social Policy," in *Crime and Justice: A Review of Research,* edited by Michael Tonry (Chicago: University of Chicago Press, 1997).

28. Mary P. Koss, "The Underdetection of Rape: Methodological Choices Influence Incidence Estimates," *Journal of Social Issues 48* (1992): 61-75; Mary P. Koss, "The Measurement of Rape Victimization in Crime Surveys," *Criminal Justice and Behavior 23* (1996): 55-69.

29. Victoria L. Pitts and Martin D. Schwartz, "Promoting Self-Blame in Hidden Rape Cases," *Humanity and Society 17*(4) (1993): 383-98.

30. Elizabeth Ehrhardt Mustaine and Richard Tewksbury, "A Routine Activity Theory Explanation of Women's Stalking Victimizations," *Violence Against Women 5*(1) (1999): 43-62.

31. Mustaine and Tewksbury provide no definition of stalking. Instead, to operationalize stalking, surveyed respondents were asked whether, during the prior 6 months, they had been a victim of behavior that they defined as stalking.

32. Tjaden and Thoennes, *Stalking in America.*

33. Ibid.

34. Of the 696 incidents, in 11 incidents the respondents refused to discuss the incident, and in 13 incidents the respondents did not tell us the form(s) of the stalking behavior. Reported percentages are based on 672 incidents.

35. Ibid.

36. Gilbert, "Advocacy Research and Social Policy."

37. Fisher and Cullen, *Violent Victimization Among College Women.*

23

Where Should We Intervene?

Dynamic Predictors of Sexual Offense Recidivism

———■———

R. KARL HANSON
ANDREW J. R. HARRIS
Department of the Solicitor General of Canada

When the specific goal is to prevent sexual offense recidivism, there is almost no empirical foundation for identifying treatment targets or determining whether interventions have been successful (Hanson, 1998). All those who provide treatment, community supervision, or risk assessments for sexual offenders must, nevertheless, identify the factors that they believe are related to sexual offense recidivism. This is a difficult task. Experienced clinicians are frequently unable to differentiate between sexual offenders who benefited from treatment and those who did not (Dix, 1976; Rice, Quinsey, & Harris, 1989; Ryan & Miyoshi, 1990).

Hanson and Bussière's (1998) review of 61 studies found that long-term recidivism was best predicted by static (e.g., offense history) or highly stable factors (e.g., personality disorders). Historical factors may indicate an ongoing potential to offend, but future offenses can only be prevented by addressing problems that are currently present (i.e., criminogenic needs or dynamic risk factors) (see Andrews & Bonta, 1998; Bonta, 1996).

Authors' Note: This research would not have been possible without the help of all the probation and parole officers who so generously shared their experience and their time. The highly professional work of the field researchers, Glenn Gray, Elham Forouzan, Andrew McWhinnie, and Maureen Osweiler, was greatly appreciated, as was Tanya Rugge's efficiency in managing data collection and entry. Vernon Quinsey, Jean Proulx, Danielle Paris, Susan Cox, and Jim Bonta provided valuable comments on earlier versions of this article, as did the three not-so-anonymous reviewers. The authors would like to thank the senior management of the Department of the Solicitor General for their support. The authors hope that their investment paid off. The views expressed are those of the authors and do not necessarily reflect the views of the Solicitor General of Canada. Correspondence concerning this article should be addressed to R. Karl Hanson, Corrections Research, Department of the Solicitor General of Canada, 340 Laurier Ave. West, Ottawa, Ontario, K1A 0P8, Canada; e-mail: hansonk@sgc.gc.ca.

This article first appeared in *Criminal Justice and Behavior,* Vol. 27 No. 1, February 2000, pp. 6-35. Copyright © 2000 American Association for Correctional Psychology.

Dynamic risk factors are characteristics that can change and, when changed, result in a corresponding increase or decrease in recidivism risk. Dynamic risk factors can be further subdivided into stable dynamic factors and acute dynamic factors. Stable dynamic risk factors are expected to remain unchanged for months or years (e.g., alcoholism). Consequently, interventions aimed at creating enduring improvements need to target stable dynamic factors. In contrast, acute dynamic factors, such as alcohol intoxication or negative mood, change rapidly (days, hours, and even minutes). Acute dynamic risk factors are related to the timing of reoffending, but they may have little relationship to long-term risk potential.

Empirical work on nonsexual criminals has found that dynamic risk factors predict recidivism as well as or better than static, historical variables (Gendreau, Little, & Goggin, 1996; Zamble & Quinsey, 1997). However, the dynamic risk factors that predict general criminal recidivism may not predict sexual offense recidivism (Hanson, Scott, & Steffy, 1995).

The lack of research evidence connecting dynamic factors to sexual recidivism does not mean that these factors are unimportant; instead, it may simply indicate the need for a different type of research design when studying sexual recidivism. Long-term follow-up studies are more likely to identify stable risk factors than rapidly changing risk factors. Consequently, this study aimed to improve our understanding of dynamic risk factors for sexual offenders by using research procedures specifically designed to target changeable factors.

OVERVIEW OF STUDY

The specific design of our study followed the procedure successfully employed by Quinsey, Coleman, Jones, and Altrows (1997) in their research on dynamic risk factors for mentally disordered offenders. This procedure involved retrospective comparisons of offenders who recidivated while on community supervision with offenders who did not recidivate. Our study involved approximately 400 sexual offenders, evenly divided among rapists, boy-victim child molesters, and girl-victim child molesters.

For the recidivists, information was collected at two time periods: 6 months (T1) and 1 month (T2) before recidivating. Information was collected at equivalent time periods for the nonrecidivists, with T2 identified as the month before data collection. For both time periods, information was collected through detailed interviews with the supervising officers and by file review. Such a design can provide information on the stable dynamic factors that distinguish recidivists from nonrecidivists and information on the acute dynamic factors that immediately precede reoffending.

The recidivism risk factors targeted in this study were based on previous research (Pithers, Kashima, Cummings, Beal, & Buell, 1988; Proulx, McKibben, & Lusignan, 1996) and social cognitive theory (e.g., Bandura, 1977; Fiske & Taylor, 1991; Johnston & Ward, 1996; Laws, 1989). In this model, recidivistic sexual offenders would be expected to hold a deviant schema or habitual patterns of thought and action that facilitate their offenses. The likelihood that an offender would invoke or enact such a schema would increase if the schema were well-rehearsed, were triggered by commonly occurring circumstances, were considered socially acceptable in the offender's environment, and were consistent with the offender's personality and values. In addition, those offenders who lacked realistic self-management strategies (e.g., exposing themselves to high-risk situations) would be expected to have the most difficulty inhibiting deviant schema.

Negative affect and deviant sexual schema have been linked in previous research. McKibben, Proulx, and Lusignan (1994) (see also Proulx et al., 1996) found that deviant sexual fantasies tended to follow episodes in which offenders felt stressed or upset. Similarly, Pithers and his colleagues reported that negative emotional states were common precursors to reoffending for both rapists and child molesters (Pithers, Beal, Armstrong, & Petty, 1989; Pithers et al., 1988). Hanson and Bussière (1998), however, found that subjective distress was unrelated to long-term recidivism. It is possible that distress is an acute dynamic risk factor but not a stable dynamic risk factor.

For dynamic risk factors to be useful to therapists or community supervision officers, the factors must be observable. Consequently, the risk factors targeted in our study were informed not only by theory and previous research, but also by extensive consultation (interviews, focus groups, and pilot testing) with more than 60 community supervision officers across Canada.

METHOD

Subject Selection

Offenders were selected from all Canadian provincial correctional systems (except Prince Edward Island) and all regions of the Correctional Service of Canada (the federal service). Given the different community supervision agreements across provinces, the offenders were supervised by provincial probation officers, provincial parole officers, or federal parole officers. The number of offenders per province was approximately proportional to each province's population.

All offenders had been convicted of a sexual offense involving physical contact with the victim (pure voyeurs and exhibitionists were excluded) and had served, or were serving, part of their sentence in the community (probation, parole, mandatory supervision, and/or statutory release). Offenders who targeted only their biological or stepchildren were also excluded.

The recidivists had committed a new sexual offense (including noncontact offenses, e.g., exhibitionism) while on community supervision. Most of the recidivists (68%) had new charges for a sexual offense, although in 25% of the cases, the offenders' sexual misbehavior only resulted in a parole violation or a breach of probation. In 12 cases (6%), the offender was charged with a nonsexual offense, but the intent of the offense was clearly sexual (e.g., sexual homicide, attempting to abduct a child who escapes). One offender was counted as a recidivist when he self-disclosed in treatment that he had been stalking a particular woman while engaging in rape fantasies.

The nonrecidivists were selected from sexual offenders who had successfully completed at least 6 months of community supervision. On average, the nonrecidivists had completed 24 months in the community, whereas most of our recidivistic offenders had reoffended within 15 months. Our sample procedure required matching the recidivistic and nonrecidivistic offenders on previous offense history, victim type, and jurisdiction. The coders began by identifying a recidivist, then they searched for a nonrecidivist matched on the above criteria. If several nonrecidivists were available that met the essential matching criteria, the coders selected the nonrecidivist most similar to the recidivist. Consequently, the recidivists and nonrecidivists tended to be matched on many salient characteristics (e.g., age, schizophrenia). The quality of the informal matching was not explicitly recorded, but, as documented below, it tended to be rather close.

File Review Variables

A standardized coding manual was used to record background information for each case (i.e., static factors). This information was based on complete file reviews and national criminal history records obtained from the Royal Canadian Mounted Police. The background information included basic identifying information, detailed sexual offense histories, and a number of variables used to estimate preexisting or enduring risk for recidivism. Many of the coded items formed parts of established objective risk assessment instruments. Not all information was available for all offenders.

Objective Risk Scales

Statistical Information on Recidivism (SIR). The SIR Scale (Bonta, Harman, Hann, & Cormier, 1996; Nuffield, 1982) is an objective risk measure developed for use by the Correctional Service of Canada and the National Parole Board. Items include age, marital status, and 11 items related to criminal history (e.g., history of assault, break and enter, prior imprisonment). The SIR has been a consistent predictor of recidivism among general criminal populations (Cormier, 1997). Although there has been little research using the SIR with sexual offenders, the available research suggests that it is a good predictor of general recidivism among sexual offenders ($r = .41$) but a poor predictor of sexual offense recidivism ($r = .09$) (Bonta & Hanson, 1995). SIR Scale scores were available for 84 recidivists and 90 nonrecidivists. (SIR scores were not routinely available for provincial offenders.)

Hare Psychopathy Checklist-Revised (PCL-R). The PCL-R (Hare, 1991) was constructed to provide a reliable and valid measure of the psychopathic personality described by Cleckley (1976). Hare's 20-item measure has two correlated factors: The first factor taps core personality traits of impulsivity, irresponsibility, and callousness; and the second factor addresses antisocial behavior. As in other studies (e.g., Harris, Rice, & Quinsey, 1993; Wong, 1984), PCL-R scores were assessed through file review. The PCL-R has been a reliable predictor of general (Wong, 1984) and violent recidivism (Serin, 1996). Although previous research has not found large, direct relationships between psychopathy and sexual offense recidivism, these studies have found high rates of recidivism among those offenders who rated highly on both psychopathy and sexual deviance (Gretton, McBride, & Hare, 1995; Rice & Harris, 1997).

Because relatively complete file information is required to code the PCL-R, scores were only available for 190 recidivists and 162 nonrecidivists.

Violence Risk Appraisal Guide (VRAG). The VRAG (Quinsey, Harris, Rice, & Cormier, 1998) was originally developed to predict sexual or nonsexual violent recidivism among offenders referred to a maximum-security psychiatric institution (Harris et al., 1993). The VRAG has attracted considerable interest as an actuarial predictor of violence (Borum,

1996). Its 12 items include the PCL-R, other personality disorders, early school maladjust-ment, age, marital status, criminal history, schizophrenia, and victim injury. An application of the VRAG to a replication sample of 159 sexual offenders (Rice & Harris, 1997) found that it correlated .47 with violent recidivism (sexual and nonsexual violence) but only .20 with sexual offense recidivism. Due to incomplete files, VRAG scores were available for 146 recidivists and 121 nonrecidivists.

Rapid Risk Assessment for Sexual Offense Recidivism (RRASOR). The RRASOR (Hanson, 1997) is a brief actuarial risk scale designed to predict sexual offense recidivism. The RRASOR contains four items: (a) officially recorded sexual offenses, (b) any unrelated victims, (c) any male victims, and (d) age less than 25 years. Averaged across eight different follow-up studies (N = 2,592), the RRASOR has demonstrated moderate accuracy in pre-dicting sexual offense recidivism (r = .27, Receiver Operating Characteristic area = .71).

Other Risk Factors From File Review

In addition to the established risk scales, we coded a number of individual variables that research has suggested should be related to recidivism risk (Hanson & Bussière, 1998). These variables included the following.

Sexual Offense History. Detailed information was collected on all known sexual of-fenses (index, recidivism, and priors). This information included the victim's age, gender, and relationship to offender; the specific sex acts committed (e.g., fellatio, touching over clothes); weapons use; brutality; and victim injury. We also coded the lifetime total number of victims and the age of the offender at the first known sexual offense (whether adjudicated or not).

Sexual Deviance. Sexual deviance was assessed by considering the diversity of sexual acts committed and by direct reports of deviant sexual interests or activities. Reports of phallometric assessment (Launay, 1994) were available for 30% of the sample. We also coded whether offenders appeared to have arranged their lifestyle to facilitate, or be con-gruent with, their sexual deviance (e.g., moves in with single mothers, works in an adult bookstore).

Treatment History. We recorded the number of treatment programs attended before the index offense, including sexual offense specific treatments, alcohol programs (e.g., Alcoholics Anonymous), and general counseling. Indices of treatment failure, compliance, and motivation were combined into a 13-item scale (alpha = .85). (The complete scale is available on request.)

Antisocial Personality Disorder (APD). File information was used to diagnose APD (American Psychiatric Association, 1994) according to the criteria set in *DSM-IV.*

Miscellaneous Variables. Official reports of physical, sexual, or emotional abuse were recorded along with whether the offender had ever been taken into the care of child protec-tion services. We noted indices of psychiatric diagnoses, personality disorder, and intellectual ability. No attempt was made to arrive at independent psychiatric diagnoses, except for the diagnoses of psychopathy and APD noted above.

Interview Variables

Social Influences

During the interview, community supervision officers were asked to list all the important people in the offender's life who were not paid to be with the offender. Professionals such as welfare case workers, probation officers, and psychotherapists were excluded because relationships voluntarily initiated and maintained by the offender were considered to be more informative than relationships imposed by the state. The officers rated whether each significant individual was a positive, negative, or neutral influence on the offender. Officers were asked whether offenders were released into relatively controlled, moderately controlled, or uncontrolled environments in terms of access to victims, drugs, and alcohol.

Problems Evident During Supervision

Officers were asked to report on any problematic behavior or warning signs that they noticed during the course of supervision. For the recidivists, questions focused on the 6-month period just before the known recidivism event. For the nonrecidivists, officers described the 6 months before the interview (all the nonrecidivists were currently on community supervision). The specific factors (e.g., employment, sexual preoccupations) examined are reported in the results section.

Case Note Coding

The officers' supervision notes were coded for the same variables examined in the interview. All reports, case notes, and summaries that applied to the T1 and T2 time periods were used, provided that the materials were written before knowing that the offender had recidivated. Each separate mention of a problem area was counted separately; however, because there were few problems indicated in the case records, only dichotomous scores were analyzed (any problem mentioned or no problem mentioned).

Procedure

Four field researchers working under the supervision of the project manager (Andrew Harris) collected the data. To enhance reliability, the field researchers received a week of group training before data collection began. The project manager accompanied each researcher during his or her first week in the field and revisited each of them for 1 to 2 weeks during the course of data collection. Periodic teleconferences were held to resolve ongoing problems and to reduce rater drift.

The project received ethics approval from the relevant review boards (14 in total) and from the correctional managers involved.

Interview

Before being interviewed, each community supervision officer signed an informed consent indicating that participation was voluntary, the information was for research purposes only, and no personal or identifying information would appear in reports of the project. The interviews, lasting approximately 1 hour, were conducted in the officer's normal place of work during working hours. Of the officers with cases appropriate for this study, fewer than 1% declined participation.

The officer interview began with general questions about the officers' experience with sexual offenders and an overview of the case to be discussed. Next, officers were asked to make overall judgments of the offender's lifestyle based on their complete knowledge of the case. The officers were then asked about observed changes during the course of supervision. To aid their recall, officers were first presented with a time graph representing the course of supervision. The interviewers marked off two time periods: T2, the month before reoffending (for the recidivists) or the month before the interview (for the nonrecidivists); and T1, the month that fell 6 months before T2. The length of these month-long time periods was allowed to vary somewhat (4 to 6 weeks) due to holidays and the timing of reports and office visits. To further orient the officers to the time periods of interest, they were asked about specific events or changes (e.g., office moves, Christmas holidays) present during each of the time periods.

Officers indicated whether each problem area had ever been a concern during the whole course of supervision, and if so, whether the problem was worse at T1 or T2. For each time period (ever, T1, and T2), officers rated each risk factor as 0 (no, never a problem), 1 (very slight or possible problem or concern), or 2 (yes, some problem).

File Coding

The field researchers coded the file material before or after the interview, depending on the availability of the officer. The file coding was based on all available information and typically took 3 to 5 hours. The researcher who coded the files also conducted the corresponding interview.

Reliability

Approximately 10% of the cases (43) were coded separately by two raters in order to estimate reliability. Overall agreement was calculated separately for each of the 50 general content areas (e.g., demographics, characteristics of index offense) (18 content areas for file coding, 19 for interview ratings, and 13 for case note codes). Each content area typically contained between 5 and 15 items that were either categorical (any boy victims) or interval (total number of victims). Percentage agreement was used as a convenient measure of rater agreement. To protect against artificial inflation from low frequencies, reliabilities were only calculated when at least one rater coded something (i.e., instances of no information were not included in the reliability calculations).

There were high levels of agreement for all content areas. The average percentage of agreement was 95% for the static file coding, 97% for the interview ratings, and 94% for the supervision case notes. The interrater reliability was consistently high for all coders in the study.

Data Reduction

Because information was collected on a large number of individual variables (the complete list is available on request), the variables were organized into internally consistent scales (available on request). Scale construction began by identifying conceptually similar items. Next, the internal consistency of these items was calculated using Cronbach's alpha (Ghiselli, Campbell, & Zedeck, 1981). Items with low item-total correlations were eliminated or analyzed separately. If a proposed scale contained eight or more items and the internal consistency of the scale was low to moderate, exploratory factor analyses were conducted to identify possible subscales. Following Cattell (1966), the scree test was used to determine the number of factors to extract. The resulting factors were rotated orthogonally (Varimax in SPSS), and the internal consistencies of the resulting scales were reevaluated using Cronbach's alpha. Overall, the goal of the data reduction was to minimize redundancy while maintaining sufficient detail to identify useful distinctions between recidivists and nonrecidivists.

The scale construction and data reduction stage organized the 128 individual items from the officer interview and note codes into 22 scales. For example, the Victim Access Scale (alpha = .72) included 6 items: general victim access, cruising/creating opportunities to reoffend, grooming of victims, bicycle/4x4/motorcycle/flashy car, computer/surfing the net, and child-oriented hobbies. Each of the 22 scales contained between 2 and 10 items (median = 5). Overall, the reliability of the scales was acceptable (median alpha = .72), with only four scales having internal consistencies less than .65 (psychiatric symptoms, life stress, general social problems, and association with sexual offenders). Eight constructs were assessed with single items (unemployed, problems at work, anti-androgen use, uncontrolled release environment, no opportunities for fun/relaxation, using spirituality as a shield, attends group treatment, attends one-on-one counseling).

RESULTS

Information was collected on a total of 208 recidivists and 201 nonrecidivists. Following the predetermined sampling frame, the study examined approximately equal numbers of rapists, boy-victim child molesters, and girl-victim child molesters (see Table 23.1). When offenders had diverse victims, they were classified according to their predominant victim type. The cells were not precisely equal as some of the offenders needed to be reclassified when additional information became available.

Comparisons on Static Risk Factors

The first stage of the analysis examined static, historical variables that influence the offenders' preexisting recidivism risk. As can be seen in Table 23.1, the recidivists and the nonrecidivists were well matched on many variables. The groups did not differ on marital status, race, employment status, or age at index offense. The recidivists, however, were somewhat younger (36.3 years) than the nonrecidivists (39.1 years) when they began community supervision.

Although there were no significant differences in the number of known victims or officially recorded offenses (sexual or otherwise), the recidivistic group appeared more

TABLE 23.1 Comparison of Recidivists and Nonrecidivists on Static, Historical Variables

Measure	Recidivist	Nonrecidivist	Significance
Sample Size	208	201	
Median release date (range)	1994	1996	
	(84 to 97)	(81 to 97)	
Months in community (time at risk)	15.4	24.0	< .001
	(17.1)	(24.8)	
Demographic factors			
Mean age at index *(SD)*	34.2	34.9	n.s.
	(11.0)	(11.6)	
Mean age at exposure to risk *(SD)*	36.3	39.1	< .05
	(11.2)	(11.6)	
Ever married, in percentage	59.2	62.8	n.s.
Minority race, in percentage	14.0	11.5	n.s.
Unemployed at index, in percentage	55.6	50.3	n.s.
Sexual offense history			
Number of predominant victim type			
Adult women (rapists)	71	66	
Boys	61	61	
Girls	76	74	
Total known victims			
Mean *(SD)*	9.4	7.8	n.s.
	(20.1)	(27.2)	
Median	5	3	
Ever offended against, in percentage			
Adult females	55.1	46.2	n.s.
Adult males	6.4	4.5	n.s.
Boys	40.9	37.5	n.s.
Girls	60.4	50.7	n.s.
Diverse victim types, in percentage	53.8	33.3	< .001
Relationship to victim, in percentage			
Only related	0.4	8.0	< .001
Any acquaintances	80.8	73.0	n.s.
Any strangers	50.2	35.0	< .01
Sexual deviance			
Any juvenile sex offenses, in percentage	37.7	21.7	< .001
Any diagnosis of deviant sexual preferences, in percentages	51.0	43.0	n.s.
Phallometric assessments, in percentage			
Conducted (deviant or not)	30.8	29.9	n.s.
Deviant age preference (children)	23.6	20.9	n.s.
Deviant activity preference (e.g., violence)	14.4	14.9	n.s.
Number of paraphilias (e.g., voyeurism, exhibitionism, fetishes, etc.) *(SD)*	1.5	1.0	< .001
	(1.5)	(1.1)	
Lifestyle congruent with sexual deviance, in percentage	60.6	50.2	< .05

(continued)

TABLE 23.1   (Continued)

Measure	Recidivist	Nonrecidivist	Significance
Sex offender treatment history			
Ever attended, in percentage	76.3	77.1	n.s.
Number of different programs *(SD)*	2.1	1.9	n.s.
	(1.8)	(1.4)	
Number of poor treatment candidates	2.6	−1.2	< .001
(low motivation, dropout) *(SD)*	(6.4)	(6.8)	
Family background			
Physical abuse, in percentage	46.8	40.5	n.s.
Sexual abuse, in percentage	61.3	44.2	.001
Other abuse (emotional/neglect), in	54.8	36.8	.001
percentage			
Apprehended by child protective services,	26.9	14.9	.01
in percentage			
Any long-term separation from parents	42.8	28.9	.01
before age 16, in percentage			
Negative relationship with mother, in			
percentage			
During childhood	33.7	20.9	.01
As an adult	23.1	20.4	n.s.
Score of the overall negative childhood	2.6	1.8	.001
environment (6-item scale) *(SD)*	(1.9)	(1.7)	
Criminal record			
Number of prior offenses *(SD)*			
Sexual	2.4	2.2	n.s.
	(3.8)	(4.1)	
Nonsexual violent	1.5	1.7	n.s.
	(2.4)	(3.8)	
Nonviolent	7.7	6.4	n.s.
	(10.3)	(15.1)	
Total	11.6	10.3	n.s.
	(12.8)	(17.6)	
Number of index/current offenses *(SD)*			
Sexual	3.1	3.2	n.s.
	(3.8)	(3.3)	
Nonsexual violent	0.56	0.77	n.s.
	(1.6)	(2.4)	
Nonviolent	0.48	0.33	n.s.
	(1.3)	(0.8)	
Total	4.2	4.3	n.s.
	(4.6)	(4.4)	
Clinical assessment[a]			
IQ *(SD)*	94.4	100.1	< .001
	(14.6)	(14.5)	
PCL-R psychopathy			
Mean *(SD)*	23.4	16.7	< .001
	(6.8)	(8.7)	

(continued)

TABLE 23.1   (Continued)

Measure	Recidivist	Nonrecidivist	Significance
Percentage greater than 29	20.5	8.0	
Antisocial personality, in percentage	64.4	49.3	.01
Any personality disorder mentioned in file, in percentage	40.9	35.8	n.s.
Any psychotic disorder, in percentage	5.3	5.0	n.s.
Objective risk scales[b]			
SIR *(SD)*	1.6	7.2	.001
	(9.0)	(8.8)	
Sample size	84	90	
VRAG *(SD)*	10.9	4.3	.001
	(8.6)	(9.0)	
Sample size	146	121	
RRASOR *(SD)*	2.6	2.3	n.s.
	(1.3)	(1.3)	

a. PCL-R = Hare Psychopathy Checklist-Revised.
b. SIR = Statistical Information on Recidivism; VRAG = Violence Risk Appraisal Guide; RRASOR = Rapid Risk Assessment for Sexual Offense Recidivism.

sexually deviant on several indices. In comparison to the nonrecidivists, the recidivists had more diverse victims (in age and/or gender), fewer related victims, more strangers as victims, more juvenile sexual offenses, and more paraphilias. The recidivists (61%) were judged more likely than the nonrecidivists (50%) to have a lifestyle congruent with sexual deviance.

Both groups were equally likely to have attended specialized sexual offender treatment programs (76%); however, the recidivists were more likely than the nonrecidivists to have dropped out of treatment or to have been considered a treatment failure, $t(407) = 5.8$, $p < .001$. The extent to which the known recidivism event contributed to attrition or to the clinical ratings of treatment failure was not recorded, but it would be expected to be minimal because few of the offenders were in active treatment when they recidivated.

The early family background of the recidivists was significantly worse than that of the nonrecidivists in terms of sexual/emotional abuse, neglect, long-term separations from parents, and negative relationships with their mothers. Twenty-seven percent of the recidivists had been taken into the care of child protective services compared to 15% of the nonrecidivists ($X^2 = 8.86$, $df = 1$, $n = 409$, $p < .003$).

In adulthood, the recidivists were more likely than the nonrecidivists to meet the diagnostic criteria for APD (64% vs. 49%, $p < .002$) and psychopathy (21% vs. 8%, $p < .001$). In addition, the measured intelligence of the recidivists (Full Scale Intelligence Quotient [FSIQ] = 94.4) was lower than that of the nonrecidivists (FSIQ = 100.1), $t(314) = 3.34$, $p < .001$. The available file information revealed low frequencies of psychotic disorders in both groups (approximately 5%).

Consistent with the differences on criminal lifestyle measures (psychopathy, APD), the recidivists had significantly higher scores than the nonrecidivists on the objective criminal risk scales such as the SIR Scale, $t(172) = 4.21$, $p < .001$, and the VRAG, $t(265) = 6.14$, $p < .001$. The SIR scores (Bonta et al., 1996) indicated a low to moderate risk for general criminal recidivism (16% over 3 years for the nonrecidivists and 40% for the recidivists). The VRAG scores (Quinsey et al., 1998) suggested a 48% probability of violent recidivism over 10 years for the nonrecidivists and a 58% probability for the recidivists.

Due to deliberate matching, the objective measure of risk for sexual offense recidivism (RRASOR; Hanson, 1997) was not significantly different between the groups. Overall, the average RRASOR score indicated a moderate risk for sexual offense recidivism (21% to 37% over 10 years).

Comparisons on Dynamic Factors

Table 23.2 examines the dynamic risk factors as reported by the supervising officers. The first column of Table 23.2 displays the correlation between recidivism status (recidivist or nonrecidivist) and whether particular risk factors were ever noted during supervision. In this analysis, the risk factors noted were assumed to reflect relatively stable characteristics because neither the timing of the problems nor changes during the course of supervision were addressed.

The second column displays the correlation between recidivism status and whether risk factors were noted as changing during supervision (acute dynamic factors). Each rating was recoded as -1 (a change for the worse), $+1$ (a change for the better), or 0 (no change— continuously bad or never a problem). Some variables were not reassessed, as reliable changes were not expected. Thirty-three offenders were excluded because the officers felt that they had insufficient information to rate change (mostly because the offenders recidivated soon after release).

As an aid to interpreting the correlations, the 95% confidence interval for the correlations involving the total group ($n = 409$) is approximately .10. Correlations whose 95% confidence intervals do not overlap would be considered to be different from each other while preserving the overall Type I error rate at 5% (Schmidt, 1996). In other words, if the difference between the correlations is .20 or greater, then the correlations can be considered to be significantly different from each other. The variables were coded such that positive correlations indicate that the characteristic was more common among the recidivists than the nonrecidivists.

As can be seen in Table 23.2, there were significant differences between the recidivists and the nonrecidivists on most of the dynamic variables examined in this study. Most of the factors that were stable risk predictors were also acute risk predictors. The dynamic acute effects tended to be somewhat smaller than the stable dynamic effects; this is perhaps because there was relatively little change on the risk factors during the 6-month study period. For any individual item, 89% of the ratings indicated no change. Nevertheless, almost all the offenders (99%) showed some change on at least one item during the course of supervision. Although the effects were small, they were consistently in the predicted direction, with the nonrecidivists' behavior tending to improve and the recidivists' behavior tending to deteriorate during the course of supervision.

Compared to nonrecidivists, recidivists were more frequently unemployed ($r = .10$, $p < .05$), but neither a loss of employment ($r = -.04$) nor problems with the type of employment were a significant risk predictor for sexual offense recidivism.

The recidivists were those most likely to abuse drugs and/or alcohol during the course of supervision ($r = .17$, $p < .01$), and the amount of substance abuse increased just before recidivating ($r = .16$, $p < .01$). More recidivists (10.1%) than nonrecidivists (3.0%) had

TABLE 23.2   Stable and Acute Dynamic Risk Factors Predicting Sexual Offense
Recidivism

Measure	Correlation	
	Stable Dynamic (ever a problem)	Acute Dynamic (change for the worse)
Employment		
Unemployment	.10*	−.04
Type of employment problem	.02	.07
Drug use		
Susbstance abuse	.17**	.16**
Ever used anti-androgens	.15**	—
Started anti-androgens at T2	—	.11*
Psychological symptoms		
Negative mood	−.01	.16**
Anger	.07	.20***
Psychiatric symptoms (any)	−.03	.11*
Life stress	−.02	.06
Social adjustment		
Number of significant influences		
Positive	−.29***	—
Neutral	.07	—
Negative	.23***	—
Global problems with intimacy	.10*	—
Increased conflict with partner	—	.01
General social problems	.05	.11*
Association with sex offenders	−.04	−.00
Attitudes		
Low remorse/victim blaming	.28***	.19***
Rape attitudes	.19***	—
Child molester attitudes	.19***	—
Sexual entitlement	.29***	—

(continued)

ever used anti-androgens (sex-drive-reducing medications) ($r = .15$, $p < .01$). Of the 22
offenders who were taking anti-androgen medication at T2, 17 were recidivists ($p < .05$).
Although four of the five cases who stopped taking anti-androgens recidivated, all eight
cases who started anti-androgen medication during T2 recidivated ($p < .05$).

The recidivists and nonrecidivists were equally likely to display psychological symptoms at some point during their supervision. The recidivists' mood decreased, however, just
before committing their new offense ($r = .16$ for negative mood, .20 for anger, and .11 for
general psychiatric symptoms). The officers' reports of the offenders' general life stress
(e.g., major life change, health, and financial problems) were unrelated to recidivism.

The officers perceived the nonrecidivists' social environment to have more positive
than negative social influences (average of 2.1 vs. 0.72), whereas the pattern was reversed
for recidivists (1.3 negative vs. 1.1 positive). Similarly, intimacy problems (no intimate part-

TABLE 23.2 (Continued)

Measure	Correlation	
	Stable Dynamic (ever a problem)	Acute Dynamic (change for the worse)
Self-management		
Sees self as no risk to recidivate	.38***	.13*
Victim access	.26***	.24***
Sexual deviancy		
Sexual preoccupations	.20***	.09
Appearance		
Dirty/smelly/inappropriate	.10*	.12*
Any strong change		
for the worse	.04	.10
for the better	−.19***	.08
Lifestyle		
Antisocial lifestyle	.26***	.06
Uncontrolled release environment	.17**	—
No opportunities for fun/relaxation	.04	.06
Using religion as a shield	−.00	−.07
Cooperation with supervision		
Treatment attendence (any)	−.10	—
Started	—	.02
Ended	—	.02
Disengaged	.30***	.22***
Manipulative	.29***	.10*
No show/late for appointments	.22***	.10*
Overall cooperation	.36***	.23***

NOTE: The variables were coded such that positive correlations indicate characteristics more common among recidivists than nonrecidivists.
*$p < .05$; **$p < .01$; ***$p < .001$.

ner, relationship conflicts) were more commonly observed among the recidivists than the nonrecidivists ($r = .10, p < .05$). Contrary to expectation, there was no overall difference in the frequency with which the recidivists and nonrecidivists were known to associate with other sexual offenders ($r = −.04$).

All of the attitude measures differentiated the recidivists from the nonrecidivists. In general, the officers reported that the recidivists showed little remorse or concern for their victims, believed that sexual crimes can be justified ($r = .28$), and felt that they were entitled to express their strong sexual drive ($r = .29$). In general, there was some specialization between the type of attitudes and the type of victim (recidivistic rapists espoused rape attitudes, and recidivistic child molesters sexualized children), but the differences between the groups were not statistically significant.

The recidivists tended to view themselves as being at little risk for committing new sexual offenses and took few precautions to avoid high-risk situations ($r = .38, p < .001$). Not surprisingly, they were more likely than the nonrecidivists were to create or expose themselves to situations in which access to potential victims was likely (e.g., child-oriented hobbies and flashy cars).

The recidivists were also more likely than the nonrecidivists to engage in socially deviant (although not necessarily illegal) sexual activities such as the use of prostitutes, excessive masturbation, and self-reported deviant sexual fantasies/urges ($r = .20, p < .001$). These sexual preoccupations appeared to be a stable factor because there was no noticeable increase in sexual preoccupations before reoffending ($r = .08, p < .06$).

The physical appearance and grooming of the recidivists tended to be slightly worse overall than that of the nonrecidivists ($r = .10, p < .05$). Although strong changes in appearance were rarely noted, the nonrecidivists were more likely than the recidivists to improve their appearance during the course of supervision ($r = -.19, p < .001$).

The recidivists were more likely than the nonrecidivists to have a generally chaotic, antisocial lifestyle ($r = .26, p < .001$). The recidivists tended to use their leisure time aimlessly, to resist personal change (even when it was to their obvious benefit), and to hold strongly antisocial attitudes. In addition, the release environment of the recidivists was described as relatively uncontrolled in terms of access to victims, drugs, and alcohol ($r = .17, p < .01$). There were no differences in the rate at which the offenders took shelter in religion ($r = .00$) and in the frequency of constricted lifestyles (i.e., no opportunity for fun/relaxation). The lifestyle variables tended to be stable, and there were no significant relationships between acute lifestyle changes and recidivism.

The officers described the nonrecidivists as more cooperative with supervision than the recidivists ($r = .36, p < .001$). Although both groups attended equal numbers of treatment programs, the recidivists tended, more often, to be disengaged from treatment and community supervision ($r = .30, p < .001$); to attempt to deceive and manipulate the officers ($r = .29, p < .001$); and to miss scheduled appointments ($r = .22, p < .001$).

Not only were the recidivists generally noncooperative, their compliance deteriorated just before reoffending ($r = .22, p < .001$). Ending (or starting) treatment was unrelated to recidivism, but the officers considered the recidivists to become increasingly disengaged, absent, or generally noncooperative during the course of supervision. It is interesting to note that even the nonrecidivists tended to miss more and more appointments as supervision progressed, but recidivists missed the most appointments ($r = .10, p < .05$).

With rare exceptions, the same risk factors were considered important for rapists, boy-victim child molesters, and girl-victim child molesters. Of these three groups, the girl-victim child molesters appeared to be the most distinct. The same risk factors seemed important for all groups, but the effects were generally smaller for the girl-victim child molesters than for the rapists or boy-victim child molesters. Despite having a slightly larger sample size, only 8 out of 33 correlations for the stable dynamic factors were statistically significant for the girl-victim child molesters, compared to 17 out of 33 for the boy-victim child molesters and 19 out of 33 for the rapists. Considering the number of comparisons, it is difficult to determine the extent to which the observed differences are attributable to random fluctuation.

Case Note Coding

The officers' case notes tended to be brief, with little direct reference to the risk factors targeted in the interview. Approximately 10% of the files contained no information at all (either no notes or no content). The proportion of uninformative records was not significantly different between the recidivists and the nonrecidivists.

The case notes allowed group comparison on 24 of the 34 variables examined in the interview (intimacy deficits, the number of positive/negative/neutral social influences, attitudes tolerant of sexual assault, and the quality of the release environment were not coded).

The information coded from the case notes was only weakly correlated with the information obtained from the officer interviews. The average correlation between the scales scored from case notes and from the interview was .25 (*SD* = .08) at T1 and .27 (*SD* = .11) at T2. All the correlations were statistically significant, with the exception of the Sees Self as No Risk Scale at T2 ($r = .09, p > .05$).

Only 1 of the 24 comparisons between the recidivists and the nonrecidivists was significant at T1 (6 months before recidivating). At T1, the recidivists, in comparison to the nonrecidivists, failed to acknowledge their risk for recidivism ($r = .11, p < .05$, Sees Self As No Risk Scale). As expected, more of the T2 variables than the T1 variables were related to recidivism. Just before reoffending, the officers noted that the recidivists showed increased signs of sexual preoccupation and deviance ($r = .12, p < .05$, Sexual Preoccupations Scale); had access to potential victims ($r = .11, p < .05$, Victim Access Scale); and failed to acknowledge their recidivism risk ($r = .10, p < .05$, No Risk Scale). The recidivists showed increased anger just before sexually reoffending ($r = .11, p < .05$). Six of the seven cases in which the notes mentioned that the offender was taking anti-androgens were recidivists ($p < .05$). For an additional 15 cases, the offenders were known, by file review, to be taking anti-androgen medication at T2, but this was not recorded in the officers' T2 case notes.

Difference scores (T1 – T2) were used to examine the changes recorded just before recidivating. Of the 24 comparisons, only 2 were significant. Officers noted an increase in anger ($r = .12, p < .05$) between T1 and T2 for the recidivists, and the eventual recidivists were those most likely to start anti-androgen medication during T2 ($r = .12, p < .05$).

Unique Contribution of Dynamic Factors

The next set of analyses examined the extent to which the dynamic factors (stable and acute) contributed new information after controlling for preexisting differences in static risk factors. The three best predictors in each domain (static, stable, and acute) were selected through stepwise regression. Next, the unique contributions of each set of predictors were compared using hierarchical regression (see Table 23.3). As only cases with complete information were included, the sample size was substantially reduced ($n = 180$).

Static Predictors

The three best static predictors were the VRAG, IQ, and sexual deviance (a composite measure with one point given for any juvenile sexual offenses; any paraphilias, for example, exhibitionism and cross-dressing; any stranger victims; and having a diverse age/gender of victims). Overall, these static variables produced a multiple correlation R of .40 ($p < .001$) with sexual recidivism.

Stable Predictors

The best three stable predictor variables (Sees Self as No Risk, Poor Social Influences, and Sexual Entitlement) from the officer interview strongly differentiated the groups ($r = .53, p < .001$).

TABLE 23.3   The Unique Contribution of the Best Three Static, Stable, and Acute Risk Factors

Predictor Variable	r	Beta[a]	R (for set)	Unique R^2 (for set)
Static				
VRAG	.32**	.02	.40***	.035*
Sexual deviance	.24**	.12		
IQ	−.24**	−.16*		
Stable				
Sees self as no risk	.47***	.27**	.53***	.141***
Poor social influences	.39***	.15*		
Sexual entitlement	.37***	.10		
Acute				
Access to victims	.28***	.12	.32***	.035*
Noncooperation with supervision	.25***	.13		
Anger	.19**	−.01		

NOTE: The sample consists of 86 recidivists and 94 nonrecidivists. VRAG = Violence Risk Appraisal Guide.
a. Beta values are when all nine predictors are included in the analysis.
*$p < .05$; **$p < .01$; ***$p < .001$.

Acute Predictors

Similarly, the three best interview acute variables (Access to Victims, Noncooperation with Supervision, and Anger) produced an R of .32 ($p < .001$).

When the variables from each set were combined, the multiple R increased to .60 ($p < .001$). Not all of the individual variables were significant in the final regression equation. Nevertheless, each set of predictors contributed unique variance (using Equation 3.27 from Pedhazur, 1982). When entered last in the regression equation, R^2 increased by .035 ($p < .05$) for the static factors, .141 ($p < .001$) for the stable factors, and .035 ($p < .05$) for the acute factors.

Because the interview data were vulnerable to retrospective recall bias, separate analyses compared the static and dynamic risk factors using only file information. The static variables were the same as shown above (VRAG, IQ, and sexual deviancy), but the values change slightly due to the increased sample size ($n = 219$). Only two of the dynamic factors (Anger and Sexual Preoccupations at T2) from the note codes contributed unique variance in stepwise regression ($R = .21$, $p < .01$). The case note variables only marginally contributed variance over that covered by the static variables (R^2 increased by .018, $p < .08$, two-tailed). The case note Sexual Preoccupations Scale, however, significantly predicted recidivism after controlling for the three best static predictors (beta $= −.12$, $p < .05$) (overall $R = .45$; $df = 5, 213$; $p < .001$).

DISCUSSION

The purpose of this study is to identify dynamic risk factors that could be useful for the treatment and community supervision of sexual offenders. Overall, substantial differences were observed between the 208 sexual offenders who sexually recidivated while on community supervision and a comparison group of 201 nonrecidivists. The recidivists were considered to have poor social supports, attitudes tolerant of sexual assault, antisocial lifestyles, and poor self-management strategies. Not surprisingly, the officers considered the recidivists to have displayed poor cooperation with supervision, as indicated by being disengaged, manipulative, or absent. Recidivists and nonrecidivists had equivalent levels of life stress and negative affect, but the recidivists tended to show an increase in anger and subjective distress just before reoffending. In other words, psychological symptoms appeared as acute dynamic, but not as stable dynamic, risk factors. The same risk factors generally applied to both rapists and child molesters.

The interview-based results were informative but open to alternative interpretations. The first concern is that the supposedly dynamic problems observed during the course of supervision could be proxies for enduring (static or highly stable) risk factors. Despite our efforts to match the recidivists and nonrecidivists on many static predictors, the background characteristics of recidivists remained the most problematic. In particular, the recidivists were more likely than the nonrecidivists to have chronic antisocial lifestyles, long histories of diverse sexually deviant behavior, prior treatment failure, low intelligence, and poor childhood environments. Nevertheless, even after statistically controlling for many preexisting group differences, the dynamic variables continued to be strongly associated with recidivism. The recidivists were generally more problematic than the nonrecidivists, and their behavior deteriorated just before recidivating.

The second concern is the extent to which the findings were influenced by retrospective recall bias. Both the officers and the field researchers were fully aware of who had, or had not, recidivated. Consequently, old information may take on new significance once the offender is known to have reoffended. Such hindsight biases were of particular concern for the officer interviews, because in some cases, the officers were asked to recall events that transpired 4 to 5 years earlier.

Rater bias was a concern. Although the coders were instructed to separate the information related to the recidivism offense from the rest of the file information, such a separation was often difficult, if not impossible (e.g., extracting information from summary reports that included both index and recidivism information). In addition, the PCL-R was explicitly scored using all file information, which would have artificially increased the PCL-R (and the VRAG) scores of the recidivists.

This study attempted to control for retrospective recall biases by examining the case notes completed by the officers before they knew of the recidivism event. This strategy was only partially successful due to the limited information available in the case notes. Nevertheless, the major dynamic risk factors reported in the interview were also present in the contemporaneous case notes. The officers recorded concerns about sexual preoccupation/compulsivity, poor self-management strategies (sees self as no risk), increased victim access, and increased anger in the 4 to 6 weeks before recidivating. The effects were small, but the consistency of these findings with the interview results suggests that the interview results cannot be completely attributed to recall bias.

The dynamic risk factors identified in this study were similar to those identified by research on (predominantly) nonsexual criminals (Quinsey et al., 1997; Zamble & Quinsey, 1997). Quinsey et al. (1997) found that the strongest predictor of violent recidivism among mentally disordered offenders was a dimension they called dynamic antisociality. The components of dynamic antisociality (e.g., complains about the staff, no remorse, ignores previous violent acts, unrealistic discharge plans) were similar to our measures of negative attitudes, poor self-management, and lack of cooperation with supervision (e.g., No Risk, Low Remorse/Victim Blaming, Antisocial Lifestyle, and Victim Access). Quinsey et al. (1997), however, found much larger effects in the case notes ($R = .61$) than we did ($R = .21$). The larger effects may be attributable to better record-keeping, different scoring procedures, or differences in sampling procedures. Quinsey et al. (1997) eliminated from their yoked comparison groups offenders who had already eloped or offended while under supervision, which would increase the differences between their recidivistic and non-recidivistic groups. In contrast, 40% of our nonrecidivist comparison group had previously failed on conditional release.

Whereas Quinsey et al. (1997) focused primarily on nonsexual recidivism, Pithers et al. (1988) looked specifically for the precursors of sexual recidivism. Because no comparison group was used, it is difficult to know whether the factors considered by Pithers et al. were more common among recidivists than nonrecidivists. Nevertheless, it is interesting to note that those factors deemed to be important in at least 70% of Pithers et al.'s (1988) cases (anger, cognitive distortions, low victim empathy, and offense planning) were similar to the factors that differentiated the recidivists and the nonrecidivists in both the current study and that of Quinsey et al. (1997).

Although the study assessed offender behavior as independent from the behavior of their supervising officers, in practice, the two are highly related. Our measures of cooperation with supervision would be influenced not only by the offenders' behavior but also by the officers' capacity to establish rapport with difficult clients. Similarly, the association between observed dynamic risk factors and recidivism should be reduced when officers are able to effectively intervene in high-risk cases.

Of the three main types of risk factors (static, stable dynamic, and acute dynamic), the stable dynamic factors most strongly differentiated the recidivists from the nonrecidivists. This finding is partially a function of the research design, which matched the groups on many static variables. It was impossible, for example, for RRASOR scores (Hanson, 1997) to differentiate the groups because we explicitly matched the offenders on these variables. The finding that some static factors continued to differentiate the groups supports the tenacity of historical variables.

Hanson and Bussière's (1998) meta-analytic review found that sexual offense recidivism was most strongly related to sexual deviancy, and to a lesser extent, general criminality. In contrast, this study found that criminal lifestyle variables (e.g., the VRAG scores) tended to be stronger predictors than measures of sexual deviancy. Although this pattern may simply reflect random variation, there are two features of the sampling procedure that would reinforce the salience of general criminality. First, the offenders were closely matched on historical measures of sexual deviancy, which would reduce the relative contribution of sexual deviancy variables. Second, the nonrecidivists were selected from offenders who had successfully served at least 6 months of their community sentence. Consequently, serious nonsexual recidivists would be eliminated from the comparison group.

The study found similar risk factors for the different types of sexual offenders, but fewer factors were significant for the girl-victim child molesters than for the rapists or the boy-victim child molesters. Assuming that this pattern is more than a statistical anomaly, it may be that girl-victim child molesters follow a different offense cycle than other sexual offenders. One possibility is that the girl-victim child molesters may be less socially and sexually deviant. Rather than sharing the courtship disorder of the rapists (Freund, 1990; Freund, Seto, & Kuban, 1997) or the deviant victim choice of the boy-victim child molesters, some girl-victim child molesters may simply occupy the low end of a continuum of normal age preference. Similarly, some men may choose to have sex with girls when their preferred sexual partners (mature females) are not immediately available. Until the effects are replicated, any interpretation of the relative unpredictability of girl-victim child molesters is, at best, tentative.

An interesting finding of this study is the striking failure of anti-androgen medications to prevent sexual offense recidivism. Uncontrolled case studies have typically found anti-androgen use to be associated with a decreased sexual drive and reduced temptations to re-offend (Fedoroff, Wisner-Carlson, Dean, & Berlin, 1992; Money & Bennett, 1981). The finding in this study that a greater number of recidivists than nonrecidivists were taking sex-drive-reducing medications can probably be explained by the officers' desire to intervene in the highest risk cases. Given that all the offenders who started anti-androgens (most typically, cyproterone acetate) recidivated, hormonal intervention was clearly insufficient. It is possible that anti-androgens could increase the risk if their introduction is associated with decreased vigilance on the part of the offender and/or his supervising officer. This study was not designed to test the efficacy of anti-androgen medication, and the sample size was too small to make strong conclusions. Nevertheless, officers should be aware that sexual offenders still present a considerable risk for sexual offense recidivism after the introduction of sex-drive-reducing medication.

Conclusions and Recommendations

Low recidivism base rates present special challenges to prospective designs. The recidivism rate in this study was artificially set at 50%, which would be considerably higher than the 10% to 15% sexual offense recidivism rates typically found after 4 to 5 years in the community (Hanson & Bussière, 1998). Prospective designs provide the best information, but they require either long follow-up periods (5 years minimum), large sample sizes, or exceptionally high-risk offenders. Researchers interested in retrospective matched designs (as in this study) may want to begin by ensuring that the quality of case records is sufficient for their purposes.

Despite the study's limitations, this research provides some guidance to those interested in improving the treatment and community supervision of sexual offenders. Many of the stable dynamic risk factors identified in this study are useful treatment targets. In addition, dynamic risk factors should be routinely evaluated during supervision. The results suggest that offenders are most at risk for reoffending when they become sexually preoccupied, have access to victims, fail to acknowledge their recidivism risk, and show sharp increases in dysphoric moods such as anger, in particular. By carefully monitoring the offender's risk indicators, we may be able to provide graduated and responsive interventions well before the point of no return.

24

Strange Bedfellows

Is Sex Offender Notification
a Form of Community Justice?

————◾————

LOIS PRESSER
ELAINE GUNNISON
University of Cincinnati

Sex offender notification, also called community notification, is the law in all but a few American states (Pearson, 1998). The ubiquity of notification laws is matched only by the controversy surrounding them. Their fairness and consequences have been hotly contested in the courts and in the press. Following suit, criminologists have examined notification almost exclusively in terms of fairness and consequences, the latter being a matter of speculation rather than empirical inquiry (Finn, 1997; Freeman-Longo, 1996). Questions about underlying principles have received little scholarly attention.

Sex offender notification is commonly aligned with the contemporary trend toward community justice. Supporters of notification claim that the laws empower private citizens to protect themselves. They refer to notification as "community management of offenders" (Beatty, 1997, p. 20) and "a form of community policing" (Lieb, 1996, p. 299). Yet the extent to which notification truly is community justice has not been examined.

Though the term *community justice* is used broadly, it is possible to identify two unifying principles. First, community justice helps citizens increase their own safety (Moore, 1992; Zehr, 1995). Second, community justice looks to the roots of crime problems, seeking to prevent crime before it occurs (Office of Justice Programs [OJP], 1998; Oliver, 1998).

Authors' Note: The authors gratefully acknowledge the suggestions and support of Francis T. Cullen, Bonnie S. Fisher, Emily Gaarder, Lorraine Green Mazerolle, and Paul Mazerolle. Direct correspondence to Lois Presser, Division of Criminal Justice, University of Cincinnati, P.O. Box 210389, Cincinnati, OH 45221-0389; e-mail: pressel@email.uc.edu.

On the surface, sex offender notification legislation seems like a community justice initiative. The laws allegedly involve citizens in crime prevention by supplying them with information about known sex offenders (Beatty, 1997; Goodman, 1996). However, the alliance between sex offender notification and community justice is an odd one. The supporter of notification seems more like a retributivist than a problem solver.

This article examines what sex offender notification shares with community justice and what it does not. We contend that notification is not community justice, though it has appropriated some of its rhetoric. Sex offender notification differs from community justice in terms of the following: (1) views of crime, (2) the nature of citizen participation, (3) problem-solving orientations, (4) treatment of victims' needs, (5) willingness to understand offenders, (6) shaming of offenders, and (7) extension of state control.

The first section of the article examines the respective histories of the two social movements and provides a basis for understanding their rhetorical similarities and conceptual differences that are examined in the second section. Implications of the analysis are discussed in the third section of the article. Importantly, the analysis sheds light on the current failure of the community justice movement to adequately address sex crimes.

BACKGROUND

Restorative Community Justice

Restorative justice is a branch of the community justice movement. The two movements are so closely related that the term *restorative community justice* is popular (Young, 1995), and our discussion of community justice will center on restorative justice.

Restorative justice stresses the need to repair the harms caused by crime and to reintegrate victims, offenders, and communities. Programs based on restorative justice include victim-offender mediation, family group conferencing, and sentencing circles. To varying degrees, all involve healing dialogue and communal participation.

Victim-offender mediation was first implemented in 1974 in Ontario, Canada. Today, there are more than 1,000 such programs in North America and Europe (Umbreit, Coates, & Roberts, 1997). Legislation passed in 1989 in New Zealand calls for restorative justice interventions in most juvenile cases. By 1996, at least 24 American states had adopted or were considering adopting juvenile codes or administrative procedures based on the restorative justice concept (National Criminal Justice Reference Service [NCJRS], 1996).

Sex Offender Notification

The sex offender notification movement is a more recent development than restorative justice, though its historical antecedents include sweeping legislation against rape beginning in the late 1970s (Caringella-MacDonald & Humphries, 1991). Washington State was the first to pass a notification statute in 1989. The notification movement gained momentum with the 1994 enactment of New Jersey's Megan's Law, a legislative response to the rape and murder of 7-year-old Megan Kanka by a paroled sex offender (Goodman, 1996; Rudin, 1996). The New Jersey law also provided for involuntary civil commitment for the most serious offenders, a DNA database, and similar "containment" strategies (Goodman,

1996). The nationwide influence of the New Jersey law was so great that notification laws are now known generically as Megan's Laws.

Notification laws were a supplement to registration laws, which require offenders just released from prison to register with local law enforcement agencies. A "perception that registration alone is inadequate to protect the public against released sex offenders" prompted notification of community members (Finn, 1997, p. 2). That perception was fed by heinous cases, such as the victimization of Megan Kanka. The Kanka case roused citizen activism to "prevent a recurrence of such a tragedy" (Brooks, 1996, p. 56). A federal Megan's Law followed in May 1996. The law mandated the public release of information about offenders by the states, in part by relaxing confidentiality restrictions.

Two types of procedures are invoked by notification laws: one for assessing offender risk and one for disseminating information about offenders. Risk is assessed differently across the states. Some states (e.g., California) rely solely on criminal history. Some defer to the determination of one law enforcement official, such as the county prosecutor (Pearson, 1998). Some (e.g., Georgia) automatically subject certain sex offenders, such as pedophiles, to notification requirements. Finally, some states use actuarial risk assessment instruments (Canestrini, 1998; Goodman, 1996). However risk is assessed, a three-tier risk typology is commonly applied that consists of low (Tier 1), moderate (Tier 2), and high (Tier 3) risk (Goodman, 1996).

Methods of notification vary across states and communities, as local law enforcement officials devise "their own notification plan based on the offender's criminal behavior and the makeup of the community" (Finn, 1997, p. 5). There are roughly three notification categories: active notification, limited disclosure, and passive notification, which roughly correspond with the three risk tiers (Goodman, 1996). For the Tier 3 offender, only active notification delivers information to citizens without their asking for it. The public is notified through virtually any available means, including clothing labels, visits from police officers, newspaper ads, and the Internet. With limited disclosure, generally for the Tier 2 offender, only some organizations (like schools) are notified. For the Tier 1 offender, passive notification requires citizens to obtain information themselves.

According to federal law, persons convicted of any criminal offense against a minor, or a sexually violent offense against any victim, are subject to registration and notification for 10 years. The sexually violent predator, so classified by the court and a board of experts, is subject to these requirements for life (Feinberg, 1998).

Sex Offender Notification and the Restorative Justice Ideal

The sex offender notification movement draws ideologically from a restorative justice ideal, which states that a more just society will be achieved through community problem solving. In addition, the benefits of community justice will be reaped at the local level (Van Ness & Strong, 1997). The language of the notification movement underscores these two basic concepts: community and problem solving.

In the notification literature, it is "everyday citizens" who will "build a world worthy of our children" (Wetterling, 1998, p. 6). Teir and Coy (1997) observe that notification "relies solely upon self-help" (p. 406), thus downplaying the role of government. Public safety is supposedly achieved "through the sharing of information and education" by community members (Center for Sex Offender Management [CSOM], 1997, p. 5). Communities are held responsible for sex offender recidivism; when it occurs, the families of victims "are left questioning whether the community and *its* [italics added] criminal justice system let them down" (Teir & Coy, 1997, p. 405).

Sex offender notification is designed to allow citizens to "actively participate in re-claiming the safety of their neighborhoods, cities and towns" (Beatty, 1997, p. 20). Legislation is sometimes tied to community-building activities. The Megan Kanka Foundation, which provides information on notification policies, also offers scholarships to high school students who "show leadership in community service" (Megan Nicole Kanka Foundation, 1997). Notification laws occasion greater dialogue between citizens and criminal justice personnel, such that "a problem-solving relationship develops between criminal justice professionals and local residents" (CSOM, 1997, p. 5).

The ideology of communities obtaining justice has been adopted, but has restorative justice been achieved? To answer this question, we compare restorative justice and sex offender notification in terms of seven conceptual themes.

THEMES OF RESTORATIVE COMMUNITY JUSTICE AND SEX OFFENDER NOTIFICATION

Views of Crime

Supporters of both the restorative justice and the sex offender notification movements allege that certain truths about crime are the starting point of their efforts. Community justice deals with particular conflicts between people, rejecting abstract views of crime (Zehr, 1995). Notification advocates claim that they have taken a good, hard look at the facts about sexual violence and, particularly in view of recidivism data, they have designed realistic policies (see Wetterling, 1998).

We contend that the notification movement has focused on some realities about sex crime to the exclusion of others. The process by which offenders are deemed dangerous is problematic. Standardized assessment instruments are frequently used, but they tend to overestimate risk (Van Ness & Strong, 1997; Wright, Clear, & Dickson, 1984). Inaccurate determinations have resulted, such that the New Jersey Supreme Court ruled that these assessment tools should not be relied on exclusively (Cooper, 1998).

Moreover, the classification process pares the identity of the sex offender down to offending alone. That is, other life roles that the offender might play (e.g., parent or friend) are discounted. Sex offender becomes a master status; the diversity of behaviors and identities of those persons labeled sex offender are obscured. The master status is difficult to escape, and, most often, the offender must actively seek relief from notification requirements. The label may have lasting effects, as there are no "ceremonies to decertify deviance" before the community (Braithwaite & Mugford, 1994, p. 141).

Reports of high recidivism rates that are impervious to treatment (e.g., Furby, Weinrott, & Blackshaw, 1989) are used by notification supporters to justify the extreme measures that have been proposed for dealing with sex offenders, such as chemical castration. In 1997, when the U.S. Supreme Court ruled that states can indefinitely confine sex offenders, the majority opinion was that some of these persons "suffer from a volitional impairment rendering them dangerous beyond their control" (Mishra, 1997, p. 2). Yet recent research suggests that treatment, especially cognitive-behavioral approaches coupled with relapse prevention, can be effective in reducing recidivism (Marshall & Pithers, 1994). Furthermore, recidivism rates may be lower than is commonly believed. Lotke (1996) reports that untreated sex offenders sentenced to prison have a recidivism rate of 18.5 percent, compared with 25 percent for drug offenders and 30 percent for (nonsexually) violent offenders.

Another myth nurtured by notification advocates is that sex offenses are carried out by persons who are strangers to the victims. But in nearly 75 percent of sexual assault and rape cases and in 90 percent of those involving children, the victim knew the offender (Greenfeld, 1997). Forty-three percent of victims under age 12 were assaulted by family members (Chaiken, 1998). With an emphasis on "outing" the dangerous stranger, notification laws perpetuate a false sense of security that all sex offenders are known to the authorities (Finn, 1997) and ignore the social and family structures within which most offenders live. The idea that "people who harm us are not of us" justifies notification and other divisive policies (Clear, 1994, p. 149).

Citizen Participation

Citizen participation in crime control is central to the rhetoric of both movements. However, their rationales for participation and the forms it has taken differ markedly.

Rationale for Participation. In the restorative justice model, citizen participation in crime control strengthens communities. Crimes create opportunities for citizen involvement in matters of personal importance and for clarification of social norms (Christie, 1977). Community building is as important a goal as problem solving (Harris, 1991; McKnight, 1995).

In contrast, notification assumes a strictly utilitarian rationale for citizen participation. The community represents "more eyes monitoring released offenders" (Beatty, 1997, p. 20). Lawmakers and law enforcement officials set the boundaries for formal processes of notification, and citizens are expected to act on the information provided. According to notification advocates, government is not to blame if offenders are denied jobs and housing, for these are "the normal societal consequences of committing a heinous crime" and not "requirements of or the intent of notification laws" (Sacco, 1998, pp. 51-52). The state thus disowns responsibility for postnotification community conduct. Citizens determine most of the ways in which offenders are responded to day-to-day, and the government only steps in to restore peace. It is neither the duty nor the concern of citizens to achieve peace. This recipe for community action is the virtual opposite of that proposed by restorative justice, where citizens restore peace between victims and offenders and the government supervises how offenders are treated (Van Ness & Strong, 1997, pp. 38-39).

Participation of Victims, Offenders, and Other Citizens. The involvement of victims is central to the restorative justice model, which explicitly calls for "comprehensive changes to expand victim involvement in the criminal justice process" (Van Ness & Strong, 1997, p. 150). These changes include new, formal roles for victims from investigation to postsentence supervision of offenders. By comparison, though victims helped launch notification legislation in some states, their involvement soon became superfluous. For example, in Washington State, the early influence of victims' groups was great, but their policy preferences were later ignored (Scheingold, Olson, & Pershing, 1994, p. 747).

Offenders are essential actors in both restorative justice and notification processes. Restorative justice programs ask offenders to perform community service, pay restitution, and/or apologize to their victims and communities. Notification requires only that offenders register with the government, which is easy to avoid. A California study found that 75 percent of sex offenders in the state had failed to register (Montana, 1996).

Restorative justice has evolved from the grass roots; that is, the work of community members (e.g., victims' and offenders' friends and neighbors) and organizations (e.g., churches) has been as instrumental in its development as the government. Citizens design programs, act as mediation or conference facilitators, arrange community service for offenders, and offer aid to victims and offenders (Van Ness & Strong, 1997).

Conversely, notification laws maintain the dominance of the criminal justice system. Particular agents of the system assess the risk that an offender poses (Goodman, 1996), after which information is disclosed or withheld by public officials. Activism stirred by notification laws has taken several forms. Most commonly, it involves organized campaigns to alert the community to the presence of a sex offender. Citizens have also organized protests against the individual, involving a range of activities, both nonviolent and violent. Offenders and their families have been "picketed, leafleted, stoned, pummeled with eggs, threatened, or had signs posted outside their residences" (Rudin, 1996, p. 7). A lesser number have been victims of vigilante attacks (Stadler, 1995). These different forms of participating all seek the goal of exiling the offender. Rather than a means to "social cohesion," citizen participation is "an instrument of divisiveness" (Grabosky, 1992, p. 267).

Problem Solving

Notification laws are a proactive and apparently new response to a social problem, so they seem like solutions. But in fact, the sex offender is defined as the problem to be solved. Because the offender is allegedly unalterable, so too is the problem (see Furby et al., 1989; Mishra, 1997). Strategies for dealing with the sex offender problem emphasize containment (English, Pullen, & Jones, 1997; Myers, 1996). The problem can only be checked and its effects mitigated rather than averted. A sense of hopelessness thus shapes notification policies, which offer little in the way of suggested action for concerned citizens. Whereas notification laws "clearly affirm the desire for protection from assaultive and predatory behavior . . . they do not suggest what communities should do once they are notified that sex offenders live in their neighborhoods" (CSOM, 1997, p. 7).

Restorative justice approaches to sex crimes aspire to eradicate the root causes of those crimes. They have been influenced by feminist thought, which holds that the problem of sex crime is rooted in general cultural codes; thus, it is these codes that must be transformed (Carrington & Watson, 1996). Rather than a more effective crackdown on particular incidents, policing sexual violence demands the dispelling of oppressive myths and the development of new norms. Myths that facilitate sex crimes include the idea that, absent clear and abundant evidence of coercion or resistance, participation in sexual activity was probably consensual. Such beliefs are widespread. For example, most junior high school students surveyed in a Rhode Island study agreed that it is acceptable for a man to force a woman to have sexual intercourse under certain circumstances, which included spending money on a date, having dated one person exclusively for more than 6 months, and being married (Caringella MacDonald & Humphries, 1991, pp. 101-102). These findings contradict "the perception that rape is an isolated problem amenable to security and criminal justice solutions" (Caringella-MacDonald & Humphries, 1991, p. 106). As Braithwaite and Mugford

(1994) note, "Attacking deeper structures of inequality is more important" (p. 156) than individual intervention.

Sex offender notification fails to consider the societal basis of the offender's conduct, with the result that the problem of sexual violence is left unexamined and unchanged. Notification not only neglects the root causes of sexual violence but also diverts attention away from them. The public "is relieved of having to make connections between the root causes of antisocial and sexually violent acts and the kind of social-change alternatives that actually could make our communities more just and safe" (Knopp, 1991, p. 183). In fact, controlling sexual violence by making life miserable for the offender is a contradiction, because sexual violence and notification laws share the logic of dominating and harming another (Clear, 1994; Harris, 1991). The "oppressive institutions of patriarchy and . . . punishment" are inseparable (Knopp, 1991, p. 181).

The sex offender notification movement has attended to neither causes nor, for that matter, solutions. Notification laws were passed hastily, without planning (Rudin, 1996). Pallone (1995) describes how New Jersey legislators enacted Megan's Law without hearings on alternative proposals or "even a cursory reconstructive analysis" (p. 10) of the events that led to Megan Kanka's victimization to inform action.

It is true that vigilantism has been widely condemned by notification advocates (Beatty, 1997; Hanley, 1998). However, official reports tend to frame vigilantism as the result of misinformation about the laws (Hanley, 1998). Sacco (1998) speculates that "the likelihood of vigilantism will decrease as notification becomes more common" (p. 51). On the other hand, a view is emerging of vigilantism as a "logical outcome of telling people that an evil menace lurks next door" (Prentky, 1996, p. 296). The compatibility of notification law with violent responses is noted by opponents and proponents alike (Allen, 1998). Notification law, so prescriptive about other procedures, offers few suggestions as to what citizens should do about sexual violence, with the possible result that tolerance of vigilantism is fostered.

Helping Victims

Restorative justice and sex offender notification share a concern about the crime victim. In the restorative model, sanctions for offenders should be designed to meet victims' needs (Zehr, 1995). Notification laws were lobbied for by victims' groups (Scheingold et al., 1994), and some were named after victims of sexual violence (Rudin, 1996; Wetterling, 1998). But in fact, the notification movement offers little aid to victims.

Like offenders, victims of sex crimes need to be reintegrated into society. In addition to damage to self-image, relationships, and employability (Van Ness & Strong, 1997), sex crime victims are prone to "shame, self-blame, fear, developmental crises, [and] post-traumatic stress disorder" (English et al., 1997, p. 3). When restorative justice entails an apology from the offender and community condemnation of the crime, victims receive "powerful affirmation of the respect for (him or her) as a person" (Braithwaite & Mugford, 1994, p. 155). Clear (1994) suggests that condemning the offender as opposed to the offense can negatively affect the victim, upholding "the idea that moral worth is a product of judgements" (p. 133) and thus that the victim's worth is similarly prone to degradation by others.

Sex crimes cause particular harm to children (English et al., 1997), who then need special services, especially when incest has occurred. Kreindler and Armstrong (1983) point out that "incest is a family affair rather than just the expression of one family member's psychopathology" (p. 555). They highlight the discrepancy between what the child and his or her family need and what they inevitably receive. Treatment should be "as non-threatening as possible" for all involved, or "the intervention may be more damaging than the experience itself, particularly if the child ends up in care, the father in prison, and the family on welfare" (Kreindler & Armstrong, 1983, p. 560). Often, when incest is discovered and the offender is incarcerated, the child victim is made a scapegoat for the family's resultant problems, which, in turn, instills guilt and self-hatred. It should also be noted that incest victims are themselves publicly identified by notification, causing a second form of violation (Pearson, 1998).

Female rape victims are often held responsible for the violation. In court, their character and behavior are considered relevant (Spears & Spohn, 1997). Sex offender notification laws have done nothing to change the sociolegal context within which the female victim's credibility is questioned. Ironically, this is the context in which sex offender notification might effect change, because notification is a legal practice.

Notification laws do not directly address the needs of victims after the crime has occurred (Klein, 1998), except by prohibiting offender contact with victims (Shapiro, 1998). This neglect might be explained by the legal context of notification. The focus of criminal law remains firmly on the offender and protection of society, not the assistance to victims (Dow, 1989, p. 373). Neglect of victims also follows from the warlike mentality of notification law. Victims are not people with needs but rather recruits into battle, "used by the prosecution for their own adversarial purposes" (Knopp, 1991, p. 182).

Understanding Offenders

Trying to understand offenders is part of the problem-solving orientation of community justice. In stark contrast, an effort to understand sex offenders is not part of the notification agenda, which is primarily focused on exiling them.

Understanding why offenders offend allows for effective interventions. For example, many sex offenders were themselves victims of sexual assault, and "addressing the psychological harm done to offenders in the past may help to reduce the harm they inflict on others in the future" (Lotke, 1996, p. 1). Compassionate treatment approaches do not preclude efforts to encourage offenders to take responsibility for their offending. Rather, acceptance of responsibility is a first step in the most promising treatments. The second step involves "understanding the sequence of thoughts, feelings, events, high-risk circumstances, and arousal stimuli that (precede) their sexual assaults" (Knopp, 1991, p. 191). This understanding is followed by training on how to interrupt the cycle and the teaching of new attitudes and behaviors.

By contrast, the notification movement considers the offender the enemy in a battle of rights and interests (Shapiro, 1998). In this light, notification laws represent mastery over dark forces. Megan's Law "tips the balance in favor of the innocent victims of sex crimes rather than the perpetrators" (Goodman, 1996, p. 797). The efforts that followed Megan Kanka's victimization are constructed as "an inspiring story of tragedy fueling a passionate fight for the protection of children from sexual predators" (Megan Nicole Kanka Foundation, 1997, p. 1). Paradoxically, with the whole community poised for battle against the offender, he or she is more likely to try to distance himself or herself psychologically from the offense. Responsibility is avoided as "unconsciously or even consciously (offenders) work to insulate themselves from the victim" (Zehr, 1995, p. 41). Notification facilitates that insulating process by positioning the offender as adversary. To relieve the discomfort of constant shame, the offender likewise may "reject the rejectors," viewing the law-abiding community as adversaries (Braithwaite & Mugford, 1994; see also Sherman, 1993).

Shaming Offenders

Both notification and restorative justice processes shame the offender. Braithwaite (1989) commends the sort of shaming used by restorative justice programs, in which offenders are subsequently reintegrated into the community. Offenders are shown that "they are not what they do (hence) they can be better than what they do" (Wylie, 1998, p. 57). Conversely, notification rebukes both offender and offense, which may foster "adoption of a delinquent identity" (Braithwaite & Mugford, 1994, p. 146).

Notification draws a line not only between neighbors and offender, but also between neighbors and anyone who offers the offender much needed support, including relatives, friends, and employers (Montana, 1996; Nieves, 1998; Rudin, 1996). Vigilantism has been directed at both the offender and the people who help him or her.

Clinical knowledge about sexual deviance suggests that notification is likely to be counterproductive. Censure may encourage retreat into denial and defensiveness (Kreindler & Armstrong, 1983; see also Braithwaite & Mugford, 1994; Kear-Colwell & Pollock, 1997; Sherman, 1993). Pedophiles in particular may respond to notification by reoffending, because they are often loners who find companionship in children instead of adults. Montana (1996) notes that "by ostracizing sex offenders, community members may reinforce their attraction toward children" (p. 585). Furthermore, the stress of public exposure may provoke reoffense, and its threat may keep offenders from seeking treatment (CSOM, 1997).

Social Control

Both restorative justice and sex offender notification negotiate new combinations of social control. Restorative justice purportedly substitutes informal for formal social control over offenders (Christie, 1977; Stuart, 1997). The notification movement seeks a net increase in both formal and informal social control over offenders.

Restorative justice may lead to more control over more people, despite its professed intentions. First, the net of social control may be widened if persons whom the formal justice system would have dismissed (e.g., petty offenders) are sanctioned (Dittenhoffer & Ericson, 1983; Levrant, Cullen, Fulton, & Wozniak, 1999). Second, by adding restorative conditions to probation terms, more opportunities are provided to "fail" and to be incarcerated for violation. Third, state control is exercised if parties to mediation are pressured to reconcile with one another (Brown, 1994; Levrant et al., 1999; Pavlich, 1996).

Net widening is regarded as a potential problem by many restorative justice advocates (Immarigeon & Daly, 1997; Umbreit & Zehr, 1995-1996; Van Ness & Strong, 1997). Others minimize the seriousness of net widening on the grounds that, whatever the systemic effect, "it is just and right for the offender to be confronted with the personal impact of her or his crime" (Coates & Gehm, 1989; see also Braithwaite & Daly, 1994; Stuart, 1997).

For the notification movement, extending social control over sex offenders is the manifest goal. Notification generalizes the incapacitative functions of the prison beyond the prison and, indeed, beyond the dominion of government. Empirical evidence of net widening as a result of notification laws is not available, though it seems highly likely that it does occur. Probation and parole conditions are directly widened by the legislation. There is no shortage of volunteers to police those conditions (see Nieves, 1998, p. 17). With neighbors alert to any presumed evidence of criminality, the offender stands a good chance of returning to court on a violation. It is not at all clear that society is better off with this brand of justice or if its main accomplishment is simply to "ensure that their problems will have solutions" (Feeley & Simon, 1992, p. 456).

SUMMARY AND CONCLUSIONS

Sex offender notification is a flawed strategy for controlling sex crime. It reflects a skewed view of sex offenders, and, lacking a plan for problem solving, it encourages citizen action in the form of vigilantism. Notification relies on stigma, such that offenders are likely to retreat into denial and eventually to recidivate (Kear-Colwell & Pollock, 1997).

Notification has been promoted as a community justice initiative. The insight that notification shares little with community justice highlights the fact that something is missing in the restorative community justice movement. Namely, it is not meeting the needs of communities threatened by sexual violence. Harris (1987) articulates the movement's general strategy: to do what is possible and postpone the toughest challenges. She advises fellow advocates to "not allow the most difficult cases to stand in the way of more rapidly evolving better approaches for the rest" (p. 35).

That pragmatic strategy was a good one for a time, considering the movement's broad goals and formidable obstacles. Following this plan, community groups are "doing *something* [italics added]" (Caringella-MacDonald & Humphries, 1991, p. 109). However, there is now an urgent need for programs for sex offenders: The notification movement makes this clear. Most mediation programs in the United States exclude violent cases (Hughes & Schneider, 1989; Lerman, 1984; Rowe, 1985). Treatment is critical, but restorative justice programs have often failed to consider current knowledge about offender treatment (Levrant et al., 1999). If restorative justice cannot change serious sex offenders, then incapacitation—through confinement or registration and notification—would seem the only legitimate means available for protecting society.

Though restorative programs for sex offenders are in short supply, a few have been developed that emphasize both treatment and restorative justice principles. One such program is The Safer Society, sponsored by an association of churches, which calls for offender-specific interventions including "restraint of the few" very serious sex offenders (Knopp, 1991, p. 185). The restraint used should be "the least restrictive and most humane option for the shortest period of time in the most remedial and restorative environment" (Knopp, 1991, p. 186). Above all, The Safer Society emphasizes early intervention with youth who show signs of sexual aggression and educational programs that teach nonsexist values.

Other innovations are on the horizon. Some victim-offender mediation programs in Canada and England have surrogate victims meet with sex offenders so that certain benefits of encounter are realized without added trauma to victims (Zehr, 1995, p. 206). Victim-sensitive sex offender therapy, developed by Walter Berea, considers the victim's needs at each of three offender treatment phases (Zehr, 1995, p. 207). Finally, Braithwaite and Daly (1994) call for a pyramid of responses to rape and other violence between intimates that applies family group conferencing in combination with law enforcement responses. A succession of responses, both formal/legal and informal/communitarian, is "more practical and more decent" than formal sanctions alone (Braithwaite & Daly, 1994, p. 201). What these interventions to sex crime have in common is a practical agenda for meeting the needs of victims, offenders, and communities, often using community resources.

Research on effective treatment for sex offenders of all types should be a priority of government and the scientific community. Too little is known about what works with sex offenders (Quinsey, 1998, p. 415). In addition, the effects of notification on positive community outcomes, such as citizens' sense of empowerment, should be studied to reveal what the notification movement is doing right. These aspects of the notification movement can help shape new programs more consistent with peacemaking. Though strange bedfellows, sex offender notification and restorative community justice might become friends yet.

25

Criminal Profiling

Real Science or Just Wishful Thinking?

———————

DAMON A. MULLER

University of Melbourne

The subject of criminal profiling has caught the public's imagination in recent times, with references to it appearing in all forms of media. The most well-known example of criminal profiling in the popular media is in the film *Silence of the Lambs,* based on the Thomas Harris novel of the same name. Several television shows have also recently been based around the premise of criminal profiling, including *Millennium, Profiler,* and even *The X-Files.* It is interesting to note that all of these popular portrayals of profiling are somewhat inaccurate because they suggest that profiling is a magical skill somewhat analogous to a precognitive psychic ability.

Those who practice criminal profiling have claimed that it is alternatively a science or an art, depending on who you listen to. Even those who confess that it is more an art than a science (e.g., Ressler & Shachtman, 1992) still point to supposedly scientific studies to support their claims that it is, in fact, worth using. Yet one of the biggest hurdles standing in the way of acceptance of criminal profiling is that there is very little authoritative material on it, and almost nothing in the way of scientific studies to support the claims of the profilers.

Many of the law enforcement agencies around the world are still quite skeptical of the work of criminal profilers. Holmes and Holmes (1996) observe that an offender profiler is usually only called in when the police have exhausted all other leads, sometimes including psychics and astrologers. Techniques such as forensic DNA analysis have become essential to modern criminal investigation, possibly because one can point to the strong scientific basis on which they are founded. Yet most people have no idea how effective profiling is, let alone how it works, apart from what they have picked up from the media.

The aim of this article is to look beyond the ubiquitous media hype that surrounds profiling and critically examine the reality. Initially, the two main approaches to profiling will be examined in some detail, highlighting the differences and similarities of the approaches.

Author's Note: This article first appeared in *Homicide Studies,* Vol. 4 No. 3, August 2000, pp. 234-264. Copyright © 2000 Sage Publications, Inc. Used with permission.

Profiling is usually conducted on serial offenders, which will also be examined, along with some of the research findings and controversies surrounding serial offenders. The approaches to criminal profiling will then be examined in light of two criteria for a science: the need for a paradigm and the requirement of falsifiability. The empirical support and problems with each of the approaches will be discussed, as will the studies that have empirically examined profiling. It is concluded that the current approaches to profiling do not yet have any substantial empirical support, but that they do have the potential to be scientific if they are worked on.

WHAT IS CRIMINAL PROFILING?

Definitions

Criminal profiling is the process of using available information about a crime and crime scene to compose a psychological portrait of the unknown perpetrator of the crime.[1] The information that the criminal profiler uses is often taken from the scene of the crime and takes into account factors such as the state of the crime scene, what weapons (if any) were used in the crime, and what was done and said to the victim. Other information used in criminal profiling can include the geographic pattern of the crimes, how the offender got to and from the crime scene, and where the offender lives. The actual process of profiling differs from one profiler to another (depending on the training of the profiler), but the aim remains the same: to deduce enough about the behavioral, personality, and physical characteristics of the perpetrator to catch him.[2]

According to Holmes and Holmes (1996), psychological profiling has three major goals to provide the criminal justice system with the following information: a social and psychological assessment of the offender(s), a psychological evaluation of relevant possessions found with suspected offenders, and consultation with law enforcement officials on the strategies that should be used when interviewing offenders. Not all profiles involve all of these three aspects, with the role of the profiler usually being dictated largely by the needs of the law enforcement officials for whom he or she is consulting. Also, not all crimes are suitable for profiling. Holmes and Holmes state that profiling is only appropriate in cases in which the unknown offender shows signs of psychopathology or the crime is particularly violent or ritualistic. Rape and arson are also considered by Holmes and Holmes to be good candidates for profiling.

A profile will rarely by itself solve a crime or catch a criminal, but is designed to be an aid to the investigating police (Wilson & Soothill, 1996). The profile will rarely be so accurate as to suggest a certain individual as being responsible for the crime, but should point the police in the right direction and help reduce the possible number of subjects. When the police have no leads, a profile might suggest some potentially helpful area that the police might have overlooked. Despite what the movies might suggest, profilers do not go running around the countryside solving crimes for hapless local police or rescuing hostages from dangerous psychopaths.

It is important to note that criminal profiling is not just one technique and that there are several distinct approaches to profiling. Wilson, Lincon, and Kocsis (1997) list three main paradigms of offender profiling: diagnostic evaluation (DE), crime scene analysis (CSA), and investigative psychology (IP). Other approaches to profiling exist, such as geographic profiling (Holmes & Holmes, 1996), but these will not be discussed in this article. The two latter approaches, both of which have been adapted and modified somewhat by various practitioners depending on their needs, will be discussed in the current report. The first method, DE, is not so much a discipline as the adaptation of psychotherapeutic (largely Freudian psychoanalytic) theory to crime by individual practitioners. As the DE approach relies mainly on clinical judgment, and as it is approached by each practitioner in a different way, there is no one body of work that can be examined to determine whether it is scientific, and as such will not be discussed here (for a more in-depth description of one approach to DE, see Copson, Badcock, Boon, & Britton, 1997). The more widely known of the remaining two approaches, CSA, was developed by the Behavioral Science Unit (BSU) of the American Federal Bureau of Investigation (FBI). It is the FBI approach to profiling that has been popularized by films such as *Silence of the Lambs* and television shows such as *Profiler*. The other, less publicly well-known approach was developed by Professor David Canter, a British academic psychologist. Canter's theories are IP and owe more to environmental psychology than to traditional criminal investigation. Although these methods have similarities, they are different enough to warrant separate treatment.

CSA

As mentioned above, the FBI approach is the more popular approach to criminal profiling. Although it is true that many people will have heard of criminal profiling and will associate it with the FBI, until recently there has been very little publicly available information as to what it actually is and how it works. Within the past few years, however, those who developed profiling with the FBI have written several popular books. Former BSU agents Ressler (Ressler & Shachtman, 1992) and Douglas (Douglas & Olshaker, 1995, 1997) have written books with journalists describing their experiences as profilers. Yet despite these books, which are more biographical than anything else, there is little authoritative information on the actual mechanics of the FBI profiling process.

Holmes and Holmes (1996) provide what is probably the best description of the underlying rationale that the FBI uses to profile offenders. The CSA approach, which is primarily applicable to serial murderers, places offenders into two broad categories on the basis of their crime and the crime scene. The two types of offenders are the disorganized asocial offender and the organized nonsocial offender, although in recent times the FBI tends to refer to these as simply disorganized and organized offenders, respectively (e.g., Ressler, Burgess, & Douglas, 1988). Ressler states that the simplistic dichotomy was to enable police who had little or no knowledge of psychological jargon to understand what the BSU thought was a basic differentiation between two distinct groups of offenders (Ressler & Shachtman, 1992). Holmes and Holmes (1996) note that this categorization is particularly applicable to crimes such as rape, sexual assault, mutilation, and necrophilia.

The disorganized offender will usually be of low intelligence, often demonstrating some sort of severe psychiatric disturbance, and will have probably had contact with the mental health system. He will often be socially inept with few interpersonal relationships outside his immediate family, and will be sexually incompetent if he has any sexual experience at all. The crime scene of the disorganized offender will often show little or no premeditation, with whatever is at hand used for a weapon and usually left at the crime scene. The victim (selected more or less at random) will have been quickly overpowered and killed, with the killing often showing extreme overkill and brutality (what the FBI refer to as a "blitz attack"; see Douglas & Olshaker, 1995). The victim's face will often be severely beaten in an attempt to dehumanize her, or she will be forced to wear a mask or blindfold. If the victim is sexually assaulted, it will often be postmortem, with mutilation to the face, genitals, and breasts not uncommon. The body will often be left at the murder scene, but if it is removed, it is more likely that the offender wants to keep it as a souvenir than to hide evidence (Holmes & Holmes, 1996; Ressler, Burgess, & Douglas, 1988; Ressler & Shachtman, 1992).

The types of offenders who make up the organized and disorganized dichotomies are relatively straightforward and are, as the names suggest, organized and disorganized personalities. The organized offender is usually reasonably intelligent but an underachiever with a sporadic education and employment history. He is often married and socially adept, at least at face value, but usually has an antisocial or psychopathic personality. The crime scene left behind by an organized offender will show signs of planning and control. The offender will often bring his own weapons and restraints, which he will then take with him after the crime. The victim will be a targeted stranger, very often female, with the offender searching for either a particular sort of victim or merely a victim of convenience. The victim will often be raped, and the offender will control the victim by using threats and restraints. The offender will usually torture the victim, killing in a slow, painful manner, which the killer will have fantasized about extensively beforehand. The body will also usually be hidden, often transported from the place where the killing occurred, and may be dismembered by more forensically aware killers to delay identification.

From the analysis of the crime scene, the investigator should then be able to determine some characteristics of the perpetrator, which will be of use to the investigating police. According to Ressler et al. (1988), criminal profiling is a six-stage process. The first stage is referred to as Profiling Inputs, and concerns the collection of all of the information that might be pertinent to solving the crime.[3] This includes photos of the crime scene, the preliminary police report, information about the victim, and all of the collected forensic information. The second stage is the Decision Process Models, in which the information is organized and a preliminary analysis is conducted. In this stage, the homicide type and style are determined (e.g., whether it is a single, mass, spree, or serial murder). Several other important factors are determined in this stage, such as the intent of the offender (e.g., whether homicide was the primary objective or whether it was secondary to another crime); the risk status of the victim (a prostitute would be an example of a high-risk victim, whereas a married woman who lived in a middle-class area would probably be a fairly low-risk victim); and the risk the offender would have been putting himself in to commit the crime. The length of time that was taken to commit the offense is determined and information about the locations (such as where the offender was abducted and where the killing was actually performed) is also investigated.

The third stage of the profiling process, Crime Assessment, is presumably the inspiration for the title of Douglas's book, *Journey Into Darkness* (Douglas & Olshaker, 1997), as it is where the profiler attempts to reconstruct the crime in his or her head. This is where the profiler attempts to "walk in the shoes" of both the victim and the offender, or what the media like to refer to as "getting into the mind of the killer." It is at this stage that the crime is categorized as organized or disorganized, as the profiler tries to determine how things happened, how people behaved, and how the offender planned and executed the crime. Also considered is the offender's motivation for the crime, such as what the offender hoped to achieve with the crime. The selection of a victim is considered, as is whether the offender staged the scene (modified the crime scene to confuse police). Common elements of the crime scene that are thought to have significance for identifying certain types of offenders, such as types and locations of wounds and the positioning of the body, are also examined.

It is not until the fourth stage, the Criminal Profile, that the profiler ties all of the above information together and the profile is actually constructed. The profiler attempts to describe the person who committed the crime and proposes strategies that might be most effective in apprehending that particular offender. The profiler constructs the profile by examining all of the information pertinent to the crime in the light of his or her experiences with other, similar crimes. The finished profile will contain anywhere between a few para graphs and several pages of information about the unknown offender, depending on how much material about the crime was forwarded to the profiler. The following elements are commonly found in a profile: the age, race, gender, and general appearance of the offender; the offender's relationship status and any notable points about his relationship history; his likely occupation; and any notable features of his employment, education, or military re- cord. The profiler also includes whether the offender lived in or was familiar with the area, the behavior of the offender both before and after the crime, some basic features about the offender's personality (including whether he has an organized or disorganized personality), and significant belongings that the offender may own, such as pornography. It also contains suggested strategies for interrogating, identifying, and apprehending the victim.

The fifth stage, the Investigation, is where the profiler submits a written report to the agency investigating the crime, which is added to their investigative efforts. If a suspect is identified and a confession is obtained, then the profile is judged to have been successful. If any additional information becomes available (e.g., new evidence or another connected murder), the new information is given to the profilers so that the profile can be reevaluated in light of the new data. The sixth stage is the Apprehension, and assumes that the correct offender has been caught. The profile and the profiling process are evaluated in terms of the actual offender so that future profiles might be even more accurate.

IP

Unlike CSA, IP is more a collection of related theories and hypotheses than a compre- hensive methodology. As mentioned previously, IP originated in Britain, mainly due to the work of David Canter, an environmental psychologist who was then the head of the psy- chology department at the University of Surrey (Canter, 1989). Canter (1994) reports that he was first approached in 1985 by British police, who were interested in determining whether psychology had anything to offer police to help them apprehend criminals. Although he observes that police are often very resistant to anything new or to any outsiders telling them how they should do their jobs, Canter's advice proved very helpful to the police in catching John Duffy. Duffy, who was dubbed the "Railway Rapist" by the media, committed approximately 25 rapes and three murders in London between 1982 and 1986 (Nowikowski, 1995). Since that case, Canter has worked on over 60 murder and rape cases in the United Kingdom (Casey, 1993).

Canter (1989) claims that psychology is directly applicable to crime, as crime can be seen as an interpersonal transaction in which criminals are performing actions in a social context (often just between themselves and their victims). He argues that our methods of psychological interaction are ingrained into our personalities, and reasons that the actions the criminal performs while engaging in a crime are direct reflections of the way they will act in other, more normal, circumstances. He postulated five broad approaches with which psychology can be used to profile offenders.

The first is interpersonal coherence, which proposes that actions performed by criminals make sense within the criminals' own psychology. For instance, the offender will select victims that are consistent with the important characteristics of people who are important to the offender. For example, there is some anecdotal evidence that serial killers only attack those of the same ethnicity as themselves in the United States (Canter, 1989). Therefore, the psychologist should be able to determine something about the offender from the victim and the way the offender interacted with the victim (where this can be determined, such as with rape). The second approach is the significance of place and time. The locations the offender chooses in which to commit the offenses will usually have some sort of significance to the offender. People are unlikely to murder or rape in locations that are unfamiliar to them, as these are crimes of control, and the offender will not be able to feel completely in control in a strange environment. Therefore, if all of the crimes are committed in a certain geographic location, there is a high chance that the offender lives or works around the area. The third approach, criminal characteristics, involves looking at crimes and offenders and seeing if differences can lead to classifications of offenders into categories and subcategories. Canter does not actually provide an example of such a classification, but one attempt to do this has been the FBI's *Crime Classification Manual* (Douglas, Burgess, Burgess, & Ressler, 1992). Douglas and Olshaker (1995) state that "we set about to organize and classify serious crimes by their behavioral characteristics and explain them in a way that a strictly psychological approach such as *DSM* [*Diagnostic and Statistical Manual of Mental Disorders*] has never been able to do" (p. 346). Canter (1994), however, is quite critical of the FBI approach—especially the organized-disorganized dichotomy used by the FBI—arguing that there is too much overlap between the two categories for it to be helpful and that they have no theoretical backing. It will be interesting to see an attempt to derive a system like this by the proponents of IP and see what similarities to and differences from the CSA system they come up with.

The fourth approach, criminal career, seeks to take advantage of the observation that criminals do not change the way they commit crimes throughout their criminal career, although they may escalate the crimes. Even escalation, though, may be a result of what has happened to the offender while committing earlier crimes, and it may be possible to negatively extrapolate back to earlier crimes committed by the offender where more evidence might be available. The fifth and final approach is forensic awareness. When a serial offender takes steps to cover his tracks, such as forcing his rape victim to take a bath or combing her pubic hair to remove any of his own hair, it is a clear sign that he has had some previous contact with police. The particular type of forensic awareness displayed by the offender should be a direct indication of the offender's previous police contact, and should help narrow the range of offenders to those with records for particular prior offenses.

Although this has been a fairly brief overview of some of Canter's suggestions, one particular area, that of space and time, has received a reasonable amount of attention and has been empirically tested. Wilson et al. (1997) report that the "circle hypothesis" (as it is referred to in Canter, 1994) is one of the more prominent of the IP theories. This approach is built on the hypothesis that serial offenders will tend to operate within an area where they feel comfortable (e.g., close to their own homes) and has many similarities to the independently developed field of geographic profiling (Holmes & Holmes, 1996). In a recent paper, Godwin and Canter (1997) investigated the spatial behavior of 54 U.S. serial killers, each of whom had killed at least 10 times. They investigated the relationship of the offender's home to the locations at which he encountered and then dumped the bodies of his victims and the changes over time. Godwin and Canter found that the serial killers in the sample were likely to encounter and abduct nearly all of their victims close to their own homes. The offender would then travel some distance, usually in a different direction for each offense, to dump the body. They also found, however, as the number of offenses progressed, the offender was more likely to dump the bodies close to home, reflecting perhaps a growing confidence with his ability to remain undetected.

The study by Godwin and Canter (1997) clearly demonstrates that experimental psychology, and IP in particular, does have something to offer police investigating serial crimes. Although psychological profiling alone will not catch an offender, the aim is to supplement police investigative efforts and give the police additional information that might focus their investigation.

Serial Murderers

One of the concepts most frequently associated with criminal profiling is that of the serial offender. This is partly due to some of the conditions under which profiling is most useful, but more to do with the fact that whenever profiling is mentioned in the popular media, it is usually in the context of profiling a serial killer. As discussed later, serial offenders have had considerable input into the development of profiling, and any discussion of profiling would be amiss if it were not to discuss serial offenders.

In addition to making good newspaper headlines, serial killers are excellent candidates for criminal profiling. Unlike most offenders, serial killers often spend a great deal of time fantasizing about and executing their crime. The fact that they kill multiple times, generally mutilating their victims, and often demonstrate some sort of psychopathology means that there is frequently a lot of material for profilers to work with (Wilson et al., 1997). These killers generally have no obvious motive for the killing, are the hardest offenders to apprehend, and their crimes are the ones that profiles are most often sought for (Holmes & Holmes, 1996).

Although serial murder has recently captured public attention, it is by no means a new phenomenon. The most well-known serial killer, who has been extensively profiled in recent times, was probably Jack the Ripper, who killed at least five women in the Whitechapel area of London in 1888 (Jenkins, 1994). Yet the term *serial killer,* popularized by Ressler (Ressler & Shachtman, 1992), is a relatively recent one, and the definition is still the subject of some debate.[4] We might think of a serial murderer as an individual who commits a series of homicides over an extended period of time, with at least a few days in between at least some of the killings. This distinction of time between the killings is important to distinguish serial killing from mass murder, in which one person kills many people in a spree, such as the recent Port Arthur massacre in Tasmania.

One of the initial hurdles in defining serial murder is how many people need to be killed before an individual is classified as a serial murderer. This has important implications for research and for the development of profiling. Some believe that two murders are enough to justify the label of serial murder (Holmes & Holmes, 1996), whereas others would argue that up to four murders are necessary (Jenkins, 1994). Whatever cutoff point is chosen, the important question should be whether serial murder (and by extension, serial murderers) is qualitatively and quantitatively different from other murders. Is it simply the number of people that are killed that defines an offender as a serial killer, or is there some fundamental difference between serial killers and all other murderers?

The motive of the serial killer is a subject that is still open to some debate. As mentioned above, many serial killings appear to lack a clear motive, with the victims often not known to the offender and seemingly chosen at random. Ressler et al. (1988) suggest that almost all serial murders are sexual in nature, although their use of the term *sexual* in this case seems to be inspired by the Freudian notion of psychosexual development. A more current view of both serial murder and serial rape is that it is not about sexual gratification per se, but rather about the exercise of power and control over the victim (Canter, 1994; Egger, 1997). In fact, it seems that there is little difference between serial rape and serial murder, with Egger (1997) observing that it does not take much to turn a violent rape into a murder. Thus, the term *sexual* might be interpreted in the context of the killer's attempt to sexually control and dominate his victim.

It is important to know the extent of the problem that serial killers pose because they generally require a great deal of effort to apprehend. If serial killers are really a rare phenomenon, then it may not be worth focusing all these resources into profiling them. The problem is, it is not even known with any confidence how many serial killers there are or how many people are the victims of serial killers. In Australia, for example, it seems that serial murderers are reasonably rare, but then there are not that many murders in Australia of any sort. For example, in Australia from 1991-1992 there were 312 murders, with 309 identified suspects/offenders and 42 incidents for which an offender was not identified (Strang, 1993). This is relatively low when we consider that Washington, D.C., a single North American city, has over 500 reported homicides each year (Chappell, 1995). To confuse matters, when a serial killer is suspected, the associated murder attracts much more attention than any other. One of the more infamous of the Australian serial killers was John Wayne Glover, the "Granny Killer" who killed six elderly women in 1989 and 1990 in Sydney's North Shore district. According to Hagan (1992), these killings prompted one of the most extensive police investigations in Australia's history.

Serial murder usually involves the killing of a stranger and is therefore hidden somewhere in the crime statistics under the category of stranger homicide. The question is, What proportion of the stranger homicides can be attributed to serial murder? Egger (1990a) notes that it is very difficult to tell, but the FBI often tends to take the pessimistic view that most of the stranger homicides are due to serial killers (Ressler et al., 1988). The FBI is probably not a very impartial judge in these matters, because as Jenkins (1996) notes, they have a vested interest in making serial offending seem to be much worse than it is. A more reasonable explanation might be to use the suggestion of Polk (1994) that the majority of these stranger homicides are so-called "honor contests" in which fights between mainly young men, often over a trivial incident, lead to death. Kapardis (1992) also notes that there are at least five separate categories of stranger homicide, and that serial and mass murder only make up an extremely small proportion of stranger killings in Victoria, Australia.

PROFILING AND SCIENCE

What Is Meant by Scientific?

In this article, a relatively loose definition of science will be used, if for no other reason than to give profiling the benefit of the doubt. As profiling claims to be an application of behavioral science, the definition of science will be drawn from those that are often used in psychology, and will revolve around the theories of Thomas Kuhn and Karl Popper.

The Need for a Paradigm

Kuhn (1962), originally a historian of science, observed that in many sciences, the state of knowledge progressed in a standard way. Rather than a science accumulating knowledge cumulatively, with old knowledge building on the new, he believed that science progressed through leaps of knowledge, or scientific revolutions. When a discipline has only recently been formed, it is characterized by a number of seemingly irreconcilable theories that have no underlying basis. As the discipline progresses, a paradigm (a theoretical foundation on which the theory rests) is eventually formed. Once a paradigm is established, work in the discipline is mainly problem solving, or experimentation within the paradigm to make known phenomena fit within the bounds of the paradigm. Unfortunately, everything will not fit as nicely as people would like, so eventually some people will begin to recognize the inadequacies of their dominant paradigm and start to formulate the basis of a new one. Once the new paradigm has gained enough support (a sort of critical mass), the new paradigm will replace the old one completely (with the old one being abandoned) in a scientific revolution. Once the new paradigm is in place, the process will begin again.

What we are interested in here is not so much the scientific revolution, but rather the concept of the paradigm. Paradigm has become one of the most overused words in social science, and is used to describe everything from a particular experimental method to an individual's conception of the world. In this article, it will be used to describe the theoretical underpinnings of a discipline, as it is this theoretical underpinning that is upended when a discipline undergoes a paradigm shift. Without a paradigm, without some coherence tying together the work within a discipline, it is impossible to be a science.

The Importance of Falsifiability

The legacy of Popper is quite simple at face value, but the reasoning behind it is somewhat more sophisticated. As discussed at length in Chalmers (1976), Popper was concerned that in science, there was a tendency toward inductive reasoning. As an example, if we heat some water and observe that it boils at 100°C and then repeat the experiment 10, 100, or 1,000 times and each time water boils at the same temperature, we are likely to conclude that water will always boil at 100°C. That assumption, although usually safe, is logically flawed, and we can, in fact, never actually prove that water boils at 100°C. But although we can never actually prove anything by experimentation, we can disprove it quite easily. For example, if we hypothesize that water will always boil at 100°C and then heat water on top of a high mountain, when the water boils at a temperature somewhat lower than 100°C, we have successfully disproved the hypothesis.

Popper therefore believes that for us to have any faith in our science, we should not attempt to prove anything but should construct hypotheses and rigorously attempt to disprove them. If we are unable to disprove a hypothesis, we still cannot say we have proved it, but we are probably justified in placing some faith in the hypothesis for the time being. This approach to science is called hypothetico deductivism, and involves creating theories that are falsifiable and using experimentation to attempt to falsify them. Thus, to be scientific, a discipline must be able to propose hypotheses that are empirically testable.

The concept of falsifiability is also important because of its legal implications. If a profile is going to be used in a court of law, either by the prosecution trying to demonstrate they have the right offender, or by the defense claiming they have the wrong one, it would need to be submitted as expert evidence. While the precedents surrounding the submission of expert evidence vary from country to country and even from state to state, one of the more significant developments was a 1993 U.S. Supreme Court case, *Daubert v. Merrell Dow Pharmaceuticals, Inc.* In this case, the Court decided that a scientific theory could be said to be reliable under four conditions. The first and most important of these conditions was whether the theory could be tested, and to be able to be tested, it had to meet Popper's criterion of falsifiability (Odgers & Richardson, 1995).

IS PROFILING SCIENTIFIC?

CSA

CSA relies heavily on the experience and intuition of the profiler, both of which are difficult to empirically test. One of the main problems with a scientific analysis of CSA is that its proponents have never felt the need to have it scientifically verified. Yet as shall be seen, there are various aspects of this technique that may be amenable to investigation.

Presence of a Paradigm

The proponents of CSA maintain that there is something of a paradigm underlying their approach, even if they do not use that particular term. Although serial offenses are apparently motiveless, the assumption that CSA is based on is that there is always a motive underlying them. That motive will be reflected in the crime scene, and by understanding that motive, investigators will have a better understanding of the offender and a greater chance of solving the crime. As Ressler et al. (1988) state, "We theorize that these men are motivated to murder by their way of thinking. Over time their thinking patterns emerged from or were influenced by their life experiences" (p. 34).

The paradigm behind CSA postulates that if certain conditions are present in childhood, such as lack of good role models and childhood abuse, then the individual will turn to fantasy for stimulation and gratification. If the individual has access to pornography or violent fiction, these fantasies might start to include violence and control. The fantasies will eventually dominate the individual's life to such an extent that the individual will act them out. When the actual offense is not as perfect as the fantasy, the individual will continue to offend until it becomes perfect (which is unlikely to happen) or he is apprehended (Ressler et al., 1988).

A paradigm implies some sort of theory, and one of the most fundamental aspects of CSA, that of offenders being organized or disorganized, is completely atheoretical. At no point, as far as the author is aware, is any difference stated in the developmental precursors that lead to the different types of offenders, with the exception possibly of major psychiatric disturbance. Even if one accepts the more current view that there is a continuum between organized and disorganized offenders (Wilson et al., 1997), what is it that pushes an offender one way rather than the other? Similarly, what is it that will lead one mentally disordered person to be peaceful and harmless and another to be a killer?

Falsifiability

Freudian psychoanalysis is concerned with unconscious processes that are often not observable or testable, and has been long criticized because many of the assertions that it makes in this area cannot be falsified (Odgers & Richardson, 1995). Many of the claims of CSA sound much like those of psychoanalysis, with talk of fantasies and sexual motivations, and, like psychoanalysis, these claims do not seem to be falsifiable in most cases. Take, for example, the following statement: "Although some of the murderers in our study did not report fantasies in a conscious way, their description of the murders they committed reveal hidden fantasies of violence" (Ressler et al., 1988, p. 52). We may be left wondering when FBI agents became experts in interpreting the unconscious fantasies of others. If one claims that a violent murder is a sign of violent fantasies—even if the murderer does not report any violent fantasies—then how is one to falsify the hypothesis that all murderers have violent fantasies?

As it stands, the CSA approach is not a good candidate for falsifiability, primarily due to the nature of the ideas that it is based on. A further problem is that those involved have had little interest in their work being empirically substantiated. One of the problems is that of operationalizing the variables. As mentioned previously, Ressler et al. (1988) claim that many serial offenders have had troubled childhoods and have had an abnormally strong interest in pornography. Although it would be possible to create a falsifiable hypothesis that all serial offenders had a difficult childhood and were interested in pornography, this would be of little use unless you were also able to state the levels at which these things became important to their development as serial offenders. It would also be helpful to have some sort of theoretical reason that these variables would lead to the outcome of serial offending.

Problems

CSA does have the potential to be scientific (with some work), but the main problem seems to be that it does not want to be scientific. Douglas, the FBI agent who was responsible for hiring profilers for the BSU, states that in a profiler, "degrees and academic knowledge [are not] nearly as important as experience and certain subjective qualities" (Douglas & Olshaker, 1997, p. 30). Jenkins (1996) states that criminal profiling is the FBI's special area of expertise, something that they believe that they do better than anyone else in the world. In essence, in the United States at least, the FBI has a monopoly on criminal profiling, and it does not look like they are about to endanger that by telling anyone else how it works—or even if it works.

Although there might be some validity to the argument that revealing too much about how profiling is done might reveal to offenders ways in which they can avoid being apprehended (assuming, of course, that serial offenders read psychology or criminology journals), the dangers of not having the techniques open to investigation are even more serious. Canter (1994) states quite succinctly that "a doctor is not expected to operate on hunch and intuition, to learn his trade merely from hearing how others have treated patients in the past, to have no firmly established principles to operate on" (p. 275). Although the experience of police officers is certainly valuable and should not be overlooked, if we have no way of measuring the effectiveness of this approach, we may be missing something important.

IP

Unlike CSA, IP was designed from the beginning with science in mind, but this does not mean that it is a science in itself. Canter and his colleagues have attempted to use established psychological principles and research methodology to create a discipline that is empirically sound and open to peer review. IP has a great deal of potential to become a science, but it still has a long way to go before it will be recognized as a discipline in itself.

Presence of a Paradigm

There is something of an underlying theme present in IP, but it is not nearly coherent enough to be called a paradigm. The theme is that of a narrative or a story that people create for themselves and that contains information on how they understand and interact with the world. Once an offender (like any other person) has formed this narrative, it will be reflected in everything that he does, including any offenses that he commits. From this comes the assumption that we can learn something about an offender by looking at his crimes and how he commits them. This may give us information about the geographical areas that the offender frequents, about how the offender interacts with other people in his day-to-day life, and about the sort of offenses that the offender might have been convicted of in the past. An example of a hypothesis derived from this paradigm is that offenders will operate in an area in which they are most familiar, as an offender's mental map of a geographical area is part of his narrative. This hypothesis has been tested and supported by both Canter (e.g., Godwin & Canter, 1997) and others outside IP (Holmes & Holmes, 1996), thus lending support to the paradigm.

Falsifiability

The benefit of working within an established science such as psychology or criminology is that there are accepted ways in which to perform research. Furthermore, research that is performed is usually published and submitted to peer review to get input from the widest possible audience. As such, most of the theories that have been formulated as part of IP are constructed in such a way that they can be easily falsified. Canter (1989) made a specific point of stating that all of the main claims that are made by IP "lead themselves to specific hypotheses that can be tested against empirical data before being used within an investigation" (p. 16).

The underlying paradigm of the criminal narratives, as opposed to some of the hypotheses that it has inspired, is actually quite difficult to falsify. Admittedly, a paradigm itself does not need to be falsified, only to generate hypotheses that can be falsified. For example, one of the hypotheses that the paradigm has generated is that the experience of the criminal will be reflected in his crime. To test this hypothesis, one could look at the activities of offenders who had previously been apprehended and incarcerated and the activities of those who had not. If the offenders who had not been apprehended previously showed the same level of forensic awareness as the offenders who had, then that particular aspect of the hypothesis will have effectively been falsified.

Problems

Wilson et al. (1997) claim that one of the main problems with the IP approach to profiling is that it does not actually tell us anything new, except to propose new avenues to explore. This is probably a somewhat extreme view, as applying the application of psychological knowledge to criminal investigation potentially has great value. Canter has shown that the application of psychological principles and methodologies can, for example, help identify where the offender might live and what his job might be (e.g., Godwin & Canter, 1997). It is very easy for those in academia to remain aloof and remote from the real world, yet this is an attempt to make some practical use of psychology by applying it to genuine social problems.

Even within Great Britain, Canter is not without his critics. Copson et al. (1997) state that "it seems to have been assumed by some observers that Canter's is the only systematic approach to profiling in use in Britain, not least because he says so" (p. 13).[5] Copson and his colleagues, proponents of the DE model of profiling, claim that statistical approaches to profiling (such as those used in IP) are only reliable so long as the data set that they are based on is reliable. As has been mentioned previously, it is extremely difficult to determine even how many serial killers there are, let alone get reliable statistics on their activities and characteristics. They argue that until a more reliable database is built up, the clinical judgment of practitioners is a more reliable way to construct a criminal profile. Although it is true that there is a lack of reliable data on serial offenders, criminologists have spent years collecting data on "normal" (i.e., nonserial) rapes and murders, which may be able to contribute to profiling. What is not known, however, is how applicable these data are to serial offenders.

STUDIES CONDUCTED ON PROFILING

CSA

If profiling is to be thought of as a science and a science is defined by the studies that examine its theories, then the defining study for the FBI approach would be that published under the title of *Sexual Homicide: Patterns and Motives* (Ressler et al., 1988). This study is basically the foundation on which the scientific basis of the FBI approach to profiling rests. The fact that there have been so few published studies on the FBI approach means that the scientific credibility of the FBI approach rests solely on this study.

The study, which attempts to determine the antecedents of serial murder, presents both qualitative and quantitative data. In the sample examined, the researchers find a large amount of support for their hypothesis that the serial offender is the result of a developmental process, with most of the subjects reporting that they had troubled childhoods. For example, 69% of the respondents reported a history of alcohol abuse in their families while growing up, and 74% reported that they were psychologically abused (Ressler et al., 1988). The authors also provide quotes from the offenders that seem to support their hypothesis that most serial homicides are sexual in nature. Unfortunately, this study does have some fundamental flaws, which call into question the legitimacy of the approach.

One of the first things that any social science researcher learns is the danger of using retrospective self-report studies. These studies ask subjects to look back at their life and comment on what they remember they did or what they were like at a certain point. This research methodology is open to considerable abuse and can be very inaccurate. For example, using the present topic, if you are talking to a person who was a neighbor of a serial killer when he was young, then the subject will be quite likely to selectively recall information that they think will be of interest to the researcher. There is also a very real danger of subjects' lying (e.g., to impress the researcher) and there is often no way to verify the veracity of the data.

The study conducted by Ressler et al. (1988) consisted mainly of interviews with 36 convicted serial killers who were in prison. Most, if not all, serial killers would be classified under *DSM-IV* (American Psychiatric Association, 1994) as suffering from antisocial personality disorder (Egger, 1997). In the mass media, this usually translates into their being referred to as psychopaths or sociopaths. According to Davison and Neale (1994),

> The adult antisocial personality shows irresponsible and antisocial behaviour by not working consistently, breaking laws, being irritable and physically aggressive, defaulting on debts and being reckless. He or she is impulsive and fails to plan ahead. In addition, he or she shows *no regard for truth* [italics added] nor remorse for misdeeds. (p. 271)

Surely the psychopathic serial killer is the least suitable person on whom to conduct retrospective self-report research. Furthermore, the study included only convicted and imprisoned serial offenders who were willing to participate in the study, which most criminologists would consider to be an unacceptably biased sampling procedure (Wilson et al., 1997). For example, there may be some fundamental difference between those serial offenders who get caught and those who are able to evade capture. Thus, the profiling based on the imprisoned serial offender may not be appropriate for catching all serial offenders.

One of the most important factors of the CSA model of criminal profiling is the dichotomous categorization of offenders as organized or disorganized offenders, but how useful is this distinction? Holmes and Holmes (1996), for example, state that these categories are more useful in "lust killings" than in other sorts of serial murder that do not show evidence of sexual motives. Although the concepts of the organized and disorganized offenders are discussed at length in Ressler et al. (1988), they do not attempt to use the data from the offenders in their sample to support or explain this typology. Ressler and Shachtman (1992) hypothesize that about one third of all serial killers are disorganized offenders and the remaining two thirds are organized offenders, but offer no data to support the claims. Wilson et al. (1997) claim that it is actually more of a continuum between organized and disorganized than two distinct types, with many offenders falling into the mixed category that displays features of both the organized and disorganized offenders.

The real truth is that we simply do not know. As far as the author knows, there have never been any published empirical studies on the differences between various subtypes of serial offenders. The organized/disorganized typology is the brainchild of the BSU, and although they have published information about it, they have never actually articulated any theoretical basis for the typology on which a study might be based.

Ressler et al. (1988) provide an excellent example of how politics and ideology may influence one's objectivity. The FBI, as North America's premier law enforcement organization, is a bastion of White, middle-class, conservative views, a fact admitted by many of the agents themselves (e.g., Douglas & Olshaker, 1995; Ressler & Shachtman, 1992). Is it then surprising that the FBI experts believe that serial killers often come from broken homes (where they are often raised by a single mother) and report daydreaming, masturbation, confusion about sexual preference, and an interest in pornography as features of their childhood?

It is also important to remember that the only thing that has been determined so far is a correlation between factors such as abuse or neglect in childhood and serial killers. This does not imply that serial offending is causally related to an individual's having a difficult childhood or an obsession with pornography. Egger (1997) describes one serial killer, Arthur Shawcross, who did not show any evidence of coming from a dysfunctional or violent family. Rather than the antecedents of Shawcross's offending being environmental, as CSA might argue, they appeared more to be biological, with Shawcross being involved in a number of serious accidents, some of which involved cerebral concussion. Examples such as this tend to cast doubt on the validity of the CSA paradigm of the development of serial offending.

IP

The most obvious of the studies conducted on IP, in which Godwin and Canter (1997) investigated the spatial patterns of serial murderers in the United States, has been described in some detail previously. Professor Canter and many of his colleagues have a history in experimental psychology, and several other studies have been published in the psychological and criminological literature. As yet, there has not been a great deal of experimental work on the core features of IP, that of the narrative of the offender and how it is reflected in the crimes. Some of the other research that the IP department at the University of Liverpool is working on includes the decision-making process of detectives, psychological autopsies (investigating the course of actions that leads to an assault), and investigative interviewing ("What Is Investigative Psychology?" 1997).

Although the overall paradigm itself has not been experimentally tested, some of the theories that contribute to IP have. In one example, Canter and Kirby (1995) look at the conviction history of child molesters. This study investigated the validity of the common assumption that child molesters will have a history of sexually deviant behavior and assaults on children, and that these men will escalate their offending from minor to more serious sexual offenses. Interestingly, they found that these assumptions, which are often held by police officers, had no empirical basis. They found that these offenders were more likely to have had a history of convictions for theft, burglary, and violent offenses than for prior minor sexual offenses. They also found that there was little evidence to suggest escalation from less serious offenses. For example, very few of the men who were child molesters had any history of indecent exposure.

The Canter and Kirby (1995) study has very obvious implications for profiling sexual offenders, as it suggests strategies for narrowing the range of potential suspects by suggesting the offenses that the offender is more likely to have been convicted of in his past. A less obvious implication of this study is for CSA, where the assumptions and preconceptions that the profilers have about certain offenders greatly influence the profile. This study suggests that in the case of child molesters, these assumptions are likely to lead the profile astray.

An interesting point to note about the Canter and Kirby (1995) study is that it does not seem to fit within the paradigm of the criminal narrative. This could be taken as evidence that IP is not scientific, as the paradigm is not broad or thorough enough to cover all of the work in the area. Another way to look at it, however, is as providing a less direct support for the paradigm. Canter (1994) does not just believe that criminals have narratives but that all people do, and that these narratives are developed by the individual's experiences of interacting with the world. Canter (1994) notes that police officers also tend to have rather limited narratives, with their explanations of how criminals operate formed mainly from their experience of police work and by what they observe in the courts. What Canter and Kirby (1995) have demonstrated is that, at least in regard to sex offenders, the narratives that the police have to explain the behavior of sex offenders may be too limited and are, in some cases, misleading. Although this does not directly support the idea of criminal narratives, it does provide some support for the narrative per se, and thus does fit within the paradigm of IP.

Other Related Studies

The studies mentioned so far are those that apply specifically to either CSA or IP. As mentioned earlier, another form of profiling that is used is known as DE. DE derives mainly from the clinical experience of the profiler, who is usually primarily a psychologist or a psychiatrist. The DE profile is usually a one-off event and as such does not lend itself to empirical testing. Some profilers do not owe allegiance to any of these camps exclusively, and pick and choose aspects of each that suit them best. Various researchers have also empirically investigated these more eclectic approaches.

Wilson and Soothill (1996) review three cases in which various approaches to profiling had been used to help police. They state that of the three cases examined, the profiles were generally fairly accurate, although in the first two they were not actually used by the police to assist in the investigation. In the third case, the "Granny Killings" mentioned earlier, the profile was quite accurate except for one crucial characteristic—the killer was actually 40 years older than the profile said he would be.

In probably the most comprehensive experimental study on profiling conducted to date, Pinizzotto and Finkel (1990) examined profiles conducted by professional profilers, detectives, psychologists, and students for a series of cases. The study was looking at whether the accuracy of the profiles differed between the groups and whether there was a qualitative difference between the profilers and the nonprofilers in the process in which the profile was constructed. The accuracy of the profilers varied depending on the case, with the profilers more accurate than all of the other groups combined in the sex offender case, but these same profilers were not especially accurate for the homicide. With regard to the sex offender case, the profilers were significantly more accurate for items such as the gender, age, and education of the offender. In the homicide case, however, the detectives were significantly more accurate than the profilers in regard to the offender's employment and the relationship of the offender's residence to the crime scene. It was also found that the profilers wrote richer, more detailed reports than the nonprofilers, and that the profilers recalled more details that were necessary to generate the profile. There are, of course, some problems with the study. The psychologists and students used, for instance, had no special interest in policing or profiling, so it would be expected that those who have to construct profiles for a living were both better prepared and more invested in the process, and thus tried harder than the nonprofilers (Pinizzotto & Finkel, 1990).

Does It Actually Work?

In asking profiling to be scientific, we are trying to establish with some reliability whether profiling is of any use to us. Many police officers have shown a great deal of skepticism about profiling, partly due to the fact that they see apprehending offenders as their particular area of expertise, but also because it is still such a poorly developed field (e.g., Davies, 1994). As has been discussed above, the experimental evidence is still not overwhelming, but studies such as those conducted by Pinizzotto and Finkel (1990) suggest that profiling might have some validity. Experimental verification is not what will win the police over, however. Police still persist in using psychics to help them solve difficult cases, although Wiseman and West (1997) have shown experimentally that there is absolutely no validity to the claims made by psychics in regard to criminal investigations.

The real test of profiling is not experimental studies in the laboratory, but evaluations on how well profiling actually performs in practice. Wilson et al. (1997) suggest, somewhat naively, that after looking at the track record of profiling so far, the suggestion is that it works. They base this claim on a case study of selected high-profile crimes, but do not give any references or source for the data. The main problem with this claim is that it is purely anecdotal. Related to that is the problem of reporting bias, as we are only likely to hear about cases in which profiling has been used if the case was successfully resolved and the profile was accurate.

Organizations such as the FBI are, understandably, reluctant to release figures on the successes and failures of the profiles that they provide. Although figures such as an 80% success rate have been circulated (e.g., Ressler & Shachtman, 1992), there has yet to be any data put forward to substantiate this claim. According to Ressler et al. (1988), the accuracy of each profile is looked at after an offender has been apprehended so that the profilers may learn from their errors. The evaluation is not performed in public, and most people have no knowledge of how accurate profiles actually are. This is becoming increasingly important, as more private individuals are commissioning profiles themselves (or requesting that the investigating police do) for cases in which they have an interest. We would not tolerate other participants in criminal investigations (such as forensic DNA analysts) withholding data on the effectiveness of their techniques, so why do we tolerate it with psychological profiling?

There is also the question as to how accurate a profile actually has to be to be of help to the investigating authorities. Obviously, an incorrect profile has the potential to mislead the investigation, but this may only be a problem if the police place a greater amount of faith in the profile than they do in their own investigative skills. Pinizzotto (cited in Wilson et al., 1997), for example, found that from 192 requests for profiles, only 17% actually were used to help identify the suspect. More positively, 77% of the respondents reported that the profile had helped them to focus their investigation. Overall, however, if profiles are consistently found to be incorrect in at least some aspects, police will quickly lose faith in their worth.

CONCLUSIONS

Offender profiling, in all its various guises, is still very much a discipline that is yet to be proved. Unlike much of psychology or criminology, the accuracy of an offender profile may have profound implications. If a profile of an offender is wrong or even slightly inadequate, police may be misled, allowing the offender to escape detection for a little while longer—and innocent people may be dead as a result. This is not to say that we should ignore profiles or that police should not use them, but that we should approach profiling with caution. We should not blindly accept or rely on something that may not have any relationship to the truth.

This article has demonstrated that, of the two main approaches to offender profiling, IP is easily more scientific than CSA. Whereas IP has produced testable hypotheses and has several empirical studies to back up its claims, CSA is based mainly on experience and intuition of police officers and is not particularly amenable to testing. We cannot say which approach is more successful (defining successful as providing information that results in more arrests) as there is no reliable published information on the effectiveness of the various approaches. There is a great deal of anecdotal evidence supporting CSA, and it is more widely depicted in the press than IP; yet this is not enough to indicate that it is significantly more successful than IP. Clearly, the effectiveness of the approaches is a subject in which more investigation is needed.

Building a solid scientific basis on which profiling can stand and empirically testing profiling in the lab and the field should not be too difficult. The scientific basis for IP is already present, and rethinking CSA so that it can produce testable hypotheses should not be impossible. However, as long as the FBI has a monopoly on profiling (which it does in most western nations except Britain) and they decline to share any information, it will be very difficult to prove that it is worthwhile. Yet as psychologists and criminologists, we are more qualified than police officers to put profiling to the test, and maybe if there is to be a change, it must begin with us.

If there is to be any hope to create a science out of profiling, the first step is to establish greater cooperation between those organizations that have an interest in it. The history of profiling seems to be littered with mistrust and contradictions between some of the key players, as has been alluded to several times in this article. The most readily available information sources about profiling are probably the books by Douglas (Douglas & Olshaker, 1995, 1997) and Ressler (Ressler & Shachtman, 1992), both of whom were integral to the development of the CSA approach to profiling in North America. Yet it is amazing how often these two authors, who worked together in the FBI, blatantly contradict each other. These contradictions tend to be not about fundamental issues but more about self-glorification. For example, Ressler (Ressler & Shachtman, 1992) states that although the agents of the BSU assisted in making the film *Silence of the Lambs* by letting the director observe them working for some time, none of the characters was actually based on particular people. Both the killers and the agents were based on amalgams of case files and active or retired agents. Yet Douglas (Douglas & Olshaker, 1997) quite distinctly states that one of the characters in the film, an FBI agent, was directly inspired by him. Although this might seem inconsequential to the validity of profiling, it may serve to call into question the professionalism of profilers and profiling in general. Rather than trying to sell books, make money, and acquire fame, the parties involved should be more concerned with improving profiling and demonstrating that it works.

Egger (1997) provides examples of serial killings in many countries around the world, all of which could possibly benefit from the input of profiling. By having profiling data and theories readily available and open to peer review, police forces that do not have the resources or knowledge to develop profiling techniques of their own will have access to information that may help them. Furthermore, an open approach to profiling will allow professionals and academics with a wide range of expertise and knowledge to contribute to the development of profiling.

The public and the media have long had a fascination with crime and all things related to it, which extends at least as far back as Arthur Conan Doyle's famous 19th-century detective, Sherlock Holmes. It is not uncommon to see an entire section in a book shop devoted to the category "True Crime," with dozens of books telling the stories of significant crimes from both Australia and overseas. It is beyond the scope of this article to hypothesize why people have such an interest in hearing about the actions of the most depraved section of society, yet it is clear that this infatuation is not about to suddenly die away. When considering a subject such as criminal profiling, it is easy to get lost in the hype and difficult to distinguish the fact from the fiction.

Frank Black, the main character in the television show *Millennium*, has psychic visions of the murder being committed when he visits a crime scene. If profiling worked like that in real life, it would probably simplify matters, with the ability to profile being just a special talent that some people had. Unfortunately, it does not work like that in real life. The reality of profiling is that without some solid theoretical and empirical basis on which to build a profile of an offender, we may as well just base it on psychic visions. If we are to help the most people and realize the potential of profiling, then we must accept that profiling requires much more work and an open approach.

NOTES

1. In this article, the terms *criminal profiling, offender profiling,* and *psychological profiling* will be used somewhat interchangeably. Within law enforcement circles, an unknown offender is referred to as the UNSUB, for "unknown subject" (Douglas & Olshaker, 1995).

2. In this article, it will be assumed that the perpetrator is male. Almost all identified serial killers have been male, and all of the research on serial killers has focused exclusively on male killers. Although female serial killers may exist (Hale & Bolin, 1998), they will not be considered in the present article.

3. The Behavioral Science Unit (BSU) profilers do not generally visit a crime scene. All of the information is usually sent to the Federal Bureau of Investigation (FBI) center in Quantico, Virginia, where the profile is constructed (Douglas & Olshaker, 1995).

4. Egger (1997) states that although Ressler claims that he coined the phrase, several others disagree with him. This is a prime example of how ego tends to confuse the issues in profiling.

5. Paul Britton and David Canter seem to have something of a running feud going on between them. It is therefore difficult to state how objective their assessments of each other are (e.g., see Wilson & Soothill, 1996).

References

Abbey, A. (1991). Acquaintance rape and alcohol consumption on college campuses: How are they linked? *Journal of American College Health, 39,* 165-169.

Abel, G. G. (1995). *The Abel Questionnaire for Boys.* (Available from Abel Screening, 1280 Peachtree Street NW, Suite 100, Atlanta, GA 30309)

Abel, G. G., Becker, J. V., Mittelman, M. S., Cunningham-Rathner, J., Rouleau, J. L., & Murphy, W. D. (1987). Self-reported sex crimes of nonincarcerated paraphiliacs. *Journal of Interpersonal Violence, 2,* 3-25.

Abel, G. G., Mittelman, M. S., & Becker, J. V. (1985). Sexual offenders: Results of assessment and recommendations for treatment. In H. Ben-Aron, S. I. Hucker, & C. D. Webster (Eds.), *Clinical criminology* (pp. 191-205). Toronto, Canada: M. M. Graphics.

Abel, G. G., & Osborn, C. (1992). The paraphilias: The extent and nature of sexually deviant and criminal behavior. *Clinical Forensic Psychiatry, 15,* 675-687.

Abel, G. G., & Osborn, C. (in press). The paraphilias. In M. G. Gelder, J. J. Lopez-Ibor, Jr., & N. C. Andreasen (Eds.), *New Oxford textbook of psychiatry.* New York: Oxford University Press.

Adams, M. (1998). *Hustlers, escorts and porn stars: The insider's guide to male prostitution in America.* Las Vegas, NV: Insider's Guide.

Adler, P. (1985). *Wheeling and dealing: An ethnography of an upper level drug dealing and smuggling community.* New York: Columbia University Press.

Ahrens, C. E., & Campbell, R. (2001). The effects of assisting victim recovery from rape. *Journal of Interpersonal Violence, 15,* 959-986.

Ahrens, C. E., Campbell, R., Wasco, S. M., Aponte, G., Grubstein, L., & Davidson, W. S. (2001). Sexual Assault Nurse Examiner programs: An alternative approach to medical service delivery for rape victims. *Journal of Interpersonal Violence, 15,* 921-943.

AIMS Media. (1995). *The correctional officer: Recognizing and preventing closed-custody male sexual assaults* (No. 8856). Chatsworth, CA: Author.

Alarid, L. F. (1996). *Women offenders' perceptions of confinement: Behavior code acceptance, hustling, and group relations in jail and prison.* Unpublished doctoral dissertation, Sam Houston State University, Huntsville, TX.

Alarid, L. F. (1999, November). *Understanding women prison subcultures using the case study approach.* Paper presented at the annual conference of the American Society of Criminology, Toronto, Canada.

Alarid, L. F. (2000). Sexual orientation perspectives of incarcerated bisexual and gay men: The county jail protective custody experience. *The Prison Journal, 80*(1), 80-95.

Alexander, P. (1988). Prostitution: A difficult issue for feminists. In F. Delacoste & P. Alexander (Eds.), *Sex work: Writings by women in the sex industry* (pp. 184-214). London: Virago.

Allen, M. (1998, August 28). Killing shows Connecticut the limits of its "Megan's Law." *New York Times*, p. A19.

Allgeier, E. R., & Lamping, J. C. (1998). Theories, politics, and sexual coercion. In P. B. Anderson & C. Struckman-Johnson (Eds.), *Sexually aggressive women* (pp. 49-75). New York: Guilford.

American Association of University Women. (1993). *Hostile hallways: The AAUW survey on sexual harassment in America's schools.* Washington, DC: Author.

American Medical Association. (1995). *Sexual assault in America.* Retrieved from http://www.ama-assn.org/public/releases/assault/action.html

American Psychiatric Association. (1980). *Diagnostic and statistical manual of mental disorders* (3rd ed.). Washington, DC: Author.

American Psychiatric Association. (1987). *Diagnostic and statistical manual of mental disorders* (3rd ed., rev.). Washington, DC: Author.

American Psychiatric Association. (1994). *Diagnostic and statistical manual of mental disorders* (4th ed.). Washington, DC: Author.

Amnesty International. (1999). *Not part of my sentence: Violations of the human rights of women in custody.* New York: Author. Retrieved from http://www.amnesty-usa.org/rightsforall/women/index.html

Anderson, P. B. (1998). Women's motives for sexual initiation and aggression. In P. B. Anderson & C. Struckman-Johnson (Eds.), *Sexually aggressive women* (pp. 79-93). New York: Guilford.

Andrews, D. A., & Bonta, J. (1998). *The psychology of criminal conduct* (2nd ed.). Cincinnati, OH: Anderson.

APBnews.com. (1999, October 10). Sex with guards rampant at women's prison. Retrieved January 30, 2000, from the World Wide Web: http://www.apbnews.com/cjsystem/behind_bars/1999/10/10/guards

Archer, J. (1984). Gender roles as developmental pathways. *British Journal of Social Psychology, 23*, 245-256.

Arnone, K. (2000, Spring). Megan's Law and habeas corpus review: Lifetime duty with no possibility of relief? *Arizona Law Review, 42*, 157.

Atchison, C., Fraser, L., & Lowman, J. (1998). Men who buy sex: Preliminary findings of an exploratory study. In J. E. Elias, V. L. Bullough, V. Elias, & G. Brewer (Eds.), *Prostitution: On whores, hustlers, and johns* (pp. 172-203). Amherst, NY: Prometheus.

Atkeson, B. M., Calhoun, K. S., & Morris, K. T. (1989). Victim resistance to rape: The relationship of previous victimization, demographics, and situational factors. *Archives of Sexual Behavior, 18*, 497-507.

Austin, R. (1992). The Black community, its lawbreakers, and a politics of identification. *Southern California Law Review, 65*, 1769-1817.

Awad, G. A., & Saunders, E. B. (1991). Male adolescent sexual assaulters. *Journal of Interpersonal Violence, 6*, 446-460.

Bachman, R. (1994). *Violence against women: A national crime victimization survey report* (No. NCJ-145325). Washington, DC: Bureau of Justice Statistics.

Bachman, R., & Saltzman, L. (1995). *Violence against women: Estimates from the redesigned survey* (No. NCJ-154348). Washington, DC: Bureau of Justice Statistics.

Bachman, R., & Taylor, B. M. (1994). The measurement of family violence and rape by the redesigned National Crime Victimization Survey. *Justice Quarterly, 11,* 499-512.

Badgett, M. V. L. (1995). The wage effects of sexual orientation discrimination. *Industrial and Labor Relations Review, 48,* 726-739.

Baker, T., Skolnik, L., Davis, R., & Brickman, E. (1988). The social support of survivors of rape: The differences between rape survivors and survivors of other violent crimes and between husbands, boyfriends, and women friends. In A. Burgess (Ed.), *Rape and sexual assault II* (pp. 105-123). New York: Garland.

Bandura, A. (1977). *Social learning theory.* Englewood Cliffs, NJ: Prentice Hall.

Barbaree, H., Seto, M., Serin, R., Amos, N., & Preston, D. (1994). Comparisons between sexual and non-sexual rapist subtypes. *Criminal Justice and Behavior, 21,* 95-114.

Barker, A. F. (1994). *Arson: A review of the psychiatric literature.* New York: Oxford University Press.

Barnard, M. (1993). Violence and vulnerability: Conditions of work for streetworking prostitutes. *Sociology of Health and Illness, 15,* 683-705.

Barnett, W., & Spitzer, M. (1994). Pathological firesetting 1951-1991: A review. *Medicine, Science, and the Law, 34,* 4-20.

Baro, A. L. (1997). Spheres of consent: An analysis of the sexual abuse and sexual exploitation of women incarcerated in the state of Hawaii. *Women and Criminal Justice, 8*(3), 61-84.

Barry, K. (1979). *Female sexual slavery.* New York: New York University Press.

Barry, K. (1995). *The prostitution of sexuality.* New York: New York University Press.

Barthalow, B. N., Doll, L. S., Joy, D., Douglas, J. M., Bolan, C., Harrison, J. S., Moss, P. M., & McKiman, D. (1994). Emotional, behavioral, and HIV risks associated with sexual abuse among homosexual and bisexual men. *Child Abuse & Neglect, 18,* 753-767.

Bartol, C. R. (1995). *Criminal behavior: A psychosocial approach.* Englewood Cliffs, NJ: Prentice Hall.

Beatty, D. (1997). Community notification—It's the right thing to do. *Corrections Today, 59,* 20.

Beck, A. J. (2000). *Prison and jail inmates at midyear 1999* (Bureau of Justice Statistics Bulletin, NCJ 181643). Washington, DC: U.S. Department of Justice.

Beck, A. J., & Mumola, C. J. (1999). *Prisoners in 1998* (Bureau of Justice Statistics Bulletin NCJ 175687). Washington, DC: U.S. Department of Justice.

Becker, J. V., Cunningham-Rathner, J., & Kaplan, M. S. (1986). Adolescent sexual offenders: Demographics, criminal and sexual histories, and recommendations for reducing future offenses. *Journal of Interpersonal Violence, 1,* 431-445.

Becker, J. V., Harris, C. D., & Sales, B. D. (1993). Juveniles who commit sexual offenses: A critical review of research. In G. C. Nagayama Haall, R. Hirschman, J. R. Graham, & M. S. Zaragoza (Eds.), *Sexual aggression: Issues in etiology, assessment, and treatment* (pp. 215-228). Washington, DC: Taylor & Francis.

Bell, A. P., & Weinberg, M. S. (1978). *Homosexualities: A study of diversity among men and women.* New York: Simon & Schuster.

Bell, L. (Ed.). (1987). *Good girls/bad girls: Feminists and sex trade workers face to face.* Seattle, WA: Seal Press.

Bennett, W. W., & Hess, K. M. (1984). *Investigating arson.* Springfield, IL: Charles C Thomas.

Berger, R. J., Searles, P., & Neuman, W. L. (1988). The dimensions of rape reform legislation. *Law and Society Review, 22,* 329-357.

Berk, R. A., Berk, S. F., Loseke, D. R., & Rauma, D. (1983). Mutual combat and other family violence myths. In D. Finkelhor, R. J. Gelles, G. T. Hotaling, & M. A. Straus (Eds.), *The dark side of families* (pp. 197-212). Beverly Hills, CA: Sage.

Berkman, T. (1996). Responses to the international child sex trade. *Boston College International and Comparative Law Review, 19,* 397-416.

Berrill, K. T. (1990). Anti-gay violence and victimization in the United States: An overview. *Journal of Interpersonal Violence, 5,* 274-294.

Bevacqua, M. (2000). *Rape on the public agenda: Feminism and the politics of sexual assault.* Boston: Northeastern University Press.

Binder, R. L. (1981). Why women don't report sexual assault. *Journal of Clinical Psychiatry, 42,* 437-438.

Bindman, J. (1998). An international perspective on slavery in the sex industry. In K. Kempadoo & J. Doezema (Eds.), *Global sex workers: Rights, resistance, and redefinition* (pp. 65-68). New York: Routledge.

Black, D. (1983). Crime as social control. *American Sociological Review, 48,* 34-45.

The Black Coalition Fighting Back Serial Murders. (n.d.). *Counting women's lives: Organizing for police accountability in black communities.* Los Angeles: Author.

Blake, D. D. (1994). Rationale and development of the Clinician-Administered PTSD Scales. *PTSD Research Quarterly, 5*(2), 1-2.

Blake, D. D., Weathers, F. W., Nagy, L. M., Kaloupek, D. G., Charney, D. S., & Keane, T. M. (1996). *The Clinician-Administered PTSD Scale for DSM-IV: One Week Symptom Status Version (CAPS-SX).* Unpublished scale. (Available from second author at the National Center for PTSD, Boston, MA)

Blake, D. D., Weathers, F. W., Nagy, L. M., Kaloupek, D. G., Klauminzer, G., Charney, D. S., & Keane, T. M. (1990). A clinician rating scale for assessing current and lifetime PTSD: The CAPS-1. *Behavior Therapist, 13,* 187-188.

Blount, A. G., Sheahan, T. C., Johnson, D. M., & Chard, K. M. (in press). Personality disorders and coping styles in female treatment seeking childhood sexual abuse survivors. *Psychology Research and Practice.*

Blumberg, N. H. (1981). Arson update: A review of the literature on firesetting. *Bulletin of the American Academy of Psychiatry and the Law, 9,* 255-265.

Boer, D. P., Wilson, R. J., Gauthier, C. M., & Hart, S. D. (1997). Assessing risk for sexual violence: Guidelines for clinical practice. In C. D. Webster & M. A. Jackson (Eds.), *Impulsivity: Theory, assessment, and treatment* (pp. 326-342). New York: Guilford.

Bograd, M. (1984). Family systems approaches to wife battering: A feminist critique. *American Journal of Orthopsychiatry, 54,* 558-568.

Boles, J., & Garbin, A. (1974). The strip club and stripper-customer patterns of interaction. *Sociology and Social Research, 58,* 136-144.

Boney-McCoy, S., & Finkelhor, D. (1995). Psychosocial sequelae of violent victimization in a national youth sample. *Journal of Consulting and Clinical Psychology, 63,* 726-736.

Bonta, J. (1996). Risk-needs assessment and treatment. In A. T. Harland (Ed.), *Choosing correctional options that work* (pp. 18-32). Thousand Oaks, CA: Sage.

Bonta, J., & Hanson, R. K. (1995, August). *Violent recidivism of men released from prison.* Paper presented at the 103rd Annual Convention of the American Psychological Association, New York.

Bonta, J., Harman, W. G., Hann, R. G., & Cormier, R. B. (1996). The prediction of recidivism among federally sentenced offenders: A re-validation of the SIR scale. *Canadian Journal of Criminology, 38,* 61-79.

Bordt, R. (1997). *The structure of women's non-profit organizations.* Bloomington: Indiana University Press.

Borum, R. (1996). Improving the clinical practice of violence risk assessment: Technology, guidelines, and training. *American Psychologist, 51,* 945-956.

Bourduin, C. M., Henggeler, S. W., Blaske, D. M., & Stein, R. J. (1990). Multisystemic treatment of adolescent sex offenders. *International Journal of Offender Therapy and Comparative Criminology, 34,* 105-113.

Bourget, D., & Bradford, J. (1987). Fire fetishism, diagnostic and clinical implications: A review of two cases. *Canadian Journal of Psychiatry, 32,* 459-462.

Bourget, D., & Bradford, J. (1989). Female arsonists: A clinical study. *Bulletin of the American Academy of Psychiatry and the Law, 17,* 293-299.

Bourgois, P., & Dunlap, E. (1993). Exorcising sex-for-crack: An ethnographic perspective from Harlem. In M. S. Ratner (Ed.), *Crack pipe as pimp: An ethnographic investigation of sex-for-crack exchanges* (pp. 97-132). New York: Lexington.

Bowker, L. H. (1981). Gender differences in prisoner subcultures. In L. H. Bowker (Ed.), *Women and crime in America* (pp. 409-419). New York: Macmillan.

Bowker, L. H. (1982). Victimizers and victims in American correctional institutions. In R. J. Johnson & H. Toch (Eds.), *The pains of imprisonment* (pp. 63-76). Beverly Hills, CA: Sage.

Boxer, A. M., Cook, J. A., & Herdt, G. (1991). Double jeopardy: Identity transitions and parent-child relations among gay and lesbian youth. In K. Pillemer & K. McCartney (Eds.), *Parent-child relations throughout life* (pp. 59-92). Hillsdale, NJ: Lawrence Erlbaum.

Boyes, R. (1996, August 22). How the sex tourists evade justice. *The Times.*

Bracey, D. H. (1983). The juvenile prostitute: Victim and offender. *Victimology, 8,* 149-162.

Bradford, J., Ryan, C., & Rothblum, E. D. (1994). National Lesbian Health Care Survey: Implications for mental health care. *Journal of Consulting and Clinical Psychology, 62,* 228-242.

Bradford, J. M. W. (1982). Arson: A clinical study. *Canadian Journal of Psychiatry, 27,* 188-193.

Bradford, J. M. W. (1985). Arson: A review. In M. H. Ben-Aron, S. J. Hucker, & C. D. Webster (Eds.), *Clinical criminology: The assessment and treatment of criminal behavior* (pp. 97-106). Toronto, Canada: M. and M. Graphics Ltd.

Braithwaite, J. (1989). *Crime, shame and reintegration.* Cambridge, UK: Cambridge University Press.

Braithwaite, J., & Daly, K. (1994). Masculinities, violence, and communitarian control. In T. Newburn & B. Stanko (Eds.), *Just boys doing business? Men, masculinity and crime* (pp. 189-213). London: Routledge.

Braithwaite, J., & Mugford, S. (1994). Conditions of successful reintegration ceremonies. *British Journal of Criminology, 34,* 139-171.

Brannon, J. M., & Troyer, R. (1991). Peer group counseling: A normalized residential alternative to the specialized treatment of adolescent sex offenders. *International Journal of Offender Therapy and Comparative Criminology, 35,* 225-234.

Breaking the silence on prison rape and AIDS. (1995, July). *Corrections Compendium, 20,* 14.

Breedlove, W., & Breedlove, J. (1970). *Swingers.* San Francisco: Covertal Press.

Brickman, J., & Briere, J. (1984). Incidence of rape and sexual assault in an urban Canadian population. *International Journal of Women's Studies, 7,* 195-206.

Briere, J., & Runtz, M. (1989). The Trauma Symptom Checklist (TSC-33): Early data on a new scale. *Journal of Interpersonal Violence, 4,* 151-163.

Briere, J., & Runtz, M. (1993). Childhood sexual abuse: Long-term sequelae and implications for psychological assessment. *Journal of Interpersonal Violence, 8,* 312-330.

Briere, J. N. (1992). *Child abuse trauma: Theory and treatment of the lasting effects.* Newbury Park, CA: Sage.

Briere, J. N., & Elliott, D. M. (1994). Immediate and long-term impacts of child sexual abuse. *Future of Children, 4*(2), 54-69.

Briggs, L., & Joyce, P. R. (1997). What determines posttraumatic stress disorder symptomatology for survivors of childhood sexual abuse? *Child Abuse & Neglect, 21,* 575-582.

Brimnier, L. D. (1995). *Being different: Lambda youths speak out.* New York: Franklin Watts.

Brooks, A. D. (1996). Megan's Law: Constitutionality and policy. *Criminal Justice Ethics, 15,* 56-66.

Brown, J. G. (1994). The use of mediation to resolve criminal cases: A procedural critique. *Emory Law Journal, 43,* 1247-1309.

Brown, N. (1966). *Love's body.* New York: Random House.

Brown, S. L., & Forth, A. E. (1997). Psychopathy and sexual assault: Static risk factors, emotional precursors, and rapist subtypes. *Journal of Consulting and Clinical Psychology, 65,* 848-857.

Browne, A., & Finkelhor, D. (1986). Impact of child sexual abuse: A review of the literature. *Psychological Bulletin, 99*(1), 66-77.

Bruno, A. (1993). *The iceman.* New York: Dell.

Brush, L. D. (1990). Violent acts and injurious outcomes in married couples: Methodological issues in the National Survey of Families and Households. *Gender & Society, 4,* 56-67.

Brussa, L. (1998). The TAMPEP project in Western Europe. In K. Kempadoo & J. Doezema (Eds.), *Global sex workers: Rights, resistance, and redefinition* (pp. 246-259). New York: Routledge.

Bumiller, K. (1990). Fallen angels: The representation of violence against women in legal culture. *International Journal of the Sociology of Law, 18,* 125-142.

Bureau of International Labor Affairs. (1996). *Forced labor: The prostitution of children.* Washington, DC: U.S. Department of Labor.

Bureau of Justice Statistics. (1995). *The nation's jails hold record 490,442 inmates* (DOJ 95-027A). Washington, DC: U.S. Department of Justice.

Bureau of Justice Statistics. (1999). *Women offenders.* Washington, DC: U.S. Department of Justice.

Bureau of Justice Statistics. (2000). *Sourcebook of criminal justice statistics, 1999* (NCJ 184989). Washington, DC: U.S. Department of Justice.

Burge, S. K. (1983). Rape: Individual and family reactions. In C. Figley & H. McCubbin (Eds.), *Stress and the family II: Coping with catastrophe* (pp. 103-119). New York: Brunner/Mazel.

Burgess, A. W. (1975). Family reaction to homicide. *American Journal of Orthopsychiatry, 45*(3), 391-398.

Burgess, A. W., & Lottes, I. (1988). Overview of child sexual abuse. In A. W. Burgess & C. W. Grant (Eds.), *Children traumatized in sex rings* (pp. 1-6). Arlington, VA: National Center for Missing and Exploited Children.

Bushman, B. J., & Cooper, H. M. (1990). Effects of alcohol on human aggression: An integrative research review. *Psychological Bulletin, 107,* 341-354.

Butler, J. (1990). *Gender trouble.* New York: Routledge.

Byington, D. B., Martin, P. Y., DiNitto, D. M., & Maxwell, M. S. (1991). Organizational affiliation and effectiveness: The case of rape crisis centers. *Administration in Social Work, 15,* 83-103.

Byrne, A., & Walsh, J. B. (1989). The epileptic arsonist. *British Journal of Psychiatry, 155,* 268.

Calder v. Bull, 3 U.S. 386 (1798).

Calhoun, T. C. (1992). Male street hustling: Introduction processes and stigma containment. *Sociological Spectrum, 12*(1), 35-52.

Campagna, D. S., & Poffenberger, D. L. (1988). *The sexual trafficking in children: An investigation of the child sex trade.* Dover, MA: Auburn House.

Campbell, R. (1996). *The community response to rape: An ecological conception of victims' experiences.* Unpublished doctoral dissertation, Michigan State University, East Lansing.

Campbell, R. (1998a). The community response to rape: Victims' experiences with the legal, medical, and mental health systems. *American Journal of Community Psychology, 26*, 355-379.

Campbell, R. (1998b). Invisible men: Making visible male clients of female prostitutes in Merseyside. In J. E. Elias, V. L. Bullough, V. Elias, & G. Brewer (Eds.), *Prostitution: On whores, hustlers, and johns* (pp. 155-171). Amherst, NY: Prometheus.

Campbell, R., & Ahrens, C. E. (1998). Innovative community services for rape victims: An application of multiple case study methodology. *American Journal of Community Psychology, 26*, 537-571.

Campbell, R., Baker, C. K., & Mazurek, T. (1998). Remaining radical? Organizational predictors of rape crisis centers' social change initiatives. *American Journal of Community Psychology, 26*, 465-491.

Campbell, R., & Bybee, D. (1997). Emergency medical services for rape victims: Detecting the cracks in service delivery. *Women's Health, 3*, 75-101.

Campbell, R., Sefl, T., Barnes, H. E., Ahrens, C. E., Wasco, S. M., & Zaragoza-Diesfeld, Y. (1999). Community services for rape survivors: Enhancing psychological well-being or increasing trauma? *Journal of Consulting and Clinical Psychology, 67*, 847-858.

Canestrini, K. (1998). The method of risk assessment used for the New York State Sex Offender Registration Act. *National Conference on Sex Offender Registries Proceedings.* Washington, DC: Bureau of Justice Statistics.

Cannon, A. (1996, May 15). Mother perseveres in Megan's Law effort. *Philadelphia Inquirer,* p. B01.

Canter, D. (1989, January). Offender profiles. *Psychologist, 2*, 12-16.

Canter, D. (1994). *Criminal shadows: Inside the mind of the serial killer.* London: HarperCollins.

Canter, D., & Kirby, S. (1995). Prior convictions of child molesters. *Science and Justice, 35*, 73-78.

Caringella-MacDonald, S., & Humphries, D. (1991). Sexual assault, women, and the community. In H. E. Pepinsky & R. Quinney (Eds.), *Criminology as peacemaking* (pp. 98-113). Bloomington: Indiana University Press.

Carlisle, A. (1993). The divided self: Toward an understanding of the dark side of the serial killer. *American Journal of Criminal Justice, 17*(2), 23-36.

Carmen, A., & Moody, H. (1985). *Working women: The subterranean world of street prostitution.* New York: Harper & Row.

Carr, C. (1994). *The alienist.* New York: Random House.

Carr, C. (1997). *The angel of darkness.* New York: Random House.

Carrington, K., & Watson, P. (1996). Policing sexual violence: Feminism, criminal justice and governmentality. *International Journal of the Sociology of Law, 24*, 253-272.

Carter, C. (Executive Producer). (1996-1999). *Millenium.* Los Angeles: 20th Century Fox Television.

Carter, D. L. (1995, July). Computer crime categories: How technocriminals operate. *FBI Law Enforcement Bulletin,* pp. 21-26.

Casey, C. (1993). Mapping evil minds. *Police Review, 101*, 16-17.

Castro, K. G., Lieb, S., Jaffe, H. W., Narkunas, J. P., Calisher, C. H., Bush, T. J., & Witte, J. J. (1988). Transmission of HIV in Belle Glade, Florida: Lessons for other communities in the United States. *Science, 239*(4386), 193-197.

Cattell, R. B. (1966). The scree test for the number of factors. *Multivariate Behavioral Research, 1*, 245-276.

Center for Sex Offender Management (CSOM). (1997). *An overview of sex offender community notification practices: Policy implications and promising approaches.* Silver Spring, MD: Author.

Chaiken, J. M. (1998). Sex offenders and offending: Learning more from national data collection programs. *National Conference on Sex Offender Registries Proceedings.* Washington, DC: Bureau of Justice Statistics.

Chalmers, A. F. (1976). *What is this thing called science? An assessment of the nature and status of science and its methods.* St. Lucia, Australia: University of Queensland Press.

Chancer, L. S. (1993). Prostitution, feminist theory, and ambivalence: Notes from the sociological underground. *Social Text, 37,* 143-171.

Chappell, D. (1995). How violent is Australian society? In D. Chappell & S. Egger (Eds.), *Australian violence: Contemporary perspectives II* (pp. 13-29). Canberra: Australian Institute of Criminology.

Chard, K. M. (2000). *Cognitive processing therapy for sexual abuse: A treatment manual.* Manuscript in preparation.

Chard, K. M., Weaver, T. L., & Resick, P. A. (1997). Adapting cognitive processing therapy for child sexual abuse survivors. *Cognitive and Behavioral Practice, 4,* 31-52.

Charmaz, K. (1983). The grounded theory method: An explication and interpretation. In R. M. Emerson (Ed.), *Contemporary field research: A collection of readings* (pp. 109-126). Boston: Little, Brown.

Chen, R. K. (1996, Fall). Symposium on Megan's Law: Constitutional challenges to Megan's Law: A year's retrospective. *Boston University Public Interest Law Journal, 6,* 57.

Chodorow, N. (1989). *Feminism and psychoanalytic theory.* New Haven, CT: Yale University Press.

Chonco, N. (1989). Sexual assaults among male inmates. *The Prison Journal, 68*(1), 72-82.

Christie, N. (1977). Conflict as property. *British Journal of Criminology, 17,* 1-15.

Clark, C. S. (1994). Prison overcrowding: Will building more prisons cut the crime rate? *Congressional Quarterly Researcher,* 97-120. Retrieved November 15, 1999, from the World Wide Web: http://webspirs4.silverplatter.com:8100/c11824

Clear, T. R. (1994). *Harm in American penology: Offenders, victims, and their communities.* Albany: State University of New York Press.

Cleckley, H. (1976). *The mask of sanity* (5th ed.). St. Louis, MO: Mosby.

Cleveland, H. H., Koss, M. P., & Lyons, J. (1999). Rape tactics from the survivors' perspective: Contextual dependence and within-event independence. *Journal of Interpersonal Violence, 14,* 532-547.

Coates, D., Wortman, C. B., & Abbey, A. (1979). Reactions to victims. In I. H. Frieze, D. Bar-Tal, & J. S. Carrol (Eds.), *New approaches to social problems* (pp. 21-52). San Francisco: Jossey-Bass.

Coates, R. B., & Gehm, J. (1989). An empirical assessment. In M. Wright & B. Galaway (Eds.), *Mediation and criminal justice: Victims, offenders and community* (pp. 251-263). London: Sage.

Cochran, S. D., & Mays, V. M. (1996). Prevalence of HIV-related sexual risk behaviors among young 18- to 24-year-old lesbian and bisexual women. *Women's Health: Research on Gender, Behavior, and Policy, 2*(1-2), 75-89.

Cohen, L., & Roth, S. (1987). The psychological aftermath of rape: Long-term effects and individual differences in recovery. *Journal of Social and Clinical Psychology, 5,* 525-534.

Cohen, M. A., Aladjem, A. D., & Bremin, D. (1990). Firesetting by patients with the acquired immunodeficiency syndrome (AIDS). *Annals of Internal Medicine, 112,* 386-387.

Coker, A. L., Walls, L. G., & Johnson, J. E. (1998). Risk factors for traumatic physical injury during sexual assaults for male and female victims. *Journal of Interpersonal Violence, 13,* 605-620.

Collins, B. G., & Whalen, M. B. (1989). The rape crisis movement: Radical or reformist? *Social Work, 34,* 61-63.

Collins, J. J., & Schlenger, W. E. (1988). Acute and chronic effects of alcohol use on violence. *Journal of Studies on Alcohol, 49,* 516-521.

Comstock, C. D. (1991). *Violence against lesbians and gay men.* New York: Columbia University Press.

Conte, J. R., & Berliner, R. (1988). The impact of sexual abuse on children: Empirical findings. In L. Walker (Ed.), *Handbook of sexual abuse on children* (pp. 72-93). New York: Springer.

Cooley, C. (1964). *Human nature and the social order.* New York: Schocken. (Originally published in 1902)

Coomaraswamy, R. (1997, February 12). *Report of the Special Rapporteur on Violence Against Women: Its causes and consequences.* Paper presented at the 53rd Session of the United Nations Economic and Social Council.

Coomaraswamy, R. (1999). *Report on the mission of the United States of America on the issue of violence against women in state and federal prisons* (E/CN.4/1999/68/Add.2). Geneva, Switzerland: United Nations High Commissioner. (May be accessed on the U.N. High Commissioner for Human Rights, Geneva, Switzerland Web site: http://www.unhchr.ch/ Huridocda/Huridoca.nsf/ TestFrame/7560a6237c67bb118025674c0 04406e9?Opendocument)

Cooper, B. (1989). Prostitution: A feminist analysis. *Women's Rights Law Reporter, 11,* 99-119.

Cooper, S. A. (1998). Community notification and verification practices in three states. *National Conference on Sex Offender Registries Proceedings.* Washington, DC: Bureau of Justice Statistics.

Copson, G., Badcock, R., Boon, J., & Britton, P. (1997). Editorial: Articulating a systematic approach to clinical crime profiling. *Criminal Behaviour and Mental Health, 7,* 13-17.

Cormier, R. B. (1997). Yes, SIR! A stable risk prediction tool. *Forum on Corrections Research, 9,* 3-7.

Cornell, D., Hawk, G., & Warren, J. (1996). *Assessment of aggression in violent criminal defendants.* Retrieved from http://ness.sys.virginia.edu/ilppp/airavcd.html

Cornell, D., Warren, J., Hawk, G., Stafford, E., Oram, G., & Pine, D. (1996). Psychopathy in instrumental and reactive violent offenders. *Journal of Consulting and Clinical Psychology, 64,* 783-790.

Cotton, D. J., & Groth, A. N. (1982). Inmate rape: Prevention and intervention. *Journal of Prison and Jail Health, 2*(1), 47-57.

Cotton, D. J., & Groth, A. N. (1984). Sexual assault in correctional institutions: Prevention and intervention. In I. R. Stuart (Ed.), *Victims of sexual aggression: Treatment of children, women, and men* (pp. 127-155). New York: Van Nostrand Reinhold.

Coutorie, L. E. (1995). The future of high technology crime: A parallel Delphi study. *Journal of Criminal Justice, 23*(1), 13-27.

Cramer, D. W, & Roach, A. J. (1988). Coming out to Mom and Dad: A study of gay males and their relationships with their parents. *Journal of Homosexuality, 15*(3-4), 79-92.

Cranston, K. (1991). HIV education for gay, lesbian, and bisexual youth: Personal risk, personal power, and the community of conscience. *Journal of Homosexuality, 22*(34), 247-259.

Crowe, L. C., & George, W. H. (1989). Alcohol and human sexuality: Review and integration. *Psychological Bulletin, 105,* 374-386.

Cunnington, S. (1984). Aspects of violence in prostitution. In J. Hopkins (Ed.), *Perspectives on rape and sexual assault* (pp. 25-36). London: Harper & Row.

Dakof, G. A., & Taylor, S. E. (1990). Victims' perceptions of social support: What is helpful from whom? *Journal of Personality and Social Psychology, 58*(1), 80-89.

Dallou, M. (1996). Fighting prison rape: How to make your facility safer. *Corrections Today, 58*(7), 100-106.

Daubert v. Merrell Dow Pharmaceuticals, Inc., 509 U.S. 579 (1993).

D'Augelli, A. R. (1991). Gay men in college: Identity processes and adaptations. *Journal of College Student Development, 32,* 140-146.

D'Augelli, A. R. (1992). Lesbian and gay male undergraduates' experiences of harassment and fear on campus. *Journal of Interpersonal Violence, 7,* 383-395.

D'Augelli, A. R. (1993). Preventing mental health problems among lesbian and gay college students. *Journal of Primary Prevention, 13*(4), 1-17.

D'Augelli, A. R. (1996). Enhancing the development of lesbian, gay, and bisexual youths. In E. O. Rothblum & L. Bond (Eds.), *Prevention of heterosexism and homophobia* (pp. 124-150). Thousand Oaks, CA: Sage.

D'Augelli, A. R., & Dark, L. I. (1995). Vulnerable populations: Lesbian, gay, and bisexual youth. In L. O. Eron, I. H. Gentry, & P. Schlegel (Eds.), *Reason to hope: A psychosocial perspective on violence and youth* (pp. 177-196). Washington, DC: American Psychological Association.

D'Augelli, A. R., & Hershberger, S. L. (1993). Lesbian, gay, and bisexual youths in community settings: Personal challenges and mental health problems. *American Journal of Community Psychology, 21,* 421-448.

D'Augelli, A. R., Hershberger, S. L., & Pilkington, N. W. (in press). Lesbian, gay, and bisexual youths and their families: Disclosure of sexual orientation and its consequences. *American Journal of Orthopsychiatry.*

Davies, A. (1994). Editorial: Offender profiling. *Medicine, Science and Law, 34,* 185-186.

Davies, P. M., Weatherburn, P., Hunt, A. I., Hickson, F. C. I., McManus, T. J., & Coxon, A. P. M. (1992). The sexual behavior of young gay men in England and Wales. *AIDS Care, 4,* 259-272.

Davis, A. J. (1968, December). Sexual assaults in the Philadelphia prison system and sheriffs' vans. *Trans-Action,* pp. 8-16.

Davis, G., & Leitenberg, H. (1987). Adolescent sex offenders. *Psychological Bulletin, 101,* 417-427.

Davis, J., & Bernstein, M. (1996). *Prevalence of voyeurism in San Diego County.* Unpublished report.

Davis, J. A. (1992). *Forensic psychology, psychiatry and the law: The public order offenders* [Lecture]. San Diego, CA.

Davis, J. A. (1996). *Criminal investigative analysis: Criminal and psychological profiling* [Lecture]. San Diego, CA.

Davis, J. A., & Milton, M. (1997). A psychological analysis of bombers and arsonists. *Journal of Forensic Examination, 6,* 18-23.

Davis, L., McShane, M., & Williams, F. P. (1995). Controlling computer access to pornography: Special conditions for sex offenders. *Federal Probation, 59*(2), 43-48.

Davis, N. J. (Ed.). (1993). *Prostitution: An international handbook on trends, problems, and policies.* Westport, CT: Greenwood.

Davis, R., Taylor, B., & Bench, S. (1995). Impact of sexual and nonsexual assault on secondary victims. *Violence & Victims, 10,* 73-84.

Davis, R. C., & Brickman, E. (1996). Supportive and unsupportive aspects of the behavior of others toward victims of sexual and nonsexual assault. *Journal of Interpersonal Violence, 11,* 250-262.

Davis, R. C., Brickman, E., & Baker, T. (1991). Supportive and unsupportive responses of others to rape victims: Effects of concurrent victim adjustment. *American Journal of Community Psychology, 19,* 443-451.

Davison, G. C., & Neale, J. M. (1994). *Abnormal psychology* (6th ed.). New York: Wiley.

Day, K. (1990). Mental retardation: Clinical aspects and management. In R. Bluglass, P. Bowden, & N. Walker (Eds.), *Principles and practice of forensic psychiatry* (pp. 399-418). Edinburgh, UK: Churchill Livingstone.

Dean, L., & Meyer, I. H. (1995). HIV prevalence and sexual behavior in a cohort of New York City gay men (aged 18-24). *Journal of Acquired Immune Deficiency Syndromes, 8,* 208-211.

Dean, L., Wu, S., & Martin, I. L. (1992). Trends in violence and discrimination against gay men in New York City: 1984-1990. In G. M. Herek & K. T. Berrill (Eds.), *Hate crimes: Confronting violence against lesbians and gay men* (pp. 46-64). Newbury Park, CA: Sage.

Delacoste, F., & Alexander, P. (1987). *Sex work: Writings by women in the sex industry*. Pittsburgh: Cleis Press.

Demme, J. (Director). (1991). *Silence of the Lambs* [Film].

Department of Justice. (1980). *Crime in the U.S.: FBI Uniform Crime Reports for the U.S., annual for 1979*. Washington, DC: Government Printing Office.

Department of Justice, Bureau of Justice Statistics. (1999). *National Crime Victimization Survey, 1992-1997. Part 38: 1992-1996 Incident-Level Rape Subset* (7th ICPSR ed.) [Computer file]. Ann Arbor, MI: Inter University Consortium for Political and Social Research [Producer and Distributor].

De Young, M. (1984). Ethics and the lunatic fringe: The case of pedophile organizations. *Human Organizations, 43*(1), 72-74.

Diana, L. (1985). *The prostitute and her clients: Your pleasure is her business*. Springfield, IL: Charles C Thomas.

DiMaggio, P. J., & Powell, W. W. (1991). Introduction. In W. W. Powell & P. J. DiMaggio (Eds.), *The new institutionalization in organizational analysis* (pp. 1-38). Chicago: University of Chicago Press.

Dittenhoffer, T., & Ericson, R. V. (1983). The victim/offender reconciliation program: A message to correctional reformers. *University of Toronto Law Journal, 33*, 315-347.

Dix, G. E. (1976). Differential processing of abnormal sex offenders. *Journal of Criminal Law, Criminology, & Police Science, 67*, 233-243.

Dixon, D. (1985b). Perceived sexual satisfaction and marital happiness of bisexual and heterosexual swinging husbands. *Journal of Homosexuality, 11*, 209-222.

Dixon, J. (1985a). The commencement of bisexual activity in swinging married women over age thirty. *Journal of Sex Research, 11*, 115-124.

Dobash, R. E., & Dobash, R. P. (1977-1978). Wives: The "appropriate" victims of marital violence. *Victimology: An International Journal, 2*, 426-442.

Dobash, R. E., & Dobash, R. P. (1979). *Violence against wives: A case against the patriarchy*. New York: Free Press.

Dobash, R. E., Dobash, R. P., Wilson, M., & Daly, M. (1992). The myth of sexual symmetry in marital violence. *Social Problems, 39*, 71-91.

Doezema, J. (1998). Forced to choose: Beyond the voluntary v. forced prostitution dichotomy. In K. Kempadoo & J. Doezema (Eds.), *Global sex workers: Rights, resistance, and redefinition* (pp. 34-50). New York: Routledge.

Doll, L. S., Joy, D., Barthalow, B. N., Harrison, J. S., Bolan, C., Douglas, J. M., Saltzman, L. E., Moss, P. M., & Delgado, W. (1992). Self-reported childhood and adolescent sexual abuse among adult homosexual and bisexual men. *Child Abuse & Neglect, 16*, 855-864.

Donaldson, S. (1993). *Prisoner rape education program: Overview for administrators and staff*. Brandon, VT: The Safer Society Press.

Donaldson, S. (1995). *Rape of incarcerated Americans: A preliminary statistical look*. Retrieved June 22, 2000, from the World Wide Web: http://www.spr.org/docs/stats.html

Donaldson, S., Dumond, R., Knopp, F., Struckman-Johnson, C., & Thompson, L. (1995). *Training Americans to rape: The role of our jails, prisons, and reformatories*. Retrieved June 22, 2000, from the World Wide Web: http://www.spr.org/docs/usatoday.html

Doren, D. M. (1998). Recidivism base rates, predictions of sex offender recidivism, and the "Sexual Predator" commitment laws. *Behavioral Sciences and the Law, 16*, 97-114.

Douglas, J., & Olshaker, M. (1995). *Mindhunter: Inside the FBI elite serial crime unit*. New York: Scribner.

Douglas, J., & Olshaker, M. (1997). *Journey into darkness*. London: Heinemann.

Douglas, J. E., Burgess, A. W., Burgess, A. G., & Ressler, R. (1992). *Crime classification manual*. New York: Lexington Books.

Dow, D. R. (1989). Individuals, government, and rights: A reply to Cathleen Herasimchuk. *South Texas Law Review, 30,* 369-385.

Dressel, P., & Petersen, D. (1982a). Becoming a male stripper: Recruitment, socialization, and ideological development. *Work and Occupations, 9*(3), 387-406.

Dressel, P., & Petersen, D. (1982b). Gender roles, sexuality, and the male strip show: The structuring of sexual opportunity. *Sociological Focus, 15*(2), 151-162.

Due, L. (1995). *Joining the tribe: Growing up gay and lesbian in the 90's*. New York: Anchor.

Dumond, R. W. (1992). The sexual assault of male inmates in incarcerated settings. *International Journal of the Sociology of Law, 20*(2), 135-157.

Dumond, R. W. (1994). *Training curriculum: Rape awareness and intervention*. Medfield: Massachusetts Department of Correction, Division of Staff Development.

Dumond, R. W. (1995, August). *Ignominious victims: Effective treatment of male sexual assault in prison*. Paper presented at the 103rd annual conference of the American Psychological Association, New York.

Dunkel-Schetter, C. (1984). Social support and cancer: Findings based on patient interviews and their implications. *Journal of Social Issues, 40*(4), 77-98.

Dunkel-Schetter, C., & Wortman, C. B. (1981). Dilemmas of social support: Parallels between victimization and aging. In S. B. Kiesler, J. N. Morgan, & V. K. Oppenheimer (Eds.), *Aging: Social change* (pp. 349-381). New York: Academic Press.

Durkin, K. F. (1996). *Accounts and sexual deviance in cyberspace: The case of pedophilia*. Unpublished doctoral dissertation, Virginia Polytechnic Institute and State University, Blacksburg.

Durkin, K. F., & Bryant, C. D. (1995). Log on to sex: Some notes on the carnal computer and erotic cyberspace as an emerging research frontier. *Deviant Behavior, 16*(3), 179-200.

Dutton, M. A., & Rubinstein, F. L. (1995). Working with people with PTSD: Research implications. In C. R. Figley (Ed.), *Compassion fatigue: Coping with secondary traumatic stress disorder in those who treat the traumatized* (pp. 82-100). New York: Brunner/Mazel.

Eberle, A. J. (1989). Klinefelter syndrome and firesetting behavior. *Pediatrics, 83,* 649.

Eberth, L. D. (1989). *The psychological impact of rape crisis counseling on volunteer counselors*. Unpublished doctoral dissertation, The Wright Institute.

Edgley, C. (1989). Commercial sex: Pornography, prostitution, and advertising. In K. McKinney & S. Sprecher (Eds.), *Human sexuality: The social and interpersonal context* (pp. 370-424). Norwood, NJ: Ablex.

Egger, S. A. (1990a). Serial murder: A synthesis of literature and research. In S. A. Egger (Ed.), *Serial murder: An elusive phenomenon* (pp. 3-34). Westport, CT: Praeger.

Egger, S. A. (1990b). *Serial murder: An elusive phenomenon*. New York: Praeger.

Egger, S. A. (1997). *The killers among us: An examination of serial murder and its investigation*. Upper Saddle River, NJ: Prentice Hall.

Eigenberg, H. (1989). Male rape: An empirical examination of correctional officers' attitudes toward rape in prison. *The Prison Journal, 68*(2), 39-56.

Eigenberg, H. M. (1994). Male rape in prisons: Examining the relationship between correctional officers' attitudes toward male rape and their willingness to respond to acts of rape. In M. C. Braswell, R. H. Montgomery, Jr., & L. X. Lombardo (Eds.), *Prison violence in America* (2nd ed., pp. 145-165). Cincinnati, OH: Anderson.

Ellis, L. (1987). Relationship of criminality and psychopathy with eight other apparent behavioral manifestations of sub-optimal arousal. *Personality and Individual Differences, 8,* 905-925.

Elmer-Dewitt, P. (1995, Spring). Welcome to cyberspace. *Time* (Special Issue), pp. 4-11.

Emm, D., & McKenry, P. C. (1988). Coping with victimization: The impact of rape on female survivors, male significant others, and parents. *Contemporary Family Therapy, 10*(4), 272-279.

Enck, G. E., & Preston, J. (1988). Counterfeit intimacy: A dramaturgical analysis of an erotic performance. *Deviant Behavior, 9,* 369-381.

English, K., Pullen, S., & Jones, L. (1997). *Managing adult sex offenders in the community—A containment approach* (National Institute of Justice Research In Action). Washington, DC. National Institute of Justice. Retrieved from http://www.ncjrs.org/txtfiles/sexoff.txt

Enloe, C. (1989). *Bananas, beaches, and bases: Making feminist sense of international politics.* Berkeley: University of California Press.

EPCAT (End Child Prostitution in Asian Tourism). (1997, April 20). The paedophile's club. *The Sunday Leader.*

Erdman, H. P., Klein, M. H., & Greist, J. H. (1985). Direct patient computer interviewing. *Journal of Consulting and Clinical Psychology, 51,* 760-773.

Erickson, D. J., & Tewksbury, R. (2000). The gentlemen of the club: A typology of strip club patrons. *Deviant Behavior, 21*(3), 271-293.

Estep, R. E., & Waldorf, D. (1989). *Safe sex among male street hustlers and call men.* Paper presented at the annual meetings of the American Sociological Association.

Estrich, S. (1987). *Real rape.* Cambridge, MA: Harvard University Press.

Evans, N. J., & D'Augelli, A. R. (1995). Lesbians, gay men, and bisexual people in college. In R. C. Savin-Williams & K. M. Cohen (Eds.), *The lives of lesbians, gays, and bisexuals* (pp. 201-226). New York: Harcourt Brace Jovanovich.

Fagan, T. J., Wennerstrom, D., & Miller, J. (1996). Sexual assault of male inmates: Prevention, identification and intervention. *Journal of Correctional Health Care, 3*(1), 49-65.

Fairstein, L. A. (1993). *Sexual violence: Our war against rape.* New York: William Morrow.

Faller, K. (1990). *Understanding child sexual maltreatment.* Newbury Park, CA: Sage.

Fang, B. (1976). Swinging: In retrospect. *Journal of Sex Research, 12,* 220-237.

Father says he raped girl to teach her about sex. (2001, April 9). Retrieved from www.apbnews.com/newscenter/breakingnews/2001/04/09/story_man_rapes_his_daughter.html

Federal Bureau of Prisons. (1997). *PS 5324.04 sexual abuse/assault prevention and intervention programs.* Retrieved August 15, 1999, from the World Wide Web: http://www.bop.gov/progstat/53240104.html

Federal Emergency Management Agency. (1988). *Fire in the United States* (7th ed.). Emmitsburg, MD: Author.

Fedoroff, J. P., Wisner-Carlson, R., Dean, S., & Berlin, F. S. (1992). Medroxy-progesterone acetate in the treatment of paraphilic sexual disorders. *Journal of Offender Rehabilitation, 18,* 109-123.

Feeley, M. M., & Simon, J. (1992). The new penology: Notes on the emerging strategy of corrections and its implications. *Criminology, 30,* 449-474.

Feinauer, L. (1982). Rape: A family crisis. *American Journal of Family Therapy, 10,* 35-39.

Feinauer, L., & Hippolite, D. L. (1987). Once a princess, always a princess: A strategy for therapy with families of rape victims. *Contemporary Family Therapy, 9,* 252-261.

Feinberg, D. (1998). Justice Department guideline changes and clarifications. *National Conference on Sex Offender Registries Proceedings.* Washington, DC: Bureau of Justice Statistics

Feldman, C. (1997, May 6). *Parents' protests, new laws keep sex offenders on move.* Retrieved from http://www.cnn.com/US/9705/06molester.moves/index.html

Feldman, D. (1997). The "Scarlet Letter laws" of the 1990s: A response to the critics. *Albany Law Review, 60,* 1081.

Fenichel, O. (1945). *The psychoanalytic theory of neurosis.* New York: Norton.

Ferree, M. M., & Martin, P. Y. (1995). Introduction. In M. M. Ferree & P. Y. Martin (Eds.), *Feminist organizations: Harvest of the new women's movement.* Philadelphia: Temple University Press.

Figley, C. R. (1983). Catastrophes: An overview of family reactions. In C. Figley & H. McCubbin (Eds.), *Stress and the family II: Coping with catastrophe* (pp. 3-20). New York: Brunner/Mazel.

Figley, C. R. (1995). Compassion fatigue as secondary traumatic stress disorder: An overview. In C. R. Figley (Ed.), *Compassion fatigue: Coping with secondary traumatic stress disorder in those who treat the traumatized* (pp. 1-20). New York: Brunner/Mazel.

Fink, B. (1995). *The Lacanian subject.* Princeton, NJ: Princeton University Press.

Finkelhor, D., & Dziuba-Leatherman, J. (1994). Victimization of children. *American Psychologist, 49,* 173-183.

Finkelhor, D., Hotaling, G., Lewis, I. A., & Smith, C. (1990). Sexual abuse in a national sample of adult men and women: Prevalence, characteristics, and risk factors. *Child Abuse & Neglect, 14,* 19-28.

Finn, P. (1997). *Sex offender community notification.* Washington, DC: National Institute of Justice.

Fischer, K. (1989). Defining the boundaries of admissible expert testimony on rape trauma syndrome. *University of Illinois Law Review,* pp. 691-734.

Fiske, S., & Taylor, S. (1991). *Social cognition* (2nd ed.). New York: McGraw-Hill.

Flowers, B. R. (1998). *The prostitution of women and girls.* Jefferson, NC: Macfarland.

Foa, E. B., Riggs, D. S., Dancu, C. V., & Rothbaum, B. O. (1993). Reliability and validity of a brief instrument for assessing posttraumatic stress disorder. *Journal of Traumatic Stress, 6,* 459-473.

Follingstad, D., Wright, S., Lloyd, S., & Sebastian, J. (1991). Sex differences in motivations and effects in dating violence. *Family Relations, 40,* 51-57.

Forrest, G. G. (1994). *Alcoholism and human sexuality.* Northvale, NJ: Jason Aronson.

Forth, A. E., Hart, S. D., & Hare, R. D. (1990). Assessment of psychopathy in male young offenders. *Psychological Assessment: A Journal of Consulting and Clinical Psychology, 2,* 342-344.

Forth, A. E., & Kroner, D. (1995). *The factor structure of the Revised Psychopathy Checklist with incarcerated rapists and incest offenders.* Unpublished manuscript.

Foundation Against Trafficking in Women, International Human Rights Law Group, and Global Alliance Against Traffic in Women. (1999). *Human rights standards for the treatment of trafficked persons.* The Netherlands: Global Alliance Against Traffic in Women.

Frank, E., Anderson, B., Stewart, B., Dancu, C., Hughes, C., & West, D. (1988). Immediate and delayed treatment of rape victims. *Annals of the New York Academy of Sciences, 528,* 296-309.

Frazier, P. A., & Haney, B. (1996). Sexual assault cases in the legal system: Police, prosecutor, and victim perspectives. *Law and Human Behavior, 20,* 607-628.

Freeman-Longo, R. E. (1996). Feel good legislation: Prevention or calamity? *Child Abuse & Neglect, 20,* 95-101.

Freud, S. (1932). The acquisition of the power over fire. *International Journal of Psychoanalysis, 13,* 405-410.

Freud, S. (1938). Three contributions to the theory of sex. In A. A. Brill (Ed.), *The basic writings of Sigmund Freud.* New York: The Modern Library.

Freud, S. (1989). Three essays on the theory of sexuality. In P. Gay (Ed.), *The Freud reader* (pp. 239-292). New York: Norton.

Freund, K. (1990). Courtship disorders. In W. L. Marshall, D. R. Laws, & H. E. Barbaree (Eds.), *Handbook of sexual assault: Issues, theories, and treatment of the offender* (pp. 195-207). New York: Plenum.

Freund, K., Seto, M. C., & Kuban, M. (1997). Frotteurism and the theory of courtship disorder. In D. R. Laws & W. O'Donohue (Eds.), *Sexual deviance: Theory, assessment, and treatment* (pp. 111-130). New York: Guilford.

Friedman, K., Bischoff, H., Davis, R., & Person, A. (1982). *Victims and helpers: Reactions to crime.* Washington, DC: U.S. Department of Justice, National Institute of Justice.

Frieze, T. H., Hymer, S., & Greenberg, M. S. (1987). Describing the crime victim: Psychological reactions to victimization. *Professional Psychology, 18,* 299-315.

Fritz, M. (1999, June 3). The politics of parental grieving. *Los Angeles Times,* p. A1.

Frohmann, L. (1991). Discrediting victims' allegations of sexual assault: Prosecutorial accounts of case rejections. *Social Problems, 38,* 213-226.

Frohmann, L. (1997). Discrediting victims' allegations of sexual assault: Prosecutorial accounts of case rejections. In P. A. Adler & P. Adler (Eds.), *Constructions of deviance* (2nd ed., pp. 211-228). Belmont, CA: Wadsworth.

Fulero, S. M. (1995). Review of the Hare Psychopathy Checklist-Revised. In J. C. Conoley & J. C. Impara (Eds.), *Twelfth mental measurements yearbook* (pp. 453-454). Lincoln, NE: Buros Institute.

Furby, L., Weinrott, M., & Blackshaw, L. (1989). Sex offender recidivism: A review. *Psychological Bulletin, 105,* 3-30.

Gamson, W. A. (1990). *The strategy of social protest* (2nd ed.). Belmont, CA: Wadsworth.

Gamson, W. A. (1992). *Talking politics.* New York: Cambridge University Press.

Gaquin, D. (1977-1978). Spouse abuse: Data from the national crime survey. *Victimology, 2,* 632-643.

Gardner, J. J. (1986, June). Attitudes about rape among inmates and correctional officers. *Dissertation Abstracts International, 47*(12), 4514-A.

Garnets, L. D., Herek, C. M., & Levy, B. (1990). Violence and victimization of lesbians and gay men: Mental health consequences. *Journal of Interpersonal Violence, 5,* 366-383.

Gebhard, P. H., Gagnon, J. H., Pomeroy, W. B., & Christensen, C. V. (1965). *Sex offenders.* New York: Harper & Row.

Geller, J. L. (1984). Arson: An unforeseen sequela of deinstitutionalization. *American Journal of Psychiatry, 141,* 504-508.

Geller, J. L. (1987). Firesetting in the adult psychiatric population. *Hospital and Community Psychiatry, 38,* 501-506.

Geller, J. L. (1992a). Arson in review. *Psychiatric Clinics of North America, 15,* 623-645.

Geller, J. L. (1992b). Communicative arson. *Hospital and Community Psychiatry, 43,* 76-77.

Geller, J. L., Erlen, J., & Pinkus, R. L. (1986). A historical appraisal of America's experience with "pyromania": A diagnosis in search of a disorder. *International Journal of Law and Psychiatry, 9,* 201-229.

Gemme, R., Murphy, A., Bourque, M., Nemeh, M. A., & Payment, N. (1984). *A report on prostitution in Quebec* (Working Papers on Prostitution and Pornography, Report No. 11). Ottawa: Department of Justice.

Gendel, W. S., & Bonner, E. J. (1984). Gender identity disorders and paraphilias. In H. H. Goldman (Ed.), *Review of general psychiatry.* Rockville, MD: Lange.

Gendreau, P., Little, T., & Goggin, C. (1996). A meta-analysis of the predictors of adult offender recidivism: What works! *Criminology, 34,* 575-607.

George, L. K., Winfield, I., & Blazer, D. G. (1992). Sociocultural factors in sexual assault: Comparison of two representative samples of women. *Journal of Social Issues, 48,* 105-125.

Ghiselli, E. E., Campbell, J. P., & Zedeck, S. (1981). *Measurement theory for the behavioral sciences.* San Francisco: W. H. Freeman.

Gidycz, C. A., & Koss, M. P. (1990). A comparison of group and individual sexual assault victims. *Psychology of Women Quarterly, 14,* 325-342.

Giobbe, E. (1991). Prostitution and sexual violence. *Center for Advanced Feminist Studies (University of Minnesota), 8,* 6-7.

Glover, E. (1943). *The psychopathology of prostitution.* London: Institute for the Study and Treatment of Delinquency.

Godwin, M., & Canter, D. (1997). Encounter and death: The spatial behavior of U.S. serial killers. *Policing: An International Journal of Police Strategy and Management, 20,* 24-38.

Goffman, E. (1959). *The presentation of self in everyday life.* New York: Anchor Press/Doubleday.

Goffman, E. (1963). *Stigma: Notes on the management of spoiled identity.* Englewood Cliffs, NJ: Prentice Hall.

Golding, J. M., Siegel, J. M., Sorenson, S. B., Burnam, M. A., & Stein, J. A. (1989). Social support sources following sexual assault. *Journal of Community Psychology, 17,* 92-107.

Goldstein, P. J., Ouellet, L. J., & Fendrich, M. (1992). From bag brides to skeezers: A historical perspective on sex-for-drug behavior. *Journal of Psychoactive Drugs, 24,* 349-361.

Goodman, E. A. (1996). Megan's Law: The New Jersey Supreme Court navigates uncharted waters. *Seton Hall Law Review, 26,* 764-802.

Gornick, J., Burt, M. R., & Pittman, K. J. (1985) Structure and activities of rape crisis centers in the early 1980s. *Crime & Delinquency, 31,* 247-268.

Grabosky, P. N. (1992). Law enforcement and the citizen: Non-governmental participants in crime prevention and control. *Policing & Society, 2,* 249-71.

Graves, R. E. (1993). *Conceptualizing the youthful male sex offender: A meta-analytic examination of offender characteristic by offense type.* Unpublished doctoral dissertation, Utah State University.

Greenfeld, L. A. (1997). *Sex offenses and offenders: An analysis of data on rape and sexual assault.* Washington, DC: Bureau of Justice Statistics.

Greenwald, H. (1970). *The call girl.* New York: Ballantine.

Greif, G. L., & Porembski, E. P. (1988). Implications for therapy with significant others of persons with AIDS. *Journal of Gay and Lesbian Psychotherapy, 1*(1), 79-86.

Greissman, A. V. (1996, September). The fate of "Megan's Law" in New York. *Cordozo Law Review, 18,* 181.

Gretton, H., McBride, M., & Hare, R. D. (1995, October). *Psychopathy in adolescent sex offenders: A follow-up study.* Paper presented at the Annual Conference of the Association for the Treatment of Sexual Abusers, New Orleans, LA.

Gretton, H., McBride, M., Lewis, K., O'Shaughnessy, R., & Hare, R. D. (1994, March). *Patterns of violence and victimization in adolescent sexual psychopaths.* Paper presented at the biennial meeting of the American Psychology-Law Society (Division 41 of the American Psychological Association), Santa Fe, NM.

Gross, L., & Aurand, S. K. (1992). *Discrimination and violence against lesbian women and gay men in Philadelphia and the Commonwealth of Pennsylvania.* Philadelphia: Philadelphia Lesbian and Gay Task Force.

Gross, L., Aurand, S. K., & Adessa, R. (1988). *Violence and discrimination against lesbian and gay people in Philadelphia and the Commonwealth of Pennsylvania.* Philadelphia: Philadelphia Lesbian and Gay Task Force.

Grossman, A. H. (1994). Homophobia: A cofactor of HIV disease in gay and lesbian youth. *Journal of the Association of Nurses in AIDS Care, 5,* 39-43.

Groth, N., & Burgess, A. (1980). Male rape: Offenders and victims. *American Journal of Psychiatry, 137*(7), 806-819.

Gunasekera, R. (1996, October 27). *Sri Lanka says orphanages used in child-sex trade.* Reuters World Service.

Haapasalo, J. (1994). Types of offense among the Cleckley psychopaths. *International Journal of Offender Therapy and Comparative Criminology, 38,* 59-67.

Hagan, M. (1992). Special issues in serial murder. In H. Strang & S. Gerull (Eds.), *Homicides: Patterns, prevention and control: Proceedings of a conference held 12-14 May 1992* (pp. 135-138). Canberra: Australian Institute of Criminology.

Hale, R., & Bolin, A. (1998). The female serial killer. In R. M. Holmes & S. T. Holmes (Eds.), *Contemporary perspectives on serial murder* (pp. 33-58). Thousand Oaks, CA: Sage.

Hall, G. C. N. (1995). Sexual offender recidivism revisited: A meta-analysis of recent treatment studies. *Journal of Consulting and Clinical Psychology, 63,* 802-809.

Hall, J. R., Jr. (1990). Fire in the U.S.A. and Japan. *International fire comparison report no. 1.* Quincy, MA: National Fire Protection Association.

Hammelman, T. L. (1993). Gay and lesbian youth: Contributing factors to serious attempts or considerations of suicide. *Journal of Gay and Lesbian Psychotherapy, 2,* 77-89.

Hammett, T. M., Harmon, P., & Maruschak, L. M. (1999). *1996-1997 update: HIV/AIDS, STDs and TB in correctional facilities: Issues and practices.* Washington, DC: U.S. Department of Justice. Retrieved August 25, 1999, from the World Wide Web: http://www.ncjrs.org/txtfiles1/176344.txt

Hammond, W. R., & Yung, B. (1993). Psychology's role in the public health response to assaultive violence among African American men. *American Psychologist, 48,* 142-154.

Hanley, R. (1998, June 18). Attorney general seeks to combat vigilantism: Effort to clear up "Megan's Law" confusion. *New York Times,* p. B5.

Hanson, R. K. (1997). *The development of a brief actuarial risk scale for sexual offense recidivism* (User Report No. 1997-04). Ottawa: Department of the Solicitor General of Canada.

Hanson, R. K. (1998). What do we know about sex offender risk assessment? *Psychology, Public Policy and Law, 4,* 50-72.

Hanson, R. K., & Bussière, M. T. (1998). Predicting relapse: A meta-analysis of sexual offender recidivism studies. *Journal of Consulting and Clinical Psychology, 66,* 348-362.

Hanson, R. K., & Scott, H. (1994, July). *Sexual and non-sexual recidivism of child molesters and other criminals.* Paper presented at the Canadian Psychological Association convention, Penticton, British Columbia, Canada.

Hanson, R. K., Scott, H., & Steffy, R. A. (1995). A comparison of child molesters and non-sexual criminals: Risk predictors and long-term recidivism. *Journal of Research in Crime and Delinquency, 32,* 325-337.

Hare, R. D. (1980). *The Psychopathy Checklist–Revised.* Victoria, BC: Author.

Hare, R. D. (1991). *Manual for the Hare Psychopathy Checklist-Revised.* Toronto, Ontario, Canada: Multi-Health Systems.

Hare, R. D. (1992). *A model program for offenders at high risk for violence.* Ottawa: Correctional Services of Canada.

Hare, R. D. (1996). Psychopathy: A clinical construct whose time has come. *Criminal Justice and Behavior, 23,* 25-54.

Hare, R. D. (1998). Psychopathy, affect, and behavior. In D. Cooke, A. Forth, & R. Hare (Eds.), *Psychopathy: Theory, research, and implications for society* (pp. 105-137). The Netherlands: Kluwer.

Hare, R. D., & McPherson, L. M. (1984). Violent and aggressive behavior by criminal psychopaths. *International Journal of Law and Psychiatry, 7,* 35-50.

Harris, G. T., & Rice, M. E. (1984). Mentally disordered firesetters: Psychodynamics versus empirical approaches. *International Journal of Law and Psychiatry, 7,* 19-34.

Harris, G. T., & Rice, M. E. (1996). A typology of mentally disordered firesetters. *Journal of Interpersonal Violence, 11,* 351-363.

Harris, G. T., Rice, M. E., & Cormier, C. A. (1991). Psychopathy and violent recidivism. *Law and Human Behavior, 15,* 625-637.

Harris, G. T., Rice, M. E., & Quinsey, V. L. (1993). Violent recidivism of mentally disordered offenders: The development of a statistical prediction instrument. *Criminal Justice and Behavior, 20,* 315-335.

Harris, M. K. (1987, Fall). Exploring the connections between feminism and justice. *National Prison Project Journal,* pp. 33-35.

Harris, M. K. (1991). Moving into the new millenium: Toward a feminist vision of justice. In H. E. Pepinsky & R. Quinney (Eds.), *Criminology as peacemaking* (pp. 83-97). Bloomington: Indiana University Press.

Harris, T. (1981). *The red dragon.* New York: Putnam.

Harry, I. (1989a). Parental physical abuse and sexual orientation. *Archives of Sexual Behavior, 718,* 251-261.

Harry, I. (1989b). Sexual identity issues. In *Report of the Secretary's Task Force on Youth Suicide* (DHHS Publication No. ADM 89-1622, Vol. 2, pp. 131-142). Washington, DC: Government Printing Office.

Hart, S. D., & Hare, R. D. (1997). Psychopathy: Assessment and association with criminal conduct. In D. M. Stoff, J. Brieling, & J. Maser (Eds.), *Handbook of antisocial behavior* (pp. 22-35). New York: Wiley.

Hart, S. D., Kropp, P. R., & Hare, R. D. (1988). Performance of psychopaths following conditional release from prison. *Journal of Consulting and Clinical Psychology, 56,* 227-232.

Harvey, M. (1985). *Exemplary rape crisis program: Cross-site analysis and case studies.* Washington, DC: National Center for the Prevention and Control of Rape.

Hatty, S. (1989). Violence against prostitute women: Social and legal dilemmas. *Australian Journal of Social Issues, 24,* 235-248.

Hazelwood, R. R., Dietz, P. E., & Warren, J. I. (1995). The criminal sexual sadist. In R. R. Hazelwood & A. W. Burgess (Eds.), *Practical aspects of rape investigation: A multidisciplinary approach.* Boca Raton, FL: CRC Press.

Hazelwood, R. R., & Warren, J. I. (1995a). The relevance of fantasy in serial sexual crime investigation. In R. R. Hazelwood & A. W. Burgess (Eds.), *Practical aspects of rape investigation: A multidisciplinary approach.* Boca Raton, FL: CRC Press.

Hazelwood, R. R., & Warren, J. I. (1995b). The serial rapist. In R. R. Hazelwood & A. W. Burgess (Eds.), *Practical aspects of rape investigation: A multidisciplinary approach.* Boca Raton, FL: CRC Press.

Healy, M. A. (1995). Prosecuting child sex tourism at home: Do laws in Sweden, Australia, and the United States safeguard the rights of children as mandated by international laws? *Fordham International Law Journal, 18,* 1852-1871.

Hemphill, J. F. (1992). *Recidivism of criminal psychopaths after therapeutic community treatment.* Unpublished master's thesis, University of Saskatchewan, Saskatoon, Canada.

Hemphill, J. F., Hare, R. D., & Wong, S. (1998). Psychopathy and recidivism: A review. *Legal and Criminological Psychology, 3,* 139-170.

Herbert, T. B., & Dunkel-Schetter, C. (1992). Negative social reactions to victims: An overview of responses and their determinants, In L. Montada, S. Filipp, & M. J. Lerner (Eds.), *Life crises and experiences of loss in adulthood* (pp. 497-518). Hillsdale, NJ: Lawrence Erlbaum

Herdt, C. H. (1989). Gay and lesbian youth: Emergent identities and cultural scenes at home and abroad. *Journal of Homosexuality, 17*(1-2), 1-42.

Herdt, C. H., & Boxer, A. M. (1993). *Children of horizons: How gay and lesbian teens are leading a new way out of the closet.* Boston: Beacon.

Herek, G. M., Gillis, J. R., Cogan, J. C., & Glunt, E. K. (1997). Hate crime victimization among lesbian, gay, and bisexual adults: Prevalence, psychological correlates, and methodological issues. *Journal of Interpersonal Violence, 12,* 195-215.

Herek, G. M., & Glunt, E. K. (1988). An epidemic of stigma: Public reactions to AIDS. *American Psychologist, 43,* 886-891.

Herman, J. L. (1992). Complex PTSD: A syndrome in survivors of prolonged and repeated trauma. *Journal of Traumatic Stress, 5*(3), 377-389.

Hershberger, S. L., Pilkington, N. W., & D'Augelli, A. R. (1997). Predictors of suicidality among gay, lesbian, and bisexual youths. *Journal of Adolescent Research, 12,* 477-497.

Hetnick, E. S., & Martin, A. D. (1988). The stigmatization of the gay and lesbian adolescent. *Journal of Homosexuality, 15*(1-2), 163-183.

Hickey, E. (1997). *Serial killers and their victims.* Pacific Grove, CA: Brooks/Cole.

Hill, R. W., Langevin, R., Paitich, D., Handy, I., Russon, A., & Wilkinson, L. (1982). Is arson an aggressive act or a property offense? A controlled study of psychiatric referrals. *Canadian Journal of Psychiatry, 27,* 648-654.

Hoigard, C., & Finstad, L. (1992). *Backstreets: Prostitution, money and love.* University Park: Pennsylvania State University Press.

Holmes, R. M. (1988). A model of personal violence. *Kentucky Research Bulletin, 2,* 1-5.

Holmes, R. M., & DeBurger, J. (1985). Profiles in terror: The serial murderer. *Federal Probation, 39,* 29-34.

Holmes, R. M., & DeBurger, J. (1988). *Serial murder.* Newbury Park, CA: Sage.

Holmes, R. M., & Holmes, S. T. (1994). *Murder in America.* Thousand Oaks, CA: Sage.

Holmes, R. M., & Holmes, S. T. (1996). *Profiling violent crimes: An investigative tool* (2nd ed.). Thousand Oaks, CA: Sage.

Holmes, R. M., & Holmes, S. T. (1998a). *Contemporary perspectives on serial murder.* Thousand Oaks, CA: Sage.

Holmes, R. M., & Holmes, S. T. (1998b). *Serial murder* (2nd ed.). Thousand Oaks, CA: Sage.

Holmstrom, L. L., & Burgess, A. W. (1979, July). Rape: The husband's and boyfriend's initial reactions. *The Family Coordinator,* pp. 321-329.

Holtzen, D. W., Kenny, M. E., & Mahalik, J. R. (1995). Contributions of parental attachment to gay and lesbian disclosure to parents and dysfunctional cognitive processes. *Journal of Counseling Psychology, 42,* 350-355.

Hoover, D. R., Munoz, A., Carey, V., Chmiel, J. S., Taylor, J. M. C., Margoloic, J. B., Kingsley, L., & Vermund, S. H. (1991). Estimating the 1978-1990 and future spread of HIV in subgroups of homosexual men. *American Journal of Epidemiology, 134,* 1190-1205.

Horowitz, M. J., Wilner, N., & Alvarez, W. (1979). Impact of Events Scale: A measure of subjective distress. *Psychosomatic Medicine, 41,* 209-218.

Hudson, M. (1998, January 25). Megan's Law deceptive, experts say "it tends to give people a false sense of safety." *Roanoke Times.* Retrieved from http://www.vachss.com/av_dispatches/megan_2.html

Hughes, S. P., & Schneider, A. L. (1989). Victim-offender mediation: A survey of program characteristics and perceptions of effectiveness. *Crime & Delinquency, 35*, 217-233.

Hull, J. G., & Bond, C. F. (1986). Social and behavioral consequences of alcohol consumption and expectancy: A meta-analysis. *Psychological Bulletin, 99*, 347-360.

Human Rights Watch. (1996). *All too familiar: Sexual abuse of women in U.S. state prisons.* New York: Author.

Human Rights Watch. (1998). *Nowhere to hide: Retaliation against women in Michigan state prisons.* New York: Author. (Summary can be accessed on the Human Rights Watch Web Site at http://www.hrw.org/hrw/reports98/women/Mich.htm)

Hunter, I., & Schaecher, R. (1987). Stresses on lesbian and gay adolescents in schools. *Social Work in Education, 9*, 180-190.

Hunter, J. (1990). Violence against lesbian and gay male youths. *Journal of Interpersonal Violence, 5*, 295-300.

Hunter, J., & Santos, D. (1990). The use of specialized cognitive-behavioral therapies in the treatment of adolescent sexual offenders. *International Journal of Offender Therapy and Comparative Criminology, 34*, 239-247.

Immarigeon, R., & Daly, K. (1997, December). Restorative justice: Origins, practices, contexts, and challenges. *International Community Corrections Association (ICCA) Journal on Community Corrections,* pp. 13-18.

Inciardi, J. A. (1970). The adult firesetter: A typology. *Criminology, 8*, 145-155.

Inciardi, J. A. (1989). Trading sex for crack among juvenile drug users. *Contemporary Drug Problems, 16*(4), 689-700.

Inciardi, J., Lockwood, A. D., & Pottieger, A. E. (1993). *Women and crack cocaine.* New York: Macmillan.

Irigaray, L. (1985). *This sex which is not one* (C. Porter, Trans.). New York: Cornell University Press.

Irving, G., Bor, R., & Catalan, J. (1995). Psychological distress among gay men supporting a lover or partner with AIDS: A pilot study. *AIDS Care, 7*(5), 605-617.

Jackson, H. F., Glass, C., & Hope, S. (1987). A functional analysis of recidivistic arson. *British Journal of Clinical Psychology, 26*, 175-185.

Jacobs, B. (1999). *Dealing crack: The social world of street corner selling.* Boston: Northeastern University Press.

Jacobson, R., Jackson, M., & Berelowitz, M. (1986). Self-incineration: A controlled comparison of inpatient suicide attempts: Clinical features and history of self-harm. *Psychology and Medicine, 16*, 107-116.

James, E. (1991). *Catching serial killers.* Lansing, MI: International Forensic Services.

James, J. (1978). The prostitute as victim. In J. R. Chapman & M. Gates (Eds.), *The victimization of women* (pp. 175-201). Beverly Hills, CA: Sage.

Janoff-Bulman, R. (1989). Assumptive worlds and the stress of traumatic events: Applications of the schema construct. *Social Cognition, 7*, 113-136.

Janoff-Bulman, R., & Frieze, I. H. (1983). A theoretical perspective for understanding reactions to victimization. *Journal of Social Issues, 39*(2), 1-17.

Jenkins, P. (1994). *Using murder: The social construction of serial homicide.* New York: Aldine de Gruyter.

Jenkins, P. (1996). The social construction of serial homicide. In J. E. Conklin (Ed.), *New perspectives in criminology* (pp. 2-14). Boston: Allyn & Bacon.

Jenkins-Hall, K. D. (1989). Cognitive restructuring. In D. R. Laws (Ed.), *Relapse prevention with sex offenders* (pp. 207-215). New York: Guilford.

Jenks, R. (1995). Swinging: A test of two theories and a proposed new model. *Archives of Sexual Behavior, 14,* 517-527.

Jenness, V. (1993). *Making it work: The prostitutes' rights movement in perspective.* New York: Aldine de Gruyter.

Jensen, G. F., & Karpos, M. (1993). Managing rape: Exploratory research on the behavior of rape statistics. *Criminology, 31,* 363-385.

Johnson, D. M., Pike, J. L., & Chard, K. M. (in press). Factors predicting PTSD, depression, and dissociative severity in female treatment-seeking childhood sexual abuse survivors. *Child Abuse & Neglect.*

Johnson, H. (1996). *Dangerous domains: Violence against women in Canada.* Toronto: Nelson Canada.

Johnson, S. D., Gibson, L., & Linden, R. (1978). Alcohol and rape in Winnipeg, 1966-1975. *Journal of Studies on Alcohol, 39,* 1887-1894.

Johnston, L., & Ward, T. (1996). Social cognition and sexual offending: A theoretical framework. *Sexual Abuse: A Journal of Research and Treatment, 8,* 55-80.

Joinson, C. (1992). Coping with compassion fatigue. *Nursing, 22,* 116-122.

Jones, R. S., & Schmid, T. J. (1989). Inmates' conceptions of prison sexual assault. *The Prison Journal, 68*(1), 53-61.

Kaban, E. (1996, November 12). *ILO says 250 million children are workers.* Reuters World Service.

Kahn, T. J., & Lafond, M. A. (1988). Treatment of the adolescent sexual offender. *Child and Adolescent Social Work, 5,* 135-148.

Kamel, G. W. L. (1983). *Downtown street hustlers: The role of dramaturgical imaging practices in the social construction of male prostitution.* Unpublished doctoral dissertation, University of California, San Diego.

Kanka, M. (2000, March 28). *How Megan's death changed us all: The personal story of a mother and anti-crime advocate.* Retrieved from http://www.apbnews.com/safetycenter/family/kanka/2000/03/28/kanka0328_01.html

Kantrowitz, B., King, P., & Rosenberg, D. (1994, April 14). Child abuse in cyberspace. *Newsweek,* p. 40.

Kapardis, A. (1992). Killed by a stranger in Victoria, January 1990-April 1992: Locations, victims' age and risk. In H. Strang & S. Gerull (Eds.), *Homicides: Patterns, prevention and control: Proceedings of a conference held 12-14 May 1992* (pp. 121-132). Canberra: Australian Institute of Criminology.

Kappeler, S. (1986). *The pornography of representation.* Minneapolis: University of Minnesota Press.

Karter, J. J., Jr. (1990). Fire loss in the United States during 1989. *Fire Journal, 5,* 56-65.

Kattoulas, V. (1995, November 30). *World tourism industry dodges child sex-tour issue.* Reuters North American Wire.

Katz, P. A., & Ksansnak, K. R. (1994). Developmental aspects of gender role flexibility and traditionality in middle childhood and adolescence. *Developmental Psychology, 30,* 272-282.

Katzenstein, M. F. (1987). Comparing the feminist movements of the United States and Western Europe: An overview. In M. F. Katzenstein & C. M. Mueller (Eds.), *Women's movements of the United States and Western Europe: Consciousness, political opportunity, and public policy* (pp. 3-20). Philadelphia: Temple University Press.

Keane, T. M., Caddell, J. M., & Taylor, K. L. (1988). Mississippi Scale for Combat-Related Posttraumatic Stress Disorder: Three studies in reliability and validity. *Journal of Consulting and Clinical Psychology, 56,* 85-90.

Keane, T. M., Malloy, P. F., & Fairbank, J. A. (1984). Empirical development of an MMPI subscale for the assessment of combat-related posttraumatic stress disorder. *Journal of Consulting and Clinical Psychology, 52,* 888-891.

Kear-Colwell, J., & Pollock, P. (1997). Motivation or confrontation: Which approach to the child sex offender? *Criminal Justice and Behavior, 24,* 20-33.

Kempadoo, K. (1998). Introduction: Globalizing sex workers' rights. In K. Kempadoo & J. Doezema (Eds.), *Global sex workers: Rights, resistance, and redefinition* (pp. 1-28). New York: Routledge.

Kempadoo, K., & Doezema, J. (Eds.). (1998). *Global sex workers: Rights, resistance, and redefinition.* New York: Routledge.

Kilpatrick, D. G. (1988). Rape aftermath symptom test. In *Dictionary of behavioral assessment techniques* (pp. 366-367). Oxford, UK: Pergamon.

Kimmerling, R., & Calhoun, K. S. (1994). Somatic symptoms, social support, and treatment seeking among sexual assault victims. *Journal of Consulting and Clinical Psychology, 62,* 333-340.

Kindermann, C., Lynch, J., & Cantor, D. (1997). *Effects of the redesign on victimization estimates.* Washington, DC: Bureau of Justice Statistics.

Klaus, P. A., & Rand, M. R. (1984). *Family violence.* Washington, DC: Bureau of Justice Statistics.

Klein, L. (1998). Do ask, do tell: Assessing implications of community notification requirements within sexual offender legislation. In L. J. Moriarity & R. J. Jerin (Eds.), *Current issues in victimology research* (pp. 177-191). Durham, NC: Carolina Academic Press.

Knopp, F. H. (1991). Community solutions to sexual violence. In H. E. Pepinsky & R. Quinney (Eds.), *Criminology as peacemaking* (pp. 181-193). Bloomington: Indiana University Press.

Knowles, G. J. (1996). Male prison rape: A search for causation and prevention. In *Sociological Abstracts* (#96532301). San Diego, CA: Cambridge Scientific Abstracts.

Kosid-Uthe, J. (1992). Considerations in obtaining and using expertise search warrants in cases of preferential child molesters. In K. V. Lanning (Ed.), *Child molesters: A behavioral analysis* (3rd ed., pp. 45-59). Arlington, VA: National Center for Missing and Exploited Children.

Koson, D. F., & Dvoskin, J. (1982). Arson: A diagnostic study. *Bulletin of the American Academy of Psychiatry and the Law, 10,* 39-49.

Koss, M. P. (1985). The hidden rape victim: Personality, attitudinal, and situational characteristics. *Psychology of Women Quarterly, 9,* 193-212.

Koss, M. P. (1990). The women's mental health research agenda: Violence against women. *American Psychologist, 43,* 374-380.

Koss, M. P. (1992). Defending date rape. *Journal of Interpersonal Violence, 7,* 122-126.

Koss, M. P. (1993a). Detecting the scope of rape: A review of prevalence research methods. *Journal of Interpersonal Violence, 8,* 198-222.

Koss, M. P. (1993b). Rape: Scope, impact, interventions, and public policy responses. *American Psychologist, 48,* 1062-1069.

Koss, M. P., Dinero, T. E., Seibel, C. A., & Cox, S. L. (1988). Stranger and acquaintance rape. *Psychology of Women Quarterly, 12,* 1-24.

Koss, M. P., Goodman, L. A., Browne, A., Fitzgerald, L. F., Keita, G. P., & Russo, N. F. (1994). *No safe haven: Male violence against women at home, at work, and in the community.* Washington, DC: American Psychological Association.

Koss, M. P., & Harvey, M. R. (1991). *The rape victim: Clinical and community interventions.* Newbury Park, CA: Sage.

Kosson, D. S., Kelly, J. C., & White, J. W. (1997). Psychopathy-related traits predict self-reported sexual aggression among college men. *Journal of Interpersonal Violence, 12,* 241-254.

Kreindler, S., & Armstrong, H. (1983). The abused child and the family. In P. D. Steinhauer & Q. Rae-Grant (Eds,), *Psychological problems of the child in the family* (2nd ed., pp. 545-564). New York: Basic Books.

Kuhn, T. S. (1962). *The structure of scientific revolutions.* Chicago: University of Chicago Press.

Kupers, T. A. (1997). Men, prison and the American Dream. *Tikkun, 12*(1), 60-61, 74, 79.

Kurz, D. (1989). Social science perspectives on wife abuse: Current debates and future directions. *Gender & Society, 3,* 501-513.

Kurz, D. (1990). Interventions with battered women in health care settings. *Violence and Victims, 5,* 243-256.

Kurz, D. (1993). Physical assaults by husbands: A major social problem. In R. J. Gelles & D. R. Loseke (Eds.), *Current controversies on family violence* (pp. 88-104). Newbury Park, CA: Sage.

Lalumière, M. L., & Quinsey, V. L. (1996). Sexual deviance, antisociality, mating effort, and the use of sexually coercive behaviors. *Personality and Individual Differences, 21,* 33-48.

Lande, S. D. (1980). A combination of orgasmic reconditioning and covert sensitization in the treatment of a fire fetish. *Journal of Behavior Therapy and Experimental Psychology, 11,* 291-296.

Lane, K. E., & Gwartney-Gibbs, P. A. (1985). Violence in the context of dating and sex. *Journal of Family Issues, 6,* 45-59.

Laner, M. R., & Thompson, J. (1982). Abuse and aggression in courting couples. *Deviant Behavior, 3,* 69-83.

Langen, P. A., & Innes, C. A. (1986). *Preventing domestic violence against women.* Washington, DC: U.S. Department of Justice.

Lanning, K. V. (1992). *Child molesters: A behavioral analysis* (3rd ed.). Arlington, VA: National Center for Missing and Exploited Children.

Launay, G. (1994). The phallometric assessment of sex offenders: Some professional and research issues. *Criminal Behavior and Mental Health, 4,* 48-70.

Laws, D. R. (Ed.). (1989). *Relapse prevention with sex offenders.* New York: Guilford.

Leck, C. (1994). Politics of adolescent sexual identity and queer responses. *High School Journal, 77,* 186-192.

Ledray, L. (1999). *Sexual Assault Nurse Examiners (SANE): Development and operations guide.* Washington, DC: Department of Justice, Office for Victims of Crime.

Lemp, C. F., Hirozawa, A. M., Givertz, D., Nieri, C. N., Anderson, L., Lindegren, M. L., Janssen, R. S., & Katz, M. (1994). Seroprevalence of HIV and risk behaviors among young homosexual and bisexual men. *Journal of the American Medical Association, 272,* 449-454.

Leong, G. B. (1992). A psychiatric study of persons charged with arson. *Journal of Forensic Sciences, 37,* 1319-1326.

Lerman, L. G. (1984). Mediation of wife abuse cases: The adverse impact of informal dispute resolution on women. *Harvard Women's Law Journal, 7,* 57-113.

Lester, D. (1975). *Unusual sexual behavior: The standard deviations.* Springfield, IL: Charles C Thomas.

Levin, J., & Fox, J. (1985). *Mass murder: America's growing menace.* New York: Plenum.

Levine, P. (1988). *Prostitution in Florida: A report presented to the Gender Bias Study Commission of the Supreme Court of Florida.* Tallahassee: Florida Supreme Court.

Levrant, S., Cullen, F. T., Fulton, B., & Wozniak, J. F. (1999). Reconsidering restorative justice: The corruption of benevolence revisited. *Crime & Delinquency, 45,* 3-27.

Lewin, B. R. (1996). *The assessment of the cognitive and affective antecedent conditions to assist in the prediction of aggressive and violent behavior.* Unpublished manuscript, California State University, San Diego.

Lewinsohn, P. M., Rohde, P., & Seeley, J. R. (1996). Adolescent suicide ideation and attempts: Prevalence, risk factors, and clinical implications. *Clinical Psychology: Science and Practice, 3*, 25-46.

Lewis, I. (1998). Learning to strip: The socialization experiences of exotic dancers. *Canadian Journal of Human Sexuality, 7*(1), 51-66.

Lewis, N., & Yarnell, H. (1951). Pathological firesetting (pyromaniac). *Nervous and Mental Disease Monographs, 2.*

Lewis v. United States, 385 U.S. 206, 208-209 (1966).

Lieb, R. (1996). Community notification laws: "A step toward more effective solutions." *Journal of Interpersonal Violence, 11*, 298-300.

Liebman, F. (1989). Serial murderers. *Federal Probation, 53*(4), 41-45.

Lim, L. L. (Ed.). (1998). *The sex sector: The economic and social bases of prostitution in southeast Asia.* Geneva: International Labor Organization.

Linnoila, M., DeJong, J., & Virkkunen, M. (1989). Monoamines, glucose metabolism, and impulse control. *Psychopharmacology Bulletin, 25*, 404-406.

Lisak, D., & Ivan, C. (1995). Deficits in intimacy and empathy in sexually aggressive men. *Journal of Interpersonal Violence, 10*, 296-308.

Lockwood, D. (1978). *Sexual aggression among male prisoners.* Ann Arbor, MI: University Microfilms International.

Lockwood, D. (1980). *Prison sexual violence.* New York: Elsevier North-Holland.

Lockwood, D. (1985). Issues in prison sexual violence. *The Prison Journal, 62*, 73-79.

Lockwood, D. (1994). Issues in prison sexual violence. In M. C. Braswell, R. H. Montgomery, Jr., & L. X. Lombardo (Eds.), *Prison violence in America* (2nd ed., pp. 97-102). Cincinnati, OH: Anderson.

Loewy, A. (1987). *Criminal law in a nutshell.* St. Paul, MN: West.

Lonsway, K. A. (1996). Preventing acquaintance rape through education: What do we know? *Psychology of Women Quarterly, 20*, 229-265.

Lotke, E. (1996, April). Sex offenders: Does treatment work? *Issues and Answers: Research Update.* Washington, DC: National Center on Institutions and Alternatives.

Louis Harris and Associates, Inc. (1993). *The health of American women.* New York: Author.

Lowman, J. (1990). Notions of formal equality before the law: The experiences of street prostitutes and their customers. *Journal of Human Justice, 1*, 55-76.

Lowman, J., & Fraser, L. (1995). *Violence against persons who prostitute: The experience in British Columbia* (Technical report). Canada: Department of Justice.

Luckenbill, D. F. (1984). Dynamics of the deviant sale. *Deviant Behavior, 5*(4), 337-354.

Luckenbill, D. F. (1986). Deviant career mobility: The case of male prostitutes. *Social Problems, 33*(4), 283-296.

Lunde, D. (1976). *Murder and madness.* New York: W.W. Norton.

Lurigio, A. J., Jones, M., & Smith, B. E. (1995). Child sexual abuse: Its causes, consequences, and implications for probation practice. *Federal Probation, 59*(3), 69-76.

MacDonald, J. M. (1977). *Bombers and firesetters.* Springfield, IL: Charles C Thomas.

Madigan, L., & Gamble, N. (1991). *The second rape: Society's continued betrayal of the victim.* New York: Lexington Books.

Maguire, K., & Pastore, A. L. (Eds.). (1997). *Sourcebook of criminal justice statistics 1997.* Washington, DC: Bureau of Justice Statistics.

Maher, L. (1997). *Sexed work: Gender, race, and resistance in a Brooklyn drug market.* New York: Oxford University Press.

Makepeace, J. M. (1981). Courtship violence among college students. *Family Relations, 30*, 97-102.

Makepeace, J. M. (1983). Life events stress and courtship violence. *Family Relations, 32,* 101-109.

Makepeace, J. M. (1986) Gender differences in courtship violence victimization. *Family Relations, 35,* 386-388.

Malcolm, P. B., Andrews, D. A., & Quinsey, V. L. (1993). Discriminant and predictive validity on phallometrically measured sexual age and gender preferences. *Journal of Interpersonal Violence, 8,* 486-501.

Markoff, J. (1992, March 22). Sex by computer: The latest technology fuels the oldest drives. *New York Times,* p. A5.

Marshall, S. (1995, September 14). On-line child pornography busted. *USA Today,* p. A1.

Marshall, W. L. (1997). Pedophilia: Psychopathology and theory. In D. Laws & W. O'Donahue (Eds.), *Sexual deviance: Theory, assessment, and treatment* (pp. 152-174). New York: Guilford.

Marshall, W. L., & Pithers, W. D. (1994). A reconsideration of treatment outcome with sex offenders. *Criminal Justice and Behavior, 21,* 10-27.

Marsiglio, W. (1993). Attitudes towards homosexual activity and gays as friends: A national survey of heterosexual 15- to 19-year-old males. *Journal of Sex Research, 30,* 12-17.

Martin, A. D. (1982). Learning to hide: The socialization of the gay adolescent. *Adolescent Psychiatry, 10,* 52-65.

Martin, P. Y. (1990). Rethinking feminist organizations. *Gender & Society, 4,* 182-206.

Martin, P. Y. (1997). Gender, accounts, and rape processing work. *Social Problems, 44,* 464-482.

Martin, P. Y. (1999). *Rape processing work in organization and community context.* Unpublished manuscript, Florida State University, Department of Sociology.

Martin, P. Y., & DiNitto, D. (1987). The rape exam: Beyond the hospital ER. *Women and Health, 12,* 5-28.

Martin, P. Y., DiNitto, D., Byington, D., & Maxwell, M. S. (1992). Organizational and community transformation: The case of a rape crisis center. *Administration in Social Work, 16,* 123-145.

Martin, P. Y., DiNitto, D., Harrison, D., & Maxwell, S. M. (1985). Controversies surrounding the rape kit exam in the 1980s: Issues and alternatives. *Crime & Delinquency, 31,* 223-246.

Martin, P. Y., & Powell, M. R. (1994). Accounting for the second assault: Legal organizations' framing of rape victims. *Law and Social Inquiry, 19,* 853-890.

Martin, R. J. (1996, Fall). Symposium on Megan's Law: Introduction: Pursuing public protection through mandatory community notification of convicted sex offenders: The trials and tribulations of Megan's Law. *Boston University Public Interest Law Journal, 6,* 29.

Martin, S. E., & Bachman, R. (1998). The contribution of alcohol to the likelihood of completion and severity of injury in rape incidents. *Violence Against Women, 4,* 694-712.

Masters, W., & Johnson, V. (1970). *Human sexual inadequacy.* Boston: Little, Brown.

Matoesian, G. M. (1993). *Reproducing rape: Domination through talk in the courtroom.* Chicago: University of Chicago Press.

Matthews, N. A. (1994). *Confronting rape: The feminist anti-rape movement and the state.* New York: Routledge.

Mavromatis, M., & Lion, J. (1977). A primer on pyromania. *Diseases of the Nervous System, 38,* 954-955.

McCall, G. J. (1993). Risk factors and sexual assault prevention. *Journal of Interpersonal Violence, 8*(2), 277-295.

McCann, I. L., & Pearlman, L. A. (1990). Vicarious traumatization: A framework for understanding the psychological effects of working with victims. *Journal of Traumatic Stress, 3,* 131-149.

McCann, I. L., Sakheim, D., & Abrahamson, D. (1988). Trauma and victimization: A model of psychological adaptation. *Counseling Psychologist, 16,* 531-594.

McCleod, E. (1982). *Women working: Prostitution now.* London: Croom Helm.

McCoy, C. B., & Inciardi, J. A. (1995). *Sex, drugs, and the continuing spread of AIDS.* Los Angeles: Roxbury.

McElroy, W. (1995). AXV *A woman's right to pornography.* New York: St. Martin's.

McGirk, T. (1996, May 12). Their latest holiday destination. *The [Colombo, Sri Lanka] Independent.*

McKeganey, N. (1994). Why do men buy sex and what are their assessments of the HIV-related risks when they do? *AIDS Care, 6*(3), 289-301.

McKeganey, N., & Barnard, M. (1996). *Sex work on the streets: Prostitutes and their clients.* Buckingham, UK: Open University Press.

McKibben, A., Proulx, J., & Lusignan, R. (1994). Relationships between conflict, affect and deviant sexual behaviors in rapists and child molesters. *Behaviour Research and Therapy, 32,* 571-575.

McKnight, J. (1995). *The careless society: Community and its counterfeits.* New York: Basic Books.

McLeer, S. R., & Anwar, R. (1989). A study of battered women presenting in emergency departments. *American Journal of Public Health, 79,* 65-66.

McLeod, M. (1984). Women against men: An examination of domestic violence based on an analysis of official data and national victimization data. *Justice Quarterly, 1,* 171-193.

McNeely, R. L., & Mann, C. R. (1990). Domestic violence is a human issue. *Journal of Interpersonal Violence, 5,* 129-132.

McNeely, R. L., & Robinson-Simpson, G. (1987). The truth about domestic violence: A falsely framed issue. *Social Work, 32,* 485-490.

Mechanic, M., & Resick, P. (1993, October). *The Personal Beliefs and Reactions Scale: Assessing rape-related cognitive schemata.* Paper presented at the 9th annual meeting of the International Society for Traumatic Stress Studies, San Antonio, TX.

Megan Nicole Kanka Foundation. (1997). *Abuse/incest support.* Trenton, NJ: Author.

Meredith, W. H., Abbott, D. A., & Adams, S. L. (1986). Family violence: Its relation to marital and parental satisfaction and family strengths. *Journal of Family Violence, 1,* 299-305.

Metzner, J. L., & Ryan, G. D. (1995). Sexual abuse perpetration. In G. P. Sholevar (Ed.), *Conduct disorders in children and adolescents* (pp. 119-144). Washington, DC: American Psychiatric Press.

Meyer, I. H., & Dean, L. (1995). Patterns of sexual behavior and risk taking among young New York City gay men. *AIDS Education and Prevention, 7*(Suppl.), 13-23.

Michaud, S., & Aynesworth, H. (1983). *The only living witness.* New York: Signet.

Mies, M. (1986). *Patriarchy and accumulation on a world scale: Women in the international division of labor.* London: Zed.

Miles, M., & Huberman, M. (1984). *Qualitative data analysis: A sourcebook of new methods.* Beverly Hills, CA: Sage.

Miller, E. M. (1986). *Street woman.* Philadelphia: Temple University Press.

Miller, E. M. (1991, August). *Thinking about prostitution discourse as a way of thinking about gender as a principle of social organization.* Paper presented at the annual meeting of the American Sociological Association, Cincinnati, OH.

Miller, J. (1993). Your life is on the line every night you're on the streets: Victimization and resistance among street prostitutes. *Humanity & Society, 17,* 422-446.

Miller, J. (1995a). Gender and power on the streets: Street prostitution in the era of crack cocaine. *Journal of Contemporary Ethnography, 23,* 427-452.

Miller, J. (1995b). Sex tourism in Southeast Asia. In A. Thio & T. Calhoun (Eds.), *Readings in deviant behavior* (pp. 278-283). New York: HarperCollins.

Miller, J. (1997). Victimization and resistance among street prostitutes. In P. A. Adler & P. Adler (Eds.), *Constructions of deviance* (2nd ed., pp. 500-515). Belmont, CA: Wadsworth.

Miller, J. (1999). *The commercial sex industry in Sri Lanka: Some preliminary observations.* International Centre for Ethnic Studies Lecture Series, Colombo, Sri Lanka.

Miller, J., & Schwartz, M. D. (1995). Rape myths and violence against street prostitutes. *Deviant Behavior, 16*(1), 1-23.

Miller, M. E., & Sulkes, S. (1988). Firesetting behavior in individuals with Klinefelter's syndrome. *Pediatrics, 82,* 115-117.

Miller, M. W., Geddings, V. J., Levenston, G. K., & Patrick, C. J. (1994, March). *The personality characteristics of psychopathic and non psychopathic sex offenders.* Paper presented at the biennial meeting of the American Psychology-Law Society (Division 41 of the American Psychological Association), Santa Fe, NM.

Miller, W. R., Williams, A. M., & Bernstein, M. H. (1982). The effects of rape on marital and sexual adjustment. *American Journal of Family Therapy, 10,* 51-58.

Mishra, R. (1997, July 15). What can be done? Society struggles with the treatment of sex offenders. *Detroit Free Press.* Retrieved from http://www.freep.com/news/health/qsex15.htm

Mitchell, M. E. (1991). A family approach and network implications of therapy for victims of violence as applied in a case of rape. *Journal of Family Psychotherapy, 2,* 1-13.

Money, J., & Bennett, R. G. (1981). Post-adolescent paraphilic sex offenders: Anti-androgenic and counseling therapy follow-up. *International Journal of Mental Health, 10,* 122-133.

Montana, J. A. (1996). An ineffective weapon in the fight against child sexual abuse: New Jersey's Megan's Law. *Journal of Law & Policy, 3,* 569-604.

Montgomery, H. (1998). Children, prostitution, and identity: A case study from a tourist resort in Thailand. In K. Kempadoo & J. Doezema (Eds.), *Global sex workers: Rights, resistance, and redefinition* (pp. 139-150). New York: Routledge.

Moore, J. M., Thompson-Pope, S. K., & Whited, R. M. (1996). MMPI-A profiles of adolescent boys with a history of firesetting. *Journal of Personality Assessment, 67,* 116-126.

Moore, M. H. (1992). Problem-solving and community policing. In M. Tonry & N. Morris (Eds.), *Modern policing: Crime and justice, a review of research* (Vol. 15, pp. 99-158). Chicago: University of Chicago Press.

Morse, B. (1995). Beyond the Conflict Tactics Scale: Assessing gender differences in partner violence. *Violence and Victims, 10,* 251-272.

Morse, E. V., Simon, P. M., Balson, P. M., & Osofsky, H. J. (1992). Sexual behavior patterns of customers of male street prostitutes. *Archives of Sexual Behavior, 21*(4), 347-357.

Morse, E. V., Simon, P. M., Baus, S. A., Balson, P. M., & Osofsky, H. J. (1992). Cofactors of substance use among male street prostitutes. *Journal of Drug Issues, 21*(4), 977-994.

Morse, E. V., Simon, P. M., Osofsky, H. J., Balson, P. M., & Gaumer, H. R. (1991). The male street prostitute: A vector for transmission of HIV infection into the heterosexual world. *Social Science and Medicine, 32*(5), 535-539.

Motiuk, L. L., & Belcourt, R. L. (1997). *Homicide, sex, robbery, and drug offenders in federal corrections: An end-of-1996 review.* Ottawa: Research Branch, Correctional Service of Canada.

Muehlenhard, C. L., & Linton, M. A. (1987). Date rape and sexual aggression in dating situations: Incidence and risk factors. *Journal of Counseling Psychology, 34,* 186-196.

Mueller, C. M. (1987). Collective unconsciousness, identity transformation, and the rise of women in public office in the United States. In M. F. Katzenstein & C. M. Mueller (Eds.), *Women's movements of the United States and Western Europe: Consciousness, political opportunity, and public policy* (pp. 89-108). Philadelphia: Temple University Press.

Murray, A. (1998). Debt-bondage and trafficking: Don't believe the hype. In K. Kempadoo & J. Doezema (Eds.), *Global sex workers: Rights, resistance, and redefinition* (pp. 51-64). New York: Routledge.

Myers, J. E. B. (1996). Societal self-defense: New laws to protect children from sexual abuse. *Child Abuse & Neglect, 20,* 255-258.

Nacci, P., & Kane, T. (1983). The incidence of sex and sexual aggression in federal prisons. *Federal Probation, 47,* 31-36.

Nacci, P., & Kane, T. (1984). Sex and sexual aggression in federal prisons: Inmate involvement and employee impact. *Federal Probation, 48,* 46-53.

Nagle, J. (Ed.). (1997). *Whores and other feminists.* New York: Routledge.

National Broadcasting Company. (1999, September 11). *Women behind bars* [Documentary].

National Commission on Correctional Health Care. (1997). *Standards for health services in prisons.* Chicago: Author.

National Criminal Justice Reference Service (NCJRS). (1996). Balanced and Restorative Justice Project (BARJ). *Office of Juvenile Justice and Delinquency Prevention (OJJDP) Fact Sheet #42.* Retrieved from http://www.ncjrs.org/txtfiles/91415.txt

National Gay and Lesbian Task Force Policy Institute. (1994). *Anti-gay/lesbian violence, victimization, and defamation in 1993.* Washington, DC: Author.

National Victim Center and the Crime Victims Research and Treatment Center. (1992). *Rape in America: A report to the nation.* Arlington, VA: Author.

Nelson, A., & Robinson, B. W. (1996). *Gigolos and madames bountiful: Illusions of gender, power, and intimacy.* Toronto: University of Toronto Press.

Nielsen, J. (1970). Criminality among patients with Klinefelter's syndrome and the XYY syndrome. *British Journal of Psychiatry, 117,* 365-369.

Nieves, E. (1998, January 4). Watching "Megan's Law" in practice. *New York Times,* p. 17.

Nisonoff, L., & Bitman, I. (1979). Spouse abuse: Incidence and relationship to selected demographic variables. *Victimology, 4,* 131-140.

Norris, J., & Birnes, W. (1988). *Serial killers: The growing menace.* New York: Dolphin.

Nowikowski, F. (1995). Psychological offender profiling: An overview. *Criminologist, 19,* 225-226.

Nuffield, J. (1982). *Parole decision-making in Canada: Research towards decision guidelines.* Ottawa, Canada: Ministry of Supply and Services.

O'Brien, D. (1988). *Two of a kind: The Hillside Stranglers.* New York: Signet.

Ochs, E. P., Meana, M., Pare, L., Mah, K., & Binik, Y. M. (1994). Learning about sex outside the gutter: Attitudes toward a computer sex expert system. *Journal of Sex and Marital Therapy, 20,* 86-102.

O'Connor, J. J. (1987). *Practical fire and arson investigation.* New York: Elsevier.

Odem, M. E., & Clay-Warner, J. (1998). *Confronting rape and sexual assault* (Worlds of Women Series, No. 3). Wilmington, DE: Scholarly Resources.

Odgers, S. J., & Richardson, J. T. (1995). Keeping bad science out of the courtroom: Changes in American and Australian expert evidence law. *University of New South Wales Law Review, 18,* 108-129.

Office for Drug Control and Crime Prevention, United Nations Interregional Crime and Justice Research Institute, and Center for International Crime Prevention. (1998). *Global programme against trafficking in human beings: An outline for action.* Geneva: United Nations.

Office of Justice Programs (OJP). (1998). *Attorney general encourages community leaders to focus on community justice.* Washington, DC: Author.

Ogletree, R. (1993). Sexual coercion experience and help-seeking behavior of college women. *Journal of American College Health, 41,* 149-153.

Ogloff, J., Wong, S., & Greenwood, A. (1990). Treating criminal psychopaths in a therapeutic community program. *Behavioral Sciences and the Law, 8,* 81-90.

Oliver, W. M. (1998). *Community-oriented policing: A systematic approach to policing.* Upper Saddle River, NJ: Prentice Hall.

Orbuch, T., Harvey, J., Davis, S., & Merbach, N. (1994). Account-making and confiding as acts of meaning in response to sexual assault. *Journal of Family Violence, 9,* 249-264.

Orcutt, J. D., & Faison, F. (1988). Sex-role change and reporting of rape victimization, 1973-1985. *Sociological Quarterly, 29,* 589-604.

O'Shaughnessy, P. (1995, July 30). Megan Kanka has become a symbol of the right to know about rapists and molesters living nearby. *New York Daily News,* p. 6.

O'Sullivan, E. A. (1978). What has happened to rape crisis centers? A look at their structure, members, and funding. *Victimology, 3,* 45-62.

O'Sullivan, G. H., & Kelleher, M. J. (1987). A study of firesetters in the southwest of Ireland. *British Journal of Psychiatry, 151,* 818-823.

Overall, C. (1992). What's wrong with prostitution? Evaluating sex work. *Signs, 17,* 705-724.

Owen, B. (1998). *In the mix.* Albany: State University of New York Press.

Paglia, C. (1990). *Sexual persona.* New York: Vintage.

Paglia, C. (1994). *Vamps and tramps.* New York: Vintage.

Pallone, N. J. (1995). A view from the front line. *Criminal Justice Ethics, 14,* 9-11.

Paris, F., Yuille, J. C., Walker, L., & Porter, S. (1999). *Sex offenders' reasoning on ethical issues: Moral blindness or developmental delay?* Manuscript submitted for publication.

Pavlich, G. (1996). The power of community mediation: Government and formation of self-identity. *Law & Society Review, 30,* 707-733.

Pearl, J. (1987). The highest paying customers: America's cities and the costs of prostitution control. *Hastings Law Journal, 38*(4), 769-800.

Pearson, E. A. (1998). Status and latest developments in sex offender registration and notification laws. *National Conference on Sex Offender Registries Proceedings.* Washington, DC: Bureau of Justice Statistics.

Pedhazur, E. J. (1982). *Multiple regression in behavioral research: Explanation and prediction* (2nd ed.). New York: Holt, Rinehart & Winston.

Pendleton, E. (1997). Love for sale: Queering heterosexuality. In J. Nagle (Ed.), *Whores and other feminists* (pp. 73-82). New York: Routledge.

Pernanen, K. (1991). *Alcohol in human violence.* New York: Guilford.

Petersen, D., & Dressel, P. (1982). Equal time for women: Social notes on the male strip show. *Urban Life, 11*(2), 185-208.

Peterson, R. (1980). Social class, social learning, and wife abuse. *Social Service Review, 50,* 390-406.

Phongpaichit, P. (1982). *From peasant girls to Bangkok masseuses.* Geneva: International Labor Office.

Pilgrim, C. W. (1885). Pyromania (so-called), with a report of a case. *American Journal of Insanity, 41,* 456-465.

Pilkington, N. W., & D'Augelli, A. R. (1995). Victimization of lesbian, gay, and bisexual youth in community settings. *Journal of Community Psychology, 23,* 33-56.

Pinizzotto, A. J., & Finkel, N. J. (1990). Criminal personality profiling: An outcome and process study. *Law and Human Behavior, 14,* 215-233.

Pithers, W. D., Beal, L. S., Armstrong, J., & Petty, J. (1989). Identification of risk factors through clinical interviews and analysis of records. In D. R. Laws (Ed.), *Relapse prevention with sex offenders* (pp. 77-87). New York: Guilford.

Pithers, W. D., Kashima, K., Cummings, G. F., Beal, L. S., & Buell, M. (1988). Relapse prevention of sexual aggression. In R. Prentky & V. Quinsey (Eds.), *Human sexual aggression: Current perspectives* (pp. 244-260). New York: New York Academy of Sciences.

Pleck, E., Pleck, J. H., Grossman, M., & Bart, P. (1977-1978). The battered data syndrome: A comment on Steinmetz's article. *Victimology, 2,* 131-140.

Plumridge, E. V., Chetwynd, S. J., Reed, A., & Gifford, S. J. (1996). Patrons of the sex industry: Perceptions of risk. *AIDS Care, 8*(4), 405-416.

Pocket Criminal Code, 1999. (1998). Scarborough, Ontario, Canada: Carswell.

Polk, K. (1994). *When men kill: Scenarios of masculine violence.* Melbourne, Australia: University of Cambridge Press.

Pollock-Byrne, J. M. (1990). *Women, prison and crime.* Pacific Grove, CA: Brooks/Cole.

Popiel, D. A., & Suskind, E. C. (1985). The impact of rape: Social support as a moderator of stress. *American Journal of Community Psychology, 13,* 645-676.

Porter, S. (1996). Without conscience or without active conscience? The etiology of psychopathy revisited. *Aggression and Violent Behavior, 1,* 179-189.

Posner, R. A. (1992). *Sex and reason.* Cambridge, MA: Harvard University Press.

Prasad, M. (1999). The morality of market exchange: Love, money, and contractual justice. *Sociological Perspectives, 42,* 181-198.

Prendergast, W. E. (1991). *Treating sex offenders in correctional institutions and outpatient clinics: A guide to clinical practice.* New York: Haworth.

Prentky, R. A. (1996). Community notification and constructive risk reduction [Commentary]. *Journal of Interpersonal Violence, 11,* 295-298.

Prentky, R. A., Burgess, A. W., Rokous, F., Lee, A., Hartman, C., Ressler, R., & Douglas, J. (1989). The presumptive role of fantasy in serial sexual homicide. *American Journal of Psychiatry, 146*(7), 887-891.

Prentky, R. A., & Knight, R. A. (1991). Identifying critical dimensions for discriminating among rapists. *Journal of Consulting and Clinical Psychology, 59,* 643-661.

Prentky, R. A., Lee, A. F. S., Knight, R. A., & Cerce, D. (1997). Recidivism rates among child molesters and rapists: A methodological analysis. *Law and Human Behavior, 21,* 635-659.

Prescod, M. (1990, June). Paper presented at the annual meeting of National Women's Studies Association, Akron, OH.

Pride, A. (1981). To respectability and back: A ten-year view of the anti-rape movement. In F. Delacoste & F. Newman (Eds.), *Fight back: Feminist resistance to male violence.* Minneapolis, MN: Cleis.

Prins, H. (1986). *Dangerous behavior, the law, and mental disorder.* London: Tavistock.

Prins, H. (1987). Up in smoke—the psychology of arson. *Medico-Legal Journal, 55,* 69-84.

Prins, H., Tennent, G., & Trick, K. (1985). Motives for arson (fire raising). *Medicine, Science and the Law, 25,* 275-278.

Proulx, J., McKibben, A., & Lusignan, R. (1996). Relationships between affective components and sexual behaviors in sexual aggressors. *Sexual Abuse: A Journal of Research and Treatment, 8,* 279-289.

Prus, R., & Irini, S. (1980). *Hookers, rounders, and desk clerks.* Toronto: Gage.

Puri, B. K., Baxster, R., & Cordess, C. C. (1995). Characteristics of firesetters: A study and proposed multiaxial psychiatric classification. *British Journal of Psychiatry, 166,* 393-396.

Queen, C. (1997). Sex, radical politics, sex-positive feminist thought, and whore stigma. In J. Nagle (Ed.), *Whores and other feminists* (pp. 125-135). New York: Routledge.

Quinsey, V. I. (1998). Treatment of sex offenders. In M. Tonry (Ed.), *The handbook of crime & punishment* (pp. 403-425). New York: Oxford University Press.

Quinsey, V. L., Chaplain, T. C., & Upfold, D. (1989). Arsonists and sexual arousal to firesetting: Correlation unsupported. *Journal of Behavior Therapy and Experimental Psychology, 20,* 203-209.

Quinsey, V. L., Coleman, G., Jones, B., & Altrows, I. (1997). Proximal antecedents of eloping and reoffending among supervised mentally disordered offenders. *Journal of Interpersonal Violence, 12,* 794-813.

Quinsey, V. L., Harris, G. T., Rice, M. E., & Cormier, C, A. (1998). *Violent offenders: Appraising and managing risk.* Washington, DC: American Psychological Association.

Quinsey, V. L., Rice, M. E., & Harris, G. T. (1995). Actuarial prediction of sexual recidivism. *Journal of Interpersonal Violence, 10,* 85-105.

Rabwin, P., & Caulfield, B. (Producers). (1993-2000). *The X-Files.* Los Angeles: 20th Century Fox Television.

Rand, M. R. (1997). *Violence-related injuries treated in hospital emergency departments* (No. NCJ 156921). Washington, DC: Bureau of Justice Statistics.

Rapoport, I. C. (Producer). (1996-1999). *Profiler.* Burbank, CA: NBC Studios.

Rappaport, R. (1988). The serial and mass murderers. *American Journal of Forensic Psychiatry, 9*(1), 39-48.

Rasanen, P., Hakko, H., & Vaisanen, E. (1995). Arson trend increasing—a real challenge to psychiatry. *Journal of Forensic Sciences, 40,* 976-979.

Rasmussen, P. K., & Kuhn, L. H. (1976). The new masseuse: Play for pay. In C. A. B. Warren (Ed.), *Sexuality, encounters, identities, and relationships.* Beverly Hills, CA: Sage.

Ratner, M. S. (Ed.). (1993). *Crack pipe as pimp: An ethnographic investigation of sex-for-crack exchanges.* New York: Lexington Books.

Ray, I. (1844). *A treatise on the medical jurisprudence of insanity* (2nd ed.). Boston: William D. Tickner.

Reese, J. T. (1979). Obsessive compulsive behavior: The nuisance offender. *FBI Law Enforcement Bulletin.*

Remafedi, C. (1987a). Adolescent homosexuality: Psychosocial and medical implications. *Pediatrics, 79,* 331-337.

Remafedi, C. (1987b). Homosexual youth: A challenge to contemporary society. *Journal of the American Medical Association, 258,* 222-225.

Remafedi, C. (1987c). Male homosexuality: The adolescent's perspective. *Pediatrics, 79,* 326-330.

Remafedi, C. (1994). Predictors of unprotected intercourse among gay and bisexual youths: Knowledge, beliefs, and behavior. *Pediatrics, 94,* 163-168.

Remafedi, C., Farrow, J. A., & Deisher, R. W. (1991). Risk factors for attempted suicide in gay and bisexual youth. *Pediatrics, 87,* 869-875.

Remer, R., & Elliott, J. E. (1988). Characteristics of secondary victims of sexual assault. *International Journal of Family Psychiatry, 9,* 373-387.

Resick, P. A., Nishith, P., & Astin, M. C. (1996, November). Preliminary results of an outcome study comparing cognitive processing therapy and prolonged exposure. In P. A. Resick (Chair), *Treating sexual assault/sexual abuse pathology: Recent findings.* Symposium conducted at the 30th annual convention of the Association of the Advancement of Behavior Therapy, New York.

Resick, P. A., & Schnicke, M. K. (1993). *Cognitive processing therapy for rape victims: A treatment manual.* Newbury Park, CA: Sage.

Resick, P. A., Schnicke, M. K., & Markway, B. G. (1991, November). *Personal Beliefs and Reactions Scale: The relation between cognitive content and posttraumatic stress disorder.* Paper presented at 25th annual convention of the Association of the Advancement of Behavior Therapy, New York.

Reske, H. J. (1994, December). Computer porn a prosecutorial challenge: Cybersmut easy to distribute, difficult to track, open to legal questions. *ABA Journal,* p. 40.

Ressler, R. K., Burgess, A. W., & Douglas, J. E. (1988). *Sexual homicide: Patterns and motives.* Lexington, MA: Lexington Books.

Ressler, R. K., & Shachtman, T. (1992). *Whoever fights monsters.* New York: Pocket Books.

Rice, M. E., & Harris, G. T. (1991). Firesetters admitted to a maximum security psychiatric institution. *Journal of Interpersonal Violence, 6,* 461-475.

Rice, M. E., & Harris, G. T. (1995). *Cross-validation and extension of an actuarial instrument for the prediction of recidivism among sex offenders* (Research Report, Vol. 12, No. 2). Penetanguishene, Ontario, Canada: Penetanguishene Mental Health Centre.

Rice, M. E., & Harris, G. T. (1996). Predicting the recidivism of mentally disordered firesetters. *Journal of Interpersonal Violence, 11,* 364-375.

Rice, M. E., & Harris, G. T. (1997). Cross-validation and extension of the Violence Risk Appraisal Guide for child molesters and rapists. *Law and Human Behavior, 21,* 231-241.

Rice, M. E., Harris, G. T., & Cormier, C. A. (1992). An evaluation of a maximum security therapeutic community for psychopaths and other mentally disordered offenders. *Law and Human Behavior, 16,* 399-412.

Rice, M. E., Harris, G. T., & Quinsey, V. L. (1990). A follow-up of rapists assessed in a maximum security psychiatric facility. *Journal of Interpersonal Violence, 4,* 435-448.

Rice, M. E., Quinsey, V. L., & Harris, G. T. (1989). *Predicting sexual recidivism among treated and untreated extrafamilial child molesters released from a maximum security psychiatric institution* (Research Report No. VI-III). Penetanguishene, Ontario, Canada: Mental Health Centre.

Rider, A. O. (1980). The firesetter: A psychological profile. *FBI Law Enforcement Bulletin, 49,* 7-13.

Riggs, D. S., & Kilpatrick, D. G. (1997). Families and friends: Indirect victimization by crime. In R. C. Davis, A. J. Lurigio, & W. F. Skogan (Eds.), *Victims of crime* (pp. 120-138). Thousand Oaks, CA: Sage.

Rix, K. J. B. (1994). A psychiatric study of adult arsonists. *Medicine, Science, and the Law, 34,* 21-35.

Robboy, H. (1985). *Emotional labor and sexual exploitation in an occupational role.* Paper presented at the annual meetings of the Mid South Sociological Society, Little Rock, AR.

Robinson, B. E., Walters, L. H., & Skeen, R. (1989). Response of parents to learning that their child is homosexual and concern over AIDS: A national survey. *Journal of Homosexuality, 18*(1-2), 59-80.

Rodkin, L. I., Hunt, E. J., & Cowan, S. D. (1982). A men's support group for significant others of rape victims. *Journal of Marital and Family Therapy, 8*(1), 91-97.

Roesler, T., & Deisher, R. W (1972). Young male homosexuality. *Journal of the American Medical Association, 219,* 1018-1023.

Rofes, E. E. (1989). Opening up the classroom closet: Responding to the educational needs of gay and lesbian youth. *Harvard Educational Review, 59,* 444-453.

Rofes, E. E. (1994). Making our schools safe for sissies. *High School Journal, 77,* 37-40.

Ronai, C. R. (1992). The reflexive self through narrative: A night in the life of an erotic dancer/researcher. In C. Ellis & M. Flaherty (Eds.), *Investigating subjectivity: Research on lived experience* (pp. 102-124). London: Sage.

Ronai, C. R., & Ellis, C. (1989). Turn-ons for money: Interactional strategies of a table dancer. *Journal of Contemporary Ethnography, 18*(3), 271-298.

Rotheram-Borus, M. J., Hunter, I., & Rosario, M. (1994). Suicidal behavior and gay-related stress among gay and bisexual male adolescents. *Journal of Adolescent Research, 9,* 498-508.

Rotheram-Borus, M. J., Hunter, I., & Rosario, M. (1995). Coming out as lesbian or gay in the era of AIDS. In G. M. Herek & B. Greene (Eds.), *AIDS, identity, and community: The HIV epidemic and lesbians and gay men* (pp. 150-168). Thousand Oaks, CA: Sage.

Rotheram-Borus, M. J., Rosario, M., & Koopman, C. (1991). Minority youth at high risk: Gay males and runaways. In M. E. Colten & S. Gore (Eds.), *Adolescent stress: Causes and consequences* (pp. 181-200). New York: Aldine de Gruyter.

Rotheram-Borus, M. J., Rosario, M., Meyer-Bahlburg, H. F. L., Koopman, C., Dopkins, S. C., & Davies, M. (1994). Sexual and substance use acts of gay and bisexual male adolescents in New York City. *Journal of Sex Research, 371,* 47-57.

Rowe, K. (1985). The limits of the neighborhood justice center: Why domestic violence cases should not be mediated. *Emory Law Journal, 34,* 855-910.

Rubenstein, C. M. (1996, March). Internet dangers. *Parents,* pp. 145-149.

Rubin, G. (1975). The traffic in women: Notes on the "political economy" of sex. In R. Reiter (Ed.), *Toward an anthropology of women* (pp. 157-210). New York: Monthly Review Press.

Rubin, G. (1984). Thinking sex: Notes for a radical theory of the politics of sexuality. In C. Vance (Ed.), *Pleasure and danger: Exploring female sexuality.* London: Pandora.

Ruch, L. O., & Chandler, S. M. (1983). Sexual assault trauma during the acute phase: An exploratory model and multivariate analysis. *Journal of Health and Social Behavior, 24,* 174-185.

Ruch, L. O., & Leon, J. J. (1983). Sexual assault trauma and trauma change. *Women and Health, 8,* 5-21.

Rudin, J. B. (1996). Megan's Law: Can it stop sexual predators—and at what cost to constitutional rights? *Westlaw Criminal Justice, 11,* 1-18.

Russell, D. E. H. (1982a). The prevalence and incidence of forcible rape and attempted rape of females. *Victimology: An International Journal, 7,* 81-93.

Russell, D. E. H. (1982b). *Rape in marriage.* New York: Macmillan.

Russell, D. E. H. (1984). *Sexual exploitation: Rape, child sexual abuse, and workplace harassment.* Beverly Hills, CA: Sage.

Ryan, G. (1997). Juvenile sex offenders: Defining the population. In G. D. Ryan & S. L. Lane (Eds.), *Juvenile sexual offending: Causes, consequences, and correction* (pp. 3-8). San Francisco: Jossey-Bass.

Ryan, G., & Miyoshi, T. (1990). Summary of a pilot follow-up study of adolescent sexual perpetrators after treatment. *Interchange, 1,* 6-8.

Ryan, G., Miyoshi, T. J. O., Metzner, J. L., Krugman, R. D., & Fryer, G. E. (1996). Trends in a national sample of sexually abusive youth. *Journal of the Academy of Child and Adolescent Psychiatry, 35,* 17-25.

Sacco, D. T. (1998). Arguments used to challenge notification laws—and the government's response. *National Conference on Sex Offender Registries Proceedings.* Washington, DC: Bureau of Justice Statistics.

Sales, E., Baum, M., & Shore, B. (1984). Victim readjustment following assault. *Journal of Social Issues, 40,* 117-136.

Salutin, M. (1971). Stripper morality. *Transaction, 8,* 12-22.

Samarasinghe, M. (1996, October 30). *Sri Lanka cracking down on child sex abuse.* Reuters World Service.

Samarasinghe, M. (1997, February 11). *Sri Lanka deports Swiss facing child abuse charges.* Reuters World Service.

Sanchez, L. E. (1998). Boundaries of legitimacy: Sex, violence, citizenship, and community in a local sexual economy. *Law and Social Inquiry, 22*(3), 543-580.

Saum, C. A., Surratt, H. L, Inciardi, J. A., & Bennett, R. E. (1995). Sex in prison: The myths and realities. *The Prison Journal, 75,* 413-430.

Saunders, D. G. (1986). When battered women use violence: Husband-abuse or self-defense? *Violence and Victims, 1,* 47-60.

Savin-Williams, R. C. (1990). *Gay and lesbian youth: Expressions of identity.* Washington, DC: Hemisphere.

Savin-Williams, R. C. (1994). Verbal and physical abuse as stressors in the lives of lesbian, gay male, and bisexual youths: Associations with school problems, running away, substance abuse, prostitution, and suicide. *Journal of Consulting and Clinical Psychology, 62,* 261-269.

Savin-Williams, R. C. (1995). Lesbian, gay male, and bisexual adolescents. In A. R. D'Augelli & C. J. Patterson (Eds.), *Lesbian, gay, and bisexual identities across the lifespan* (pp. 165-189). New York: Oxford University Press.

Sawyer, S., Rosser, B. R. S., & Schroeder, A. (1998). Brief psychoeducational program for men who patronize prostitutes. *Journal of Offender Rehabilitation, 26*(3/4), 111-125.

Scacco, A. M. (1975). *Rape in prison.* Springfield, IL: Charles C Thomas.

Scacco, A. M. (Ed.). (1982). *Male rape: A casebook of sexual aggression.* New York: AMS Press.

Scarpitti, F. R., & Andersen, M. L. (1989). *Social problems.* New York: Harper & Row.

Schauben, L. J., & Frazier, P. A. (1995). Vicarious trauma: The effects on female counselors of working with sexual violence survivors. *Psychology of Women Quarterly, 19,* 49-64.

Schechter, S. (1982). *Women and male violence.* Boston: South End Press.

Scheingold, S. A., Olson, T., & Pershing, J. (1994). Sexual violence, victim advocacy, and republican criminology: Washington State's Community Protection Act. *Law & Society Review, 28,* 729-763.

Schmidt, F. L. (1996). Statistical significance testing and cumulative knowledge in psychology: Implications for training of researchers. *Psychological Methods, 1,* 115-129.

Schmitt, F., & Martin, P. Y. (1999). Unobtrusive mobilization by an institutionalized rape crisis center: All we do comes from victims. *Gender & Society, 13,* 364-384.

Schneider, C. (1997, June 26). Impact of Megan's Law. *Atlanta Journal and the Atlanta Constitution,* p. B3.

Schneider, S. C., Farberow, N. L., & Kruks, C. N. (1989). Suicidal behavior in adolescent and young adult gay men. *Suicidal and Life-Threatening Behavior, 19,* 381-394.

Schopf, S. (1995, Fall). Megan's Law: Community notification and the Constitution. *Columbia Journal of Law and Social Problems, 29,* 117.

Schulman, M. (1979). *A survey of spousal violence against women in Kentucky* (Study No. 792701, conducted for Kentucky Commission on Women, sponsored by the U.S. Department of Justice, Law Enforcement Assistance Administration). Washington, DC: Government Printing Office.

Schulman, S. (1994). *My American history: Lesbian and gay life during the Reagan/Bush years.* New York: Routledge.

Schupe, A., Stacey, W. A., & Hazelwood, L. R. (1987). *Violent men, violent couples: The dynamics of domestic violence.* Lexington, MA: Lexington Books.

Schwartz, M. D. (1987). Gender and injury in spousal assault. *Sociological Focus, 20,* 61-75.

Schwartz, M. D., & DeKeseredy, W. S. (1997). *Sexual assault on the college campus: The role of male peer support.* Thousand Oaks, CA: Sage.

Schwartz, P., & Rutter, V. (1998). *The gender of sexuality.* Thousand Oaks, CA: Pine Forge.

Scibelli, P. (1987). Empowering prostitutes: A proposal for international legal reform. *Harvard Women's Law Journal, 10,* 117-157.

Scott, D. (1974a). *Fire and fire-raisers.* London: Gerald Duckworth.

Scott, D. (1974b). *The psychology of fire.* New York: Charles Scribner's Sons.

Scully, D. (1990). *Understanding sexual violence: A study of convicted rapists.* Boston: Unwin Hyman.

Searles, P., & Berger, R. J. (1995). *Rape and society: Readings on the problem of sexual assault.* Boulder, CO: Westview.

Sears, D. (1994). *To kill again: The motivation and development of serial murder.* Wilmington, DE: Scholarly Resources.

Serin, R. C. (1991). Psychopathy and violence in criminals. *Journal of Interpersonal Violence, 6,* 423-431.

Serin, R. C. (1996). Violent recidivism in criminal psychopaths. *Law and Human Behaviour, 20,* 207-217.

Serin, R. C., Malcolm, P. B., Khanna, A., & Barbaree, H. E. (1994). Psychopathy and deviant sexual arousal in incarcerated sexual offenders. *Journal of Interpersonal Violence, 9*(1), 3-11.

Seto, M. C., & Kuban, M. (1996). Criterion-related validity of a phallometric test for paraphilic rape and sadism. *Behaviour Research and Therapy, 34*(2), 175-183.

Shapiro, F. (1998). The big picture of sex offenders and public policy. *National Conference on Sex Offender Registries Proceedings.* Washington, DC: Bureau of Justice Statistics.

Sherman, L. W. (1993). Defiance, deterrence, and irrelevance: A theory of the criminal sanction. *Journal of Research in Crime & Delinquency, 30,* 445-473.

Siegel, J. M., Sorensen, S. B., Golding, J. M., Burnam, M. A., & Stein, J. A. (1989). Resistance to sexual assault: Who resists and what happens? *American Journal of Public Health, 79,* 27-31.

Signorile, M. (1993). *Queer in America: Sex, the media, and the closets of power.* New York: Random House.

Sijuwade, P. (1995). Counterfeit intimacy: A dramaturgical analysis of an erotic performance. *Social Behavior and Personality, 23*(4), 369-376.

Silbert, M. H., & Pines, A. M. (1981). Occupational hazards of street prostitutes. *Criminal Justice and Behavior, 8*(4), 395-424.

Silbert, M. H., & Pines, A. M. (1982). Victimization of street prostitutes. *Victimology, 7*(1-4), 122-133.

Silver, R. C., Wortman, C. B., & Crofton, C. (1990). The role of coping in support provision: The self-presentational dilemma of victims of life crises. In I. G. Sarason, B. R. Sarason, & G. R. Pierce (Eds.), *Social support: An interactional view* (pp. 397-426). New York: Wiley.

Silverman, D. C. (1978). Sharing the crisis of rape: Counseling the mates and families of victims. *American Journal of Orthopsychiatry, 48,* 166-173.

Silvestre, A. J., Kingsley, L. A., Wehman, P., Dappen, R., Ho, M., & Rinaldo, C. R. (1993). Changes in HIV rates and sexual behavior among homosexual men, 1984 to 1988. *American Journal of Public Health, 83,* 578-580.

Skipper, J., & McCaghy, C. (1970). Stripteasers: The anatomy and career contingencies of a deviant occupation. *Social Problems, 17,* 391-404.

Skoloff, B. (2001, March 23). Man convicted of murder, rape in death of 13-year-old boy. Retrieved October 9, 2001 from http://www.apbnews.com/newscenter/breakingnews/2001/03/23/story_brown_convicted.html

Smith, B. (1998). *An end to silence: Women prisoners' handbook on identifying and addressing sexual misconduct.* Washington, DC: National Women's Law Center.

Smith, N., & Batiuk, M. (1989). Sexual victimization and inmate social interaction. *The Prison Journal, 68,* 29-38.

Smucker, M. R., Dancu, C., Foa, E. B., & Niederee, J. L. (1995). Imagery rescripting: A new treatment for survivors of childhood sexual abuse suffering from posttraumatic stress. *Journal of Cognitive Psychotherapy: An International Quarterly, 9*(1), 3-17.

Snell, C. L. (1995). *Young men in the street: Help-seeking behavior of young male prostitutes.* Westport, CT: Praeger.

Spalter-Roth, R., & Schreiber, R. (1995). Outsider issues and insider tactics: Strategic tensions in the women's policy network during the 1980s. In M. M. Ferree & P. Y. Martin (Eds.), *Feminist organizations: Harvest of the new women's movement* (pp. 105-127). Philadelphia: Temple University Press.

Spears, J. W., & Spohn, C. C. (1997). The effect of evidence factors and victim characteristics on prosecutors' charging decisions in sexual assault cases. *Justice Quarterly, 14,* 501-524.

Stadler, M. (1995, November 7). Stalking the predator. *New York Times,* p. A23.

Staggenborg, S. (1995). Can feminist organizations be effective? In M. M. Ferree & P. Y. Martin (Eds.), *Feminist organizations: Harvest of the new women's movement* (pp. 339-355). Philadelphia: Temple University Press.

Stall, R., Barrett, D., Bye, L., Catania, J., Frutchey, C., Hennessey, J., Lemp, C., & Paul, J. (1992). A comparison of younger and older gay men's HIV risk-taking behaviors: The Communication Technology 1989 Cross-Sectional Survey. *Journal of Acquired Immune Deficiency Syndromes, 5,* 682-687.

Stanko, E. (1985). *Intimate intrusions: Women's experience of male violence.* New York: Routledge Kegan Paul.

Stark, E., Flitcraft, A., & Frazier, W. (1979). Medicine and patriarchal violence: The social construction of a "private" event. *Internal Journal of Health Services, 9,* 461-493.

Steinbach, G. (1986). Les differentes conceptions du droit en matiere d'incendie et les generalities criminologiques sur les incendiarires. *Neuropsychiatric de l'Enfance et de l'Adolescence, 34,* 33-38.

Steinmetz, S. K. (1977-1978). The battered husband syndrome. *Victimology, 2,* 499-509.

Stekel, W. C. (1924). *Peculiarities of behavior.* New York: Boni and Liveright.

Stewart, B., Hughes, C., Frank, E., Anderson, B., Kendall, K., & West, D. (1987). The aftermath of rape: Profiles of immediate and delayed treatment seekers. *Journal of Nervous and Mental Disease, 175,* 90-94.

Stewart, L. A. (1993). Profile of female firesetters. *British Journal of Psychiatry, 163,* 248-256.

Stone, G. L. (1995). Review of the Hare Psychopathy Checklist-Revised. In J. C. Conoley & J. C. Impara (Eds.), *Twelfth mental measurements yearbook* (pp. 454-455). Lincoln, NE: Buros Institute.

Stone, K. (1980). The second victims: Altruism and the affective reactions of affiliated males to their partner's rape. *Dissertation Abstracts International, 41,* 5-B. (University Microfilms No. 1933)

Stop Prisoner Rape. (1993). *Motion and brief of Stop Prisoner Rape: Amicus curiae in support of petitioner, Dee Farmer in Dee Farmer, Petitioner v. Edward Brennan, Warden, et al. respondent, 511 U.S. 825* (No. 92-7247). New York: Author.

Strang, H. (1993). *Homicides in Australia: 1991-92.* Canberra: Australian Institute of Criminology.

Straus, M. A. (1977-1978). Wife beating: How common and why? *Victimology, 2,* 443-458.

Straus, M. A. (1990a). Injury and frequency of assault and the representative sample fallacy in measuring wife beating and child abuse. In M. A. Straus & R. J. Gelles (Eds.), *Physical violence in American families: Risk factors and adaptions to violence in 8,145 families* (pp. 75-91). New Brunswick, NJ: Transaction Books.

Straus, M. A. (1990b). Measuring intrafamily conflict and violence: The Conflict Tactics (CTS) Scales. In M. A. Straus & R. J. Gelles (Eds.), *Physical violence in American families: Risk factors and adaptions to violence in 8,145 families* (pp. 29-47). New Brunswick, NJ: Transaction Books.

Straus, M. A. (1993). Physical assaults by wives: A major social problem. In R. J. Gelles & D. R. Loseke (Eds.), *Current controversies on family violence* (pp. 67-87). Newbury Park, CA: Sage.

Straus, M. A., & Gelles, R. J. (1986). Societal change and change in family violence from 1975 to 1985 as revealed by two national surveys. *Journal of Marriage and the Family, 48,* 465-479.

Straus, M. A., Gelles, R. J., & Steinmetz, S. K. (1980). *Behind closed doors: Violence in the American family.* New York: Doubleday.

Strommen, E. F. (1989). Hidden branches and growing pains: Homosexuality and the family tree. *Marriage and Family Review, 24,* 9-34.

Struckman-Johnson, C. J., & Struckman-Johnson, D. L. (1999, November). *Pressured and forced sexual contact reported by women in three midwestern prisons.* Paper presented at the annual meeting of the Society for the Study of Sexuality and the American Association of Sex Educators, Counselors, and Therapists, St. Louis, MO.

Struckman-Johnson, C. J., & Struckman-Johnson, D. L. (2000, March). *Sexual coercion rates in ten prison facilities in the Midwest.* Paper presented at the annual meeting of the Academy of Criminal Justice Sciences, New Orleans, LA.

Struckman-Johnson, C. J., Struckman-Johnson, D. L., Rucker, L., Bumby, K., & Donaldson, S. (1995, May). *A survey of inmate and staff perspectives on prisoner sexual assault.* Paper presented at the annual meeting of the Midwestern Psychological Association, Chicago, IL.

Struckman-Johnson, C. J., Struckman-Johnson, D. L., Rucker, L., Bumby, K., & Donaldson, S. (1996). Sexual coercion reported by men and women in prison. *Journal of Sex Research, 33*(1), 67-76.

Stuart, B. (1997). *Building community justice partnerships: Community peacemaking circles.* Ottawa, Canada: Report of the Ministry of Justice.

Styles, J. (1979). Outsider/insider: Researching gay baths. *Urban Life, 8*(2), 135-152.

Sullivan, E., & Simon, W. (1998). The client: A social, psychological, and behavioral look at the unseen patron of prostitution. In J. E. Elias, V. L. Bullough, V. Elias, & G. Brewer (Eds.), *Prostitution: On whores, hustlers, and johns* (pp. 134-154). Amherst, NY: Prometheus.

Swisher, K. (1995, September 14). On-line child pornography charged as 12 are arrested. *Washington Post,* pp. A1, A13.

Sykes, O., & Matza, D. (1957). Techniques of neutralization: A theory of delinquency. *American Journal of Sociology, 22,* 664-670.

Tabachnick, B., & Fidell, L. (1996). *Using multivariate statistics* (3rd ed.). New York: HarperCollins.

Tattleman, I. (1999). Speaking to the gay bathhouse: Communicating in sexually charged spaces. In W. L. Leap (Ed.), *Public sex/gay space* (pp. 71-94). New York: Columbia University Press.

Teir, R., & Coy, K. (1997). Approaches to sexual predators: Community notification and civil commitment. *New England Journal of Criminal & Civil Confinement, 23,* 405-426.

Teske, R. H. C., & Parker, M. L. (1983). *Spouse abuse in Texas: A study of women's attitudes and experiences.* Newark, NJ: Criminal Justice/NCCD Collection, John Cotton Dana Library.

Testa, M., & Parks, K. A. (1996). The role of women's alcohol consumption in sexual victimization. *Aggression and Violent Behavior, 1,* 217-234.

Tewksbury, R. (1989a). Fear of sexual assault in prison inmates. *The Prison Journal, 69,* 62-71.

Tewksbury, R. (1989b). Measures of sexual behavior in an Ohio prison. *Sociology and Social Research, 74,* 34-39.

Tewksbury, R. (1990). Patrons of porn: Research notes on the clientele of adult bookstores. *Deviant Behavior, 11*(3), 259-271.

Tewksbury, R. (1994a). Male strippers: Men objectifying men. In C. L. Williams (Ed.), *Doing "women's work": Men in nontraditional occupations* (pp. 168-181). Thousand Oaks, CA: Sage.

Tewksbury, R. (1994b). Dramaturgical analysis of male strippers. *Journal of Men's Studies, 2*(4), 325-342.

Tewksbury, R. (1995). Adventures in the erotic oasis: Sex and danger in men's same-sex, public sexual encounters. *Journal of Men's Studies, 4*(1), 9-24.

Thomas, R. M., Plant, M. A., & Plant, L. L. (1990). Alcohol, AIDS risks, and sex industry clients: Results from a Scottish study. *Drug and Alcohol Dependence, 26,* 265-269.

Thompson, W., & Harred, J. (1992). Topless dancers: Managing stigma in a deviant occupation. *Deviant Behavior, 13,* 291-311.

Tobin, D. L., Holroyd, K. A., Reynolds, R. V., & Wigal, J. K. (1989). The hierarchical factor structure of the coping strategies inventory. *Cognitive Therapy and Research, 13,* 343-361.

Toch, H. (1992). *Mosaic of despair: Human breakdowns in prison* (rev. ed.). Washington, DC: American Psychological Association.

Tonkonogy, J. M., & Geller, J. L. (1992). Hypothalamic lesions and intermittent explosive disorder. *Journal of Neuropsychiatry and Clinical Neurosciences, 4,* 45-50.

Truong, T. (1990). *Sex, money, and morality: Prostitution and tourism in southeast Asia.* London: Zed.

Tyra, P. A. (1979). *Volunteer rape counselors: Selected characteristics, empathy, attribution of responsibility, and rape counselor syndrome.* Unpublished doctoral dissertation, Boston University School of Education.

Ullman, S., & Siegel, J. (1995). Sexual assault, social reactions, and physical health. *Women's Health: Research on Gender, Behavior, and Policy, 1,* 289-308.

Ullman, S. E. (1996a). Do social reactions to sexual assault victims vary by support provider? *Violence and Victims, 11,* 143-156.

Ullman, S. E. (1996b). Social reactions, coping strategies, and self-blame attributions in adjustment to sexual assault. *Psychology of Women Quarterly, 20,* 505-526.

Ullman, S. E. (1996c). Correlates and consequences of adult sexual assault disclosure. *Journal of Interpersonal Violence, 11,* 554-571.

Ullman, S. E. (1997a). Attributions, world assumptions, and recovery from sexual assault. *Journal of Child Sexual Abuse, 6,* 1-19.

Ullman, S. E. (1997b). Review and critique of empirical studies of rape avoidance. *Criminal Justice and Behavior, 24,* 177-204.

Ullman, S. E. (1999). A comparison of gang and individual rape incidents. *Violence and Victims, 14,* 123-134.

Ullman, S. E., & Brecklin, L. R. (in press). Alcohol and adult sexual assault in a national sample of women. *Journal of Substance Abuse.*

Ullman, S. E., Karabatsos, G., & Koss, M. P. (1999a). Alcohol and sexual aggression in a national sample of college men. *Psychology of Women Quarterly, 23,* 673-689.

Ullman, S. E., Karabatsos, G., & Koss, M. P. (1999b). Alcohol and sexual assault in a national sample of college women. *Journal of Interpersonal Violence, 14,* 603-625.

Ullman, S. E., & Knight, R. A. (1991). A multivariate model for predicting rape and physical injury outcomes during sexual assaults. *Journal of Consulting and Clinical Psychology, 59,* 724-731.

Ullman, S. E., & Knight, R. A. (1993). The efficacy of women's resistance strategies in rape situations. *Psychology of Women Quarterly, 17,* 23-38.

Umbreit, M. S., Coates, R., & Roberts, A. W. (1997, December). Cross-national impact of restorative justice through mediation and dialogue. *ICCA Journal on Community Corrections,* pp. 46-53.

Umbreit, M. S., & Zehr, H. (1995-1996). Family group conferences: A challenge to victim-offender mediation? *VOMA Quarterly, 7,* 4-8.

United States v. Russell, 411 U.S. 423 (1973).

University of Washington. (1996). *Sexological dictionary.* Retrieved from ftp://ftp.u.washington.edu/public/sfpse/sex/sexdict.txt

Uribe, V., & Harbeck, K. M. (1991). Addressing the needs of lesbian, gay, and bisexual youth: The origins of Project 10 and school-based intervention. *Journal of Homosexuality, 22*(34), 9-28.

U.S. Department of Justice. (1999a). *Crime in the United States, 1998.* Washington, DC: Federal Bureau of Investigation.

U.S. Department of Justice. (1999b). *National Institute of Corrections Solicitation for a cooperative agreement on the development of a training curriculum for investigating allegations of staff sexual misconduct with inmates.* Washington, DC: Author. (may be accessed at the NCIC Web site at http://www.nicic.org/inst/coop-miscondcurr99.htm)

U.S. Department of Justice. (1999c). *Summary findings for correctional populations.* Washington, DC: Author. Retrieved August 29, 1999, from the World Wide Web: http://www.ojp.usdoj.gov/bjs/correct.htm

U.S. General Accounting Office. (1999). *Women in prison: Sexual misconduct by correctional staff.* United States General Accounting Office Report to the Honorable Eleanor Holms Norton (GAO/GGD-99-104). Washington, DC: Author. (may be accessed on the GAO Web site at http://www.gao.gov/new.items/gg99104.pdf)

U.S. House of Representatives, Select Committee on Children, Youth, and Families. (1989). *Down these mean streets: Violence by and against America's children.* Washington, DC: Government Printing Office.

Van der Poel, S. (1992). Professional male prostitution: A neglected phenomenon. *Crime, Law and Social Change, 18*(3), 259-275.

Van Ness, D., & Strong, K. H. (1997). *Restoring justice.* Cincinnati, OH: Anderson.

Virkkunen, M., DeJong, J., Bartko, J., & Linnoila, M. (1989). Psychobiological concomitants of history of suicide attempts among violent offenders and impulsive fire setters. *Archives of General Psychiatry, 46,* 604-606.

Virkkunen, M., Nuutila, A., Goodwin, F. K., & Linnoila, M. (1989). Relationship of psychobiological variables to recidivism in violent offenders and impulsive fire setters. *Archives of General Psychiatry, 46,* 600-604.

Vito, G. F., & Holmes, R. M. (1994). *Criminology: Theory, research, and policy.* Belmont, CA: Wadsworth.

Vizard, E., Monck, E., & Misch, P. (1995). Child and adolescent sexual abuse perpetrators: A review of the research literature. *Journal of Child Psychology and Psychiatry and Related Disciplines, 36,* 731-756.

von Krafft-Ebing, R. (1965). *Psychopathia sexualis.* New York: Scarborough.

Vreeland, R. G., & Levin, B. M. (1980). Psychobiological aspects of firesetting. In D. Canter (Ed.), *Fires and human behavior.* New York: John Wiley.

Walkowitz, J. (1980). *Prostitution and Victorian society.* Cambridge, UK: Cambridge University Press.

Wardell, L., Gillespie, D. L., & Leffler, A. (1983). Science and violence against wives. In D. Finkelhor, R. J. Gelles, G. T. Hotaling, & M. A. Straus (Eds.), *The dark side of families: Current family violence research* (pp. 69-84). Beverly Hills, CA: Sage.

Warren, J., Reboussin, R., & Hazelwood, R. (1996). *The temporal sequencing and cognitive mapping of serial rapists.* Retrieved from http://ness.sys.virginia.edu/ilppp/serialrape.html

Wasco, S. M., & Campbell, R. (2000). *Emotional reactions of rape victim advocates: The roles of anger and fear in helping rape victims.* Manuscript submitted for publication.

Wasco, S. M., Campbell, R., Barnes, H., & Ahrens, C. E. (1999, June). *Rape crisis centers: Shaping survivors' experiences with community systems following sexual assault.* Paper presented at the Biennial Conference of the Society for Community Research and Action, New Haven, CT.

Weathers, F. W., & Litz, B. T. (1994). Psychometric properties of the Clinician-Administered PTSD Scale, CAPS-1. *PTSD Research Quarterly, 5*(2), 2-6.

Webster, C. D., Harris, G. T., Rice, M. E., Cormier, C., & Quinsey, V. L. (1994). *The Violence Prediction Scheme: Assessing dangerousness in high risk men.* Toronto, Canada: University of Toronto Press.

Weinrott, M. R. (1996). *Juvenile sexual abuse: A critical review.* Unpublished manuscript.

Weinrott, M. R., & Saylor, M. (1991). Self report of crimes committed by sex offenders. *Journal of Interpersonal Violence, 6,* 286-300.

Weisburg, D. K. (1985). *Children of the night: A study of adolescent prostitution.* Lexington, MA: Lexington Books.

Weiss, C., & Friar, D. J. (1974). *Terror in the prisons: Homosexual rape and why society condones it.* Indianapolis, IN: Bobbs-Merrill.

Wenninger, K., & Ehlers, A. (1998). Dysfunctional cognitions and adult psychological functioning in child sexual abuse survivors. *Journal of Traumatic Stress, 11,* 281-300.

West, D. J. (1998). Male prostitution: Gay sex services in London. In J. E. Elias, V. L. Bullough, V. Elias, & G. Brewer (Eds.), *Prostitution: On whores, hustlers, and johns* (pp. 228-235). Amherst, NY: Prometheus.

Wetterling, P. (1998). The Jacob Wetterling story. *National Conference on Sex Offender Registries Proceedings.* Washington, DC: Bureau of Justice Statistics.

What is investigative psychology? (1997). Retrieved from http://www.liv.ac.uk/Psychology/Groups/IP/whatinps.html

Whitaker, C. J., & Bastian, L. D. (1991, May). *Teenage victims* (Tech. Rep. No. 128129). Washington, DC: U.S. Department of Justice, Office of Justice Programs, Bureau of Justice Statistics National Crime Survey.

White, D. H. (1988). *Governor's Task Force on Bias-Related Violence: Final report.* Albany: New York Governor's Office.

White, P. N., & Rollins, J. C. (1981). Rape: A family crisis. *Family Relations, 30,* 103-109.

Wijers, M., & Lap-Chew, L. (1997). *Trafficking in women, forced labour and slavery-like practices in marriage, domestic labour and prostitution.* Netherlands: Foundation Against Trafficking in Women.

Wiklund, N. (1987). *The motives for arson.* Stockholm: The Swedish Fire Protection Association.

Williams, F. P., & McShane, M. (1995). *Erotica and the Internet.* Paper presented at the annual meeting of the Academy of Criminal Justice Sciences, Boston, MA.

Williams, J. E. (1984). Secondary victimization: Confronting public attitudes about rape. *Victimology, 9,* 66-81.

Williams, L. (1989). *Hard core: Power, pleasure, and the frenzy of the visible.* Berkeley: University of California Press.

Wilsnack, S. C., Vogeltanz, N. D., Klassen, A. D., & Harris, T. R. (1997). Child sexual abuse and women's substance use: National survey findings. *Journal of Studies on Alcohol, 58,* 264-271.

Wilson, P., Lincon, R., & Kocsis, R. (1997). Validity, utility and ethics of profiling for serial violent and sexual offences. *Psychiatry, Psychology and Law, 4,* 1-11.

Wilson, P., & Soothill, K. (1996, January). Psychological profiling: Red, green or amber? *Police Journal, 69,* 12-20.

Winick, C. (1962). Prostitutes' clients' perceptions of the prostitutes and of themselves. *International Journal of Social Psychiatry, 8*(4), 289-299.

Wiseman, R., & West, D. (1997, January). An experimental test of psychic detection. *Police Journal, 70,* 19-25.

Wong, S. (1984). *The criminal and institutional behaviour of psychopaths* (User Report No. 1984-87). Ottawa: Ministry of the Solicitor General of Canada.

Wong, S. (1988). Is Hare's Psychopathy Checklist reliable without the interview? *Psychological Reports, 62,* 931-934.

Wood, R. E. (1981). The economics of tourism. *Southeast Asia Chronicle, 78,* 2-12.

Wooden, W. S., & Parker, J. (1982). *Men behind bars: Sexual exploitation in prison.* New York: Plenum.

Wright, K. N., Clear, T. R., & Dickson, P. (1984). Universal applicability of probation risk-assessment instruments: A critique. *Criminology, 22,* 113-134.

Wyatt, G., Notgrass, C., & Newcomb, M. (1990). Internal and external mediators of women's rape experiences. *Psychology of Women Quarterly, 14,* 153-176.

Wylie, M. S. (1998, November/December). Secret lives: Pedophilia and the possibility of forgiveness. *Family Therapy Networker,* pp. 39-59.

Yalom, I. D. (1960). Aggression and forbiddenness in voyeurism. *Archives in General Psychiatry, 3,* 305-319.

Young, M. A. (1995). *Restorative community justice: A call to action.* Washington, DC: National Organization for Victim Assistance.

Zamble, E., & Quinsey, V. L. (1997). *The criminal recidivism process.* Cambridge, UK: Cambridge University Press.

Zausner, M. (1986). *The streets: A factual portrait of six prostitutes as told in their own words.* New York: St. Martin's.

Zeegers, M. (1984). Criminal firesetting: A review and some case studies. *Medicine and the Law, 3,* 171-176.

Zehr, H. (1995). *Changing lenses: A new focus for crime and justice.* Scottdale, PA: Herald Press.

Zielbauer, P. (2000, May 22). Sex offender listings on web set off debate. *New York Times.* Retrieved from http://www.nytimes.com/library/tech/00/05/biztech/articles/22abus.html

Index

About the Editors

———■———

Ronald M. Holmes is Professor of Justice Administration at the University of Louisville. He is the author of several books, among them *Profiling Violent Crimes, Sex Crimes,* and *Serial Murder.* He is also the author of more than 50 articles appearing in scholarly publications. He is Vice President of the National Center for the Study of Unresolved Homicides and has completed more than 500 psychological profiles for police departments across the United States. He received his doctorate from Indiana University.

Stephen T. Holmes is Assistant Professor of Criminal Justice at the University of Central Florida. Prior to this position, he was a social science analyst for the National Institute of Justice in Washington, D.C. He has authored six books and more than 15 articles dealing with policing, drug testing, probation and parole issues, and violent crime. He received his doctorate from the University of Cincinnati.